D0060861

The Sociology of the Kibbutz

Studies of Israeli Society
Volume II

SHANAHAN LIBRARY
MARYMOUNT MANHATTAN COLLEGE
221 EAST 71 STREET
NEW YORK, NY 10021

HN
660
.A8
S83
v.2

The Sociology of the Kibbutz

Studies of Israeli Society
Volume II

Editor: **ERNEST KRAUSZ,** Bar-Ilan University
Assistant Editor: **DAVID GLANZ**

Editorial Board:

JOSEPH BEN-DAVID, The Hebrew University, Jerusalem
ELIHU KATZ (Chairman), The Hebrew University, Jerusalem
BILHA MANNHEIM, Technion—Israel Institute of Technology, Haifa
YONATHAN SHAPIRO, Tel-Aviv University
ALEX WEINGROD, Ben-Gurion University of the Negev

Publication Series of the Israel Sociological Society

SHANAHAN LIBRARY
MARYMOUNT MANHATTAN COLLEGE
221 EAST 71 STREET
NEW YORK NY 10021

Transaction Books

New Brunswick (U.S.A.) and London (U.K.)

Sponsored by the Schnitzer Foundation for Research on the Israeli Economy and Society—Bar-Ilan University
© 1983 by Israel Sociological Society

All rights reserved under International and Pan-American Copyright Conventions. No part of this book may be reproduced or transmitted in any form or by any means, electronic or mechanical, including photocopy, recording, or any information storage and retrieval system, without prior permission in writing from the publisher. All inquiries should be addressed to Transaction Books, Rutgers—The State University, New Brunswick, New Jersey 08903.

Library of Congress Catalog Number: 79-93045
ISBN: 0-87855-455-6 (cloth), 0-87855-902-7 (paper)
ISSN: 0734-4937
Printed in the United States of America

Library of Congress Cataloging in Publication Data
(Revised for volume 2)
Main entry under title:

Studies of Israeli society.

  (Publications series of the Israel Sociological Society)
  Vol. 2: Editor, Ernest Krausz; assistant editor, David Glanz.
  "Bibliography of social research on Israel, 1970–76 [by] Ron Lahav": v. 1, p. 255–308.
  Includes bibliographies.
  Contents: v. 1. Migration, ethnicity, and community.—v. 2. The sociology of the kibbutz.
  1. Israel—Social conditions—Addresses, essays, lectures—Collected works. 2. Israel—Emigration and immigration—Addresses, essays, lectures—Collected works. 3. Israel—Ethnic relations—Addresses, essays, lectures—Collected works. 4. Kibbutzim—Israel—Addresses, essays, lectures—Collected works. I. Krausz, Ernest. II. Glanz, David. III. Israel Sociological Society. Publication series of the Israel Sociological Society.
HN660.A8S83   306'.095694   79-93045
ISBN 0-87855-455-6 (cloth), 0-87855-902-7 (paper)

Fried. 29.95/26.96 / 7/22/83

Table of Contents

Preface

The best of Israeli social science is scattered in a very large variety of international journals. The object of this publishing venture is to identify the major themes which occupy research in Israel and focus attention on one such theme in each volume. The selection of previously published materials is accompanied by original integrative essays, the overall objective being that of generating discussion, reassessment, and further research.

The contents of this volume are concerned with the sociology of a unique Israeli social institution, the kibbutz. The kibbutz is recognized throughout the world, as Melford Spiro notes in the introduction, as an important laboratory for the investigation of problems and issues of perennial concern to the social sciences. These questions of the concept and historical development of the kibbutz, social differentiation and socialization, and work and production within the kibbutz possess a significance far beyond their immediate social context. Does the kibbutz offer a model for an alternative, communal lifestyle for the modern world? How has the kibbutz changed over the past decades within the context of a rapidly modernizing Israeli society? The articles collected here attempt to provide the concerned reader with some of the answers social researchers on the kibbutz have reached.

A special feature of this volume is a comprehensive bibliography of articles on the kibbutz which should serve as a significant resource for readers interested in studying the topic further. Shimon Shur and David Glanz, who produced this bibliography, both deserve our thanks for their efforts. Thanks are due as well to Professor Erik Cohen who was particularly helpful with the selection of material. We would also like to thank Eliette Orchan for preparing the special statistical appendix on the kibbutz.

First and foremost we are most grateful to the Schnitzer Foundation for Research on the Israeli Economy and Society, Bar-Ilan University, for its generous support in sponsoring this volume. In addition we are grateful to the office of the president of Bar-Ilan University and the Institute for Research of the Kibbutz and the Cooperatiave Idea of Haifa University, who helped support this publication. Thanks are also due to the Sociological Institute for Community Studies of Bar-Ilan University and the Sociology and Anthropology Department of Tel-

Aviv University, without whose assistance this publishing venture would not have been possible. We must also mention two individuals who gave freely of their time and advice, the chairman of the Israel Sociological Society, Professor Ephraim Yuchtman-Yaar, and Ruth Bokstein, the society's secretary.

It is a pleasant task to thank the contributors of the original essays for their kind cooperation—Professor Melford Spiro and Professor Menachem Rosner, who was also involved in the selection process, as well as the authors and publishers who have permitted us to reprint their articles.

Acknowledgments

We also wish to gratefully acknowledge the permission to use copyrighted material granted by the following journals and publishers:

"An Experiment That Did Not Fail," in *Paths in Utopia*, by Martin Buber (1949): 139–149. © Macmillan Publishing Company, Routledge and Kegan Paul, Ltd.

"The Kibbutz and the Moshav," in *Agricultural Planning and Village Community*, ed. J. Ben-David (1964): 45–57. © Unesco.

"Integration, Effectiveness and Adaptation in Social Systems: A Comparative Analysis of Kibbutzim Communities," *Administration and Society*, vol. 6 (1974/5): 283–301; 416–421 (with omissions). © Sage Publications.

"The Structural Transformation of the Kibbutz," in *Social Change*, ed. G. K. Zollschan and W. Hirsh (1976): 703–742. © Schenkman Publishing Company.

"Legality and Ideology in the Kibbutz Movement," *International Journal of the Sociology of Law*, vol. 9 (1981): 279–302. © Academic Press.

"Some Observations on Historical Changes in the Structure of Kibbutzim," *Hakibbutz*, vol. 6–7 (1978/9): 389–391. © Federation of the Kibbutz Movements.

"Social Stratification in a 'Classless' Society," *American Sociological Review*, vol. 16, no. 6 (1951): 766–774. © American Sociological Association.

"Functional Differentiation of Elites in the Kibbutz," *American Journal of Sociology*, vol. 64, no. 5 (1959): 476–487. © University of Chicago Press.

"Reward Distribution and Work-Role Attractiveness in the Kibbutz: Reflections on Equity Theory," *American Sociological Review*, vol. 37 (1972): 581–595. © American Sociological Association.

"Dynamics of Social Stratification in Kibbutzim," *International Journal of Comparative Sociology*, vol. 21, no. 1–2 (1979): 88–100. © E. J. Brill Publishers.

"Is Direct Democracy Feasible in Modern Society?" in *Problems of Integrated Cooperatives in the Industrial Society: The Example of the Kibbutz*, ed. K. Bartolke, Th. Bergman, and L. Liegle (1980). © Van Gorcum Publishing Co.

"Is the Family Universal?—The Israeli Case," in *A Modern Introduction to the Family*, ed. N. W. Bell and E. F. Vogel (1968): 68–79. © American Anthropological Association.

"The Family in a Revolutionary Movement," in *Comparative Family Systems*, by M. F. Nimkoff (1965): 259–286. © Houghton Mifflin Company.

"Kibbutz and Parental Investment," in *Small Groups*, ed. P.A. Hare et al. (1981). © John Wiley and Sons, Ltd., London.

"Relations Between Generations in the Israeli Kibbutz," *Journal of Contemporary History*, vol. 5, no. 1 (1970): 73–86. © The Institute of Contemporary History.

"Socialization Practices of Parents, Teachers, and Peers in Israel: The Kibbutz Versus the City," *Child Development*, vol. 45 (1974): 269–281. © Society for Research in Child Development.

"The Committed: Preliminary Reflections on the Impact of the Kibbutz Socialization Pattern on Adolescents," *The British Journal of Sociology*, vol. 26, no. 3 (1975): 343–353. © Routledge and Kegan Paul, Ltd.

"Structural Differentiation, Production Imperatives, and Communal Norms: The Kibbutz in Crisis, *Social Forces*, vol. 40 (1962): 234–242. © University of North Carolina Press.

"Kibbutz and Colony: Collective Economies and the Outside World," *Comparative Studies in Society and History*, vol. 14 (1972): 456–483. © Cambridge University Press.

"Industrialization in Advanced Rural Communities: The Israeli Kibbutz," *Sociologia Ruralis*, vol. 17 (1977): 59–72. © European Society for Rural Sociology.

"Organizational Effects of Managerial Turnover in Kibbutz Production Branches," *Human Relations*, vol. 31, no. 2 (1978): 1001–1018. © Plenum Publishing Company.

Introduction: Thirty Years of Kibbutz Research

Melford E. Spiro

The papers brought together in this volume represent an excellent sample of the social research undertaken on the kibbutz movement over the past thirty years. Together they should give the social science reader a genuine understanding of the wide range of topics investigated, the different methods used, and the theoretical concerns of the investigators, all of which underscore the point that kibbutz society (as has so often been remarked) constitutes an especially important laboratory for the investigation of a variety of problems and issues that have been of perennial concern to the social sciences.

For the general reader this volume will also provide a great deal of information and insight about a rather unique social system which also represents one of the most important achievements of Zionism. A kibbutz is a particular type of socialist community, and the papers in this volume address a variety of issues that characterize the structure and functioning of that type. But the kibbutz was created at a particular juncture in the history of European Jewry, a juncture which saw the development of Zionist colonization from within, and the rise of Communism, Fascism, and Nazism from without. The kibbutz movement came into being not only as a human response, but as a specifically Jewish response to those great historical events, occupying (in its own eyes) the avant-garde position of Zionism. The achievements of the kibbutz movement can only be understood in the context of the Zionist élan which informed its creation and development, just as its failures are to be understood in the context of the establishment of a Jewish state and the "Ingathering of the Exiles."

Those—politicians as well as historical and political theorists—who view human beings as actors in a historical drama, believe that the kibbutz movement, having fulfilled its "historical Zionist mission," will soon retire from the historical stage. This prediction is made both by those who admire the achievements of the kibbutz but view its demise (which they lament) as historically inevitable, as well as by those who have consistently opposed its extra-Zionist (social and political) goals and who, seizing upon its failures, look forward to (if not actively

1

work for) its end as the desirable consummation of a misguided experiment. Thus far, that experiment is one (to borrow from the title of Martin Buber's lead-off chapter in this volume) "that did not fail," and in my view its predicted demise, like the report of Mark Twain's death, has been greatly exaggerated.

To fully understand the papers in this volume, it is important to place the historical origin of the kibbutz not only in its Zionist context, but in its utopian context as well. The founders of the kibbutz movement were inspired by a twin vision: a vision not only of an old people reborn, but of a new society to be created. While the following chapters address some of the characteristics and dimensions of that society, I would like to say a few words about the vision that inspired its creation.

Although seldom included in any catalogue or list of characteristics which mark human beings as a unique species, I would nevertheless propose that the capacity to imagine an ideal state of existence is one of them. That this capacity is manifested in such diverse expressions as the fantasies of individuals, the theories of philosophers, the creations of novelists, and the myths and eschatologies of all religions, suggests that individuals and groups have a need to construct a vision of an ideal reality in which the perceived deficiencies of their immediate reality are temporarily overcome, if not permanently transcended. Both the capacity and the need comprise two of the distinctive attributes of *human* nature.

When the vision of such an ideal reality is projected as a group (and not merely as an individual) goal, conceived to be attainable by human (rather than divine) action, and believed to be achievable in the natural (rather than in a supernatural) order, it is usually designated as a *utopia*. Defined in that manner, the kibbutz movement had its origin in a utopian vision.

Most utopian visions share three characteristics. First, they seem to be a peculiarly Western phenomenon. Second, despite the proliferation of utopian visions in the West (certainly since the Enlightenment), there have been few attempts to actualize them. Third, the vast majority of utopian actualizations have been short-lived, coming to an end if not during, then shortly after the lifetime of their founder(s). Given these characteristics of utopian visions, the kibbutz founders were rare (if not unique) in attempting to actualize their vision, making their attempt in the East (although admittedly their vision had its origin in the West), and rather than coming to an end during their lifetime, the kibbutz movement (which initially, at least, embodied that vision) continues to survive in the third (and, in some cases, even the fourth) generation.

Realizing that their new society could not be successful unless its institutions were anchored in social actors whose values and motivational dispositions were radically different from those prevailing in the European society they had ideologically rejected and physically abandoned, the founders of the kibbutz developed a utopian vision which comprised nothing less than the creation of a "new man." Viewing human nature as essentially "good," they believed it was only necessary to strip Western man of the morally corrupting effects of bourgeois culture and urban civilization for the uncorrupted characteristics of human nature to be uncovered. (Like all other Zionist pioneers they too were innocent of the characteristics of Eastern man, an innocence whose historical and political consequences continue to reverberate in the State of Israel to this very day.) When the corrosive excrescences of capitalism and urbanism are removed—indeed, when capitalism and urbanism are replaced by socialism and a rural life—the essential characteristics of human nature, they believed, would be uncovered. These characteristics include love and kindness, fellowship and altruism, a placing of the good of the group over the good of the self.

To uncover those characteristics, the kibbutz founders created or at least attempted to create a socio-cultural system in which, consistent with their vision, science ("reason") rather than institutionalized religion ("superstition") informed its world view; cooperation, based on sentiments of brotherhood, was the dominant mode of social relations; goods and services were distributed according to the guiding principle of "from each according to his ability, to each according to his needs"; radical egalitarianism was practiced; social classes were abolished by the abolition of both hired labor and private property; pure democracy was practiced, and the rotation of leadership roles precluded anyone or any group from acquiring formal power over others; and in which children were freed from the domination of parents, and wives of husbands, through revolutionary changes in the institutions of marriage and the family.

To what extent those institutions were indeed put into effect, and to what extent the utopian vision was in fact implemented by these institutions, can be gauged to a considerable degree by the data presented in the following chapters. An equally important question—one which is not addressed in this volume—is the degree to which the kibbutz founders were successful in transmitting that vision and those institutions to their children and grandchildren. That an increasing number of the younger generation are leaving the kibbutz movement is well known. What is not known very well, are their motives for leaving. One can be committed to the original vision and the institutions of the kibbutz without, however, wanting to live in a small village, with one's parents, far from an urban center, together with the small group of people one has known intimately from birth, or in a community in which it is not always possible to pursue one's preferred profession or occupation, and so on. Whether the increasing resignations from the kibbutz are motivated by a rejection of kibbutz society as such, or by the wish to fulfill needs that are frustrated by the kibbutz characteristics which are tangential to its vision and institutions, is not very well known. Nor is it known to what extent the surrounding social environment—the 97 percent of the Israeli population who do not live in kibbutzim—has affected the motivation of the children and grandchildren of the kibbutz founders to remain in kibbutz society and to perpetuate either its vision or its institutions.

With the founding of the State of Israel and the process of "normalization," the hopes and disillusionments alike that were aroused by the Six-Day War, the conquest of and the need to rule over a hostage Arab population of the West Bank and Gaza, the absorption of a large non-Western immigrant population (that has now become a majority)—with all of these and more, Israel has undergone dramatic social and cultural changes that culminated in and are symbolized by the rise to political power of Menachem Begin and the Likud party.

Whatever one might think of these changes (or of their recent political expression) in the macro-social system of Israel, they have had a serious impact on the kibbutz movement and the self-image of their members. The cynosure of the Jewish population of Palestine and of the world Zionist movement (not to mention its symbolic importance for the European and American Left), the kibbutz movement has been the object of a radical shift in attitudes since the establishment of the State of Israel, ranging from indifference (many Israelis have never even visited a kibbutz) to derision (by those who view this movement as a relic of a never-to-be-recaptured past) to downright hostility (as was evidenced, especially on the part of the Sephardic populations of development towns, in the 1981 national elections). How these attitudinal changes affect the 3 percent of the population that lives in kibbutzim, and the even smaller percentage that comprises the second and third generations, is simply not known.

Still, whatever their effects on the increasing resignations from the kibbutz movement, and the soul-searching that its members have been undergoing as a result, it is nevertheless the case that this movement has been a highly successful enterprise by virtue of its longevity (compared to almost every other utopian movement), as well as any other criterion by which the success of social systems is judged. Expanding from one kibbutz with a few score members in 1910, to 240 kibbutzim with 100,000 members today, the kibbutz movement has proven to be an adaptive and a highly creative enterprise. Although comprising only 3 percent of the population of Israel, it produces 33 percent of the gross national farm product, 5 percent of the industrial product (even though industrialization is a relatively new phenomenon in the kibbutz movement) and 12 percent of the gross national product. Moreover, it has provided a disproportionately large percentge of Israel's military officers, members of parliament, and cabinet ministers. It has also created the best school system in the country, and has contributed more than its share to the country's pool of novelists, poets, artists, and the like, not to mention social scientists (some of whom are represented in this volume) and has "contributed" much less than its share to the delinquent and criminal population of Israel.

To return to the utopian vision that informed the establishment of the kibbutz movement, I wish to emphasize that many of the elements comprising that vision have undergone change. Whether the kibbutz has survived because of or in spite of those changes is a matter of debate, both within the movement as well as within the small group of scholars who have studied the kibbutz. Without entering into that debate, let me record some of those changes, some of which are addressed in the following chapters.

1. Kibbutz society has changed in many respects from a *Gemeinschaft* to a *Gesellschaft*, if not in structure, then in orientation. This is partly a function of an increasing size, and in part a function of the departure from the "group-dynamics" orientation (as I once called it) of the kibbutz founders, an orientation in which the group and its welfare were overriding values, and in which group interaction was a value in itself. To be with one's fellows at all times—to work with them during the day, dance and sing at night, and to share one's thoughts and feelings always—was of intrinsic importance in the early kibbutz. This group-dynamics orientation was manifested in and symbolized by the kibbutz dining room, the focus for and center of kibbutz life. The dining room was where one went (of course) to eat, but also—and more important—to listen to the one kibbutz radio, to play chess, to attend a concert, to read a newspaper, to be informed of one's work assignment for the next day, to dance (and in dance to express feelings and longings otherwise inhibited and unacknowledged), and above all to express one's need for and solidarity with one's fellows.

   Today that group-dynamics orientation is gone. With the replacement of the one-room by a three-room apartment (complete with stove, refrigerator, television set, hi-fi stereo, and comfortable and modern furniture), the dining room has lost its social function, and group-dynamics has been replaced by the dynamics of friendship (and kinship), whose expressions take place not in the public dining room but in the private apartments.

2. Kibbutz society has changed from an instrument—for Zionist and socialist revolution—to an end in itself. Very few younger members of a kibbutz will say, as the kibbutz founders said, that they live in a kibbutz to foster the goals of these two revolutionary movements. Rather, they say, they live there because it is home, that is where they were born and raised, and where they feel most comfortable.

3. Following from the above, kibbutz society has changed from an anticonsumption, indeed an ascetic, society, to a consumption-oriented society. Material comforts—in dress, housing, food, and in leisure activities—are actively sought rather than rejected as "bourgeois" goals unworthy of serious socialists. Indeed, one of the characteristics of the contemporary kibbutz—which is reflected in the image it has in the larger Israeli society— is its remarkably high standard of living.

4. Kibbutz society has changed from a nature-oriented to a production-oriented society. To work on and live by the produce of the land was the most important economic goal of the founders of the kibbutz movement. The land symbolized nature, and to work with one's hands on the land was the antithetic experience of the long Jewish diaspora which the kibbutz founders turned their backs on. The early kibbutz was rural and agricultural, and also non-technolgical and anti-industrial. That has all changed. Although

the kibbutz economy is still importantly agricultural, it is thoroughly technological, and rather than opposing industrialization, most kibbutzim have at least one industrial enterprise. The kibbutz industrial plant has replaced one or more of its agricultural branches, while the productivity of the machine has replaced the mystique of nature in the kibbutz *Weltanschauung*.

5. Kibbutz society has changed from one large ideo-emotional "family" to a society comprised of separate biological families. Rejecting their parents' values, the kibbutz founders physically abandoned them when they emigrated to Palestine. Family and kinship based on biological ties were replaced by comradeship based on ideological ties, and in some essential ways the kibbutz community became a surrogate "family." Again, all of that has changed. Marriage has become an increasingly important relationship; for many, the nuclear family has become a focal institution, and the ties of bilateral kinship have become centrally important both in informal social relationships as well as in pressure group politics.

6. Finally, kibbutz society has changed from its former emphasis on self-realization (*hagshama atzmit*) to the contemporary emphasis on self-actualization (*mimush atzmi*). Self-realization denotes a commitment to the implementation of the goals of Zionism and socialism by the act of joining a kibbutz and thereby realizing in oneself the achievement of those overriding group goals, even if it means the abandonment of personal ambitions. Self-actualization denotes, rather, the achievement of personal ambitions, and the kibbutz is valuable insofar as it is an effective instrument for the realization rather than the abandonment of those ambitions.

There are some who view these changes as destructive to the kibbutz vision and, hence, to the kibbutz itself. Others view them as an abandonment of the utopian elements in that vision and, therefore, the enhancement of the survival of kibbutz society and its core values. These changes, the latter claim, have occurred without any changes in those core values, viz., a commitment to equality, freedom, mutual aid, full democracy, and to a classless society. Which of these views is correct only the future will tell. For the present the chapters in this volume provide the basic information for judging which of these views more accurately characterizes the kibbutz today.

Social Research, Change, and the Kibbutz

Menachem Rosner

The twenty-two articles collected in this volume represent only a small fraction of the impressively large, and constantly growing, body of scholarly publications based on social scientific research on the Israeli kibbutz.[1] While the bulk of this research is relatively recent, it is possible to distinguish between studies employing different theoretical and methodological approaches in anthropology, sociology, and social psychology, and focusing on diverse aspects of the kibbutz as a unique social institution. This essay presents an analysis of these differences as they appear in the articles herein collected and in the social research on the kibbutz in general. In addition, this presentation is based on the assumption that beyond differences resulting from such disciplinary considerations, a significant factor shaping the nature of social research on the kibbutz has been the rapid changes in both the internal structure of the kibbutz and its relationship to the surrounding general society. Consequently, this introductory article seeks to link the discussion of the major changes in the kibbutz since the creation of the State of Israel with its analysis by social science researchers.[2]

The first comprehensive and organized research efforts to study the kibbutz were initiated in the early 1950s by two separate groups. During this period, a number of American anthropologists studied different kibbutzim quite independently of each other. In 1954, the Hebrew University Department of Sociology was invited to conduct a large-scale research project for the Ichud Hakibbutzim Federation under the direction of the late Yonina Talmon-Garber. A number of clear differences between these two research endeavors may be noted. The American anthropologists tended to focus on specific kibbutzim and on particularly problematic subjects. Melford Spiro, who presented one of the most comprehensive descriptions and analyses of the kibbutz system in his community study (1956), concentrated primarily on the study of the family (1954) and of education in the kibbutz (1960). Eva Rosenfeld's work (1951, 1957) focused on the study of stratification and changes in consumption patterns. R. D. Schwartz

7

dealt with the lack of formal law within the kibbutz (1954). Stanley Diamond (1957) compared the kibbutz culture with that of the small Eastern European Jewish *shtetl* (village) against which the founding generation of the kibbutz had rebelled.

The project directed by Yonina Talmon-Garber was designed to compare twelve kibbutzim characterized by distinct variations in the basic kibbutz social structure and value orientation. This study did not concentrate exclusively on specific subjects, but tried to develop a comprehensive and holistic approach to kibbutz society by studying the interrelation between the different institutional sectors within the kibbutz.

Methodologically, the anthropologists used primarily participant observation techniques, while the sociological study employed mainly survey research methods based on random sampling, questionnaires, etc.

For the anthropologists, the kibbutz was seen as a social laboratory in which the universality of particular social institutions could be tested. The best examples of this approach are represented in this volume by Spiro's attempt to test the universality of the family, and Rosenfeld's similar attempt—although based on opposite assumptions (as we will show later)—to test the universality of social stratification.

Yonina Talmon-Garber's theoretical orientation was that of historical sociology. As a student of Martin Buber, she saw the kibbutz as one link "in man's long chain of human efforts to realize in the 'here and now' a model of a good society." Her interest in the kibbutz was, therefore, a part of her larger interest in utopian and millenarian movements as well as in the sociology of religion.

The kibbutz's relative longevity and its social and economic achievements give it a special place among other historical and contemporary utopias and intentional communities or, as Buber puts it, "as an experiment that did not fail." However, the primary distinction between the kibbutz experience and such other communities and movements is the central role played by the kibbutz in the process of nation-building in Israel. This pattern of involvement and openness toward the surrounding society stands in stark contrast to the strategy of isolation, insulation and closure which most of the communal and utopian movements have deliberately chosen in order to assure their survival and the "pure" implementation of their values and ideals.

Talmon-Garber conceived of the kibbutz as a revolutionary movement—both national and social—and the framework for her study was Max Weber's theory of the routinization of charisma. Social change in the kibbutz is thus analyzed as a case of institutionalization of revolutionary values and ideologies, and as part of the common theoretical framework for the analysis of social change in specific institutions.

While the orientation of the American group was primarily theoretical, and the studies, published in English only, had no impact on kibbutz members, the

Talmon-Garber study was intended to assist the kibbutz federation, that cooperated in the study, in planning and guiding social change. In spite of this important difference, these two types of studies have an important common denominator which distinguishes them from many more recent studies. Both reflect a period in the kibbutz history that is characterized by doubts, self-questioning, and a sense of imminent crisis—a period which lasted from the establishment of the State of Israel, in 1948, until the early sixties.

During the years preceding the establishment of the state and especially during the War of Independence, the kibbutz played a prominent role in the process of nation building. From the middle of the thirties, most of the rural settlements established were kibbutzim. Their collective form of organization and their idealistic commitment were perceived as being particularly well suited to the conditions of insecurity and to the economic and environmental hardships to which they were exposed at that time. During the war, several kibbutzim came to be perceived as national symbols of heroism. Kibbutz members and those youths educated in the kibbutz-related movement played central roles both in the ghetto revolts and the partisan movements in Europe and in the Jewish underground-army in Palestine—the "Haganah" and the "Palmach"—before and during the War of Independence. In addition, a large part of the immigration of Jewish refugees from Europe after World War II was organized by kibbutz members as part of the struggle for independence. In 1948, the percentage of kibbutz residents in the Jewish population reached its highest point at 7 percent, thereby surpassing the 3–4 percent which was the peak during the thirty years following the establishment of the first kibbutz.

This situation changed dramatically during the fifties. The newly created state bureaucracy gradually took over the responsibility for the tasks in the areas of defense, settlement, and immigrant absorption, tasks that kibbutz members had previously performed within their unique framework of voluntary organization. These changes were considered as part of a trend toward centralization of power in the state administration and a weakening of the voluntary organizations that were dominant in the prestate period.

The mass immigration that increased the Jewish population by 137 percent between 1948 and 1955, contributed only to a limited extent to the growth of the kibbutzim during this period (by some 45 percent). Moreover, in the later stages of the postwar immigration, following the establishment of the state, the overwhelming majority of immigrants came from Arab countries and its masses practically passed over the kibbutz movement.

Between 1956 and 1962, the kibbutz population did not grow, and its relative size in the total Israeli population declined to 3.7 percent. Most of the new immigrants from Arab countries, who were not prepared to join kibbutzim, were settled in new moshavim, a much looser form of cooperative village (see the article by Joseph Ben-David). Toward the end of the fifties there was a rapid expansion of rural-agricultural settlement activities, with indications of an agricultural surplus, combined with a growing scarcity of production factors such as suitable land and water. Consequently, economists and political leaders concluded that the central national goal in the future should be industrialization—a process traditionally linked with urbanization. This change in national priorities had a direct impact on the traditional function of the kibbutz movement of transforming highly educated youths into farmers and agricultural workers. Furthermore, while in the past the majority of the immigrants to Israel had come with a middle-class and professional background, raising the question of who would perform the nonskilled physical work in the country, the new mass immigration created a surplus of nonskilled workers.

This dramatic shift in the occupational structure also had its impact on the stratification structure of the Israeli society at large. In the past, the surplus of professionals as well as ideological considerations, created a rather egalitarian distribution of income that was also consistent with the egalitarian principles of the kibbutz and was perceived as one of the traits of Israeli socialism. At the end of the fifties, the increase of nonskilled laborers, mainly of oriental origin, and the growing demand for college-educated professionals as part of the processes of modernization and industrialization, created the background for the legitimization of demands for a growing inequality in salaries.

These processes were the catalysts for questions from both inside and outside the kibbutzim during this period. Could the kibbutz movement still fulfill a central pioneering role? Some of the traditional roles of training educated youths for agricultural and manual labor now seemed superfluous. Moreover, it seemed possible that government bodies and other forms of settlements such as the moshav or development towns might be more successful in assuring secure borders, absorbing immigrants, and in creating new settlements.

In the past, the development of the kibbutz movement was facilitated by its membership in a widespread network of voluntary organizations and institutions connected with the Histadrut, the Jewish Federation of Labor, which formed a kind of safety belt around the kibbutz. At the end of the fifties, however, it seemed that the position of these labor organizations had weakened and that their commitment to communal and egalitarian principles had been replaced by a trade-unionist struggle for higher wages on an unequal basis.

Given these developments, another fundamental question was added to those mentioned earlier: would it prove possible to maintain and develop an egalitarian and communal subculture in a society losing its special pioneering and egalitarian attributes and developing toward a "normal" capitalist state?

This type of self-examination and doubts about the future viability were not limited to the relationship between the kibbutz and the surrounding society. In the fifties, significant internal changes occurred in many kibbutzim as a result of growing heterogeneity and processes of internal differentiation. Most of the kibbutzim started as small groups of young people, mainly bachelors, who were highly committed to the ideology and the collective goals of the kibbutz with its nondifferentiated, primarily agricultural occupational structure.

In the fifties, several social subgroups based on age and country of origin could be distinguished in many kibbutzim. The family also evolved as an important social unit, and a more permanent division of labor and professional differentiation emerged in the still predominantly agricultural economy. Analytically, these two steps have been "constructed" as two different ideal types of social structure—the *Bund* versus the *Commune* (Talmon-Garber, 1972).

The doubts concerning the role of the kibbutz in the Israeli society and its future, as well as the influx of new immigrants as members who were not socialized in the kibbutz youth movements, resulted, in some kibbutzim, in a lowering of commitment toward the basic kibbutz value structure and in a different interpretation of these values. In some of the older kibbutzim, efforts towards economic development and achievement came to be perceived as the new primary form of making a "pioneering" contribution to the economic independence of the new state, while the younger kibbutzim were still occupied in performing the traditional pioneering roles of settlement, defense, and so on.

Questions related to the character of Israeli society—state initiative versus voluntarism, socialism versus capitalist normalization, and the like—stressed the importance of political issues. Thus, in the early fifties, a split, based on political differences, occurred in one of the main federations as well as in a number of individual communities. This split contributed to a further weakening of the status of the kibbutz in the Israeli society, as well as of the collective self-image of kibbutz members themselves. Such was the historical background against which several of the first studies on the kibbutz were conducted.

In his analysis of the kibbutz, Martin Buber stressed the "nonfailure" of this experiment, contrasting it with many socialist, cooperative, and communal experiments that clearly did fail. He emphasized that the primary reason for this "nonfailure" was the nondogmatic character of the kibbutz ideology. "The men did not, as everywhere else in the history of cooperative settlements, bring a plan with them, a plan which the concrete situation could only fill out, but not modify. Their ideal gave an impetus but no dogmas; it stimulated but did not dictate."

This nondogmatic character, the ability to adapt structures and institutions to changing conditions, while preserving the essential values, was not always perceived by social scientists studying the kibbutz during the crisis or transition period. Trying to test several theories in the kibbutz setting sometimes leads to extreme conclusions, such as Melford Spiro's early suggestion that the "kibbutz constitutes an exception to the generalization concerning the universality of the family, structurally viewed." This exception was possible, he suggested, since kibbutz members perceived each other psychologically as kin, and the kibbutz functioned, therefore, as one large extended family. Several years later, Spiro published an addendum in which he offered an alternative interpretation suggesting that Murdock's definition of marriage, that served as his starting point, should be revised, and that the social unit of cohabiting adults of opposite sex in the kibbutz should be called "marriage" even if one of Murdock's criteria was missing.

While Spiro saw marriage and family in the kibbutz as an exceptional case which might lead to a modification of general theoretical propositions, another American researcher studying kibbutzim in the same period came to different conclusions. According to Eva Rosenfeld's interpretation, the processes of internal differentiation and institutional change in the kibbutz support the functional theory of stratification. Despite the egalitarian ideology of the kibbutz, at least two distinct social strata can be observed. Paradoxically, although there is equality in the distribution of material rewards, a kind of class struggle can be discerned, leading to institutional change. The development of social strata according to the functional position is related to both the differential functional importance of social roles and the scarcity of personnel able to fulfill the more important positions. Shortly after the publication of Rosenfeld's article, doubts began to be raised about the interpretation of these findings. Yonina Talmon-Garber stated, on the basis of her much larger and more comprehensive study, that attempts to analyze her research material in terms of a division between elite and nonelite failed completely (Talmon, 1972). Nevertheless, even in a recent study, Rosenfeld's article is cited as an important empirical test of the universal functional need for stratification (Treiman, 1977).

Yet, while Spiro was underestimating the processes of social differentiation and Rosenfeld perhaps exaggerating its significance, another American researcher, Ivan Vallier, stressed the opposition between the trends of social differentiation, at least in the economic area, and the basic values and structure of the kibbutz. In Vallier's opinion, "these communes because of a unique historical situation, illustrate a sociological problem which may be referred to as 'value pattern inappropriateness'." The moral values on which the kibbutz is based are the polar opposites of values that are functional for a production unit. The implicit conclusion is, therefore, that if the kibbutzim wish to preserve their original values they will not be able to perform as efficient production units. On the other hand, giving priority to production makes the hiring of outside labor imperative, introduces hierarchy, formality, and specialization, leading to deviation from the basic kibbutz values and to a change in the communal pattern.

The common denominator of the three aforementioned articles is the anthropological method, and in each case only a single kibbutz was studied. Despite this very severe constraint, the researchers sought to test, or at least to reach for, general theoretical conclusions.

Two other articles dealing with the same historical period, by Yonina Talmon-Garber and Amitai Etzioni, who participated in the same research project, are based on survey data in which a large number of individual members were interviewed in a sample of twelve kibbutzim from one of the major kibbutz federations. One of the striking differences in the results was that while Spiro considered the kibbutz community as an extended family and questioned the existence of nuclear families, Talmon-Garber detected a growing familistic trend. She even hinted that this might endanger the integration of the community and the authority of the communal institutions in areas such as education, consumption, and the like. Analyzing the trend toward growing familism, Talmon-Garber stressed the sociological roots of the phenomenon both inside and outside the kibbutz. She argued that the decline in intensity of collective identification leads to an increasing significance of the family which is being perceived as a major source of emotional gratification. This, she suggested, is part of a more general trend toward the increasing legitimization of the autonomy of subgroups, among them the family. The improvement of material conditions and the growing number of children increased the number of common tasks and responsibility of family members.

Talmon-Garber's analysis of the familistic trend, however, is not deterministic and uni-directional. On the contrary, she stressed that certain mechanisms were introduced deliberately by kibbutzim to satisfy what was viewed as legitimate needs of kibbutz members. Such steps were also taken to limit the fulfillment of basic individual needs by familial solutions instead of within the kibbutz's joint community framework. A good example of this is the improvement of the communal dining facilities intended to avert the move from the dining room to the family apartment. Talmon-Garber claimed that despite the strength of the familistic trend, there were notable instances where reorganization—or secondary institutionalization—had led to its partial reversal.

The sociobiological explanation of the trend toward the family, represented in this volume by Joseph Shepher and Lionel Tiger's essay, fits into the framework of the earliest group of studies, although it deals with the interpretation of research done in the 1960s and 1970s. We take this position since Shepher and Tiger use the kibbutz as do Spiro and Rosenfeld, as a social laboratory for universal theories. It is worthwhile to note that in addition to Tiger and Shepher, several of their critics (Mednick, 1975) also see a test case in the kibbutz, while others (Kanter, 1976; Rosner and Palgi, 1982) stress the uniqueness of the historical, economic, and social conditions of the kibbutz and the difficulty of generalizing from its experience. As in their previous book, *Women in the Kibbutz* (1975), the authors perceive the women in the kibbutz as the main instigators of the familial process. They explain women's attitudes by means of biological factors. In their book, the "biogrammar" of women was their basic explanatory variable for the biological argument. After reconsideration, the authors have retreated from their earlier, more extreme position. In their later essay, they stress that the higher parental investment of women—a result of mammilarian physiology—is the primary explanatory variable for the "double phenomenon of polarization of sexual division of labor and familialization.'' These socio-biological interpretations have initiated a fierce and a continuing debate and controversy among social scientists that is beyond the scope of this essay. One school of critics of the sociobiological interpretation is mentioned here. Alternative critiques have been offered by Gerson (1978) and Buber-Aggasi (1979). On the other hand, Spiro (1979) has offered an interpretation that is basically similar to the sociobiological position of Shepher and Tiger.

Amitai Etzioni's study of the processes of elite differentiation in the kibbutz uses the theoretical framework of functional differentiation developed by Talcott Parsons in studying the development of organizational structures in the kibbutz. While Etzioni's first and more detailed (Hebrew) version of this article had an applied intention in guiding the kibbutzim in ''organizational development,'' the article included in this volume analyzes the different stages of elite differentiation. The author's conclusion is that while elite roles emerge and differentiate according to ''functional'' requirements, the ''specialization'' of kibbutz members into different types of elite roles occurs in a later stage. Similar to the above-mentioned statement by Talmon-Garber, that no clear division between elite and nonelite members can be discerned, Etzioni's conclusion is that in most kibbutzim the holding of elite roles has not become a basis for the formation of solidaric ties and subcollectivities.

While the articles mentioned up to now deal with the first above-mentioned historical period, most of the other articles in this collection deal with the developments in the second period that brought fundamental changes both in the internal structure of the kibbutz and in its status within the fabric of the larger Israeli society.

In contrast to the period of self-examination and crisis during the fifties, the first years of the sixties showed signs of being a turning-point in the kibbutz adaptation to the new conditions and changes in its social and economic structure. Their first expression was the growth of population, primarily as a result of the increasing number of kibbutz-born adults who joined the kibbutz as regular members, following their military service.

Between 1962 and 1967, the kibbutzim population increased by 13 percent and the number of members by 20 percent. From the beginning of the sixties onwards, most of the kibbutzim were becoming multigeneration communities with members of different generations and age-groups living together in a relatively small community, and maintaining equality in all spheres of social life, as well as in the decision-making process accomplished by the general assembly and by the various committees. This integration was often accompanied by internal tensions within the kibbutz movement, expressed mainly on the ideological plane. However, this tension also contributed substantially to the regeneration of the movement and to the efforts to overcome the crisis.

These tensions have been interpreted by some observers as a conflict between the attitudes and values of the second generation—which deviate from the original ideology—and the "dogmatic" ideological conservatism of the founding generation. Erik Cohen and Menachem Rosner, however, offer an alternative interpretation, arguing that the original ideology, far from being a monolithic and well-integrated whole, actually contained many inconsistencies and contradictions. The second generation can therefore be seen as playing a creative role in the process of ideological clarification and reformulation which is functional in the adaption of the kibbutz to changing social conditions. The second generation places a much stronger emphasis on the kibbutz as a home rather than a social experiment, on human content rather than institutional forms, the individual rather than the collective. The authors stress the difference between the structural factors in the social background of the founders who had rejected the existing "outside" society by creating the kibbutz and the second generation who perceive the kibbutz as a fact, as a way of life like any other and struggle to endow their lives with meaning within the setting of a socialist, communitarian movement.[3]

In this connection, Reuven Kahane's essay is particularly relevant. He stresses the contribution of the kibbutz educational system in developing the particular approach of pragmatic idealism prevalent among the kibbutz-born generation, and based on a mixture of individualistic and collectivistic orientations. He suggests that a certain inconsistency exists in the educational goals, and that a multiplicity of socialization agents stress different orientations. The resulting tensions, he concludes, may help to explain the high need for achievement among the kibbutz-born youths.

The stress on achievement and independence in kibbutz education is also one of the unanticipated findings in the research done by Edward Devereux and his colleagues, comparing socialization practices in the kibbutz with those in the Israeli city. The authors connect these traits of the kibbutz educational system with its capacity to produce committed, cooperative kibbutzniks, and also a very large share of the nation's political and military leadership.

The "pragmatic idealism" of the second generation and its strong achievement orientation apparently contributed to the rapid process of kibbutz industrialization that started in the sixties. About 80 percent of the 290 existing kibbutz enterprises were established beginning with the early sixties. At this time, too, a new direction in the selection of types of industry could be discerned. Priority was accorded to capital-intensive and science-based industries, since the number of workers demanded by them was much more compatible with the ability of the kibbutzim to supply them from within its own membership. (The majority of outside employees hired by kibbutz industries are therefore still concentrated in enterprises established before this period.)[4]

The success of the process of industrialization in the kibbutzim offered rural employment to the growing population in the face of the above-mentioned limitations imposed upon agricultural development. Thus, the desertion of villages—a common occurrence in countries undergoing accelerated industrialization—was prevented. Consequently, the percentage of the kibbutz in the Jewish rural population again began to increase continuously (from 21 percent in 1961 to 35.6 percent in 1976). The industrialization process, together with the increasing rate of productivity in agricultural branches, where the number of workers has hardly grown, augmented the portion of the kibbutz in the gross national product to a degree greatly outweighing their share in the population (33 percent of the agricultural output and 6 percent of the industrial output against only 3.3 percent of the Jewish population).

Industrialization also enhances the contribution of the kibbutz economy to the struggle of Israel for economic independence. While the part of kibbutz industry in export significantly outweighs its part in production, the kibbutz industry production developed until 1976 at a rate surpassing that of Israeli industry as a whole and continues to grow.

The accelerated industrialization process is documented and analyzed by David Barkin and John W. Bennett as an example of the ability of the kibbutz movement to respond to both outside economic pressures and internal demographic and social changes. This ability of the kibbutz to adapt to changes in the surrounding society is compared with the isolationist ideology of the American Hutterite colonies. The change in attitudes toward higher education for members is presented as another example of the difference between the Hutterite attempts to "isolate" themselves from the surrounding society and the kibbutz orientation toward involvement in it. This dramatic change occurred at the end of the sixties in response to both the aspirations of second generation members toward self-realization and development, and the requirements of changing agricultural technologies and of the growing industrialization.

Between 1969 and 1973, the number of students in higher education institutions increased four-fold. Every year about 5 percent of the kibbutz members receive post-secondary school education compatible with their personal wishes and the needs of the kibbutz. In the past, the general assumption was that higher education would alienate members from fulfilling roles in the kibbutz labor framework, increase the number of people working outside the kibbutz and eventually even leaving it. It has become clear, however, that most of the students are reintegrated into kibbutz roles on returning from their studies, and that the number of students who leave is even lower than the general percentage of members leaving.

The processes of growth and inter-generational differentiation as well as of internal role differentiation connected to industrialization and professionalization, raise the question of the possibility of maintaining the communal character of the kibbutz and its egalitarian and direct democratic institutions in this changing environment.

Erik Cohen's article further develops the structural typology of kibbutzim that was originally conceived by Talmon-Garber in the comparison between different kibbutzim. Talmon-Garber based her typology on Toennies's classical distinction between *Gemeinschaft* ("commune") and *Gesellschaft* ("association") but assumed that there are no kibbutzim of the association type. She, therefore, differentiated only three subtypes of "communes" among the more mature kibbutzim—unified, federated and segmentary. In addition to this she used the ideal-type of *Bund* ("communion"), developed by Schmalenbach (1961) to characterize young kibbutzim in their first stage of development. Erik Cohen assumes that the mature and large kibbutzim are in a process of transition from "commune" towards "association": that corresponds with Toennies's *Gesellschaft* ideal-type. "The very economic and organizational success of the kibbutz led to a thorough-going transformation of its social structure, of its way of life and of the relationship between its members. As an ongoing enterprise, the modern kibbutz is a success but it is not the realization of the original utopia."

The differences between this evaluation, written in the early seventies, and that of Ivan Vallier's article, written a decade earlier, is striking. While Vallier emphasizes the inability of the kibbutz to operate successfully as an economic unit because of basic "value pattern inappropriateness," Erik Cohen stresses the problems related to the very economic success of the kibbutz that Vallier had denied as possible.

The social processes of growing complexity, specialization and professionalization are analyzed from different theoretical perspectives by Ephraim Yuchtman and Eliezer Ben-Rafael. Yuchtman assumes that the processes of role differentiation and professionalism may lead to a transition from equality to equity in the distribution of rewards. His interpretation is based on his empirical findings showing that "kibbutz branch managers, despite enjoying greater intrinsic and extrinsic rewards, tend to be less attracted than the rank and file to their jobs." The author assumes that while equality prevails in the distribution of material rewards, the likelihood of equity increases "as the group becomes more preoccupied with external problems of adaptation and goal attainment and as considerations of rationality, objectivity and efficiency dominate."

Ben-Rafael defines the kibbutz in the framework of stratification theory as a primary community constituting a collective entrepreneur and belonging to a sectional status group within the Israeli society. According to him a major tension in the kibbutz stratification system stems from the fact that the aspirations of kibbutz members to increase their collective wealth create internal power and prestige differentiations inside the kibbutz community. He considers that this tension constitutes, in the final analysis, a particular case only of a more general problem common to all modern and free societies, namely, the basic contradiction between democratic and egalitarian values and the "spirit of capitalism."

The meaning of the "spirit of capitalism" in Ben-Rafael's conceptualization is different from the more general concepts of rationalization, modernization, functional differentiation, and economic efficiency used by Vallier, Cohen, Yuchtman, and others. But despite these differences in formulation and in the theoretical framework applied, the assumption of an inherent conflict between economic progress and success and the communal values of equality and democracy is held by all the above-mentioned authors.

An alternative approach to this fundamental problem can be found in the contributions of Leviatan and of Rosner and Cohen. Uri Leviatan examines the phenomenon of managerial personnel turnover and its effects upon the conduct of kibbutz farm branches and industrial plants. His major findings are that organizations that practice rotation are no less, and perhaps are even more, efficient than those that do not. This startling conclusion argues that workers in such enterprises tend to be more involved, knowledgeable, and creative than those in nonrotating kibbutzim. These findings seem to contradict the above-mentioned, almost universally held, belief about the conflict between the implementation of kibbutz values and economic efficiency. At least within the special framework of the kibbutz, the conformity to the egalitarian norm of managerial rotation seems to be positively correlated with economic success.

The article by Menachem Rosner and Nissim Cohen deals with the assumption that growing internal differentiation and complexity might lead to a "degeneration" of the central element in the mechanism of kibbutz direct democracy—the weekly general assembly. A comparison between two groups of kibbutzim with relatively high and low attendance at the assembly shows that these differences can be explained by differences in the degree of members' ideological commitment and of the kibbutz's social solidarity, and are independent of structural differentiation and technological rationality. Well-functioning general assemblies were found in some of the largest, most complex, and differentiated kibbutzim when these conditions did exist.

Therefore, the authors conclude that in the kibbutz, the degree of implementation of egalitarian and democratic values is not necessarily sacrificed for the processes of modernization and rationalization. Kibbutz ideology plays an active and a creative role in the choice of technologies and organizational patterns adopted.

While assumptions based on a universal logic of modernization and industrialization are implicit in some of the articles as to the future development of the kibbutz, a series of steps that were taken during the sixties and especially the seventies point in opposite directions. The choice of technologies and products that are most often adopted are increasingly compatible with the aspirations of kibbutz members and do not require the employment of outside-hired labor. The continuing decline in employment of such outside-hired labor and the development of democratic and nonhierarchic patterns of industrial management based on sociotechnical criteria are examples of such steps. In many cases, this growing conformity to kibbutz values did not result in loss of economic efficiency but even enhanced it, as was stated recently by an Israeli economist: "The secret of the economic success of the kibbutz is its ideology" (Don, 1981).

Some of these results might be related to the special kibbutz conditions in which the lack of individual material rewards enhances the importance of intrinsic job satisfaction, participation in decision making, etc. as motivational factors, and might, therefore, be interpreted in the framework of contingency theory (Perrow, 1972). According to this theory, no single organizational model will be optimal in all situations. While the contingency factors—stressed in organizational theory—to which the organization has to adapt are mainly technology, work force characteristics, and market structure, the unconventional kibbutz conditions stress the importance of values and social structure. Another possible interpretation of these kibbutz findings attributes to them a more universal significance. New organizational theories and more general theories of postindustrial society question the functionality of the conventional bureaurcratic and hierarchical organization model based on centralization, narrow specialization, standardization, etc. The kibbutz model of organization, based on its original values and adapted to modern conditions, may therefore be seen as a forerunner of more general trends towards participatory democracy, nonbureaucratic organization, and improved quality of working life.[5] These developments are also relevant to the changing role of the kibbutz in the Israeli society.

The most astonishing development in kibbutz life has been its economic success and the rise in its standard of living. In the fifties, most of the kibbutzim had to struggle with economic hardships, and the standard of living was lower than the average of the general population. The dramatic improvement of its collective economic status has had an ambivalent impact on the general status of the kibbutz in the society. In terms of the positive values placed on economic achievement in the Israeli society, one could expect a rise in prestige of the kibbutz. On the other hand, this success highlights the contradiction between the ideological self-definition and perception of the kibbutz as part of the working class, its organizational affiliation with socialist labor parties and the General Federation of Labor, and its objective status in the upper brackets of the income hierarchy as well as being the owners, although collectively, of means of production.

This inconsistency is exacerbated by the ethnic factor which has become increasingly salient in Israeli society's class structure. While today most of the workers in agriculture and industry in Israel are from oriental Sephardi communities, kibbutz members who work in the same occupations are predominantly of western Ashkenazi origin. A threefold cleavage exists threfore between the kibbutz and a large part of the Israeli working class. The kibbutz members are of different ethnic origin, enjoy a relatively high standard of living, and are owners of means of production who sometimes employ hired labor.

The fact that the kibbutzim have an important role in the socialist worker parties that ruled Israel in its first thirty years of existence, has also reinforced the image of the kibbutz as part of the ruling establishment, consisting mainly of those of Ashkenazi origin.

In recent years, efforts have been made to increase the consistency between the ideological self-definition of the kibbutzim and their social and economic actions. The decrease in the number of hired workers, deliberate efforts toward cooperation with the neighboring development towns—mostly of oriental origin—and toward recruitment of members of oriental origin are steps in this direction. But although in the last four years the Labor party has been in the opposition, the 1981 elections showed that the kibbutzim continue to be perceived by their neighbors as part of the establishment.

These developments raise several serious questions concerning the future role of the kibbutz movement in the Israeli society. The economic success of the kibbutzim has demonstrated that they are not a conservative force held over from the prestate period but fulfill an important economic function.

On the other hand, while the economic success of the kibbutzim is widely known, large portions of the Israeli population are not aware of the "postindustrial" character of the kibbutz values and its organizational structure, as stressed in this volume by Naphtali Golomb and Daniel Katz. This lack of awareness is surely related to the actual stage of development of the Israeli society. While Golomb and Katz stress the above-mentioned trend of large-scale organizations to develop in the direction of kibbutz principles of egalitarianism, voluntarism and democracy, the prevaling trend in Israeli society seems to be toward inequality, bureaucratic centralism and nonparticipatory democracy.

Future developments in Israeli society will determine whether the kibbutz will have to continue competing in the economic market to assure the survival of its noneconomic and unconventional values, or if it will once again be able to assume an important role in shaping the future of the Israeli society.

The articles included in this volume present analyses of the developments in different areas of the kibbutz society during the first thirty years of the existence of the State of Israel. Despite the different disciplines and divergent theoretical orientations employed, there is a high degree of consensus as to the basic difficulties faced by the kibbutz in the past and present. There is, however, less agreement about future trends. We hope that these analyses will contribute to a better understanding both of the unique features of the kibbutz society and of the more general sociological lessons that can be learned from this experience. While the articles included in this book cover most aspects of kibbutz life, other aspects such as aging, consumption, and relations with the Israeli society have not been included due to lack of space or lack of studies done in these fields.

This volume can, therefore, serve both as an introduction to the growing scientific literature on the kibbutz and as a challenge to study new or neglected areas.

Notes

1. The recently published bibliography on the kibbutz, of scientific works in languages other than Hebrew (Shur et al., 1981), comprises 951 items, while the bibliography of scientific publications in Hebrew (Shur, 1980) comprises 585 items.
2. The first sociological study on the kibbutz (Landshut, 1944) was published 34 years after the foundation of Degania, the first kibbutz.
3. Most of the theoretical assumptions expressed in this article have been empirically corroborated in the large research on the second generation that started in the late sixties and early seventies (Rosner et al., 1978).
4. The percentages of hired workers in kibbutz factories decreased between 1969 and 1977 from 52 to 41%, while the number of factories increased from 164 to 287. (In the factories belonging to the Ichud Federation employing the largest number of hired workers, the development during this period was even more dramatic: the percentage of hired workers decreased from 76 to 61 percent, while the number of factories increased from 45 to 97.) The same trends continue up until now. A detailed analysis of this change in the industrialization process is presented in Leviatan and Rosner (1980).
5. An international conference has been centered around this relationship between the kibbutz experience and the above-mentioned general trends (Cherns, 1980). The assumption of the relevance of the kibbutz experience for advanced industrial society has also influenced the recent institutionalization of the scientific interest in the kibbutz: witness the creation of an Academic Council for Kibbutz Studies in the United States and the Project for Kibbutz Studies at Harvard University. This approach is also expressed in a recent comprehensive study of one kibbutz-community (Blasi, 1980).

Bibliography

Blasi, Joseph R. (1980). *The Communal Future: The Kibbutz and the Utopian Dilemma.* Norwood, Pa.: Norwood Editions.

Buber-Agassi, Judith (1979). "Kibbutz and sex roles." *Crossroads* 4:145-75.

Cherns, Albert (ed.) (1980). *Quality of Working Life and The Kibbutz Experience.* Proceedings on an International Conference in Israel. Norwood, Pa.: Norwood Editions.

Diamond, Stanley (1957). "Kibbutz and shtetl: the history of an idea." *Social Problems* 5(2):71–99.

Don, Yehuda (1981). *The Economics of Transformation from Agricultural to Agro-Industrial Production Cooperatives (The Case of the Israeli Kibbutz).* Ramat-Gan: Bar-Ilan University, Department of Economics.

Gerson, Menachem (1978). *Family, Women and Socialization in the Kibbutz.* Lexington, Mass.: Lexington Books.

SHANAHAN LIBRARY
MARYMOUNT MANHATTAN COLLEGE
221 EAST 71 STREET
W YORK, NY 1002?

Kanter, Rossabeth M. (1976). "Interpreting the results of a social experiment." *Science* 192:662–63.

Landshut, Sigfried (1944). *The Kibbutz Community*. Jerusalem: The Institute for Zionist Education (Hebrew).

Leviatan, Uri; Rosner, M. (eds.) (1980). *Work and Organization in Kibbutz Industry*. Norwood, Pa.: Norwood Editions.

Mednick, Martha T. Shuch (1975). "Social change and sex role inertia: the case of the kibbutz." In Mednick, M.T.S., Tangri, S., and Hoffman, L. W., *Women and Achievement: Social and Motivational Analysis*. New York: Wiley & Sons.

Perrow, Charles (1972). *Complex Organizations*. Glencoe, Ill.: Scott Foresman.

Rosenfeld, Eva (1951). "Social stratification in a classless society." *American Sociological Review* 16(6): 766–74.

Rosenfeld, Eva (1957). "Institutional change in the kibbutz." *Social Problems* 5(2):110–36.

Rosner, Menachem; Palgi, Michal (1982). "Equality of sexes in the kibutz—regression or new meaning?" In Palgi, M., Blasi, J., Rosner, M., and Saphir, M. (eds.), *Sex-Role Equality in the Kibbutz: The Test of the Theories?* Norwood, Pa.: Norwood Editions. In press.

Rosner, M.; Ben-David, J.; Avnat, A.; Cohen, N.; Leviatan, U. (1978). *The Second Generation*. Tel-Aviv: Sifriat Hapoalim (Hebrew).

Schmalenbach, Herman (1961). "The Sociological Category of Communion." In Parsons, T., et al. (eds.), *Theories of Society*, vol. I. Glencoe, Ill.: Free Press.

Schwartz, Richard D. (1954). "Social factors in the development of legal control: a case study of two Israeli settlements." *Yale Law Journal* 63(4):471–91.

Shur, Shimon; Beit-Hallahmi, B.; Blasi, J. R.; Rabin, A. L.; (1981). *The Kibbutz: A Bibliography of Scientific and Professional Publications in English*. Norwood, Pa.: Norwood Editions.

Spiro, Melford E. (1954). "Is the family universal?" *American Anthropologist* 56:839–46.

Spiro, Melford E. (1956). *Kibbutz: Venture in Utopia*. Cambridge, Mass.: Harvard University Press.

Spiro, Melford E. (1965). *Children of the Kibbutz*. New York: Schocken.

Spiro, Melford E. (1979). *Gender and Culture: Kibbutz Women Revisited*. Durham, N.C.: Duke University Press.

Talmon-Garber, Yonina (1972). "Differentiation and elite formation." In Talmon. Y., *Family and Community in the Kibbutz*. Cambridge, Mass.: Harvard University Press.

Tiger, Lionel; Shepher, Joseph (1975). *Women in the Kibbutz*. New York: Harcourt, Brace & Jovanovich.

Treiman, Donald J. (1977). *Occupational Prestige in Comparative Perspective*. New York: Academic Press.

THE CONCEPT AND DEVELOPMENT OF THE KIBBUTZ

An Experiment That Did Not Fail

Martin Buber

THE era of advanced Capitalism has broken down the structure
of society. The society which preceded it was composed of
different societies; it was complex, and pluralistic in structure.
This is what gave it its peculiar social vitality and enabled it to
resist the totalitarian tendencies inherent in the pre-revolu-
tionary centralistic State, though many elements were very
much weakened in their autonomous life. This resistance was
broken by the policy of the French Revolution, which was
directed against the special rights of all free associations. Thereafter centralism in its new, capitalistic form succeeded where
the old had failed: in atomizing society. Exercising control over
the machines and, with their help, over the whole society,
Capitalism wants to deal only with individuals; and the modern
State aids and abets it by progressively dispossessing groups of
their autonomy. The militant organizations which the proletariat
erected against Capitalism—Trades Unions in the economic
sphere and the Party in the political—are unable in the nature of
things to counteract this process of dissolution, since they have
no access to the life of society itself and its foundations: production and consumption. Even the transfer of capital to the
State is powerless to modify the social structure, even when
the State establishes a network of compulsory associations,
which, having no autonomous life, are unfitted to become the
cells of a new socialist society.

From this point of view the heart and soul of the Co-operative Movement is to be found in the trend of a society towards
structural renewal, the re-acquisition, in new tectonic forms,
of the internal social relationships, the establishment of a new
consociatio consociationum. It is (as I have shown) a fundamental error to view this trend as romantic or utopian merely

because in its early stages it had romantic reminiscences and utopian fantasies. At bottom it is thoroughly topical and constructive; that is to say, it aims at changes which, in the given circumstances and with the means at its disposal, are feasible. And, psychologically speaking, it is based on one of the eternal human needs, even though this need has often been forcibly suppressed or rendered insensible: the need of man to feel his own house as a room in some greater, all-embracing structure in which he is at home, to feel that the other inhabitants of it with whom he lives and works are all acknowledging and confirming his individual existence. An association based on community of views and aspirations alone cannot satisfy this need; the only thing that can do that is an association which makes for communal living. But here the co-operative organization of production or consumption proves, each in its own way, inadequate, because both touch the individual only at a certain point and do not mould his actual life. On account of their merely partial or functional character all such organizations are equally unfitted to act as cells of a new society. Both these partial forms have undergone vigorous development, but the Consumer Co-operatives only in highly bureaucratic forms and the Producer Co-operatives in highly specialized forms: they are less able to embrace the whole life of society to-day than ever. The consciousness of this fact is leading to the synthetic form: the Full Co-operative. By far the most powerful effort in this direction is the Village Commune, where communal living is based on the amalgamation of production and consumption, production being understood not exclusively as agriculture alone but as the organic union of agriculture with industry and with the handicrafts as well.

The repeated attempts that have been made during the last 150 years, both in Europe and America, to found village settlements of this kind, whether communistic or co-operative in the narrower sense, have mostly met with failure.[1] I would apply the word "failure" not merely to those settlements, or attempts at settlements, which after a more or less short-lived existence either disintegrated completely or took on a Capitalist complexion, thus going over to the enemy camp; I would also

[1]Of course, I am not dealing here with the otherwise successful "socio-economic organizations, used by governmental or semi-governmental agencies to improve rural conditions" (Infield, *Co-operative Communities at Work*, p. 63).

apply it to those that maintained themselves in isolation. For the real, the truly structural task of the new Village Communes begins with their *federation*, that is, their union under the same principle that operates in their internal structure. Hardly anywhere has it come to this. Even where, as with the Dukhobors in Canada, a sort of federative union exists, the federation itself continues to be isolated and exerts no attractive and educative influence on society as a whole, with the result that the task never gets beyond its beginnings and, consequently, there can be no talk of success in the socialist sense. It is remarkable that Kropotkin saw in these two elements—isolation of the settlements from one another and isolation from the rest of society—the efficient causes of their failure even as ordinarily understood.

The socialistic task can only be accomplished to the degree that the new Village Commune, combining the various forms of production and uniting production and consumption, exerts a structural influence on the amorphous urban society. The influence will only make itself felt to the full if, and to the extent that, further technological developments facilitate and actually require the decentralization of industry; but even now a pervasive force is latent in the modern communal village, and it may spread to the towns. It must be emphasized again that the tendency we are dealing with is constructive and topical: it would be romantic and utopian to want to destroy the towns, as once it was romantic and utopian to want to destroy the machines, but it is constructive and topical to try to transform the town organically in the closest possible alliance with technological developments and to turn it into an aggregate composed of smaller units. Indeed, many countries to-day show significant beginnings in this respect.

As I see history and the present, there is only one all-out effort to create a Full Co-operative which justifies our speaking of success in the socialistic sense, and that is the Jewish Village Commune in its various forms, as found in Palestine. No doubt it, too, is up against grave problems in the sphere of internal relationships, federation, and influence on society at large, but it alone has proved its vitality in all three spheres. Nowhere else in the history of communal settlements is there this tireless groping for the form of community-life best suited to this particular human group, nowhere else this continual trying and trying again, this going to it and getting down to it, this critical awareness, this sprouting of new branches from the same stem and out of the same formative impulse. And no-where else is there this alertness to one's own problems, this constant facing up to them, this tough will to come to terms with them, and this indefatigable struggle—albeit seldom expressed in words—to overcome them. Here, and here alone, do we find in the emergent community organs of self-knowledge whose very sensitiveness has constantly reduced its members to despair—but this is a despair that destroys wishful thinking only to raise up in its stead a greater hope which is no longer emotionalism but sheer work. Thus on the soberest survey and on the soberest reflection one can say that, in this one spot in a world of partial failures, we can recognize a non-failure—and, such as it is, a signal non-failure.

What are the reasons for this? We could not get to know the peculiar character of this co-operative colonization better than by following up these reasons.

One element in these reasons has been repeatedly pointed out: that the Jewish Village Commune in Palestine owes its existence not to a doctrine but to a situation, to the needs, the stress, the demands of the situation. In establishing the "Kvuza" or Village Commune the primary thing was not ideology but work. This is certainly correct, but with one limitation. True, the point was to solve certain problems of work and construction which the Palestinian reality forced on the settlers, by collaborating; what a loose conglomeration of individuals could not, in the nature of things, hope to over-come, or even try to overcome, things being what they were, the collective could try to do and actually succeeded in doing. But what is called the "ideology"—I personally prefer the old but untarnished word "Ideal"—was not just something to be added afterwards, that would justify the accomplished facts. In the spirit of the members of the first Palestinian Communes ideal motives joined hands with the dictates of the hour; and in the motives there was a curious mixture of memories of the Russian *Artel*, impressions left over from reading the so-called "utopian" Socialists, and the half-unconscious after-effects of the Bible's teachings about social justice. The important thing is that this ideal motive remained loose and pliable in almost every respect. There were various dreams about the future: people saw before them a new, more comprehensive form of the family, they saw themselves as the advance guard of the

Workers' Movement, as the direct instrument for the realization of Socialism, as the prototype of the new society; they had as their goal the creation of a new man and a new world. But nothing of this ever hardened into a cut-and-dried programme. These men did not, as everywhere else in the history of co-operative settlements, bring a plan with them, a plan which the concrete situation could only fill out, not modify; the ideal gave an impetus but no dogma, it stimulated but did not dic-tate.

More important, however, is that, behind the Palestinian situation that set the tasks of work and reconstruction, there was the historical situation of a people visited by a great exter-nal crisis and responding to it with a great inner change. Fur-ther, this historical situation threw up an élite—the "Chaluzim" or pioneers—drawn from all classes of the people and thus beyond class. The form of life that befitted this élite was the Village Commune, by which I mean not a single note but the whole scale, ranging from the social structure of "mutual aid" to the Commune itself. This form was the best fitted to fulfil the tasks of the central Chaluzim, and at the same time the one in which the social ideal could materially influence the national idea. As the historical conditions have shown, it was impossible for this élite and the form of life it favoured, to become static or isolated; all its tasks, everything it did, its whole pioneering spirit made it the centre of attraction and a central influence. The Pioneer spirit ("Chaluziuth") is, in every part of it, related to the growth of a new and transformed national community; the moment it grew self-sufficient it would have lost its soul. The Village Commune, as the nucleus of the evolving society, had to exert a powerful pull on the people dedicated to this evolution, and it had not merely to educate its friends and associates for genuine communal living, but also to exercise a formative structural effect on the social periphery. The dynamics of history determined the dy-namic character of the relations between Village Commune and society.

This character suffered a considerable setback when the tempo of the crisis in the outer world became so rapid, and its symptoms so drastic, that the inner change could not keep pace with them. To the extent that Palestine had been turned from the one and only land of the "Aliyah"—ascent—into a country of immigrants, a quasi-Chaluziuth came into being alongside the genuine Chaluziuth. The pull exerted by the Commune did not abate, but its educative powers were not adapted to the influx of very different human material, and this material sometimes succeeded in influencing the tone of the community. At the same time the Commune's relations with society at large underwent a change. As the structure of the latter altered, it withdrew more and more from the transforming influence of the focal cells, indeed, it began in its turn to exert an influence on them—not always noticeable at first, but unmistakable to-day—by seizing on certain essential elements in them and assimilating them to itself.

In the life of peoples, and particularly peoples who find themselves in the midst of some historical crisis, it is of crucial importance whether genuine élites (which means élites that do not usurp but are called to their central function) arise, whether these élites remain loyal to their duty to society, establishing a relationship to it rather than to themselves, and finally, whether they have the power to replenish and renew themselves in a manner conformable with their task. The historical destiny of the Jewish settlements in Palestine brought the élite of the Chaluzim to birth, and it found its social nuclear form in the Village Commune. Another wave of this same destiny has washed up, together with the quasi-Chaluzim, a problem for the real Chaluzim élite. It has caused a problem that was always latent to come to the surface. They have not yet succeeded in mastering it and yet must master it before they can reach the next stage of their task. The inner tension between those who take the *whole* responsibility for the community on their shoulders and those who somehow evade it, can be resolved only at a very deep level.

The point where the problem emerges is neither the individual's relationship to the idea nor his relationship to the community nor yet to work; on all these points even the quasi-Chaluzim gird up their loins and do by and large what is expected of them. The point where the problem emerges, where people are apt to slip, is in their relationship to their fellows. By this I do not mean the question, much discussed in its day, of the intimacy that exists in the small and the loss of this intimacy in the big Kvuza; I mean something that has nothing whatever to do with the size of the Commune. It is not a matter of intimacy at all; this appears when it must, and if it is lacking, that's all there is to it. The question is rather one of openness. A real community need not consist of people who are perpetually together; but it must consist of people who, precisely because they are comrades, have mutual access to one another and are ready for one another. A real community is one which in every point of its being possesses, potentially at least, the whole character of community. The internal questions of a community are thus in reality questions relating to its own genuineness, hence to its inner strength and stability. The men who created the Jewish Communes in Palestine instinctively knew this; but the instinct no longer seems to be as common and alert as it was. Yet it is in this most important field that we find that remorselessly clear-sighted collective self-observation and self-criticism to which I have already drawn attention. But to understand and value it aright we must see it together with the amazingly positive relationship—amounting to a regular faith—which these men have to the inmost being of their Commune. The two things are two sides of the same spiritual world and neither can be understood without the other.

In order to make the causes of the non-failure of these Jewish communal settlements sufficiently vivid, in Palestine, I began with the non-doctrinaire character of their origins. This character also determined their development in all essentials. New forms and new intermediate forms were constantly branching off—in complete freedom. Each one grew out of the particular social and spiritual needs as these came to light—in complete freedom, and each one acquired, even in the initial stages, its own ideology—in complete freedom, each struggling to propagate itself and spread and establish its proper sphere—all in complete freedom. The champions of the various forms each had his say, the pros and cons of each individual form were frankly and fiercely debated—always, however, on the plane which everybody accepted as obvious: the common cause and common task, where each form recognized the relative justice of all the other forms in their special functions. All this is unique in the history of co-operative settlements. What is more: nowhere, as far as I see, in the history of the Socialist movement were men so deeply involved in the process of differentiation and yet so intent on preserving the principle of integration.

The various forms and intermediate forms that arose in this

way at different times and in different situations represented different kinds of social structure. The people who built them were generally aware of this as also of the particular social and spiritual needs that actuated them. They were not aware to the same extent that the different forms corresponded to different human types and that just as new forms branched off from the original Kvuza, so new types branched off from the original Chaluz type, each with its special mode of being and each demanding its particular sort of realization. More often than not it was economic and suchlike external factors that led certain people to break away from one form and attach themselves to another. But in the main it happened that each type looked for the social realization of its peculiarities in this particular form and, on the whole, found it there. And not only was each form based on a definite type, it moulded and keeps on moulding this type. It was and is intent on developing it; the constitution, organization and educational system of each form are—no matter how consciously or unconsciously— dedicated to this end. Thus something has been produced which is essentially different from all the social experiments that have ever been made: not a laboratory where everybody works for himself, alone with his problems and plans, but an experimental station where, on common soil, different colonies or "cultures" are tested out according to different methods for a common purpose.

Yet here, too, a problem emerged, no longer within the individual group but in the relation of the groups to one another; nor did it come from without, it came from within— in fact, from the very heart of the principle of freedom.

Even in its first undifferentiated form a tendency towards federation was innate in the Kvuza, to merge the Kvuzoth in some higher social unit; and a very important tendency it was, since it showed that the Kvuza implicitly understood that it was the cell of a newly structured society. With the splitting off and proliferation of the various forms, from the semi-individualistic form which jealously guarded personal independence in its domestic economy, way of life, children's education, etc., to the pure Communistic form, the single unit was supplanted by a series of units in each of which a definite form of colony and a more or less definite human type constituted itself on a federal basis. The fundamental assumption was that the local groups would combine on the same principle of solidarity and mutual help as reigned within the individual group. But the trend towards a larger unit is far from having atrophied in the process. On the contrary, at least in the Kibbuz or Collectivist Movement, it asserts itself with great force and clarity; it recognizes the federative Kibbuzim—units where the local groups have pooled their various aspirations— as a provisional structure; indeed, a thoughtful leader of their movement calls them a substitute for a Commune of Communes. Apart from the fact, however, that individual forms, especially, for instance, the "Moshavim" or semi-individualistic Labour Settlements—though these do not fall short of any of the other forms in the matter of communal economic control and mutual help—are already too far removed from the basic form to be included in a unitary plan, in the Kibbuz Movement itself subsidiary organizations stand in the way of the trend towards unification which wants to embrace and absorb them. Each has developed its own special character and consolidated it in the unit, and it is natural that each should incline to view unification as an extension of its own influence. But something else has been added that has led to an enormous intensification of this attitude on the part of the single units: political development. Twenty years ago a leader of one of the big units could say emphatically: "We are a community and not a Party." This has radically changed in the meantime, and the conditions for unification have been aggravated accordingly. The lamentable fact has emerged that the all-important attitude of neighbourly relationship has not been adequately developed, although not a few cases are on record of a flourishing and rich village giving generous help to a young and poor neighbour which belonged to another unit. In these circumstances the great struggle that has broken out on the question of unification, particularly in the last decade, is the more remarkable. Nobody who is a Socialist at heart can read the great document of this struggle, the Hebrew compilation entitled *The Kibbuz and the Kvuza*, edited by the late labour leader Berl Kaznelson, without being lost in admiration of the high-minded passion with which these two camps battled with one another for genuine unity. The union will probably not be attained save as the outcome of a situation that makes it absolutely necessary. But that the men of the Jewish Communes have laboured so strenuously with one another and against one another for the emergence of a *communitas communi-*

tatum, that is to say, for a structurally new society—this will not be forgotten in the history of mankind's struggle for self-renewal.

I have said that I see in this bold Jewish undertaking a "signal non-failure". I cannot say: a signal success. To become that, much has still to be done. Yet it is in this way, in this kind of tempo, with such setbacks, disappointments, and new ventures, that the real changes are accomplished in this our mortal world.

But can one speak of this non-failure as "signal"? I have pointed out the peculiar nature of the premises and conditions that led to it. And what one of its own representatives has said of the Kvuza, that it is a typically Palestinian product, is true of all these forms.

Still, if an experiment conducted under certain conditions has proved successful up to a point, we can set about varying it under other, less favourable, conditions.

There can hardly be any doubt that we must regard the last war as the end of the prelude to a world crisis. This crisis will probably break out—after a sombre "interlude" that cannot last very long—first among some of the nations of the West, who will be able to restore their shattered economy in appearance only. They will see themselves faced with the immediate need for radical socialization, above all the expropriation of the land. It will then be of absolutely decisive importance *who* is the real subject of an economy so transformed, and who is the owner of the social means of production. Is it to be the central authority in a highly centralized State, or the social units of urban and rural workers, living and producing on a communal basis, and their representative bodies? In the latter case the remodelled organs of the State will discharge the functions of adjustment and administration only. On these issues will largely depend the growth of a new society and a new civilization. The essential point is to decide on the fundamentals: a re-structuring of society as a League of Leagues, and a reduction of the State to its proper function, which is to maintain unity; or a devouring of an amorphous society by the omnipotent State; Socialist Pluralism or so-called Socialist Unitarianism. The right proportion, tested anew every day according to changing conditions, between group-freedom and collective order; or absolute order imposed indefinitely for the sake of an era of freedom alleged to follow "of its own accord". So long as

Russia has not undergone an essential inner change—and to-day we have no means of knowing when and how that will come to pass—we must designate one of the two poles of Socialism between which our choice lies, by the formidable name of "Moscow". The other, I would make bold to call "Jerusalem".

The Kibbutz and the Moshav

Joseph Ben-David

The kibbutz is a village with a population ranging from 30 to 1,500 inhabitants. The smaller, more intimate type of these villages used to be—and sometimes still is—called a 'kvutza'. The land of the kibbutz is always nationally owned, allocated to the settlers for a nominal rent. All other property is communally owned except for a few personal belongings. Work and marketing are centrally organized, directed by managers and committees, which are elected by a meeting of all members. These meetings and elections are always fairly, though informally, conducted, and each member is free to express his views on the conduct of the office holders, or to suggest candidates and vote according to his best convictions. In principle, kibbutz democracy is unlimited. In fact, however, it is limited to the internal affairs of the kibbutz, since the village as a whole is, with few exceptions, attached to one of the four kibbutz federations which are more or less closely identified with certain political parties. The members are, therefore, expected to belong to a certain political party. Dissenters are tolerated, but party rivalry for supremacy in the kibbutz is shunned, since such contests have led in the past to serious conflict and even to the breaking-up of some communities.

All adult persons of both sexes work full-time and adolescents work part-time. All children go to school until the age of 18. The family is not a unit in the division of labour; work is allocated to each individual according to the needs of the collectivity. Children are brought up in special quarters from infancy. Nowadays, however, there is an indeterminate period during which the infant stays with the mother after birth, and in most kibbutzim children occasionally sleep with their parents. The children's houses are divided according to age ; thus children of the same age from different families grow up together, while siblings of different ages live, eat, sleep and play separately. Nevertheless there are strong family ties and no doubts about family identity. Children and parents spend a great deal of their leisure time together, perhaps more than in urban families.

All income belongs to the community, and members' needs are provided for equally by communal institutions. They are allocated rooms or flatlets according to their marital status and seniority; most of the meals are taken in the common dining hall; there is a communal clothes' depot, laundry, dispensary, etc. Only for the yearly vacation and minimal personal needs do members receive a small cash allowance. While equality is maintained in the allocation of all the standard necessities of life—of course, what is considered as standard has risen considerably with time, like everywhere else—an effort is made to provide for the special needs of individuals. Kibbutzim are generous in providing for their members in case of sickness, etc., in caring for aged parents of members, and contribute considerably towards satisfying the artistic and cultural interests of their members according to individual taste.

The most important point about the kibbutz is that for the large majority of its members it is a way of life voluntarily chosen. There are as yet few second-generation kibbutzim, and most of the existing ones were founded by groups of youth movement members who prepared themselves during a period of years for settling in a kibbutz. Among immigrants who founded most of the kibbutzim this preparation usually started abroad in agricultural training centres ('hakhsharoth'). After immigration, or if the group originated in Israel right from the beginning, they worked for a period as an organized group. This group was a 'gar'in' (nucleus) of a future kibbutz with a name, institutions and elected representatives of its own. A new kibbutz was usually founded by members of one such nucleus, but subsequently it absorbed further nuclei and individuals who, after a trial period, became part of the kibbutz. This prolonged process of preparation acquainted people sufficiently with the kibbutz way of life, so that only those who really preferred this life and were closely attached to their group stayed on. [1]

The 'moshav ovdim' is also located on nationally owned land, but the land here is divided equally between the families. There is a ban on hired labour, and the farm is planned so that all the work can usually be done by the members of the household. A portion of the land, however, may remain under common cultivation. The families work their own plots separately, but have to provide work for the communally cultivated land. [2]

Marketing is co-operatively organized, and there are arrangements for mutual aid, provident funds, the provision of services, and usually also for obtaining credit and for the purchase of equipment and consumption goods. Thus the moshav self-government, working through the general meeting of members and their elected representatives (with similar titles as in the kibbutz; internal secretary, external secretary, work manager, etc.) has important functions, though not as important as those in the kibbutz.

Since, however, each family is here a separate consumption and residential unit, the communal life of the moshav is much less intensive than that of the kibbutz. Social and economic differentiation, though kept within limits, is considerable. Thus while it is impossible for one family to increase its holdings through the purchase of land, it can increase its livestock and its income through efficiency. Another source of differentiation is the presence of non-farmers, such as teachers, craftsmen, employees of the co-operative and in rare cases even a doctor. These people do not as a rule become members of the moshav, and would not be able to do so, because membership is dependent upon the possession and cultivation of an agricultural holding. In so far as these people settle in the moshav permanently, they are a further source of social inequality. [3]

Politically the large majority of moshavim are attached to one of two federations, one affiliated to Mapai (moderate Labour Party), the other to the Religious Party, and there is similar pressure towards political conformity in a moshav as in a kibbutz. But some of the arrangements of the moshav have been copied by other villages which have no political or ideological tinge, and have a non-political federation of their own. [4]

---

1. Today, recruitment of Israel youth to kibbutzim usually takes place through a special branch of the Army 'Nahal' which enables youth movement members to do their regular army service in units situated in kibbutzim where agricultural work is combined with military training. Members of such units have founded a few villages of their own, but usually those who stay on after the completion of their service are too few to establish a new village, so they are directed to existing kibbutzim.
2. There are a few moshavim where individual property is limited to the house and a small yard. In these moshavim ('moshavim shitufiyim') the organization of work is exactly like that in a kibbutz, except that the work-load of married women is reduced by a certain amount according to the size of their families and the age of their children, since they have to do their own house-work.
3. Cf. Yonina Garber-Talmon, 'Social Differentiation in Co-operative Villages', *British Journal of Sociology*, Vol. III, No. 4, 1952, p. 338-57.
   In principle such specialists can be members of a kibbutz, since membership thereof does not entail individual ownership of land. As a matter of fact, however, very few of them ever join a kibbutz. If they live in a kibbutz they present an even more difficult problem than in a moshav, since they share all the amenities with the members and are in addition paid a salary. They have, therefore, money which no kibbutz member has.
4. Officially this latter type is called simply 'moshav', while the former, socialist type is called 'moshav ovdim' (workers' settlement). In everyday speech, and in this book, 'moshav' usually refers to 'moshav ovdim'.

Furthermore, the moshav structure has of late undergone considerable transformation as a result of having been used as the standard pattern for the agricultural settlement of new immigrants. [1] Thus moshav also refers today to a variety of small villages with a variety of co-operative arrangements. The majority are officially affiliated to the socialist federations and adopt, in principle, the moshav constitution (equality, ban on hired labour, etc.), but this constitution is not very closely adhered to, especially in the newly established moshavim (cf. Chapters VI to VIII below).

As has been shown, the kibbutz is one of the most highly-organized human communities. It has a constitution which regulates more aspects of life than in any other modern community and its self-governing and legislative institutions are constantly functioning with all members—at least in principle—taking active part. Yet this most self-conscious of all communities came into being practically without any advance planning, as a result of an almost pure process of trial and error.

The first kibbutz—Degania—was formed in 1909-10, as the result of a successful experiment by seven agricultural workers (replaced later by twelve others) in working the lands given to them as a commune. This small-scale experiment was, however, an important event, closely watched by members of the world-wide Zionist Movement. [2]

One of the central ideas of the Zionist Movement was that only through the creation of a broad stratum of agricultural population could the Jews strike real roots in their homeland. Its members believed in physiocratic theories extolling primary production as the chief source of the wealth of nations, and they hoped that widely dispersed agricultural settlements would determine the Jewish character of the land. Jews in Europe and the Middle East rarely owned land and were concentrated in business and other middle-class occupations, the only ones open to them as long as they lived in the midst of other nations. In order to become an independent nation they had to perform all work necessary to a society. Agriculture, the most difficult and to Jews the most alien kind of manual work (though it had been the typical occupation of ancient Jews in their own country) became the symbol of national transformation. [3] As a result the Zionist movement embarked on a policy of buying up barren land with a view to reclaiming it for purposes of agricultural settlement.

This policy, however, could not be realized under the conditions obtaining in Palestine prior to 1910. Jewish farming until then succeeded only in the most fertile coastal areas and only as a plantation type of agriculture, where most of the work was done by cheap labour (cf. above, p. 24). The conditions of the farm labourer were very poor and only Arab *fellahin* or Yemenite Jews were willing to put up with them. The creation of a Jewish agricultural population dispersed over the whole country was therefore out of the question.

This situation was, however, for a minority, a challenge and an opportunity. To an increasing number of young Jews in Russia, and later in other Eastern and Central European countries, agricultural work in Palestine became a personal ideal. Repelled by anti-Semitism on the one hand, and by the social and religious restrictions of the traditional communities of petty traders from which they originated on the other, they rebelled against everything connected with their social environment. They came to

---

1. See Chapter VII.
2. Zionism is the Jewish nationalist movement, the main purpose of which has been the establishment of a Jewish State and the revival of the Hebrew language in Palestine. Until the nineteenth century Jews had lived in Europe and the Middle East (including Palestine) in autonomous communities which preserved Hebrew as their literary and ritual language, observed the Jewish religion and customs as they existed in Palestine about 1,500 to 2,000 years ago, and never ceased to consider themselves as a nation whose homeland was Palestine. From the nineteenth century onwards an ever-increasing number of Jews drifted back to Palestine. Until the 1880s, the immigrants were mostly religious people who regarded settlement in Palestine as a ritually desirable action and were inspired by vague Messianic hopes. Subsequently they included increasing numbers of more or less secularized Jews whose avowed purpose was the creation of a modern Jewish nation and Hebrew culture. These were the Zionists. In 1896 they founded an organization which was later officially recognized in the Palestinian Mandate given to Britain by the League of Nations.
3. Many Zionists were also influenced by Tolstoy's ideas about the redeeming qualities of agricultural work.

Palestine first as individuals, and later as members of organized groups influenced by early Russian socialism.

Their collectivist ideals were well suited to the conditions under which they had to live in the new country, since only by the pooling of resources could they surmount the difficulties and feeling of loneliness which they had to face. Even before the foundation of the first kibbutz, there sprang up a variety of workers' co-operative kitchens and other semi-formal mutual aid societies, and the young immigrants were constantly organizing themselves into groups and 'parties'. This experience of organized group life led to the experiment of the kibbutz. Its success was due to the fact that the settlers did not regard their work as a means to an end, but as an end in itself; they wanted to prove to themselves and to others that they could become agricultural workers and maintain at the same time a civilized way of life.

There was from the very beginning widespread interest in the efforts of this handful of idealists who decided to leave school, university or white-collar careers and become farm labourers. These young workers came to be called 'halutzim' (pioneers); their failures and successes were widely commented upon in the local and international Zionist press; poems and songs were written about them, and thousands of members of Zionist youth movements regarded them as heroes.

These, then, were the factors which led to the creation of the kibbutz: the Zionist organization was in search of settlers willing to settle on difficult terrain; young unmarried people, imbued with socialist ideals of equality and labour, joined organized movements and became accustomed to co-operative or communal arrangements; and great public interest was aroused among Zionists throughout the world in the agricultural settlement of the country.

The same factors which explain the emergence of the kibbutz also explain its subsequent development. It took some years before Degania assumed a permanent character.[1] Then came the First World War during which the whole settlement movement was brought to a standstill. But among the youth growing up in the country, and even more among the members of Zionist youth movements abroad, the halutzim and Degania had become legends in the meantime. Even before the war ended three small new kibbutz-type settlements had been founded. At the end of the war there was a considerable influx of members of youth movements who arrived with the intention of becoming halutzim. Of the 35,183 immigrants who came to the country between 1919 and 1923, 16,751 belonged to the labour force. Of the latter, 4,952 (i.e., nearly one-third) registered as agricultural workers.[2] Since there were practically no such workers among Jews in their countries of origin, this figure refers mainly to the halutzim who intended to become agricultural workers and had probably gone through a period of agricultural training in a hakhshara (cf. p. 46) abroad.

The relatively large numbers of immigrants broke up the intimacy characteristic of the groups of 'workers' before the First World War. Besides, the newcomers were influenced by the ideas of Russian communism, and aimed at creating a large, centralized organization of workers' socialist enterprises. In 1920 a so-called Labour Brigade was founded, which acted as contractor for work performed by communistically organized groups of workers. In the same year was founded the General Federation of Jewish Labour (Histadruth) which was to become a central organization comprising trade unions, institutions for social and sickness insurance, as well as a variety of enterprises owned collectively or co-operatively by their members (including kibbutzim and moshavim) or directly by the Histadruth.

1. In the beginning, the question arose whether the pioneers who had successfully reclaimed the land should remain on the site at all, or whether they should return it to the Zionist organization for settlers who could not undertake the arduous task of pioneering, whilst they themselves moved on to open up new areas. Cf. Joseph Baratz, *Village by the Jordan: the Story of Degania*, London, 1954.
2. Moshe Sicron, *Immigration to Israel 1948-1953: Statistical Supplement*, Jerusalem, 1957, p. 16-17, tables A 24, A 26.

The new spirit stressed large-scale and national organization and was alien to the close, quasi-family spirit of the original kvutza. There was a search for more impersonal social forms. Besides the groups of the Labour Brigade, this was shown in the creation of the moshav ovdim in 1921. Two moshavim, Nahalal and Kfar Yehesk'el, were founded in that year; among the founders were a number of former members of Degania.

Under the impact of these changed circumstances a new type of kibbutz, or more precisely the large kibbutz as distinct from the original small kvutza, came into being. This kibbutz, reflecting the ideas of the Labour Brigade, was to be open to all those applying for membership. No questions were to be asked about personal way of life and views, as long as the would-be member accepted the formal discipline of the organized community in matters of work, consumption and other things deemed necessary by the organization. Such a kibbutz was to include industry as well as agriculture, and all the kibbutzim were supposed to be organized in a central federation with ultimate and far-reaching authority over the individual settlements.

The founders of this new type of kibbutz regarded the kibbutz movement as a means for the creation of a working class and the crystallization of its politics. It had therefore to be an organized mass movement, and not something restricted to a few, spontaneously formed élite groups.

These trends towards the creation of a centralized and impersonally organized socialist economy in the country were, however, short-lived. They were supported by only a minority of the population, and had, of course, no support from the Mandatory Government which was the absolute ruler of the country. Socialist enterprise could be carried on only as part of an open economy, i.e., not as a centrally directed and compulsory organization, but as a number of separate enterprises the success of which depended on the quality and enthusiasm of their members and leaders.[1] The Labour Brigade could not last long under these circumstances, and it was dissolved after a few years. The kibbutzim, however, gained in importance and became in many ways the spearhead of political socialism in the country.

The reasons for this were as follows. Next to the promotion of Jewish immigration, the settling of the lands belonging to the Zionist organization was now even more than before the First World War the most important aim of the Zionist movement. But owing to insufficient funds this settlement was still regarded as a task which could be performed only by groups of dedicated young people acting out of idealism and not out of considerations of profit. The kibbutz, whose collective way of life and whose ideals concerning the dignity of work and equalitarian social relations had a great attraction for thousands of Zionist youth movement members abroad as well as in Palestine, still seemed the framework best suited for pioneer settlements.

Apart from establishing Jewish settlements all over the country, kibbutzim also performed an important task in the absorption of immigrants, especially in the 1930s. A great many of those who arrived in the country were neither properly prepared nor motivated for successful adjustment to conditions there. Getting away from European anti-Semitism, they hoped to live in Palestine a more dignified life than would have been possible in their countries of origin. They did not fully realize, however, that in a poor country like Palestine they would have to lower their standards of living, and that possibly they would have to exchange their middle-class occupations for working-class occupations. Nor were they aware of the difficulties of life in a 'colonial' situation, and the strain and dangers imposed by the constant strife with the Arabs. Many of these people entered a kibbutz for shorter or longer periods. There they learnt to become workers, and to endure poverty without loss of dignity; and how an organized community could withstand both physical and political adversity. Even if they later left and

---

1. This is true of economic enterprises only. In the organization of trade unions and social services, especially sickness insurance, centralization could be and was carried very far, since neither the government, nor anyone else, took any serious interest in such matters, so that the Histadruth had virtually a monopoly of these services from the beginning.

settled elsewhere, the kibbutz was the place where they received their real preparation for life in the country.

The Utopian socialist ideals of the kibbutzim became, therefore, the means for realizing the national aim of settlement. As a result, their ideas came to be regarded as the official ideology of the Yishuv. Even those who opposed socialism had to admit that the kibbutzim performed a national service and that the halutzim represented an élite. Thus the kibbutzim became the most rapidly expanding ecological structure in the country during the period of the British mandate (cf. Table 16).

TABLE 16. The growth of towns and villages in Jewish Palestine between 1922 and 1945

Year	Cities and urban settlements	Villages	Moshavim	Moshvei ovdim	Kibbutzim
		Population			
1922	68 870	11 540	550	860	1 190
1931	136 160	27 740	2 350	3 400	3 800
1936	315 360	59 530	5 830	9 910	11 840
1945	439 200	80 700	13 200	18 000	37 400
		Number of settlements			
1922	8	34	3	8	19
1931	19	42	14	16	31
1936	27	46	27	44	47
1945	27	44	35	63	116

Source: A. Gertz, (ed.), *Statistical Handbook of Jewish Palestine, 1947*, Jerusalem, 1947, p. 38.

The growth of the kibbutzim became particularly rapid between 1936 and 1945. Until 1936 the population of the kibbutzim grew at about the same rate as that of the moshavim. In that year the Arabs launched a minor war against the Jewish population which led in 1939 to the publication of a British White Paper seriously curtailing immigration and the rights of the Jewish population to settle in parts of the country. Meanwhile, persecution in Europe made immigration a matter of vital importance for the Jews. In consequence the Jewish population found itself in a state of emergency from 1936 onwards, which ended in the Jewish revolt against the British and the granting of independence to the country in 1948. During these years, the absorption of large numbers of immigrants, the expansion of settlements, and the fostering of a spirit of altruistic pioneering became matters of even greater importance than before. The growth of the kibbutzim at this time is, therefore, evidence of the successful way in which they met these challenges.

As has been already pointed out (cf. p. 48) there were genuine differences of taste as well as ideology between kibbutzim. The original kvutzoth regarded the self-perfection of the individual settlement as their paramount goal. They were no less convinced of their national mission than the others, but believed that this mission could only be fulfilled by each group of settlers autonomously finding its own identity and way of life. They played down the importance of ideologies and political platforms, as well as party organization, and believed that the renascence of the nation would be achieved by moral regeneration spearheaded by the kvutzoth.

In contrast were those brought up in the atmosphere of European socialism and communism of the early 1920s, for whom ideology and organization were of supreme importance. As a result of these differences, a federation founded in 1925 comprising all kibbutzim was dissolved after a short period of existence. In 1927 two kibbutz federations, and in 1929 a third, were founded with distinct ideologies and political programmes.

Those founded in 1927 were the Kibbutz Meuhad, which fostered large open kibbutzim tightly organized in a centralized federation (cf. p. 49 above), and the Hakibbutz Haartzi shel Hashomer Hatzair, which held up the traditions of the small and autonomous kvutza, but restricted its autonomy to economic and social affairs. In matters of politics and ideology there was complete uniformity. The Hakibbutz Haartzi, the Hashomer Hatzair youth movement and a related political party which changed its name several times (now called Mapam) adopted a doctrinaire Marxist ideology, the propagation and the realization of which was to be one of the main tasks of the kibbutz.[1]

The organization founded in 1929 was the Hever Hakvutzoth, the federation of the original, non-ideological and autonomous kibbutzim. Its foundation was to some extent a compromise with the original principles of kibbutz autonomy and opposition to ideology. It was recognized, however, that without the support of a youth movement and some representative organization these kibbutzim would lose their élite position to the organized, missionary kibbutz movements.

There was a real difference between the social atmosphere of the small kibbutzim of the Hever Hakvutzoth and the Hakibbutz Haartzi (average membership in the early 1940s was 93 and 123 respectively, not including children, parents, members of Hakhsharoth training at the kibbutz, etc.) and the larger kibbutzim of the Hakibbutz Hameuhad (average membership 264, with a much greater range of variation—one kibbutz had more than 600 members by 1942—than in the other two federations).[2]

The differences between the various federations gradually diminished, however, in the course of time. After a while it became obvious that not the particular ideologies of the federations but conditions common to the kibbutz movement as a whole determined its development. The most important of these was the pioneering function of the kibbutz.

Since, as has been pointed out, the carrying-out of pioneering tasks depended on voluntary action, the kibbutz needed people willing to undertake difficult missions. Those who had just chosen to live in a kibbutz out of preference for a collective way of life could not be absorbed in it, because they found after a while that the constant pressure for participation in the affairs of the community imposed on them too much of a strain. All kibbutzim, therefore, adopted measures for fostering youth movements, training groups (hakhsharoth), selecting candidates and furthering group cohesion and a sense of mission. Thus neither the exclusivist élite ideology of the original kvutza nor the idea of the open kibbutz could be realized in practice, and eventually similar methods of recruitment and social relations were adopted in all kibbutzim.

The relative autonomy of the kibbutz within the federation was also determined by practical considerations rather than ideology. All kibbutzim found that some sort of organization uniting a number of kibbutzim was necessary. Maintenance of contacts with youth movements abroad and in the country, the absorption of training groups, helping new kibbutzim, especially if they occupied strategically exposed positions[3] and negotiating with central organizations such as the Jewish Agency and the various economic institutions of the Histadruth—all these called for some permanent form of co-operation.

On the other hand, the idea of central direction of the individual kibbutz as conceived by the Kibbutz Meuhad could nowhere be realized in practice. Each kibbutz was a separate economic enterprise and social entity which could not be moulded according to a central plan. Central direction would therefore have been inefficient. Furthermore, it would have been incompatible with the spirit of voluntary pioneering without which the kibbutz could not have existed.

1. Individual dissent is, however, tolerated in these kibbutzim too.
2. S. Landshut, *Hakvutza*, Jerusalem, 1944, p. 76.
3. Cf. Chapter V about the importance of these matters today.

Economic considerations of the individual kibbutz also proved stronger than the ideologies of the federations in shaping kibbutz enterprise. Industries were introduced in kibbutzim belonging to all the federations, in spite of the ideology of the Hever Hakvutzoth and the Kibbutz Artzi, according to which such complex division of labour was incompatible with the spirit of equality and fraternity in the kibbutz.

Finally the size of individual kibbutzim became determined in the long run by the requirements and absorptive capacities of their economy and by natural demographic growth on the one hand, and by social requirements probably inherent in the kibbutz structure in general on the other, rather than by the strongly differing ideas of the federations about the relative desirability of the large kibbutz or the small kvutza. Today, while the largest kibbutzim with populations of about 1,500 people are to be found in the Kibbutz Meuhad, kibbutzim of this size are exceptions rather than the rule, even in that federation. If we disregard the two largest kibbutzim in the Kibbutz Meuhad and the largest kibbutz in the Ihud (a new federation, cf. p. 53), we find kibbutzim of about the same size in the three large federations. The average size of the population of the kibbutzim is also about the same in these three federations, namely 380 in the Kibbutz Meuhad, 361 in the Kibbutz Artzi and 326 in the Ihud, and the variation between the sizes and characters of different kibbutzim in each of these federations is much greater than that between the federations themselves. [1]

In view of all this one would have expected a gradual disappearance of the ideological differences between the federations, and perhaps even a merger of the federations. As a matter of fact, however, exactly the opposite happened; instead of uniting, the federations have become increasingly divided.

The causes of this development must not be sought in the internal structure of the kibbutz, but in its place within society. As pointed out, due to the pioneering mission of the kibbutz the federations had to recruit members actively and on a large scale, partly to be able to meet an ever-growing demand for the foundation of new settlements, and partly to replace the large number of members constantly leaving the kibbutzim. [2] Recruitment, however, was possible only through the creation of youth movements with ideologies justifying the particular kibbutz federation to which the movement was attached, to the exclusion of others. Competition for new recruits was only the most important means of obtaining public support for the different kibbutz federations. They also needed the support of the Zionist organization, which was a democratic body based on political parties. Thus the federations became involved in a contest for political influence.

In addition to these political interests of the kibbutz federations, there was the interest of the political parties in the federations themselves, Through their connexion with a kibbutz movement, the parties acquired an aura of pioneering, and the invaluable asset of an organized, disciplined and idealistic following. It seemed that parties which did not possess a kibbutz movement of their own would be unable to compete for public support, especially among the younger generation. [3] As a result kibbutz movements arose among all the parties with the exception of those whose ideology was entirely incompatible with the kibbutz. The most important of these smaller federations has been the Kibbutz Dathi (religious kibbutz) attached to the National Religious Party.

Thus kibbutz federations became increasingly identified with political parties. Of course, the kibbutz movement as a whole has been political from the beginning. Its aim was the creation of socialist communities as a step towards building a socialist society. But, originally, the federations made deliberate efforts to safeguard the character of the kibbutz as an autonomous social movement, and to keep away from politics. They

1. Cf. *Statistical Abstract of Israel*, No. 12, Jerusalem, 1961, p. 34, about the total population of the different kibbutz federations. Data about individual kibbutzim were obtained from the Demography Department of the Central Bureau of Statistics.
2. Of the 1,927 members of a sample of seventeen kibbutzim, nearly half had left by 1937.   (S. Landshut, op. cit, p. 61.)
3. On the political importance of the kibbutzim and agriculture in general, cf. also Amitai Etzioni, 'Agrarianism in Israel's Party System', *Canadian Journal of Economics and Political Science*, Vol. XXIII, No. 3, 1957, p. 363-75.

intended to serve the common aim of the creation of an organized working-class and, eventually, of a socialist society by preserving each its peculiar social characteristics. Thus, even though members of the Kibbutz Meuhad and of the Hever Hakvutzoth usually belonged to the same party, the federations remained separate.

With increasing political involvement all this changed, and the connexion with different political parties became the only reason for the existence of separate federations. So when in the early 1940s a split occurred in Mapai, to which the Kibbutz Meuhad was closely linked, it became increasingly difficult to maintain the unity of the federation. Eventually it was split in two. The majority which identified itself with the new party (Ahduth Ha'avoda) retained the original name Kibbutz Meuhad, while the large minority sympathizing with Mapai joined the Hever Hakvutzoth, which was also connected with the same party, forming a new federation—the Ihud Hakvutzoth Vehakibbutzim.

The function of the kibbutzim in the absorption of immigrants has practically disappeared, and their military importance has become negligible since the establishment of the State. Apart from certain border areas where kibbutzim are pioneers of settlement,[1] they have expanded very little since 1951 and not at all since 1955 (cf. Table 17). The new settlers on the land have not been inspired to create a new way of life or to be a pioneering élite, and have shown no willingness to enter kibbutzim. Most of the agricultural settlements were formed within the framework of moshavim, though, as will be seen below, in a rather modified form of moshav.

The political power positions gained by the kibbutzim during the 1930s and 1940s, have, however, been maintained. No new political ideologies to replace the socialist, halutzic myth have emerged, and only the beginnings of new organizations and cliques as well adapted to the formation of a political élite as the kibbutz movement have appeared.

A a result, active or former kibbutz members form a relatively large percentage of the members of the Knesset (Israel Parliament), and an even larger percentage of the members of the government (cf. Table 18). Two of the parties, Mapam and Ahduth Ha'avoda, are represented in the Knesset by a majority of kibbutz members. If members of moshavim are added, the representation of socialist agriculture is even higher. It has to be pointed out, finally, that kibbutz (and moshav) members are prominent in the present ruling parties, while there are none in the parties which have never participated in the government. Their political weight, therefore, is greater than their actual number in the Knesset implies.

While kibbutzim always saw themselves in the vanguard of socialist Zionism, their original aim was not to serve as cadres for leaders of political parties. Leadership fell to them only as a result of unforeseen circumstances. Their conscious intention has always been to serve their political ideals through the creation of unique socialist communities where people do their best out of loyalty to the group and its values, without any incentive of personal gain, and where a new, better way of life is created, based on a sense of belonging to the community as a whole, and on economic equality, fraternity and lack of competition.

Such Utopian values have always been attractive to a great many people all over the world, and most of the interest in the kibbutz has been due to its proneness to these values. A great number of studies have explored the extent to which the kibbutzim have succeeded in realizing their Utopian aims and resolving the problems and tensions arising out of this unique way of life.[2] The main problems seem to have been the fate

1. Cf. Chapter V.
2. Cf. S. Landshut, op. cit. ; H. F. Infield, *Co-operative Living in Palestine*, London, 1946 ; M. Buber, *Paths in Utopia*, 1949 ; E. Rosenfeld, 'Social Stratification in a Classless Society', *American Sociological Review*, Vol. XVI, No. 6, 1951, p. 766-74 ; Y. Talmon-Garber, 'The Family in Collective Settlements', *Transactions of the Third World Congress of Sociology*, Vol. IV, London, 1956, p. 116-26, and 'Differentiation in Collective Settlements', *Scripta Hierosolymitana*, Vol. III, Jerusalem, 1956 ; M. Spiro, *Venture in Utopia*, Cambridge (Mass.), 1956 ; Y. Talmon-Garber, 'Hamishpaha Vehahatzava Hatafkidith shel Bnei

of the family in the commune and the difficulty of maintaining real equality. We shall comment briefly on them.

First, what is the position of the family in the kibbutz? The rules according to which the individual has to regard the kibbutz as his family, to the extent of sharing his room and other possessions with whomever necessary, working when and where it is most useful to the community, accepting the decisions of the collective about his accommodation and general level of consumption, may be quite acceptable to the individual who voluntarily chooses the kibbutz as his home. There is something of the atmosphere of a youth camp in these arrangements, and those who join the kibbutz are people who enjoy such a life, especially since it is to promote a higher purpose. As settlers, however, grow older and/or get married and have children, there usually arises a need for more privacy, and communal arrangements are often regarded as an intolerable interference with one's private life.

Indeed it took some time before the kibbutz adjusted itself to the existence of families. Until quite recently, housing was extremely limited in the kibbutzim. It was customary for three or more people to share a room, and many lived in tents for years. Sharing a room with only one other person was, therefore, an enviable luxury which could not always be afforded. Besides, there was the feeling that privacy should really not be encouraged. Another difficulty was the children. They were maintained by the kibbutz, and there was never any question of the parents having to make any financial sacrifices for their children. On the other hand, of course, there was collective pressure on couples to limit the number of children to what the community thought it could bear. At times actual decisions were taken in such matters though sanctions were never applied.

These were difficult problems between the 1920s and 1940s when many kibbutzim went through hard times for ten to fifteen years, so that married couples had to put up with not having a room of their own and had to postpone having children or refrain from having more than one child for years. Even if they recognized that the sacrifice demanded of them was under the circumstances justified, the strain was often very great.

These problems have disappeared during the last fifteen years. Married couples now have quarters of their own, even with some rudimentary cooking facilities and an extra small room for children or guests. But once these basic needs of family life were satisfied, new ones arose. Many families want to have the evening meal at home, some want their children to stay with them permanently or occasionally and/or want to have a decisive say in matters relating to their education.

Various kibbutzim have given in to these demands, to a greater or lesser extent, but have done so with some misgivings. It is felt that there is a limit beyond which the autonomy of the family becomes incompatible with the existence of the kibbutz. Yet in spite of such qualms great changes have occurred in these matters during the last ten years, and it seems that the communal arrangements of the kibbutz can be adjusted without much difficulty to quite an intensive family life.

Secondly, in the past it was feared, especially by the kibbutzim of the Hever Hakvutzoth, that a large-size and complex division of labour would run counter to the maintenance of a real spirit of fraternity and equality. As a result they deliberately restrained the growth of kibbutzim, even at the cost of some economic inefficiency. Other kibbutzim have never shared these apprehensions, and today they have ceased to be important considerations in all kibbutzim. There is now a complex division of labour in kibbutzim belonging to all federations. This, indeed, has created more or less permanent differences in status, authority and influence among the members, especially in the larger and older kibbutzim. Since, however, economic equality is more or less maintained, such differences

Hador Hasheni Bakibbutz' (Family and occupational placement of the second generation), *Megamoth*, Vol. VIII, No. 4, Oct. 1957, p. 369-92 ; M. Spiro, *Children of the Kibbutz*, Cambridge (Mass.), 1958 ; Y. Talmon-Garber, 'Social Structure and Family Size', *Human Relations*, Vol. XII, No. 2, 1959, p. 120-46 ; A. Etzioni, 'The Functional Differentiation of Élites in the Kibbutz', *American Journal of Sociology*, Vol. LXIV, No. 5 ; M. Sarell, 'Shamranuth Vehidush Bedor Hasheni B'kibbutzim ' (Conservatism and innovation in the second generation), *Megamoth*, Vol. XI, No. 2, 1961, p. 99-123.

TABLE 17. The growth of Jewish population in types of settlement between 1945 and 1961

Type of settlement	Number of settlements					Population					
	1945	1948	1951	1955	1960	1945	1948	1951	1955	1960	1961
Total (urban population)	27	42	46	49	57	439 200	576 207	1 067 647	1 215 564	1 588 780	1 620 000
Total (rural population)	258	326	606	732	723	149 300	110 631	310 706	371 240	322 409	312 535
Large villages	44	34	29	27	24	80 700	24 160	42 942	58 481	85 975	60 902
Private moshavim	35	⎱104²⎰	42	43	52	13 200	⎱30 142²⎰	24 974	21 162	29 326	40 172
Moshvei ovdim	⎱63¹⎰	(104²)	191	273	345	⎱18 000¹⎰	(30 142²)	60 810	92 503	115 122	120 046
Moshavim shitufiyim	(63¹)	(104²)	28	27	19	(18 000¹)	(30 142²)	4 024	4 856	3 625	3 909
Kibbutzim	116	177	217	225	229	37 400	54 208	68 156	77 818	77 955	77 209
Work camps	—	—	28	20	—	—	—	8 386	6 300	—	—
Other rural settlements	—	—	13	25	—	—	—	22 666	70 084	—	—
Temporary settlements	—	—	41	23	5	—	—	75 061	30 690	2 229	2 007
Agricultural schools of large farms	—	11	17	69	47	—	2 121	3 687	9 346	8 177	6 564
Immigrant camps	—	—	—	3	—	—	12 723	26 039	—	—	—
Not known	—	—	—	—	—	—	17 117	—	—	—	—

Note: The value 63¹ (number of settlements, 1945) and 18 000¹ (population, 1945) each cover the combined rows Moshvei ovdim and Moshavim shitufiyim. The value 104² (number of settlements, 1948) and 30 142² (population, 1948) each cover the combined rows Private moshavim, Moshvei ovdim and Moshavim shitufiyim.

Source: A. Gertz (ed.), *Statistical Handbook of Jewish Palestine, 1947*, Jerusalem, 1947, p. 38; *Statistical Abstracts of Israel*, No. 9, p. 14, No. 12, p. 33, 494.

1. Includes moshvei ovdim and moshavim shitufiyim.
2. Includes all three types of moshavim.

TABLE 18. Members of Knesset and Government by party affiliation and relation to kibbutzim and moshavim, 1960

	Mapai[1]	Mapam[2]	Ahduth Ha'avoda[2]	National Religious Party[2]	Other religious parties[3]	Liberals	Heruth[3]	Arab[2] Parties	Communists[3]
Knesset total	42	9	8	12	6	17	17	4	5
Past or present members of kibbutzim	7	6	6	2	1	—	—	—	—
Past or present members of moshavim	5	—	—	1	—	—	—	—	—
Others	30[4]	3	2	9	5	17	17	4	5
Government[5] total	13	—	2	4	1	—	—	—	—
Those connected with kibbutz or moshav	5	—	2	—	1	—	—	—	—

1. Core party in all Governments since the establishment of Israel.
2. Supporting present (1960) coalition government (among the other religious parties and the Arab parties, only some support present coalition).
3. Have been permanently in opposition.
4. Including two closely identified with kibbutz and moshav movements as a result of long service in agricultural institutions of the Histadruth.
5. Includes sixteen senior and four junior ministers.

are not felt to be an affront to personal dignity. A high position in the division of labour does not automatically ensure a high status. If the person is unpopular or ideologically suspect, deference will be withheld from him, even if he has an economically important role. Status differences, therefore, are not necessarily perceived as social inequality, but as differences in popularity which do not diminish the essential equality of members. As a result differences in the congeniality of jobs, or in the formal authority which they carry, have not created permanent and rigid differences in status.

It seems, therefore, that neither family autonomy nor division of labour are necessarily disruptive of the peculiar social form of the kibbutz. Individual kibbutzim have adjusted flexibly and efficiently to these developments, and there is no proof that the strains caused have been greater than those with which families and communities normally have to put up in any given kind of social structure. The real problem of the kibbutz does not lie, therefore, in the feasibility of curtailing the autonomy of the family or in maintaining equality among its members, but in the threat to its pioneering and missionary functions. The kibbutzim did not grow just because intensive group life and equality were in themselves attractive to so many people, but because these characteristics enabled such people to endure the privations of pioneering. Kibbutzim, with few exceptions, do not undertake pioneering tasks today, and the movement has reached the stage of stagnation. It is unable to attract people from the outside, and members of kibbutzim are themselves assailed by doubts as to the value of their particular way of life. Adjustments to changing social and economic needs—which as such are not too difficult to make—are under these circumstances regarded as threatening, since even minor adjustments may prove fatal where the will to carry on does not exist.

The future of the kibbutz, therefore, depends either on finding some new national or social mission equally well suited to its peculiar structure as pioneering settlement, or else on consciously abandoning its claims to political and ideological leadership, and concentrating its efforts on perfecting its social and economic characteristics, until it becomes an attractive enough alternative to the individualistic way of life prevailing in other present-day communities.

It is unlikely, however, that this decision will be faced. Apart from the general reluctance to abandon an élite position once attained, the kibbutz movement, as has been shown (cf. p. 53 above), has become the main organizational and economic basis of two political parties, and of important sections of two other parties, one of these latter being the largest political party in the country. Furthermore, the role of the kibbutz in the history of Zionist settlement and struggle for statehood is a central theme in the socialist myth which legitimizes the rule of left-wing parties in the country. As a result the kibbutzim are not free agents in deciding their own future, because their leadership is part and parcel of political organizations that have important vested interests in perpetuating the élite position occupied by the kibbutz movement.

Many of the political leaders representing the kibbutz movement and upholding its ideology are, however, no longer active members of kibbutzim, though some of them may still retain formal membership. Altogether, it seems that the politically most active element which was attracted to the kibbutz in the first place because it was an élite group has probably deserted it by now. Former members of kibbutzim abound in high political office (cf. p. 55 above), among high-ranking government officials and army officers, and in many other positions of responsibility. [1] The present membership of the kibbutzim is, therefore, probably composed of people who are more genuinely attracted to the kibbutz as a way of life than as an élite group. This deduction is also supported by a recent attitude survey of members in a sample of kibbutzim. [2]

The kibbutzim are, therefore, under cross-pressures from the claims of a pioneering ideology on the one hand, and the claims of members concerned with making the kibbutz a fairly comfortable place to live in, on the other. The first are backed up by tradition, the rewards attaching to an élite status, and political party interests; while the second derive strength from the growth of the families in the kibbutz and the diminishing importance of agricultural pioneering in the country. As long as this situation of indecision under cross-pressures lasts, there is little prospect of a renewed expansion of the kibbutz movement.

1. Cf. Joseph Ben-David, 'The Rise of a Salaried Professional Class in Israel', *Transactions of the Third World Congress of Sociology*, London, 1956, p. 302-10.
2. Y. Talmon-Garber and Z. Stup, 'Histapkuth Bemuath—Dfusei Thmura Ideologith (Secular asceticism-patterns of ideological change), *Sefer Bussel*, 1961, p. 1-41.

Integration, Effectiveness, and Adaptation in Social Systems: A Comparative Analysis of Kibbutzim Communities

Daniel Katz and Naftali Golomb

The kibbutz system furnishes a new model of community life which emphasizes both the integrated group and the integrated individual. It is a way of life which includes within the framework of its community the full personality and avoids the fragmentation of the individual which is characteristic of most organized societies. It is a total-inclusion system in which members live, raise children, work and produce and grow old and die. A kibbutz is in fact a micro-cosmos society. It is a community which strives with considerable success to integrate technological achievements with social achievements. The discrepancy between technical advance and social progress is the crucial dilemma of modern industrial society. The kibbutz system thus is of interest not only in its own right, but in relation to more conventional social structures.

Students of comparative social organizations will be very limited, however, in their understanding of the kibbutz system if they take the traditional sociological approach with its descriptive categories derived from formal structural analysis. Often its assumptions are those of closed-system theory. Kibbutz members themselves raise questions about the applicability and relevance of much of the past research to the understanding of the kibbutz system and the dynamic issues of kibbutz life. The sociological conceptions emphasize social structural variables of descriptive character and minimize motivational and personality considerations based upon more explanatory propositions. Yet the kibbutz system is a small system based upon voluntarism, informality, face-to-face interaction, and direct democracy. There are no formal sanctions for coercing people, and there are no material incentives for maximizing individual effort. The branch teams in farm and factory are autonomous groups. The complex network of vertical and horizontal committees cutting across the community is maintained by shared expectations and norms and by the referent power of leaders and subgroups. The main social forces shaping the social realities of the kibbutz are the group forces of a socialpsychological character. The motivational dynamics of the individual in the system are crucial. Hence an approach which accepts motivational forces as *givens* or *constants* is inadequate for a study of the kibbutzim. What is needed, then, for better understanding of the kibbutz is a theoretical attack designed to deal with the integration of the individual into his group and his community, to study motivational and cognitive processes and interpersonal relations—in brief, a socialpsychological approach. Often, however, psychologists, in their concern with personality variables, neglect the social context which conditions and helps to determine human behavior. Research needs to be guided by a theory which will take account not only of the integration of the individual into his community, but of the integration of the community itself and of the relationships of the community to the larger social systems in which it is embedded.

In recent years, a new approach which cuts across traditional areas of academic specialization has been winning support in the behavioral sciences, namely, open-system theory.[1] It is especially appropriate for the study of kibbutzim in that it deals with the human inputs into a social system, the specific internal processes of the system, the outcomes and the relations of the system to its environment. It is concerned with feedback processes which regulate the system and coordinate subsystems and with the underlying communication mechanisms of types of feedback. The degrees and kinds of openness which permit adaptation to outside forces are considered in relation to the coding and filtering mechanisms which preserve system identity. An open system functions not to maintain a steady state of a static character, but rather a state of dynamic equilibrium. Thus, open-system theory would deal not only with the three levels of our analysis, but also with their interdependence. The three levels are:

(1) The Individual Level—The motivations and beliefs which attract the individual to the system, which hold him in the system, and which relate to his performance in that system.

(2) The System Level—The internal system processes and the integration of the system as a system, system effectiveness and the effects of the system upon the behavior of its members.

(3) The Supra-System Level—The relation of the kibbutz to the movement of which it is a member and to the larger Israeli society.

For a study of kibbutzim, open-system theory needs some specification to encompass the three levels of analysis. Specifically, this elaboration must take into account three crucial problem areas:

(1) The degree of integration-disintegration.

(2) The degree of effectiveness.

(3) The adaptation and creative modification of values.

Every crucial problem area of a kibbutz is operationally perceived as a criterion measurement—that is, integration, effectiveness, and creative modification are yardsticks for the evaluation of the individual, of the system, and of its relationships to its social environment. These three criteria can thus be used at all levels of analysis. Moreover, they need to be used over a time sequence and their dynamic determinants ascertained. They may differ in their degree of realization at the different levels. Consequently, it may be that the kibbutz cannot reach maximum or optimal solutions at all levels simultaneously. The March-Simon model of "satisficing" may, under certain conditions, be the more appropriate model (March and Simon, 1958). March and Simon show that, in general, systems have built-in constraints which predispose them toward a satisfactory solution rather than an optimal outcome.

In examining the three criteria as they apply to the various levels of analysis, one can expect to find considerable overlapping between the individual and the system level in the specifics of integration and effectiveness. In kibbutz life, there is much less separation between goals and the means for their attainment than in formally organized systems.

The roles of the kibbutz member are much more likely to be expressive of his personality than is the role behavior of a person living in industrial society. The formal role differentiation making for segmentalization of the person is not a common occurrence in the kibbutz. Furthermore, the goals of the kibbutz system are deemed to be the same as the goals of the individual members. There is an organic feedback loop between the individual and the system with no intervention of coercive mechanisms through which the system controls its members.

The implications of our mode of analysis will become clearer if we describe the application of criteria to the three levels of analysis.

INTEGRATION

INDIVIDUAL LEVEL

The major interest here is the degree to which the individual is fully integrated into the social system in relation to his own needs and capacities. On the negative side the apathetic, anomic, uninvolved person shows not only lack of system integration but poor personality integration as well. He is outside the system in a psychological sense with no channels of personality expression to compensate for his social isolation. The rebellious person, on the other hand, can be alienated in some respects from the major system but can still be active and expressive in his rebellion. In the kibbutz, this theoretical problem of the disaffected system person who is still a well-integrated personality is not likely to arise because of the closeness of the system to the individual. Hence alienation, as well as apathy, are indications of the failure of system integration.

Another measure of poor system integration is the degree of conflict the individual experiences between his system roles, or between his personal needs and aspirations, and his functional role as a worker. Women in the kibbutzim have some of the same frustrations between their work roles and their aspirations as in other societies, but the problem is recognized and solutions are being sought (Rosner, 1967).

On the positive side, we speak of good integration of members into the system if they are bound in, in four ways: functionally, socioemotionally, normatively, and ideologically.

(1) Functional integration refers basically to two factors: (a) whether the individual has a meaningful work role in the system, and (b) whether membership in the system brings a materially satisfying way of life.

(2) Socioemotional integration refers to the affective attachment to the system and includes identification with the community, attraction to fellow members, and positive conditioning to the social environment.

(3) Normative integration has to do with the acceptance of norms of behavior which are shared with others and which are consistent with the values of the system. These shared norms, then, are the legitimized expectations of the behavior of members. Thus the individual will conform to what he perceives as legitimate institutional demands, without feeling coerced.

(4) Ideological integration refers to more generalized values of the kibbutz movement and furnishes the broader legitimation for system norms.

The kibbutz cliché of thinking is to overestimate the normative and ideological forms of integration and to underestimate the other types. But all four are important in achieving maximum integration. Deficits in one form can be compensated for by another, but in the long run integration suffers if one type is absent or weak. The kibbutz does lack the material type of reward available to people in Israel outside the kibbutz. No one can profit at the expense of his neighbor. Nevertheless, material progress and material rewards are not without significance. People share in the common fruit of their labors and their joint efforts lead to greater returns.

These four types of integration can be separated for purposes of analysis, but in reality they exist in combination and interact with one another. Economic success is functional, or instrumental, but will add to socioemotional integration. Further, a work role that is weak in functional meaning to the individual can be strengthened by its socioemotional characteristics. In discussing kibbutz farming as an integrating mechanism, we will see how it involves functional and socioemotional features as well as ideological ones.

Moreover, functional, socioemotional, normative, and ideological involvements are the sociopsychological sources of integration. For commitment to the community, these sources have to be tied to the community system in that it is the kibbutz that is the agency responsible for insuring the satisfaction of needs. Thus it is not enough to have people finding gratification in their work or in their attachment to their physical environment. They conceivably could find similar meaningful work roles in other systems or they could still like their surroundings in a non-kibbutz setting. Hence, mechanisms of integration develop which link the individual to the particular community through symbols reflecting a common way of life, a common history, and a common fate. We shall discuss these mechanisms in the following description of socioemotional integration.

Socioemotional integration refers to the identification of the individual with his community, to his rootedness in his environment, to his sense of belonging to his group. There are many mechanisms which operate to produce integration of this sort. In the first place, physical separation of the community from the surrounding society makes possible the emotional attachment to a physically bounded space, its people and its objective environment (buildings, land, hills and valleys, trees). Furthermore, physical boundaries are critical for a contra-culture which could be overrun by the many constant forces from the dominant society. Kibbutzim that did start in the outskirts of urban centers were not able to survive in the setting when the cities grew and enveloped them. It is extremely difficult to set up a cooperative commonwealth in an urban backyard of a capitalistic community. The development and preservation of system identity requires boundaries and, in this case, physical separation in order to provide the necessary conditions both for cultural distinctiveness and for emotional identification with the new system.

Second, ceremonials, festivals, public singing and dancing, and celebrations of the birthday of the kibbutz all provide the basis for an affective conditioning to the community. Nor should the heavy social reinforcement of these occasions be underestimated. The interstimulation of people engaged in common celebrations builds up in a circular fashion. The Hora dancing includes all members of the community in a common joyous dance, in contrast to modern individual dancing. Kanter includes these types of group activities as one of the mechanisms making for communal commitment, and her study of American utopian communities reports that such commitment is associated with the success or failure of the system (Kanter, 1968).

Third, decision-making also can contribute heavily to the emotional cohesion of the group, though there are occasions when it may detract from group solidarity. The continuity of personal association is paralleled by the historical continuity of the culture which, as one of its forms of expression, has made Hebrew its accepted language. The feeling of togetherness and sense of community grow out of a common way of life and a common history and are fostered by symbolic and functional activity. The result of these many processes has been the creation of a cultural island.

Socialization practices for the second and third generations which emphasize the distinctiveness of kibbutz culture are productive of integration for those who have not selected themselves for the kibbutz.

The commitment of the children growing up in the kibbutz will differ in some respects from that of the founding kibbutzniks, but the strength of their attachment may be just as great. The use of peer groups to develop a collective sense of responsibility in communal activities and growing up in a psychologically rewarding environment with unique characteristics tie the younger generation to their communities. This is attested by the fact that the great majority of the kibbutz second generation, after contact with the outside world through service in the armed forces, returns to the kibbutz—either to their own community or to the kibbutz of the spouse. The low attrition rate is all the more remarkable in view of the greater affluence and the more comfortable way of life outside of the kibbutz and the greater variety of stimulation provided by the urban environment.

It should also be noted that farming as a way of life helps to bind the individual to his community. The general trends in most societies toward urban concentration can obscure the real attractions of farming as an occupation. People leave the land in good part because of the difficulty of competing as small farmers and because of the economic rewards and stimulation of the city. Those who take jobs in factories and in many service organizations in the city are not, however, moving to more gratifying work. In fact, many farmers in Western countries cling to their farms long past the point of economic solvency. Apart from monetary considerations, farming holds many intrinsic satisfactions. The individual can shape and control his environment, can watch the results of his labor take form, and can have direct experience with the world of nature. In other words, his work can be an integrating pattern in which his needs for accomplishment, for individuality and for aesthetic enjoyment of nature, can all find fulfillment. The kibbutzim have presented a contra-cultural trend in societal development in utilizing farming as an important means for mobilizing the energies of people of a relatively high level of education for community living. This has been accomplished by avoiding the extreme of the individual farmer working on his own and the opposite extreme of the large-scale farm with its hierarchical organization. The kibbutzim with their cooperative farming teams provide ample opportunity for meaningful interaction among the members. Yet every individual is a key performer and his individuality is not lost in routinized fragmented role-taking. Thus the kibbutz has utilized the natural advantages of farming in a social framework of mutual support and responsibility as a mechanism of integration. In addition, of course, the ideology of the founders placed a high value upon a back-to-the-land movement so that we are dealing with a combination of forces the relative weights of which are difficult to ascertain.

In a voluntary system like the kibbutz, then, there is a state of instability in integration if there is insufficient coverage of all four types of involvement. It is well known that many kibbutz members who are strong in their ideological integration are weak in functional integration or in socioemotional integration and in time some of them may depart from their kibbutz. As we have already indicated, one problem for women in the kibbutz is their functional integration.

Thus the kibbutz as a voluntary, all-inclusive society faces special problems in the integration of its members. It must be especially attractive to recruit and hold members because joining a kibbutz is a crucial act which has to take into consideration one's whole life span. Joining a kibbutz is not like joining other organizations such as business enterprises, public agencies, labor unions, and so on. Potential members, in reaching a decision to join, must explore factors transcending the usual considerations involved in entering other organizations. They must be prepared to accept the kibbutz as a way of life where they will establish their families, raise children, and become full-fledged participants in the community. There is the implicit commitment to perpetuate the system from one generation to another and to insure its growth. This means that the self-selection process, while it does not guarantee integration, can work to facilitate the binding-in of members possessing common values and prior commitment. Self-selection, however, does not assure functional integration, as the history of utopian communities attests. In the past, some American utopian groups have attracted people with a common ideology but with no experience and little capacity for farming or business activities. In spite of their attractiveness as intellectual discussion centers, they failed as economic enterprises.

In Israel, there is an uneven state of competition between the kibbutzim and the larger society in attracting and holding members. The kibbutz as a voluntary system cannot hold its members against their wishes and they are always free to move to the larger society. They are prepared to manage for themselves, even in urban environments. Dissatisfied kibbutz members thus have the alternative of moving to the cities, but dissatisfied urban dwellers, in most cases, lack the socialization and training which would make the kibbutz a realistic alternative for them. This one-sided state of affairs operates to reduce the growth rate of the kibbutzim, but it also works to increase the degree of integration of self-selected members into the kibbutz system.

SYSTEM LEVEL

At the level of the system, we are interested in the unity and cohesiveness of the kibbutz community. Do the groups such as the work teams, educational groupings, and age groups crosscut or overlap all along the system in relation to their values, cultural backgrounds, and political orientations? If cleavage exists in the system, then there is the fear that, in such a small community where relationships are so close, the break will be intensified strongly. It may lead to personalization of issues and may split the community into rival parties. This has happened on a few occasions in the past.

Diversities and differences of groups making up the kibbutz are not inevitably a force making for disintegration. Diversities and differences are helpful in breeding a cross-fertilized social system, nourished by varying cultural streams in reference to age, sex, country of origin, profession, and status. Experience indicates that the best communities seem to be those which became melting pots of people from many cultures. In the long run, these communities seem preferable, because of the richness of their cultural base, to those deriving from a mono-culture with members coming from a single country of origin. Although this is commonly accepted as a sound generalization, it is nevertheless true that melting-pot processes may temporarily cause difficulties before adequate communication is achieved.

Differences among groups can be helpful if these differences focus on only one issue and are not cumulative across many crucial questions affecting the system. If, however, members of a group differ from members of another group on a series of issues, there is reinforcement of their divergent approaches and polarization of the community is a likely outcome. In the kibbutz, for example, the differences between the younger and older generations could become a critical problem if the young people were not readily absorbed into the management structure. Hence, divergencies in values of the generations need not be reinforced by their occupying different positions in the decision-making hierarchy as is true in the United States. Nevertheless, the kibbutz is vulnerable to polarization of opposed groupings in that it is separated from the larger society with relative lack of outside communication and with many relationships among the same people in the community. As has been already noted, differences in points of view can become intensified through personalization. The very closeness of the community, however, can be its own remedy. Since one has to live and work with people with whom one has disagreed, there is the practical necessity of keeping communication channels open. This is consistent with the observation of

Newcomb (1947) that the breakdown of communication increases autistic hostility.

If we look at the four bases of integration (functional, socioemotional, normative, ideological), then we have a means for evaluating the unity of the kibbutz. In the first place, functional arrangements work in the direction of integration. Groups within the community are not split along lines of material reward, since they share equally in the outcomes of system functioning. Moreover, though there are some differences with respect to the meaningful character of jobs, these are relatively minor compared to most societies. Differences do exist in that service roles are seen as less rewarding psychologically than other positions and carry less status—a differentiation which runs counter to the old utopian concept of egalitarianism. One solution has been the rotation of less desirable jobs, which does not occur in conventional societies where people are bound into intrinsically unrewarding tasks. Nevertheless, as professional and specialized roles develop, the kibbutz may face more of a problem in the future than it has in the past.

Second, socioemotional attraction to a subgroup is not likely to be a cause of friction between groups as in ethnic divisiveness in the United States. Opportunities for friendship patterns are provided by the small work groups and other associations in the kibbutz. It is not necessary for a member to love every one of his fellows in the community. What is necessary is that socioemotional attractions and repulsions do not become channelled along lines of functional groups or ideological factions. Again, the nature of kibbutz arrangements does not facilitate such divisiveness.

Third, for community cohesiveness, there should not be conflicting norms for different groups. There are a number of devices which minimize normative conflict. For one thing, norms governing behavior derive very closely from the participation of all members of the community in the interpretation of accepted practices. For another, the rotation of officers for all activities prevents cleavage between the manager and rank and file members. Again, it is possible that normative conflict may assume more importance in the future with increasing professionalization.

Fourth, though there may be ideological differences in the kibbutz among its members, there are seldom strong group differences based upon commitment to discrepant value systems. Some kibbutzim in the past did split on political issues and actively carried the fight through to a separation into two communities. This, however, is a great exception in the history of the kibbutzim. Probably the greatest source of value conflict has to do with the distribution of resources between the economic and social subsystems. There are those who want to see any surplus reinvested in farming and production, and those who would give more emphasis to utilizing the returns for a better way of life. Since this is a relative question of emphasis, it does not make for disintegration of the community at the ideological level.

Another reason why ideological conflict is not a major source of divisiveness in the kibbutzim is the nature of the ideological beliefs of many members. They see their values as capable of being operationalized rather than as existing on a symbolic level with little reference to experience. Particularly striking to the observer visiting the kibbutzim is the highly pragmatic orientation of a people committed to ideological doctrines. He finds ideologists who not only discuss all types of issues at considerable length, but who are also heavily task-oriented; when it comes to practical problems, their words resemble those of the graduates of an American engineering school. They have a capacity for immediately translating an issue into its problem characteristics, identifying the dimensions of the problem, and moving ahead to its solution.

The explanation of this orientation has three sources. The original migrants who founded the community were a highly select group with respect to their varied experiences, intellectual sophistication, and motivation to build their own communities. A second reason is the nature of the objective environment. The circumstances facing the settlers were harsh, but capable of transformation. To survive required a high degree of sacrifice and pragmatism, but meaningful attacks upon economic problems yielded substantial returns. Hence, efforts at problem solution were rewarded. The third reason has to do with the nature of the ideology. The beliefs themselves were more functional than those of religious utopias which are often of a negative, prohibitive character. The ideas of cooperative effort and sharing, and of the full use of human resources in attacking community problems, whether economic or social, were not so much symbolic ideals as highly useful weapons.

This is not to say that the average member of the kibbutz of either the old or the new generation is a model of integration in fusing the Marxian ideals of theory and practice. Most members probably would show a gap between their declared values and their operational values. And the younger generation would be less concerned with the older expressed values and would be more involved in the operational norms of the system. Nonetheless, the values of the kibbutz system, like most democratic ideologies, would have more objective reference and receive more pragmatic testing than the codes of revealed truth, absolutistic morality, or symbolic traditionalism.

Basically, then, most kibbutzim show a high degree of community integration compared to other social systems. There are no economic lines of cleavage. There are some problems of conflict associated with work roles but these are relatively minor. There is a heavy sharing of norms about the many roles and activities of members. Though there are some differences in values, there is a great deal of ideological agreement based upon both self-recruitment into the system and choices made to remain within the system. The fact that roles are not as divorced from personal expression as in a complex formal organization does permit more personalization of conflict between people and more carry-over of differences from one setting to another. But by and large, the differences that do occur do not accumulate and reinforce one another along group lines.

The real test of kibbutz integration, however, is to be found in its turnover and growth. Net growth furnishes a critical operational measure of kibbutz integration in attracting and holding people, especially since the utopian community is a small contra-culture group. If there is group unity and a correspondence between individual needs and values and group norms and ideology, then people will not leave the system. Moreover, it should be attractive not only to its older members, but also to the new young people who come to visit and to do volunteer work.

INTEGRATION WITH THE SOCIAL ENVIRONMENT

No community can remain closed to its larger social environment, namely, the society in which it exists. The kibbutzim interact with society, are affected by it, and in turn affect the larger culture. The drastic changes occurring in Israel in the last decade necessarily have led to adaptation processes on the part of the kibbutzim in relating to the larger system. Yet the kibbutzim in some ways represent a contra-culture to the culture of Israel, which legitimizes private enterprise, formalized religion, and large-scale organizations. The question is whether the kibbutzim might meet the fate of the utopian communities of the nineteenth century.

Can the kibbutzim reach a dynamic equilibrium between integration and separation with respect to the larger society? One fact which argues that that outcome is probable is the pluralistic character of Israeli society. Pluralistic society is the breeding life-space of utopian communities. Israeli society has many different social forms in its farming, industry, and military establishments. The military represents not only some traditional patterns, but also a citizens' army and an internal Peace Corps. A tolerance, then, for different organizational forms and for different value systems does exist in Israel today. Within this pluralistic framework, however, there must be an openness across subsystems so that, for example, the kibbutzim will accept new members from other sectors of Israeli life and, in turn, allow its members the freedom to leave the kibbutzim for other subsystems. The autonomy of a subsystem does not permit it to keep its borders closed.

The concept of pluralistic society has two dimensions. One refers to the tolerance for various social forms such as cooperative communities, and publicly and privately owned and operated farms; the other refers to the number of relatively independent power groups having the same essential social form. The kibbutzim exist in a society which is pluralistic in both senses. Israeli society has many private enterprises with no domination by one or two industrial giants. Moreover, it is unusual in the variety of types of social structures it legitimizes. At one extreme is the privately owned and operated company. At the other extreme is the communal cooperative of the kibbutz. In between are still other forms. The moshavim are cooperative communities with family-owned farms. There are publicly or governmentally owned and operated enterprises. In addition, the labor movement owns some plants which are run as conventional, private, profit-making businesses. But the labor movement also has cooperative units of an industrial or service character, owned by individual workers who operate them with considerable autonomy with respect to the Histadrut, or overall labor organization. The Histadrut not only is in private business, but also is the administrative tent for various types of cooperative enterprises. Capitalistic and socialistic forms are thus intermingled in Israeli society. The 1960 contributions of the various sectors of the domestic economy are illustrated in Table 1. In the United States, private enterprise contributes over 80% of the gross national product. In Israel, 95% of the workers belong to labor unions. In the United States, only 28% of the workers are union members. The pluralism

TABLE 1
THE SECTOR DISTRIBUTION OF ISRAELI ECONOMY

Net Domestic Products of Israel in 1960	
State Sector	21.1
Labor-controlled sector	20.4
Total Public	41.5
Total Private	58.5

SOURCE: Sixth Report of the Falk Institute, Hein Barkay.

of Israel is thus much more favorable to the survival and growth of cooperative communities than is that of the United States.

The fact that the kibbutzim are not as contra-cultural in Israel as they would be in the United States does not mean that the more balanced society represents a harmonious state of affairs. As counter forces approach equality, the situation that develops resembles more a tug of war than integration. A pluralistic system thus has built-in sources of system strain. The kibbutzim would not like to see the balance in Israel shifted toward the private sector. On the contrary, their members view their substystem as a microcosm of the larger society toward which the larger structure should move. They wish to modify Israeli institutions in the direction of egalitarian and cooperative values. In turn, some of the proponents of private property and traditional modernization would like to see the decline of the egalitarianism of the cooperative movements.

The fourfold bases of integration at the individual level still have some relevance for the relationship of the kibbutz to the larger society. The subsystem will be tied into the larger structure if it can furnish needed products and services to the national state and in return can receive the resources it needs. In other words, functional interdependence is an important aspect of societal integration. As will appear in greater detail in subsequent discussion, the kibbutzim, though dependent upon Israel for their well-being, make contributions of critical importance to the economic and political life of Israel.

Socioemotional attraction to the Israeli people as a whole is fostered by threats and dangers to Israel. The continuing conflict with Arabs has unified the people of Israel so that distinctions between kibbutzniks and non-kibbutzniks are of less importance. Though there are differences in norms governing behavior in the kibbutz and in other parts of Israel, norms associated with the assumption of national roles are the same. The members of the kibbutz are staunch supporters of the national state. They play active political roles in voting and serving in office. Their young people willingly accept the required years of military service, and the kibbutzim furnished more than their share of volunteers in combat units in the Six Days' War. Normatively, the people of the kibbutzim are tied into the national system as responsible citizens.

Ideologically, there are real differences between the values of the socialist direct democracy of the kibbutz and those of other parts of the Israeli society. But there is agreement on such ideological goals as democracy, humanitarianism, equality of opportunity and upon the need for an independent homeland for the Jewish people.

The basis for the relationship between the kibbutzim and Israeli society is one of social exchange, and this concept will be elaborated in more detail later. In brief, however, there is a trade-off between the resources and autonomy permitted to the kibbutzim and their contributions to the economy of the nation, to its defense system, power structure, cultural revival, and so on. In contrast to the utopian communities, which were concerned only with their own salvation and tried to be fully isolated from the larger society, the kibbutzim are integrated into Israel through their multifunctional roles. Kibbutz members have participated in significant roles in Israel far beyond their proportion in the population. This heavy contribution was obvious in the prestate period, but its vitality and dynamics in serving Israel in the poststate period are nonetheless still true if one consults objective records.

There is a swinging pendulum of trends in the adaptation of the kibbutzim to the changes that occur in the larger society, and also in the adaptation (radiation) of the larger society to the kibbutz way of life. The equilibrium between the Israeli society and the kibbutzim is dynamic, and it is related to the qualitative and quantitative changes in the role of kibbutzim. Three periods should be noted.

In the prestate period, the majority of the people in the larger society recognized the kibbutzim as an elite group serving the larger society, and kibbutz members were perceived with pride. In the early years of Israel's statehood, however, there were drastic changes of attitude in the large society toward the kibbutzim. These communities during this period were perceived as an outmoded social form, and as contradictory to the normalization needed for the economic growth of Israel. The role of kibbutzim in the past was respected. As Israel gained its statehood, people thought that the role of voluntary organizations, and especially the kibbutzim, had passed. Many saw the kibbutz as being quite rigid and unadaptive to technological innovations. Its basic foundations, they believed, prevented it from competing with the family farm and private industry. Jewish people, having thirsted for 2,000 years to gain their statehood, achieved their goal. The reaction was to believe that the state, through its institutions would solve all problems. There was no need for the roles of voluntary organizations and this was especially seen as true for the kibbutzim. In this period, the pendulum was at the lowest point in comparison to its heights in the prestate period. Also expressed was the ideological justification that egalitarian principles were contradictory to the normalization of Israel's economy.

Over time, it became more and more clear to the objective observer that the kibbutzim were no less adaptable than other social forms and were capable of meeting the needs of accelerated environmental changes in modern Israeli industrial society. The interesting phenomenon is that they have reached a creative modification of the kibbutz human organization which is still consistent with its major values.

Consequently, in the third period, which carries us into the present time, the kibbutzim are seen as playing an important role in modern Israeli society. But there have been qualitative and quantitative changes in the roles of the kibbutzim in Israel compared to the prestate period. Thus, the pendulum is again swinging toward the top, but not following its previous path. The kibbutzim are now seen in a more differentiated way, both with respect to their contributions to various areas of life, and to the societal inputs provided by Israel. A more balanced approach is in evidence. This approach, both by the society at large and by the kibbutz people, is necessary for recognizing that subcultures are less strong and thus more adaptive to the larger society. The parts played by the subsystem and the supersystem must be seen in the right proportion. In Israeli society and its governmental agencies, people realize the importance of voluntary organizations in contributing to the functions of a structured, institutionalized society. Never can a state solve its problems without the help of many diversified forms of voluntary organizations. Israel has become more sober and after so many centuries of oppression, has already passed the period of emotional drunkenness which occurred with the achievement of statehood.

During the past five years, the kibbutzim have kept pace with the larger society by an average annual growth rate of three percent. The prevailing dynamics of growth of egalitarian communities in the inegalitarian pluralistic society of Israel is the survival model of gradual growth that preserves its percentage share in population growth of the past years. This corresponding rate of population increase can be viewed as a *satisficing* solution to the built-in dilemma of a contra-culture surviving in a dominant culture.

The hypothesis would be that it cannot grow disproportionately compared to the larger society without creating great system strain. Yet it would be unsafe to project parallel growth curves for the years ahead because the assumption of a pattern of stable relationships between the size of a subsystem and the larger system is questionable in the dynamic society of Israel. There are some facts which contradict it. The limitations of water and land are now much greater than in previous years and affect the urban areas less heavily than the rural sections. To continue their growth rate, kibbutzim must accordingly develop in new economic directions. Then, too, the influx of Oriental Jews has affected the composition of the kibbutz and non-kibbutz populations differentially. Whereas Oriental Jews comprised only 10% of the population of Israel in 1948, they are now a little more than 50% of the population. But in the kibbutzim of 1969 they are only 7% or 8% of the membership. In short, there are dynamic forces affecting the society and its subsystems in different ways so that evenness of growth across the system may require a self-fulfilling prophecy on the part of many leaders.

We have jumped from the kibbutz as a community to the larger Israeli society and neglected the integration between these levels achieved through the larger groupings and movements such as regional cooperation, the kibbutz movements, the overall kibbutz federation, and the labor movement. These interstitial networks operate as a two-way street through which the kibbutz becomes involved in the larger society and in turn is strengthened by its belonging to larger groupings. In some respects, the kibbutz is a cultural island in its physical separation, in its relatively high degree of autonomy, and in its own norms and practices, but it is an island with many bridges to nearby islands and to the mainland.

Regional cooperation, though not the major basis of societal integration, is significant in its own right. In addition to linking several kibbutzim together in establishing and maintaining a common high school, regional cooperation takes other interesting forms. In a given geographical area, the kibbutzim will maintain common facilities for processing and marketing agricultural products. This arrangement will also include the moshavim or cooperative farms in the area. Kibbutzniks are thus brought together, not only with their fellows from other kibbutzim, but also with outsiders from the cooperative farms. The economic cooperation which results benefits both groups.

All kibbutzim belong to one of five organized movements or federations. There is a high degree of cooperation among the communities in these movements, and a large movement can support research and training centers for its members. In this fashion, some of the advantages of technical, specialized, and professional training present in a larger system can be realized by the participation of the small communities in their movement. Each movement has its own bank to provide economic assistance and loans. Other services, such as the skills of architects for designing new buildings, are also provided. Moreover, decisions about the allocation of manpower are made at the federation level. Applicants for membership from the outside are assigned to given kibbutzim. If a new kibbutz is set up, the manpower to be furnished by individual communities is discussed and decided by the federation. Finally, though the ideological differences between the movements are no longer as great as during the founding years, the values of a given kibbutz receive support both in their maintenance and their operation through interaction in their own movement. The movements also serve to tie the kibbutzim to the larger society as well, as will appear presently in our discussion of the labor movement.

The kibbutzim have moved toward even greater cooperation through a single federation, which is the organization of the five movements or federations. The overall organization has many educational, research, and training institutions. The major centers are Oranim, a teachers' college for kibbutz educators; the Rupin Institute for agriculture; Rehovat, for graduate training in agriculture; and the Economic Advisory Research Center. The Rupin Institute, an institution of higher education for managers, agricultural workers, and other technicians, illustrates how the federation ties the kibbutzim into the larger society. For this Institute, in some of its operations, is officially an agency of the Israeli government though operated by the federation. The government contributes to the budget of the Institute, as in the case of the Kibbutz Management Center, which is a joint venture of the Ministry of Farming and the federation. The Institute utilizes many faculty members from the universities of Israel. As part of its technical assistance program, the government sends foreign students, mainly from Asia and Africa, to the Institute for special programs of study. Thus this federation activity provides a network of communication and activity connecting the kubbutzniks with the larger society. Similarly, at Oranim the federation maintains a teachers' training college primarily for kibbutz teachers, which also has government support, utilizes lecturers from Israeli universities, and links kibbutz people to Israeli society.

All members of the kibbutzim are also members of the labor movement in Israel. The founding fathers were in the majority of cases Socialists, many of whom were active in the labor movements in their own country, and later in Israel. They helped to establish the fairly powerful labor organization known as the Histadrut, and some officers of the Histadrut came from kibbutzim. Again, this involvement of kibbutzniks in activities outside their communities ties them into other systems. It furnishes ideological reinforcement for their value orientation and in turn relates outside labor to the kibbutzim as a source of support. In fact, the social exchange means that there is more ideological input into the labor movement from the kibbutzim than from the labor movement into the kibbutzim.

The relationship between the labor movement and utopian communities finds reflection in political activities. Many kibbutzniks are members of one of the labor parties. They are not merely formal members but activists, and frequently stand for election to public office. In the past, Parliament members from kibbutzim held about 15% of the seats and about a third of the Cabinet posts in spite of the fact that they constitute only 4% of the population. Hence, the activities of the kibbutz members in the labor movement and in the related political parties involves them heavily in Israeli society. Elected and appointed political officers maintain their kibbutz membership and make possible effective communication in the kibbutzim about national affairs. Though these people have held strategic positions in government, they have not utilized their posts to advance the kibbutz cause, though they are sometimes subject to criticism by some kibbutzniks for the divorcing of their two roles.

We have made passing reference to the support of kibbutzim values from their ties to their own movement and to the labor movement. The ideological integration of the kibbutz member thus has a broad base because he is not only tied to the norms of his own community, but he is also identified with the values of collectivities which transcend his immediate group. He has a sense of belonging to the socialist movement in his country and to related ideological groupings the world over. The interest of kibbutzniks in Japanese groups attempting to set up cooperative commonwealths is a case in point. There has been another trend, however, not as universal, but still not particularistic in its implications, namely the identification with Zionism—belief in the necessity of a Jewish homeland to preserve the physical and cultural integrity of the Jewish people. This was an important force in founding the kibbutzim and in the ideological integration of their members. Continuing immigration into Israel of refugees helps to sustain this stream of influence. The younger generation of kibbutzniks were relatively less affected by this type of value orientation, but the continuing threat of the Arabs to the existence of Israel has made Zionism more salient for them as well.

MODERNIZATION AND
THE SURVIVAL OF THE KIBUTZIM

Some sociologists regard the kibbutzim as anachronisms in a modern society and predict their demise as Israel moves toward modernization. The argument, in somewhat exaggerated form, runs as follows. In the prestate period, the egalitarian ideology and the collective enterprises of the pioneering kibbutzim played a functional role in the motivation, morale, and effective struggle for achieving an independent state. The dedication of individuals to the community of interest in the absence of formalized structure was critical in the early days. With the establishment of the state, however, the movement is of questionable usefulness. In fact, the traditional collective of prestate history is a conservative and restricting factor in Israel's development and egttarianism has become an ideological stereotype without real meaning. Modernization in developing countries has a number of essential characteristics.

First, the growth of Weberian bureaucracy with elaborated role systems replaces traditional and personal relationships as the basis of social organization. Universalistic rules and roles become the reliable conditions for societal maintenance and growth, rather than particularistic relationships. The rule of law replaces the rule of men. Coordination and planning of societal activities and the meeting of the needs of all cannot be predicated upon the specific interpersonal relationships within the small groups. The kibbutzim, with their emphasis upon informal social structure, voluntarism, and direct democracy, are no longer in the mainstream of the universalistic trends of a large, developing industrial society. They will either decline in membership or lose their distinctive character as utopian communities.

Second, the growth of mass media and mass communication sounds the death knell for small groups in maintaining their distinctive values, modes of limited communication, and entertainment. Information relevant to the whole society is readily available to all citizens and provincial interests take second place. Values and ideals common to the society are directly and indirectly instilled through newspapers, the radio, and television.

Third, urban centers providing many types of services from medical care to theaters grow at the expense of the rural environment. The diversification of activity in employment is paralled by greater opportunities for cultural and social stimulation in the urban setting. Increasingly, the kibbutzim and moshavim, as small rural communities, cannot compete with the cities in professional and job opportunities and in a culturally rich life.

Fourth, as modernization proceeds, it makes available certain types of freedom for many individuals in that they are not tied to a given set of people or a given geographical area. They are not confined to the work situation for establishing friendships, they may join the political groups they wish, and they may find compatible associates for their hobbies. They can shift jobs and places of residence. In the first stages of industrial development, such opportunities may be relatively few, but with the development of a more affluent society, they are becoming more abundant. The rules of the bureaucratic game have their own restrictions, but they do not tie the individual inevitably to a single subsystem; nor does membership in one subsystem necessarily dictate membership in another system. Some individuals may feel lost in such an impersonal world, but many find freedom in escaping personal surveillance by an enclosing primary group around the clock. Since self-expression and self-realization depend upon the individual's ability to choose for himself, he may well prefer the freedom to manipulate an organizational environment to fitting himself into the more restricting mold of a small rural community.

There is merit in this contention that the kibbutzim represent too much of a contra-culture to survive the modern trends in a developing society. Basically, however, this view is a great oversimplification and fails to see the many aspects of modernization, dealing with past trends in large industrial societies rather than their present dilemmas. Modernization has not been the same for the United States, which lacked the traditional institutions, as for England with its historical and cultural traditions. Nor has it been the same in Sweden, with its compromises between socialism and capitalism, as in the United States. The factor of size alone is of significance. Small collective farms or industrial establishments might not be competitive in producing for a huge market in the United States. In Israel, the small market does not demand the economy of scale of the American scene. In fact, kibbutz farming and moshav farming have been more productive in Israel than has the farming of the private sector of the economy.

The major weakness in the doctrine of modernization as outmoding the kibbutzim, however, is the critical problem now encountered by post-industrial bureaucratic society. There is a fictitious component in the assumption that universalistic rules and roles and a government of laws rather than of men supplants particularistic arrangements among people. The sociological abstraction covers over the working out of the system in terms of human interaction. The great question in the highly developed bureaucratic systems is how to reform the structure to break down its formalization and to involve people in its operation and management. Large-scale organizations are threatened by revolt from within and the changes under consideration are in the direction of the kibbutzim principles of egalitarianism, voluntarism, and democracy. Thus the kibbutzim, instead of being a conservative force holding over from a prestate period, may be ahead of the present trends of normalization and modernization. The question, then, may be whether or not a country necessarily has to go through a period of bureaucratic modernization before it is ready to achieve democratic decentralization. Leon Trotsky's law of leaping development would predict that not every society has to go through the same evolutionary stages, but may be able to skip a given stage. In other words, it may not be necessary for Israel to become a set of a few centralized bureaucracies before permitting decentralization and autonomy to its subsystems.

Large bureaucratic structures are confronted by the difficulties of centralization in their control processes. The de jure centralization is often de facto decentralization, with a rubber stamping of decisions made down the line. Industrial organizations often move toward decentralization in order to have their component units face the test of competing directly in the marketplace. One great advantage of the small unit like the kibbutz is the ready mobilization of resources to solve an urgent problem and the economy of this mobilization. A large structure has difficulty in responding to immediate challenges, and by the time it can make the necessary rearrangements, the opportunity for effective action is gone. Hence, the large organization often fights the old war, not the present conflict. The expense, moreover, of making adjustments to meet changing demands is inordinately high for big structures, compared to the small unit.

Nor is there any compelling reason for assuming that a small country like Israel cannot continue to develop as a pluralistic society. There are genuine strengths in its pluralism which can have the advantage of both bureaucratic structures and voluntaristic subsystems. The advantage of the latter is the high degree of dedication and motivation of the members. This dynamic force has been directed at national goals of defense production, political leadership, and cultural activity. Such dedication is necessary in a small country where manpower is not expendable. It is as necessary now as in the prestate period. The growth of larger bureaucratic structures in Israel may make this need more rather than less salient.

Since a large system cannot operate through direct democracy, it is important to know what forms of indirect democracy are most functional for effectiveness and member satisfaction. We would suggest that the relationship between the kibbutzim and the Israeli nation furnishes a possible model. The kibbutzim, as subsystems of Israel, provide the psychological integration at the small-group level through direct democracy and maximum involvement of their people. They are, moreover, represented in the larger system through the election of their people to public office and the selection of their people for government posts. This mechanism ties them into the larger structure as does their identification with national goals. The representative democracy of the whole may have some of its vitality furnished by units which are not simple pieces of the larger bureaucracy but subsystems in their own right. Larger nations like the United States have problems in achieving such integration because the subunits, which could develop lives of their own and still be tied to the larger structure, are lacking. Individual states of the union may have once presented such possibilities. They no longer do. Israel is not only small, but it is unified by immediate and common danger. Hence it needs to maintain its pluralism, vitality, and dynamism, and here its cooperative communities are highly functional.

NOTE

1. The development of this theory as it applies to social systems by D. Katz and R. L. Kahn provides a useful framework for the analysis of the kibbutzim.

REFERENCES

ALLPORT, F. H. (1934) "The J-curve hypothesis of conforming behavior." *Journal of Social Psychology* 5: 141-183.

———(1933) *Institutional Behavior.* Chapel Hill: Univ. of North Carolina Press.

ASCH, S. (1952) *Social Psychology.* Englewood Cliffs, N.J.: Prentice-Hall.

BETTELHEIM, B. (1969) *Children of the Dream.* New York: Macmillan.

BUBER, M. (1949) *Paths in Utopia* (R.F.C. Hull, trans.). London: Routledge & Kegan Paul.

COHEN, E. (1969) "Comparative Study of the political institutions of collective settlements in Israel." Hebrew University Department of Sociology Report.

DURKHEIM, E. (1947) *Division of Labor in Society.* New York: Free Press.

KANTER, R. M. (1968) "Commitment and social organization: a study of commitment mechanisms in utopian communities." *American Sociological Review* 33: 499-517.

KATZ, D. and R. L. KAHN (1966) *Social Psychology of Organizations.* New York: John Wiley.

KELLEY, H. H. and J. W. THIBAUT (1954) "Experimental studies of group problem solving and process." In *Handbook of Social Psychology,* G. Lindzey and B. Aronson (eds.). Reading Mass.: Addison-Wesley. Vol 2, pp. 735-785.

MARCH, J. G. and H. A. SIMON (1958) *Organizations.* New York: John Wiley.

MELMAN, S. (n.d.) "Industrial efficiency under managerial vs. cooperative decision making." (mimeo)

NEWCOMB, T. M. (1947) "Autistic hostility and social reality." *Human Relations* 1: 69-86.

ROSNER, M. (1967) "Women in the kibbutz: changing status and concepts." *Asian and African Studies* (Annual of the Israel Oriental Society) 3: 35-68.

YUCHTMAN, E. and S. E. SEASHORE (1967) "A system resource approach to organizational effectiveness." *American Sociological Review* 32: 891-903.

The Structural Transformation of the Kibbutz[1]

Erik Cohen

Introduction

The collective movement in Israel is now more than 60 years old. From the days when a small group of people established the first "Kvutza" (collective) at Um Jumi (later to become Degania Alef) to the present day, the kibbutz movement has come a long way indeed. In 1969, there were 231 kibbutzim with about 84,670 inhabitants, about half of them full members. The kibbutz is by now famous throughout the world and

[1] This essay should have been written by the late Yonina Talmon-Garber, to sum up many years of work on the collective movement. But her premature death prevented her from writing in a comprehensive form the many single findings and insights of her work. So it happened that, though Mrs. Talmon always talked in terms of a structural typology of kibbutzim and its internal dynamics, she never put her ideas on this central theme of the sociological study of the kibbutz into written form (except in a summary fashion in [25]; this summary has been reprinted in [32]). It is a sad task for me, and one which I approach with much reluctance, to make up for that deficiency.

As I worked so closely with Yonina Talmon it is hard to point out exactly which ideas are hers and which are my own. I shall try, however, to indicate, wherever possible, where I am using Mrs. Talmon's ideas in my analysis.

The ideas presented in this paper were largely developed on the basis of the Research Project on Social Structure and Social Change in Collective Settlements, conducted at the Department of Sociology, Hebrew University, from 1954-1968; the study was directed by the late Yonina Talmon-Garber, and, in its later stages, by the author. I am indebted to Professor D. Katz, Dr. H. Meier-Cronemeyer and Dr. M. Rosner for their useful comments.

has been much studied, though only seldom copied.[2] It is one of the most prospering sectors of the Israeli economy, its agriculture ultramodern, though industry is gradually dominating its economy and beginning to provide the main source of its income. Among its members figure politicians, scientists, artists, managers of large public enterprises, etc. Nevertheless, at present, it experiences a deep internal crisis, caused, in part, by its very success. How has all this come about? What was the underlying process of transformation and what are the sources of the contemporary situation? We shall not attempt to give an exhaustive answer to this problem. But we shall try to uncover the basic sociological dynamics of the process of structural transformation of the kibbutz and indicate some of the factors at the root of the present crisis.[3]

Structural typologies of social development are among the most common tools of macrosociological analysis. Beginning with F. Toennies' conceptualization of social evolution in terms of "Gemeinschaft" and "Gesellschaft" (36), through the more refined typologies of Becker (1), Redfield (23), and many others, modern sociologists have attempted to provide a general paradigm of overall social change and transformation.[4]

Particularly relevant for our purpose is the attempt of the German sociologist, H. Schmalenbach to amend the basic Gemeinschaft-Gesellschaft typology by the addition of a new type, the Bund.[5] Schmalenbach's much neglected concept can be applied to many of the social and religious movements which, nourished by the discontent of contemporary life, strive to renew and rejuvenate society through a complete abandonment of its established institutions and through a radical or revolutionary transformation of its values and ways of life. Schmalenbach conceived of the Bund as a voluntary, and essentially transient, type of social structure. It is characterized by intensive emotional bonds between the members, and a strong attachment to the ideals which inspire them. The members of this Bund live in a state of heightened emotionality. The Bund is formed by similarly minded adults, who join each other by free choice and as a consequence of personal decision; they do not possess any common primordial attributes prior to joining the Bund. The Bund is, then, essentially a universalistic structure. In this respect it differs fundamentally from Toennies' "Gemeinschaft."

Schmalenbach's contribution makes possible the introduction of a

---

[2] There exist several bibliographies of publications on the Kibbutz: those by Horigan (18), Cohen (6), and Schur (30) are the most comprehensive ones.

[3] The theme of the contemporary crisis in the kibbutz is taken up in a more philosophical form in another paper by the author (7).

[4] For one of the best analytical discussions of these typologies see (24, Ch. VL).

[5] Schmalenbach's seminal essay was originally published in German (28); parts were translated into English under the title "The Sociological Category of Communion" (22, pp. 331–347).

radical change into the historical model of Toennies: the Gemeinschaft-Gesellschaft model is a linearly-evolutionary one, leading from a social past rooted in blood and soil to an ever more rationalized, uprooted, and individualistic future society. The addition of the Bund leads to a change of the model. Schmalenbach talked of the possibility of the Bund emerging from both the Gemeinschaft and the Gesellschaft as well as turning into each of these. For our purpose, however, it is important to point out that his analysis leads to an essentially cyclical model of social development. The full cycle could be presented schematically as Gemeinschaft turning into Gesellschaft, Gesellschaft being rejuvenated through the appearance of the Bund, the Bund striking roots and becoming through institutionalization a new Gemeinschaft, which again turns into Gesellschaft, etc. The fateful unilinearity of Toennies' conception is thus substituted by a cyclical model which emphasizes oscillation between institutionalization and rejuvenation. We shall see in the following that such a model serves well for the analysis of the structural transformations of the kibbutz.

The concept of the Bund was further refined by E. Shils (29, p. 138), who, on the basis of differentiation between ideological and personal primary groups, claimed that it is possible to differentiate, accordingly, two types of Bund — the ideological and the personal Bund. This insight provided another very useful lead for our own analysis.

The general conceptual scheme outlined here was applied by Yonina Talmon, at the early stages of our investigation, to the study of the social dynamics of the kibbutz. Mrs. Talmon dealt with these dynamics on two separate levels: phylogenetically the kibbutz movement as a whole undergoes a historical process of transformation from the Bund to the Commune (her term for the Gemeinschaft); orthogenetically each individual kibbutz undergoes such a transformation, irrespectively of the particular point in time when it was founded — though those kibbutzim which were founded at a relatively advanced point in the development of the movement will never exemplify fully the characteristics of the Bund and will pass quickly this stage of development. The transition from Bund to Commune is irreversible. Mrs. Talmon, however, conceived of the transition in terms of a multilateral scheme, and defined several constructed types of Communes into which a Bund may pass.

My own approach to the structural dynamics of the kibbutz is based on Mrs. Talmon's scheme but I attempt to amplify and amend it in two ways: firstly, I have further refined the typology and brought it in tune with reality through the addition of several new subtypes, discovered in the process of our analysis. Secondly, I have tried to bring the analysis up to date by conceptualizing some of the recent transformations in the largest and most mature kibbutzim in terms of a transition to a new structural type, the Association (my term for "Gesellschaft"). I have also tried to indicate the first stirrings towards a movement of internal rejuvenation in terms of the rebirth of the Bund through the strivings of some second-generation members of these mature kibbutzim.

The Underlying Variable: Mode of Integration

Figure 1 presents in the most concise as well as comprehensive form the various structural types of our typology as well as the dynamic interrelationships between them. The terms in bold-faced type represent the basic types; the others represent the constructed subtypes. This typology has been derived by way of abstraction from a variety of concrete findings as well as from several partial typologies which had been developed in the course of our study, embracing such aspects as types of institutionalization (4), family structure (33), structure of the sphere of work (5), etc. Our study lasted for about 14 years; during

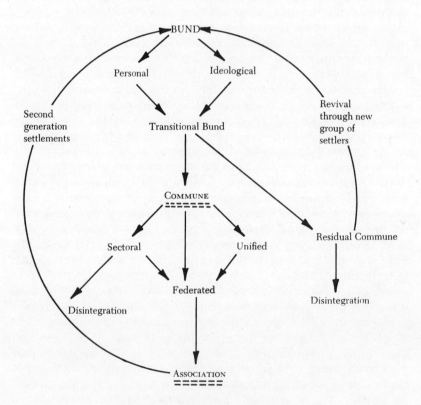

FIGURE 1: The Paradigm of Structural Types

that time structural types were provisionally conceptualized and then again reconceptualized under the impact of new findings and of a fuller view of the interrelationships between the various spheres of life on the kibbutz. The typology here presented represents only the last stage of this process of constant reformulation. It is thus possible that it will be further refined as additional data accumulate and as the kibbutz undergoes new historical changes.[6]

Our types are of necessity composed of a wide variety of characteristics. Though most of these are empirically derived, I do not claim that every kibbutz which can be categorized under one of the types will necessarily exhibit *all* the traits characteristic of that type. However, the various characteristics of a type usually cluster together and will appear whenever there are no strong local historical, geographical, or social conditions which work to the contrary. Whenever such conditions become a common factor influencing significantly a number of kibbutzim, an additional constructed type had been added to the typology.

Though empirically derived, our types are not unsystematic congeries of empirical traits. The various features of each type are logically interrelated. The focal theoretical variable of our typology is the characteristic manner in which each of the various types achieves social integration.

The concept of "mode of integration"[7] refers to the fundamental principle through which a community coheres and forms a unified whole. In each of the three main types of kibbutzim, the Bund, Commune and Association, a different mode of integration predominates:

(1) The integration of the Bund focuses on the *level of values*. The members of the Bund adhere to a common set of intensely lived "ultimate values" which give a transcendent though vaguely-defined meaning to every act of their daily life and to every aspect of their social relationships. The social integration of the Bund derives from the intensive and common attachment to values on part of all the members. The close personal ties between the members derive from that universalistic common attachment. Integration through common attachment to values will be most pronounced in the "ideological Bund," though the "personal Bund" is also essentially integrated in the same way; only the values, and the consequences of the value-attachment, are different: whereas in the "ideological Bund" the value emphasis is on the tasks of the kibbutz in the world beyond the community (e.g., pioneering for the broader Zionist movement), in the "personal Bund" the value emphasis is turned principally to the community itself — to the ideals of human relationships the members are expected to live up to.

---

[6] For comparative purposes, see an early statement of the typology in (33, pp. 123–127 and 25).

[7] I use this concept as defined by Holzner (17).

(2) The integration of the Commune focuses on the *level of social relations*. The members of the Commune are closely attached to more or less well-defined subgroups within the broader community. These particularistic attachments are permitted and valued for their own sake as well as accepted as a means through which the individual is integrated into the broader social framework. Integration of the community is achieved through the interlacing of the subgroups through increasingly formalized processes of arbitration and mutual adaptation between the subgroups. Some degree of allegiance of the members to the ultimate values is still essential for the smooth functioning of the Commune, though this allegiance is now much less intensive than it had been in the Bund.

(3) The integration of the Association focuses on the *level of formal institutions*. These institutions, of which there is a wide variety in the large and complex modern kibbutz, allocate to the individual members their tasks and roles on the one hand and services and rewards on the other, and thus function as the principal means of regulation of life in the Association. The set of formal institutions is supported on the one hand by a degree of value consensus through which the institutions and their principal functionaries are legitimized, and on the other by the complex of primary relations and social groupings which still continue to exist in the Association, though they cease to be the principal mechanism of integration.

The Structural Types: The Bund

The Bund, like the kibbutz movement in general, is the result of the interplay of a variety of factors: firstly, it was a reaction of young Jews against traditional, stagnant Jewish society in the Diaspora (12); as such it constituted the extreme form of revolutionary Zionism. Secondly, it was a revolutionary reaction of idealistic Jewish youths against the social malaise of Western bourgeois, capitalistic, urban society; in this respect it was one of the varieties of the European youth movement of the twenties, akin in ideas and spirit to such movements as the German *Wandervogel*, which inspired Schmalenbach to formulate the concept of the Bund in the first place.[8] Finally, it was a tool for the realization of broader Jewish national aims in Palestine, a form of life deemed most suitable for the difficult and often hostile natural and social conditions with which he pioneers had to struggle in the early period of Jewish settlement in Palestine.

The values of the early kibbutz had, then, two chief points of reference: on the one hand they were inward-directed, towards the improvement

[8] On the Jewish youth movement in Germany see (21); for a comparison of Jewish and non-Jewish youth movements in Germany see (20).

of man and society through the whole-hearted acceptance of a set of humanistic and socialist ideals; on the other hand they were outward-directed, towards the broader society, through the acceptance of the precepts of pioneering Zionism which allotted the kibbutz the role of the spear-head of Jewish settlement in Palestine. The kibbutz was conceived at one and the same time as an end in itself, as well as a means towards broader societal ends; it was an ideological creation, but unlike other utopian movements it was also expected to fulfill national tasks and, hence, had to adapt itself effectively to changing conditions. This fact prevented its early petrification and endowed it with a dynamism absent from the other utopian movements (3).

The relative emphasis on the internal versus the external point of reference of the kibbutz values led to important ideological differences between the various federations of kibbutzim, which in turn caused significant variations in the social structure between the settlements associated with each Federation. On one end of the continuum is the federation with which the earliest-established kibbutzim were associated, the Chever Hakvutzot, which gave primary emphasis to humanistic values, such as personal freedom and self-accomplishment, and hence advocated small, loosely organized settlements (called kvutzot, from Hebrew "Kvutza," a group). From this federation stem the best examples of the "personal" Bund. On the opposite end of the continuum is Hakibbutz Hameuchad, the movement which gave primary emphasis to the values of pioneering Zionism and considered the settlements primarily as tools for national goals. Hence it advocated the creation of large kibbutzim (19), endowed from the start with a higher degree of formal organization than that typical of the early settlements of the other movements.[9] From this movement stem the best examples of the "ideological" Bund. Socialist values, which attempt to harmonize personal ideals with ideals of social service, were most emphasized by the Hashomer Hatzair movement, which takes an intermediate position between the two other federations. The small Religious Kibbutz Federation came closest to the Chever Hakvutzot in the secular aspects of its ideology, but in addition to them also kept to the precepts of the orthodox Jewish religion; some of its leaders even tried to derive the collective principles of life from their religious convictions.

The ideal type of the Bund was most closely realized by some of the earliest established kibbutzim for a relatively long period of time. These settlements were founded in the wake of an intensive Jewish social and ideological awakening in the Diaspora. They had to struggle against highly adverse conditions in Palestine, with very meagre resources, while enjoying only limited support from Jewish national institutions.

[9] For a sociological analysis of the development of Hakibbutz Hameuchad see (39, Ch. III and VI).

Only a very strong commitment to the cause helped them to persist in their efforts. The kibbutzim which had been founded in later periods, and especially after the establishment of the State of Israel, resembled the ideal type of the Bund less completely. The intensity of their communal experience was somewhat muted by the institutionalized process of establishing new kibbutzim by powerful and well-organized institutions. The value-commitment of their members was no longer as absolute as that of the founders of the first collectives. They underwent a structural transformation more quickly. The pace of structural transformation also seems to have been generally quicker in the "ideological" Bunds than in the "personal" ones. Whereas the "personal" Bund tends to change into a more or less stable Commune, there are already strong pressures within the "ideological" Bund towards an early transformation into an Association. The reason for this difference is that the "ideological" Bund puts a greater premium on objective, instrumental achievements, and hence is more amenable to quick growth and formal institutionalization than the "personal" Bund, where direct and spontaneous person-to-person relationships are more highly valued. Since in our investigation we dealt with movements such as Chever Hakevutzot and Hashomer Hatzair where the "personal" Bund predominated in the early stages, we shall deal primarily with this variant of the Bund.

As mentioned before, the integration of the Bund is based, primarily, on the common and intensive commitment of its members to a set of ultimate values. However, though the commitment is intensive, the precise social meaning of the values for various concrete situations is still vague. The Bund is not an institutionalized form of life and hence no precise social norms, referring to expected behavior in concrete situations, have yet been formulated. Moreover, in the "personal" Bund there is a particularly strong opposition against any attempt at such a formulation. Social order is expected to derive from mutual understanding, not from rules of conduct.

This fact in itself would suffice to produce a very intensive activity in the Bund around matters of public concern. Such activity has in fact been even more intensified, and sometimes became extremely hectic, owing to a fundamental characteristic of the ideological orientation of the members of the early Bund: they were convinced that they participated in a social experiment which, to their mind, might be crucial for the future of Jewish society in Palestine, or even prototypical for a new, communal world order in the future. Hence every aspect of life, every decision on the way in which things were managed, became endowed with an existential, almost transcendent importance. Every detail of life was seen "sub specie aeternitatis," and otherwise prosaic problems had to be dealt with in most fundamental terms. All areas of life were judged directly from the point of view of the ultimate values. Since no specific norms were yet institutionalized, no segregation of subspheres which would enjoy relative isolation from the basic precepts had yet taken place. There existed no secondary sets of values, no functional independence, no relative autonomy. In this respect, the Bund comes close to the early stages of formation of a religious sect, the life of which is completely and rationally permeated by a set of basic religious precepts (37, p. 331–343). In religious-sociological terms it might be said that life in the prototypical Bund had been endowed with a "sacred" quality; there was nothing merely instrumental, merely secular. Everything had a broader, symbolic meaning. Therefore, no special "sacred" period is set aside from the ordinary flow of time for ceremonies or festivities, except those directly concerned with the expression of the solidarity of the collective (for example, the commemoration of the day the settlement was established). The Bund abolished most traditional distinctions in the reckoning of time, kept neither the sabbath nor most other Jewish religious festivals.[16] In the celebration of those festivals which it still kept, national or natural themes were emphasized, while the religious themes were completely disregarded.

In the Bund, the collective assembly was the only political authority. It ruled the community and decided on matters large and small. In the early Bund, each member could convene the assembly at will to discuss a grievance. The collective had no officials or functionaries. Gradually, however, several such roles, initially with very limited authority and ill-defined responsibilities, appeared: the "work-coordinator," a technical role concerned with the allocation of workers to jobs; the secretary, a role which later split into the roles of the internal secretary, concerned mainly with social and personal matters within the community, and of the external secretary, dealing with relationships of the kibbutz with institutions and other communities; and the "production-manager," concerned with the over-all coordination of production. At first, such public roles had to be performed in the member's spare time. Time for such work was allocated later.

In the economic sphere, work in the Bund was organized by production and service branches. The economy was diversified and the branches were small. However, heterogeneity did not imply occupational specialization: members were not yet permanently attached to any branch, but rotated freely between branches, according to their shifting needs. The branches had initially no formal leaders; only with time did the role of the branch-manager emerge, initially as a role concerned mostly with the technical ties of the branch with the kibbutz, such as care for the supply of manpower and materials, despatch of products, etc. This role was also performed in the member's free time, after he worked a full workday in the branch like any other worker.

---

[10] The Protestant sects also disregarded feasts and festivals and reduced their number radically.

Social life in the Bund focused on the collective. The dining hall, the communal green and the public shower were the most common meeting places. The importance of the family was reduced to a minimum — in the secular kibbutz movement, marriage was informal and expressions of conjugal love and of solidarity of the married couple were shunned. Children were delegated to the children's home, where they received all the personal services as well as education. Relations with the parents were very restricted (34). The whole community formed one undifferentiated body, and ideally there were no factions or social subdivisions within it.

Integration of its members around a set of strongly felt ultimate values is the basic strength of the Bund. However, such a form of social integration is essentially an unstable one. There is a fundamental conflict or dilemma inherent in the social structure of the Bund, between the pressure to conform and thus to preserve collective solidarity as against the liberty of each member to interpret freely the basic precepts of kibbutz life. Members of the Bund are asked to achieve full agreement on any issue facing the collectivity. Still, there exists no well-defined institutional mechanism through which such an agreement could be achieved. Hence, public life in the early Bund tended to be hectic. The constant and intensive social interaction, concerning matters large and small, required a great mental and physical effort from all the members. With time they tired,, and discussion on principles sometimes degenerated into personal conflicts. This led to breakdowns in relations and often also to the desertion of the kibbutz by dissatisfied members. The intensity of the discussion was not necessarily related to the functional importance of the matter on hand or to the personal interest of the participants. Rather, it had to do with the symbolic significance of sometimes small matters for the overall design of a utopian society. This very fact also endowed acts of personal behavior with exceptional importance: hence, the demand to lead an "exemplary" life, without clear and unequivocal norms of conduct and without formal sanctions, often created strong inner tension in the individual, who constantly forced himself to live up to the model of exemplary behavior held forth by his group. Though I possess no precise data, I suspect that there were several cases of "altruistic" suicide (14) in the kibbutz, due to overly intensive concern of the members with the demand to comply with all too highly set standards of personal conduct, strongly supported by informal but all-pervasive public opinion. These cases of suicide might serve as the most extreme indications of the sometimes severe psychological pressure under which the individual in the Bund had to labor.

As long as the kibbutz is still small, socially homogeneous, functionally undifferentiated and enjoying a measure of external support from the kibbutz Federation to which it belongs, or from the national institutions, it is generally within its powers to overcome its internal strains. As conditions change, however, its stability becomes jeopardized by its internal conflicts. The mode of integration typical of the Bund, common adherence to a set of ultimate values, does not suffice any more to prevent change or even disintegration.

The Structural Types: The Transitional Bund

Virtually every Bund experienced a period of crisis some time after its establishment. Internal dissent, disenchantment, and lack of sufficient economic and organizational support on part of the national institutions actually led to the disintegration of several kibbutzim established in the early stages of the collective movement. In the later stages, most such disintegrating settlements have been physically salvaged through the efforts of the national institutions and the kibbutz federation. Only very few places were completely abandoned. However, many such settlements remained socially unstable for prolonged periods of time, as we shall see in our discussion of the Residual Commune. Nevertheless, most Bunds succeeded in overcoming the initial crisis and in making the transition to the Commune. The period of transition might last a considerable time, and hence we often find an intermediary type of kibbutz which is not any more a Bund, neither yet a Commune. We called it the "Transitional Bund."

The tension caused in the original Bund by the lack of criteria for an agreed upon translation of ultimate values into concrete norms for daily behavior, aggravates as the kibbutz matures. In the early stages of its existence the members are immersed in a state of "primaeval experience," an enthusiasm of pioneering and creation which enables them to overcome, or overlook, the difficulties of daily life. As time goes on this primaeval enthusiasm gradually ebbs and a more prosaic, practical approach to the many problems of life in a young, small, and remote agricultural settlement becomes necessary. The point of crisis is usually reached when a new group of settlers is sent to the kibbutz to complement it.[11] This group of newcomers is often similar to the founders in ideological outlook, but younger and comes from a different country of origin. This introduces a degree of strangeness between the two groups. However, the main difficulty stems from the differential perspective of the two groups towards the kibbutz: the newcomers did not partake in the "primaeval experience," and though they might be as enthusiastic about collective life as the founders, their initial collective experience is usually not as intensive and profound as that of the founders had been.

Moreover, a degree of differentiation is liable to take place with the

[11] Such groups, sent by the federation to which the kibbutz pertains, are called in Hebrew "Hashlama" (complement) and hence we shall refer to them in the following as "complements."

coming of the new members. Whereas until now all members had approximately the same knowledge and experience in the management of collective affairs and were rotated among all roles as a matter of principle, now a difference in the level of knowledge and experience appears: the newcomers are much less knowledgeable and experienced in kibbutz affairs than the founders. For a time, at least, the more skilled and responsible jobs have to be performed by the founders. The question as to when and to what degree responsibilities will be shared with the newcomers often becomes one of the chief points of conflict between the two groups.

The kibbutz at this stage is still permeated by a spirit of overall unity, and hence considerable effort is spent to integrate the newcomers completely into the original Bund. If this effort succeeds, the kibbutz is likely to preserve for an additional period its Bund-like qualities. However, it will not remain unchanged indefinitely since other factors act for transition. The most important of these is, perhaps, the life-cycle of the members. At foundation, most members are young and still single. As families are created and children born, a new focus of interest and identification emerges — the nuclear family. The original Bund used to be hostile to the nuclear family group and tended to restrict its functions and its social importance to the minimum. The members viewed the family from the perspective of their own youth experience: as members of a youth movement, they rebelled against their own parents and started a new and revolutionary way of life. However, as the new families expand and children grow up, a gradual shift of perspective takes place in the outlook of at least part of the members. In the Transitional Bund there is, typically, an open conflict between the emergent family solidarity and the efforts of the collective to safeguard the total allegiance of its members. This conflict is one of the chief sources of tension in this type of settlement; it achieves resolution only with the redefinition of the role of the family in the fully-fledged Commune.

The demographic change is usually accompanied by a crisis in the economic and organizational structure of the kibbutz. At foundation, the kibbutz usually enjoys financial support from the colonizing institutions. Such support enables it to overcome the hardship inherent in settlement in a new and often hostile region. It is initially not utterly dependent for its livelihood upon the market value of its products, and hence able to devote itself to some social experimentation. This includes, among else, the attempt to realize directly some of its values in the sphere of work: for example, the rejection of functional authority or specialization as means for the realization of the values of equality and full personal development. Such rigorous application of these values in the sphere of work is not necessarily conducive to high productive efficiency.

As the kibbutz matures, external financial support is gradually phased out. The kibbutz is expected to become economically viable as quickly as possible. Viability has to be proved in terms of income, in an essentially capitalistic, competitive economy. Since the kibbutz is often located on an economically disadvantageous site, only extreme efficiency in production will ensure viability. Pressures for specialization, mechanization, rational organization, and definition of authority are thus created. Such pressures often coincide with the period of social crisis in the Bund mentioned above. The strain upon the system is thereby considerably increased and many kibbutzim find themselves on the verge not only of social, but also of economic and organizational breakdown. In more recent times, many Transitional Bunds had to receive extensive support, financial and organizational, from their federation, or from the Settlement Department of the Jewish Agency, to enable them to survive the crisis.

As the Transitional Bund strives to overcome its difficulties it passes through a process which we shall call the "struggle of institutionalization." In this process day-to-day conduct in the economic sphere — and gradually also that in other institutional spheres — becomes separated from the ultimate values of collective life, through a series of new normative arrangements, often against the wishes of the more orthodox members of the community.

Under pressure for efficiency and increased production, old branches expand and become mechanized and new ones are added. Work becomes more specialized and more and more members have to acquire some basic training and experience in order to be able to perform the more skilled jobs. Hence, rotation of members among jobs gradually decreases and most members become permanently attached to their branches. As work in the branch becomes more complex, a greater need for coordination arises. Hence, an increase in the branch-manager's authority takes place. Concomitantly, there is more need for overall organization. The administrational and organizational structure of the kibbutz becomes strengthened, and the importance and authority of central functionaries increases. These functionaries feel most strongly the tensions resulting from the conflict between the concept of an absolutely egalitarian, nondifferentiated society and the need for functional authority and specialization. They often pay the price of their organizational success in terms of loss of solidary ties with their fellow members. As in the case of the nuclear family, so too in the sphere of work, reintegration is achieved only in the Commune where functional authority achieves a degree of legitimation.

However, it would be wrong to consider the struggle of institutionalization as a simple, unilinear translation of ultimate but vague values into concrete, unequivocal norms. The vagueness of the ultimate values permits a multiplicity of interpretations and the normative translation of these values implies a decision as to their "correct" meaning. The struggle of institutionalization, though caused by the tension between direct allegiance to ultimate values and the exigencies of existence, actually brings to the fore some of the fundamental dilemmas in the value system itself. I shall illustrate this problem through the analysis of the implications of one central value, that of equality, for one sphere of life, that of consumption, in which the dilemma is particularly acute.[12]

The value of equality was one of the chief foci of social integration in the original Bund. Its practical implications, however, were often vague. In the sphere of consumption, it was at first applied as meaning "to each according to his needs." Since there were very few goods to be distributed at this early stage, and since the strong future-orientation of the members diminished the saliency of consumption, the system at first worked well. A member would approach the communal clothing store, for example, and ask for an item of clothing; he would be given the object *bona fide*, provided that it was available. Even so, there was some informal social control; the members' "needs" were rudimentary and similar and hence, he would not, or could not ask for any fancy goods (which in any case were not available). If he did, he would be ridiculed or admonished by his peers.

However, as conditions changed with the entrance of new complements of members, the emergence of families and of children and the growing present-orientation of the members, the sphere of consumption gained in importance. More and more disputes occurred with the manager of the clothing store about who "really" needs what, and social tensions increased. The struggle of institutionalization started with the growing pressure to define the idea of equality in consumption. However, there were two equally valid definitions: "essential equality" would recognize the inherent differences between members, implying differential needs; equality would be then achieved through the equal *relative* satisfaction of differential needs: whoever needs more, gets more. "Mechanical equality" would allocate to everyone an equal share of goods, notwithstanding the "real" needs. The original method of distribution embodied the concept of essential equality. Since this concept is not amenable to institutionalization, pressure was building up towards a more mechanical concept of equality. The community decided upon what the needs of a member "really" were and formalized them concretely in terms of a "norm of distribution," which specified how much of the various goods a member should receive during a given period of time ("norm of time") or how many articles (e.g., shirts or underwear) a member is entitled to possess at any given moment of time ("norm of quantity").

This new arrangement led to the achievement of a degree of stability in the Transitional Bund and in the early Commune. However, it curtailed the members' opportunity to satisfy individual needs and preferences in consumption. As the kibbutz prospered and the level of con-

---

[12] E. Rosenfeld (27) presents an interesting and detailed account of the struggle of institutionalization in the sphere of consumption.

sumption rose, new pressures for freedom of choice and expression of personal taste in consumption built up. The system of "norms" could not respond to such pressures: hence, new mechanisms of distribution such as a "personal budget" or a system of "points" had to be introduced. These mechanisms provided again, some leeway to personal choice, albeit within financial limits. Thereby, an element inherent in the conception of "essential equality," the adaptation of consumption to personal needs and preferences, was again introduced into the distributive mechanism. The pendulum, therefore, moved again away from mechanical equality and in the direction of qualified "essential equality." The demand, voiced in some quarters, to permit complete freedom of consumption in an ever increasing number of areas as the kibbutz becomes affluent, points in the same direction.

This example shows very clearly the possibility of alternative interpretations of an ultimate value and the way in which emphasis moves with changing conditions from one interpretation to another, without ever doing full justice to every possible legitimate interpretation of that value. I think that this pendulum-like movement in the interpretation of values forms the basic characteristic of the ideological dynamics in the kibbutz.

The Structural Types: The Residual Commune

Before turning to the description of the Commune, a few words should be said on the Residual Commune, a type of settlement lacking integration and stability, which results from an unsuccessful transition from the Bund to the fully developed Commune. The Residual Commune has lost its integration around a set of intensely felt ultimate values, but at the same time has not achieved a new and stable integration through a well-developed network of social ties, characteristic of the Commune. It is a small kibbutz, the growth of which had been arrested and hence failed to "take off."

The Residual Commune is not larger or even smaller than the Bund. However, it is not socially homogeneous, but composed of a series of residua of groups which passed through the settlement at various periods of time. The typical process through which such a situation arises is the following: a few years after a Bund has been founded, a serious internal crisis of transition induces many of its founders to leave the settlement. Among those who leave are often individuals who have been the pillars of the community. The settlement, therefore, remains without leaders. The new complement sent to reinforce the settlement finds nothing to hang on to and usually disintegrates quickly. The kibbutz federation at this moment often starts a losing game. As the danger arises that the young kibbutz will completely disintegrate, the federation is forced to send additional reinforcements. As these successive waves of reinforcements disintegrate in their turn, the typical social structure of the Residual Commune emerges: each group of members sent to the kibbutz — the founders included — leaves behind a tiny residuum. The community thus becomes a patchwork of small, separate, ill-integrated subgroups. Such a social framework cannot provide the necessary support for the absorption of newcomers and often not even for the retention of those already living in it. Plagued by social as well as functional problems, the Residual Commune shows a strong tendency to disintegrate completely.

The phenomenon of the Residual Commune became relatively frequent in the period immediately following the establishment of the state, when the kibbutz movement as a whole suffered its major internal crisis and when the kibbutz federations were yet unable to deal effectively with the challenge presented by the new circumstances. The federations learned gradually that they cannot resolve the problem of the instability of the Residual Communes through the dispatchment of more and more reinforcements, since they thereby only dissipated their meager resources. They initiated a new strategy: several settlements were left to disband almost completely and were then settled anew by a large nucleus, thereby virtually recreating a Bund. Other such settlements have been "adopted" by larger and more mature kibbutzim, who nurtured them out of their difficulties (35). Many of the younger, relatively small kibbutzim of our days are not Bunds any more, but such Residual Communes which achieved a degree of stability through the joint efforts of the kibbutz federations and of the colonizing institutions. A special term has been coined to designate these settlements: "Hakibbutz Haza'ir" ("the tiny kibbutz"). After achieving a degree of stability the tiny kibbutz finally starts on a belated transition to the Commune.

The Structural Types: The Commune

Most kibbutzim, particularly in the earlier periods, successfully accomplished the transition to the Commune. The Commune represents a new point of stability, in which the focus of integration is transferred from the level of ultimate values to the network of social ties between the members of the community. The overall solidarity of the collective, characteristic of the original Bund, is permanently weakened during the struggle of institutionalization in the Transitional Bund. Various kinds of subgroups appear in the community. Efforts to realise the ultimate values completely and directly in every sphere of daily life are also weakened. Social differentiation and institutionalization introduce a sober, profane quality into kibbutz life. The original enthusiasm disappears, but so do also the incessant internal struggles. Members settle down to business. Vaguely defined general ideological and national goals of the kibbutz movement are translated into concrete, localised terms: the economic and social independence and development of the individual community gains precedence over all other concerns. Success of the movement as a whole is often judged in terms of the economic prosperity of the kibbutz.

The newly won, partial autonomy of various institutional spheres from overall ideological regulation makes possible the efficient solution of functional problems in the spheres of work, organization, consumption, education etc. It is interesting to note, however, that at the same time that life in the kibbutz has lost its "sacred" quality, there is renewed interest in purely symbolic activities, and a concomitant gradual revival of rituals and celebrations — particularly, the reintroduction of religious marriage ceremonies and the observation of Jewish religious festivals. The content of the latter is often adapted to serve the symbolic needs of the kibbutz. Such symbolic activities reinforce overall social cohesion and allegiance to basic values, which might be weakened through total preoccupation in daily, routine activities.

The personal motivations of the members to live in the kibbutz also change: if previously they chose kibbutz life out of a deep attachment to the collective ideal and the task of the kibbutz as the spearhead of a future society, they now shift to more mundane, concrete considerations. Chief among these are job-satisfaction, attachment to the community as such and particularly, social involvement with their peers. The nuclear family serves as an important integrating mechanism: since most members are married, they are attached to the kibbutz not only through their personal social ties but also through the various social ties of the other members of the nuclear family. The young, unattached member of the Bund could easily leave everything and give up kibbutz life if his initial enthusiasm turned into disenchantment. The middle-aged member of the Commune, who had lived in the kibbutz for most of his adult life, in addition to his ideological commitment is involved with it through a multiplicity of ties.

Social ties, not idealistic allegiance, thus become the chief focus of integration of the Commune, the force which holds its members together and motivates them to work for the common good. Different types of subgroups, with varying degrees of cohesion, emerge in the kibbutz. According to the nature of such subgroup we differentiate three subtypes of Communes: [13]

The Unified Commune exemplifies most fully the mode of integration typical of the Commune: its integration rests almost completely on the network of personal relations among its members. This is less true of the other subtypes. The Unified Commune is socially homogeneous, lacking a clear-cut division into several clearly differentiated subgroups. However, it has also lost the strong, overall cohesion of the early Bund. The social

---

[13] The subtypes have been defined by Mrs. Talmon in (25). In the following discussion I have drawn heavily upon her work.

ties typically form a network of interrelated and intertwined small sub-groups. The pivotal points of this network are the nuclear families and the penumbra of other kinship ties which become the more numerous as the settlement matures and gains a three-generation depth. Other types of small groups which appear in the Unified Commune are groups of common origin, age groups, solidary work-groups, neighborhood groups, groups of members with common cultural interests, etc. Though the family predominates among these various subgroups, none of them is either strong enough or comprehensive enough to divide the com-munity along clear-cut lines. Integration is, then, achieved through the intersection of subgroups, and the appearance of a complex, dense, all-embracing network of relationships much in the way typical of the Gemeinschaft.

The Unified Commune often originated from a slowly growing Bund, which made the transition without serious social upheavals. However, though this subtype of Commune is closest to the Bund, the social dynamics of the Unified Commune differ considerably from those of the Bund. Since the community is homogeneous and grew without major perturbations, it often develops a body of local customs, almost a tradi-tion, supported by considerable consensus, which guides daily life. There is little dissent and social life is ordinarily quiet. As a result, the Unified Commune develops a tendency to apathy — members withdraw into their narrow circles of kin and acquaintances and take only a lim-ited interest in matters of importance to the community as a whole. They tend to delegate authority to decide on such matters to the elected public bodies and officials, the secretary, the production manager, or the secretariat, since there is ordinarily no basic conflict of interest between the groups in the community. The officials are the representatives of the common consensus. The Unified Commune may, as a result, develop a group of official role-bearers who, though not expressly an "elite" in the ordinary sense of the term, nevertheless bear considerable responsi-bility and hence possess a high degree of authority in many matters of public concern.

In the sphere of work, the Unified Commune is characterized by a con-siderable degree of autonomy of the various branches of production, the members of which usually work together for long periods of time and characteristically form a cohesive primary group (15). Though work in the Unified Commune is more formally organized than in the Bund, the mechanisms of control are still rather loose and most of the actual coordination of production is carried out through informal, personal contacts between the various role-bearers. The extent and manner of development of various branches depends largely on the personal ability and zeal of its workers. The overall economic development of the Unified Commune is, hence, chiefly the result of the various forces operative in its individual branches. As yet, there exists but little overall planning and rational direction.

Social life centers on the family group. In the mature Unified Commune, the network of kinship ties is often of considerable scope. Large kinship groups often form corporate groups. The dominance of family ties over other types of social relations may occasionally lead to a situation in which the community is dominated by a coalition of several such groups which are powerful enough to impose their will upon the collective in most matters of importance regarding the daily life of the members. Such groups sometimes act in unison in matters of direct personal concern to the members or to their offspring, such as the distribution of important articles of consumption, allocation of work-places or opportunities for higher education for the children. The corporate kinship groups may act in such matters as pressure groups, using their influence in communal institutions, presenting a common front in the communal assembly, etc. Sometimes severe, though covert, conflicts between such groups might disturb the usually placid atmosphere of the Unified Commune. This may lead to a family-based factionalism, which is essentially foreign to the non-familistic spirit of the kibbutz ideology.

The Federated Commune. This subtype of the Commune is composed of several large, clearly distinct subgroups, each of which provides a primary focus of identification to its member. The individual member is integrated into his community through attachment to his subgroup. Overall integration is achieved through the interplay between the subgroups, though the Federated Commune relies less on direct, personal relations than the Unified Commune and more on formalized institutional relationships.

Whereas in the Unified Commune the complements of new members are gradually absorbed by the community, and lose their distinctiveness, in the Federated Commune they keep their separate identities. It is difficult to state the precise reasons for these differing paths of social development. It seems that two main factors are operative here: the differences in origin and in cultural background between the subsequent groups of settlers, and the period of time which elapses between the entrance of each group into the kibbutz. If new members come from different countries and cultural backgrounds and arrive after lengths of time so that there exists a considerable difference in the age of members of the various groups, the probability of mutual assimilation diminishes considerably. When the second generation grows up in the kibbutz it often, though not necessarily always, forms a separate subgroup in the community. The main criteria of differentiation between subgroups in the Federated Commune are, then, one or several of the following: country of origin, cultural background, length of stay in the community, age and generation. The larger the number of criteria which differentiate the subgroups from each other, and the greater the differences in each criterion, the sharper the social segregation between the subgroups and the stronger the impact of the segregation upon all spheres of social life. For example, in those Federated Communes where the differences between the criteria were many and considerable, the social cohesion of workgroups in the branches is affected: the branches tend then either to be composed only of members of the same subgroup, or several solidary cliques, composed of members of various subgroups, appear in the branch (15).

The subgroups provide the chief framework of the day-to-day life of the Federated Commune. The majority of the friends and acquaintances of a member are found in his subgroup. Many of his neighbours also belong to his subgroup, since dwelling units are allocated to members in accordance with their length of stay in the kibbutz. Most matters of communal interest are discussed first within the subgroup before they are dealt with formally by the communal assembly or by another public institution of the kibbutz. The subgroup resembles to some degree the original Bund, but its social life and the commitment of the members are less intensive. Still, the subgroup serves as a mediating framework between the individual member and the collective — the member's ties to the subgroup are the chief social mechanism which safeguards his attachment to the community. The family, which used to be all-important in the Unified Commune, loses some of its importance in the Federated Commune; it becomes secondary to the subgroup (25, p. 15).

Relations between members of different subgroups are cooler and more formal than those within the subgroups. A good deal of competition between subgroups is quite common; this may focus on spheres such as public offices, norms for the allocation of goods (particularly dwellings and furniture, which are mostly allocated by length of stay in the kibbutz) and allocation of jobs in the branches. Sometimes serious crises may break out on such matters and a considerable amount of tension may be generated. However, the subgroups do not ordinarily fight with each other, and there is no thorough-going "class-conflict" between them.[14]

Since the Federated Commune is more heterogeneous than the Unified one, there exist fewer points of overall agreement between its members. The members of the subgroups perceive the possibility of conflict on various issues and are hence more aware of matters of public importance, particularly those which might concern them individually, than are members of the Unified Commune. There is less apathy on part of the rank and file and less readiness to leave matters to the functionaries to de-

[14] For an opposite view see (26).

cide. Instead, their authority tends to become more formally defined, and their behavior more tightly controlled.

In the sphere of work there is also more centralization. The branches lose part of their independence vis-à-vis the central institution. The process of production, for instance, is centrally controlled. Overall rational planning of investments and of the development of the economy is gradually introduced.

Whereas in the Unified Commune there is a tendency towards "traditionalization" — institutionalization of various customs — in the Federated Commune there is a tendency towards increasing formalization — institutionalization through explicit and fixed rules and regulations. The Federated Commune is more bureaucratized, centralized, and rationalized than the Unified Commune. Many of its basic characteristics point already towards the transition to the Association.

The Sectorial Commune. Before we discuss the emergence of the Association as a social type of kibbutzim, short consideration should be given to a deviant type of the Commune, the Sectorial Commune.[15] Like the Federated Commune, this subtype is also divided into a few subunits, which we call sectors. The sectors differ from the subgroups of the Federated Commune in the nature of their cohesion. In the Federated Commune the focus of cohesion is *internal,* the emotional attachment of the members is the basis of their subgroup. The focus of cohesion of the sectors is *external,* the sectors are formed through mutual opposition of groups of members. But they do not enjoy a high degree of internal cohesion. The sectors are essentially power or pressure groups, contending with each other over the distribution of resources and rewards in the community. The allegiance of the members to their sector does not derive principally from their emotional attachment to it, but from the necessity to ally themselves with people of similar interests in opposition to those whose interests are different. The Sectorial Commune is, then, involved in continuous social conflict often accompanied by a disregard of the basic norms of kibbutz life.

The Sectorial Commune is not only a deviant type of the Commune from the point of view of kibbutz values — in its "pure" form, it is not a viable community. The Sectorial Commune is too ridden with dissent and socially disjointed to be able to mobilize much support for institutional arrangements intended to regulate its social life and help it to overcome its difficulties. Without such support, formal arrangements malfunction. A certain amount of anomie is hence endemic to this subtype of the Commune. In extreme cases, the Sectorial Commune will collapse since the kibbutz does not possess the mechanisms necessary

---

[15] This subtype was called by Mrs. Talmon the Split or Factional Commune (25, p. 13).

to contain and regulate the perpetual internal struggle. Such extreme cases, however, are rare. Most concrete examples of the Sectorial Commune which came up in our study only approximated the theoretical case here described. Still, a few of these reached the verge of collapse at some points in their past. They were generally saved from total collapse by the emergence of a group of rather authoritative leaders, usually central functionaries of the kibbutz, who entered the social and institutional vacuum and imposed their will upon the community in an effort to save it. These leaders tended to concentrate in their hands the control over the most important social, political and economic processes and decisions and thereby endowed the kibbutz with a measure of order and continuity in the performance of essential tasks, which would otherwise be completely lacking. This group of functionaries usually belonged to the dominant sector in the community. Its members enjoyed personal authority in the community. The ability to control people and processes has been the principal reward for their efforts. In some cases the functionaries may also have enjoyed a few personal material benefits from such control, but these are at best of secondary importance. Nevertheless, in the kibbutz situation personal authority and authoritarian control over people are considered highly illegitimate forms of behavior, and though these functionaries managed to hold the community together by their actions, they nevertheless generated a considerable amount of antagonism, particularly on the part of the opposing sector. However, the functionaries held on to their offices, often for considerable periods of time and in spite of opposition, owing to the fact that most members were unwilling to accept any kind of public office. The majority was apathetic towards community-wide issues and mainly concerned with their personal advantages and problems.

The tendency toward individualistic self-concern has spread even into family life (25, p. 15). Attendance at the collective assembly is ordinarily low, except when issues of personal interest to the members are on the agenda. Cohesion of work-groups is low. Work tasks are accomplished primarily through the application of close personal control by the branch manager and other office bearers on the workers. The organization of work is deficient and work often inefficient. Members' attention is given predominantly to the sphere of consumption while their commitment to collective goals is generally low.

The Sectorial Commune emerged as a result of weakening of social ties within the various contingents of members constituting the kibbutz accompanied by a rise of antagonism between those contingents. Historically, such conditions were created by the aftermath of the schism in one of the kibbutz federations, Hakibbutz Hameuchad, in 1951. After the schism — the causes of which were ideological and political — groups of dissenting members left the kibbutzim of Hakibbutz Hameuchad and joined the former Chever Hakvutzot federation which now became

Ichud Hakevutzot Ve'Hakibbutzim. The schism shift was a traumatic experience: in some cases several groups of dissenting members were sent by their new federation to establish a new kibbutz. In others, a group of dissenters joined an old, established kibbutz of the Chever Hakvutzot, which had been in need of reinforcement. Most such settlements suffered serious social convulsions. Most members who switched federations were not enthusiastic youngsters looking for new experiences, but middle-aged disenchanted individuals, who were forced to change their kibbutz affiliation for political reasons. The conditions of life in the new settlements were mostly much below the standards which the members had enjoyed previously. Hence, the primary concern of many has been to achieve improvements in their individual standard of living. They were less interested in the common good of the new collective. People who knew each other from before united and formed "sectors" which acted as power groups. The clash between the sectors was produced through their conflicting interests, particularly in the sphere of distribution of commodities and other rewards.

Most Sectorial Communes seem to have been created through the historic accident of the schism in one of the kibbutz federations. Others might have emerged through different social processes though such cases seem to be rare.

Obviously, the various subtypes of Communes which we have described, do not appear in reality in their "ideal-typical" form. Many kibbutzim represent combinations of traits characteristic of two or even all three subtypes. Moreover, transition from one type to the other is common. Though, in principle, such transition can take place from each of the types into all the others, the most common process is the transition from the Unified, or Sectorial, Commune into the Federated Commune. As a Unified Commune matures, a new group of settlers, or more often the emergent second generation, may introduce internal, social differentiation into the community and transform it into a Federated Commune. As a Sectorial Commune matures and overcomes its crisis, internal cohesion of the various sectors increases and relations between them become less strained, so that the kibbutz gradually becomes a Federated Commune. All the large, mature Communes tend, therefore, to become federated. Only very few pass into maturity preserving the essential traits of a Unified Commune. None can remain indefinitely as a Sectorial Commune. Developmentally, as well as structurally, the Federated Commune forms the type of transition to the Association.

The Structural Types: The Association

The Commune represents a point of equilibrium in the social development of the kibbutz movement. Indeed, Mrs. Talmon, working on the data of a large-scale comparative study conducted in the middle fifties, conceptualized the process of social change in the kibbutz merely as a transition from the Bund to the Commune. She had not detected in her data any indication of a further major step in the process of structural change.

However, since the middle fifties considerable changes have taken place in the kibbutz (particularly in the large, mature and developed Communes) as well as in the position of the kibbutz itself in Israeli society. These changes had important repercussions on the social structure of the kibbutz. It is necessary to introduce a new ideal type, the Association, which will present in a coherent, theoretical form the emergent social characteristics of the mature kibbutz of our days. It has to be emphasized that no systematic study has yet been conducted of the kibbutzim which approximate the type of the Association. Hence, my analysis of the forces of transition to the Association as well as of its structural characteristics will of necessity be somewhat sketchy.

The transition from the Commune to the Association differed in some important respects from the process of transition from the Bund to the Commune. The latter has to do primarily with the internal crisis of the kibbutz in the early stages of its growth and the pangs of adaptation to its immediate environment. This process of transition takes place on an individual basis, each kibbutz undergoing it, in a more or less similar manner, as a step in its own development. The transition from Commune to Association is also connected with far-going internal changes in the kibbutz, particularly with its enormous economic and organizational success (7). However, the economic and organizational changes which took place in the kibbutz reflect in themselves a major change in the relationship between the kibbutz and the national society.

The first kibbutzim were established to serve as spearheads of development in a socially and economically largely backward country. The kibbutz considered itself as performing a pioneering role in the development of a new society. With the establishment of the state the pioneering functions of the kibbutz were greatly reduced and confined mostly to the outlying regions of the country. The mature, older Communes lost much of their society-wide importance and prestige; they turned to their own affairs and became primarily preoccupied with their economic advancement. This change, however, coincided with major developments on the national scene. Since the establishment of the state, and especially in the last 10 or 15 years, Israel underwent a rapid process of economic development and modernization, during which the country became industrialized with an increasingly large number of the population becoming urbanized. The mature kibbutzim came to participate actively in this process of development and modernization, and in some areas, such as the industrialization of agriculture, served as its spearhead. The kibbutz itself thus became industrialized and its way

of life partly urbanized.[16] The functional interdependence between
the kibbutz and the broader society grew considerably and its ideological separation from other sectors of that society decreased in importance.
The individual settlements became economically and culturally involved with their regions as well as with national institutions and frameworks to an unprecedented degree.

One can only speculate on what would have happened to the kibbutz
if Israeli society reached an advanced stage of development much before
the transition from Bund to Commune was completed in most kibbutzim,
so that the still highly solidary and ideologically oriented Bunds had to
face a modern, complex society. In my opinion, the kibbutz would
either crack up under the impact of external forces penetrating most
spheres of life of the yet tender collectives; or, alternatively, it would
seal itself off hermetically from outward influences and come to resemble other utopian communities in the Western world. The stabilizing
effect of the transition to the Commune, made the further transition to
the Association feasible. The mature kibbutzim led the way and assisted
the younger and less developed ones to come to terms with the new
conditions. Our discussion will follow the developments in mature
kibbutzim. But we have to keep in mind that almost all contemporary
kibbutzim are affected by the external factors which are at work in
the transition to the Association and tend to show some traits of the
Association.

The Association, unlike the Bund or the Commune, is to a large extent
an "urbanized" community, in the cultural sense of the term. Not only
is its economy geared to the general forces of the market but its whole
way of life is increasingly influenced by standards and values which
derive from the broader society.[17] This reorientation can be seen in
several spheres of life: members of the large, mature kibbutz tend increasingly to look upon Jewish, middle-class, urban society as a reference
group in matters of living standards or even of life styles. As the kibbutz became more affluent it could strive realistically to emulate urban
living standards. In the process, the attempt to create a distinctive
kibbutz "style of life" fell into oblivion. The same process can be seen
even more clearly in the sphere of cultural activity and the arts. During
the early stages the kibbutz put great emphasis upon a distinctive
kibbutz style in the creative arts and in music, upon the organic
interdependence of the artist and his community. In recent years, as
artistic creativity in the kibbutz proliferated and the artists became
increasingly professionalized, their primary reference group became

16 The first to draw attention to this point was Weinryb (38).

17 For a description of a similar process of transition from local to general cultural
standards in American society, see M. Stein's reanalysis of the Lynds' studies of
Middletown (31, p. 60 ff.).

other artists and artistic movements outside the kibbutz.[18] The direct
communication between the artist and his community became of secondary importance, particularly as the artistic taste of the members
themselves underwent differentiation. Whereas previously the kibbutz
would publicly exhibit the work of a member because the members
liked it, now it is exhibited because the artist is esteemed *outside* the
kibbutz.

This process can also be followed in the area of occupational and professional activities of the members; as more and more members receive
a special professional education, the focus of their interest at work
changes subtly: though contribution towards the success of the branch
or enterprise remains the primary goal of most members, the evaluation
of individual performance by other members is increasingly based on
general professional criteria. The reference group of the professionalized
worker becomes other professionals outside the kibbutz. This means,
in terms of our value analysis, that the performance of roles in various
institutional spheres is now made subject to values and norms which
often hail from other value-systems and are only remotely related to
the original values of the kibbutz. The values of the broader society,
then, penetrated into the kibbutz and introduced a degree of value-
pluralism which reflects the pluralism existent in the broader society.

Our argument leads to the conclusion that the social boundaries
between the kibbutz, particularly the large mature ones, and the surrounding society have been considerably weakened under the impact of
internal as well as external forces.[19] The boundaries have not been
abolished completely — the large kibbutz of today continues to be a
corporate entity maintained by the contributions of members, but the
breadth of common ties has been narrowed considerably and the effort
of the members to develop the kibbutz economically or even culturally
contributes to the further narrowing of these ties.

The processes of interpenetration and dependence are particularly
strong in the economic sphere where they are chiefly a consequence
of the enormous increase in the scale of production and differentiation
of economic activities which took place in the last few years. The
branches of production and services grew considerably and became internally differentiated. A large number of workers with special skills
are necessary to maintain these highly developed branches. A process
of professionalization set in, accompanied by the provision of specialized
training outside the kibbutz in courses provided by the kibbutz movements or in national educational institutions. High premium was set
on efficiency, profitability of production, and the ability of the kibbutz

[18] On this point see the interesting discussion in (2, p. 82).
[19] On the concept of social boundaries and the problems of their relative strength
or weakness, see (11).

economy to compete on the national and sometimes even international markets. The kibbutz, always innovation-prone, underwent a "scientific revolution." The most advanced agricultural techniques were introduced into the branches and agriculture became gradually industrialized.

The original kibbutz was an agricultural settlement. The modern kibbutz introduced industrial enterprises at the beginning, as a means to process its agricultural products. Later, industry was intended chiefly to absorb the manpower unsuitable for agricultural work, particularly the aging members. Ultimately, industrial development became an economic goal in its own right, until it reached such proportions as to vie with agriculture as the primary source of the income.

Efficiency and profitability now became primary criteria for economic decisions to the detriment of all other considerations, such as the ideological or the traditional agricultural ones, which were previously profoundly influential. Henceforth, the kibbutz will engage in those pursuits which promise the highest rate of return. Such considerations lead it to move even further away from agriculture into secondary and even tertiary processes of production. As industry comes to dominate the economic life of the kibbutz, commercialized personal services such as guest-houses within the community and commercial outlets for products, located in the big cities, gain increasing importance as a major source of income.

As specialization and mechanization of productive processes increased, the individual settlement is often unable to provide the investments and managerial resources for large scale enterprises. The remedy in such cases is often sought in outside economic alliances: large-scale regional cooperation, economic ventures common to a number of kibbutzim or to a kibbutz and a private investor, sub-contracting parts of the production process to other enterprises, and so on. The most important form of outside involvement is regional cooperation in which kibbutzim of the same region or several adjoining regions establish a series of regional enterprises. These are predominantly of two types: processing plants for agricultural products and mechanical services to agriculture (9). The boundaries of the individual kibbutz as a productive unit are gradually blurred as outside involvement grows.

There is a growing tendency towards regional and interregional economic integration between kibbutzim. As regional cooperation in the economic sphere advances, regional frameworks in other spheres have been established. Of particular importance are regional frameworks of adult education, some of which have recently become regional colleges. The forces which led to such development were similar to those which started economic regional cooperation in the first place: the demand for an increasingly higher level of education which the individual kibbutz could not provide. These developments culminated in the proposal to establish a "kibbutz-university" on the national scale, which is at present being seriously considered.

The rising level of professionalism and the general education of members of the Association in conjunction with greater personal freedom of occupational choice leads to another phenomenon: the highly skilled professional who lives on the kibbutz but works in the city as a university teacher, high-level governmental employee, or is independently employed (for example, freelance graphic designer). Though few people as yet engage in the free trades, their appearance is an important indication of the economic "opening up" of the Association.

The growth and increasing complexity of the economy, accompanied by similar but not quite as far-reaching changes in other areas of kibbutz life, has led to considerable changes in the organizational structure of the kibbutz.

The individual kibbutz more and more resembles a corporation with the central functionaries serving as executives for a series of semi-independent but coordinated enterprises within and outside the kibbutz. The decision-making process has been rationalized: basic decisions on investments, planning, and coordination are preserved for the central decision-making bodies of the kibbutz. The various branches and industrial enterprises achieved a considerable degree of autonomy within the limits of basic decisions. Changes are also taking place in the branches themselves: the branch manager and most of the members who work steadily in the branch are now mostly professionals, semi-professionals or skilled workers. Many of the unskilled jobs are relegated to hired workers or other workers who are not full members of the community. In many cases, mechanization or automation does away with many or all unskilled functions. The highly specialized nature of most economic or organizational decisions prevents the rank and file members from participating meaningfully in the decision-making processes outside their sphere of competence. Several kibbutzim of the Association type established a new political institution: an intermediate public body between the secretariat or other committees and the general assembly, called a "council." Many members of the council are current or ex-functionaries of communal institutions and understand the problems and the language of management. The general assembly is, in such kibbutzim, relegated to the ratification of basic decisions and meets relatively infrequently. In order to close or narrow the communication gap with the assembly, the Association introduces modern techniques of mass-communication for the explanation of complex matters in relatively simple language. Though this enables the rank and file to gain a degree of participation in important decisions, the formation of their opinion becomes dependent upon the way information is presented to them, and hence is subject to manipulation. Moreover, the general tendency of the rank and file is to move away from economic and organizational matters and concern itself mainly with social and personal matters.

Effective power over decisions lies more and more with the trained manager and professional. Even though the functionaries continue to be elected by the general assembly, the assembly's choice becomes narrowed by educational requirements. Only those with prior training and experiences are in fact eligible for the top jobs. The principle of rotation is still adhered to, but the circle of potential top functionaries becomes fairly limited.

A large part of the membership continue even in the Association to perform important and meaningful economic tasks as managers, professionals, or skilled workers. However, in spite of increasing mechanization and automation, there remains a group of members who perform only routine, uninteresting tasks. They often find compensation in increased leisure time activities, which include adult education programs and many varieties of creative activities such as acting, painting, dancing, participation in home study groups and so on. The over all tendency in the Association is, hence, towards increased differentiation of interests and activities, with some of the members being chiefly work-oriented and others leisure-oriented. Still, not all the members are deeply involved with either work or some creative leisure activity — there is a growing margin of passive and alienated members.

The increasing demographic complexity and social heterogeneity in the Association leads to a growing differentiation of needs and tastes; coupled with the growing influence of the Association, this differentiation leads to important changes in the pattern of consumption.

Consumption remains one of the chief areas of concern of the members of the Association, but its focus changes. Previously the controversy focused on items of daily material consumption, such as clothing and furnishings. With prosperity, the supply of such items became ever more plentiful and variety increased. Simultaneously, however, tastes and levels of aspiration changed. The member of the Association demanded increased freedom of choice, not only *within* each of the principal areas of personal consumption (safeguarded, for example, by the personal budget arrangements, which appropriated limited sums of money for clothing, shoes, books, etc.), but also in the allocation of his appropriations *between* these areas. Several large kibbutzim were therefore forced to adopt the "comprehensive budget," which consists of an allocation of a lump sum of money to members without limitation as to the areas in which it might be used. Though such sums are still relatively small, and though the amount allocated is not dependent upon the tasks performed by the member in the kibbutz, such arrangements come very close to the payment of an actual yearly salary to the members. They may, indeed, use the resources allocated to them to their best advantage, but a large part of the sphere of personal consumption thereby becomes almost completely de-institutionalized, the collective virtually losing control over its members.

The personal budget, even the comprehensive one, still covers only a small part of the members' total consumption. Not only are food and all personal services within the kibbutz excluded from the budget, but so are living facilities, education outside the kibbutz and foreign travel. As goods of personal consumption become abundant, the focus of interest in the sphere of consumption shifts to these other areas. Members demand improved personal services within the community. They press for larger dwelling units with more rooms and better amenities. The distribution of such amenities is usually well regulated in the mature kibbutz. The case of foreign travel and higher education is different. Only a small percentage of members can as yet be sent to travel abroad. Though some order of priority has usually been established, the matter still causes considerable tension and controversy, since many of the younger members resent having to wait a long time for their turn to travel. The demand for higher education grew enormously in recent years. This demand points to an increasingly individualistic tendency in the modern kibbutz. Second-generation members, in particular, tend to pursue their personal interests in higher studies and are often not inclined to adapt their studies to the needs of their community. Since the kibbutz did not develop any clear guidelines to regulate the provision of higher education outside the kibbutz, this matter is also the subject of considerable controversy and dissatisfaction. The inability of young people to get the kind of education they aspire to is probably the chief major factor in the decision of those who leave the kibbutz.

The processes of social and economic changes heretofore described have important repercussions upon the structure of social ties in the Association. Though these repercussions have not been systematically studied, it appears that there are two interrelated tendencies involved: the loosening up of the federated structure which ordinarily preceded the Association, and the emergence of a complex, shifting, pluralistic or even individualistic pattern of social relations, on the one hand; and the increasing social involvement of the members outside their proper settlement, on the other.

The criteria of origin, age and seniority which provided the basis for the differentiation of subgroups within the first generation in the Federated Commune, lose much of their importance as most of first generation members become older and the kibbutz grows numerically. Even the generational criterion becomes less cutting: whereas earlier the second generation tended to be a homogeneous, cohesive subgroup, age groups now form within the second generation. The arrival of the third generation provides the kibbutz with a continuous, three-generational structure in which all ages are represented. This smoothes the edges of generational and age differentials as a basis for social differentiation.

On the other hand, new criteria for the formation of groups, in accordance with the professional orientation or the personal interests of members, arise: these "functional" groups cut across the old subgroup boundaries within the kibbutz. However, these new group formations seem to be of a less permanent, less cohesive, as well as less comprehensive character than the subgroups which preceded them. They are mostly restricted to a certain sphere of interest or type of activity. It seems that the characteristic patterns of social relations in the Association are loose networks, rather than distinct, cohesive groups. The element of individual choice of personal relations grows in importance. Concomitantly, the member is less completely integrated into the social setup of the Association than he was in the Commune.

The Federated Commune, not unlike the Bund, is a closed society: only few of the significant social ties of the members stretch beyond the confines of their community. Such ties are mostly of a political nature: relations with the kibbutz federation, the political party with which the federation is associated, or with the youth movement of the federation in the cities. The Association, however, opens up socially. Professional or cultural interest groups are formed on the regional level. Members participate in professional, cultural or scientific activities and associations on the regional level. Here, they can find people who speak their language and share their interests, which are often too specialized to find much response within the confines of their own relatively small community. Since they tend to choose their friends and acquaintances in accordance with their tastes, members may entertain close social ties with people living in cities and other localities who are not necessarily close to the kibbutz and its ideology. As the initial rejection of relatives outside the kibbutz gradually dies out and new ties of kinship between the kibbutz and the outside society are formed through intermarriages, relations with kin become an important focus of outside attachments (39, p. 281). As in any other highly differentiated and highly specialized society, the social allegiances to the members of the Association tend to change from local to functional ones: many associate less with members of their own community and more with people with whom they have common interests and inclinations, wherever these may live. Such a process of realignment of social ties is well known from modern urban societies. The fact that we find the same process in the contemporary kibbutz attests to the extent to which the Association is diametrically opposed to the Bund, which emphasized undifferentiated internal solidarity and the rejection of the surrounding society.[20]

Owing to the complexity of the institutional structure of the Associa-

[20] For the connection between internal differentiation and weakening of boundaries of social systems, see (11, p. 111).

tion as well as to the loosening of the network of social ties between the members, integration ceases to rest primarily on the network of social relations. The focus of integration, instead, moves to the formal institutional structure. The chief mechanism through which a member becomes attached to his community now becomes the set of formally defined rights and obligations of membership, roles and relationships. The member is expected to fulfill his duty toward the community. In exchange, he and his offspring receive a broad array of communal services. Still, the distribution of rewards, particularly of material ones, remains even in the Association dissociated from the individuals' contribution to the community. There are still no formal sanctions which could be applied in case a member does not comply with the rules. Social control is, then, still predominantly informal, though it is guided by the formal rules of the community, fed by the media of mass-communication emanating from the formal institutions and often directed by public functionaries.

Life in the Association lacks many of the original attractions of kibbutz life, such as the intensive communal experience of the Bund or the cosy togetherness of the Commune. But as life in the kibbutz becomes less attractive socially, it provides more opportunities for personal development and self-fulfilment than ever before, both in the professional sphere and in the sphere of leisure activities. Though the member does not receive any personal material rewards for his work, he still contributes to the general affluence and thus indirectly enjoys the fruits of his efforts. Indeed, the level of consumption and services in the Association quickly approximates, and sometimes even surpasses, those enjoyed by the urban middle class. The member of the Association, hence, sacrifices much less than before in terms of personal comfort and opportunities, and many of the factors which would previously attract him to the city lose some of their appeal. The Association can provide most of the advantages of urban living, while sparing the member many of its disadvantages. Under these conditions the kibbutz becomes increasingly an alternative form of life in a modern and industrialized society.

Though the modern Association in general functions adequately, its emerging institutional structure finds it hard to resolve some of the problems called forth by its very size and complexity. The most important problem is the growing marginality of part of the membership: as the processes of specialization and increasing complexity proceed, the differences between members who participate actively in the economic, organizational, political, social and cultural life of the community and those who do not become even more pronounced. Thus, almost no one can any longer participate in *all* spheres and many do participate in *some*, to the neglect of others. But a group of members gradually emerges who participate in almost no sphere of activity. The growing individualization of the Association and concomitant lack of concern with participation enables these members to live on the kibbutz without really constituting an integral part of the community. Closely connected with this problem is that of anomie. We have already mentioned the decline of informal social control in the loosely-knit Association. However, the increased formalization of social control is unable to prevent really serious deviation, since the kibbutz, as a voluntary community, does not possess a set of legitimate informal sanctions to be applied to those cases in which informal controls prove ineffective. Nor is there a system of differentiated rewards which would compensate members for extra efforts or for extra time spent for the common cause. Hence, the performance of functions depends, even in the Association, on the personal motivation of members. Important changes in motivation have taken place, and the devotion to a common cause has largely receded into the background and been substituted by the aspiration to achieve individual professional success and to derive a broad spectrum of intrinsic job-satisfactions provided by interesting and creative tasks in production. Though such motivations are supported by the institutional system and though members are encouraged to strive for professional achievement, on which their standing in the community largely depends, there still exists no means to *force* them to succeed. Hence, if a member is not positively motivated to work, he can easily carve out a corner for himself in the complex structure of the large Association where he can subsist indefinitely without contributing any real efforts to the common cause. Conversely, those members who are most active and contribute most to the common good are also often able to arrange special rewards for themselves such as increased personal use of common facilities (for example, cars) which are, strictly speaking, illegitimate by kibbutz standards.

Finally, and again closely related to the above points, the Association obviously runs the danger of losing its ideological compass. Value-change was a characteristic of the kibbutz throughout its history. But the problem now is that the members of the Association might gradually abandon even the basic ideological assumption of the kibbutz movement, which up till now provided a common bond among them, as well as a most important dividing line between them and the rest of Israeli society. The members might then turn each to his private conception of life and society, and thereby blur or even abolish one of the last boundaries which separate the kibbutz as a corporate entity from its surroundings. Such a state of things has not yet developed, but the probability of such a development increases progressively.

Our analysis so far points to a basic dilemma of the contemporary kibbutz, which can be felt to various extents in every kibbutz settlement but is most prominent in the large Association: the very economic and organizational success of the kibbutz led to a thorough-going transformation of its social structure, of its way of life, and of the relationships between members. As an ongoing enterprise, the modern kibbutz is a success. But it is not the realization of the original utopia. Moreover, it is not at all clear whether the basic institutional arrangements of the kibbutz are capable to contain the tendency of continuous growth and expansion. We have seen some indications of emergent problems and strains which the Association finds extremely hard to resolve.

Most members of the generation of founders accept this transition to the Association as perhaps unfortunate but necessary; the alternative would be an ossified, underdeveloped, small community, out of touch with modern reality, resembling some of the religious utopian communities of the Western world. Members of the kibbutz-born second generation often find themselves in a dilemma in this respect. They were brought up on the utopian ideals of the early days. But the only kibbutz they really know is often the modern Association. Most react to the dilemma by a selective interpretation of the basic precepts of kibbutz life.[21] But there are variations. On one extreme are those who tend towards the introduction of additional changes and innovations into the kibbutz, which would make it resemble even further the modern, urban society.[22] On the other extreme are those second generation members who, though they were raised on the modern, large and complex kibbutz, still hanker after the days of its inception. They revolt against the encroaching urbanization and the increasing complexity and anonymity of the contemporary kibbutz. These youths react to the modern kibbutz in two diametrically opposed ways: for some, the kibbutz has already lost its distinctive value and so they quit and move to the cities, mostly in search of higher education. Others seek to experience anew the spirit of excitement of pioneering, like that of the early days. In the late fifties and early sixties, when no new kibbutzim were established, some of these quit the kibbutz, and settled in moshavim or new towns which were being established in the newly developing regions of the country. Several new moshavim were based on nuclei of second-generation youths from the kibbutz. Such youths were also prominent in the nucleus of first settlers in Arad, a new town in the Judean Desert. Other second-generation members found the excitement of a fresh start when they were sent by their federation to help out small, new kibbutzim, which suffered from serious social and economic problems and tended to become Residual Communes. However, only few second-generation members stayed on beyond the one-year period of service to the Federation (35). The members of the parent settlement

---

[21] For a fuller discussion of the dilemmas which the second generation faces see (10).

[22] For example, at a recent convention of second-generation members of one of the movements it was proposed to remunerate the principal economic functionaries for their work, thereby abolishing the principle of separation between work and consumption; the proposal was, however, rejected.

are usually opposed to the idea that second-generation members settle in the new kibbutzim or even establish kibbutzim of their own. They see the chief task of the new generation to continue the life work of their parents in the kibbutzim in which they were born.

Indeed, until recently no new kibbutzim had been established by second-generation members, though the idea was often discussed and had been attractive to many of them. Only in the last few years have a few such kibbutzim emerged. After the Six Day War, particularly, second-generation youths participated in the establishment of new kibbutzim in the occupied areas, such as the Golan Heights, for instance. The new kibbutz settlements are located in underdeveloped and outlying areas, and their atmosphere resembles to an extent that of the early kibbutz. This development could thus be considered as a re-emergence of the Bund, but this did not grow out, as the original Bund had, as a revolt against the bourgeois society of the Diaspora, but as a reaction to the way of life in the large and complex, urbanized contemporary kibbutz. It seems then, that with this development the structural transformation of the kibbutz completed a full cycle: it started with the Bund, moved to the Commune and later to the Association; while lately a few new Bunds are established by or through the active participation of second-generation members. One should not, however, expect that the return to the Bund among second-generation youths will take major proportions in the near future. It will stay confined to a select few, in the same way in which the pioneering Zionism of the generation of founders of the kibbutz movement embraced only a small fraction of the Jewish society in the Diaspora. The very re-emergence of the Bund among the second generation, however, attests both to the underlying dilemma as well as to the continuing vitality of the kibbutz movement.

Prospects for the Future

In this paper I used a historical-typological approach in order to trace the major social transformation of the kibbutz and to analyze the dynamic forces, both internal and external to the kibbutz movement, which brought about these transformations. The analysis enables us now to identify the sources of the spiritual crisis experienced by the contemporary kibbutz, and exemplified most clearly by the Association type. We find that the kibbutz has become more vigorous than ever before through the processes of industrialization, modernization, and urbanization. Nowadays, it forms an integral and important sector of Israeli society. However, these developments also changed profoundly the nature of the institutional arrangements and social relations in the kibbutz and thus put into question its ability to preserve its unique social characteristics. The large and mature kibbutz may easily become just another form of modern urban life, distinguished from other such forms merely by some peculiar arrangements and institutions, but losing most of its historically distinguishing characteristics as a revolutionary communal and corporate entity. The crisis of the contemporary kibbutz does not result from weakness or disorganization, as did the crisis which characterizes the Transitional Bund. Rather, it is a crisis called forth by material success which has not been paralleled by the establishment and internalization of new spiritual goals. The crisis in the kibbutz is in this respect strikingly similar to the general crisis of contemporary Western society. The question, then is: What are the alternatives for the future of the kibbutz? More specifically, are there any alternatives for the kibbutz which do not exist for the rest of modern society?

In the past, questions of this sort were often discussed in terms of the "viability" of the kibbutz.[23] Such an indiscriminate approach to the problem is obviously beside the point. In the course of our discussion we have dwelt upon some forms of kibbutz life, like the "Residual Commune," which suffer from serious functional problems and, if these are not rectified, are probably doomed to extinction. These, however, are extreme and exceptional cases. There is no question whatever that in the future the viability and growth of the kibbutz is secure. The loss of distinctiveness and uniqueness in the way of life is sufficiently compensated for by material well-being, professional opportunities and possibilities for self-fulfillment. Granting, then, that the kibbutz will continue to exist, the question is often asked whether it will preserve its "essential" characteristics. The answer to this question depends upon one's conception of what these "essential" characteristics actually are. One has to remember that the kibbutz is not a religious movement and did not intend to realize on earth a "sacred" community, reflecting a transcendental order of things. Though the values of the early kibbutz had a "sacred" quality, they were essentially secular values. Hence, neither the values nor the arrangements based on them are immutable. There exist no fixed, accepted criteria by which to judge the success or failure of the kibbutz in a transcendental sense. Whatever the conception of the kibbutz maintained by the "Founding Fathers" might have been, it is perfectly legitimate, within the framework of a secular conception of values, for members of successive generations to alter its values, goals and institutional arrangements. The only legitimate question about the future of the kibbutz, then, is the one relating to the kinds of alternatives which one could conceive of for its future development and the probabilities attached to each of them.

The concrete problem at hand is whether the transition to the Association will continue in the future or whether a reaction against this development will set in and curb or reverse it. The forces which push towards the Association are unquestionably very strong and impinge upon the kibbutz movement as such, and not only upon the large and mature kibbutzim, though in the latter these forces are particularly strongly felt. Nevertheless, several forces are already at work in the kibbutz movement which act to attenuate the present trend, though it is doubtful whether they will be strong enough to reverse it.

First, the present trend towards increasing social differentiation and interpenetration with the surrounding society, two of the chief character- istics of the Association, could be attenuated in the future. As the kib- butz depends less and less on the influx of new members from the out- side and grows more and more through natural increase, the kibbutz-born members are becoming the predominant, and might even later become the only, group of origin in the community. This is an element of homogeneity which endows the kibbutz with bonds of common descent and separates it from the surrounding society. As such, this demographic trend works against the "Eclipse of Community" tendency, character- istic of the transition to the Association.[24] Still, we have to keep in mind that the kibbutz participates increasingly in the marrage market of the broader society and hence, many of the spouses of second-generation members of any kibbutz will not be kibbutz-born.

Secondly, the kibbutz is characterized by a considerable degree of self- consciousness and self-criticism and by an uncanny ability to adapt its social arrangements to changing circumstances, so as to keep them in tune with those values of the basic ideology which are still meaningful to its members. The young second-generation members who long for the experience of the original Bund, are by no means the only ones who dis- like the atmosphere created by the transition to the Association. Many thoughtful old-timers and many leaders of the movement are aware of the fact that the very material success of the kibbutz might undermine the realization of some of their most cherished values. Though the problem is the subject of frequent discussions and much controversy, the effective measures taken to countervail the trend towards individualiza- tion and the weakening of social ties are as yet few. Among the most effective is the establishment of "Members' Social Centers" (Mo'adon Le'chaverim) as a means to provide a novel and attractive focus of social interaction. Another is the establishment of community radio stations, which have been attempted in at least one of the largest kib- butzim. Other measures were taken on the regional or even national level: as mentioned, the kibbutzim are in the process of establishing a series of regional colleges and it has also been proposed to establish a nationwide "University of the Kibbutz." These institutions enable members to receive highly specialized professional training as well as

[24] I am indebted to Mr. Y. Shatil on this point.

general education of a high quality within frameworks controlled by the kibbutz movement. Such institutions serve, then, to counter the tendency towards increased interpenetration with the general society. The educational programs of such institutions also take into account the special needs and problems of the kibbutz and thereby serve to ameliorate the impact of professionalization and diversification of interests on community life.

Another series of measures intends to smooth out the raw edges left by the tendencies towards increased specialization and formalization, particularly in the spheres of work and of public activities. The growing emphasis upon the human relations approach, particularly in industry, and the constant effort to improve communication between the institutions and the rank and file members attest to efforts to overcome some of the obstacles to good relations and to full participation of members in increasingly more complex processes. In this connection, the rising interest in organization and development and similar techniques should be noted. Some of these countervailing mechanisms, however, are not without dangers of their own: after all, "social engineering" of various kinds has been applied in the modern Association-like society, to manipulate people as well as to counter tendencies to passivity, social atomism and alienation. There is no guarantee that they will not be used in this way in the kibbutz as well, though we have to keep in mind that there is no fundamental opposition of interests between the leadership and the general membership of the kibbutz and that leaders are still rotated at a relatively high, though declining, rate (8).

Whatever the usefulness of these various measures discussed earlier, they are, to my mind, mainly palliatives which do not cut to the heart of the matter. If the kibbutz is really set to achieve a reversal of present trends, it will probably have to decide in the future on some very radical changes in the allocation of its resources, both material and human. In the past, the necessity to achieve economic consolidation and prosperity led the kibbutz to give primary emphasis to the instrumental sphere. The large and mature kibbutzim have already achieved considerable affluence. Therefore, some of the settlements at least could allow themselves even to forego a degree of technological or economic advance in order to realize more fully some social and humanistic values. A trend in this direction can already be discerned among some of the leaders. If it prevails, an interesting change of emphasis might occur in the kibbutz. If the fifties were an epoch of rapid technological change and the sixties an epoch of economic and organizational consolidation, the seventies might become an epoch of social renaissance of kibbutz-life. Almost paradoxically, such a development would seem to coincide with a parallel trend in modern, post-industrial society — a trend which often points to the kibbutz as to a model of the "good life."

BIBLIOGRAPHY

1. Becker, H. "Sacred and Secular Societies: Retrospect and Prospect," in: H. Becker (ed.) *Through Values to Social Science*, pp. 248–280. Durham, N.C.: Duke University Press, 1950.

2. *Bein Tze'irim (Among the Young)* (in Hebrew) Tel Aviv: Am Oved, 1969.

3. Buber, M. "Epilogue — An Experiment that Did Not Fail," in M. Buber, *Paths In Utopia*. Pp. 139–149. Boston: Beacon Press, 1950.

4. Cohen, E. "Patterns of Institutionalization in the Sphere of Work in the Kibbutz." *Niv Hakvutsa*, 7, (3), 1958, pp. 519–530 (in Hebrew).

5. Cohen, E. "Changes in the Social Structure of the Sphere of Work in the Kibbutz." *Riv'on Lekalkala (The Economic Quarterly)*, 10, 1963 (in Hebrew).

6. Cohen, E. *Bibliography of the Kibbutz*, Tel Aviv: Giv'at Haviva, 1964.

7. Cohen, E. "Progress and Communality: Value Dilemmas in the Collective Movement." *International Review of Community Development*, No. 15–16, 1966, pp. 3–18.

8. Cohen, E. and E. Leshem. "Public Participation in Collective Settlements," *International Review of Community Development*, No. 19/20, 1968, pp. 251–270.

9. Cohen, E., and E. Leshem. *Survey of Regional Cooperation in Three Regions of Collective Settlements*. Publications on Problems of Regional Development, No. 2, Rehovot: Settlement Study Center, 1969.

10. Cohen, E. and M. Rosner. "Relations Between Generations in the Israeli Kibbutz." *Journal of Contemporary History*, 5(1), 1970, pp. 73–86.

11. Cohen, Y. A. "Social Boundary Systems." *Current Anthropology* 10 (1) 1969, pp. 103–126.

12. Diamond, S. "Kibbutz and Shtetl: The History of an Idea." *Social Problems* 5(2), 1957, pp. 71–99.

13. Diamond, S. "The Kibbutz: Utopia in Crisis." *Dissent*, 4, 1957, pp. 132–140.

14. Durkheim, E. *Suicide*. Glencoe, Illinois: Free Press, 1951.

15. Etzioni, A. "Solidaric Work Groups in Collective Settlements." *Human Organization*, 16(3), 1957, pp. 2–7.

16. Halpern, B. "Comments on Science and Socialism." *Dissent*, 4, 1957, pp. 140–146.

17. Holzner, B. "The Concept of 'Integration' in Sociological Theory." *The Sociological Quarterly*, 8(1), 1967, pp. 51–62.

18. Horigan, F. D. *The Israeli Kibbutz*. Psychiatric Abstract Series No. 9, National Institute of Health, Public Health Service, U.S. Dept. of Health, Education and Welfare, 1962. (mimeo.)

19. Lavi, Ch. "Hakvutza Hagdolah" (The Large Kvutzah) in Sh. Gadon (ed.) *Netivei Hakvutza VeHakibbutz* (The Path of the Kvutzah and the Kibbutz), Am Oved, Tel Aviv, 1958, pp. 351–356 (in Hebrew).

20. Meier-Cronemeyer, H. "Die Politik der Unpolitischen," *Koelner Zeitschrift fuer Soziologie und Sozial-Psychologie,* 7, 1965, pp. 833–854.
21. Meier-Cronemeyer, H. "Juedische Jugendbewegung." *Germania Judaica* 8, 1969.
22. Parsons, T., et al. (eds.). *Theories of Society.* New York: Free Press, 1961.
23. Redfield, R. *The Folk Culture of Yucatan.* Chicago, Illinois: University of Chicago Press, 1941.
24. Reissman, L. *The Urban Process.* New York: Free Press, 1964.
25. *Research Report,* No. 3, 1959-1963, Dept. of Sociology, Hebrew University, Jerusalem, 1964.
26. Rosenfeld, E. "Social Stratification in a Classless Society," *American Sociological Review,* 16, 1951, pp. 766–774.
27. Rosenfeld, E. "Institutional Change in the Kibbutz," *Social Problems,* 5(2), 1957, pp. 118–136.
28. Schmalenbach, H. "Die soziologische Kategorie des Bundes," *Die Dioskuren,* 1, 1922.
29. Shils, E. "Primordial, Personal, Sacred and Civic Ties," *British Journal of Sociology,* 8, 1957.
30. Shur, S. H. *Kibbutz Bibliography* . The Van Leer Foundation, Jerusalem, Dept. for Higher Education, Kibbutz Artzi, Tel Aviv, and Social Research Center on the Kibbutz, Giv'at Haviva, 1971.
31. Stein, M. *The Eclipse of Community.* New York: Harper and Row, 1960.
32. Talmon-Garber, Y. *Family and Community in the Kibbutz.* Cambridge, Mass.: Harvard University Press, 1972.
33. Talmon-Garber, Y. "Social Structure and Family Size," *Human Relations,* 12(2), 1959, pp. 121–145.
34. Talmon-Garber, Y. "The Family in a Revolutionary Movement: The Case of the Kibbutz in Israel," in: M. Nimkoff (ed.); *Comparative Family Systems,* pp. 259–286. Boston: Houghton Mifflin and Co., 1965.
35. Talmon-Garber, Y., and E. Cohen. "Collective Settlements in the Negev," in Y. Ben David (ed.): *Agricultural Planning and Village Community in Israel,* UNESCO, Paris, 1964, pp. 69–82.
36. Toennies, F. *Gemeinschaft und Gesellschaft.* 8th Ed., Leipzig: 1935.
37. Troeltsch, E. *The Social Teachings of the Christian Churches.* New York: Harper and Row, 1960.
38. Weinryb, B. D. "The Impact of Urbanization in Israel," *Middle East Journal,* 11(1), 1957, pp. 23–36.
39. Weintraub, B., M. Lissak, and Y. Azmon. *Moshava, Kibbutz and Moshav.* Ithaca, N.Y.: Cornell University Press, 1960.

The Religious Kibbutz: Religion, Nationalism, and Socialism in a Communal Framework*

Aryei Fishman

The Religious Kibbutz Federation (RKF), *Hakibbutz Hadati*, comprising fifteen settlements in 1980,[1] is represented in this article as a Zionist movement of religious renewal within Orthodox Judaism, at a communal level. The purpose of this article is to show how the RKF was able to take the kibbutz life-structure, which had evolved and been shaped by the three central kibbutz federations within a secular nationalist and socialist framework and, through its religious ideology, turn it into a social instrument for the creation of a modern self-contained community governed by the *halakha* (Torah law). In this respect, as we shall see, the religious kibbutz embodies a directed response to a challenge, namely, to work out the mutual accommodation between halakha and the exigencies of a modern national community. The national and socialist parameters of the kibbutz life-structure were to set up the "laboratory" conditions for working out that accommodation.

The Religious Community

Though the religious kibbutz was formed in the ideological mold of the secular kibbutz, it is rooted in a distinct matrix of Jewish religious culture and history. In Judaism, the local religious community is envisaged as the Jewish people writ small, and serves as a carrier of the transformative ethos with which the people were charged by the Sinai covenant: to carry out the will of God in history by performing the precepts of halakha, thereby restructuring the world religiously.[2] Jewish communal life, accordingly, acquires its basic religious legitimation through its ordering by Torah law.[3] This law prevailed universally in Jewish communal life until traditional Jewish society disintegrated under the impact of emancipation, in the early nineteenth century. When the Western European state awarded equal civil rights to its Jewish inhabitants and authorized their participation in

115

its institutions, it nullified, at the same time, the authority of Torah law in most spheres of communal life. The authority of the Jewish community contracted, and was limited mainly to the religious-ritual sphere.[4]

The RKF emerged in the early 1930s. Its creation was motivated primarily by national values, but also by the nebulous idea of utilizing the structure of the kibbutz settlement to revive religious community life, in the sense of restoring *all* spheres of life, in which Jews participated, to the framework of the religious community.[5] This idea was to be clarified and attain articulate ideological expression in the late 1930s, when religious kibbutzim began to settle on the land.

At that time, there was a sizeable gap between the normative demands of a modern self-contained community as represented by the kibbutz settlement, and normative halakha. Halakhic legislation had all but come to a standstill since the end of the eighteenth century, and the Rabbinate, whether in the Land of Israel or in the diaspora centers of learning, was generally insensitive to the problems that arose in regard to the autonomous functioning of a modern national community, and made no efforts to come to grips with them. In effect, this meant not only that observant Jews were unable to assume all the responsibilities for the community's existence, but that it was impossible to maintain such a community according to halakha.

This was the challenge that the establishment of kibbutz settlements posed for the RKF. By applying religious law to a pioneering community that encompassed and integrated the major social institutions necessary for maintaining a self-contained communal life, the RKF sought to bridge the gap between national-pioneering norms and halakha, thus restoring the broad scope of the religious community, according to the prototype of the traditional community.

Modification of the Traditional Outlook

The religious community that the Orthodox pioneers established differs, however, from the traditional community in its attitude toward the world and history. Whereas the traditional community dissociated itself from universal society and its institutions, confining its meaningful world within particularist boundaries, the kibbutz religious community identifies itself with society at large, and its meaningful world blends traditional religious and general human values. Moreover, while the traditional community repudiated purposeful active Jewish participation in history, thereby restraining the Sinaitic ethos, the kibbutz religious community approves such participation. Finally, the traditional community hardly recognized the present as an autonomous, religiously significant dimension of time, viewing the religious valence of the present as deriving primarily from its continuity with the contiguous past. In contrast, the kibbutz religious community conceives of the present as a distinct period of historic time, charged with its own religious valence. These three differences between the preemancipation traditional community and the kibbutz religious community signal the fundamental change in the image of the Jewish people which took place within Orthodox Jewry, as a positive response to emancipation and national renascence, and created modern, as opposed to traditionalistic, Orthodoxy.

We cannot deal here with the earlier modernizing movements within Orthodox Jewry that legitimated a drastic modification of the traditional religious view, and prepared the ground for the RKF. The reference is to the movements of Torah-im-Derekh-Eretz[6] and Religious Zionism.[7] We only note briefly that each movement sought in its own way to evolve a new meaningful unity for modern Jewish life after the traditional order had been undermined, by synthesizing traditional and universal cultures, and favoring the active participation of the Jewish people in history within the framework of a modern state. Whereas Torah-im-Derekh-Eretz sought to attain this goal through the integration of the observant Jew within the life of a non-Jewish European state, religious Zionism sought to attain it within a Jewish national state.

The special quality of the RKF, compared with the above-mentioned modernizing movements, was its ability to actualize in its pioneering settlements the synthesis of the traditional and universal cultures, by participating in history within an autonomous religious community. For the structure of the religious kibbutz comprises three analytic community-wide components: a national collectivity, a socialist collectivity, and a halakhic order.[8] The secular kibbutz had already integrated the national and socialist collectivities into one community, and had thus created a potent social vehicle for active participation in history, through identification with both modern Jewish and universal values. The RKF, in adopting the kibbutz form of life, was to join the integrated national and socialist collectivities with the halakhic order and to stimulate their interaction. On the one hand, the two collectivities were to serve as social carriers of the halakhic order, and thus provide the substance of daily life in a modern religious community. On the other hand, the halakhic order was to be impressed on the national and socialist collectivities, thus completing and realizing the religious community. It follows that the interaction between the two integrated collectivities and the halakhic order within a closed system was to create the dynamics of a modern religious community taking a consciously active part in history.

Indeed, the settlement activity of the RKF created the real conditions for the actualization of such a community. The majority of the religious kibbutzim, especially those established in the prestate years, took part in the expansion of the political borders of the national community as a whole, and in the defense of those borders.[9] Just as the kibbutz movement as a whole, at least until the creation of the state, may be regarded as the spearhead of modern Jewish national participation in history, the RKF may be regarded as the preeminent expression of an active Jewish religious orientation to history in the context of national renascence.

The Religious-National Collectivity

Let us proceed to specify the relationship between the national collectivity and the halakhic order within the perspective of the RKF. We have intimated that the national-religious role which the RKF assumed was the closing of the gap between the normative demands of a pioneering settlement constituting a micro-national community, and those of halakha. Not only was the autonomous settlement to extend the basis of Jewish community life beyond the confines of the traditional religious community, but its closed social framework was to form a limited arena for staging a direct confrontation between national pioneering and halakhic norms, thus "forcing" a solution to the problems that would arise. As was stated in 1942:

> We maintain micro-communities that take part in all spheres of life and at the same time we observe the halakhic framework . . . . By filling our roles in all these spheres, we confront halakha with all the problems deriving from the reality of our life. . . . The gap that exists today between halakha and reality . . . will disappear only when these two elements confront each other in public life . . . and clash. Our creation as a community makes this clash possible.[10]

According to this ideological outlook, the "clash" between the two sets of norms was eventually to close the gap between them, allowing them to become mutually compatible. While the pioneering norms were to create and maintain a viable national collectivity, the halakhic norms were to provide fundamental religious legitimation for the national collectivity, without impairing its orderly operation.

Halakha and History

The faith that inspired the religious pioneers to believe that the Torah could bridge the gap between normative halakha and the normative requirements of the national collectivity, was nourished by the attribution of a religious valence to the national collectivity and by the vision of restoring halakha to what was considered its proper role in history. The religious consciousness, aroused by national revival, reverted to the golden, preexilic, age, when the creative power of the Torah flowered in the form of Oral Law with its broad relevance to changing social institutions.[11] Jewish life in the golden age was contrasted with life in the diaspora, in which the Torah did not relate to all spheres of life, and its creativity could not attain its fullest viable expression. According to this view, "Inasmuch as the people ceases to create its own life . . . an antagonism is created between the Torah and life." On the other hand, political independence implied controlling the objective conditions of Jewish life, thus enabling the elimination of the contrasts between the Torah and that life. National revival, whereupon, involved "understanding the Torah anew, reviving it and restoring it to the role it played before the Jewish people went into exile.'' If follows that the merger of the creative power of the Torah and the political power of nationalism would create conditions for arousing the inner dynamics of halakha, so that Oral Law could again maintain the unity between the Torah and developing historical reality.

According to the religious pioneering conception, there is a qualitative relationship between the Torah and the everyday world, the basic intention of the Torah being to mold the world by impressing its stamp of sacredness on it, through halakhic precepts. Inasmuch as social institutions undergo transformation in the course of historical development, judicial formulations should also be modified within the framework of Oral Law, so that halakha can apply its stamp of sacredness on these instititutions.[12] The new institutions do not lead to the creation of new rulings, but to the unfolding of new formulations potentially contained in the sources, for the Oral Law merely expresses explicitly that which was revealed *in nuce* at Sinai. Guided by rational investigation in accordance with the logical rules of hermeneutics,[13] new halakhic formulations, in accordance with changing historical reality, would materialize. In 1938, this was expressed as follows:

> In our view, the Torah does not contain laws and ordinances for one generation alone, but it is an absolute imperative for the entire Jewish people wherever they are in every generation . . . . We do not regard the Torah as a summary of a certain period in the development of mankind or even in the development of the Jewish people. . . . It was surely the intent of the Torah to order and perfect the life of our people in the period in which it was given; nevertheless, we find in it not only detailed laws and ordinances, but also general guidelines for generations to come. This is the basis for Oral Law. Every generation finds its own rationale in the Torah, reflecting its responsibilities and special needs. Furthermore, it finds in the Torah possibilities of application that were not, nor could not have been, apparent in former generations, although these possibilities were potentially contained therein.

In 1951 this belief was restated: ''Jewish religion . . . aspires to contain within its framework every new reality that develops in the course of time and establishes itself in the world . . . Oral Law within the system of the Torah implies providing an answer for the new.''

According to this line of thought, the qualitative relationship between halakha and changing historical reality necessitates the creation of new halakhic rulings. For that purpose one must be closely familiar with existing and changing social institutions, so that halakha could shape historical reality. Thus, the relationship between a new reality and halakha was conceived as dialectic. While the new reality was perceived as capable of instigating the creation of new halakhic formulations, halakha was conceived as subjecting this reality to the authority of its norms. In this relationship the halakhic legislator was given the task of directing ''the dialogue between Torah and life.'' He was to familiarize himself with the new social institutions, to ascertain how to apply halakha to these institutions, and to formulate new halakhic rulings so as to order the changing reality by religious norms.

Thus the RKF took the innovating ethic inherent in theoretical halakha,[14] expressed in the concept of *hidushei Torah* (Torah innovations), and extended it beyond the confines of the study-house. With this ethic it sought to revive halakhic legislation within a living pioneering environment, in order to fructify "not only the wasteland, but the laws of the Torah as well." Since the Torah was conceived as "a Torah of life which encompasses every facet of life and makes life possible," halakha was believed to be potentially compatible with the normal functioning of a pioneer Jewish settlement.

The faith of the RKF in the potential compatibility of halakhic and pioneering norms was put to practical test when settlement began. The religious pioneers had anticipated that they would be faced with problematic situations because of the clash between the two sets of norms. But such situations did not deter them from plunging into the reality which they perceived as disarrayed, in that autonomous communal living and halakhic observance precluded one another, in order to solve the problems that would come up. The religious feeling inspiring the religious pioneers is exemplified in the discussion that preceded the establishment of the RKF's first mountain kibbutz, Kfar Etzion, in the early forties. According to the agricultural know-how of the period, the economic viability of mountain settlements depended on the cultivation of orchards. However, only hybrid fruit trees could grow in the moutain soil, and hybrids are forbidden by the Torah.

> The question of hybrids faces us in all severity. Again we have to ask ourselves: will we be able to rise to the task? Isn't it more realistic to postpone the plan for a mountain settlement? However, this is not the course for a religious pioneering movement. . . . Questions of that sort will not be solved . . . as long as they are not put to practical test. We are the religious group . . . upon whom their solution depends.

The belief that the Torah could provide an answer for any problematic situation in which normative halakha prevented the regular functioning of an autonomous modern Jewish settlement, led the religious pioneers to perceive themselves as pathfinders, innovating halakha in the pioneering reality.

The Religious-Socialist Collectivity

What was the religious conception of the socialist collectivity inherent in the religious kibbutz community, according to the RKF ideology? On one level of meaning, the socialist collective was regarded as an intrinsic religious value expressing "the intention of the Torah" in ordering social life. The life of cooperation and equality was conceived as a way of life for realizing the intention of the Torah with regard to the organization of economic interpersonal relations.

On a second level of meaning, the socialist collectivity was conceived as an instrumental religious value. We have seen that the religious-national collective was conceived as a closed arena in which would be staged the confrontation between pioneering and halakhic norms so as to reveal the formula for their operative compatibility. The socialist collective was conceived as an intermediate agency in the pursuit of that goal. That is, the socialist collective, having a central authority which could control the allocation of all economic resources including manpower, could control and direct the national collective in testing various solutions to the problem arising from the clash between pioneering and halakhic norms—and it could do so far more efficiently than a community fragmented into many social and economic units. In that sense, the kibbutz was described in an incisive statement (1942), as "a consolidated community which undertook to conduct a directed experiment . . . to fashion a Torah community in modern circumstances. A directed social experiment is possible only in a directed society."

The Charismatic-Religious Community

Our discussion has focused on the relationship between halakha and the adaptive environment of an autonomous pioneering religious community, with the community seeking to accommodate itself to the environment and to dominate it. We have not specified the problematic situations in which clashes took place between national pioneering and halakhic norms, nor have we dealt with the solutions to such situations.[15] In effect, the solutions depended on the Rabbinate, whose authority the RKF recognized in principle with regard to the exegesis of halakha. But the Rabbinate did not always come up with solutions that were compatible with the ideological frame of reference of the RKF. This is not the place to consider the complex attitude of the RKF to the Rabbinate, other than to note that there were situations in which the RKF acted autonomously, with the self-awareness of bearing nonformal religious authority—which may be defined as charismatic authority— to operate as a community.[16] From this point of view, the socialistic framework of the kibbutz sensitized the inter-psychic affinity of the kibbutz members to the point where they felt they were operating as one personality, so to speak, and, infused with primary religious power, possessed the authority to act on their own communal authority. This awareness was remarked upon retrospectively in 1951:

> We assumed the authority to determine . . . practices even though they were not always in accord with what is written in the *Shulhan Arukh* . . . . We did this . . . because of our religious feeling . . . that a community is able to withstand the violation of an accepted religious practice. If an individual transgresses that which is written in the *Shulhan Arukh*, his religious outlook might be utterly destroyed. However, a religious community that lives a communal life with col-

lective responsibility could assume responsibility in this sphere too. Only thus can we explain to ourselves how we dared to touch areas which, from the formal point of view, we were unqualified to touch.

Perhaps the outstanding example of the sense of communal charismatic authority is the approach of the RKF to the problems of defense on the Sabbath. When the first religious kibbutz, Tirat Tzvi, settled on the land in 1937, halakha did not permit carrying out on the Sabbath the various activities needed to ensure the security of an autonomus Jewish settlement. That alone made the establishment and continued existence of a religious settlement questionable. Nevertheless, Tirat Tzvi plunged into that halakhically-disarrayed reality. When, *ex post facto*, security problems arose which jeopardized its very existence, it became possible in the course of time to obtain dispensations from the Rabbinate for Sabbath activities on which the security of such a settlement might depend.[17] In other words, there were times when the religious community, inspired by the sense of bearing charismatic authority, leaped the gap between pioneering and halakhic norms and temporarily bridged it by this authority, until eventually it was possible to close the gap at the religious institutional level.

Conclusion

The religious ideology of the RKF was developed chiefly in the formative period of the religious kibbutz movement in the 1930s and 1940s. We have seen how the RKF community, through this ideology, projected the Sinaitic-charged transformative ethos to the world at large, with the intent of restructuring it through halakhic patterns. We have also noted how the RKF transmuted the achievement orientation inherent in the innovative ethic of theoretical halakha, with the aim of rendering it applicable to the workaday life of a modern community. It would seem that the religious impulses generated by the community-oriented halakhic ethic gave rise to unanticipated forces in workaday life. Studies conducted in the 1970s on the relative economic success of all kibbutzim indicate that, as a group, those of the RKF excel.[18] This economic success may be explained in terms of the "transformative potential"[19] of Judaism, as expressed specifically in the capability of the motivational and structural traits inherent in the halakhic ethic to stimulate economic institutions in a collective framework.[20] But that is a theme for a separate article.

Notes

*I am grateful to Elihu Katz and Ernest Krausz for their helpful comments on an earlier version of this article. I also wish to thank Priscilla B. Fishman for her editorial suggestions.
1. There are two Orthodox kibbutzim affiliated with the Poalei Agudat Israel movement that are not members of Hakibbutz Hadati. The religious ideology discussed in this article does not apply to them.

2. For the local Jewish community embodying the Jewish people in miniature, see, for example, M.P. Golding, "The juridical basis of communal association in medieval rabbinic legal thought," *Jewish Social Studies* 28 (1966): 77–78. For Judaism as an historical religion charged with the Sinaitic transformative ethos, see especially R.J. Zwi Werblowsky, "Hannouca et Noël, ou Judaisme et Christianisme," *Revue de l'Histoire des Religions* 145 (1954): 30–68, particularly pp. 60–65.

3. See, for example, M. Elon, "Mishpat Ivri," *Encyclopedia Judaica*, vol. 12, Jerusalem: Keter, 1971, p. 124.

4. Elon, "Mishpat Ivri," pp. 140–41.

5. For the initial period of the RKF ideology, see A. Fishman, "On the formation of the religious kibbutz movement," *Hakibbutz* 6–7 (1978–79): 69–87 (Hebrew).

6. Literally "Torah and civic life." For this movement see, for example, M. Breuer, *The "Torah-Im-Derekh-Eretz" of Samson Raphael Hirsch.* Jerusalem–New York: Feldheim, 1970.

7. For this movement, see, for example, M. Waxman, *The Mizrachi, Its Aims and Purposes.* New York: Mizrachi Bureau, 1918.

8. For these three communal components in the religious kibbutz, see M. Unna, "The elements of the religious kibbutz," in A. Fishman (ed.), *The Religious Kibbutz Movement.* Jerusalem: World Zionist Organization, 1957, pp. 27–30.

9. For a brief history of the RKF until 1966, see A. Fishman, "Hakibbutz Hadati," *Encyclopedia of Zionism*, vol. 1. New York: Herzl Press, 1971, p. 452.

10. The reader interested in the sources for the quotations in this article is referred to the Hebrew version of the article that appeared in *Petahim* 39 (June 1977): 21–26.

11. For the relationship between Written and Oral Law, see for example, M. Elon "Mishpat Ivri," pp. 115–23.

12. See S. Friedman, in A. Fishman, *The Religious Kibbutz Movement,* pp. 38–39.

13. For these rules, see L. Jacobs, "Hermeneutics," *Encyclopedia Judaica*, vol. 8, pp. 366–72.

14. Cf. M. Breuer, "Pilpul," *Encyclopedia Judaica*, vol. 13, pp. 524–27.

15. For the specification of many of the problematic situations and their solutions, see S. Friedman, "The Extension of the scope of halakha," in A. Fishman, *The Religious Kibbutz Movement*, pp. 37–50; and T. Admanit, "The observance of the agricultural mitzvot today," in A. Fishman, *The Religious Kibbutz Movement*, pp. 119–26.

16. For the concept of a charismatic community, see Max Weber, *Economy and Society*, ed. G. Roth and C. Wittich. New York: Bedminster, 1968, pp. 243, 1119; and G. Roth, "Sociohistorical model and developmental theory." *American Sociological Review* 40 (1975), especially pp. 151–52.

17. See, for example, M. Or, "The first Shabbat in Tirat-Tzvi," in A. Fishman, *The Religious Kibbutz Movement*, pp. 105–8.

18. Y. Goldschmidt and L. Shashua, "Economic success, equality, and central intervention in the kibbutz sector." *Hakibbutz* 3–4 (1976): 218–19 (Hebrew).

19. For this concept referring to the capacity of original religious impulses to undergo transformation and to produce thereby unintended changes in the social life, see S. N. Eisenstadt, "The implications of Weber's sociology of religion for understanding processes of change in contemporary non-European societies and civilizations," in Charles Y. Glock and P. E. Hammond (eds.), *Beyond the Classics? Essays in the Scientific Study of Religion.* New York: Harper and Row, 1973, p. 136.

20. See A. Fishman, *The Religious Kibbutz: a Study in the Interrelationship of Religion and Ideology in the Context of Modernization.* Unpublished Ph.D. dissertation, Jerusalem: Hebrew University, 1975 (Hebrew).

Legality and Ideology in the Kibbutz Movement

Michael Saltman

Introduction

A case study is worth no more than its illustrative contribution in dealing with a wider problem. In looking at changing legal thought in the *kibbutz* movement, the subject matter does not in itself constitute the final object. The wider context, in which the *kibbutz* data are to be analyzed, derives from those variables and conditions governing the concept of legality. The present paper adopts Skolnick's position,

> . . . my statement that sociologists ought to explore the nature of legality means that sociologists ought to study the conditions under which men consider rules to be lawful and how men create, interpret and transform principles and associated rules within institutions (Skolnick, 1966, p. 27).

It is not the intention of this paper to further the polemical issue between Skolnick and Auerbach (1966), nor is the paper primarily concerned with taking sides between conflicting ideologies underlying the concept of "legality", be they natural or positivist. The basic assumption is, however, that any ideology of legality is by definition a social phenomenon, and, therefore, is capable of explanation by reference to other social variables. The main question, to which this paper is addressed, is by what criteria does law draw its premise of legality in the social setting of the *kibbutz?*

The fieldwork on which this article is based is ongoing and was started in March 1979. Most of the fieldwork has been conducted in one *kibbutz*. The reasons for selecting that specific *kibbutz* were more personal than academic. The writer has a number of friends, as well as a number of former students, living in that *kibbutz*, all of whom paved the way to gain access to data which normally the *kibbutz* would be reluctant to publicize. Data were collected by means of observations, open ended interviewing and the examination of archival material; comparative data were also collected at a few additional *kibbutzim*, but these were invariably in connection with a defined issue and did not entail participant observation.

In the somewhat sparse literature on the subject, the main argument to date appears to be between Schwartz (1954, 1976) and Shapiro (1976). Schwartz's argument, succinctly stated, is that in the absence of formal sanctions, the lack of "legal control" has resulted from the effectiveness of non-legal public opinion. Shapiro contends that there has always been a measure of "legal control" exercised through the judicial functions of the *kibbutz* General Assembly; that the principle of individualized generality "is a necessary attribute of a legal system, whose major area of activity is the performance of an allocative function". Both Schwartz and Shapiro allude to the relevance of ideology to the *kibbutz* situation. Neither of them develops this point further in establishing the connection between ideology and legality, which, in the present writer's opinion is the crux of the problem. It is suggested here that the form of "legal control", as a problem, is distinct from and subservient to the question of "legal validity". What Schwartz terms informal sanctions based on public opinion might in actual fact constitute highly formal sanctions in the given ideological context. Furthermore, Schwartz's mechanically functional explanation of "informality" in terms of its efficiency is questionable. According to Schwartz (1976, pp. 439–442), the status of ideology, *vis-à-vis* informality, is reduced to a post-factum rationalization. The present paper assumes quite the contrary, to the effect that what is apparently informal is the systematic product of an ideological position. There are few societies in the history of mankind that can rival the *kibbutz* for its ideological self-awareness. The history of decision-making in the *kibbutz* movement has been inextricably linked to ideological debate. The pragmatic needs of the time have been constantly measured against the yardstick of ideological positions, and the latter have tended to adapt to the requirements of the former without radically changing its basic premises. How relevant ideology remains in the contemporary scene is an important issue for the present paper. But the point being stressed here is that Schwartz is quite wrong in divorcing the issue of "legal control" from ideology.

Within this broad context, the paper specifically addresses itself to two relevant issues. In the first place, it contests Schwartz's conclusion that there is no law in the *kibbutz*, while allowing that by any positivist definition of law Schwartz is probably correct. The present paper, however, will utilize an alternative model of law, by means of which it will be demonstrated that the *kibbutz* rationally and systematically applies principles of law in order both to maintain order and to remedy deviations. Secondly, the paper will demonstrate a trend or shift towards increased formalization of law from an initial consensus, based on normative statements as to how people "ought" to behave, to the formulation of written, law-like propositions, governing behaviour in certain domains.

Ideology and Structure

The prototype of the *kibbutz* was the *kvutza*, founded in Degania in 1910. Its ideological premises are to be found, in part, in the writings of Busel, Baratz and Gordon (1960; 1944 and 1948; 1927 to 1929, respectively). But this ideology is not monolithic. It draws on several sources and provides a synthesis of the anti-clericalism of the Jewish Enlightenment movement and its ensuing Zionist concomitants, the naturalism and altruism of Tolstoy and the social radicalism stemming from the Russian Revolution of 1905. The confirmed Marxists arrived in Palestine after the first world war and founded *kibbutzim* during the 1920s.

The first *kvutza* settlers were not a random group of people who established a community and thereafter rationalized their life-style in ideological terms. From the outset, they had a clear view of the type of organic society they wished to construct. It is also erroneous to assume that the *kibbutz* has evolved from a simple to a complex entity. The *kvutza* was complex and sophisticated in ideological terms from its inception. Its ideological tenets were based on the idea of a small group extending beyond the accepted conceptual boundaries of the family, while maintaining the intimacy of familial relationships. In one of his few references to deviant behaviour within this framework, A. D. Gordon advocates that just as a family does not normally expel its deviant members, neither should the *kvutza* expel its deviants but rather should strive to educate them.

This initial group can be described, in Schmalenbach's (1961) terms, as a Bund. An element of almost mystical communion brought the founders together on the basis of a total commitment to the shared values of the group. While their self-image was that of a single family, they had to contend with the problem of the incompatibility of that premise with the concept of the nuclear family. As long as there was no generation of children, this problem was soluble. But in the presence of a second generation and the influx of new members over the years, compromises had to be reached to enable the institutional coexistence between the familial values of the collectivity on the one hand and the nuclear family on the other. The initial Bund assumed the form that Tönnies has described as *gemeinschaft*.

The characteristic economic structure of the *kibbutz* is linked to an ideological premise that negates the ownership of private property. All property is owned collectively by the *kibbutz* and is redistributed in kind to all its members on an egalitarian basis. The individual member contributes his labour to the communal effort. Economic policy is determined by the General Assembly of the *kibbutz* and is implemented through its elected committees. While economic homogeneity has been maintained consistently over the years and the *kibbutz* has remained a classless society, it should be pointed out that there are differential statuses within the *kibbutz*. The high value placed on the work ethic produces an ideal type of personality, a person who physically contributes above and beyond his normative share. Add to this other favourably regarded characteristics such as asceticism, active involvement in decision making bodies, cultural activities and a tendency to maintain good relationships with all and sundry, this ideal personage will enjoy a degree of relatively high status within the community. This will not necessarily accord him material benefits, but his prestige will stand him in good stead to influence decision making. These people function as individuals and their existence does in no way imply even the incipient formation of a class structure. The small scale demographic nature of the *kibbutz* favours the effective application of direct democracy. All members have equal voting rights in the General Assembly which meets on a weekly basis to discuss and decide on all matters pertinent to the community. The General Assembly is the sovereign body of the *kibbutz*, performing both legislative and judicial functions, in addition to which it elects the *kibbutz* executive functionaries and committees that implement its decisions.

While committees are formally elected and their spheres of activities are defined by nothing more formal than their title, economic committee, work committee, education committee, etc., their powers are not formally defined in any written document. On the other hand, the powers and the procedures of the General Assembly, in most *kibbutzim*, are reflected within a written document. Each *kibbutz* composes its own document and variations between these documents may even be viewed as a sort of "common law" that has arisen over time in a specific place. In comparing two such documents from two *kibbutzim* within the Kibbutz Ha'artzi movement – Sha'ar Ha'amekim and Mishmar Ha'emek, – the opening paragraphs referring to the subject of authority read slightly differently. In the first respective instance it reads "The General Assembly is the highest institution of the *kibbutz*, and its authority is not to be curtailed in any way." The document of the second *kibbutz* reads as follows, "The General Assembly is the highest institution handing down decisions on matters dealing with all spheres of *kibbutz* life". The second paragraph is perhaps more illuminating in expressing not only procedural differences, but would also indicate the relative degree of bureaucratization in the decision-making process of either *kibbutz*. In the Sha'ar Ha'amekim example it states, "The General Assembly can discuss and decide upon any question brought before it by a member or a committee *after it has passed through the stages of an initial inquiry at the level of the appropriate institutions and the secretariat.* No institution can prevent a member from bringing a problem before the "General Assembly" (Author's emphasis). The Mishmar Ha'emek example, in its second paragraph, categorizes the subjects of the general assembly's competence into 13 sub-sections and makes no mention of a precondition of prior stages of inquiry. The other paragraphs in both documents refer mainly to procedural issues, participants, agenda, voting procedures on different types of problems and appeals. A number of sections, particularly in the Sha'ar Ha'amekim document, appear to have been designed to protect the individual member from any over-zealousness on the part of committees.

It is true that neither document spells out specific judicial functions for the General Assembly. Even on the procedural level, there are no rules of evidence, cross-examination, application of precedent and certainly no mention of sanctions. By any formal definition of law, Schwartz is entirely correct in pointing out that there is no "law" in the *kibbutz*. That the General Assembly performs a judicial function without recourse to a formal definition of law is, however, a proposition worth evaluating. An alternative model to a formal legal system was presented by Karl Llwellyn in his work *The Common Law Tradition*, which, in turn, has been excellently analyzed by Twining (1973). Llwellyn addressed himself to two styles of law, the one termed Grand Style and the other, Formal Style. Presented as models, which function as descriptive tools rather than as explanatory devices, it is suggested here that Llwellyn's concept of Grand Style would describe in large measure the operation of the General Assembly in its judicial capacity. One factor, that is important to bear in mind during the following argument, is that the General Assembly is also the supreme legislative body of the *kibbutz* and thus is aware of the legislative intent, when it is called upon to interpret its own rules in a judicial capacity.

It is perhaps tempting to compare this simple structure with that of simple societies described in the ethnographic literature. But in clear distinction to these traditional primitive societies, the *kibbutz* has to be seen as a voluntary, conscious and planned association into a *gemeinschaft*.

The internalized norms of the *kvutza* were initially the product of a constant ideological discussion. The attitude adopted towards law displayed a curious combination of aspects of natural law, on the one hand, with features of the anti-law school of early Soviet jurisprudence on the other. This latter school, under the leadership of Pashukanis, envisaged that the future communist society meant "not the victory of socialist law, but the victory of socialism over any law . . . Public law is a bourgeois ideological weapon having its highest development under capitalism". (Pashukanis, 1951, pp. 127–129.) This statement was echoed in the deliberations of the *kibbutz* founders, when they met at Tel Yosef in 1924 to debate a draft of proposed Articles of Association. Shapiro, who has researched the historical data in this instance, quotes one of the speakers at that meeting.

> We have a certain natural opposition to law. Our taste is to be beyond the framework of laws, and it is pleasant for us; for strong in us is the impression of law in capitalistic society, law that exists in absolute contradiction to the feeling of justice we have inside us. And through opposition to the existing society we have transferred part of our hatred to law as such . . . Many of the values most precious to us we acquired only because we throw off the yoke of the accepted law (Shapiro, 1976).

There is no evidence to suggest any direct linkage between the founders of the *kibbutz* movement and Pashukanis' school of jurisprudence. The people, who established Degania in 1910, were in their late teens at the time of the 1905 revolution and their political philosophy synthesized elements of both social radicalism and anarchism. It was only with the advent of the third wave of immigration, coming into Palestine from Russia after the first world war, that the *kibbutz* was seriously influenced by communist ideology. Certainly the lowest common denominator recognized by both Pashukanis and the *kibbutz* founders was that law as an ideology did not represent the interests of the proletariat. Had there been any expectations, common to Pashukanis and to some of the *kibbutz* founders, that the law would simply "wither away" over time, they were not met either in the *kibbutz,* or in the Soviet Union, even though the directions taken in either instance were different. Early on in the Stalin period of rule, Pashukanis was disposed of both intellectually and physically and law developed in accordance with the ideology of the dictatorship of the proletariat.

Returning to the same speaker at the 1924 Tel Yosef meeting, quoted above by Shapiro, he goes on to state the following in the next sentence,

> . . . and with this we forget that law as such in the role of an instrument for the organization of a society and the existence of its members, is a good and necessary thing without which no society could exist. All depends on the contents of the laws, their intention and the way of realizing them in life.

The ambivalence, implicit in this speaker's ideas, is still tolerable within the *kibbutz* setting. The *kibbutz* remains a small-scale society. Its internal autonomy has not been significantly imposed upon by the State, neither as a social unit in the Ottoman Empire, under the British Mandate, nor in the independent State of Israel.

The Ideology of Resource Allocation

The nature of "law", as such, in the *kibbutz* derives in part from the ideological principles underlying the allocation of resources. In addition to the *kibbutz* having negated the private ownership of property, *kibbutz* justice in its allocative capacity is ideally linked with Marx's statement: "from each according to his ability, to each according to his needs" (Marx, 1875, 1955). In his *Critique of the Gotha Programme*, Marx categorically relates this precept to the precondition of the disappearance of bourgeois law. Any utilitarian principle of allocation, as for example "to each in accordance with his contribution" lends itself well to the formation of formal legal precepts governing the consequences of this type of allocation. Under these conditions there will be differentially treated classes of persons, acts, things and circumstances. Hart (1961, p. 121) has emphasized the generality of the classifications which the law makes, and that these classifications are essentially the basis of any kind of formal legal system. The Marxist precept, as adopted and adapted by the *kibbutz*, conversely, does not lend itself easily to classifications and enactments. An injunction to the effect that all able-bodied persons in the kibbutz will work for 8 to 9 hours/day is untenable since some persons may not be capable of doing so. It is equally meaningless to state that all persons with seniority over 15-years will have television sets in their houses, since it is not beyond the realm of possibility that someone may not want a television set in his or her house.

The interpretation of the precept has been neither identical nor dogmatic in all *kibbutzim*. There are four *kibbutz* movements in Israel [1]. Of the four movements, the Kibbutz Ha'artzi has been prominent in maintaining an orthodox interpretation of Marxism, certainly until the mid 1960s. It viewed itself as the "true" mirror of communism. This point emerged time and time again in those debates that drew on comparisons between the *kibbutz* and the Soviet *kolkhoz*. While the same precept was also fundamental to the other movements, it was certainly not within the same political context. In the other movements the vestiges of anarchy from the original Bund-type *kvutza* provided an alternative source of interpretation that specifically recognized the factor of individuality, implicit in Marx's statement. Furthermore, as shall be demonstrated below, the notion of individualism has a significant influence over the application or non-application of precedent in the resolution of conflicts of interest. What on face value might appear as inconsistency in the application of precedents or the simple blatant disregard of precedent, is in fact quite consistent with the initial ideological premise.

The *kibbutz*, however, is not anarchic and social control is judiciously exercised so as to maintain a state of order. As Kamenka and Tay have put it (1975, p. 136) in a *gemeinschaft* "the emphasis is on law and regulation as expressing the will, the internalized norms and traditions". Honoré (1973, pp. 2–7) has used a more effective term in this instance, "shared understandings", that can subsume under it "will, the internalized norms and traditions". In that same article Honoré makes two points that are relevant and important for the present paper. Firstly:

> The (shared) understanding must relate to prescription. No prescription is necessary to tell people to do as they please. Natural liberty is the state of affairs existing in the absence of prescriptions. The understanding must relate to something which involves the curtailment of liberty.

Honoré's second point is that "the existence of group understanding as to how certain things are to be done is one thing; how they came to exist and how they now continue in existence quite another". It is in the sense of both these points that Marx's principle has been clarified in the *kibbutz* context. One of the principal movements, the Kibbutz Ha'artzi, restated the principle at a meeting in Kibbutz Ein Hashophet in 1958,

> The foundations of co-operative life in the *kibbutz* rest on the principle that each member gives to the society to the best of his ability and the *kibbutz* cares for the needs of each member in accordance with its economic ability and the decisions of the movement. This basic formula of our communal life is indivisible. Only if the member gives to the *kibbutz* to his fullest capacity can the ability of the *kibbutz* to care for the member be guaranteed (Kibbutz Ha'artzi Movement, 1964, Chapter III, p. III).

The essence of Marx's formula is that there is no stated conditional or utilitarian linkage between the two clauses, even though the interpretation of a linkage remains implicit. The restatement by the Kibbutz Ha'artzi makes the linkage more explicit, introducing a utilitarian factor into the sense or spirit of the formula, as well as recognizing the principle of the relative scarcity of resources. Two questions emerge here. Why was it necessary to make these additional qualifications? And what are the consequences of the new formula? Honoré's distinction between different kinds of questions is recognized here and while a hypothetical answer may be given to the first question, the main scope of the present paper relates to an examination of the latter question. One may formulate a hypothesis that the implicit relationship between the two clauses of Marx's original proposition, as expressed in the internalized norms of the *kibbutz*, could not cope with the growing number of hard cases over time, thus necessitating a new shared understanding of the original precept.

This has taken the form of a printed booklet of some 100 pages, divided into sections and sub-sections. Its format and style is roughly equivalent to a Restatement of Customary Law, in so far as it codifies normative statements. This booklet has been produced by the Department of Social Affairs of the Kibbutz Ha'artzi and while many of the paragraphs are based on decisions taken by the movement, the compendium as such has no intrinsic legal status. Its contents are not binding on the individual *kibbutzim* that make up the movement. The authors have taken great pains to point out in their introduction that the booklet is neither "Mosaic law, nor a constitution in any sense of the word". Its stated function is to provide guidelines for the *kibbutz* member in organizing his activities and to help him to make decisions on the various spheres of activities within the *kibbutz* context. Most of the sections in the compendium implicitly qualify the two clauses of Marx's formula. The contribution of the member to the collective is less complex than the sections referring to what the *kibbutz* gives to the member. It describes a normal daily workload, conditions for working overtime, working on Saturdays and holydays, duty rosters, vacations and reduced workload norms for older members and women after childbirth. These are descriptive passages, the phraseology of which is far removed from legal phraseology. There is no mention of sanctions in the event that these norms are in any way contravened. The sections referring to the allocation of resources are also descriptive in their formulation. Basic commodities, such as food and clothing, are distributed on a wholly egalitarian basis, while also taking into account individual preferences. For example, the issue of clothing is dealt with as set out below.

(1) All clothing requirements of the member will be met in the framework of the budget and with maximal regard to the desire and taste of the member. Within different kinds and categories of clothes, determined by the departments of the Kibbutz Ha'artzi, the member can express his preference for a given item as opposed to another on the basis of norms

determined by the movement.

(2) The council expresses its opposition to a personal clothing allowance, either in money or in credit points. In order to supply special needs of members, the budget of the clothing store and the clothing committee may be reinforced.

(3) The *kibbutz* may elect a clothing committee, the function of which is to clarify and decide upon special problems, demands or enquiries as well as ensuring the maintenance of the professional abilities of the (clothing store) staff.

Other commodities, under conditions where either the demand exceeds the supply, or where there is a significant quality differential in the nature of the commodity, i.e. quality of housing, furniture, vacations abroad, are distributed unequally on a short-term basis, but ultimately equally on a long-term basis. The distribution of these items is governed by a waiting list based on relative seniority of membership. This principle will be elaborated below in the section referring to precedent.

These above mentioned domains of allocation are not problematic. They are common knowledge to all *kibbutz* members; the consensus around them is solid and since there are rarely "hard cases" on these issues, their presentation in the compendium is matter-of-fact and descriptive. In turning, however, to those areas that in the past have produced "cases", the formulation of the relevant passages is transformed from descriptive norms into what Hart has termed, "primary rules of obligation" (1961, pp. 79–88). These take the form of either prescriptions or prohibitions. A clear example of this may be seen in the section referring to property from outside sources.

(1) All property received by a member from outside sources, such as inheritances, payments for artistic and literary creations, reparations etc., is the sole property of the *kibbutz*.

(2) The member is not allowed to ensure for himself an income by means of additional work in any sphere.

(3) The member is not allowed to waive his rights over family property (e.g. inheritance) to the benefit of relatives outside the *kibbutz*. This property belongs to the *kibbutz*, and the member is obliged to claim it and transfer it to the *kibbutz*.

What is being suggested here is that as long as the norms derive their legitimacy from the ideological consensus based on internalized values, there is no need for rule-making. As soon as there are a significant number of deviations from this consensus, there is a corresponding movement to compensate for these deviations by formulating unambiguous rules of obligation. It must be stressed, however, that these rules do not constitute laws in a positivist sense, since they lack the ingredient of any statement as to what is to be done in the event that the rule is contravened. What appears to be taking place in the *kibbutz* is the institutionalization of norms into customs within a general trend towards the formulation of laws. What seems to be applicable in this instance as in other cases of such "double institutionalization" (Bohannan, 1965, pp. 33–42) is the factor of greater precision in statement. The second stage of reinstitutionalization, according to Bohannan, is a function of the presence or absence of legal institutions in the society. This second aspect of legitimacy becomes the second focal point of this paper.

Tensions, Deviations and Remedy Agents

The normal gamut of interpersonal tensions, such as arguments between neighbours, petty jealousies, the consequences of the violation of sexual norms, etc., is to be found in the *kibbutz*. Given the basic premise of equality, tensions and deviations will also arise as a consequence of any act that negates this premise. It is public knowledge in a small-scale society when a person consistently shirks his responsibilities and duties or receives greater benefits and privileges than others. If, as described above, the legitimacy of actions derives from a shared ideological understanding, then it follows from this that under conditions of the weakening of the shared understandings, remedy agents of a formal nature may emerge. In the *kibbutz* context there is a justifiable degree of idealism in such a hypothesis, justifiable in so far as the *kibbutz's* ideological self-awareness of its *raison d'etre* has been a potent force in its development. Furthermore, it is difficult to point out any significant internal structural changes within the *kibbutz* that might have precipitated this process of formalization. Thus, *the process is affected not so much by structural change as by the changing circumstances in which the kibbutz finds itself vis-à-vis the outside world.* The *kibbutz* has to deal with the capitalist society within which it is located. There is more money circulating in the *kibbutz* than at any previous time; the managers of *kibbutz* industries have to have expense accounts in their business dealings, whether in Tel-Aviv or in Tokyo, and the number of kibbutz "professionals", employed outside the *kibbutz,* is constantly growing. It must be emphasized, however, that the formalization of the rules has emerged in order to protect the ideology rather than to foster the interests of specific groups.

The judicial function of the General Assembly has been cited as an example of a formal remedy agent. There are, however, alternative remedy agents which also serve to maintain the efficacy of prescriptions. If the rules of obligation, either in explicit statement or in the form of a shared understanding, are based on consensus, it is proposed here that some of the mechanisms for rectifying deviance from these rules are also based on shared understandings.

Within the *kibbutz* there are gradations of public opinion and its expression can take a variety of forms. Its exercise is not an arbitrary process and public opinion is to be observed in one form or another in the light of the severity of the incident, the relative degree of sensitivity of the member, and his relative standing in the community. There is in fact an element of regularity in the mustering of public opinion, which can be seen in terms of escalation of pressure on the deviant member. Again, the small-scale nature of the society heightens the effectiveness of labeling. The ultimate sanction is to transform the member into a complete outsider by expelling him from the community.

At the lowest levels of mustering public opinion against a deviant, close relatives or friends may point out to him in private conversations the wrongness of his attitude. This happened to A, who was renowned for the abrasiveness in his social interactions with others. Alternatively, we find another mode at this level, the judicious use of the joking relationship. An old man, B, who in accordance with the norms worked a relatively reduced work-load, refused to work even at this minimal level. He was constantly subjected to the gentle ribbing of a joking relationship by his work group, peer group, and others. In the anthropological literature, the joking relationship is often cited as a mechanism for containing hostility. Its application in this instance was effective, in so far as the incident (the refusal of an old man to work) was not particularly grave; the man in question was sensitive to the reaction and his veteran standing in the community could not tolerate the application of a severer sanction. Moving up the continuum there can be varying degrees of social ostracism, ranging from partial to total. An ex-*kibbutz* member, whose studies at the University up to the level of doctorate were financed by the *kibbutz*, demonstrated a growing inclination to embark on an academic career. This was totally unacceptable to that particular *kibbutz*. According to his description, he was subjected to the whole gamut of shades of ostracism. This involved, in the first instance, the proferring of advice by mediators; the ever-increasing reserve on the part of his peers in their interaction with him; cessation of mutual visiting; people shying away from vacant seats at his table in the communal dining-hall; and, at a later stage, people doing their utmost to avoid conversing with him. At the point where it became clear that he was not prepared to sacrifice his academic career, he became fully ostracized, and, consequently left the *kibbutz*.

There is a point, beyond the non-formal sanction application, where public opinion merges with the decision-making of the constituted bodies of the *kibbultz*, be they the *kibbutz* secretariat, various committees or, in the final instance, the General Assembly of the *kibbutz* sitting in its judicial capacity. There are various techniques that have the clear effect of a sanction. If the case is sufficiently serious or the person in question is clearly recalcitrant, the *kibbutz* may publish in its internal newspaper that that person was called in for a "clarificatory discussion" with the *kibbutz* secretariat. This is generally understood as a serious move. Other techniques, bearing implicit sanction, refer to the selective placement of members in different work situations, whereby some jobs are seen as being preferable to others on an internal prestige ranking scale. In the case of A, mentioned above, he found himself working as a gardener, which is both solitary and low prestige work. At a later stage A was further relegated as an assistant to the woman who was in charge of the foreign volunteers in the *kibbutz*, a position that removed him even further from social contact with his fellow members. This arrangement allowed for a reasonable *modus vivendi*.

Case Material

Cases will be used here primarily for the purposes of the apt illustration of contentions in this paper. No attempt will be made in this paper to render a statistical analysis of cases.

The case of the unwanted member

X, who had been invalided out of the 1948 War of Independence, was not a popular member of the *kibbutz*. It was felt over the years that despite his disability, he was not pulling his weight sufficiently in the *kibbutz*, in addition to which he was generally disagreeable in his social relationships with other people. His social standing in the *kibbutz* could be described as "low". When, a number of years ago, he left the *kibbutz* voluntarily, nobody was particularly upset. After 10 years of being outside the *kibbutz*, at which point his wife died, he reapplied for membership. The *kibbutz*, taking into account his heroism from the War of Independence, the fact that his wife had died, and his sincere professions of commitment to the *kibbutz* way of life, having been "outside" for 10 years, reaccepted him. During the ensuing years, he did not succeed in improving his status. It was then discovered that X had been receiving a disability allowance from the Ministry of Defence over the years, which he had been using to pay off his debts from his 10 year period outside the *kibbutz* and also to help purchase an apartment for his daughter, who lived outside the *kibbutz*. It was also generally assumed that he had been collecting this disability allowance even prior to his having left the *kibbutz*. The matter was brought before the *kibbutz* secretariat, which saw no alternative but to bring it before the General Assembly. X defended himself before the General Assembly, by claiming that his late wife had incited him not to declare these earnings and by also professing regret over his action. This was in no way convincing. Several members demanded his expulsion. Nobody asked him to remain. Some people, however, were bothered by the fact that his second wife was now dying of cancer and that formal expulsion at this stage would be unnecessarily cruel. The situation became clear to X that he was *persona non grata* in the *kibbutz* and drawing the correct conclusion, he left voluntarily, which was exactly the effect that the *kibbutz* had wished to achieve.

The case of the wanted member

Y was a veteran member of the same *kibbutz*. He was well respected and had "good" social standing. Over the years Y had received substantial reparations from Germany which he had transferred to the account of the *kibbutz*. His daughter married a young man from abroad, who was a successful graduate student. On completion of his doctorate, he was offered a job in the United States. One of the factors influencing the young couple to accept the American offer was their financial inability to purchase an apartment in Israel. The young man's father abroad had other financial commitments which rendered him unable to assist the young couple. Y decided to dock a substantial portion of the reparations' money remitted to the *kibbutz* in favour of his daughter to enable her to purchase an apartment and thus not leave Israel. During the following months the *kibbutz* received the reduced remittance. This was quite intolerable for the *kibbutz*. Y was called before the *kibbutz* secretariat, which censored him for this action. Y remained firm in his intention towards continuing to help his daughter remain in Israel. The secretariat suggested that the *kibbutz* would take on the responsibility of helping the daughter, but this of course would be at a much lower rate of financial assistance. Y refused on the grounds that this was his individual problem and not the problem of the *kibbutz* (note this ideological confrontation). It became obvious that the *impasse* could only be broken at the level of the General Assembly. While the possibility of expulsion was an option, nobody wanted to expel Y by virtue of his veterancy and "good" social standing, as well as taking into account as a peripheral factor the contribution to the *kibbutz* over many years of the very substantial reparations from Germany. At the same time the grounds for expulsion were quite explicit. The General Assembly decided to call in an arbitrator from the Movement. It is of course understood that the arbitrator's decision is binding. The arbitrator found against Y who was obliged to cease docking money from the reparations, but was not obliged to reimburse the considerable sums remitted to his daughter over the year. There was no need even to consider the possibility of expelling Y. Y is still a respected member of the community, even sitting on important committees. However, a number of members of his peer group now interact with him with a considerable amount of reserve even to the extent of a degree of hostility.

These two cases in juxtaposition raise a number of interesting problems. Although the latter case preceded the former chronologically, it makes no difference, since no connection was established between them at any level of remedy agent. The fact that no cognitive connection exists here plus the fact that the outcomes were different despite the existence of an unambiguous rule of prohibition would, on face value, militate strongly against the existence of any kind of consistent legal thinking in the *kibbutz*. But legal thought, of a kind, is very much present, not in terms of abstract formal criteria of justice, but as a substantive effort to resolve a particular case in a given social context. When, in the *kibbutz*, the individual comes into a confrontation either with the community or with another individual, it is not in the capacity of an abstract configuration of rights and duties, but, in the words of Kamenka and Tay

(1975), as a "whole man, bringing with him his status, his occupation and his environment, all of his history and social relationships".

Following from this, the framework of reference, that might best serve to reconcile the apparent inconsistencies, is that of the legal realism discussed by Llwellyn and others. The most important attributes of Llwellyn's Grand Style, that might prove relevant in so far as the functioning of the *kibbutz* General Assembly is concerned, are as follows.

(1) There is no mandatory outcome to remedy a given situation. The outcome is based on pragmatic considerations, either for a variety of reasons, or in order to achieve different kinds of effects.

(2) Rules in the *kibbutz* do not constitute the basic premise of a syllogism but are general propositions embodying a policy, the function of which is to guide rather than to control interpretation.

(3) The General Assembly functions as a remedy agent, approximately in Llwellyn's terms, so as to "resolve the doubt according to wisdom, justice and situation sense within the leeways accorded by the authoritative sources" and "to provide guidance for the future".

The *kibbutz* members themselves are under no illusion that their system has achieved a higher level of justice. Quite the contrary, injustices are often perpetrated under these conditions and the members are quite aware of this fact. A case in point has been given by Evens (1975, pp. 166–209).

In analyzing the content of these two cases, it is clear that in both instances a formal model of a legal rule has not been applied. While in both cases the deviation was clear from a formal point of view, both men were handling private sources of income for private purposes, no predetermined sanction was applied. The reasoning is that the principle underlying the *kibbutz* prohibition against handling private money for private purposes is still "a general proposition embodying a policy; its function is to guide but not control interpretation". It is such, since there is no stated "interlocking principle", in Honoré's terms, which directs what is to be done when the primary rule of obligation is broken. The second factor is the question as to what is the nature of the problem involving a question of law. When Llwellyn points out that the scope of the deviation is doubtful, this is precisely applicable to this case material. The question before the General Assembly may have been precipitated by the "illegal" handling of money in both instances, but the matter being dealt with was the totality of the behaviour of X and Y, that which is designated by Kamenka and Tay as the "whole man". That remedies, bearing different values, were applied in both cases by the General Assembly in its judicial capacity, is indicative of that body's measure of social control, acting in Llwellyn's terms "to produce effects z, or for reasons z, or to remedy mischief z".

Perhaps the most important point, in clarifying the judicial role of the

General Assembly, is in determining whether it resolves "the doubt according to wisdom, justice and situation sense . . ." or is merely employing "fireside equities". A fireside equity is a factor, irrelevant to the case, that serves to evoke the sympathy of the judges, as for example in the case of X, being invalided out of the 1948 war, or the fact that X's second wife was dying. While these factors were taken into account as mitigating circumstances, they were in no way crucial to the outcome. Twining (1973) has demonstrated that what Llwellyn meant by "situation sense" is essentially a true understanding of the facts and a right evaluation of them. In any other context this could be abruptly dismissed as metaphysics. Within the *kibbutz* context it appears to be a relevant framework of reference, in which it is possible to resolve all kinds of glaring inconsistencies. The reasons have already been stated above, but are reiterated here for emphasis. The rules of communal existence are shared understandings deriving from a common ideological position. These constitute the yardstick, against which the "whole man" is constantly being measured and evaluated. Where rules have had to be restated and the General Assembly has to judge by them, there is no need to search for the legislative intent, since the General Assembly was also the legislative body. If the intentions are universally known, then a high degree of consistency can be maintained. Conversely, consistency is not maintained by case-to-case precedent.

The use of precedent is a complex issue on the *kibbutz*. Theoretically, in a society based on an ideology of equality, there should be no need for the application of precedent, since all resources and benefits are allocated on an equal basis, this essentially being the only tenable precedent. In practice, however, the *kibbutz* is forced into the application of various types of precedents, since by necessity there has to be an unequal distribution of some resources and benefits. Furthermore, the *kibbutz* has taken into account the recognition of the individuality of its members. Shapiro (1976) has stated that "individualized generality is a necessary attribute of a legal system whose major area of activity is the performance of an allocative function". An example of a relatively undisputed norm, serving as a precedent, is seniority as a criterion for the allocation of housing. Recently built buildings are of better quality and design than older buildings, and in certain instances, more spacious. Since in most *kibbutzim* children do not live at home, the principle of allocating access to better housing is seniority. Seniority also used to be a normative precedent for the allocation of work roles, the "subjectively" better or more prestigious jobs within the *kibbutz* being allocated to long-standing members. But this precedent has been modified over the years by other principles, including economic rationale, ability, and recently, job satisfaction (this latter factor sometimes taking precedence over economic rationale). Thus, generalized principles of seniority, based on a very wide consensus, constitute sets of precedents.

On other issues, as for example vacations abroad, *kibbutzim* apply a rigid set of rules, based on a strict rotational principle of equal allocation. This is, of course, the ideal. But all kinds of specific problems emerge here. A member who has parents abroad can make a better claim for more frequent visits abroad. This is precisely the point made by Hart, that law deals with *classes* of persons, and the *kibbutz* of the field study has responded to this by declaring that people having parents aboard are entitled to visit them there every 5 years, providing the parents have not visited Israel during that period. Similar sets of well-defined rules also apply to the private use of *kibbutz* motor-vehicles, including the liability of the driver involved in a traffic offense. On such mundane issues as the latter example, one finds the highest degree of formalization both in the promulgation and the application of these rules. Traffic offenses of the private driver, and sometimes the driver who is on *kibbutz* business, may involve coercive sanctions, in so far as at least part of the fine is docked from the member's annual allowance for private expenditure.

These are not the most problematic domains. There are some spheres wherein precedent is rejected *a priori*, since it makes for "bad" precedent or creates a conflict of interest, either on an interpersonal level or between the individual and the *kibbutz*. One such problem is that of *kibbutz* members working outside the *kibbutz*. The movement, to which each *kibbutz* is federated, engages in political, economic, educational and social activity on a national level, both at home and abroad. All these activities draw on personnel from the individual *kibbutzim*, and ceilings have been established above which the *kibbutz* need not contribute, but up to which they are expected to contribute. In addition to these functionaries, the *kibbutz* has always contributed part of its membership to public service in the national interest, regular army officers, politicians, university teachers, and others. In these latter instances, earned salaries are remitted to the *kibbutz*. In recent years, the growth of *kibbutz* industries has created regional industrial and agricultural complexes that draw on the *kibbutz* for managerial personnel. Add to all this the permanent list of *kibbutz* members waiting their turn for leave of absence to study at the universities, there is a potentially serious drain on *kibbutz* manpower resources. This is what is implied by conflict of interests, which in most cases is a conflict between the member and the *kibbutz*, but sometimes also produces an interpersonal conflict of interests in so far as certain prestigious jobs outside the *kibbutz* can create an emotional climate of rivalry and jealousy. The application of rules does not operate well in this sphere. The overall tendency seems to be that each case has to be treated on its own merits, involving a subtle interaction of criteria based on the nature of the job in question in all its aspects, the job held by the member in the *kibbutz*, the personal standing and personality of the individual involved. The *a priori* rejection of precedent is illustrated in the following case.

The case of the responsible member's burden
W was offered a job as a representative of his *kibbutz* movement in the United States. This is considered a very prestigious job and even an honour to the *kibbutz* to which the member belongs. In the past, any member being offered

such a job automatically received the requisite permission. W's present job was that of headmaster of the *kibbutz* secondary school and he fulfilled this function excellently, to the degree that nobody else was considered his equal in that respect. Prior to this, he had served in the important role of *kibbutz* secretary, and currently his wife was now serving as *kibbutz* secretary. He and his wife had very "high" social standing in the *kibbutz*. On the personal level, he was most interested in accepting the job, but despite this the *kibbutz* denied permission, thus breaking the established tradition of granting permission for such a prestigious offer. The following argument was made. Since he was needed in his present position and since he was regarded as one of the most responsible persons in the *kibbutz*, it was expected of him to decline the offer. Other members of the *kibbutz*, commenting on this case, stated quite categorically that had it been another member involved, whose personal status in the *kibbutz* and whose professional abilities were not of the same high calibre as W's, they would have approved the application. The person who was the prime mover in bringing about this decision was one of W's closest working colleagues and friends. W accepted the decision and remains on good terms with his colleague. In ruling out the possibility of any political manoeuvering against W by a person or persons in the *kibbutz* for their own reasons, W found himself in exactly the same situation the following year. W was offered the job of director-general of the teachers' training college, which belongs to the three major *kibbutz* movements. The same argument was applied again for the same reasons. The outcome, however, was slightly different this time. The movement appealed the *kibbutz's* decision at the level of the movement's court and a decision was handed down against the *kibbutz*, which in turn decided not to honour the court's decision, even at the risk of possible sanctions. Finally, a compromise was achieved through the intervention of high-ranking mediators, when it was decided that W would assume the directorship the following year and during the intervening time the *kibbutz* would have to make every effort to find a replacement for W in his capacity of headmaster.

It is not easy to understand, from the point of view of one accustomed to an Anglo-American or European system of law, why *kibbutz* members accept what we would term inequities resulting from the lack of consistent application of precedent. While some people privately express their disgruntled feelings, when they themselves feel injured, they nonetheless accept the rules of the game when they are applied to others. This does not imply inconsistency, since their views are expressed privately, if at all. Were a person to object publicly, he or she would be liable to bring upon himself or herself a considerable degree of stigma for having shaken the foundations of the ideological commitment. There is of course another alternative open to the member, which is that of leaving the *kibbutz*, the initial stage of which is the declaration of this intention. But even if this was being used for manipulative purposes only, he or she would still have to take into account his or her own social standing within the *kibbutz*, the nature of his or her denied request as parts of all those factors subsumed under the heading of situation sense. The fact that somebody else had received the same privilege which he or she had been denied, would provide neither a necessary nor a sufficient argument.

Factors Promoting Formalization

The work of E. B. Pashukanis has been cited above in a specific reference to the concept of the "withering away of law", and the fact that this process has not been realized in the *kibbutz*. This paper argues that there is a form of law in the *kibbutz*, which Pashukanis and Schwartz would presumably relegate under the rubric of a "type of social control". The early history of the *kibbutz*, however, depicts the existence of a group of people which lived according to a rigid code of behaviour that transcended the contemporary concepts of modes of production and private ownership of property. The *kibbutz* member, as a legal persona, has never been a mere legal reflection of the "economic man". Furthermore, major conflicts of interest have not emerged in the *kibbutz* as a consequence of the internal allocation of resources. Thus, it is reiterated that there is a degree of justification to the idealist contention, made above, that as the commitment to the shared understandings waned, the recourse to law-like formulations became inevitable. In the *kibbutz* instance, conflicting interests have emerged in the context of the *kibbutz's* relationships with the outside world, and it is argued here that these have brought about changes in the hither-to *gemeinschaft* legal structure.

All cases cited to this point involve factors that in one way or another originated from outside the immediate *kibbutz* setting such as jobs outside the *kibbutz* or money from external sources. The relationship between the *kibbutz* and its external environment is both complex and problematic. Far from being a hermetically sealed off community, not only does the *kibbutz* have ramified economic and political relationships with the outside world, but also social values, originating from the outside, seep into the *kibbutz*. One of the channels is the contact that the younger *kibbutz* members have with the outside world, primarily in the frameworks of either the army or the universities. Some of the newly-acquired values are highly negative, in so far as the *kibbutz* is concerned. Another source of "alien values" originates from volunteers. Each year, thousands of volunteers from European countries come to live on *kibbutzim* for short periods of time, working on labour intensive projects in exchange for board and lodging. While the *kibbutz* attempts to minimize the degree of contact between the volunteers and their equivalent age group from within the *kibbutz*, certain problems arise out of the inevitable contact that takes place. One such example is the "drug culture" as imported by the European volunteers. Other sources of this problem may be the high-school, army or university. Whatever the source of the problem, it has become sufficiently serious for certain *kibbutzim* to react. Since informal sanctions are hardly likely to prove effective in the case of a drug addict, several *kibbutzim* have responded by drawing up sets of formal by-laws to deal with the issue. Such a set of rules has recently been adopted by *kibbutz* M, in which at least 30 of its members and high-school pupils admitted to having taken drugs of one kind or another at least on one occasion.

The two paragraphs of the preamble reject the use of drugs as being antithetical to the *kibbutz* way of life. Paragraphs three to seven refer to a five-man committee elected by the General Assembly, which also includes the *kibbutz* secretary *ex officio*. In describing its functions, the committee is both investigative and judicial, having wide powers in the promotion of its functions. The following three paragraphs contain the main body of "law".

(8) A member, who is found involved in the use of drugs will be summoned before the committee and his membership will be suspended. The member will be required to co-operate and receive treatment at the discretion of the committee in consultation with professional advisers. After the lapse of one year from the time of this decision, it will be decided whether he will be readmitted to membership.

(9) A member found involved in the growing, manufacturing or supply of drugs or found encouraging the involvement of *kibbutz* youth in drug usage will be expelled from the *kibbutz*.

(10) A member who, despite measures taken against him, continues to take drugs, or returns to taking drugs, will be expelled from the *kibbutz*.

One of the options open to the committee is to report the matter to the police, or to the military police if the offender is in the army. The *kibbutz* has traditionally attempted to shield its members from police intervention when misdemeanours and, occasionally, crimes have been committed by members. This can, therefore, be regarded as a particularly severe sanction. On the other hand, a more moderate sanction is proposed for soldiers involved in the use of drugs, they will not be permitted to use *kibbutz* vehicles, nor will they be allowed to represent the *kibbutz* in sports or cultural activities.

The formal style of this document raises the question why Kibbutz M chose to deal with the problem in this particular way. In the General Assembly's debate on the issue, the rules together with their interlocking sanctions were adopted reluctantly. There was little element of doubt during the debate that their adoption was for the specific purpose of creating a deterrent factor, and it was also made quite clear that case to case precedent would have to be applied, if the document were to have any credibility whatsoever for the *kibbutz* membership.

Another external factor, that has to be taken into account, concerns decisions handed down by Israeli courts of law in respect of *kibbutz* members. To what extent are the *kibbutzim* going to have to take these decisions into account when they make their own rulings? Will court rulings become precedents within the *kibbutz* context? Prior to the establishment of the state and even in the two decades thereafter, when a member left his or her *kibbutz* either voluntarily or otherwise, she or he left with nothing much more than the clothes on his or her back. The nature of the outside society was such that he or she could find work and housing and could commence a new way of life. At that time there were still egalitarian elements in Israeli society at large, which did not impose insurmountable difficulties on the ex-*kibbutz* member seeking to adapt to outside conditions. It certainly did not enter the minds of those people to claim any kind of financial assistance from the *kibbutz* in order to embark on a new way of life. Today, the situation is radically different. The *kibbutz* member is leaving a relatively wealthy society to join a bourgeois society on the outside. These conditions establish a need, and the *kibbutz* does in fact make financial arrangements for members who leave, in order that they can make a start in a new life outside. This is not necessarily out of altruism, but rather out of consideration of a court decision that obliges the *kibbutz* to pay severance or dismissal payments in accordance with the state's labour laws. One of the effects of this external factor is that on its basis the member can certainly regard himself in a right-obligation relationship with the *kibbutz* above and beyond the basic allocative principle, which in turn is definitely alien to the kind of legal thought that has been described above.

Other court decisions, primarily in the form of injunctions, have challenged the legality of *kibbutz* decisions. A case in point from 1975 concerned a woman who requested an injunction from the court to prevent the *kibbutz* from expelling her.

The case of the reluctant spouse
The event took place in Kibbutz D. The woman, a mother of five children, was separated from her husband, who in turn had left the *kibbutz*. She refused to sign a power of attorney that would enable the *kibbutz* to claim maintenance payments from the husband, who had left the *kibbutz*. The *kibbutz* felt strongly that the husband should in fact contribute towards maintenance of his five children, sufficiently strongly to reach a decision to expel the woman in the light of her refusal. The woman took the correct legal avenue in seeking an injunction, since the court has considerable leeway in its discretion for issuing an injunction. The court ruled in its decision that "there is no social, factual or legal foundation for the secretariat's recommendation and, therefore, the General Assembly cannot decide on the recommendation to remove the woman and her children from the *kibbutz*". The point of law was not debated, since the *kibbutz* did not respond to the injunction, thus making the injunction a permanent one.

The law reporter in this instance, Mr Y. Ronen from Kibbutz Ein Harod, discusses the implications of this case. Kibbutz D based its decision on article 78 of the Movement's by-laws, which states,

> If the membership of a member is terminated for any reason and the spouse
> or ex-spouse elects to remain and keep the children in the *kibbutz* in his/her
> own right, this does not rule out the right of the *kibbutz* to sue the spouse,

whose membership has been terminated, for maintenance payments and to demand from the spouse or ex-spouse remaining in the *kibbutz* to claim, either by means of negotiation or by recourse to court, for the maintenance costs of the children by that same spouse or ex-spouse, who has left, and to transfer these monies to the account of the *kibbutz*.

The court recognized that an obligatory norm is expressed within this inelegant statement, but considered that its legal validity is dubious, given that association with a *kibbutz* is on a voluntary basis, rather than a contractual one. One conclusion arrived at by Mr Ronen, was that *kibbutz* members would in fact have to enter into a contractual relationship with the *kibbutz*, in order to prevent situations of this sort. Such a solution is obviously in absolute contradiction to the ideological basis of the *kibbutz* as such, and, therefore, impractical. But the mantle of the prophet has certainly settled on the shoulders of Mr Ronen, who states in conclusion that the *kibbutz* cannot afford to "reconcile itself with court verdicts that provide a loophole for a member not to fulfil the decisions of the General Assembly or the by-laws of the *kibbutz*, while at the same time remaining a member in contradiction to these by-laws, norms in which we believe. We should organize ourselves at this time, before decrees, which we shall not be able to oppose, fall upon us". Mr Ronen's gloom, while somewhat exaggerated, should be of some concern to the *kibbutz* movement. An ever increasing number of court decisions questioning the legality of *kibbutz* decisions must surely have a long-term effect on the decision-making process and legal thought of the *kibbutz*. Precedents, created by Israeli courts, cannot be simply ignored by the *kibbutz*, not only because of their legal implications, but also because of their social consequences, implicit in Mr Ronen's solution.

Conclusions

This paper has addressed itself to three interrelated issues. Firstly it has argued against Schwartz, by attempting to show that a system of law does in fact exist in the *kibbutz*. Secondly it has demonstrated that the tenets of the initial system have become formalized over time and thirdly it has tried to analyze some of the conditions, under which this process of formalization has taken place.

One of Schwartz's main arguments for the presence or absence of law in the *kibbutz* hinges on the corresponding presence or absence of a court. But the judicial functions of the General Assembly do not constitute the crucial issue in determining whether the *kibbutz* has a legal system or not. The works of Becker (1970, pp. 104–105) and Barkun (1968, pp. 146–148) indicate that a court is not a basic prerequisite for legality. Becker, in particular, has rightly pointed out the contradiction in Schwartz's initial study on the *kibbutz* and Schwartz and Miller's later study (1964), in which a correlation is established between societal complexity and the evolution of legal institutions. Most writers on the subject of the *kibbutz* have recognized its societal complexity. If complexity is a basic precondition for the emergence of a court, then, as asked by Becker, "why is there no court in the *kibbutz?*" Schwartz had answered this by citing the efficacy of what he terms "informal sanctions". The present paper contends that the so-called "informal sanctions" are not so informal and are calibrated to a degree of precision as a function of the gravity of the situation and the person's overall standing within the community. The main point of disagreement with Schwartz, however, is on his claim that ideology became a post-factum rationalization for the efficacy of the "informal sanctions". Schwart's conditions for falsifying this proposition are that it must be demonstrated that an anti-law ideology (and here Schwartz's meaning is anti-formal law) was in existence prior to 1910, when the first *kvutza* was founded. This is an impossible condition, since in the absence of a group, there is a corresponding absence of attitudes to the issue in question. Schwartz's proposition can only be rejected on the grounds of an alternative proposition, which might prove to be more plausible.

Legitimacy for *kibbutz* "law" derives from the shared understanding of a common ideological premise. If the kibbutz has *a priori* rejected private ownership of property, then its main institutional function is to ensure an egalitarian redistribution of its common resources. The allocative principle is based on the non-utilitarian proposition of "from each according to his ability, to each in accordance to his needs". Paradoxically this is egalitarian, even though it could, at any given point of time, lead to an unequal distribution, since in the long run every individual potentially benefits from the equal distribution. In order that this system can operate, there has to be a high degree of commitment to the ideological premise, whereby individuals voluntarily curtail their own personal liberties, rather than having their liberties curtailed through coercion. It makes no difference whether these attitudes were in existence prior to 1910 or not. This was the shared understanding of the people who established Degania in 1910, and remains in one form or another until the present day. Legality in the *kibbutz* is, therefore, inextricably linked to ideology.

Seen in its ideal context, it is not specific laws that are being violated by individual *kibbutz* members, but rather those members are deviating from their voluntary commitment. Under such circumstances the "whole man" becomes the object of scrutiny, rather than the single act being placed against the yardstick of legality. What emerges is a system based on legal realism that Llwellyn and others could not effectively apply in formally constituted law courts. Once again, on the ideal level, we are talking of a system of law, characterized by Weber as being "substantively rational", since its "law makers or finders consciously follow clearly conceived and articulated generalizations" (Rheinstein, 1954).

The formalization of rules has taken place by means of restating selected norms and principles that make up the ideological complex of shared understandings. But it is not possible to demonstrate that structural changes have taken place in the *kibbutz*, which, in turn, could show that there is a distinct trend towards the breaking down of traditional *kibbutz* homogeneity.

This has simply not been the case. The principle of private property continues to be rejected, and the allocation of resources, although somewhat modified, is still guided by the principle of "to each according to his needs". If formalization has served any purpose at all, it has been in the direction of protecting the ideological commitment, as opposed to fostering or reinforcing any vested interest groups within the community. The need for formalization has emerged primarily as a consequence of the ramification of the *kibbutz's* relationships with the outside capitalist world, both in the State of Israel and abroad, and the potentially dangerous effects of that contact for the survival of the *kibbutz* ideal.

In real terms, as distinct from the ideal type, the voluntary curtailment of personal liberty involves, by definition, the recognition of rules. This paper has attempted, in Skolnick's terms, "to explore the nature of legality . . . by studying the conditions under which men consider certain rules to be lawful". If in the first part of the paper it has been demonstrated that the specific form of legality derives from ideological considerations, the second part of the paper has addressed itself to the problem how this concept of legality has had to adapt to changing social circumstances. Restatements, formalization, bureaucratization and the potential influence of external law courts are not only symptomatic of a waning ideological commitment, but serve to teach us, again in Skolnick's terms, "how men create, interpret and transform principles and associated rules within institutions." In the final instance it also enables us to make seriously considered value judgements about the conditions, under which we live.

Acknowledgements

A preliminary draft of this paper received sound criticism from the following people, to whom I acknowledge my appreciation: Maureen Cain, Nira Reiss, Henry Rosenfeld, Menachem Rosner and Yoseph Shepher. I also wish to thank Assaf Nahir, who helped me collect the data and Allan Shapiro, whose comments and advice over the years have been particularly helpful.

Notes

1 The four movements are: Ichud Hakibbutzim allied with the Mapai party; Hakibbutz Hameuchad allied with the Achdut Ha'avoda party; Hakibbutz Ha'artzi allied with the Mapam party and the Kibbutz Hadati, which comprises all the religious *kibbutzim*. The differences between the movements are in the shades of ideological expression of the basic idea as well as in their different political affiliations. Most of the data for this paper have been collected from *kibbutzim* in the Kibbutz Har'artzi movement.

References

Auerbach, L. (1966) Legal tasks for the sociologist. *Law & Society Review* **1**.
Baratz, J. (1944) In *Sepher Yoseph Baratz*. (Shapiro, J., Ed.). Ha'va'ad hatziburi l'hotzaat hasepher Yoseph Baratz: Tel-Aviv. (*The Book of Joseph Baratz* The Public Committee for publishing the Work of Joseph Baratz).

Baratz, J. (1948) *Degania 'A'* (in Hebrew). Association of kvutzot: Jerusalem.

Barkun, M. (1968) *Law Without Sanctions.* Yale University Press: New Haven.

Becker, T. L. (1970) *Comparative Judicial Politics.* Rand McNally & Company: Chicago.

Bohannan, P. (1965) The differing realms of law. *American Anthropologist* **67,** 2.

Busel, S. (1960) In *Sepher Busel.* (Wurm, S., Ed.) Tarbut v'hinuch: Tel-Aviv. (*The Book of Busel.* Culture and Education).

Evens, T. M. S. (1975) Stigma, ostracism and expulsion in an Israeli kibbutz. In *Symbol and Politics in Communal Ideology.* (Moore, S. F. & Myerhoff, B., Eds). Cornell University Press: Ithaca and London.

Gordon, A. D. (1927 to 1929) *The Collected Writings of A. D. Gordon,* 5 Volumes (in Hebrew). The Central Committee of the Young Worker's Party: Tel-Aviv.

Gordon, A. D. (1973) *Selected Writings.* Arno Press: New York.

Hart, H. A. L. (1961) *The Concept of Law.* Oxford University Press: Oxford.

Honoré, A. M. (1973) Groups, laws, and obedience. In *Oxford Essays in Jurisprudence. Second Series.* (Simpson, A. W. B., Ed.). Oxford University Press: Oxford.

Kamenka, E. & Tay, A. E. (1975) Beyond bourgeois individualism. In *Feudalism. Capitalism and Beyond.* (Kamenka, E. & Neale, R. S., Eds). Australian National University Press: Canberra.

Kibbutz Ha'artzi Movement (1964) Asuphot: Tel Aviv (in Hebrew).

Marx, K. (1955) Critique of the Gotha Program. In *Karl Marx and Frederick Engels. Selected Works.* Foreign Languages Publishing House: Moscow.

Pashukanis, E. B. (1951) General theory of law and Marxism. In *Soviet Legal Philosophy,* (Hazard, J. N., Ed.). Harvard University Press: Cambridge, Mass.

Schmalenbach, H. (1961) The sociological category of communion. In *Theories of Society.* The Free Press: New York, pp. 331–348.

Schwartz, R. D. (1954) Social factors in the development of legal control: a case study of two Israeli settlements. *Yale Law Journal* **471.**

Schwartz, R. D. (1976) Law in the kibbutz: a response to Professor Shapiro. *Law & Society review* **1.**

Schwartz, R. D. & Miller, J. C. (1964) Legal Evolution and Societal Complexity. *American Journal of Sociology* **70.**

Shapiro, A. E. (1976) Law in the kibbutz: a reappraisal. *Law & Society Review* **1.**

Skolnick, J. H. (1966) Social research on legality: a reply to Auerbach. *Law & Society Review* **105**.

Twining, W. (1973) *Karl Llwellyn and the Realist Movement.* Weidenfeld & Nicolson: London.

Some Observations on Historical Changes in the Structure of Kibbutzim

S. N. Eisenstadt

I

It is but superfluous to emphasize that the kibbutz, from its beginning up till the present, has on the one hand undergone far-reaching changes and transformations, while on the other has, at the same time, maintained a high level of continuity in its membership, collective and institutional identity — but it seems to me that not all aspects of these changes, transformations and continuity have been given the degree of attention and emphasis that they deserve.

The single best researched aspect of these changes and transformations has been the one which stressed the growing economic growth, modernization and specialization of the kibbutz social structure in general and of the economic structure in particular, and the concomitant routinization of the ideology and ideological fervor and commitment in general and that of the second generation in particular.

The study of this aspect of changes in the kibbutz stressed also the connection between the growing institutionalization and routinization of its ideology and the attempts to contain these various structural developments within the institutional limits of the continuously changing and yet persistent ideological premises of the kibbutz and their major institutional implications — such as the stress on equality, communality — i.e., communal ownership of the means of production and control of patterns of consumption, the stress on the avoidance of dependence on hired labor and the like.

One of the more interesting outcomes of these processes of change has been the relatively very high degree of the success of many — if certainly not of all — of the kibbutzim as economic innovators and entrepreneurs who played a very important part in the transformation of Israeli agriculture into one of the most modernized and successful parts of Israeli economy, branching off even into the industrial sector.

But the full explanation of even these facts necessitates to take into account several aspects of the social structure of the kibbutz and of its transformation which go beyond the analysis of routinization of kibbutz ideology, social differentiation and economic modernization of the kibbutz economy. Above all it is necessary to go beyond the implicit premise of many of the studies of kibbutzim which often tended to look on the kibbutz as relatively closed community or series of communities not unlike some other utopian communities. In this perspective even the study of the different kibbutz movements — and of economic entreprises common to different kibbutzim or to them and to other sectors of the society — has been to a rather high degree seen and analyzed from this vantage point of the single kibbutz community.

And yet such perspective misses or at least belittles the crucial importance for the understanding of the dynamics of the kibbutz society, of the place of the kibbutz in the social structure of Israel and the nature of the linkages that have developed between the kibbutz and other sectors of this society — and of the changes in these linkages.

II

The starting point of such an analysis is the obvious, simple and yet basic fact that the kibbutz has been itself — and was seen by large, although certainly not all, sectors of Israeli society — as the epitome and symbol of the Zionist-socialist movement and ideology.

But this was not only a purely "symbolic" or ideological attitude. Its major link to the internal structure of the kibbutz and to its intitutional relations to other sectors of Israeli society has been the elitist image and self-image of the kibbutz — i.e., the fact that the kibbutz viewed itself, and was viewed by large parts of the society, as an elite group or sector — an elite epitomizing and attempting to realize, through social and cultural creativity, the ideals of national renaissance in concrete institutional settings.

This elite status of the kibbutz with the broader Israeli society was evident not only in some general vague symbolic identification and rhetoric references in ritual situations, but also in some very specific institutional repercussions.

The most important of these repercussions was, on the one hand, the relatively disproportionate numbers of the members of kibbutzim in elite position of the Yishuv and of the State of Israel; the importance of membership in youth movements which aimed at joining the kibbutz movements; and even transitory membership in kibbutzim — as channel to elite status; and, on the other hand, not only the high general prestige accorded to membership in kibbutzim, but also the relatively heavy subsidization of kibbutzim by the centers of the society. (An interesting illustration of the combination of such symbolic emulation and attachment, together with such subsidization, can be found in the Nahal formations, as well as in the direction of volunteers from youth movements and from abroad to work — as a sort of national service — for different periods of time in the kibbutzim).

But it is exactly here also that some of the most important changes — which shed very important light on the transformation of social structure of the kibbutz — can be identified and should be fully and systematically studied.

The crucial change here has been that from the concentration of such elite activities of members (mostly leaders of the kibbutzim) in top political, ideological, top-security and military (as of the Haganah in general and the Palmach in particular) positions into the direction of participation of wider membership — and less of the leadership of the kibbutzim — in more extended numbers in the different elite and continuous service military formations, such as the paratroopers — but not necessarily in top military position; and in the growing participation in various types of economic — including industrial — entrepreneurship.

This change has been very closely related to the — rather gradual, seemingly imperceptible and yet very forceful — change in the kibbutz from being the symbol of pioneering — a symbol demanding commitment, emulation and following, to a symbol of the latent, already institutionalized better aspirations of the society or some of its pristine values, commanding high respect and different forms of subsidizing — with but little direct commitment and following.

Closely related to this was the nature of the attraction of kibbutzim to new members from the outside and the parallel bases of attachment of second and third generation of children to their kibbutzim. It seems that there has here taken place a shift from attraction in terms of such pioneering commitments (although it did not disappear entirely) to one in terms of a combination of relatively high standard of living, prestigious status and quality of life — all these not unconnected with the combination of elite status with the growing emphasis on economic development and expansion of the kibbutzim.

III

How can we explain the combination of all these changes — those of the internal structure of the kibbutz and those in the nature of its (elite) status in the society?

The clue to such an explanation lies on the combination of certain aspects of the pioneering ideology of the kibbutz with that of some of the more persistent aspects of its social structure.

Thus, first of all, the elitist pioneering ethos emphasized very strongly not only the ascetic or utopian element in the kibbutz ideology, but also the pragamtic institution-building one in general, and economic in particular.

The institutional implication of these orientations have been manifold. These orientations contained within themselves both the background for development of varied entrepreneurial activities, as well as the potentiality of the transformation of the pioneering ethos into a variety of directions.

Of special importance in this context has been another aspect of the kibbutz ideology — namely its egalitarianism. This has been, from its very beginning, the internal egalitarianism of a very select elite group, almost of a sect or series of sects. While the members of these sects were in principle ready to extend such egalitarian conceptions towards other sectors of the society — yet made such extension contingent on the adherence to the elite standards of pioneering, and to acceptance of all the concrete institutional precepts of the kibbutz life. In so far as these other sectors could not live up to such standing, the kibbutzim tend to develop towards a more distant "tutelary" approach — while maitaining the relatively pristine sectarian purity — most fully manifest in their approach to new immigrants.

The most crucial aspect, from the point of view of our analysis, of the internal structure of the kibbutzim, has been the communal (non-familistic) division of labor and the relatively weak emphasis on professionalism.

The conjunction of the elitist sectarian orientation with the communal internal organization has transformed the kibbutzim in the direction of a combination of "gentleman-farmer", with some sort of non-celibate monasticism — a combination which enabled the development of a high level of motivation to perform elite functions with a high level of communal discipline.

The combination of these aspects of the pioneering ethos together with this basic characteristic of the internal structure of the kibbutz may indeed explain several of the crucial aspects of the changes in the internal structure of the kibbutz and its place in the broader Israeli social structure anlyzed above.

This is probably related — in ways which have yet to be more fully investigated — to the two factors. Thus first the relative flexibility of the pioneering ethos and the multiplicity or pluralism of institutional foci of such pioneering orientations alluded to above, and the communal (non-familistic) division of labor and the relatively weak emphasis on professionalism, have provided for members of kibbutz security which enabled the taking of risks in new directions — as well as the structural possibility of moving and shifting of manpower from one sector to another and its mobilization for new tasks — thus explaining the ability of the kibbutzim to develop diverse entrepreneurial activities and shift from one sphere of (elite) positions and activities to another.

At the same time, however, these very characteristics — as well as the different aspects of the egalitarian ethos analyzed above — enabled also the kibbutzim to maintain continuously sectarian attitudes and a high level of segregation or closure with respect to other sectors of the society, and this in face of the change of its symbolic place in Israeli society and the power and nature of their attraction to members of sectors outside themselves.

IV

This, in its turn, has greatly influenced two other aspects of the linkage between the kibbutzim and the broader Israeli society which became crucial since the establishment of the State and, in which, by the way, their difference from the moshavim stands out.

These are, first, the place of the kibbutzim in the absorption of new immigrants and the different modes of their participation in the political life of the State of Israel — as distinct from that of the Yishuv.

The story with respect to the absorption of new immigrants is very well known — the relatively small number of new immigrants absorbed in the kibbutzim and above all new kibbutzim established by new ("oriental" and "western" alike) immigrants — as against the high level of success of the moshav movement, above all to establish new settlements by immigrants who may — although not all of them — become among the most successful parts of the Israeli agricultural sector.

Closely related to this have been the different modes of participation of the kibbutzim and moshavim in the political system which developed after the establishment of the State of Israel and which, in general, has been characterized by the decline of the ideological movement, the growth of State and of a combination of populistic tendencies with development of strong patron-client patterns.

Here the kibbutzim remained — as they were with respect to the absorption of new immigrants — the upholder of the more sectarian ideological orientations — attempting often to serve as a voice of conscience or as moral guide, but building their strength more on internal coalitions within the centers of the respective parties, rather than on full participation in the middle and lower echelons of the political game, thus indirectly contributing to their growing decline in the central political elite.

All these trends and tendencies are, of course, continuously changing and in order to understand them more fully they have to be investigated more fully and systematically — but the preceding brief analysis may perhaps serve as a starting point for such investigation.

SOCIAL DIFFERENTIATION

Social Stratification in a "Classless" Society*

Eva Rosenfeld

AMERICAN sociologists are notoriously unhappy with the state of empirical research in social stratification. Yet, although numerous critical articles have been written, particularly taking to task the most prolific group of modern students of stratification—the Warner school—little, if any, cumulative effect can be detected, in spite of the great overlap in the points of attack. In the impasse which we seem to have reached, with some happily following beaten paths which others bitterly denounce, it seems to the author that a study of social stratification in social systems different from ours while yet belonging to the broad heritage of Western culture, may prove to be more provocative and contribute more to a clarification of some confused issues than another in the long series of theoretical articles.[1]

The social system in question, the collec-

tive settlements in Israel, seems to be particularly rewarding in sociological implications, whatever aspect of it might be studied; this is due mainly to its clear-cut cultural structure and to the fact that the collective settlements grew and developed for many years in a social environment which was not unfriendly and not dominant; the institutional dynamics of the collective society are thus, to a large extent, indigenous.

The presentation, which will follow, of social stratification in these collectives will, it is hoped, throw a new light on some of the old problems, and particularly on three moot questions raised by the critics of present-day research on stratification:

1. The disregard of the question of structural-functional reasons for differential prestige rank associated with various social roles, and of the selective process whereby some individuals get into the high rank positions. The forty-year-old history of the Israeli collectives reveals the process whereby social strata emerge out of an initially undifferentiated group of young adults living in an equalitarian and democratic system and bent on preventing the crystallization of fixed social strata. The fact that such strata *did* emerge, makes it imperative to raise the question of the functional importance of some social roles and the question of scarcity of personnel.[2]

---

* Revised version of a paper read at the annual meeting of the Eastern Sociological Society held in New Haven, March 31–April 1, 1951.

† The analysis of social stratification in the agricultural collectives in Israel is a part of a larger study carried out with the help of a research grant from the Social Science Research Council (1947–1950), aimed at discovering the dynamics of institutional changes in these planned communities.

[1] Form expressed a similar hope when, deploring the "failure to distinguish conceptually and empirically the types of stratification," he suggested that "One technique for (overcoming) this is to study settlements that obviously differ from the average in amount and type of stratification." William H. Form, "Status Stratification in a Planned Community," *American Sociological Review*, 10 (Oct. 1945), 605.

[2] For an admirably concise and clear theoretical analysis of these questions, see Kingsley Davis and Wilbert E. Moore, "Some Principles of Stratification," *American Sociological Review*, 10

157

2. Conceptual confusion in the use of the terms "class" (economic rank), "status" (prestige and honor rank) and "power" or "influence."[3] The Israeli collectives fall into the category of "classless" societies (together with the societies of Hutterites, Amanites, the 19th century Oneida and others). The social stratification which emerged is, therefore, free from the "confusing" economic factor.

3. The seeming bias against raising the question of conflicting interests of the various strata. In the Israeli collectives there are, as we shall see, no economic classes and, consequently, there is no "class struggle." Yet, the various strata that emerged, have different vested interests with respect to institutional change, and the roles they play in the actual process of change reveal this conflict of interests. Thus the question of the functional relation between social stratification and social change is forced into the open with great clarity.

Before proceeding to the analysis of social stratification in the Israeli collectives, some general information is in order. The first collective (or "kibutz") was established in 1910. At present, over thirty thousand adult members and another thirty thousand children, old parents and transient groups live in more than two hundred collective agricultural settlements; this comprises about six per cent of the settled Jewish population in Israel and over one-third of its settled rural population. The collectives average about 200 members or about 500 souls; there are several large ones with more than 1,500 population. With the exception of a dozen or so religious collectives, all the rest belong to either one of the three large federations of collectives and through them

to the socialist and anti-clerical General Federation of Trade Unions (the Histadrut).

With one exception, all collectives are based on farming but, increasingly, industrial branches are being developed. All property, not only the means of production, belongs to the commune, and members who leave have no claim on any part of it. There is no exchange market nor labor market within the collectives, although there is business as usual with the outside world. Members are assigned to work by an elected Work Committee. All administrative officers and branch managers are elected—by the General Meeting or by the workers in the given branch, respectively—for a period of one to two years and, although their nomination may be extended several times, there is a principle of turnover in managerial positions and of rotation of disliked tasks. The manager of the communal factory may be—and is—assigned to kitchen duty in slack season or on holidays.

Furthermore, the members' position in the administrative hierarchy is not related to their life chances for material gratifications: the basic norm is "from everyone according to ability—to everyone according to need." In principle, and in practice as well, it may happen that the manager of an important branch of the collective enterprise lives in a smaller room, has more primitive furniture, worse clothes, and eats less well than some of the unskilled workers who happen to be sickly and need special food and housing. All commodities are distributed centrally and in kind; food is eaten in the communal dining hall. Children are brought up, from birth, in communal children's homes.

Political institutions are democratic and equalitarian. All decisions of general interest are taken by a simple majority vote in the General Meeting, every member having one vote. Minor decisions are made by the Management Committee and other special committees elected by all members for one-year terms.

Thus, the social structure of the kibutz prevents the emergence of economic differentiation. Yet, differential social status ex-

(April 1945), 242–249. The findings presented in this paper support some of their generalizations, mainly that the universality of social stratification seems to be related to differential functional importance of social positions and to differential scarcity of personnel. On the other hand, as will appear below, our findings question their proposition that all types of rewards must be differentially dispensed in favor of high rank strata and their assumption that high prestige is always directly derived from high rank positions.

[8] See especially the survey article by Llewellyn Gross, "The Use of Class Concepts in Sociological Research," *American Journal of Sociology*. 54 (March 1949), 409–421.

ists in the kibutz society. Members with high and low status regard each other with a set of stereotype attitudes, and in their relations the awareness of being a distinct social type is clearly expressed. The high and low strata play distinct roles in the process of institutional change and the difference in their Weltanschauungs is well known.

Several questions demand answering:

1. How did the distinct strata emerge out of the equalitarian group of early settlers?
2. What are the criteria for locating members in one of the strata?
3. What are the characteristics of each stratum?
4. What are the relations between them and their attitudes to each other?
5. What special roles do they play in the process of institutional change?
6. What self-perpetuating processes can be observed?

To simplify matters, the following analysis is limited to first-generation full members; transient and marginal groups are excluded; the special problems of the position of the woman in the collective will also be omitted.

As to methodology, the uniformities reported in this paper were first discovered through participant observation in three of the oldest collectives over a period of a year and a half. These uniformities were subsequently checked by (1) short visits to a selected group of the oldest communes, with a systematic observation and interview guide; (2) intensive interviews with the leaders of the two important factions in the current struggle for institutional change: the "conservatives" and the "innovators" and (3) participation in nationwide meetings of the collective movement, called to discuss the pressure for change in the institutional structure.

The Emergence of Social Strata. Managerial positions of vital importance to the group are quite naturally[4] entrusted to those

members whom the group deems most capable and trustworthy. Yet, the association of a high status rank with managerial positions was not a simple process. Neither could it be said of the kibutz society that "the question of . . . why different positions carry different degrees of prestige . . . is logically prior and, in the case of any particular individual or group, factually prior . . . (to the question of) how certain individuals get into these positions."[5] In fact, it would seem that in the Israeli collectives this order of priority was reversed: managerial positions gained high prestige because of the initially high prestige of the persons who became elected to fill them.

Two structural characteristics of the kibutz society must be kept in mind: the glorification of manual "productive" work and the fierce insistence on complete equality, which made all authority unacceptable. The glorification of manual labor grew out of the general scarcity of workers and farmers among the immigrant Jews and their strategic importance in the task of building the nation anew in the deserted land. Since there was a surplus of intellectuals and white-collar workers among the Jews, the "clean" and "brainy" type of work was looked down at and the manual worker became the hero of the day. Such attitudes, particularly strong in the early years of settlement, imbued managerial tasks with deep ambiguity. On the one hand the group itself insisted on a turnover in all managerial and administrative positions—even though efficiency might suffer. On the other hand, the members elected to managerial positions felt impelled to insist on going back to "real work" after the end of their first term—even though they might have enjoyed their task. But in this secular society the pressure of the need for efficiency in time won over the cultural considerations.

In a new settlement there is much movement from bottom to top: new branches are being opened, skill and initiative are at

---

[4] "Nothing surprised me more in my investigations of the communistic societies than to discover . . . the ease and certainty with which brains come to the top . . ." concluded a 19th century observer

of communistic societies in this country (Charles Nordhoff, *The Communistic Societies of the United States,* New York: Harper & Bros., 1875, p. 392).

[5] See Davis and Moore, *op. cit.,* p. 242.

a premium and the small group quickly recognizes ability and good judgment. While, at the outset, there is usually only one skilled worker in every branch and he is naturally put in charge of the less skilled, years of work and experience often produce several self-taught capable workers in every branch. Then a system of turnover of managers may be adopted for some years. But again, as years pass, one worker usually becomes recognized as the best among the good workers and the tendency then is to re-elect him as manager for many years. Such men are usually successful in several fields. The collectives, as any pioneering society, suffer from a lack rather than abundance of men and women with talent, initiative and integrity; their scarcity puts them at a premium and gains them general recognition and high esteem. Thus there emerges a group of members whose personal status is so high that their re-election to important managerial positions is a matter of course, the benefit to the group in making best use of them being obvious to all. In the early years of settlement in Palestine, the formalities were observed more than now: managers would insist upon returning to "real, productive work" after a term in the office; but these periods of "productive work" grew shorter and shorter and the principle of turnover nowadays means, in reality, turnover within a given range of managerial positions. Simultaneously, the exigencies of managing a big enterprise and the scarcity of good managers made for a general shift in valuation from manual to "brainy" work.

In time, these correlates of personal attribute—managerial positions—became fixed in the popular mind and are used, instead of the original criterion of status, to denote the high standing of these members in the community. This substitution of status criteria became complete with the arrival of newcomers to the kibbutz, who are faced with the existence of an already stable group of highly respected leaders-managers whose personal background and attributes are hidden by time and social distance. However, within the core of oldtimers, personal attributes remain the true criterion of the esteem they bestow.

As the community grows older and the original group of pioneers becomes ever smaller in the influx of newcomers, seniority also becomes a source of prestige. The oldtimers ("vatikim") are the aristocracy of the kibbutz. They are accorded a certain amount of esteem for the attribute of seniority alone. One might call this "the charisma of the pioneering personality." And since, in most cases, the leaders, managers and "responsible workers" are recruited from among the oldtimers (newcomers are not as generously appraised as the oldtimers and they are not given as much opportunity for showing their best abilities) the attribute of seniority comes to denote not only a personal distinction of idealism and pioneering spirit, but also the correlate: the managerial position; and the managerial positions gain in prestige through the charisma of the oldtimers who hold them.

Locating Members in One of the Social Strata. The objective attributes of status are used explicitly whenever a kibbutz member is asked to describe or give information about some other member. The highest rank attribute is mentioned first; other, additional and qualifying attributes may then follow.

The highest rank is associated with a designation of "an important personality" (Yish hashoov) which, on closer questioning, reveals one of the top leaders in the kibbutz movement or a person highly skilled and specializing in some activity of general importance in the kibbutz movement. A qualification: "an important personality *in his kibbutz,*" means a local leader or branch manager who is credited for contributing to the success of the communal enterprise or to the high morale of the community. All "important personalities" are oldtimers and no mention of seniority is made, unless the member is one of the very first pioneers, the father of the kibbutz movement. The "important personalities" are the living myths of the collective ideology—they exemplify the devotion, the faith, the accomplishment which show that the system really "works."

Second in rank is, simply, "one of the first members" (ahad mihavatikim); this attribute is then followed by a designation of the special work the oldtimer is doing. In many cases, the oldtimers have a managerial position in one of the branches of the farm or specialize in some administrative tasks. If the work position is not managerial, the special branch in which the oldtimer works as a steady and "responsible" worker is stressed: "He is one of the *chief* field workers," or, "She is one of the *oldest* workers in the poultry yard" or, "She is the *head* nurse of infants."

If a member is not an oldtimer and yet not a recent arrival, the length of his stay in the community is not mentioned, only his position at work. Here, again, we find members in managerial and administrative positions who have successfully merged with the oldtimers; members who are simply "good, reliable workers" in a specific branch; and members who simply "work" in a given branch.

"Just an unskilled, moveable worker" (stam pkak) is the lowest designation. In this category one finds newcomers who are still unknown in the community and those of the older members who are not considered responsible or who are sickly, lazy, unpleasant to work with and shunned by all work groups—and who are, therefore, assigned every day to various menial jobs in whatever branch the need may be—usually the vegetable garden, orchards, services and factory (if there is any).

The concept of rank is thus based on objectively defined attributes of seniority and managerial position in work or administration. The informal leaders of the kibutz movement and within the collectives are always members who belong to this upper stratum of oldtimers-mangers. The rank and file (amho) are composed of the middle stratum of "responsible workers" (both oldtimers and middlecomers) and of the lowest stratum of "pkaks."

Within the rank and file, the ratio of steady to moveable workers varies greatly from one community to another and, within every collective, over the span of time. But the significant distinction in terms of differential life attitudes, opinions and social role played in the process of change, obtains between the upper, managerial stratum on the one hand, and the whole rank and file on the other. The numerical ratio of the lower to the middle substrata affects the relations between the upper stratum and the rank and file (see section on relations between the two strata).

The Characteristics of the Two Social Strata. Two special life conditions characterize the upper stratum of leaders-managers; one is the immunity from frustrating and humiliating experiences in dealing with central distributive and administrative kibutz institutions, and the second is the greater life chance for emotional gratifications derived from the special, ego-expanding experiences associated with their position of seniority, responsibility and leadership. These two special life conditions revolve around important areas of communal life.

One of the serious problems in collective life is the dependency of the individual, in the satisfaction of his material needs, upon the elected officers who are supposed to distribute commodities centrally, in kind and according to a general (and rather vaguely defined) concept of "need." For several reasons (into which it would be impossible to enter here) the relations between kibutz members and their distributive officers very often place the members in humiliating and frustrating situations. The kibutz "aristocracy" is spontaneously treated with more respect and deference and, therefore, very unlikely to encounter these humiliating situations. Furthermore, a sense of one's importance in the affairs of the community, and the feeling of security it generates, make their behavior in dealing with the distributive officers more poised and self-confident and this, in turn, affects the attitude of the officers so that it is very unlikely that they will release against the upper stratum members whatever irritation or hostility they may feel.

Another serious problem in the kibutz is generated by the fact that the individual does not see directly the results of his work-effort. His energy is pooled, together with that of others', in the communal enterprise and the fruits of his labor are pooled with those of the others'; so is the recognition. The sense of personal creation and an opportunity to realize one's sense of workmanship as well as the claim to the group's recognition for one's efforts, all these are lost to most members among the rank and file. Seemingly, in the kibutz, this loss is serious; especially, is the recognition by the group important to the individual.

A woman working in the kibutz dairy complained to me one day that her supervisor snapped at her "What did you do today, anyway?" and she felt very hurt and upset. I asked her, why should such a thing bother her; after all, she is an experienced, responsible worker and if her conscience is at rest, she should not mind the supervisor's remarks. She answered: "Outside, you get your money for your work and that is the main thing and the work relation ends there. Here you get no reward at all. Look at me, after 13 years of hard work in the dairy, what have I got? But we work, because we know that is the right thing to do. The only thing we want is 'iahas'— recognition."

The managers of the branches, who identify themselves with the branch and direct its policy, see the harvest as the product of their own labor. The administrative officers and the oldtimers in general, who direct the policy of the whole community, see the communal enterprise as a whole, can grasp it as a whole and identify with it; they watch the growth and development of the farm and village with pride and interest and receive therefrom emotional gratifications. Since seniority is so highly correlated with managerial and leadership positions, many members of the upper stratum have several sources of opportunities for ego-expanding experiences, while some of the rank and file have none.[6] Furthermore,

managers and administrators often have a chance to leave the settlement and go to town on some errand; they enjoy a degree of freedom of movement and the pleasure of some petty cash which they can spend to see a show or go to a café—pleasures which the rank and file are deprived of. On errands in town, the managers again experience the ego-expanding gratifications, as they represent their whole community in the dealings with banks, merchants and government agencies.

These special life conditions tend to create a special "managerial Weltanschauung" among the upper stratum. They experience less of the strain and dependency and more of the pleasures of collective living. "What is all this talk of 'dependency' I hear?" exclaimed one of the top leaders. "Why, we in the kibutz are the only people who are truly free: free from the worry and anxiety of competitive existence. I feel more free than all your Rockefellers. I do what I *really* want!"

The rank and file, on the other hand, see collective life from the disadvantageous point of daily routine, difficult and subordinate work, tensions and conflicts in many institutional relations.

The importance of emotional gratifications in the kibutz society can not be overstressed. The kibutz ideology is that of avant-guard pioneering, and the motivation is essentially that of self-denial. Material rewards for individual effort are nonexistent. The whole motivational system is based on the assump-

---

[6] Davis and Moore (op. cit., p. 243) mention three types of rewards that can be used to induce people into desired positions: those that contribute to "sustenance and comfort," to "humor and diversion" and to "self-respect and ego-expansion." They claim also that "In any social system all three kinds of rewards must be dispensed differentially accord-

ing to positions." The stratification system in the kibutz certainly supports the statement concerning the existence of special rewards, but it shows also that it is not at all necessary for any system to dispense all three kinds of rewards. Special sustenance and comfort are not associated with high prestige positions; neither is there any indication that, all other forces remaining equal, future developments will necessarily lead to preferential treatment of the managerial stratum with regard to the standard of living. To the contrary, a pressure for higher material rewards comes from the rank and file who are underprivileged in "humor and diversion" as well as in "self-respect and ego-expansion." The former type of rewards is sought by them as a compensation for the lack of the latter two.

tion that the members derive emotional gratifications in the course of communal life. This assumption is in turn based on the existence of identification of the members with their work, the village, the group, the communal future. If the society does not provide any basis for identification, or if the members are not prepared to identify with the community, no emotional gratifications are forthcoming and the whole motivational system collapses.

Relations between the Managerial Stratum and the Rank and File. Social relations among all members are completely informal. Among the older members no overt signs of deference exist. A certain degree of social distance is, however, introduced by newcomers through their spontaneously deferential attitude towards the managerial stratum. One may observe a newcomer stepping aside to let the "big leader" pass through the door; in addressing the "important personalities" the newcomers speak more politely and quietly than with other newcomers. This deferential attitude on their part springs from the fact that they actually are strangers to the oldtimers and are incapable of ever achieving the degree of familiarity obtaining among the oldtimers; their deferential attitude towards the managers is brought from the outside world. The newcomer is faced with a fixed correlate of personal status—managerial position—and he often does not sense the initial criterion of status—personal attributes—which, historically and logically, stands behind these occupational correlates. This attitude of restraint and deference on the part of the newcomers tends to increase the gulf between the upper stratum and the rank and file and interferes with the proper functioning of communication and with mutual understanding of each stratum's viewpoints and problems.

In a summer rest-home maintained by the kibutz, a girl newcomer became friendly with one of the oldtimers. "How I enjoy being able to talk with you," she exclaimed once. "Back home, I would never dare to speak to you—you always seemed so formidable and distant." The oldtimer was bewildered at her feeling of

distance. He felt that he was always open to approach by anyone in the kibutz.

In reality, the two strata regard each other with a set of stereotype attitudes. The managers-leaders are respected for their contribution to the communal enterprise as leaders, organizers, managers of farm and shops, but they are not loved. (On the part of some insufficiently motivated newcomers the respect is not even genuine.) The special character of their life conditions is recognized and they are privately—and sometimes publicly—accused of not really knowing "what kibutz life tastes like." "These people don't lead our lives," say the rank and file. The managers and leaders, on the other hand, feel slightly contemptuous of and discouraged with the rank and file for their inadequate enthusiasm, their lack of interest and participation in group life, their demands for a higher standard of living and less self-denial. It seems clear that the managers-leaders do not grasp the difference in the life conditions of the rank and file and the impact it must make on their image of and attitude toward the collective society. An incident in which the author participated will illustrate the nature of the differences between the two strata and the relations between them:

I was chatting with an oldtimer in the tiny switchboard-post office-armory room where his job was to answer telephone calls and take care of the mail. "Tell me," he said, "you've been around long enough to know what the score is. You know what is bad in our system and I know it too, so let's not talk about that. But tell me, what, in your mind, are the good things in kibutz life?" I started hesitantly but then warmed up and talked about the deep emotional gratifications many people seem to receive from identifying themselves with a big, expanding, to them meaningful enterprise. As I talked, the manager of the local factory stuck his head through the window and listened. His face warmed up with a smile and when I finished he exclaimed: "Let me shake your hand! It is all true, very true, what you just said!" But the first man flared up: "Oh, that's him again," he cried, dismissing the other with an impatient gesture (though not an unfriendly one; they were both oldtimers). "I know your song—and it is not the whole song, my friend. True, people in central positions, who can influence life around them, do feel all that. But most of the people do the dirty work and they feel nothing of the sort. To the contrary, they ask themselves: 'What the hell am I breaking my neck for? What do I get out of this?'"

The Distinctive Roles of the Two Strata in the Dynamics of Institutional Change. The managerial stratum, strongly identified with the communal enterprise and immune from many tensions, acts as a whip for inducing greater effort in work and maintaining the austerity in consumption. The rank and file, on the other hand, press for the elimination of the discomfort and dependency inherent in some of the institutional structures, and for a higher standard of living. The pressure of the rank and file towards readjustments in the institutional structure is strongly opposed by the leadership, who use several means in their effort to restrain the "innovators." Among the means used by them is, first, intimidation through ridicule in the General Meetings; secondly, administrative obstacles put in the way of an initiator who insists on placing an issue on the agenda for a public discussion or wants to publish an article in the kibbutz newspaper or periodical (secretaries and editors are members of the "upper" stratum); thirdly, the invitation of top leaders—men who have a charismatic appeal and are experienced "whipper-uppers" for a pep talk; more generally, a systematic attempt is being made · at strengthening the ideological motivation through special seminars, literature, lectures, etc.

The different roles played by the two strata are clearly visible at the General Meetings where leaders and managers call for ever greater effort and self-sacrifice and the rank and file resist more or less passively. During the informal gathering which always follows after the official meeting is closed, the resentment of the rank and file members is openly voiced: the leader-stratum is labelled "fanatics," "saints" and "conservatives." The only means used by the rank and file are passive resistance in the form of general apathy, loss of interest and refusal to participate in meetings, committee work and other communal activities. It is only when the passive resistance of the rank and file seriously threatens group morale that the leaders reluctantly give in to the pressure from below. Even then, the central secretariat of the kibbutz federation may exert its constraining pressure and threaten the "deviating" settlement with expulsion. The innovations are felt to be a retreat from the pure collective system and are feared eventually to lead to a destruction of the very foundations on which this system rests.

Thus the differences in life conditions and the resulting differences in each stratum's image of and attitude toward the collective society create two types of vested interests with regard to the question of institutional change: those more directly exposed to the dysfunctional consequences of the collective system have a stake in the pressure for change, while those experiencing more directly the functional aspects and less exposed to the tensions and strain fight to preserve the system in its entirety; they identify themselves with and act as the guardians of the system as a whole and of the status quo. Thus in these times of "sturm und drang" the leadership is not best qualified to lead in the search for solutions—its function is mainly conservative.

The question arises as to the *self perpetuating forces in the existing social stratification.* It is too early yet to make definite statements in this respect. The oldest of the sons and daughters of the first generation are still in their twenties and all of them are children of the early pioneers—the kibbutz aristocracy. Few have become active in communal affairs. Two tendencies may, however, be observed: (1) to sons and daughters of the top leaders and managers, their parents' intelligence and abilities (and often also personal integrity and a very high standard of values) are often transmitted, whether through heredity or through personal contact and influence. Since special training and higher education are offered by the community on the basis of intellectual promise, special ability and loyalty to kibutz values, these sons and daughters of the upper stratum have a better chance to be given additional training and to be placed in positions of trust and responsibility. In some cases two and three children of an "important personality" show great promise and special talent, and all are given special educational opportunities. (2) In addition, some of the "halo effect" of the parents does fall on their children. The sons and daughters of "big shots" in the kibutz movement are regarded as the aristocracy among the growing crop of second-generation youths. There is a vague aura of prestige clinging to the "big name." They are very desirable as marriage partners and a marriage of children of "big shots" is a popular event in the kibutz society, while marriages of others pass unnoticed. Still, the community applies the initial criteria of status—intelligence, ability, devotion to collective values and good work performance—to the second-generation members, just as it originally did in the small group of pioneers with respect to each other.

Conclusions. The very special type of social stratification in the Israeli collectives is distinguished by the following features which may now be related to the several theoretical questions raised at the beginning of this paper:

1. A distinct relation between the prestige of personality attributes and the prestige of social position. Scarcity puts a premium on capable and trustworthy members with initiative and leadership ability. Functional necessity forces the group to keep these highly valuable and esteemed members within a narrow range of important, managerial positions. Prestige becomes associated with these positions which are, then, used as an index of high social status.

2. A divorce between material and nonmaterial rewards. High status positions do not bring economic rewards. Members in managerial positions enjoy extensive (long range) emotional rewards (some due to their personalities; particularly, an ability to identify with larger entities and with the future of the group; and some due to the tasks they perform) and these rewards make them more satisfied with their lot than the rank and file. The latter, deprived of these emotional gratifications, demand immediate (short range) material gratifications and reduction in institutional strain.

3. A conflict of interests obtains with regard to institutional change, which is not related to economic exploitation or inequality, but to what might be termed "spiritual exploitation" or an unequal distribution of seemingly crucial, emotional gratifications. The managerial stratum upholds the collective ideology and the status quo. Their special life conditions and resulting managerial Weltanschauung, interfere with effective communication between the strata; they are accused of not knowing what collective life "really" is. Their efforts at grappling with the growing demands of the rank and file take the form of "ideological education" which, they hope, will increase the people's emotional gratifications.

These features of social stratification in the kibutz explain the seeming paradox of "class struggle" in a "classless" society.

The Functional Differentiation of Elites in the Kibbutz[1]

Amitai Etzioni

I. FUNCTIONAL ANALYSIS OF ELITES

Every social system, perhaps every system of action, is confronted with four basic functional problems. When simple social systems become more complex, when a *Gemeinschaft* becomes a *Gesellschaft*, four distinct subsystems emerge, each predominantly devoted to one of the major functions. Thus many processes of change can be analyzed as processes of functional differentiation. These ideas, formulated by Professor Parsons in 1953,[2] have been fruitfully applied in the analysis of a large number of social as well as non-social systems, including the social structures of task-oriented groups,[3] of families,[4] and of economies;[5] the processes of socialization and social control;[6] and the

history of culture, especially religion and the structure of the legal system.[7] This paper attempts to show that, after some minor additions, this conceptual scheme can be very helpful in analyzing the social structure and the differentiation of elites. The discussion is based on a study of elites in communal settlements (*kibbutzim*) in Israel.[8]

The four universal functional problems are: (1) the need of the system to control the environment; (2) gratification of the system's goals; (3) maintenance of solidarity among the system units; and (4) reinforcement of the integrity of the value system and its institutionalization. In the rest of the discussion these functional problems will be referred to as "adaptive," "goal-attainment," "solidaric," and "normative," respectively. Following Parsons' suggestion the adaptive and goal-attainment functions will be labeled "external" and the solidaric and normative "internal." The adaptive and normative will be labeled "instrumental" and the goal-attainment and solidaric functions "consummatory"[9] (see Table 1).

[1] This paper is based on the author's Ph.D. dissertation, "The Organizational Structure of the *Kibbutz*" (University of California, Berkeley, 1958). He is indebted to Professors S. M. Lipset and Philip Selznick, and to Professor Talcott Parsons for criticism of an earlier version and especially to Dr. Y. Talmon-Garber. The data were collected at the Israeli Institute of Productivity.

[2] See Talcott Parsons, "A Revised Analytical Approach to the Theory of Social Stratification," in R. Bendix and S. M. Lipset (eds.), *Class, Status and Power* (Glencoe, Ill.: Free Press, 1953), pp. 92–128; and Talcott Parsons, Robert F. Bales, and Edward A. Shils, *Working Papers in the Theory of Action* (Glencoe, Ill.: Free Press, 1953).

[3] Parsons *et al., op. cit.,* pp. 63–268, esp. 111–61.

[4] Talcott Parsons, Robert F. Bales, *et al., Family Socialization and Interaction* (Glencoe, Ill.: Free Press, 1955).

[5] Talcott Parsons and Neil J. Smelser, *Economy and Society* (Glencoe, Ill.: Free Press, 1956).

[6] *Family, Socialization and Interaction,* pp. 36, 38–39, 40–45, 140–41, 200–216.

[7] Discussions of Professor Parsons in a seminar, Berkeley, spring, 1958.

[8] A preliminary report on this study was published in Hebrew (see Amitai Etzioni, "The Organizational Structure of the *Kibbutz*," *Niv HaKevutza*, VI, No. 3 [August, 1957], 412–33, and VI, No. 4 [November, 1957], 658–82).

[9] Talcott Parsons, "The Role of General Theory in Sociological Analysis" (paper presented to the American Sociological Society, Washington, D.C., 1957).

In every social system at least some social situation, roles, or, in more complex structures, collectivities are devoted mainly to one of the major functions. When the social systems become complex and internally differentiated, we would expect to find in each subsystem some roles or collectivities which specialize in initiating, directing, and/or regulating the activities of each subsystem. We shall refer to these roles and collectivities as "elites." Thus we would expect to find in each complex social system four elites, one for each subsystem.

TABLE 1

	Instrumental	Consummatory
External	A Adaptive	G Goal attainment
Internal	Latent (Normative) L	Solidarity I

We suggest calling the adaptive elite—the elite of the specialists or experts, the goal-attainment elite—the politicians or managers (depending on the context); the elite of integrative activities—the social leaders, and the elite of the normative subsystem—the "cultural" (as defined by Parsons) leaders, including philosophers, ideologists, religious leaders, and others. This nomenclature can be justified by showing that the activities of experts, managers, and social and cultural leaders, using these designations approximately as they are generally understood, are cognate with the activities of the four functional subsystems discussed above, if both types of activities are analyzed in terms of pattern variables. The pattern variables of the four subsystems have been specified by Parsons as shown in Table 2.[10]

We shall turn now to specify the various elite activities in these terms. The experts are adaptive because their activities are specific and universalistic. They deal with

[10] *Working Papers*, p. 182.

knowledge, science, and technology. They are interested in the objective features of the environment from the point of view of the specific system problem they attempt to solve. The political or managerial elites (managers are in a certain sense the politicians of their organizations) are affective and performance oriented. They direct activities toward the system goals (this is the affective element) and are interested in motion toward these goals rather than in maintaining the quality of the system (this is the performance orientation). The social leaders (often "informal leaders") are particularistic and diffuse in their orientation. Their focus of interest is the particular system of which they are leaders, and their influence as well as their involvement are not limited to segmental spheres of their group activity but encompass the whole group sphere of action. The cultural leaders deal with symbols and values which determine the normative quality of the system. Creation of new meanings, integration of new meanings with the old ones, reinterpretation of systems of

TABLE 2

A		G
	Universalism Specificity	Affectivity Performance
	Quality Neutrality	Diffuseness Particularism
L		I

meaning, creating and maintaining value commitments—all these activities undertaken by cultural leaders have one common requirement: some independence and detachment from the social system and a certain degree of neutrality toward it.

This typology of elites should be seen as an analytical scheme. Concrete elites can be analyzed according to the specific ways in which the analytical elements are combined. Thus industrial elites are often managerial-expert; many politicians are political-integrative (social) oriented, and the secondary orientations of many members of the cultural elites seem to be expert orientations (e.g., most academicians). Thus a relatively more sophisticated classification of elites can be achieved only when the analytical scheme is applied at least twice and the predominant as well as the subordinate orientations of elites determined.

II. THE PROCESS OF FUNCTIONAL DIFFERENTIATION

In a very simple and uninstitutionalized social system, as, for instance, friendship between two people who have about equal status and similar involvement in the relationship, there may be no elite positions. But in somewhat larger (e.g., experimental groups) or more institutionalized (e.g., the family) systems, specialized roles of initiation and control will tend to develop. At first, or at very low levels of complexity, these elite positions will tend to be *multifunctional,* that is, the same role-holders will initiate and control action in all major areas of activities. In friendship between a veteran and a recruit, one, say the veteran, may be the "expert" on adapting to the environment (he knows the "ropes"), have a determining influence on the nature of the activities (to go have a beer or watch a movie), and at the same time be the one who maintains the harmony of the relationship (gives in) and reinforces its norms. Thus the veteran has a multifunctional elite position in the friendship system. In some primitive societies the chief and his court, seen as one unit, is such a multifunctional undifferentiated elite.

At somewhat more complex levels elite roles and elite groups become differentiated. The separation of the religious elite from the political-bureaucratic elite is perhaps the most significant and well-known case to the student of modern societies. Industrial sociologists focus on a vital differentiation of line-staff functions (manager-expert functions) which emerges as industrialization develops. The formal-informal leadership distinction, essential to organizational sociology, is a differentiation between managerial-oriented and solidaric-oriented leaders.

We shall turn now to a detailed account

of a case study of the process of functional differentiation of the elite of a community. The functional differentiation of the elite will be related to changes in the structure of a community which becomes more and more complex and more and more institutionalized.

III. NATURAL HISTORY OF THE "KIBBUTZ" AND ELITE DIFFERENTIATION

The elites we studied are the elites of the communal settlements in Israel, the *kibbutzim.*[11] There are about 225 *kibbutzim,* most of which follow a fundamentally similar life-pattern. The groups which eventually establish *kibbutzim* are conceived in the youth movements, grow up in the training camps, mature into autonomous young *kibbutzim,* and settle down to the routine life of an older *kibbutz.* We shall discuss the nature of the social system at each stage and then relate the process of elite differentiation to the changes in the nature of the social system. We shall attempt to find support for the following hypotheses in the data we collected: (*a*) with increasing complexity of the social system the elite becomes differentiated, that is, various functions are carried out by separate roles and different people; (*b*) differentiation is not random but follows a certain predictable pattern, multifunctional elites becoming differentiated according to functional lines; (*c*) once differentiated, a hierarchy of elites tends to develop, in which specialized (mono-functional) elites are at or near the bottom, dual elites are at the middle levels, and collectivity oriented elites are at the top; and (*d*) the process through which a new social system is created and gradually gains functional autonomy is analyzed and related to the differentiation of the elites. In the sociologi-

[11] For some excellent general discussions of the *kibbutz* see Melfrod E. Spiro, *Kibbutz: Venture in Utopia* (Cambridge, Mass.: Harvard University Press, 1956); M. Weingarten, *Life in a Kibbutz* (New York: Reconstructionist Press, 1955); Henrik F. Infield, *Cooperative Living in Palestine* (New York: Dryden Press, 1944); and Esther Tauber, *Molding Society to Man* (New York: Bloch Publishing Co., 1955).

cal literature there are very few discussions of the emergence of new social systems larger than small groups.

A. ELITES IN A PARTIAL SYSTEM

Most new *kibbutzim* grow out of groups of young people who are recruited from outside the *kibbutz* movement. Usually these groups crystallize in some collectivistic-oriented social movements like the pioneering youth movements in Israel and some Zionist youth movements in the Diaspora.[12] These young people generally live in their parents' homes, study or work during the day, and meet in the evenings and week ends in order to create a social group which later will become a *kibbutz*.

These youth-movement groups, called *gariinim*,[13] are sporadic and partial social systems, dominated by normative and integrative orientations; sporadic, because between periods of activity the whole group becomes latent, and partial because they depend on parents, schools, work places, youth-movement headquarters, and other external institutions for the fulfilment and regulation of some basic functions. Particularly, the external functions of adapting to the environment (e.g., making a livelihood) and allocating the available facilities among the group members are fulfilled for the group by members of outside social systems.

The group is a relatively autonomous system as far as the internal functions are concerned. Activities are mainly of two types: (1) normative—studying the writing of Marx, Lenin, Borkhov, and other European and Israeli socialists and discussing *kibbutz* literature and Israel's politics; and (2) integrative—dancing, communal singing, and trips and parties. Much emphasis is put on holidays and various Boy Scout–like rituals.

The groups are small, coeducational, and highly homogeneous in terms of age, ethnic, and socio-economic status as well as educational background. This homogeneity, the lack of external functions, and the emphasis on internally oriented activities tend to create highly solidaric groups whose social structure is based almost completely on informal social control.

Elites at this stage are restricted to internal functions. Most external activities are initiated and controlled by elites in other systems. Parents determine when younger members can go to the youth-movement center, how much time they can spend, if they may join a trip, etc. Schools or employers have similar controlling functions. A youth guide nominated by the youth-movement headquarters directs and limits many of the activities conducted by the group. The *gariin* has some "self-government" through two channels: elected committees and informal leadership. But the scope of this self-regulation is very limited. Informal leaders are easily co-opted, and committees tend to become inactive shortly after their election.

There is no elite differentiation at this stage. The youth guide controls both normative and integrative activities. The informal leaders, as far as we can tell, have similar positions in both realms of activity. Many local branches of the youth movements have only one committee which often discusses and decides on issues of both kinds, interchangeably.

B. ELITES IN THE TRANSITORY PERIOD

The second stage in the natural history of the *kibbutz* begins when the *gariinim* leave their sheltered homes and city life for intensive training, usually after graduation from high school. There are several alternative training arrangements: some training takes place in agricultural colleges which are also boarding schools,[14] some in *moshavot*. Often the training for farm work and *kib-*

---

[12] See J. Ben David, "Report of the Research Project on Youth Movement in Israel," *Transactions of the Second World Congress of Sociology* (London: International Sociological Association, 1954), Vol. I; S. N. Eisenstadt, *From Generation to Generation* (Glencoe, Ill.: Free Press, 1956).

[13] Literary, "pits"; also "core." The term is used to designate that these groups are seeds of future *kibbutzim*.

[14] These schools are discussed by Amitai Etzioni, "The Organizational Structure of 'Closed' Educational Institutions in Israel," *Harvard Educational Review*, XXVII, No. 2 (Spring, 1957), 107–25.

butz life is combined with service in the army. In most cases the training takes place in an older *kibbutz*. We shall follow the development of the *gariin* and its elites when this alternative is chosen.

With the transfer to the training place, the *gariin* becomes a permanent social group called *hachshara,* which means "training." The group settles in one of the *kibbutz* quarters. Interaction becomes continuous, and contact among members is very frequent. For the first time the group obtains a common external base. All *gariin* members work for the same "employer," an older host *kibbutz,* and are trained by its members. The members obtain all their supplies and accommodations from the communal services of the host *kibbutz.*

At the same time the *hachshara* becomes much more autonomous. It gains a high degree of self-control over internal functions and some control over externally oriented activities. The controlling functions of the youth guide are internalized. The group has to initiate and regulate by itself all social and cultural activities. Functionaries of the older *kibbutz* give some "expert" advice on these issues (e.g., help to obtain a lecturer) and set some limits to self-regulation (e.g., a trip planned for Passover has to be delayed because the *hachshara* help is needed for an early harvesting). But, in general, the older *kibbutz* interferes only rarely in the *hachshara's* internal activities.

Externally oriented activities of the *hachshara* still take place in systems not under its control. The members work in the host *kibbutz* farm and services and receive accommodation from it. They are assigned to jobs mainly according to the *kibbutz* needs and by its work assigner. He usually determines which members will be assigned to what jobs, thus leaving the *hachshara* little control over the division of labor within it.

The increase in internal control is revealed in the considerable increase in scope and significance of committee activities. In the *gariin* period most issues were decided through informal group discussions; in the *hachshara* it is done in the general assembly, which usually meets once a week and decides almost all the issues. It also elects committees which function in its name and report to it about their activities.

There is a cultural committee in charge of normative functions and also of some integrative functions.[15] It organizes lectures, a library, supply of newspapers and political information, etc., as well as parties and rituals on Friday and holiday evenings. There is a members' committee in charge of integrative and some normative activities. It has same judicial functions (e.g., it settles serious conflicts among members). Its representatives hold intimate informal discussions with *hachshara* members who have "personal" problems, who are suspected of intending to desert the group, and who deviate from this or that *kibbutz* norm. At this stage the members' committee has only limited control over the allocation of material rewards, which are supplied by the host *kibbutz* mainly to individuals in the *hachshara* and not to the *hachshara* as a group.

There is a work committee which represents the *hachshara* toward the host *kibbutz* work assigner. It bargains with him over the ratio of *hachshara* members assigned to skilled and semiskilled jobs to unskilled workers, reports about members who are sick, on applicants for vacations, etc. Thus at this stage it is a committee with an external-representative function.

The first signs of differentiation can be recognized at this stage. There is a role differentiation among the three or more committees but little differentiation among the elite personnel. While some members are considered as having greater aptitudes for this or that elite role, specialization is not encouraged. Active members are often switched from one committee to another and often are members of two at a time.

As noted, there are some signs of role

[15] The committees in the *kibbutz* are described and discussed in the studies mentioned above (see n. 11) and in Maurice Pearlman, *Collective Adventure* (London: William Heinmann Ltd., 1938), and Ben-Shalom Avraham, *Deep Furrows* (New York: Hashomer Hatzair Organization, 1937).

differentiation on the elite level but very little specialization of elite personnel. In earlier stages of differentiation tasks which have hereto been organized in one role become separated and invested in two or more separate roles. Such role differentiation does not mean that a parallel differentiation of personnel occurs automatically. The same people can go on carrying out the now separate tasks (this happens when the work unit becomes separated from the family unit), or there can be a high turnover among the carriers of the separate roles, so that most people will carry each role for some time, and only little specialization will occur. The young *kibbutzim* come close to this model for a short period, maintaining considerable differentiation of elite roles with little differentiation of elite personnel.

C. ELITES IN AN AUTONOMOUS COLLECTIVITY

The third step in the natural history of the *kibbutz* takes place when the training is completed. The *hachshara* leaves the host *kibbutz* and establishes a new one. Not all *hachsharot* (plural of *hachshara*) reach this stage. Some disintegrate, and some join an existing *kibbutz*. We shall follow the development of the elites where the *hachshara* establishes a *kibbutz* of its own.

The major change from *hachshara* to *kibbutz* is the internalization of control over the adaptive and managerial functions. At this stage members work in a farm at services which belong to and are controlled by themselves. the older *kibbutzim* send often a guide or two to help out during the first months, but they are generally considered strictly experts, sources of advice, and not partners in the structure of control. The general assembly controls production, division of labor, and allocation of material rewards (consumption), as it controlled the social and cultural activities in the *hachshara*.

The elite, which heretofore consisted of a few committees and informal leaders, expands rapidly and becomes much more elaborated and specialized. A whole organizational structure with a center of decisions

(the secretariat), division of tasks and authority as well as some hierarchization, develops. The first full-time functionaries are elected. A large number of new, mainly external-oriented committees are created, following the model of the older *kibbutzim*.

The most important new committee is the farm committee, which is in control of the externally oriented subsystem, the work system. It is a managerial-expert committee which plans and regulates the allocations of means of production, including labor, machines, other types of equipment, soil, water, fertilizers, technological knowledge, and financial means.

The work committee now distributes the workers according to the needs of their farm and its services as well as their personal needs; thus control over work becomes internalized. The farm committee is helped by various expert committees, including a planning committee for planning of the new *kibbutz* site, construction, and farm; a crop committee, which works out the details of the agricultural planning, including crop rotation; and some other committees which vary from *kibbutz* to *kibbutz*.

An important change takes place in the functions of the members' committee. In the *hachshara* days it had only integrative-normative functions (see above); now a new medium of integration is added. The committee determines the allocation of various material rewards and handles the integrative problems emerging from it.

The committees have limited significance compared with the functionaries, who are elected for the first time at this stage. While the committees meet once or twice per week after working hours, the functionaries are part or full-time organizers who devote a considerable part of their working day as well as much of their leisure time to organizational activity. At this stage there are usually five functionaries: the general farm manager, usually also the chairman of the farm committee, who actually directs the work system of the *kibbutz;* the treasurer, who is the *kibbutz* representative in the city in financial and marketing matters; the shopping agent, who makes purchases for the *kibbutz* in the city; and the secretary, whose role is a combination of the clerk of the *kibbutz*, its representative to the authorities, and the only functionary active in internal activities. He is often chairman of the members' committee. Most of the new *kibbutzim* have also part-time work assigners. In others work is assigned by the work committee members in their free time. The last important addition are branch managers. The *kibbutz'* farm and communal services (communal kitchen, laundry, children's houses, clothing store, etc.) are organized into work units called "branches." At this stage most branches are established, and branch managers are elected or nominated.

At this point a hierarchy of elites develops for the first time. At the top is the secretariat, to which all other committees are subordinated. Most functionaries are members of the secretariat; otherwise they are subordinated to it as well. The most developed hierarchy is found in the new organizational branch of the external activities. From bottom to top we find the following levels: workers, branch managers, farm committee and the general farm manager, the secretariat, and, finally, the general assembly.

By now, there is a considerable differentiation of elites as to role. The strongest differentation is between the externally and internally oriented elites. On the one hand, we find the cultural committee, members' committee, and the secretary; on the other, the farm committee, other externally oriented committees, as well as four functionaries (all except the secretary) and the branch managers. There is some differentiation along the four functional lines. In the internal wing the cultural committee is predominantly normatively oriented, and the members' committee and the secretary are predominantly integratively oriented. (This differentiation basically existed already in the *hachshara* days, but it becomes more emphasized.) In the external branch the farm committee and the general farm manager are predominantly managerially

oriented, and the advisory committees (the planning committee, the crop committee, and others) are predominantly expert-oriented. The branch managers of small branches are more expert-oriented; the branch managers of larger branches are managerial-oriented.

D. ELITES IN A COMPLEX SYSTEM

The change from a young *kibbutz* to an older one is a change from a relatively simple monolithic collectivity to a complex commune. The solidaric ties to the *kibbutz* as a collectivity are weakened with the increase of the significance of the solidaric ties to the subcollectivities. In earlier stages the *kibbutz* was mainly a group of young bachelors. By now most of its members have established a family, which becomes a significant unit of activity and loyalty.[16] A second focus of solidarity is often found in the new groups which join *kibbutz* after the first years. The young *kibbutzim* are small (forty to eighty members), homogenous groups. But soon the groups are not large enough for the various needs of the *kibbutz*, mainly for a rational organization of the farm and defense system. New groups join, unlike it in age, educational background, and/or ethnic origin and socioeconomic status. In most cases some social differentiation is maintained along these lines.[17] As the *kibbutz* becomes older, the children often constitute a social subcollectivity of their own. At last, to close the circle, the *kibbutz* plays host to a *hachshara*, which is preparing itself for the day it will establish its own *kibbutz*. In *kibbutzim* where there is little differentiation of loyal-

[16] On the increasing significance of the family as a cohesive unit in the *kibbutz* see Y. Talmon-Garber, "The Family in Israel," *Marriage and Family Living*, XVI, No. 4 (November, 1954), 348, and Y. Talmon-Garber, "The Family in Collective Settlements" (stenciled).

[17] On the development of social differentiation in the *kibbutz* see Eva Rosenfeld, "Social Stratification in a 'Classless' Society," *American Sociological Review*, XVI, No. 6 (December, 1951), 766–74; Yonina Talmon-Garber, "Differentiation in Collective Settlements," *Scripta Hoerosolymitana* (Hebrew University, Jerusalem), III (1956), 153–78.

ties on status bases (e.g., old-timers versus newcomers; ethnic origins) often loyalties are woven along functional lines of work units (called "branches").[18] But the elites themselves almost never constitute a basis for crystalization of a solidaric group (see below).[19]

The organizational structure itself does not change in any basic way, although it becomes considerably larger and more elaborate. At a relatively early stage an educational committee is added which is responsible for the socialization of the children, a normative function. As the number of the children increases, subcommittees for various age groups are introduced. In order to maintain normative primacy of the committee, larger *kibbutzim* elect special educational subcommittees for administrative and technical tasks. The members' committee usually establishes an increasing number of subordinated committees which deal with specific allocations like a housing committee, an equipment committee, a health committee, and many others.

The number of functionaries and the time allocated to them are increased, but no new tasks are formed. Functionaries are first released from regular work for an hour a day (known in the *kibbutz* as an "eight," i.e., eighth part of the working day). The time allocated for organizational activity is gradually increased. While in the new *kibbutz* usually only one or two functionaries have a full-time office, in the older *kibbutz* most functionaries are old full-time officers; in large *kibbutzim* two full-time functionaries fulfil tasks earlier carried out by one part-time functionary. Thus, *in toto*, there is mainly an increase in the volume of elite activity but little additional differentiation on

[18] See Amitai Etzioni, "Solidaric Work-Groups in Collective Settlements," *Human Organization*, XVI, No. 3 (1958), 2–6.

[19] On lack of social ties between elite members see Y. Talmon-Garber, "Differentiation in Collective Settlements," *op. cit.*, p. 117. On the concept of social circulation see H. D. Lasswell, D. Lerner, and C. E. Rothwell, *The Comparative Study of Elites* (Stanford: Stanford University Press, 1952), pp. 8–9.

the role level. The reason is, we suggest, that basic functional differentiation has already been reached at the earlier stage.

The main change as far as the elite structure is concerned lies now on a different level. Specialization takes place now on the personnel level. Until now we saw a process of increasing differentiation on the role level, while elite members were switched frequently from role to role, although there was some concern about specialization of personnel, as noted earlier. At this last stage members are increasingly specialized in one function, yet elite members frequently hold more than one office, this being less true as the institution ages.

We studied the offices held simultaneously by elite members of two *kibbutzim;* a young *kibbutz*, COT, established in 1949 and an older COT and forty-one "additional" offices in BAH. By additional offices we mean the offices a member holds simultaneously with his basic office. From the point of view of the present argument and the statistics supplied, it does not make any difference which role is designated as "base" and which as "additional"; what matters is the number of offices held by one person and the types of combination.

Obviously, the number of cases is too small to allow for a fourfold functional analysis. But if we divide the offices into externally and internally oriented offices (we have suggested that the external-internal differentiation develops earlier), we can see significant differences between the two *kibbutzim* (see Table 3).

The data support the suggestion made above. In the younger *kibbutz* there are more members who hold offices in elites of different functional subsystems than in the older; while in the young *kibbutz* 33 per cent of the combinations of offices are cross-functional, less than 10 per cent are so in the older *kibbutz*. In support of this conclusion from other *kibbutzim*, it may be said that in Benjamin, a young *kibbutz*, the treasurer, who plays an adaptive-dominated role, was also the ideological leader of the *kibbutz*. In Simon (a young *kibbutz*) the general farm manager was at the same time also the chairman of the educational committee. We do not know about any similar combinations in older *kibbutzim*. Some probably exist, but they seem to be considerably less frequent.

IV. ELITES AND INSTITUTIONALIZED BRIDGES

Differentiated societies have separate subsystems devoted to the major functions. Thus the work system is devoted to adaptation, family and education to socialization (normative dominancy), the legal system mainly to integration, and what is often referred to as decision-making can be termed, in the conceptual frame of reference applied here, a managerial subsystem. The activities

interstitial units are certain types of elites. While most are *specialized*, some are dual-oriented and others collectivity oriented. The *dual* elites serve two subsystems simultaneously; the *collectivity* oriented elites serve the whole. By integrating and co-ordinating differentiated activities, both contribute to the cohesiveness and effectiveness of the system.

We would expect to find specialized elites at the bottom or close to the bottom of organization and stratification structures, dual elites at the middle level, and collectivity oriented at the top level. But while organizational structures almost always have one center of decision (i.e., a top elite), in stratification and political structures of so-

TABLE 3

DISTRIBUTION OF ADDITIONAL OFFICES

	External-* External Offices	External-Internal or Internal-External Offices	Internal-Internal Offices
COT (young *kibbutz*)	8	6	4
BAH (older *kibbutz*)	27	4	10

* The first term designates the office of the elite member; the second, the additional offices. Thus external-internal, for instance, means that a member in an external committee (e.g., farm committee) is also a member of an internal committee (e.g., educational committee).

of these various subsystems have to be integrated if the system is to be maintained and its ability to reach its goals is to be preserved. To some degree this is performed by the regular functioning of the various subsystems, especially the integrative and normative subsystems. To some degree the ties among the various subsystems are maintained by special intersystem (interstitial) sectors. Some professions and many cross-class social groups and voluntary associations seem to have this function.

We would expect interstitial units to lack a dominant unidimensional orientation and their structure to reflect the orientational nature of the subsystems they bridge. Thus, if we see a vocational school as a typical interstitial unit, we would expect it to combine the normative orientation of the family and primary school with the external orientations of the occupational system.

Among the most important categories of

cieties it varies considerably. While totalitarian states have a centralized top elite, in feudal societies and some democratic societies, notably the United States, top-level elite structure is much more complicated.[20]

The *kibbutz* gives us an opportunity to study a society which has a top collectivity oriented elite which to a large degree coincides with the elites institutionalized in the organizational structure and also to study a dual elite. The work committee in both the young and the older *kibbutz* is a dual elite; the secretariat is collectivity oriented.

The work committee assigns members to jobs. Two types of considerations impinge equally on the decisions to assign members:

[20] See Raymond Aron, "Social Structure and the Ruling Class," in Bendix and Lipset (eds.), *op. cit.*, pp. 567–77; C. Wright Mills, *The Power Elite* (New York: Oxford University Press, 1956); Talcott Parsons, "The Distribution of Power in American Society," *World Politics*, X, No. 1 (October, 1957), 123–43.

the needs of the farm and services and the needs of the *kibbutz* as a solidaric unit. In pattern variables the first set of considerations is universalistic, specific, and performance- and neutrality-dominated. The factors taken into consideration are economic, technological, and physical require-

tive system, on the other—a difficult thing, since the conflicting needs of the two sub-systems are considerable. *Kibbutz* members often refuse to serve on the work committee, especially to be work assigners. While, in general, committee members are elected for one or two years, work assigners

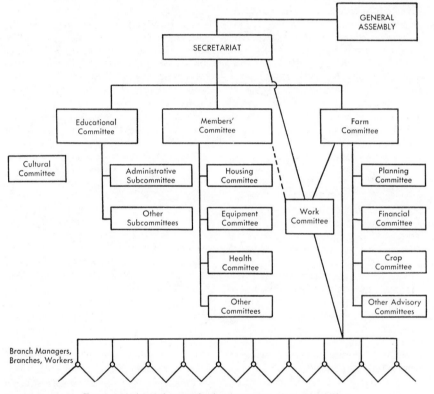

Fig. 1.—Model of the organizational structure of an older *kibbutz*

ments, aptitudes, managerial expediency, efficiency, and optimal distribution of means of production. The second set of considerations is particularistic, diffuse, quality and affectively oriented. The members' preferences about jobs, team mates, positions in the *kibbutz*, character, and similar factors are taken into account.

The task of the work committee is to work out solutions which will not undermine the work system, on one hand, and the integra-

are elected for shorter periods, in most *kibbutzim* for three months.

The interstitial character of the work committee is revealed by the hierarchical nature of the organization (Fig. 1). Most elite roles in the organizational structure of the *kibbutz* are clearly in one line of authority. Thus the branch managers are subordinated to the general farm managers; the housing, equipment, and health committees to the members' committee; and the members of the educational subcommittees to the educational committee. But the work committee and work assigner are not clearly subordinated to any committee and are often directly represented in the top committee, the secretariat (see below). While the work assigner often works in close cooperation with the general farm manager and is under considerable influence from his managerial (universalistic) demands, he is also under pressure of the health committee, members' committee, and secretary to take into account "human factors." In some *kibbutzim* one member of the work committee is an ex-officio representative of the members' committee. Former members of the work committee seem to be more likely to become active members of internally oriented committees than holders of any externally oriented role, and former members of internal committees seem to be more like work-committee members than do those of any external committee.

Organizational structures are characterized among other things by a single center of direction. The nature of this top unit reflects to some degree the nature of the whole system. Thus, if the system is characterized by a dominancy of the normative function, for instance, we would not be astonished to find a strong representation of normative-oriented actors in the top elite of the system. But, on the other hand, the top elite of any organization cannot be a specialized elite in the dominant function of the organization, because other functions of the organization may be neglected. Since the organization is a social system, its effective functioning and, in the long run, its very existence depend on representation of all major functions—directly or indirectly—at the top level. Thus top management of successful industries includes "managers" as well as experts, engineers as well as salespeople, economists as well as accountants.

The top elite of the organization structure of most *kibbutzim* is the secretariat. It controls the whole organizational structure and is responsible before the general assembly for the functioning of the various commit-

tees and functionaries. In cases of conflict among the various committees, the issue is often decided by the secretariat or by the general assembly, which may act on recommendations submitted by the secretariat.[21] The agenda of the general assembly is prepared by the secretariat, and one of its members is the chairman of the general assembly in most *kibbutzim*. While members of the other committees often develop quite strong loyalties to one realm of activity, the secretariat is considered to be the "cabinet" of the whole *kibbutz*, and its members are particularly expected to have "the general welfare" of the *kibbutz* as their primary focus of interest and loyalty.

The secretariat is well adapted to its functions as a top, collectivity oriented elite. All major functions are represented in it. It includes usually the treasurer, the general farm manager, the chairman of the members' committee, the chairman of the educational committee, and often the work assigner. The secretary is the nominal chairman of the committee. In addition to the functional representatives, one or two members are usually elected to "represent the public." These are sometimes the most influential members of the secretariat. They are not committed to one function and thus help the secretariat to reach agreed upon policies. Thus, while most committees include only specialists of one or two kinds, the secretariat includes representatives of all major functions and some unspecialized members. It is a multifunctional body which represents the collectivity as a unit versus the various subsystems.

DISCUSSION

At every stage of change (especially from the *gariin* to the *hachshara* and from the *hachshara* to a young *kibbutz*) involves, on the one hand, an expressive crisis for the organization and, on the other hand, en-

[21] On the democratic process in the *kibbutz* see R. D. Schwartz, "Democracy and Collectivism in the Kibbutz," in *Social Problems,* special issue on the *kibbutz,* S. Diamond (ed.), Vol. V, No. 2 (Fall, 1957).

hanced ritualistic activity. The crisis is expressed in considerable reorganization and in high turnover of members. The "rituals" —especially when a *hachshara* reaches maturity and a new *kibbutz* is established— are highly institutionalized. The analogy between it and the socialization of the child may lead as well to intriguing insights into organizations and institutionalization.

Elites emerge and develop in a patterned process. First there are elite situations (informal discussions which include decision-making in the youth movement), then elite roles emerge. The third step occurs when elite roles differentiate, without a necessary parallel differentiation of the elite personnel taking place. Often a more or less parallel differentiation occurs later on the personnel level; this could be designated as specialization. The last stage, which seems not to have developed in most *kibbutzim*, occurs when the various elites become subcollectivities (i.e., bases for formation of solidaric ties).

It was pointed out by Parsons that differentiation of social (and non-social) systems do not develop randomly but take place along predictable lines of the fourfold func-

tional scheme. The differentiation of elites seems, at least in our case, to follow along the same lines.

In analyzing the various elite roles and the process of change, we found that certain concepts and patterns of relationships have to be added to the scheme which was our starting point. We found that concurrently with the process of differentiation a process of integration (not a process of merging!) takes place. On the one hand, "primitive," multifunctional, undifferentiated elites give way to a set of specialized elites; on the other hand, interstitial elites emerge which integrate the activities of either two subsystems or of the collectivity as a whole. These elites are placed in the political and stratification structure of the organization and society studied here, so as to allow them, to some degree, to regulate the activities of the specialized elites and thus to integrate the whole system. It remains to be explored if these concepts and suggestions can be usefully applied to the study of elites in different contexts.

COLUMBIA UNIVERSITY

Reward Distribution and Work-Role Attractiveness in the Kibbutz: Reflections on Equity Theory

Ephraim Yuchtman

The problematic nature of role attractiveness among office-holders in Israeli Kibbutzim is examined by comparing a representative sample of managers and workers of a typical production unit in the Kibbutz. The results indicate that, despite enjoying greater intrinsic and extrinsic rewards, managers tend to be less attracted than the rank-and-file to their jobs. This finding is explained by equity theory, i.e., the managers do not get out of the job what they should on the basis of what they have put into it. The apparent penetration of equity to the egalitarian-oriented Kibbutz is explained in light of its continuous processes of role differentiation and professionalization. The relevance of such processes for the equity argument is further indicated by the analysis of related data. The article concludes with some suggestions concerning possible extensions of the equity principle and the social conditions of its applicability.

THE differential allocation of rewards has been a major factor accounting for variations in the attractiveness of different roles for individuals. To be sure, the social psychological processes underlying the operation of rewards are not yet fully understood, and different parameters have been offered as mediating the effects of rewards on attitudes and behaviors. The concepts of value importance (Vroom, 1964; Evans, 1969; Mobley and Lock, 1970), status consistency (Homans, 1961; Brandon, 1965; Sampson, 1968), expectancy (Vroom, 1964; Lawler, 1971) and equity (Homans, 1961; Jacques, 1961; Blau, 1964; Adams, 1965) illustrate the importance of such variables, particularly as they apply to the work situation. Yet, the general positive influence exerted by rewards on attitudes toward roles with which they are associated is commonly accepted

[1] This study was partly supported by the Ruppin Institute, Israel. I wish to thank professors Michael Inbar of the Hebrew University, and Michael Flynn and William Gamson of the University of Michigan, for their insightful comments on an earlier draft of this paper. The present paper was read at the August 1972 American Sociological Association meeting in New Orleans.

on both theoretical and empirical grounds. Thus, the finding of a positive relationship between attraction to work roles and their occupational or organizational levels is largely explained by the greater rewarding potential of roles of higher positions (Herzberg, 1957, 1958; Vroom, 1964; Robinson et al., 1969; Quinn et al., 1971).

In view of these general trends it is interesting to note that members of Israeli Kibbutzim are not particularly attracted to higher positions in the community (Garber-Talmon, 1956; Spiro, 1956; Darin-Drabkin, 1962; Ben-Yosef, 1963; Leon, 1969). Furthermore, it has been claimed that candidates for central roles (usually managerial) often attempt to avoid their nomination, and public pressure is sometimes required for the candidate to take the job (Garber-Talmon, 1956). Indeed, expressed dissatisfaction among candidates to and occupants of higher positions may contain elements of ritualistic behavior. But students of the Kibbutz generally agree that, while instances of ceremonial disinterestedness do occur, their overall importance should not be exaggerated. Thus, it remains to be explained why the expected positive relationship between the hierarchical position of the work role and its attractiveness is not obtained in the Kibbutz.

On first examination this peculiar phenomenon seems to be simply explained by the egalitarian nature of the Kibbutz. The principle of economic and social equality has been a vital ingredient of the Kibbutz' value-system since its beginning. At the societal level this principle is expressed in the collective structure of the community in general and in its virtually complete abolition of the institution of private property in particular.[2] A crucial mechanism for maintaining this egalitarian structure has been the denial of a different allocation of material and economic rewards for occupational and organizational positions (Rosen-

feld, 1951; Aurbach, 1953, Spiro, 1956; Talmon-Garber, 1956; Darin-Drabkin, 1962; Vallier, 1962; Ben-David, 1964; Weintraub et al, 1969). Thus, one of the most important sets of incentives of higher level jobs is absent in the Kibbutz. Furthermore, as several researchers note (Spiro, 1956; Talmon-Garber, 1956; Rosner, 1964), office holders in the community tend to experience unpleasant encounters and difficulties causing them high levels of strain. Typical examples are the frequent exposure to criticism from fellow workers, including subordinates; the need to depend on committee consensus for important decisions; the need to rely almost exclusively on skills of personal persuasion and informal leadership, since formal sanctions are scarce; and labor days which spread into the night. These instances of negative outcomes built into higher positions, can be viewed as costs reducing the attractiveness of such jobs (Rosner and Abend, 1968).

This argument is much weakened, however, by evidence which indicates that office holding in the Kibbutz carries significant privileges and rewards. Several studies show that leaders usually enjoy great influence, authority, and esteem (Rosenfeld, 1951; Diamond, 1957; Schwartz, 1957; Darin-Drabkin, 1962). Some investigators suggest, in fact, that this hierarchical reward differentiation has formed an elite stratum in the Kibbutz (Revusky, 1945; Rosenfeld, 1951; Aurback, 1953; Etzioni, 1959; Vallier, 1962). Other researchers, while rejecting this argument (Talmon-Garber, 1956; Darin-Drabkin, 1962), still acknowledge the significant rewards of office holding in the Kibbutz.

In addition to the social rewards, attention has been given to the intrinsic sources of gratification in higher positions. The latter tend to be more interesting and challenging, to provide better opportunities for using and developing skills and knowhow, and to allow for greater autonomy and responsibility on the job. Increased complexity in the division of labor in the Kibbutz, and the concommitant processes of specialization and professionalization have increased differentiation in the work role hierarchy for both social rewards and their task incentives.

---

[2] During its earlier period the Kibbutz implemented the idea of collective sharing vigorously in both the production and consumption spheres (Diamond, 1957; Rosenfeld, 1957; Talmon-Garber and Stupp, 1970). The emphasis on total communal sharing of consumption goods has gradually been weakened (Rosenfeld, 1957; Rabkin and Spire, 1970), though the collective ownership of all means of production has been fully maintained.

In view of this evidence one cannot argue simply that higher positions in the Kibbutz are relatively unattractive because they lack meaningful rewards and incentives. Previous research is far from conclusive on whether office holders are remunerated more or less than the rank-and-file workers. The ambivalence toward this issue is illustrated by the following two statements of Spiro (1956):

> There is no class structure in Kiryat Yedidim, and there is no differential reward system for different kinds of labor based on some ranking technique. Some kinds of work, as has already been observed, are valued more highly than others; but those who occupy the more highly valued jobs receive no greater reward than the others. The important psychological fact about the Kibbutz culture is that everyone, regardless of his work, is viewed as a worker, with the same privileges and responsibilities as anyone else (pp. 23–4).

> Although the various Kibbutz offices are held on a temporary and a rotation basis, those who happen to hold these offices do enjoy considerable power. Moreover, as is noted below, though the tenure of office is limited to two or three years, only a small number of chaverim possess the necessary skills required to cope with the complexities of such offices . . . so that in effect these offices rotate among a small core of twelve to fifteen persons (p. 25).

The relation of role attractiveness to reward structure is difficult to understand for two related reasons. First, the relationship between reward distribution and job satisfaction has been examined only indirectly, with the relevant variables as yet empirically unassessed. Inadequate or unreported sampling procedures weaken the significance of many of these studies. In one exception (Rosner, 1964), a sample of managers and rank-and-file workers were carefully compared; but the degree of role attractiveness among the two groups was not similarly measured. Second, the tendency has been to treat managerial and other higher positions homogeneously. However, considerable vertical and horizontal differences exist among these roles (Talmon-Garber, 1956; Cohen, 1963; Rosner and Abend, 1968). Thus, an examination of each type of office is required for meaningful generalizations to be made about both problems of role attrac-

tiveness and reward distributions of higher positions in the Kibbutz.

The present study attempts to overcome these difficuties and to understand the relation of reward distribution to role attractiveness in the Kibbutz. At the empirical level, the investigation compares a representative sample of managers and rank-and-file workers of a widely-spread production unit —the poultry branch [3]—with respect to the amount and types of rewards enjoyed as well as the degree of role attractiveness reported. From a theoretical view, the study examines the socio-psychological principles which may underlie the effect of the work role's rewards on its attractiveness for incumbents. The hope was that the empirical data would shed light on whether the egalitarian principle, successfully institutionalized in the economic sphere, is similarily accepted as the rule of reward distribution for non-material rewards. The importance of this question goes beyond its relevance for the study of the Kibbutz. Recent advancements in exchange theories (Thibaut and Kelley, 1959; Gouldner, 1960; Homans, 1961; Blau, 1964; Adams, 1965; Meeker, 1971) have renewed the interest in justice as a crucial dimension of the reward distribution process. Most empirical research in this area, however, has concentrated on Adams' concept of equity as the predominant principle in modern societies, though we do not know as yet how universal it is. Some researchers point to limiting conditions of its applicability (Gamson, 1964; Weik, 1966, 1967; Sampson, 1968; Goodman and Friedman, 1971). Both Gamson and Sampson propose that equality rather than equity may, under certain conditions, be the prevailing rule. In light of this debate the present investigation, and the

---

[3] The economic structure of the Kibbutz consists of various organizational units—known as "branches"—each specializing in the production of certain goods or services. A typical Kibbutz includes several agricultural branches, such as field crops or plantations, and service units, like the kitchen or the clothing. In addition, many Kibbutzim have one or more factories, as well as a few more unique branches. Each unit is headed by a manager nominated by the appropriate community organs. While the nomination process may vary from one Kibbutz to another, it almost always involves the implicit consensus of workers in that branch.

study of the Kibbutz in general may help develop general theories of social exchange.

Method

Population. The data for the present investigation are based on a probability sample representing the entire population of the poultry branch in the Kibbutz movement, with the exception of branches comprising single full-time workers. The sample consists of twenty-six Kibbutzim (one poultry branch per Kibbutz) and comprises 130 respondents, divided into twenty-six managers and 104 workers, all full timers and members of the Kibbutz.[4] Data were collected via self-administered questionnaires delivered personally to all the workers who could be located and who agreed to cooperate. A little over 80% of the original sample returned complete, or nearly complete, questionnaires.

The choice of this particular population was not determined by the subject matter of the present paper. It should be noted, however, that the poultry is one of the most widely-spread branches in the Kibbutz movement, existing in over 75% of the total of some 230 Kibbutzim. In addition, there is little variation in the technology of the branch across Kibbutzim, a fact which contributes to this branch's similarity of tasks and organizational structure in different Kibbutzim.[5] This organization was found to be rather simple, consisting usually of a branch manager and rank-and-file workers.

The size of the poultry branch is also typical, averaging about five full-time workers. In the few groups where the number of workers exceeds ten, the organizational structure is slightly more complex, including an intermediate level of supervisory roles. Since few such cases exist and both managers and rank-and-file workers judge them as unimportant, we decided to use the dual distinction between managers and workers.

Variables

A. *Reward Distribution.* On the basis of previous research on the Kibbutz, including a pilot study, three clusters of rewards, each comprising three specific outcomes, were selected for comparing managers and workers:

1. *Intrinsic job satisfaction;*
   1a. the opportunities to learn new things
   1b. the opportunities to actualize personal ideas
   1c. the opportunities to make use of skills and knowhow
2. *Power-related rewards;*
   2a. degree of influence over what is going on in the branch
   2b. degree of authority over other persons
   2c. degree of independence in the work process
3. *Socio-emotional rewards;*
   3a. amount of esteem received by fellow workers
   3b. amount of consideration shown by fellow workers
   3c. the quality of social relations in the branch [6]

The above nine outcomes were measured by close-ended questions, having five alternatives ranging from "very high" to "very low." These questions were intended to measure the amount of rewards obtained by each individual in his view.

In addition, another form of measurement was used to examine the validity of the findings. All the respondents were presented with a list of various potential outcomes and asked to rank-order the three most often associated with the role of the branch manager. An alternative indicating that the managers enjoy no special advan-

---

[4] In most Kibbutzim there exist, in addition to regular workers, several other categories of employees. For example, children of the Kibbutz spend several hours a day at work in various branches. Similarly, in many Kibbutzim one finds non-members, such as volunteers from abroad. Hired labor, used by many Kibbutzim, is quite rare in the poultry branch. In any case, all these categories of workers, who comprise a small fraction of the labor force of this branch, were excluded from the investigation.

[5] The poultry branch is a market-oriented organization, based on the application of scientific know-how and modern technology, including various types of machinery, semi-automated equipment, quality control procedures and an elaborated system of medication—all of which require relatively sophisticated technical, administrative and marketing skills. Hence, in the medium and large branches these functions are fulfilled by full-time managers.

[6] This is an indirect question, based on the assumption that the perception of the quality of social relations in the group reflects, to a large degree, the social position of the person in it.

tages was also provided. The list of outcomes is given below:

1. higher esteem
2. greater job variety
3. more independence
4. better opportunities for social contacts
5. better opportunities to make use of and develop skills
6. better opportunities to make use of and develop knowhow
7. more influence in the branch

Note that unlike the first, the second form of measurement explicitly focuses the respondents' attention on the issue of reward distribution in general, and on the manager's relative advantage with regard to this distribution in particular.

B. *Work-Role Attractiveness.* Following Thibaut and Kelley (1959), role attractiveness was conceived in terms of two related but distinct aspects. The first is implied by their concept of "comparison level." Accordingly, the amount of satisfaction derived from a given interaction reflects the gap between the actual outcomes and those expected on the basis of a subjective yardstick developed by the person for that interaction. The second concept— "comparison level for alternatives"—implies another subjective yardstick used by the individual to evaluate his outcomes. This yardstick determines the gap between the actual outcomes and those expected from

the best available alternative. Thus, a person may be dissatisfied with his role in terms of the comparison level but still prefer to stay in it since his outcomes are positive in terms of the comparison level for alternatives.

The questions used to measure these two aspects of the role attractiveness were formulated as follows:

1. "All and all, how satisfied are you with your job?" The five alternatives of response range from "very much satisfied" to "very little satisfied."

2. "To what extent do you prefer to stay or leave this branch?" The alternatives to this question ranged from "definitely prefer to stay" to "definitely prefer to leave."

A product-moment correlation of 0.56 was obtained between the two measures, indicating the common factor they share as well as their distinct aspects. In view of this result and the conceptual distinction it reflects, we decided to keep the two measures separate rather than combine them in a single index.

Results

The distribution of rewards. Table 1 compares the managers and workers with respect to the distribution of intrinsic rewards. The findings indicate a clear advantage of managers over workers. Thus,

Table 1. Distribution of Intrinsic Rewards by Workers and Managers (%)

Rewards Degree	Opportunities to Learn New Things[1]		Opportunities to Use Personal Ideas[2]		Opportunities to Apply Skills and Knowhow[3]	
	Workers (N=97)	Managers (N=24)	Workers (N=99)	Managers (N=24)	Workers (N=100)	Managers (N=24)
Very high	10.3	29.2	11.2	25.0	12.0	29.2
High	29.9	37.5	35.3	58.3	37.0	20.8
Medium	38.1	25.0	35.3	12.5	39.0	45.8
Low	16.5	8.3	15.2	4.2	8.0	4.2
Very low	5.2	0.0	3.0	0.0	4.0	0.0
Total	100.0	100.0	100.0	100.0	100.0	100.0

[1]Gamma = 0.45   [2]Gamma = 0.56   [3]Gamma = 0.19

Table 2.   Distribution of Power-Related Rewards by Workers and Managers (%)

Rewards Degree	Authority over Other Persons[1]		Independence in the Work Process[2]		Influence in the Branch[3]	
	Workers (N=100)	Managers (N=24)	Workers (N=102)	Managers (N=25)	Workers (N=97)	Managers (N=24)
Very high	13.0	20.8	23.5	16.0	13.3	37.5
High	25.0	45.8	33.3	60.0	33.0	50.0
Medium	26.0	25.0	31.4	24.0	31.0	12.5
Low	18.0	8.4	5.9	0.0	17.5	0.0
Very low	18.0	0.0	5.9	0.0	5.2	0.0
Total	100.0	100.0	100.0	100.0	100.0	100.0

[1]Gamma = 0.46   [2]Gamma = 0.22   [3]Gamma = 0.66

about 67% of the first group perceive large, or very large, opportunities in their jobs to learn new things; while only 40% of the workers perceive their jobs in the same way. Similarly, about 83% of the managers, compared to 47% of the workers, indicate that their jobs enable them to actualize personal ideas. The differences with respect to skills and knowhow are much smaller but in the same direction as those obtained for the first two outcomes.

Table 2 presents the findings for the power-related rewards. These data reveal a pattern very similar to the previous set: the distribution of outcomes clearly favors the managers on the three measures, particularly those of authority and influence. Thus, the large majority of this group (two-thirds and over) feel that they have high degrees of authority over other persons, independence in the work-process and overall influence in the branch. The corresponding figures for the workers are much smaller. These results should be evaluated in light of the argument that insufficient authority serves as a source of role strain among office holders in the Kibbutz. At least for the managers of this branch, the present data

Table 3.   Distribution of Socio-Emotional Rewards by Workers and Managers (%)

Rewards Degree	Esteem by Co-workers[1]		Consideration and Understanding by Co-workers[2]		Quality of Social Relations in the Branch[3]	
	Workers (N=101)	Managers (N=22)	Workers (N=101)	Managers (N=25)	Workers (N=103)	Managers (N=23)
Very high	34.7	27.3	16.8	16.0	4.8	4.3
High	29.7	40.9	31.7	28.0	34.9	30.4
Medium	26.7	27.3	41.6	40.0	47.6	56.5
Low	8.9	4.5	6.9	16.0	11.7	4.3
Very low	0.0	0.0	3.0	0.0	1.0	4.3
Total	100.0	100.0	100.0	100.0	100.0	100.0

[1]Gamma = -0.01   [2]Gamma = -0.08   [3]Gamma = -0.04

Table 4.   Overall Ranking of the Advantages of Branch Managers,
by Workers and Managers (%)*

Advantages--Workers (N=98)		Advantages--Managers (N=24)	
1. Influence	52.0	1. Influence	54.2
2. Knowhow	41.8	2. Variety	45.8
3. Variety	36.7	3. Knowhow	41.7
4. Independence	35.7	4. Independence	37.5
5. Social Contacts	27.5	5. Social Contacts	20.8
6. Esteem	22.4	6. Esteem	16.7
7. Skill Development	14.3	7. Skill Development	4.2
No advantages	12.2	No advantages	16.7

*Since respondents could mention up to three advantages, the total percentage exceeds 100.

neither support nor disprove the argument.[7]

Table 3 presents the allocation of the socio-emotional rewards. The findings here differ considerably from the earlier results in that the distribution among managers and workers is nearly identical on all the three measures. Managers and workers are alike in their perceptions of the esteem and the understanding given them by fellow workers, as well as in their evaluation of the quality of social relations in the branch. Thus, the position of the managers on this dimension is lower than their standing on the other two. At the same time, these data do not show that the managers are particularly prone to experience negative interpersonal relations, or to be disliked by their fellow workers, as has been claimed. Altogether, the findings thus far indicate that the position of a manager in the poultry branch is associated with several important positive outcomes not shared to the same degree by rank-and-file workers.

Table 4 shows the results of the additional examination of the rewards of the managerial office. This table reveals three important findings:

(1) Only a small portion of respondents indicate that the managerial position is de-

[7] Thus, only 21% of the managers define their degree of authority as "very high." It is possible, therefore, that lower degrees of authority, which characterize the majority of this group, are a source of tension in it.

void of any advantage (12% and 17% of the workers and managers, respectively). (2) A high degree of agreement exists between the perceptions of workers and managers. With the exception of the alternation between knowhow and job variety, the two rankings completely overlap. In fact, the absolute figures are also very similar. (3) the findings seem to be consistent with the previous results. Power-related and intrinsic rewards appear in the upper portion—the socio-emotional in the lower portion, except for skills development.

In general, both sets of findings seem to indicate that the managers of the poultry branch, as compared with the rank-and-file, enjoy a significant increment of rewards of various kinds, particularly those related to self actualization and the exercise of influence and authority.

Work-role attractiveness. Tables 5 and 6 give the distributions of responses to the two questions concerned with role attractiveness. Both tables show that the managers are *less* attached to their work role than the workers. About 66% of the latter report high degree of satisfaction with their job, compared with 42% among the managers; and while only 17% of the workers prefer to leave the branch, 42% of the managers prefer to leave. It is interesting to note also the difference of scatter between the two tables. The responses to the measure of job satisfaction tend to concentrate around

Table 5.   Degree of Job Satisfaction
by Workers and Managers (%)*

Degree	Workers (N=101)	Managers (N=24)
Very high	21.8	8.3
High	44.6	33.3
Medium	23.7	50.0
Low	4.0	4.2
Very low	5.9	4.2
Total	100.0	100.0

*Gamma = -0.35

Table 6.   Inclination to Stay in the
Branch or Leave It by Workers
and Managers (%)*

Inclination	Workers (N=104)	Managers (N=26)
Definitely to stay	44.2	41.7
Incline to stay	31.7	12.5
Indifferent	7.7	4.2
Incline to leave	9.6	29.2
Definitely to leave	6.7	12.5
Total	99.9	100.1

*Gamma = -0.22

the middle and the adjacent upper category, while the distribution of the second variable tends to polarize among the managers. This finding can be explained by assuming that managers have better job alternatives than workers; thus, dissatisfied managers are more inclined to relinquish their jobs than dissatisfied workers. In any case, these results indicate the problematic nature of role attractiveness for leaders in the Kibbutz. To assess the scope of generality of this phenomenon we need to examine other higher positions. For the poultry branch, it appears that the managers, while enjoying more rewards than the rank-and-file, are less attracted to their work role.[8]

Discussion

The relative dissatisfaction of managers, despite their obvious advantage in rewarding outcomes vis-a-vis the workers, can be explained by the equity concept. As formulated by Adams (1965), this concept draws on earlier works, particularly those of Jacques (1956), Sayles (1958), Patchen (1959), and Homans (1961), in which the notion of justice is introduced as a critical dimension of exchange processes and their consequences for participants' attitudes and behaviors. Inequity, according to Adams,

---

[8] The significance of this apparently peculiar phenomenon may be put in question by the suggestion that the managers do not attach much importance to the outcomes they enjoy. However, additional data which will be presented later rule out this possibility.

"exists for Person whenever he perceives that the ratio of his outcomes to inputs and the ratio of Other's outcomes to Other's inputs are unequal" (1965:280). Inequity results usually in a feeling of dissatisfaction, although the theory provides for predicting additional consequences, such as the altering or cognitive distortion of outcomes and/ or inputs. Note that the bases of the comparison processes referred to in the theory are rather limited and, as Weik showed (1966, 1967), there exist several potential alternative modes of comparison, including an individual's use of his own internal standards. For the present discussion, however, the relevant theme of equity is that "people try to get out of an exchange what they think they deserve on the basis of what they have put into it" (Meeker, 1971:487). Accordingly, the managerial role has a lower degree of attractiveness for its incumbents because they put more into it than they get out. The fact that managers are rewarded better than the rank-and-file is irrelevant because the managers, whether comparing their own ratio with the workers' or using an alternative yardstick, presumably evaluate their outcomes with comparison levels of higher order. This interpretation becomes more meaningful in light of added evidence on general trends in the Kibbutz movement as well as other findings in this study.

In the last two decades the Kibbutz has undergone rapid technological and economic changes, followed by greater role differentiation in the economic and organizational spheres. These processes which were systematically described and analyzed, especially by Cohen (1963, 1966, 1972), stemmed from the Kibbutz' own goals of economic and material progress as well as from the pressing problems of economic and technological development in Israeli society. As a result, ". . . the Kibbutz was pressed to persist in the constant effort to expand, improve and modernize its technology and economy, its educational facilities and its organizational structure" (Cohen, 1966:184). An integral aspect of these processes has been the specializing and professionalizing of occupational and administrative roles. But the concern with progress and its dynamics of change have inevitably weakened the Kibbutz communal spirit. As Cohen indicated, an inherent conflict exists between the idea of progress, with its emphasis on performance, rationality and objectivity and the spirit of communality, which rests on highly personal, intimate and fraternal modes of social relations. Thus, in its preoccupation with adapting and developing, the Kibbutz could not escape the inevitable consequence of a decline in its collective spirit and a strengthening of individualism. Cohen's analysis of the dynamics of change in the Kibbutz is highly consistent with the two-factor model of social structure and behavior developed recently by Sampson (1968). One proposition derived from this model concerns the compatibility between equity and equality as alternative modes of distributive justice, on the one hand, and the group's relative emphasis on problems of adaptation and goal attainment ("mastery" in Sampson's terms) on the other.

One immediate and rather interesting implication of this formulation suggests that to the extent that task performance is directly affected by the problems of mastery, task performance will suffer *more* (at least for a time) where justice is to be accomplished through equality than where justice can be achieved through equity (Sampson, 1968:266).

Cohen's specific analysis and Sampson's conceptual framework thus indicate the social changes conducive to the emergence of equity as an alternative to equality in certain areas of Kibbutz life. The validity of this argument is revealed by examining the extent to which the Kibbutz has successfully implemented the rule of rotation. This rule has been a major mechanism in the community for maintaining the egalitarian principle. Rotation deemphasizes potential input differences by role incumbents, to allow for recruiting office holders from a large pool of candidates. With increased role differentiation, however, this rule has become harder to adhere to, particularly for technicians and managers.[9] The limited application of rotation can be viewed in two complementary ways: on the one hand, it is an outcome of the system's need to progress economically through an efficient division of labor; on the other hand, it further differentiates higher and lower positions and their occupants. Furthermore, it is reasonable to assume that as the same persons tend to hold the higher offices, they are more likely to be aware of the distinctiveness of their positions, including the requisite qualifications. In other words, they recognize that professionals are distinguished by such features as intellectual ability and technical skill. The salience of these differences enhances the likelihood of equity, rather than equality, to prevail as the mode of reward distribution.

The discussion so far suggests that the Kibbutz structure is inclined to incorporate the equity principle in its reward structure. It remains to be seen if this general analysis applies to the poultry branch. To explore this question, we will present findings on differences in input levels and manager and worker concern about outcomes.

The first two findings, shown in Tables 7 and 8, can be viewed as unobtrusive measures of both the professional level and the managers' selectivity. Table 7 compares the amount of formal technical training received by managers and rank-and-file. As this table shows, a significantly higher proportion of branch managers participated in each type of professional training available for this branch. The largest difference is obtained for the course on "branch management" which prepares technical and administrative

[9] Spiro, for example, reports that only twelve to fifteen members rotated among themselves the highest positions in the Kibbutz he studied (see quote on page 65).

Table 7. Professional Training of
Workers and Managers (%)*

Type of Training	Workers (N=104)	Managers (N=25)
Seminars	52.9	72.0
Elementary course on poultry	40.4	48.0
Advanced course in branch management	9.6	52.0
Other	20.1	28.0

*Since some respondents participated
in more than one type of training,
the percentages in the two columns
do not add up to 100.

Table 8. Participation in Offices and
Committees (%)*

	Workers (N=104)	Managers (N=25)
All types of offices	63.4	92.0
Economic committee	13.5	56.0
Secretariat	15.4	32.0
Cultural and educational committee	17.3	32.0
Chairmanship of committees	8.6	24.0

*Since some respondents participated
in more than one type of office, the
percentages in the two columns do not
add up to 100.

experts for branches in the Kibbutz [10] and
is the most advanced course for this management level. Note also that managers express a stronger desire than workers for
education and technical training. About
38% of the managers indicate a strong desire for this opportunity compared to 15%
of the workers. It appears, then, that managers are characterized by their objective
professional knowhow as well as by a desire
to improve that knowhow.

The second relevant measure pertains to
the respondents' amount of participation in
several central committees and offices typical to the Kibbutz. Nomination to these
positions is based mostly on ability and performance, thus membership in them indicates the members' high standing in terms
of these criteria. The five comparisons given
in Table 8 reveal a consistent pattern of a
higher proportion of managers who are appointed to the committees and offices.[11]
Note especially the economic committee
which demonstrates the largest gap between
the two groups. This organ is responsible
for the major economic decisions in the
Kibbutz, and its members are mostly technical and administrative experts.

The findings reported in Tables 7 and 8
indicate that the general processes in the

[10] It should be noted that the participants in
this course, which takes place in a special educational institution established by the Kibbutz movement, are sent by their Kibbutz on the basis of
their potential or actual merits as branch managers.
[11] Note that the nominations of branch managers are not ex officio.

Kibbutz of differentiation and professionalization apply, to some degree, to the poultry branch. We argued, however, that these
processes enhance awareness among office
holders of the distinctiveness of their role
qualifications.

To determine if managers have such an
awareness, we asked them along with workers, to assess the scarcity of manpower
skills required for performing their respective jobs.[12]

The distribution of responses, given in
Table 9, clearly shows that managers tend
to regard the skill requirements of their
work role more highly. Only 8% of this
group, compared to 44% of the workers,
think that most people could learn their
jobs. This finding is consistent with responses to the question which required sub-

[12] Specifically, they were asked to estimate the
proportion of members who could perform the
job, had they time enough to learn it.

Table 9. Estimation of How Many
Members Can Learn Own Job (%)

	Workers (N=100)	Managers (N=24)
Almost everyone	44.0	8.3
Many	43.0	58.4
Few	13.0	33.3
Total	100.0	100.0

Table 10.   Desirability of Intrinsic Rewards by Workers and Managers (%)

Rewards Desirability	Learning New Things[1]		Use of Personal Ideas[2]		Actualization of Skills and Knowhow[3]	
	Workers (N=98)	Managers (N=24)	Workers (N=94)	Managers (N=24)	Workers (N=91)	Managers (N=24)
Very high	32.6	50.0	21.3	33.3	24.1	50.0
High	43.9	45.8	38.3	62.5	40.7	41.7
Medium	15.3	4.2	31.9	4.2	29.7	8.3
Low	4.1	0.0	5.3	0.0	5.5	0.0
Very low	4.1	0.0	3.2	0.0	0.0	0.0
Total	100.0	100.0	100.0	100.0	100.0	100.0

[1]Gamma = 0.42   [2]Gamma = 0.53   [3]Gamma = 0.55

jects to assess the length of time needed for a person to learn his job.[13] The average length was 30.1 and 11.8 weeks, as estimated by managers and by workers, respectively. Taken together, these results tend to support the contention that managers are more professional and selective and are conscious of the higher input levels associated with their roles.

The second aspect of the equity argument treats the concern about the work role outcomes. We expected that in view of the input differences between workers and mana-

[13] The question was formulated as follows: "How many weeks are required for an average member to learn to perform your job?"

gers, the latter would attach greater importance to the rewarding outcomes of their role. Accordingly, the two groups were compared with regard to the two sets of intrinsic and power-related rewards. You will recall that the managers' advantage was demonstrated for these types of outcomes, so that to see the outcomes' significance for them is particularly germane. The results of this comparison, in Tables 10 and 11, show consistently that managers regard both sets of rewards more highly. Thus, while majorities in the two groups attach more importance to the intrinsic job rewards, this tendency is clearly stronger among the managers. A similar pattern ob-

Table 11.   Desirability of Power-Related Rewards by Workers and Managers (%)

Rewards Desirability	Authority over Other Persons[1]		Independence in the Work Process[2]		Influence in the Branch[3]	
	Workers (N=94)	Managers (N=24)	Workers (N=95)	Managers (N=24)	Workers (N=100)	Managers (N=24)
Very high	4.2	8.3	30.6	37.5	22.0	50.0
High	14.9	41.7	44.2	41.7	46.0	45.8
Medium	33.0	37.5	18.9	16.7	30.0	4.2
Low	24.5	8.3	4.2	4.2	1.0	0.0
Very low	23.4	4.2	2.1	0.0	1.0	0.0
Total	100.0	100.0	100.0	100.0	100.0	100.0

[1]Gamma = 0.58   [2]Gamma = 0.13   [3]Gamma = 0.61

tains for the desirability of power related outcomes. Note the results which treat the importance of having authority over others. This is the least preferred outcome among managers and workers, probably because of its negative ideological implications. Yet, almost three times as many managers as workers (50% vs. 19%) express strong desire for it.

Taken together, the different sets of findings strongly indicate an equity effect among managers. This group consists mainly of professionals who are aware of their higher input levels and expect, accordingly, adequate outcomes from their office. The lower degree of role attractiveness for them may be attributed, therefore, to the apparent disproportion of outcomes versus inputs. Yet, one may argue that these findings support the equity thesis only indirectly, since they pertain to the aggregate level of analysis.

To demonstrate the presence of equity more directly, one must show that, *within* the management group, variations in role attractiveness are related to differences in input and outcomes. A direct derivation from equity theory implies that the correlation between input level and role attractiveness would be negative with outcomes controlled: managers with similar outcomes would be less attracted to their office the greater their inputs. The test results for this hypothesis are presented in Table 12 which contains partial correlations between input level (indicated by skills requirements) and role attractiveness (indicated by the inclination to stay or leave the office), with the six types of outcomes separately controlled for.

As this tables shows, all six partial correlations are negative, as predicted. This latter result further demonstrates that equity considerations pervade work-role attractiveness among office holders in the present study.[14] It remains to be seen how far this

[14] An alternative method of testing the equity hypothesis is to compare the correlations between outcomes and role attractiveness with the correlations between the ratio of outcomes-to-input and role attractiveness. The correlations in the second case should be, according to equity, higher than those in the first. Such an analysis was performed and the results were highly consistent with this prediction.

Table 12. Partial Correlations between Input Level and Role-Attractiveness, Controlling for Outcomes (Managers only, N=22)

Type of Outcome	Partial Correlation
Opportunities to learn	-0.41
Opportunities to use personal ideas	-0.30
Opportunities to apply skills and knowhow	-0.27
Amount of authority	-0.30
Independence in the work process	-0.29
Amount of influence	-0.34

principle of reward distribution applies to other situations in the Kibbutz.

Conclusions and Some Implications

Any result reported here—the distribution of rewards and their importance, the attractiveness of the work role and its different inputs—can probably be accounted for by alternative theoretical principles. On the whole, however, these data appear mutually consistent and most meaningful within the framework of equity theory. At the same time, this study raises several questions unresolved by the current concept of equity. Two of these and suggestions for their clarification will be briefly discussed below.

Conditions of equity and equality. As the present discussion implies, equity and equality norms co-exist in the Kibbutz. Specifically, the Kibbutz maintains the egalitarian principle in the material sphere, and the equity principle in the non-material sphere. To understand this phenomenon, a more basic question must first be answered: Under what conditions are these two principles more likely to occur? Sampson's (1968) model and the present analysis suggest one proposition; that is, the likelihood of equity increases and that of equality decreases as the group becomes preoccupied with "external" problems of adaptation and goal-attainment, and as considerations of rationality, objectivity and efficiency dominate the group's organization and use of its human and material resources.

Gamson's (1964) analysis of coalition formations contains a complementary proposition, pointing to circumstances favorable for equality and unfavorable for equity. Among alternative models of such formations, Gamson identifies one which is characterized by its "anti-competitive theory"; namely, outcomes are allocated equally regardless of individual input differences. This process is more likely to occur when problems of group solidarity are prominent so that equal sharing is accepted to maintain group integration.

The two propositions together argue that the stronger the emphasis on external rather than internal group problems—the more likely will equity prevail. On the other hand, as the group becomes more concerned with internal maintenance problems—equality will prevail over equity. These complementary propositions can account for much research concerned with the applicability of the equity principle. Most experimental work demonstrating the presence of equity involved ad-hoc groups whose members probably cared little about the problem of solidarity. On the other hand, when the groups studied were "real," as were the classmates in Morgan and Sawyer's investigation (1967), equality rather than equity was established as the dominant rule.

The two propositions can be elaborated if one recognizes that the relative dominance of equity or equality in a given situation need not apply to all types of outcomes available in the group. Equal sharing of material rewards, for example, may be vital for integrating some social groups; whereas large variations in allocating these outcomes can be tolerated in others. The family in Western culture represents a case where the egalitarian principle regulates the allocation of material rewards, while equity applies in the spheres of authority and influence. The co-existence in the Kibbutz of equity and equality can be similarly explained. Egalitarianism is maintained in the economic sphere since members agree that it is at the core of the Kibbutz' existence.[15] At the

same time, the pressures of economic development and their implications for a rational division of labor, led to greater role differentiation and the acceptance of equity in distributing intrinsic and power-related rewards. Note also that the collective control of consumption makes it technically easier for the Kibbutz to regulate the flow of material rewards. The less tangible stuff, like intrinsic rewards or influence, is more closely attached to specific roles and less prone to central regulation.

Inconsistentcy among outcomes. Suppose we try to predict how the managers in the poultry branch can reduce their sense of inequity. Since inequity is created from a disproportional distribution between outcomes and input it follows, as Adams suggested (1965), that inequity can be reduced through increasing outcomes. In other words, so long as the ratio of outcomes to inputs is improved, inequity will decrease, regardless of the specific outcomes which are received. However, a strain toward consistency among outcomes may exist, similar to the strain toward consistency between outcomes and inputs. Under such an assumption, the pattern of available outcomes becomes highly relevant for determining how inequity can be reduced. Specifically, improving the outcomes-to-inputs ratio by increasing already large outcomes may increase rather than decrease inequity. The latter is expected to decrease only through an improvement in those outcomes toward which a person has a relatively low standing.

As for the managers in this study, two different predictions can be made for reducing inequity among them from this discussion. According to the present formulation of equity, the amount of inequity among managers will be reduced if they get more of any of the three sets of outcomes examined here. On the other hand, if the assumption about the strain toward consistency is valid, only an improvement in the socio-emotional outcomes will decrease inequity.

The theoretical relevance to each other

---

[15] In a recent convention of one of the three major sectors of the Kibbutz movement, one of the several hundred delegates proposed to introduce some form of a material incentive system for enhanced productivity. The proposal was overwhelmingly rejected.

of the concepts of consistency and equity has emerged from the studies of Branden (1965) and Kardush (1968), and been joined in the same conceptual framework by Sampson (1968). Such an approach is useful in integrating phenomena which may otherwise appear mutually independent. The extension of the equity concept, implied by the proposition advanced here, is consistent with this approach and deserves to be tested empirically.

REFERENCES

Adams, S. J.
1965 "Inequity in social exchange." Pp. 267–99 in L. Berkowitz (ed.), Advances in Experimental Social Psychology. New York: Academic Press.

Aurbach, H. A.
1953 "Social stratification in Israel's collectives." Rural Sociology 18:25–34.

Ben-David, J.
1964 "The Kibbutz and the Moshav." Pp. 45–57 in J. Ben-David (ed.), Agricultural Planning and Village Community in Israel. U.S.E.S.C.O., Paris.

Ben-Yosef, A.
1963 The Purest Democracy in the World. New York: Harzl Press.

Blau, P.
1964 Exchange and Power in Social Life. New York: Wiley.

Brandon, A. C.
1965 "The relevance of expectations as an underlying factor in status incongruence." Sociometry 28:272–88.

Cohen, E.
1963 "Changes in the social structure of work in the Kibbutz." The Economic Quarterly 10:378–388 (Hebrew).
1966 "Progress and communality: value dilemmas in the collective movement." International Review of Community Development 15–16:3–18.
1972 "The structural dynamics of Kibbutz society." In The Kibbutz Society (unpublished).

Darin-Drabkin, H.
1962 The Other Society. New York: Harcourt.

Diamond, S.
1957 "Kibbutz and Shtetl: the history of an idea." Social Problems 5:71–9.

Etzioni, A.
1959 "The structural differentiations of elites in the Kibbutz." American Journal of Sociology 64:476–87.

Evans, M. G.
1969 "Conceptual and operational problems in the measurement of various aspects of job satisfaction." Journal of Applied Psychology 53:93–101.

Gamson, W. A.
1964 "Experimental studies of coalition formation." Pp. 81–110 in L. Berkowitz (ed.), Advances in Experimental Social Psychology. New York: Academic Press.

Goodman, P. S. and A. Friedman
1971 "An examination of Adams' theory of inequity." Administrative Science Quarterly 16:271–88.

Goulder, A. W.
1960 "The norm of reciprocity: a preliminary statement." American Sociological Review 25:161–178.

Herzberg, F., B. Mausner, R. O. Peterson, and D. F. Capwell
1957 Job Attitudes: Review of Research and Opinion. Psychological Service of Pittsburgh, Pittsburgh.

Herzberg, F., B. Mausner, R. O. Peterson, and B. B. Snyderman
The Motivation to Work. New York: Wiley.

Homans, G. C.
1961 Social Behavior: Its Elementary Forms. New York: Harcourt Brace.

Jaques, E.
1965 Measurement of Responsibility. London: Tavistock.
1961 Equitable Payment. New York: Wiley.

Kardush, M.
1968 Status Congruence and Social Mobility as Determinants of Small Group Behavior. University of California, Berkeley (unpublished report).

Lawler, E. E.
1971 Pay and Organizational Effectiveness: A Psychological View. New York: McGraw-Hill.

Leon, D.
1969 The Kibbutz. A New Way of Life. Oxford: Pergamon Press.

Meeker, B. F.
1970 "Decisions and exchange." American Sociological Review 5:463–83.

Mobley, W. H. and E. A. Lock
1970 "The relationship of value importance to satisfaction." Organizational Behavior and Human Performance 5:463–83.

Morgan, W. R. and J. Sawyer
1967 "Bargaining, expectations, and the preference of equality over equity." Journal of Personality and Social Psychology 6:139–49.

Patchen, M.
1961 "A conceptual framework and some empirical data regarding comparisons of social rewards." Sociometry 24:136–56.

Quinn, R. P., S. E. Seashore, T. Mangiony, D. A. Campbell, G. L. Staines, and M. McCullogh.
1971 Survey of Working Conditions, Washington, D.C.: U. S. Government Printing Office Document #2916-0001.

Rabkin, L. Y. and M. E. Spiro
1971 "Postscript: the Kibbutz in 1970." Pp. 255–72 in M. E. Spiro, Kibbutz-Venture

in Utopia. New York: Schocken, 1971 printing.

Revusky, A.
1945 Jews in Palestine. New York: Vanguard Press.

Robinson, J.
1969 "Occupational norms and differences in job satisfaction: a summary of survey research evidence." Pp. 25-72 in J. Robinson, et al. (eds.), Measures of Occupational Attitudes and Occupational Characteristics. Ann Arbor: Survey Research Center, Institute for Social Research.

Rosenfeld, E.
1951 "Social stratification in a 'classless' society." American Sociological Review 16:766–74.

Rosner, M.
1964 "Problems and rewards in the role of the branch manager." Hedim 29:46–57. (Hebrew).

Rosner, M. and A. Abend
1968 "Determinants of the readiness to hold offices in the Kibbutz." Hedim 33:121–25. (Hebrew).

Sampson, E. E.
1968 "Studies of status congruence." Pp. 225–70 in L. Berkowitz (ed.), Advances in Experimental Social Psychology. New York: Academic Press.

Sayles, L. R.
1958 Behavior of Industrial Work Groups: Predictions and Control. New York: Wiley.

Schwartz, R. D.
1957 "Democracy and collectivism in the Kibbutz." Social Problems 5:137–47.

Spiro, M. E.
1956 Kibbutz-Venture in Utopia. Cambridge: Harvard University Press.

Talmon-Garber, Y. and Z. Stupp.
1956 "Differentiation in collective settlements." Pp. 153–78 in Scripta Hierosolymitana. Jerusalem: Hebrew University.
1970 "Secular asceticism: patterns of ideological change." Pp. 469–504 in S. N. Eisenstadt, et al. (eds.), Integration and Development in Israel. New York: Praeger and Paul Mall.

Thibaut, J. W. and H. H. Kelley
1959 The Social Psychology of Groups. New York: Wiley.

Vallier, I.
1962 "Structural differentiation, production imperatives and communal norms: the Kibbutz in crisis." Social Forces 40:233–42.

Vroom, V. H.
1964 Work and Motivation. New York: Wiley.

Weik, K. E.
1966 "The concept of equity in the perception of pay." Administrative Science Quarterly 16:271–88.
1967 "Dissonance and task enhancement: a problem for compensation theory." Organizational Behavior and Human Performance 3:400–16.
1968 "Preferences among forms of equity." Organizational Behavior and Human Performance 3:400–416.

Weintraub, D., M. Lissak, and Y. Azmon
1969 Moshava, Kibbutz and Moshav. Patterns of Jewish Rural Settlement and Development in Palestine. Ithaca: Cornell University Press.

Dynamics of Social Stratification in Kibbutzim

Eliezer Ben-Rafael

Introduction: Three Types of Collectives

The existence of stratification in kibbutzim is an issue which arises widespread differences of interpretation among researchers. According to kibbutz ideology, common ownership of the means of production, direct democracy, and collective responsibility for cultural life, education and consumption should permit the development of a strictly egalitarian setting. Thus, although stratification processes which are quite evident in kibbutz reality have been given consideration in some pieces of research (see Rosenfeld, 1951), their impact has been largely minimized by other sociologists (see, for instance, Shepher, 1974). The purpose of the following pages is to throw some light on these processes by describing and analyzing the dynamics which, in spite of the dominant egalitarian ethos, have created and institutionalized them.

However, in order to analyze stratification in the kibbutz, it is necessary to consider this structure as simultaneously belonging to three types of collectives. First, the kibbutz can be defined as a *primary community* combining features of both the primary group and the ecological community (see Scott, 1967: 213-216, 434-437). Although its population generally numbers hundreds, the channels of communication among members are direct and most individual needs are met within the framework of the community. Moreover, membership implies a wide range of mutual obligations far beyond the usual meaning of "inhabitant." Yet, as in any other type of collective, the social status of the individual member, here also, depends on his performances or conformity to norms, which produces social layers and determines paths of mobility. These processes concretize mainly within the network of face-to-face relationships, as relational rewards such as esteem, prestige, authority and power are the exclusive means of status differentiation. The extent to which these rewards effectively create social distances between members can vary from one kibbutz to another according to size or composition of the population; but, in any case, in spite of its egalitarian ethos, the kibbutz rewards these behaviours of its members which contribute most to its social cohesion and cultural order. But, on the other hand, criteria of status are also influenced by the fact that the kibbutz exemplifies the *collective type of economic entrepreneur* (Pohoryles, 1974: 205-215). This concept means not only that the members commonly own the resources from which they make their living but also that they are dominated by an outlook which constantly pressures them to amplify these resources. Accordingly, these are the performances in the domains permitting the direct amplification of the

195

kibbutz's wealth, which are the most appraised and represent the most solid status assets of a member.

The fact that a kibbutz is a collective entrepreneur signifies also that, according to its prosperity, it endows its members with a *collective socio-economic status* vis-a-vis its environment. This status is "earned" through exploitation of common resources (including work power) and through economic competition and financial transactions with the "capitalist" outside, as well as with other kibbutzim; here lies an added dimension of the kibbutz stratification system. In order to succeed in this concern, the kibbutz has to emphasize the efficiency of its internal organization, and to encourage specialization of both individual roles and institutional spheres, which means that the structural features of the kibbutz undergo permanent changes. As these changes, however, depend in the kibbutz on the direct decisions of collective bodies, the interests of individuals or groups, emerging from internal status processes may have a bearing on the decisions made and be reflected in the structural shaping of the community.

On a third level, the individual kibbutz is also a part of a sector of kibbutzim which are interrelated in numerous ways. This is partially due to the kibbutz's desire to increase its impact on society, an aim which is conditioned by its ideological self-vision as a societal model to be referred to by the outside. This feature brings into relief a dimension of social status common to members of all kibbutzim; that is, they constitute a distinct *status group* within the larger setting. Such a position if not taken for granted by the "others", may produce tension in the relations of the kibbutz sector with its social, cultural and political environment.

In sum, the discussion of the dynamics of stratification in the kibbutz includes three interrelated but distinct dimensions and at each level, problems are present which express themselves in social change.

The First Dimension: Individual Status, Group Formation and Mobility within the Primary Community

From its inception, the kibbutz movement has been dominated by an ideology inspired by classic socialism at least as much as by local conditions (Gadon, 1965). Thus the kibbutz, at least at first, imparted esteem to its members chiefly according to their devotion to the collective ideals, and was heavily dependent on a leadership capable of answering practical problems in a manner compatible with the value premises (Baratz, 1957).

On the other hand, because of its desire to establish itself as a modern setting with respect to technology and production, members were also granted prestige according to work performance (Cohen, 1967). In time, a distinction in status was to emerge between "productive" activities contributing to the accumulation of capital, and "service" activities, often looked down upon as hampering the growth of the economic basis. These early developments were not in total harmony with the ideological perspective which insisted on complete equality, but they reflected the impact of practical considerations.

Positions of authority were also present from the earliest stages though, concerned as it was with avoiding inequality, the kibbutz developed a system of decision-making, headed by a general assembly, which permitted the participation of all members. In actuality, it was to those members who were more highly respected for their work performance, ideological conformity or leadership capability that most attention was given during assembly debates; and this, in turn, facilitated their being elected to public positions. However, on the whole, reticence, evident to this day, has generally characteriz-ed the members' attitude towards formal authority and, for the sake of democracy, rotation by general elections has always been consciously stressed with regard to top executive-level positions (Etzioni, 1958). Moreoever, consciousness of this ambiguous attitude held towards formal authority has led many an esteemed kibbutz member to prefer a wide informal audience to an official position (Shepher, 1974: 275-299).

This tendency was to weaken over the course of time as the amplification of resources called for increased competence. The result was the gradual emergence of hierarchies covering a wide range of positions both in the work area and in public func-tions (Talmon-Garber, 1969: 232-263). These included the ordinary worker or com-mittee member, the foreman or chairman of a sub-committee, the manager of large branches or important committees, and, finally, the general supervisory roles. In fact, today's criteria for selection at the highest level are quite demanding and combine technical know-how, organizational competence and public relations capability. Not surprisingly, although high level offices are periodically filled by election, only a limited number of especially gifted persons are actually taken into consideration for these jobs (Spiro, 1970: 25).

The general acceptance of authority, however, has not developed evenly in all domains. An ambivalent attitude is still maintained toward public "functionaries" in non-economic spheres where the unwillingness of higher-status members to accept the "obligations of noblesse" often means that these positions are left to less prominent persons. A secretary or chairman of the education or culture committee are often chosen from the second or third level of status, and as such usually do not enjoy as secure a "grant" of authority as do the treasurer or chairman of the economic commit-tee.

The clearest hierarchical division is found within the work setting (Cohen, 1967), where each member of a crew knows his position and where any sort of confusion which could damage productivity is firmly condemned. Moreover, as the branches have grown more complex, new elements of status have emerged, such as the knowledge of the specialist, the experience of the veteran, or the special capability to handle a specific job. These elements create relations of dependency and power as members become ranked not only on the basis of their actual contributions but also as an implicit reaction to the question, "how is it possible to do without them?" (see also Davis and Moore, 1945: 242-249). On the other hand, once a person's importance is related to the collective's dependecy upon him, his position on the whole becomes less sensitive to social control and less conditioned by the acceptance of normative exigen-cies (see Blau, 1964: 19-25). This development tends to reverse the ordinary relation of dependence between the individual and the community (see also Dahrendorf, 1968: 174) and it represents a potential danger to the members' continued commitment to social norms. In fact, there exist numerous cases (some of which are quite notorious in the kibbutz movement) of people who have achieved a position of force in their com-munity, and have "liberated" themselves from many normative restrictions, using at their personal convenience facilities (cars, travels abroad, etc.) endowed to them for reasons of work.

As a whole, the phenomena described above have created in the community a complex status map characterized by both the proliferation of levels and the widening of social distance among the members. In this context one no longer feels entirely at ease with any and every member (Res. Sem., 1977) and therein lies a good reason for the weaker social cohesion one finds in many kibbutzim. Intimate subgroups are now discernible at the lunch table in the collective dining room, at social parties in private flats and even, at the general assembly, in the way people are sitting together (Talmon-Garber, 1969: 205-222). Such groupings, frequently based on seniority, origin or age, pose a contrast to the former "vertical groups, such as that of the founders, built around central personalities, or of the work crew, led by the branch manager (Etzioni, 1957) and which have been able to maintain individual conformity to norms. The multiple intimate circles which have emerged on the basis of more or less homogeneous status have, on the contrary, a much weaker hold on their members and control their opinions and behavior to a lesser extent (see also Homans, 1974: 316-335). Their impact is mainly salient in the large kibbutzim where social distances among members are especially wide. There, according to the author's personal observation, some groups at the bottom of the social ladder may even share blunt cynical attitudes towards kibbut norms and values.

Homogeneous groupings, however, may easily become foci of power. A stand of active dissent in public debates may eventually sustain claims for certain privileges or higher positions; younger groups, for instance, have sometimes demanded that people from their ranks be chosen for top responsibilities. Yet, the bargaining power of such groups fluctuates according to circumstances. For example, a recent research (for partial findings see Ben-Rafael, Tagliacozzo et al., 1975) has shown that many kibbutzim were more generous in allocating positions to their first cohorts of sons when becoming adult members of the community than to the twelfth or fifteenth cohorts. While the age gap between sons and fathers promised the first cohorts rapid access to responsibilities (when no intermediary age group exists), the younger sons were faced with older brothers and had but few chances for quick mobility. Against the background of a lack of immediate interesting prospects, the number of emigrants from this group of younger sons has frequently reached more than a third (unpublished data of the federation).

Yet, as even in the largest kibbutzim no member is altogether unknown to anybody, the "gifts" of each one gradually achieve "public notoriety". Thus there are rarely real bottlenecks for individual upward mobility in the long run, as long as such mobility does not drastically endanger the equilibrium of the general status map. This map is not enforced by any objective index comparable to that of personal income in the outside, and mobility is permitted only at a cautious rate, in order to avoid shifts which could (and sometimes do) entail crises of social relations (see also Spiro, 1970: 217-235). Of course, the very concept of individual mobility is contradictory to the egalitarian ethos, but so too is the factual differentiation of status—endowing certain people or groups with special preeminence—which exists in the community.

In this context, both balanced and unbalanced social status can be found (see Lensky, 1954). The members who enjoy a balanced status are found mainly in the middle of the social ladder, i.e., those in charge of work crews who are also known to behave generally according to social norms. Then, they "accumulate", in a more or less homogeneous manner, the middle-range prestige endowed to their job position (especially if it belongs to the "productive" sector), the extent of power and authority resulting from the level of their specific responsibility, and the esteem rewarding their conformism to social norms in general.

On the other hand, members with a greater responsibility receive broader public support, but because of their very preeminence, are also an easy target of criticism

(Rozner, 1963). When their capabilities allow them external occupations (such as in regional services, the bodies of the kibbutz movement, or political parties), the esteem they are personally granted is often mixed with an unfavorable appreciation of what is assumed to be their neglect of the kibbutz's internal needs. In addition, with the pro-liferation of subgroups, criteria of status also vary among the population of the kibbutz and the status of the individual member fluctuates under the disparate influence of the numerous circles.

Whatever its reasons, unbalance of status makes it difficult for some members to maintain solid social relationships when these do not meet their expectations. As a result of such frustration, some people tend to isolate themselves and reduce their par-ticipation in the general activity of the kibbutz. Others look to the external environ-ment and eventually have more social relationships outside the settlement than inside. A few become "tough guys", harsh in their attitude to their fellow members (Field Observations, 1978). In sum, unbalance of status tends to cause loneliness, decline of involvement in the community, and some aggressiveness in social relations.

Such consequences, it is true, are not in most cases accepted as inevitable by the kibbutzim. Some, for instance, have not hesitated to have recourse to techniques of group dynamics (without much success—see Meron, 1972: 36), with the aim of easing social relations and reducing distances among members. Others have been sensitive to specific problems directly resulting from the status "game", such as the plight of the elder member who, due to his feeble participation in the working area, has seen his social stand dramatically "devaluated". These kibbutzim have instituted a pension fund (owned by the federation of kibbutzim) to insure that the elderly remain a source of income for the community. Since the pension is directly handed over to the general treasury, and living expenses are provided to everyone anyway, this pattern has evolved mainly in order to strengthen the elderly person's status in the community. This is the very first case where money has openly served to bestow status in the kibbutz.

The Second Dimension: Collective Socio-economic Status and Institutional Changes

Status in the community has been widely influenced by the transformation of cells of pioneers into prosperous communities and, beyond status differentiation among the members, there also is a collective socio-economic status, common to all members of one kibbutz. From this viewpoint, the individual kibbutz is an entrepreneur which gains assets by competition with other entrepreneurs on the external market. Various classes of kibbutzim may be distinguished according to age, which is, in general, cor-related with size and levels of prosperity (Friedman, 1965: 45). High-status kibbutzim constitute most often real "empires" on the Israeli scale. More than fifty years old and numbering more than five hundred adult members (i.e. a population of about one thousand when children, candidates, and non-permanent inhabitants are taken into consideration), they frequently possess two or three industrial plants, several well-developed agricultural branches and modern collective services. Their population as a rule, enjoys a high standard of living.

In order to attain this prosperity, the specialization of each member in the working area has been encouraged as well as that of every sphere of activity (Cohen, 1973), while many new arrangements were implemented in the organizational scheme of the kibbutz. These, however, require decisions of the membership and, most often, do not only reflect concern for the welfare of the community and its "conciliation" with the collective's ideological values, but also, and though in a non-overt manner, general problems and specific interests emerging from internal stratification processes.

In brief, what has appeared in recent decades is that the economy and the family have become central foci of reference for many issues requiring new arrangements. The expansion of these two spheres is by no means unrelated to the widening of social distances among members and the loosening of cohesion in the community. These processes have contributed, on the one hand, to a more instrumental outlook on the part of many towards the "outcome" of the collective system (i.e., the socio-economic status it provides), and on the other, to a greater incentive to strengthen privacy by emphasizing the aspect of the family, whose internal life remains beyond the scope of collective control. Moreover, specific interests have also been behind these changes. A high status group, the "specialists", has raised the economic sector to its present position, and it is a deprived element in the community, the female population, whose efforts have increased the influence of the family.

The growing importance of the economic domain has been paralleled by a shift in the character of the economic elite (Yassour, 1976: 148-153). For the pioneers, mostly originating from the urban middle-class, it was by no means easy to become agriculturalists. Those who became efficient workers and demonstrated organizational abilities were to manage the principal branches for years. Their general influence in the community, however, was counterbalanced by that of the ideological leaders at an epoch when commitment to collective ideals was at its highest among the membership (Nahshon, 1965: 82-83). With the evolution of the economy, however, a "technocratic" elite appeared constituted by experienced professionals, engineers or economists. On the basis of its larger membership than in the past, this elite has permitted more frequent rotation in top positions, but it finds its place permanently in the upper stratum of the "productive" area. In view of the knowledge required, decision-making in general economic matters is also, in practice, left to it, and has become less and less subject to the control of non-economic organs (Friedman, 1965: 72-73). Thus, the work committee, which is responsible for allocating work days to all activities—including non-economic services—constitutes a sub-committee of the economic committee. Decisions of any committee requiring manpower or a budget, whatever its specific responsibility, must be endorsed by the economic committee, which of course is also in charge of kibbutz policy with respect to external economic and financial markets. The fact that this economic committee, though democratically elected, is, as a rule, manned by people chosen from among the "specialists" (Field Observation, 1978) indicates not only the latter's power in the community, but also the importance endowed by the members at all to the collective socio-economic status which can be theirs only through competent exploitation of common resources.

As for the family, its strength in the settlement (Talmon-Garber, 1969: 12-35) can be partially related to the changes which have occurred in the women's status (Rozner, 1967). In the context of the rational orientation dominant in the working area, the female member has been directed chiefly towards occupations assumed to be in keeping with her capability, and which are often of a lower status (the "non-productive" jobs). This situation was bound to arouse tensions in a community that had declared itself in favor of sexual equality in the most extreme terms. By returning to the traditional feminine image and abandoning her former ambitions to a position undifferentiated from that of the male member, the woman has become the agent of family "imperialism", even at the cost of shouldering a heavier burden in everyday life. Her constant efforts have made the family a most salient aspect of kibbutz life, the growing influence of which has often been at the expense of and in conflict with, collective spheres (Symposium, 1971). This process is well exemplified by the case of the evening meal. In general there are no negative feelings against the common dining-room which provides a useful meal service during the working day. However, during the evening dinner, the only meal when the members of the same family eat together, an entirely different kind of atmosphere tends to develop. Tension grows between the family's need to assert itself and the collective role of the dining room. As a result, numerous families have elected to take their evening meal (prepared by the women) in their own flats.

Similar tension has arisen between the family and the educational institution and it is expressed at night for instance, when the parents bring their children to the Children's House to sleep. The role of the nurse who works there is to end the children's day in the spirit of collective education, according to which the kibbutz is the main educational agent. Tension develops between parents who are anxious to express concern for their children's needs, and the nurse who, in contrast, worries about maintaining permanent norms (see also Bar-Yosef, 1960). This has, most often, led to a change in the nurse's role, which has been reduced to the turning off of the lights, while the parents have obtained total responsibility for ending the children's evening. What is more, in several settlements the children no longer sleep in the Children's House and accommodations have been made in the parents' home.

The influence which has been gained by the family is reflected in numerous areas. For one, weddings, contrary to the past, are now sumptuously celebrated. Economically the family has been allocated a budget with which it purchases an ever increasing number of consumption items. The educational role of parents is now fully recognized, and their flat has even become a home where several generations meet together on frequent occasions. In the new situation, the woman feels stronger *vis-a-vis* the kibbutz since she represents a social circle deeply anchored in the community, while at the same time she does not depend in any way on her husband for a living (Gerson, 1965). The case of her success, however, results not only from feelings of guilt among the males for having deprived her of her original position, but also from a general desire among the membership for increased privacy in a community which has experienced a weakening of cohesion and a great deal of tension in social relationships.

Both increased privacy and the diffusion of a pragmatic outlook towards the collective system entail a decline in the members' participation in non-economic collective spheres. This is revealed, for instance, by the frequently poor attendance at the general assembly or at cultural events (Ben-Rafael, Livneh, et al., 1973). What is at stake here is the very existence of a collective settlement which cannot be maintained, in the long run, without active many-sided cooperation among members. No wonder that a revitalization of cultural, social and political participation is on the schedule of many kibbutzim and much energy is being invested in new activities. Festivals have been created such as the settlement's day or woman's day; collective services such as the dining room, the club or the general store have been reappraised; the circulation of information of public interest has been emphasized and executive bodies have deliberately been decentralized. Such innovations taking place in the late 1970's are no longer the fruit of spontaneous initiatives but rather of rational thinking by relevant committees in an effort to bolster non-economic domains, without restricting in any substantial way the prerogatives of the economy or the family.

The Third Dimension: The Kibbutz Movement as a Status Group

The dynamics of kibbutz stratification, however, cannot be fully understood without turning to an additional aspect of the kibbutz's position in society (Weintraub, Lissak, et al., 1960). During the pre-state period, the kibbutz constituted in the eyes of many outsiders a point of reference for both its devotion to national tasks and the ideological values it represented and with which large segments of the population identified. The members themselves interpreted their endeavour as a model to be followed by society in the future and many of them were deeply involved in politics.

Depending on their specific ideological background, however, the different kibbutz federations at their beginnings variously emphasized the quality of their way of life on the one hand, and their political ambitions on the other. The most veteran of the federations, moved by humanistic socialism, was primarily committed to the normative models in its settlements and was very hesitant to initiate any political action in the outside (Katzenelson, 1965: 60-64). This federation is the only one, among the three principal, which never set up its own party. In contrast, another federation influenced by revolutionary social democracy, considered the kibbutz as a model for the "masses". Less "aristocratic" but more politically-minded than the former, it aspired to fill a leading role among the working class (Tabenkin, 1965: 66-76) and headed, for many years, its own political organization. The third main federation (Hazan, 1965: 241-252), which emerged from a youth movement, was at its outset very concerned with rigorous principles of collectivism. Later, it extended this concern to the field of political action, and set up an independent party. Under the influence of Russian Marxism, this federation embraced the Leninist theory of "proletarian vanguardism", which consistently integrated its elitist self-consciousness with its revolutionary outlook.

Only years after the creation of the state, when political militancy had decreased in society, did political parties based on kibbutz federations—having failed to achieve a large outside public following—find the way to collaborate with each other on a permanent basis. However, as the different federations had already become anchored in a great variety of power positions (like youth movements, parties or the national bureaucracy), total unification was (and still is) fraught with many difficulties (see also Ben-David (ed), 1964).

The prestige of the kibbutz movement in general was further affected by the industrial take-off (from the mid-1950's on) which reconciled Israeli society to the value of individualism, and gave a new legitimacy to the growth of a middle class. The kibbutz concomitantly experienced a sharp decline in prestige (Lissak, 1967) and it was soon to undergo an acute moral crisis (see Diamond, 1957: 132-140) entailing many internal problems. The shift in attitude from asceticism to the encouragement of consumption which came out at this epoch (the level of per-capita expenditure on consumer goods was soon to place most kibbutzim quite high in the middle class) has been interpreted by commentators (Talmon-Garber, 1969: 233-263) as a compensatory mechanism for the movement's loss of status in society. Moreover, in the new climate, the kibbutz was less able than in the past to control individual aspirations (Ben-Rafael, Tagliacozzo et al., 1975: 137-139) and a new concept much in vogue in the kibbutzim of the 1970's is that of "self-fulfillment", referring to the development of individual capabilities, unrelatedly to the community's objective requirements. As a result, new kinds of occupations, such as professional work outside the kibbutz, have become legitimized and academic higher learning among the younger generations has reached rates far beyond the direct needs of the collective (Gamzon, 1975). Although "unproductive" or external activities are still regarded ambivalently, under the new conditions, characterized as they are by strong influences from the outside as well as by weaker internal cohesion, the barriers against personal aspirations have been lowered and the kibbutz is now faced with the challenge of satisfying the goals of individuals who are less sensitive than in the past to the judgement of public opinion.

Yet, on the other hand, the kibbutz has not given up all its elitistic aspirations. By finally accepting the new "rules" of the status game in society it has launched a counter-attack over preeminence. Economic success now being a dominant criterion of prestige, the kibbutz magnifies its entrepreneur spirit not only by achieving the industrialization of the individual settlement but also by establishing regional plants by joint initiatives of several kibbutzim (Cohen & Leshem, 1969). The army now being the principal pillar of national security, the federations encouraged the sons of the kibbutz to volunteer for elite units during their military service (see Amir, 1967 and 1969; Agin, 1970). Furthermore, the federations have striven to maintain their position on the overall political, cultural and educational scene in Israel.

To be sure, the new rules of the status game bear a different significance for the kibbutz than in the past since it has been deprived now of any "guaranteed" position. Today it must compete with other groups of entrepreneurs, or with new social elites such as the military or the academics according to criteria which are by no means inherent in its own ideology (Rozner & Ovnat, 1976: 243-276; also Guivat Havivah).

Conclusions: Stratification in the Kibbutz as a Private Case of a General Problem

The three dimensions discussed in the above delineate the main features of the kibbutz system of stratification; though these dimensions interact with each other, they constitute three distinct startpoints of the system's dynamics.

The most conspicuous feature of the kibbutz as a primary community is the "neutralization" of income as a direct basis of the internal status of individuals. Up to now, concepts like salary or financial share do not exist inside the community and material goods, cultural resources or educational facilities are distributed among members unrelatedly to their social position. These facts, however, do not prevent money from playing an indirect role: to a large extent the member's contribution to the collective's income as well as the specific weight of this contribution in the work setting are by no means irrelevant to one's prestige or power in the community and these criteria join the other, less economy-oriented ones—like conformism to social norms or leadership capability—in the creating of a complex status map. Thus, though stratification in the kibbutz is but of restricted social consequences and refers mainly to the shaping of relations among members, without crystallizing social classes cross-cutting the community, the impact of status differentiation remains discernible in a whole set of phenomena such as the emergence of intimate subgroups, a variety of balanced and unbalanced types of status, the existence of diverse paths of social mobility, and the widening of social distances among people; moreover, here too there is a possibility that a powerful position could induce a "self-liberation" from normative restrictions. Thus, as a whole, the kibbutz shows that social stratification can develop on the basis of relational rewards even in the absence of "objective" economic antagonism, when ownership over productive means is common and collective responsibility rules many additional domains of social life.

The part played by financial income, however, becomes overt and dominant at the level of the socio-economic status common to all members of the same kibbutz and which is conditioned by the common exploitation of resources and facilities. This dimension of the member's status grows more and more important in his eyes not only because of the modern ethos characterizing him anyway, but also of his feebler concern, in the stratified reality, for other aspects of collective life. The more the members emphasize this dimension, the more they nourish inside the community, prestige and power differentiations as far as these refer to attributes relevant to the growth of the kibbutz's wealth. Yet, in return, the members also demand not only a high standard of living, but also ever more individual freedoms. The paradoxical phenomenon, here, is precisely the strength of pragmatic outlooks, familism and individualism in a social setting moved by a collectivistic ideology. The kibbutz is the very proof that such a possibility may exist, in given circumstances.

Another aspect of the kibbutz's relationship with the environment is the fluctuation of the social prestige of the movement as a whole. Generally stated, the loss of the movement's preeminence in recent decades has caused a decline in its self-ascribed "obligations" and has set free the members' aspirations not only to enjoy the fruit of their work but also to multiply their possibilities of personal development. These orientations have come out in a contradictory situation where most kibbutzim have solidified their socio-economic stand parallelly to the weakening of the movement's status in society. Thus, the case of the kibbutzim illustrates an inverse relation between prestige in society and economic achievements.

In the light of this evolution the question which arises is if the kibbutz, at all, has remained faithful to itself? One generation ago, the kibbutz was characterized by an aggressive ideology, well-defined organizational principles, and a preeminent position in society; today, on the contrary, the ideology has lost much of its importance in the eyes of numerous members, the organizational patterns have become diversified and the kibbutz movement is quite remote from the center of the social stage. On the other hand, however, all these changes have not yet overcome its refusal to let in money as a basis of inner social differentiation; while most changes have not been taken for granted, and new patterns have been consciously initiated with the purpose of maintaining some impact of the ideological premises. Steps have been sponsored to reduce social distances, to increase cooperation in non-economic collective spheres and to enforce the movement's status in society. The scope of these efforts, whatever their efficiency, shows that the basic premises are still influential in the structural evolution of the community. At this viewpoint, the processes undergoing the kibbutz may be considered as changes occuring "within" the system, i.e., without erasing its main principles, rather than changes "of" the system (Coser, 1965: 151-152). This system was defined here as a primary community constituting a collective entrepreneur and belonging to a sectorial status group.

It is true that the changes discussed in the above reveal processes contrasting with the community's ideological self-definition as an ideal expression of equality and cooperation; yet, it is the fact that the modern ethos, too, is a dominant characteristic of this type of setting which creates and amplifies the tensions inherent to its evolution. Thus, the stratificational model exhibited by the kibbutz, constitutes, in final analysis, but a particular case of a general problem referring to all modern and free societies, namely, the basic contradiction existing between democratic and egalitarian values, and the "spirit of capitalism".

REFERENCES

AGIN
1970   "The Sons of the Kibbutz in the Army," *Niv Hakvutzot*, vol. 19, pp. 50-55 (Heb.).
AMIR, Y.
1967   "Adjustment and Promotion of Soldiers from Kibbutzim", *Megamot*, no. 15 (Heb).
AMIR, Y.
1969   "The Effectiveness of the Kibbutz Born Soldier in the IDF", *Human Relations*, no. 22.
BARAZ, J.
1967   *Mon village en Israel*, Paris, Plon.
BEN-DAVID, J. (ed.)
1964   *Agricultural Planning and Village Community in Israel*, Paris, UNESCO.
BAR-YOSEF, R.
1960   "Socialization Patterns in the Kibbutz and their Impact on the Social Structure", *Megamot*, vol. 2 (Heb.) pp. 23-32.
BEN-RAFAEL, E.
1976   "Conflicts Sociaux Sans Antagonismes Economiques", in Rambaud, P. (ed.) *Sociologie Rurale*, Paris, La Haye, Mouton, pp. 136-142.
BEN-RAFAEL, E.
1978   "Entrepreneurs in a Collective Community: The Kibbutz Regional Industrialist", in Konopnicki, M. & Van de Walle, G., *Cooperation as an Instrument for Rural Development Communities*, London; International Cooperative Alliance, pp. 76-83.
BEN-RAFAEL, A. TAGLIACOZZO, V. KRAUS
1975   "L'Abandon du Kibbutz par les Jeunes" in *Sociologia Ruralis*, vol. XV, no. 23, pp. 131-141.
BEN-RAFAEL, E., LIVNEH and WOLFENSOHN
1973   "Democracy in the Kibbutz", *Social Res. Review*, no. 2, Haifa (Heb.).
BLAU, P. M.
1964   *Exchange and Power in Social Life*, U.S.: John Wiley & Sons, Inc.
COHEN, E.
1967   "Changes in the Social Structure of the Domain of Work in the Kibbutz", in Eisenstadt, Adler, Bar-Yosef, Kahane (eds.), *The Social Structure of Israel*, Jerusalem: Academon (Heb.).
COHEN, E.
1973   "The Structural Transformation of the Kibbutz", in N. Hirsch (ed.), *Exploration in Social Change*, 2nd ed.
COHEN, E. & E. LESHEM.
1969   *Survey of Regional Cooperation in Three Regions of Collective Settlements*, Rehovot: Settlement Study Center.
COSER, L.
1965   *The Functions of Social Conflict*, London: Routledge and Kegan Paul.
DAHRENDORF, R.
1968   "On the Origin of Inequality Among Men" in Dahrendorf, *Essays in the Theory of Society*, Stanford University Press, pp. 151-178.
DAVIS, K. & W. MOORE.
1945   "Some Principles of Stratification", *American Sociological Review*, X, No. 2, pp. 242-259.
DIAMOND, S.
1957   "The Kibbutz: Utopia in Crisis", *Dissent*, Vol. 4, pp. 132-140.
ETZIONI, A.
1957   "Solidaristic Work-groups in Collective Settlements", *Human Organization*, no. 16.
ETZIONI, A.
1958   *The Organizational Structure of the Kibbutz*, Doctoral Dessertation, Berkeley, University of California.

Field Observations of a group of kibbutz members on a six month course at the Efal Kibbutz
    College, 1978—unpublished (Heb.).
FRIEDMAN, G.
    1965   *La Fin du peuple Juif?* pp. 41-100, Paris: Nrf.
GADON, S.
    1965   *Paths of the Kwutzah and the Kibbutz*, vol. 1, Tel Aviv: Aianot (Heb.).
GAMZON, Z. F.
    1975   "The Kibbutz and Higher Education: Cultures in Collision?" Paper presented
    at the *1975 Meeting of the American Sociological Association*, San Francisco.
HAZAN, Y.
    1965   "The Kibbutz, the People, The Class" in Gadon, *op. cit.,* pp. 244-252.
HOMANS, G. C.
    1961   *Social Behaviour—Its Elementary Forms*, London: Routledge and Kegan Paul.
KATZENELSON, B.
    1965   "The Specific Character of the Kwutzah" in Gadon, *op. cit.*, pp. 60-64.
LENSKI, G.
    1954   "Status Crystallization: A Non-Vertical Dimension of Social Status", *American Socio-
    logical Review*, XIX, pp. 415-413.
LISSAK, M.
    1967   "Images of Society and Class in the Pre-State Period and in Israel," in Eisenstadt,
    Adler, Bar-Yosef and Kahana (eds.), op. cit., pp. 203-214.
MERON, H.
    1972   "The Dangers of Group Dynamics" in *Igeret Hahinuch*, No. 2, p. 36 (Heb.).
NAHSHON, E.
    1965   "From Theory to Practice", in Gadon, S., *op. cit.*, vol. 2, pp. 62-63 (Heb.).
POHORYLES, S.
    1974   "Kibbutz et Moshav Aujourd'hui et Demain", in Desroche, Konopnicki, Landau,
    Rambaud, *Societes Villageoises, Auto-Developpement et Intercooperation*, Paris, La Haye:
    Mouton, pp. 205-215.
ROSENFELD, E.
    1951   "Social Stratification in a Classless Society", *American Sociological Review*, Vol. 16,
    pp. 758-774.
ROZNER, M.
    1967   "Women in the Kibbutz: Changing Status and Concepts", *Asian and African Studies*,
    vol. 3, pp. 38-66.
ROZNER, M.
    1963   "Difficulties and Rewards in the Role of Branch Manager", *Hedim*, no. 46
    (Heb.).
ROZNER, M., A. OVNAT.
    1975   "The Position of the Kibbutz in Israeli Society", *Social Research Review*, 8,
    pp. 243-276 (Heb.).
SCOTT, W. R. (ed.)
    1967   *Social Processes and Social Structures*, New York: Holt, Rinehart and Winston, Inc.
SHEPHER, Y.
    1974   "The Kibbutz" in Weller, L., *Sociology in Israel,* Westpoint, Conn. Greenwoods
    Press, pp. 229-275.
SPIRO, M. E.
    1970   *Kibbutz—Venture in Utopia*, N.Y., Shocken Books.
    Symposium (1971) *Women in the Kibbutz*—Haifa University.
TABENKIN, J.
    1965   "A New Society—A Way for the Many" in Gadon *op. cit.*, pp. 66-76 (Heb.).
TALMON-GERBER, Y.
    1969   *Individual and Society in the Kibbutz*, Jerusalem: Magnes (Heb.).

WEINTRAUB, D., M. LISSAK, Y. AZMON.
    1960 *Moshava, Kibbutz and Moshav*, London & Ithaca, Cornell University Press.
YASSOUR, A.
    1976 "The Danger of Industrial Success to the Kibbutz. Discouraging observations of a
          Non-Professional Spectator" in Landau, Y., Konopnicki, M., Desroche, H.,
          Rambaud, P., *Rural Communities, Inter-Cooperation and Development*, N.Y. Praeger,
          pp. 148-159.

Is Direct Democracy Feasible in Modern Society? The Lesson of the Kibbutz Experience

Menachem Rosner and Nissim Cohen

Introduction

During the last decade a growing interest – both theoretical and practical – has developed in many countries regarding basic changes in the conventional patterns of decision-making and management. Concepts such as participatory democracy, industrial democracy, self-management, self-government and self-determination which were initially formulated during the 19th and early 20th century as a part of socialist and anarchist ideology, and/or of classical democratic theory regained significance and appeal for the larger public and especially for the younger generation. One of the theoreticians of self-management in France has even stated, that the goal of this movement should be defined as socialization of means of government. Self-management is the leading idea of this century in the same way as socialization of the means of production was the leading idea of the previous one (Rosanvallon, 1973). In this general framework it is understandable, that a growing interest has been shown in the experience of the 230 kibbutzim in Israel, where direct democracy is implemented not only by the weekly general assembly, which is the main focus of decision making, but also by the large dispersal of authority and influence among members through rotation of personnel in managerial positions, administration by committees and a non-bureaucratic and non-hierarchic organizational structure.

On the other hand, several scientists have used the kibbutz as a paradigm to show that direct democracy, in its different aspects, can be realized only in very special and temporary conditions and cannot be considered as a lasting social phenomenon. Dahrendorf (1959) addresses himself particularly to the institution of "rotation" and admits, that according to his definition of classes

"the fluctuation of personnel prevents the formation of classes and conflict between them" (p. 221).

But, without presenting evidence related to the kibbutz, he concludes:

"There is no reason to assume that a stable society can operate on the principle of the continuously patterned exchange of the personnel for authority positions."

209

Vallier (1962) stresses the conflict between the requirements of performance, specialization, discipline and universalism and the democratic and egalitarian norms of the kibbutz. E. Cohen (1966) stresses the conflict between the need for professional competence and expertise and non-professional democratic decision-making. The most comprehensive attempt to state the difficulties facing the implementation of direct democracy in modern society was performed by A. Meister (1973) in his analysis of the development of a large number of voluntary organizations, cooperatives and work-communities in Italy and France during a long period of history. On the basis of this analysis he developed a theory of what might be called an "iron law of degeneration of direct democracy" and claimed to find further support for this theory in the evolution of Yugoslav self-management and of kibbutz-democracy.

A similar evolution, although with different features, was found by Ostergaard and Halsey (1965) in the English retail cooperatives:

"If one looks at the practice rather than the theory, then cooperative democracy appears to be a cooperative oligarchy" (p. 219)

The main facts sustaining this assertion are: (1) the decline in members' participation in assemblies (business meetings), the reduced frequency of assemblies and their restricted functions; (2) the growing influence of employees and officials, the lengthening of the term of office of board members and the rarity of sitting members defeated in election.

Meister and Ostergaard-Halsey agree in their programmatic recommendations for the organizations they studied. Both consider a return to direct democracy a non-realistic goal and recommend to assure the functioning of the representative system mainly by a two-party system and formal devices for democratic control of the leadership's activities. Both acknowledge that their recommendations were influenced by the sociological analysis of the American International Typographical Union. This union has been presented as a deviant case, that was able to avoid the oligarchic tendencies common to other trade-unions and to maintain – on the basis of its two-party system – a well-functioning democracy with frequent changes in leadership, an active membership and a relatively small status-gap between leaders and members (Lipset, Trow and Coleman, 1962).

We shall try to present the kibbutz experience as another deviant case – deviating from the patterns established by Meister for the "degeneration of direct democracy". Analyzing the kibbutz-experience on the basis of data from recent comprehensive research and studies, we shall try to answer the following questions:

1) What is the degree of members' participation both in decision-making processes and in management and administration? What are the different

forms of participation and what are the motivations to participate? What is the authority and function of the general assembly and other self-management units (branch-assemblies, committees, etc.)?
2) Are there tendencies toward oligarchic concentration of authority and power, and if not, how have they been avoided?
3) What is the impact of contingency factors like ideological commitment and social cohesion of members, size and complexity of organization both on the participation of members and on the oligarchic tendencies?
4) What is the relationship between type of democracy – direct or representative – and degree of participation and prevention of oligarchic tendencies? What is the theoretical basis of kibbutz-democracy?

A common denominator of the doubts expressed concerning the possibility for a lasting effective functioning of kibbutz democracy (by Dahrendorf, 1959; Schoeck, 1971; Vallier, 1962 etc.) and of the more general analysis of Meister (1973) and Ostergaard (1965) rooted in Michels (1959) and Weber's theories is the assumption of an inevitable contradiction between structural differentiation and direct democracy. While on the one hand structural differentiation (specialization and expertise) is considered necessary to achieve efficiency, on the other hand it inhibits the joint decision of members on collective issues, since such decisions need specialized knowledge. It also inhibits the possibility of rotation in managerial and executive functions, since professional knowledge and expertise are needed in these positions.

While on the basis of these assumptions we can predict a negative relationship between structural differentiation and democracy, other theories predict a positive relationship between them. These theories stress mainly the strong link between structural differentiation and modernization and economic development and the level of education in different countries and the degree of democracy.

Another theoretical approach stating this positive relationship was recently developed by Hondrich (1973) on the basis of the assumption, that a higher degree of specialization causes a higher degree of inter-dependency and therefore limitations on non-democratic government.

While the first line of argument was more specifically related to direct democracy, the second one deals with democracy in general. Therefore, it will be important to explore the differences between direct democracy and the more conventional forms of representative democracy to understand more clearly their relationship with structural differentiation.

The theoretical basis of kibbutz-democracy

Is the transfer from direct to representative democracy a simple change in organizational pattern or does it imply a more basic transformation related both to philosophical assumptions and to the social structure of the organization or the community concerned? This question has special importance in the analysis of kibbutz-democracy's adaptation both to the structural changes in kibbutz-society and economy and to certain ideological changes. The latter are functions of the relationship between the kibbutz and Israeli society and of the succession of generations in the kibbutz. Some authors (Dahl, 1970) conceive the different types of democracy as points on a continuum assuming that for a given size and complexity it is necessary to choose the proper type of democracy.[1] Other authors (Schumpeter, 1950; Gellner, 1967; C. Pateman, 1970) assume that there is a basic distinction between two conceptions of democracy: (a) the classical conception based on the direct participation of citizens in decision-making and management; (b) the modern conception, where the participation of citizens is limited basically to the elections of representatives, who have legitimate authority to govern society in the name of the citizens. We agree with the later-mentioned authors, that the two conceptions are based on different sets of values and on different social conditions. The model of liberal representative democracy is implemented in different forms and degrees in the countries with democratic systems of government. Concrete examples of modern societies or even communities and organizations governed during long periods on the basis of the classical concepts of democracy are almost non-existent and the kibbutz-experience is an exceptional case.

Although no theory of kibbutz-democracy has been formulated either by the founders or by the different movements, we will try to develop a theoretical model of the kibbutz-version of classical democracy and compare it with the modern concept in its liberal version. This model is based both on opinions of kibbutz-leaders and scholars and on the analysis of the assumption behind its democratic patterns and practice.(See Chart 1).

1) We assume that the basic goal of liberal democracy is the assurance of individual rights and freedom, of a due process of electing representatives, and of controlling their activities. This goal developed from a permanent struggle between rulers and ruled, and from the attempt of the ruled to limit the possible misuse of authority by the ruler.

The basic goal of kibbutz-democracy is to overcome the division between rulers and ruled, and to avoid the possible conflict between the private needs of the members and the general needs of the kibbutz. Kibbutz-democracy is seen as an instrument towards a growing identification of the member with the community. Through his participation in the assembly and in committees the member becomes more aware of the needs of his fellow-members and of the more general needs of the kibbutz

Chart 1: Two types of democracy

	Kibbutz democracy	Liberal democracy
1 The goal	Identification with community, integration between personal needs and needs of the kibbutz	Assurance of individual rights
	Abolition of division between ruler and ruled	Limitation of misuse of authority by rulers
2 Citizens participation in decision-making	Direct participation through general assembly	Indirect participation through election of representatives
3 Relationship between different types of power	Location of legislative, executive and judiciary power in the general assembly	Separation between the three types of power to avoid domination of executive power
4 Process of decision-making	Determination of means by majority vote on the basis of value consensus. No permanent interest-groups	Fair competition between interest-groups on the basis of agreed rules of the game
5 Basis for decision-making	Particularist approach with minimum written regulations	Universalist written laws and rules
6 Distribution of authority	Dispersion of authority and rotation in offices	Hierarchy of formal authority and permanency in offices

community and its sub-units, work-branches, social groups, etc. Crystalization of individual needs and interests would be influenced by this mutual awareness.

2) According to the liberal and pluralistic conception of democracy, the democratic decision-making process, which is mainly a process of election of representatives, should assure equitable basic rules for competition between different interest-groups. These are determined by their position in the social structure and might be based on social classes, on professional interests, on ethnic origin, etc.. The essence of democracy is to assure conditions for a fair competition between different interests and the opinions or ideologies related to them.

The assumption of kibbutz-democracy is that there are no permanent interest groups in the kibbutz. Voluntary membership predicates an agreement with the basic goals of the community. The decision-making process is mainly a means for the realization of these goals. The ideal solution would be to reach consensus by mutual persuasion, but as this might be too time-consuming, decisions are made by a majority vote.

3) As a result of the need to limit the possible abuse of authority by rulers, liberal democracy is based on the separation of legislative, executive and judiciary power and on a system of checks and balances among them. The main aim of this system is to assure the independence of the legislative

and judiciary powers against possible domination by the executive body.

Since kibbutz-democracy is based on assumptions of high value – consensus and social solidarity – it is not concerned with division of power. On the contrary, the central body of kibbutz-democracy, the general assembly, performs all three functions. The legislative function is expressed by decisions on basic rules and regulations, on long-range policies and planning. The executive function is expressed by the fact that the general assembly can change or revoke any decision made by committees and branches. The judiciary function is fulfilled by the discussion and regulation of conflicts between members or between sub-units.

4) While the basic guarantees of liberal, formal democracy are written laws with a universalistic character, in the kibbutz the discussion of every issue is "substantive directed to a particular case in a particular context".[2]

There have been many attempts to introduce written regulations with a universalist character in various areas of kibbutz-life. Most of these attempts have failed and two possible explanations have been presented. a. The opposition to general universal laws is related to the particularist approach of basic kibbutz-principles: from each one according to *his* abilities and to each one according to *his* needs, where the reference is to specific individuals and not to anonymous units. This approach is rooted in an organic social structure, where members have a person to person relationship and not only a fragmented social role relationship in a social sub-system (Rosner, 1962). b. The other explanation is based on the executive function of the general assembly and on the fact, that administrative and allocative decisions cannot be based only on universalist criteria (Shapiro, 1976).

5) Thus, centrality of the general assembly and particularist approach characterize the decision-making process of kibbutz-democracy. The main difference between the two models in organizational structure is the hierarchy of authority and the permanency in authority functions characteristic of the liberal democratic model versus the dispersion of authority and the rotation of members in authority positions in the kibbutz-system.

Kibbutz-democracy is not based on a total equalization of influence among its members. As participants in the assembly they have theoretically an equal influence on the decision-making process. However, there is delegation of authority to committees and offices, and office-holders and committee-members have more authority than others in specific areas. But there is no clear-cut hierarchy of authority among committees and offices and the holding of office is time-limited in accordance with the principle of rotation. The kibbutz-principle is therefore one of dispersal of authority, that does not imply an equal amount of influence for all members at any given moment.

Structural change and its effects

The following structural factors are usually mentioned as influencing the degree of democracy: (a) size, (b) differentiation of social structure, (c) differentiation of economic structure, (d) economic affluence.

(a) Since the early sixties most of the kibbutzim have gone through a process of growth caused mainly by the absorption of members of the second and third generations and their spouses. While in the past there were few kibbutzim with more than 300 members and a population of more than 550, the number of such kibbutzim in 1976 was 76, almost a third of the total.

(b) The absorption of the younger generation caused by itself a change in the social composition, that had an impact on the structure. Related to it were the growing structural importance of the nuclear family and the development of enlarged families. Some sociologists saw in these changes a development passing through three types of social structures characterized by different types of social relations from "Bund to commune and toward association" (Cohen, 1975).

(c) The differentiation in the occupational and economic structure was caused first of all by the processes of industrialization, with the establishment of industrial plants in almost all the kibbutzim. This process was accompanied also by a growing "industrialization" of the agricultural branches caused by mechanization and professionalization. A growing diversification of services presented similar features. A certain number of members started to work outside the kibbutz both in organizations belonging to the kibbutzim (through regional enterprises or federations) or usually as professionals outside the kibbutz framework.

(d) The rising living standard was the result both of the economic development of the kibbutzim and of the diversification of the needs of a more heterogeneous population with a growing number of elderly people. It expressed itself in better housing, improved communal facilities, higher education, etc..

The following assumptions are usually made regarding the impact of structural differentiation on kibbutz-democracy: 1) growing size and complexity will demand more professional knowledge to handle it, and therefore there will be a need for more specialization and for more permanency in specialized positions; 2) growing size and complexity will produce a decrease in the involvement of the member in the different aspects and areas of the kibbutz and therefore a growing apathy to matters that do not affect him or his family. Growing affluence and more limited social relations might also facilitate the development of apathy.

On the other hand, both from the study of the kibbutz and from the list of factors cited above from Meister and others, we can identify other factors and variables, that might influence the degree of democracy without being directly related to the degree of structural differentiation. Some of these factors are related to the history of the kibbutz or its members, such as the level of education of the members, their commitment to kibbutz-ideology, their attachment to the kibbutz, or the organizational climate. We will try to explore in the following both the impact of structural changes and that of other, more independent factors on the implementation of kibbutz-democracy.

Formal authority positions and the distribution of influence

We will try to analyze the development of direct democracy in the kibbutz on the basis of the questions stated at the end of the introductory chapter. The analysis will be performed on two levels: (a) the level of the formal authority structure as expressed in the organizational structure and the distribution of authority among and within offices, committees, branches, etc. (b) the level of the general assembly as the main decision-making body of the community.

The aim of the organizational structure is to satisfy the overall needs of the members and population in almost all areas of life and activity (by provision of services, direct allocation of consumer-goods like food, clothing, furniture, etc. or the allocation of economic means to satisfy needs inside or outside the kibbutz) and to produce the economic means to finance the satisfaction of these needs. Although the individual kibbutz is a unit in a market-economy and there is no tendency to autarchy, the kibbutzim have a rather large range of autonomy in their decision-making process. Although they are integrated in larger units both in a regional framework and as part of the kibbutz federations, they enjoy a higher degree of independence, than other economic units or communities of their size.

In spite of the basic changes undergone by most of the kibbutzim in the last 15-20 years, no basic transformation of the organizational structure has taken place, and the description of the principles of this structure as opposed to the bureaucratic ideal-type (Rosner, 1973) is still accurate for most of them. As to the details of the structure (the number of committees and their subdivision, the interlocking of committees and the representation of different areas in the secretariat) there are differences between kibbutzim and even between different periods in the same kibbutz. This lack of uniformity is due to non-bureaucratic principles – the adaptation of the formal definitions of functions to the abilities and preferences of office-holders, and to different local conditions.

There are two contradictory tendencies in the process of centralization and hierarchization of the organizational structure. In some of the bigger kibbutzim a more hierarchical model has been suggested, introducing a third level between the existing two levels – the committees, each of which has authority in its designated area of responsibility, and the secretariat, the central executive body between assemblies. This third level would consist of coordinating committees, each of which would integrate and control the activities of a number of committees in a given area. A result of this tendency is usually strengthening the authority of the secretariat relative to the other committees. On the other hand, tendencies towards decentralization can be ascertained in relative strengthening of the committees' authority by allowing them to bring issues directly before the general assembly without prior discussion in the secretariat or by giving them more freedom of action in the framework of the budgets allocated to them. We have no conclusive research data on the relative strength of these two contradictory tendencies.

There is a lower degree of hierarchization in the organizational structure of the kibbutz community than in most of its industrial plants, but a striking similarity in the distribution of influence between hierarchical levels in the two settings is evident in the findings of the control-graph.[3]

Table 1: Distribution of influence in kibbutz community and industrial plant[1]   (Average scores)

| | Community[2] | | Industry[3] | |
	Actual	Ideal	Actual	Ideal
Central office-holders	4.1	4.0	4.2	4.3
Other office-holders (managerial personnel)	3.4	3.8	3.4	3.7
Members as a group	3.0	3.9	3.2	4.1

[1] The scores are based on answers to the following five-point-scaled questions:
i) How much influence do the following groups have on what happens in this kibbutz (or factory)? (actual influence).
ii) How much influence should the following groups have on what happens in this kibbutz (or factory)? (ideal influence).
[2] Unpublished data from research on the general assembly in the Kibbutz Artzi.
[3] Tannenbaum et al. (1974).

In both settings there is a quite similar gap in the actual influence between the three levels. The influence attributed to both the central office-holder and the membership is a bit larger in the industrial plant than in the whole community. The astonishing fact is, that a larger amount of influence is attributed to the plant-workers as a group, mainly through the workers assembly, than to the kibbutz-members as a group. This contradicts the assumption about the rather limited authority of the plant-assembly (Rosner, 1974). The difference might result from the fact that the number of plant-workers is usually much smaller than of kibbutz-members. There is no difference between mid-level supervisors in the plant and committee members and chairmen in the community. As to the "ideal" influence, there seems to be more legitimation for a gap of influence between plant-management and workers than between kibbutz central office-holders and members. Both in community and plant the gap in actual influence between central office-holders and other office-holders is larger than the gap between this group and workers. The increase of influence desired for the middle level is similar to that desired for the members. In the plant and in the community the data on the actual distribution of influence do not correspond to the ideal of almost equal influence between members as a group and the elected office-holders.

What kind of power?

But what is the significance of the power, that is unequally distributed? Can the existing gap be interpreted as a confirmation of Dahrendorf's (1959) statement that

"any society and indeed any social organization requires some differentiation into positions of domination and positions of subjection?" (p. 219)

We have seen that different amounts of influence have been attributed to different positions of authority. But does a distribution of authority always mean a differentiation between domination and subjection, between giving of orders and order-execution? Cannot influence be seen as a correlate of responsibility for the execution of tasks toward the attainment of collective goals, without the power to force other people to act against their will?

In the kibbutz, authority is perceived as role-specific, as a means for organizational goal-attainment, that cannot create a more general position of domination over other people. Influence necessary for administration of things in Marx' terms is positively valued and kibbutz-members in different positions desire more than they have. Authority over people, corresponding to positions of personal superiority, is negatively valued. Many people in managerial positions desire to have less of such authority than they actually have, and such non-desired surplus has a negative effect on their job-satisfaction (Rosner, 1972b). According to Lukes' (1974) definitions we should also assume that the authority of the kibbutz office-holder is not based on *power*, but on *influence*, since power is related to the existence of conflict of interest, while influence is based on persuasion, encouragement or inducement – the only means at the disposal of the kibbutz office-holders, who cannot use sanctions or material rewards. The kibbutz concept of authority and influence can be conceived therefore as a non-zero-sum concept of power, when power is seen mainly as an instrument in attaining social goals and not as an instrument in promoting the interest of one group or person in a conflict situation.

Dahrendorf also speaks of the possibility that a person in a position of domination in one sub-system or association in his terms might be in a position of subjection to another one. This situation is surely more frequent in the kibbutz, than in any other society. It is quite a usual phenomenon that the plant-manager, for example, who is in a position of "domination" towards a worker in the plant, might feel himself dependent on the decision of this worker in other areas of life; e.g., the worker might be the chairman of a committee, to whom the manager has to address himself for the satisfaction of some of his needs.

Even in the framework of the work situation, there is a relative dependency of the manager on the worker. In the kibbutz-situation, where in many branches there is a need for more workers than are available, the threat of a worker to change his work-place might have a deterrent power-effect. This effect will surely be stronger, if the worker has specialized knowledge and cannot be easily replaced. This deterrent power is reduced in the kibbutzim, that put no strict limits on the employment of hired labor. This relationship between members' deterrent power and hired labor might even be a partial explanation for the negative correlation between the number of hired workers and the degree of kibbutz-members' participation in decision-making in industrial plants (Rosner and Palgi, 1977).

Another definite limitation on the office-holder's authority is his dependence on the decisions of the general assembly, which has a veto on all his decisions. Most decisions cannot be implemented without at least the approval of the assembly.

Rotation – the implementation of norms

We will turn to the question of rotation, which was seen by Dahrendorf as test for the classlessness of kibbutz-society. He was misinformed, when stating that

> "at least originally it was stipulated that every member in turn was to occupy the position of leadership for relatively short periods of time". (p. 219)

There are almost no authority positions, for which it was assumed that every member will occupy them in turn. For almost all positions a person has to be elected and the main criterion for his election is his ability to fill the role successfully.

Regarding the frequency of rotation, there is a high correspondence between the answers to normative questions in research and the data on what is happening in most of the kibbutzim. For most of the central social, cultural and educational offices and committees the term of office is 1-2 years, while for the economic central offices – economic coordinator and treasurer – it is 3 years. Survey research data also show a high percentage of respondents' satisfaction (75%) with the degree of rotation in central offices. In the past, the situation was rather different for the position of general manager of the industrial factory. In two of the movements a majority of respondents in a study favored permanency in this role. The assumption was probably, that one needs expert knowledge to fill this position. In the meantime, in almost all industrial plants, rotation in this position, too, after 4-5 years has been implemented and recent research data show positive organizational and economic effects of this procedure (Leviatan, 1978).

How large is the number of people holding central offices? Is there a group of people going from one central position to another?

In the research on the general assembly, data on rotation were collected in 13 kibbutzim of the Kibbutz Artzi with a total membership of almost 4,000. It was found, that during the decade of 1966-1976, 200 people filled the four central positions in the kibbutz: general secretary, economic coordinator, treasurer and general manager of the industrial plant. This amounts to 5% of the membership, but since a large majority of the incumbents were men, the relevant population is the male members and then the percentage rises to 8%.

The average length of office term was 2 years. Only a very small number of persons held more than one central office in the kibbutz during these 10 years. But a larger number filled, before or after their office-holding in the kibbutz, similar roles outside the kibbutz – in the kibbutz-federation or in regional enterprises and organizations. The number of persons, who during the ten years filled such roles – in the kibbutz or outside – for more than 5 years, was 50 – or in the average less than 4 per kibbutz.[4]

These data show quite convincingly, that there is no tendency toward monopolization of central offices and that the mechanism of rotation functions in conformity with the normative principles. No decrease in the frequency of rotation can be observed in comparing these data with those of previous research from the early sixties (Rosner, 1973) in spite of the processes of industrialization, growth and structural differentiation since then. There is also no evidence of decrease in rotation in comparison with earlier periods.

The balance of rewards

How did the kibbutz avoid the tendency towards monopolization of authority positions, that was stated by Meister as almost a new iron law of oligarchy in organizations? Does the psychological mechanism stated by Michels and re-stated by Meister not exist in the kibbutz? What about the functional needs for specialization and expertise? The answer to the first question is not psychological, but sociological. The special reward structure in the kibbutz, and the social position of the office-holders create a negative balance of rewards for many offices, that are not attractive for many members or at least do not create motivations to continue for long periods in the same office.

Influence and authority cannot be exchanged for other rewards and many positions are characterized by status-incongruity, since their increased influence is not accompanied by expressions of higher esteem or higher sympathy from fellow-members.

Table 2: Groups of members with high degree of influence, esteem and sympathy, attributed by first generation respondents[1] (Percentage and rank-order)

Group	Influence		Esteem		Sympathy	
	Rank	%	Rank	%	Rank	%
Central office-holders	1	71	4	32	6	13
Branch-managers	2	38	6	26	7	9
Other office-holders	3	29	5	30	5	23
Talented members	4	26	3	35	4	29
High-achievers in work	5	22	1	60	3	34
Devoted members	6	17	2	56	1	51
High-achievers in sport or arts	7	6	7	15	2	39

[1] For reasons of space we have given only data of the first generation. No significant differences in the rank order were found between generations.

Source: Rosner et al. (1978)

Highest esteem and sympathy are attributed by respondents to categories of members, who hold no formal offices, but behave in conformity with kibbutz-values – loyal members, outstanding workers. Ability in itself deserves less esteem and sympathy, than that attributed to the two above-mentioned categories, while the highest influence is attributed to the formal office-holders according to their position in the quasi-formal hierarchy. There is no link between the holding of office and material privileges, contrary to the situation in most organizations, where a strong relationship was found between the trends towards monopolization of authority positions and growing inequality in the allocation of material rewards. Some kibbutz office-holders – mainly in economic functions and especially in industrial management – enjoy some facilities such as the use of cars, more opportunity to travel to the cities and even abroad – which can be perceived as material advantages. These, however, are subject to the social control of kibbutz public opinion and are therefore limited and surely cannot be accumulated as can material rewards in other societies.

Another, more important set of rewards, which are related to serving in office, are intrinsic rewards related to the role-content, such as the opportunity to use abilities and develop them, autonomy, variety, etc.. The degree to which such opportunities are available varies sharply between offices and in the same degree the rewards can be perceived by some persons and in some situations as positive rewards and by others as negative ones and the combination between positive and negative rewards creates the balance of rewards.

Since most of the above-mentioned rewards are not quantifiable, the balance of rewards is a theoretical construct, that cannot be objectively measured. But a set of research data shows: (a) many respondents believe that the balance of rewards is negative for many offices; (b) there is a rather strong positive relationship between the readiness of respondents to fulfill certain public offices and their perception of the ratio between positive and negative rewards related to the given office. The differences in willingness between areas of activity and levels of activity can be explained also by sex-typing, the image of the prevailing balance of rewards and the degree of attachment to the kibbutz. But an additional, important factor is personal inclination. The most frequent explanation by the more active respondents was, that they are more inclined towards such activities or that they can less withstand the pressures of the committee or the assembly, that has nominated them to office. The ability to withstand the pressure might depend both on personality factors and the degree of attachment to the kibbutz, while the inclination is probably determined both by the subjective perception of the reward-balance and the attraction or repulsion by specific positive or negative rewards.

In conclusion, it seems that the kibbutz continues to navigate between the scylla of monopolization of authority positions and the charybdis of apathy and lack of motivation to fill offices. It seems, that the danger of apathy is the more serious one and that the kibbutz also faces the problem, that the mainly psychological rewards existing in its system are not easy to manipulate. Imaginative social planning will be needed in future to avoid the danger of growing apathy as well as that of a surplus in intrinsic role-related or material rewards in certain offices.

The influence of the general assembly

The two dangers – apathy of members and centralization and mono-polization of influence in the hands of a few office-holders – are also relevant to the main institution of direct democracy in the kibbutz – the general assembly.

As stated in all the documents of the kibbutz-federations – the general assembly is supposed to be the highest authority. J. J. Rousseau's definition of the relationship between elected officeholders (the deputies)and "the people" (in his terms) can also be seen today as the normative basis for the authority of the assembly:

"They (the deputies) can conclude nothing definitively. Every law that the people have not ratified is nullified, it is not a law" (cited by Dahl, R., 1970).

The assembly has a veto-right on every decision taken by a committee, a branch or an office-holder. All basic decisions related to planning (pro-duction, investment, consumption-budget, higher education, etc.) have to be taken by the assembly. However, it deals not only with "laws" and long-range decisions. It is also the focus of discussions and decisions on different questions concerning the individual members – such as a request to take a leave from the kibbutz, to accept his relatives into the kibbutz, to let him or his relatives go to study, etc..

In spite of the high degree of authority attributed to the assembly by kibbutz-norms, we have found (by means of the control-graph) that a relatively large gap is perceived between the influence of the members as a group (expressed mainly through the assembly) and that of the central office-holders. This is not, however, the only indication of a possible discrepancy between the normatively prescribed and the actual influence of the assembly. In kibbutz-publications, various complaints are expressed concerning functioning and influence of the assembly.

These complaints can be divided into those related to: 1) failures of office-holders and 2) apathy of the members. (1) The most frequent failures of office-holders mentioned are the selection of topics for dis-cussion in the assembly, lack of prior information about these topics, authoritative style of management of the assembly and, last but not least, partial implementation of the decisions taken by the assembly. Some times those failures are attributed to a lack of ability of the office-holders to handle these areas and sometimes to their disregard of the assembly, seeing in it a waste of time and an obstacle for effective decision-making. The question of efficiency may be related also to the question of the assembly's competence to decide about complex issues that need professional knowledge. (2) The apathy of the members might express itself by a low level of attendance (passive participation), but also by a low participation in discussions (active participation), and even in voting. In some complaints a certain vicious circle is stated, where the apathy of members might reinforce the disregard of office-holders towards the assembly and vice versa.

In spite of complaints, the general assembly continues to fulfill its formal central role in every kibbutz. An attempt to abolish it and to replace it by a council of elected representatives was undertaken two years ago in one of the oldest kibbutzim, but after a trial period of a year it was decided to reconvene the general assemblies on a regular basis. There are differences between kibbutzim as to the frequency of assemblies, and in a recent survey differences between federations were also found. In 144 kibbutzim the average frequency was three times in a month. In those of the Kibbutz Artzi the average was 3.6 versus 2.7 in the two other federations (estimated by informants). In the Kibbutz Artzi attendance was around 35% of the members, versus 30% in the Kibbutz Hameuchad and 25% in the Ichud Hakibbutzim. The variance among kibbutzim was smallest in Kibbutz Artzi. But the sheer fact, that assemblies continue to convene with a relatively high frequency, does not tell us enough about the centrality of its role in the decision-making process of the community and its overall influence.

In the study of the general assembly in the Kibbutz Artzi, 40% of the respondents mentioned that it has a high amount of influence versus 12% that perceived only a low influence. A majority also stated that the decisions of the assembly expressed generally the opinions of members in spite of the fact, that only part of them attend and that the decisions are generally implemented by office-holders.

The reasons stated by the respondents for their low level of satisfaction with the assembly's influence reveal, that the average members are more blamed for this outcome than the office-holders. We have already mentioned the answer, that members are not familiar with the subjects. The next most frequent answer was, that many members are not interested or motivated (36%). The answers blaming institutions and office-holders are less frequent – lack of implementation of decisions (24%), lack of preparation of the assembly (23%) and finally disregard of the assembly by office-holders (4%).

But what are the reasons for apathy, as it is not a reaction to power-centralization and monopolization? What is its scope?

Participation in the assembly and its predictors

On the basis of research data on the general assembly in the Kibbutz Artzi we can analyze the factors influencing three dimensions of participation: presence, speaking and voting.

We have mentioned above the average of 35% of the members in Kibbutz Artzi kibbutzim that participated. In the 15 kibbutzim that participated in the research, we can provide, in addition to the general average, a measure of the turnover of members participating in the assembly. Out of 550 respondents, 23% answered that they did not participate in any of the last five meetings, 15% participated in 1-2 meetings and 62% in 3-5 meetings. There were more women than men among the non-participants (30% women versus 17% men) and the opposite among the most frequent participants. The difference between sexes is even larger in the participation in discussions. 59% of women and 29% of men do usually not participate and only 11% of men and 4% of women defined themselves as frequent speakers. The sex-patterning is even stronger concerning the topics, on which the respondents speak and is similar to the area of public activity. Men speak more frequently on economics, women on education, while the differences are smaller on social and cultural matters.

The number of participants in discussions is determined also by the time-limit. In an average meeting four different topics are discussed. The average number of participants in the discussion on a given topic is close to six. On each topic at least one of the office-holders will have to speak and at least 1 or 2 of the affected persons. The number of speakers, that do not belong to these two categories is, therefore, limited. The participation in voting is less sex-patterned and restricted – only 9% mentioned that they often abstain from vote. A much discussed issue in this area has been the introduction of the secret ballot based on the argument, that many members abstain from voting on personal matters, since they do not want to openly hurt the affected persons or their relatives and friends by voting against them. Those who opposed this innovation argued, that it is a deviation from the principles of direct democracy and a path toward formalization. Others stated that it might harm the openness of interpersonal relationship based on frankness. Eventually in a number of the older and larger kibbutzim, this change was introduced mainly for personal matters or for the election of office-holders, while on other issues and in other kibbutzim vote continues to be overt by raising hands.

What are the reasons for the variance among kibbutz-members in the different kinds of participation? Some explanations can be found in the answers to open-ended questions, while a more quantitative answer will be given by regression analysis. The respondents were asked both what their reasons are for participation in meetings and for non-participation. The main reasons for participation can be interpreted as their general attachment to the kibbutz – "to know what is going on" (54%); "to participate in decision-making", "presence in the meeting expresses attachment to the kibbutz" (38%). Another reason is more related to self-interest: "I am interested in the subjects discussed" (34%), although it does not necessarily mean that the respondent is directly affected.

Among the reasons for non-participation the most frequent are objective reasons (38%) (sickness, work) and then fatigue (25%). But 25% also mentioned as a main reason, that they are not interested in the subjects discussed, while a smaller number of respondents expressed disappointment with the assembly (17%), or argue that it has not enough influence (13%) or that the decisions are not implemented (8%).

The answers to these questions reveal a strong relationship between participation in the assembly and attachment to the kibbutz, where participation can be seen as a symbolic act expressing attachment. On the other side, a minority expressed a different approach, seeing participation in the assembly mainly as a means of satisfying personal needs both by participation in interesting discussions and in decisions, where personal interest is affected.

This more specific and pragmatic approach to the assembly (we cannot discern between interesting issues and affected self-interest) is more prevalent among the younger generation. 52% of the second generation mentioned that they participate, when the subject is interesting versus 22% of the old-timers; 51% of the old-timers see their participation as an expression of their attachment to the kibbutz versus 30% of the youngsters.

The main reasons for not speaking at the assembly seem related to a lack of self-confidence – "I am afraid of speaking before a large public" (36%), "I cannot express my thoughts clearly enough" (31%). A smaller group of respondents do not feel the need to speak (22%) or agree with others who express their opinion (15%).

Among the reasons for abstentions from voting, the most frequent is difficulty in deciding among alternatives (54%). 17% answered that they do not want to hurt other members by their vote, and 45% think, that this is an important reason, why other members abstain from voting. This again stresses the fact, that many aspects of the assembly are both affected by and influence interpersonal relations. What is the quantitative weight of different factors influencing participation in the assembly?

Table 3 shows the relationships between the three kinds of participation and series of variables measured both by zero-order correlation and by multiple regression analysis. The data show clear differences among the variables linked with the different types of participational behavior.

Table 3: Influence of different variables on forms of participation in assemblies

Variable	Attendance		Speaking		Voting
	r[1]	% variance[2]	r	% variance	r
Age	12		29	5	- 14
Sex (male = 1)	- 11		- 26	3	n.s.[4]
Level of public office (last 3 years)	19	1	28	2	n.s.
Personal influence	42	9	45	20	18
Status[3]	29		44	8	
Attachment to kibbutz	43	19	33	.	11
Attitude to general kibbutz-values	19	.	23	1	n.s.
Member's influence through assembly	35	4	n.s.	.	n.s.

[1] Pearson zero-order correlations
[2] Percent of variance explained by multiple regression
[3] Based on a measure of self-perception of status-centrality in the kibbutz
[4] Level of significance lower than .05.

Source: Unpublished data from research on general assembly in Kibbutz Artzi

The variance in assembly attendance is explained mainly by the differences in attachment to the kibbutz among members and less by the
personal influence of the respondent.[5] Speaking in assembly is determined
mainly by the status-related variables of personal influence and centrality
without any direct contribution of attachment to the kibbutz. Voting is
related mainly to personal influence and, in an unexpected direction, to
one demographic factor - age. While younger members attend and speak
less frequently than older members, they vote more frequently. Perhaps,
they are less careful and retained and perhaps more self-confident in
deciding, what alternative to choose than the more experienced oldtimers.
Another unexpected finding is, that the respondents' evaluation about the
degree of democracy in the management has almost no direct impact on
the different kinds of participation. – This analysis of the factors influencing the participatory behavior of the individual member brings us to
another issue studied in the research on the assembly – factors influencing
differences in participation among kibbutzim.

Kibbutzim with high or low participation

We have already mentioned the differences among federations in participation (presence). But even in the Kibbutz Artzi there are striking

differences between kibbutzim in the rates of attendance, that cannot be explained by simple factors such as size, age, etc.. To explore their causes, a comparison was made between six matched pairs of kibbutzim – similar in age of the kibbutz and membership, but different in the rate of participation. By the T-test, the differences between the average measure of a series of variables establish the correlates of relative high and low participation (presence) in assemblies.

Table 4: Differences between six kibbutzim with high and six with low attendance at general assemblies

Variables	High attendance		Low attendance	Significance[1] of difference
Privatization				
Size of private house	45 m²		50.5 m²	.05
T.V. set in private house	83	percent	73	.006
Members level of education				
Higher education	21.4		16.7	
less than high school	14.5		24.6	
Ideological commitment (Attitude towards values)				
General values				
High importance of equality		40		n.s.
High importance of self-labour	29		23	.05
Democratic value				
High importance of democracy	67		48	.004
High importance to have influence	73		63	.02
Preference of economic development over				
democracy	34		51	.001
Attitude toward direct democracy				
In favor of:				
Solving problems by written regulations	33		40	.06
Transferring authority from assembly to				
committees	49		60	.06
Secret ballot on personal matters	53		69	.001
Elected council replacing partly the assembly		15		n.s.
Transferring authority from secretariat to				
committees	58		46	.002
Attachment to kibbutz				
Strong attachment	49		39	.002
Satisfaction with life in kibbutz		72		n.s.
Motivations for attendance				
To know what is going on	59		46	.008
When interested in the topics	29		42	.004

Perception of democratic climate

1. High influence of members through assembly	53	38	.001
2. High personal influence	38	28	.03
3. Assemblies' decisions are implemented	30	26	.05
4. Satisfaction with rotation		76	n.s.
5. High influence of central office-holders		75	n.s.

Attributes of kibbutz assemblies

1. Satisfaction with management of assemblies	42	35	.05
2. Frequent appeals on the assembly	27	37	.03
3. No conflicts of interest in assembly	24	17	.06
4. Little need for expertise in discussions at assemblies (4 = no need)	3.15	1.95	.02
5. Speak frequently at assemblies		12	n.s.
6. Abstain frequently from votes		9	n.s.

[1] The significance of difference was calculated on the basis of average scores by T-test. For convenience mostly percentages are presented.

In Table 4 we present both objective, quantifiable attributes of the kibbutz that show significant differences and aggregates of the answers to questionnaire items or of indices formed from these items. We also present some aggregate variables, where no such differences have been found, but results are relevant to our hypotheses.

As a result of the research design, no difference can be expected as to size and age of the kibbutz, since these two variables were held constant, when matching the pairs. Data from other sources show a negative correlation between size — the number of members and candidates — and average attendance at the assembly. This correlation is stronger in the more heterogeneous sample of 147 kibbutzim of the three main federations: R = -.41, than among the kibbutzim of the Kibbutz Artzi, r = -.30. (This correlation is based on an average of data from three subsequent surveys). In the last survey, a curvilinear relationship was discovered, where the lowest attendance was found in medium-sized and medium-aged kibbutzim, which are probably going through a period of change towards more formalization of social relationships and may have difficulties of adaptation.

Among the objective attributes of the kibbutz, two findings seem to be of theoretical significance. 1) The size of private housing can be seen as related to the tendency of *privatization,*of spending more time in the private flat than in the communal meeting places (dining-room, social club, etc.). Astonishingly, there is no negative correlation between the spread of television seets and attendance. The same result was also found on the individual level, when ownership of a T.V. set did not influence attendance, contrary to the assumption of those, who opposed the introduction of T.V. in private flats. It seems therefore, that type and size of housing is a better indicator of privatization than T.V. sets. 2) The significant differences of education levels are in the expected direction and show, that even in communities with a rather high average educational level, differences in this area might influence the degree of apathy.

Values and norms

The findings regarding the attitude to values are unequivocal concerning *democratic values* and more ambiguous about *general kibbutz-values*. In the kibbutzim with more participation there is clearly more commitment to democratic values, both on a more general and a more specific level. While there are no differences in the attitude towards such basic kibbutz-values as equality, the expected differences have been found in the attitude towards a more specific value: importance accorded to self-labour and the non-employment of hired workers.

The difference between the two groups is even more consistent and striking in the attitudes toward the principles and norms of direct democracy. Although there is a general opposition against introduction of representative democracy – only 15% of both groups are in favor of an elected council, such as exists in some of the bigger kibbutzim of other movements, a weakening in the support of traditional norms can be observed in the group with lower participation. More support is expressed for formalization – both by introduction of written rules and the secret ballot, and to a limited transfer of authority from assembly to committees. We cannot establish, what is cause and what is effect – whether weaker attachment to democratic values and norms is a cause for lower attendance or vice-versa: because of the functional weaknesses of the assembly, is there a readiness to partially replace it by other mechanisms? Interestingly, the tendency toward decentralization is stronger in the kibbutzim with higher attendance. In these more respondents mentioned the traditional answers relating participation to attachment to the kibbutz and involvement in it, while in the second group the answer expressing a more pragmatic orientation and stressing self-interest was more frequent.

Perception of democratic climate

The first three variables of this set are related to the dispersion of influence among members. The index measuring members' influence through the assembly is based mainly on the questions discussed above on the assemblies' influence and members' influence. This variable can be conceived as a measure of collective influence. The influence of the assembly is evidently also related to the second variable – implementation of decisions taken by the assembly.

The differences in personal influence are less striking than those in collective influence, but they are in the expected direction. On the other hand, no significant differences were found in the variable measuring centralization of influence and monopolization of authority positions. (Monopolization was measured not only by satisfaction with rotation, but also by the objective measures cited above – and no significant difference was found.)

Differences in dispersion of influence were found, but not differences in centralization and monopolization. This reinforces the explanation given by respondents, who answered the open-ended question, why they are not satisfied with assemblies' influence. They blamed members' apathy more than office-holders.

Attributes of kibbutz-assembly

The data show, that in the group with higher attendance the assembly seems to function better. The conflicts of interest mentioned are not between members and office-holders or between permanent interest-groups. They concern concrete issues and the groups mentioned as more involved in such conflicts are: age-groups, work-branches and larger families.

Data based on participant observation of assemblies in the two groups show, that in the group with lower attendance more expertise was needed to take part in discussions. This might be a result both of differences in the selection of issues brought to the larger forum and of the means used in presentation and explanation of the subjects.

No differences were found in the frequency of speaking and voting in the two groups, and this supports the findings of the individual level analysis, that different factors affect the different types of participation. Generally, some meaningful differences can be perceived between the results of the individual level analysis and those on the kibbutz-level, by comparing Table 3 with Table 4.

Several variables with no significant influences on the individual attendance at the assembly seem to influence – when aggregated – the percentage of members participating. The most important are: education, attitude toward democratic values, perception of collective influence and of functioning of the assembly. A possible explanation is, that while the education of an individual member does not make a difference, a concentration of several members with a given level of education in a given kibbutz might make a difference. A concentration of a relatively large group of low-educated members or members with less attachment to democratic values might have a negative impact on participation in such a kibbutz. On the other hand, a member with low education or low attachment to democratic values, who is relatively isolated in his kibbutz, will perhaps tend to behave in conformity with existing norms.

Conclusion

On the basis of the above data we can examine the impact of various factors both on the degree of rotation in office – related to the dispersal of influence – and on the functioning and influence of the general assembly.

A basic limitation of our data is, that they are cross-sectional and not longitudinal. As stated above, no clear unidirectional process of degeneration of kibbutz-democracy can be established by comparing different historical periods. There were probably greater differences in the past between federations in their approach to democracy, based on different ideological conceptions. In the kibbutzim committed to a more "organic" concept of direct democracy there has been a decrease in participation in the assembly and in its influence, but participation continues to be higher in these kibbutzim. A detailed research on the topics discussed in assemblies of three kibbutzim during 35 years has not shown significant changes (Shalev, 1976). Comparative data prove, that there has even been an increase in the rate of rotation, when members of the second generation began to be active in public life. In the recent study of 12 kibbutzim there was no possibility to assess the impact of structural factors such as size, age of the kibbutz and industrialization, as these were intentionally held constant to provide the opportunity to detect the influence of other factors. Holding these factors constant might explain the lack of difference between the two groups in areas like social relations, professionalization related to size, social structure and industrialization.

On the other hand, we found clear differences in participation related to factors that are probably independent of the processes of structural differentiation and are perhaps a result of the idiosyncratic characteristics of various kibbutzim such as: social composition of membership (country of origin), critical events in the past, that might impinge on the attitude toward the assembly, etc.

Differences between kibbutzim on variables like: levels of education, degree of privatization and different components of ideological commitment such as the attitude to kibbutz-values and to democracy and, especially, attachment to the kibbutz were significantly related to differences in attendance at the general meeting. We can therefore conclude that participation in the assembly, its functioning and its centrality are related to a series of factors that are relatively independent of the factor of structural differentiation. At least in the kibbutz setting, there is no simple determinism by structural factors as expected by Dahl (1970), that on a higher level of complexity it is necessary to change the type of democracy from more direct to more representative forms. In the kibbutz, and perhaps especially in the federation studied, the transition to representative democracy can certainly not be seen as a simple formal change. The more favorable attitude toward some features of representative democracy in one group of kibbutzim seems related both to the lower participation and the impaired functioning of the assembly and to more basic factors like stronger conflicts of interests, less attachment to the kibbutz and less commitment to democratic values.

The favorable attitude toward written regulations, secret ballot and transfer of authority from assembly to committees proves, that in spite of the almost unanimous opposition to electing a council of representatives, there is a weakening of the components of the theoretical model of kibbutz-democracy. The data can be seen also as a kind of validation of the theoretical model and of our basic assumption on the link between direct kibbutz-democracy, ideological commitment (value consensus) and social solidarity (no interest groups and high identification with the kibbutz). In such a situation the outcome of a transition to representative democracy might not be a better adaptation to changing conditions, but might weaken the ideological and social foundations of the kibbutz.

These findings can be seen also in the larger framework of the basic difference between modern democratic and classical democratic theories. Kibbutz-democracy can be seen even today as a concrete embodiment o the classical theory. The link between kibbutz-democracy, ideological commitment and social solidarity probably proves, that the possibility of implementing the classical model in modern society depends not only on the degree of complexity and structural differentiation, but on ideology and social solidarity. In its special framework and even in an area with the highest degree of structural differentiation – the industrial plants – the kibbutz has shown, that there is no necessary contradiction between efficiency and ideological conformity (Rosner and Palgi, 1978). In its overall organization the kibbutz has found a way to overcome the dilemma stated by Dahl between citizen effectiveness and system-capacity. The dilemma is based on the assumption, that higher system-capacity depends on bigger size and complexity, which will necessarily decrease citizen effectiveness in influencing society and produce powerlessness. The kibbutz has succeeded in enlarging system-capacity by inter-kibbutz cooperation both on the regional and the countrywide federation level.[6] This enlargement did not cause a decrease in members' influence in the community, although there was a certain loss of autonomy to the regional organization and the federation. These are based on representative democracy, but have their roots in the direct democracy of the individual kibbutz. There are, therefore, also in these organizations clear limits to the misuse of authority.

What can be learned from kibbutz experience for other societies and organizations?

The kibbutz-experience does not deny the existence of degeneration dangers in direct and cooperative democracy. Its example demonstrates, under what conditions they can be preserved in spite of advancing structural differentiation. The three basic conditions of ideological commitment, social solidarity and equality developed in the kibbutz under specific historical conditions. Under other conditions a purposive development of these factors might counteract the oligarchic tendencies produced by a purely instrumental approach to the goals of community and organization and by an unequal distribution of rewards. Major social developments such as the rise in educational levels, increase of more sophisticated needs, that might motivate people to be socially active without material privileges, rising interdependence among people with different types of knowledge and specialization might create in other societies conditions similar to those of the "deviant" case of kibbutz-democracy.

Notes

1 Dahl (1970) distinguishes between several forms of democracy, that can be placed on a continuum: (1) primary democracy, (2) committee democracy, (3) representative democracy, (4) plebiscitary democracy, (5) polyarchia.

2 This is a citation from Kamenka and Tay's (1971) discussion of a socialist model of an organic community, that suits the kibbutz-approach very well.

3 The control graph is an instrument developed by Tannenbaum (1968), measuring the influence attributed by respondents to different groups in an organization. Analyses performed both in the kibbutz and in other settings around the world have shown a high degree of correlation between these general subjective measures and other more specific or objective measures.

4 As a result of the limited sample and its special features that will be discussed below, no significant correlation between the degree of rotation and size, industrialization and other structural variables was found. But the direction of the correlation was positive – with size (.31), with level of industrialization (.28). These findings seem to confirm the assumption, that in larger kibbutzim rotation is more frequent than in smaller ones, since there is a higher probability to find candidates who are able to fill the different offices. Size is positively correlated with industrialization.

5 High correlations have been found between personal influence measured by the control-graph method, level of office filled in the last three years and status in the kibbutz. Status was measured by the following procedure: the respondent was asked to place himself in a series of concentric circles showing a central or more peripheric position in the kibbutz.

6 This is an example of the possibility of limiting the development of structural differentiation in a given system without losing efficiency, which was worked out recently on the theoretical level by

Rueschemeyer (1977). The author questions the assumptions concerning a necessary link between structural differentiation and efficiency and stresses the possibility, that structural differentiation is encouraged by power-holders as being in their interest. The rationale for the limitation of the processes of structural differentiation in the kibbutz is not the interest of power-holders, but the need to preserve specific kibbutz-values, like democracy or equality, that might be endangered.

Summary

In contrast with the general trend of "degeneration of direct democracy" (in cooperatives, trade-unions and other voluntary organizations) the kibbutzim are governed by a weekly general assembly, and administered through committees and by rotation of personnel in managerial positions. Empirical data show that differences among kibbutzim in the degree of implementation of direct democracy can be explained by the intensity of ideological commitment of their members and the social solidarity of their kibbutz. Size and "privatization" are negatively correlated to rates of participation in the assembly, while the average level of education has a positive impact on it.

FAMILY AND SOCIALIZATION

Is the Family Universal?—The Israeli Case

Melford E. Spiro

The universality of the family has always been accepted as a sound hypothesis in anthropology; recently, Murdock has been able to confirm this hypothesis on the basis of his important cross-cultural study of kinship. Moreover, Murdock reports that the "nuclear" family is also universal, and that typically it has four functions: sexual, economic, reproductive, and educational. What is more important is his finding that no society "has succeeded in finding an adequate substitute for the nuclear family, to which it might transfer these functions."[1] In the light of this evidence, there would be little reason to question his prediction that "it is highly doubtful whether any society ever will succeed in such an attempt, utopian proposals for the abolition of the family to the contrary notwithstanding."[2]

The functions served by the nuclear family are, of course, universal prerequisites for the survival of any society, and it is on this basis that Murdock accounts for its universality.

Without provision for the first and third (sexual and reproductive), society would become extinct; for the second (economic), life itself would cease; for the fourth (educational), culture would come to an end. The immense social utility of the nuclear family and the basic reason for its universality thus begins to emerge in strong relief.[3]

Although sexual, economic, reproductive, and educational activities are the functional prerequisites of any society, it comes as somewhat of a surprise, nevertheless, that all four functions are served by the same social

From Melford E. Spiro, "Is the Family Universal?" Reproduced by permission of the American Anthropological Association from the *American Anthropologist*, LVI, No. 5, Part 1 (Oct. 1954), 839–846. This selection has been brought up to date for its insertion in the present volume.

group. One would normally assume, on purely a priori grounds, that within the tremendous variability to be found among human cultures, there would be some cultures in which these four functions were distributed among more than one group. Logically, at least, it is entirely possible for these functions to be divided among various social groups within a society; and it is, indeed, difficult to believe that somewhere man's inventive ingenuity should not have actualized this logical possibility. As a matter of fact this possibility has been actualized in certain utopian communities—and it has succeeded within the narrow confines of these communities. The latter, however, have always constituted subgroups within a larger society, and the basic question remains as to whether such attempts could succeed when applied to the larger society.

Rather than speculate about the answer to this question, however, this paper presents a case study of a community which, like the utopian communities, constitutes a subgroup within a larger society and which, like some utopian communities, has also evolved a social structure which does not include the family. It is hoped that an examination of this community —the Israeli *kibbutz*—can shed some light on this question.

A *kibbutz* (plural, *kibbutzim*) is an agricultural collective in Israel whose main features include communal living, collective ownership of all property (and hence, the absence of "free enterprise" and the "profit motive"), and the communal rearing of children. *Kibbutz* culture is informed by its explicit, guiding principle, "from each according to his ability, to each according to his needs." The family, as that term is defined in *Social Structure,* does not exist in the *kibbutz,* in either its nuclear, polygamous, or extended forms. It should be emphasized, however, that the *kibbutzim* are organized into three separate national federations, and though the basic structure of *kibbutz* society is similar in all three, there are important differences among them. Hence, the term *kibbutz,* as used in this paper, refers exclusively to those *kibbutzim* that are members of the federation studied by the author.[4]

As Murdock defines it, the family is a social group characterized by common residence, economic cooperation, and reproduction. It includes adults of both sexes, at least two of whom maintain a socially approved sexual relationship, and one or more children, own or adopted, of the sexually cohabiting adults.[5] The social group in the *kibbutz* that includes adults of both sexes and their children, although characterized by reproduction, is not characterized by common residence or by economic cooperation. Before examining this entire social group, however, we shall first analyze the relationship between the two adults in the group who maintain a "socially approved sexual relationship," in order to determine whether their relationship constitutes a "marriage."

Murdock's findings reveal that marriage entails an interaction of persons of opposite sex such that a relatively permanent sexual relationship is maintained and an economic division of labor is practiced. Where either of these behavior patterns is absent, there is no marriage. As Murdock puts it:

> Sexual unions without economic co-operation are common, and there are relationships between men and women involving a division of labor without sexual gratification . . . but marriage exists only when the economic and the sexual are united in one relationship, and the combination occurs only in marriage.[6]

In examining the relationship of the couple in the *kibbutz* who share a common marriage, and whose sexual union is socially sanctioned, it is discovered that only one of these two criteria—the sexual—applies. Their relationship does not entail economic co-operation. If this be so—and the facts will be examined in a moment—there is no marriage in the *kibbutz*, if by marriage is meant a relationship between adults of opposite sex, characterized by sexual and economic activities. Hence, the generalization that, "marriage, thus defined, exists in every known society,"[7] has found an exception.

A *kibbutz* couple lives in a single room, which serves as a combined bedroom-living room. Their meals are eaten in a communal dining room, and their children are reared in a communal children's dormitory. Both the man and the woman work in the *kibbutz*, and either one may work in one of its agricultural branches or in one of the "service" branches. The latter include clerical work, education, work in the kitchen, laundry, etc. In actual fact, however, men preponderate in the agricultural branches, and women, in the service branches of the economy. There are no men, for example, in that part of the educational system which extends from infancy to the junior-high level. Nor do women work in those agricultural branches that require the use of heavy machinery, such as trucks, tractors, or combines. It should be noted, however, that some women play major roles in agricultural branches, such as the vegetable garden and the fruit orchards; and some men are indispensable in service branches such as the high school. Nevertheless, it is accurate to state that a division of labor based on sex is characteristic of the *kibbutz* society as a whole. This division of labor, however, does not characterize the relationship that exists between couples. Each mate works in some branch of the *kibbutz* economy, and each, as a member (*chaver*) of the *kibbutz*, receives his equal share of the goods and services that the *kibbutz* distributes. Neither, however, engages in economic activities that are exclusively directed to the satisfaction of the needs of his mate. Women cook, sew, launder, etc., for the entire *kibbutz*, and not for their mates exclusively. Men produce goods, but the economic returns from their labor go to the *kibbutz*, not to their mates and themselves, although they, like all members of the *kibbutz*, share in these economic returns. Hence, though there is economic co-operation between the sexes within the community as a whole, this co-operation does not take place between mates because the social structure of this society precludes the necessity for such co-operation.

What then is the nature of the relationship of the *kibbutz* couple? What are the motives for their union? What functions, other than sex, does it serve? What distinguishes such a union from an ordinary love affair?

In attempting to answer these questions, it should first be noted that premarital sexual relations are not taboo. It is expected, however, that youth of high-school age refrain from sexual activity; sexual intercourse between high-school students is strongly discouraged. After graduation from high school, however, and their election to membership in the *kibbutz,* there are no sanctions against sexual relations among these young people. While still single, *kibbutz* members live in small private rooms, and their sexual activities may take place in the room of either the male or the female, or in any other convenient location. Lovers do not ask the *kibbutz* for permission to move into a (larger) common room, nor, if they did, would this permission be granted if it were assumed that their relationship was merely that of lovers. When a couple asks for permission to share a room, they do so—and the *kibbutz* assumes that they do so—not because they are lovers, but because they are in love. The request for a room, then, is the sign that they wish to become a "couple" (*zug*), the term the *kibbutz* has substituted for the traditional "marriage." This union does not require the sanction of a marriage ceremony, or of any other event. When a couple requests a room, and the *kibbutz* grants the request, their union is *ipso facto* sanctioned by society. It should be noted, however, that all *kibbutz* couples eventually "get married" in accordance with the marriage laws of the state—usually just before, or soon after, their first child is born—because children born out of wedlock have no legal rights according to state law.

But becoming a couple affects neither the status nor the responsibilities of either the male or the female in the *kibbutz*. Both continue to work in whichever branch of the economy they had worked in before their union. The legal and social status of both the male and the female remain the same. The female retains her maiden name. She not only is viewed as a member of the *kibbutz* in her own right, but her official registration card in the *kibbutz* files remains separate from that of her "friend" (*chaver*)— the term used to designate spouses.[8]

But if sexual satisfaction may be obtained outside of this union, and if the union does not entail economic co-operation, what motivates people to become couples? It seems that the motivation is the desire to satisfy certain needs for intimacy, using that term in both its physical and psychological meanings. In the first place, from the sexual point of view, the average *chaver* is not content to engage in a constant series of casual affairs. After a certain period of sexual experimentation, he desires to establish a relatively permanent relationship with one person. But in addition to the physical intimacy of sex, the union also provides a psychological intimacy that may be expressed by notions such as comradeship, security, dependency, succorance, etc. And it is this psychological intimacy, primarily, that distinguishes couples from lovers. The criterion of the couple relationship, then, that which distinguishes it from a relationship between adults of the same sex who enjoy psychological intimacy, or from that of adults of opposite sex who enjoy physical intimacy, is love. A couple comes into being when these two kinds of intimacy are united in one relationship.

Since the *kibbutz* couple does not constitute a marriage because it does not satisfy the economic criterion of marriage, it follows that the couple and their children do not constitute a family, economic co-operation being part of the definition of the family. Furthermore, as has already been indicated, this group of adults and children does not satisfy the criterion of common residence. For though the children visit their parents in the latter's room every day, their residence is in one of the children's houses (*bet yeladim*), where they sleep, eat, and spend most of their time.

More important, however, in determining whether or not the family exists in the *kibbutz* is the fact that the physical care and the social rearing of the children are not the responsibilities of their own parents. But these responsibilities, according to Murdock's findings, are the most important functions that the adults in the family have with respect to the children.

Before entering into a discussion of the *kibbutz* system of collective education (*chinuch meshutaf*), it should be emphasized that the *kibbutz* is a child-centered society, par excellence. The importance of children, characteristic of traditional Jewish culture, has been retained as one of the primary values in this avowedly antitraditional society. "The parents' crown" is the title given to the chapter on children in an ethnography of the Eastern European Jewish village. The authors of this ethnography write:

> Aside from the scriptural and social reasons, children are welcomed for the joy they bring beyond the gratification due to the parents—the pleasure of having a child in the house. A baby is a toy, the treasure, and the pride of the house.[9]

This description, except for the scriptural reference, applies without qualification to the *kibbutz*.

But the *kibbutz* has still another reason for cherishing its children. The *kibbutz* views itself as an attempt to revolutionize the structure of human society and its basic social relations. Its faith in its ability to achieve this end can be vindicated only if it can raise a generation that will choose to live in this communal society, and will, thus, carry on the work that was initiated by the founders of this society—their parents.

For both these reasons the child is king. Children are lavished with attention and with care to the point where many adults admit that the children are "spoiled." Adult housing may be poor, but the children live in good houses; adult food may be meager and monotonous, but the children enjoy a variety of excellent food; there may be a shortage of clothes for adults, but the children's clothing is both good and plentiful.

Despite this emphasis on children, however, it is not their own parents who provide directly for their physical care. Indeed, the latter have no responsibility in this regard. The *kibbutz* as a whole assumes this responsibility for all its children. The latter sleep and eat in special children's houses, they obtain their clothes from a communal store; when ill, they are taken care of by their "nurses." This does not mean that parents are not concerned about the physical welfare of their own children. On the contrary, this is one of their primary concerns. But it does mean that the active responsibility for their care has been delegated to a community institution. Nor does it mean that parents do not work for the physical care of their children, for this is one of their strongest drives. But the fruits of their labor are not given directly to their children; they are given instead to the community which, in turn, provides for all the children. A bachelor or a couple without children contribute as much to the children's physical care as a couple with children of their own.

The family's responsibility for the socialization of children, Murdock reports, is "no less important than the physical care of the children."

> The burden of education and socialization everywhere falls primarily upon the nuclear family. . . . Perhaps more than any other single factor collective responsibility for education and socialization welds the various relationships of the family firmly together.[10]

But the education and socialization of *kibbutz* children are the function of their nurses and teachers, and not of their parents. The infant is placed in the infants' house upon the mother's return from the hospital, where it remains in the care of nurses. Both parents see the infant there; the mother when she feeds it, the father upon return from work. The infant is not taken to its parents' room until its sixth month, after which it stays with them for an hour. As the child grows older, the amount of time he spends with his parents increases, and he may go to their room whenever he chooses during the day, though he must return to his children's house before lights-out. Since the children are in school most of the day, however, and since both parents work during the day, the children—even during their school vacations—are with their parents for (approximately) a two-hour period in the evening—from the time that the parents return from work until they go to eat their evening meal. The children may also be with their parents all day Saturday—the day of rest—if they desire.

As the child grows older, he advances through a succession of children's houses with children of his own age, where he is supervised by a nurse. The nurse institutes most of the disciplines, teaches the child his basic social skills, and is responsible for the "socialization of the instincts." The child also learns from his parents, to be sure, and they too are agents in the socialization process. But the bulk of his socialization is both entrusted, and deliberately delegated, to the nurses and teachers. There is little doubt but that a *kibbutz* child, bereft of the contributions of his parents to his socialization, would know his culture; deprived of the contributions of his nurses and teachers, however, he would remain an unsocialized individual.

As they enter the juvenile period, pre-adolescence, and adolescence, the children are gradually inducted into the economic life of the *kibbutz*. They work from an hour (grade-school students) to three hours (high-school seniors) a day in one of the economic branches under the supervision of adults. Thus, their economic skills, like most of their early social skills, are taught them by adults other than their parents. This generalization applies to the learning of values, as well. In the early ages, the *kibbutz* values are inculcated by nurses, and later by teachers. When the children enter junior high, this function, which the *kibbutz* views as paramount in importance, is delegated to the "homeroom teacher," known as the "educator" (*mechanech*), and to a "leader" (*madrich*) of the inter-*kibbutz* youth movement. The parents, of course, are also influential in the teaching of values, but the formal division of labor in the *kibbutz* has delegated this responsibility to other authorities.

Although the parents do not play an outstanding role in the socialization of their children, or in providing for their physical needs, it would be erroneous to conclude that they are unimportant figures in their children's lives. Parents are of crucial importance in the *psychological* development of the child. They serve as the objects of his most important identifications, and they provide him with a certain security and love that he obtains from no one else. If anything, the attachment of the young children to their parents is greater than it is in our own society. But this is irrelevant to the main consideration of this paper. Its purpose is to call attention to the fact that those functions of parents that constitute the *conditio sine qua non* for the existence of the "family"—the physical care and socialization of children—are not the functions of the *kibbutz* parents. It can only be concluded that in the absence of the economic and educational functions of the typical family, as well as of its characteristic of common residence, that the family does not exist in the *kibbutz*.

It is apparent from this brief description of the *kibbutz* that most of the functions characteristic of the typical nuclear family have become the functions of the entire *kibbutz* society. This is so much the case that the *kibbutz* as a whole can almost satisfy the criteria by which Murdock defines the family. This observation is not meant to imply that the *kibbutz* is a nuclear family. Its structure and that of the nuclear family are dissimilar. This observation does suggest, however, that the *kibbutz* can function without the family, because it functions as if it, itself, were a family; and it can so function because its members perceive each other as kin, in the psychological implications of that term. The latter statement requires some explanation.

The members of the *kibbutz* do not view each other merely as fellow citizens, or as coresidents in a village, or as co-operators of an agricultural economy. Rather they do view each other as *chaverim,* or comrades, who comprise a group in which each is intimately related to the other, and in which the welfare of the one is bound up with the welfare of the other. This is a society in which the principle, "from each according to his ability, to each according to his needs," can be practiced, not because its members are more altruistic than the members of other societies, but because each member views his fellow as a kinsman, psychologically speaking. And just as a father in the family does not complain because he works much harder than his children, and yet he may receive no more, or even less, of the family income than they, so the *kibbutz* member whose economic productivity is high does not complain because he receives no more, and sometimes less, than a member whose productivity is low. This principle is taken for granted as the normal way of doing things. Since they are all *chaverim,* "it's all in the family," psychologically speaking.

In short, the *kibbutz* constitutes a *gemeinschaft.* Its patterns of interaction are interpersonal patterns; its ties are kin ties, without the biological tie of kinship. In this one respect it is the "folk society," in almost its pure form. The following quotation from Redfield could have been written with the *kibbutz* in mind, so accurately does it describe the social-psychological basis of *kibbutz* culture.

> The members of the folk society have a strong sense of belonging together. The group . . . see their own resemblances and feel correspondingly united. Communicating intimately with each other, each has a strong claim on the sympathies of the others.
> . . . .
> The personal and intimate life of the child in the family is extended, in the folk society, into the social world of the adults. . . . It is not merely that relations in such a society are personal; it is also that they are familial. . . . the result is a group of people among whom prevail the personal and categorized relationships that characterize the families as we know them, and in which the patterns of kinship tend to be extended outward from the group of genealogically connected individuals into the whole society. The kin are the type persons for all experience.[11]

Hence it is that the bachelor and the childless couple do not feel that an injustice is being done them when they contribute to the support of the children of others. The children *in* the *kibbutz* are viewed as the children *of* the *kibbutz.* Parents (who are much more attached to their own children than they are to the children of others) and bachelors, alike, refer to all the *kibbutz* children as "our children."

The social perception of one's fellows as kin, psychologically speaking, is reflected in another important aspect of the *kibbutz* behavior. It is a striking and significant fact that those individuals who were born and raised in the *kibbutz* tend to practice group exogamy, although there are no rules that either compel or encourage them to do so. Indeed, in the *kibbutz* in which our field work was carried out, all such individuals married outside their own *kibbutz*. When they are asked for an explanation of this behavior, these individuals reply that they cannot marry those persons with whom they have been raised and whom they, consequently, view as siblings. This suggests, as Murdock has pointed out, that "the *kibbutz* to its members *is* viewed psychologically as a family to the extent that it generates the same sort of unconscious incest-avoidance tendencies" (private communication).

What is suggested by this discussion is the following proposition: although the *kibbutz* constitutes an exception to the generalization concerning the universality of the family, structurally viewed, it serves to confirm this generalization, functionally and psychologically viewed. In the absence of a specific social group—the family—to whom society delegates the functions of socialization, reproduction, etc., it has become necessary for the entire society to become a large extended family. But only in a society whose members perceive each other psychologically as kin can it function as a family. And there would seem to be a population limit beyond which point individuals are no longer perceived as kin. That point is probably reached when the interaction of its members is no longer face-to-face; in short, when it ceases to be primary group. It would seem probable, therefore, that only in a "familial" society, such as the *kibbutz,* is it possible to dispense with the family.

Addendum, 1958

This is, quite obviously, an essay in the interpretation, rather than in the reporting of data.[12] After rereading the paper in 1958, I realized that the suggested interpretation follows from only one conception of the role which definitions play in science. Starting with Murdock's inductive—based on a sample of 250 societies—definitions of marriage and family, I concluded that marriage and the family do not exist in the *kibbutz,* since no single group or relationship satisfies the conditions stipulated in the definitions. If I were writing this essay today, I would wish to explore alternative interpretations as well—interpretations which, despite Murdock's definitions, would affirm the existence of marriage and the family in the *kibbutz*. Hence, I shall here very briefly outline the direction which one alternative interpretation would take.

The *kibbutz,* it should be noted first, does not practice—nor does it sanction—sexual promiscuity. Each adult member is expected to form a more-or-less permanent bisexual union; and this union is socially sanctioned by the granting of a joint room to the couple. The resulting relationship is different from any other adult relationship in the *kibbutz* in a number of significant features. (1) It alone includes common domicile for persons of opposite sex. (2) It entails a higher rate of interaction than is to be found in any other bisexual relationship. (3) It involves a higher degree of emotional intimacy than is to be found in any other relationship. (4) It establishes (ideally) an exclusive sexual relationship. (5) It leads to the deliberate decision to have children. These characteristics which, separately and severally, apply uniquely to this relationship, not only describe its salient features but also comprise the motives for those who enter into it. The couple, in short, viewed either objectively or phenomenologically, constitutes a unique social group in the *kibbutz*.

What, then, are we to make of this group? Since economic co-operation is not one of its features, we can, using Murdock's cross-cultural indices, deny that the relationship constitutes marriage. This is the conclusion of the foregoing paper. In retrospect, however, this conclusion does not leave me entirely satisfied. First, although we deny that the relationship constitutes a marriage, it nevertheless remains, both structurally and psychologically, a unique relationship within the *kibbutz*. Moreover, it is, with the exception of the economic variable, similar to those distinctive relationships in other societies to which the term marriage is applied. Hence, if I were writing this paper today, I should want to ask, before concluding that marriage is not universal, whether Murdock's inductive definition of marriage is, in the light of the *kibbutz* data, the most fruitful, even for his large sample; and if it were agreed that it is, whether it ought not to be changed or qualified so as to accommodate the relationship between *kibbutz* "spouses." Here I can only briefly explore the implications of these questions.

If the stated characteristics of the *kibbutz* relationship are found in the analogous relationship (marriage) in other societies—and I do not know that they are—it is surely apposite to ask whether Murdock's definition could not or should not stipulate them, as well as those already stipulated. For if they are found in other societies, on what theoretical grounds do we assign a higher priority to sex or economics over emotional intimacy, for example? Hence, if this procedure were adopted (and assuming that the characteristics of the *kibbutz* relationship were to be found in the marriage relationship in other societies) we would, since the *kibbutz* relationship satisfies all but one of the cross-cultural criteria, term the *kibbutz* relationship "marriage."

Alternatively, we might suggest that Murdock's definition of marriage, as well as the one suggested here, are unduly specific; that cross-cultural research is most fruitfully advanced by means of analytic, rather than substantive or enumerative, definitions. Thus, for example, we might wish to define marriage as "any socially sanctioned relationship between non-sanguineally-related cohabiting adults of opposite sex which satisfied felt needs—mutual, symmetrical, or complementary." A non-enumerative definition of this type would certainly embrace all known cases now termed "marriage" and would, at the same time, include the *kibbutz* case as well.

In the same vein, and employing similar definitional procedures, alternative conclusions can be suggested with respect to the family in the *kibbutz*. Although parents and children do not comprise a family, as Murdock defines family, they nevertheless constitute a unique group within the *kibbutz*, regardless of the term with which we may choose to designate it. (1) Children are not only desired by *kibbutz* parents, but, for the most part, they are planned. (2) These children—and no others—are called by their parents "sons" and "daughters"; conversely, they call their parents—and no other adults—"father" and "mother." (3) Parents and children comprise a social group in both an interactional and an emotional, if not in a spatial, sense. That is, though parents and children do not share a common domicile, they are identified by themselves and by others as a uniquely cohesive unit within the larger *kibbutz* society; this unit is termed a *mishpacha* (literally, "family"). (4) The nature of their interaction is different from that which obtains between the children and any other set of adults. (5) The rate of interaction between parents and children is greater than that between the children and any other set of adults of both sexes. (6) The psychological ties that bind them are more intense than those between the children and any other set of adults of both sexes.

Here, then, we are confronted with the same problem we encountered with respect to the question of *kibbutz* marriage. Because the parent-child relationship in the *kibbutz* does not entail a common domicile, physical care, and social rearing—three of the stipulated conditions in Murdock's definition of family—we concluded that the family does not exist in the *kibbutz*. But, since parents and children comprise a distinct and differentiated social group within the *kibbutz*, I am now not entirely satisfied with a conclusion which seems, at least by implication, to ignore its presence. For, surely, regardless of what else we might do with this group, we cannot simply ignore it. We can either perceive it, in cross-cultural perspective, as a unique group, and invent a new term to refer to it, or we can revise Murdock's definition of family in order to accommodate it.

Should the latter alternative be preferred, it could be effected in the following way. The stipulation of "common residence" could be qualified to refer to a reference, rather than to a membership, residence; and this is what the parental room is, for children as well as for parents. When, for example, they speak of "my room" or "our room," the children almost invariably refer to the parental room, not to their room in the communal children's house. If, moreover, the educational and economic functions of the family were interpreted as responsibilities for which parents were either immediately or ultimately responsible, the *kibbutz* parent-child unit would satisfy these criteria as well. For, though parents do not provide immediately for the physical care of their children, neither do they renounce their responsibility for them. Rather, they seek to achieve this end by working jointly rather than separately for the physical welfare of all the children—including, of course, their own.

Similarly, though the parents have only a minor share in the formal socialization process, they do not simply give their children to others to be raised as the latter see fit. Rather, socialization is entrusted to specially designated representatives, nurses and teachers, who rear the children, not according to their own fancy, but according to rules and procedures established by the parents. In short, though parents do not themselves socialize their children, they assume the ultimate responsibility for their socialization. Interpreted in this way, the relationship between *kibbutz* parents and children satisfies Murdock's definition of family.

To conclude, this addendum represents an alternative method of interpreting the *kibbutz* data concerning the relationship between spouses, and among parents and children. I am not suggesting that this interpretation is necessarily more fruitful than the one adopted in the paper. Certainly, however, I should want to examine it carefully before concluding, as I previously did, that marriage and the family are not universal.

The Family in a Revolutionary Movement: The Case of the Kibbutz in Israel[*]

Yonina Talmon-Garber

Introduction

The purpose of this case study[1] is the analysis of the interrelation between changes in communal structure and modification of family organization in a revolutionary and collectivist movement.[2] We will examine closely the

[*] This is an abridged version of a paper prepared for the International Seminar of Family Research held in Washington, August, 1962. I wish to express my sincere gratitude to M. Gluckman, D. M. Schneider, and Charlotte Green-Schwartz for their critical comments.

[1] This analysis is based on a research project carried out in a representative sample of 12 of the Kibbutzin affiliated with one of the four Federations of Kibbutzim. The project has combined sociological and anthropological field methods. The data obtained from the questionnaires, from various types of interviews and from analysis of written material, were examined and carefully interpreted by direct observation. R. Bar Yoseph took an active part in the initial planning. A. Etzioni assisted me in direction of the project in its first stage. The other main research assistants were E. Ron, M. Sarell and J. Sheffer. M. Sarell and E. Cohen took over from A. Etzioni in the second stage. The main research assistants were U. Avner, B. Bonne, S. Deshen, R. Gutman-Shaku, T. Horowitz, U. Hurwitz, Z. Stup and L. Shomgar. Special thanks are due to R. Gutman-Shaku who assisted me with the collection and analysis of the material on sex-role differentiation and on aging. Z. Stup and B. Bonne assisted me with the analysis of the material on family size. U. Avner and L. Shomgar contributed much to the analysis of patterns of marriage. E. Cohen assisted me in summing up the material and made many useful suggestions.

[2] For analysis of a similar process, see R. Schlesinger, *The Family in the U.S.S.R.*

process of institutionalization of this movement and analyze the effects of this process on the position of the family in the community and on internal family role-relationships.

The main features of collective settlements or Kibbutzim are common ownership of property except for a few personal belongings, and communal organization of production and consumption. Members' needs are provided for by communal institutions on an equalitarian basis. All income goes into the common treasury; each member gets only a very small allowance for personal expenses. The community is run as a single economic unit and as one household. It is governed by a general assembly which convenes as a rule once a week. The executive agencies are a secretariat and various committees. Kibbutzim may vary in size from 40 to 50 members in newly founded settlements to more than 1000 in larger and longer established ones. The communities are usually started by a nucleus of settlers. Additional groups and individuals join the core of founders at later stages of community development. The groups of settlers are organized by youth movements and undergo a period of intensive training in longer established Kibbutzim.[3]

The process of institutionalization may be observed by an examination of the transition occurring in the collective movement as a whole, as well as by examination of the internal development in every single Kibbutz. What is the position of the family in the revolutionary stage? How does the process of differentiation and routinization affect family role relationships? We have attempted to answer these questions by comparing the patterns of family organization and role images prevalent in the Federation of the Collectives in which we conducted our study during its initial phases with the institutionalized patterns and role images most prevalent in it at present.

The Revolutionary Phase

Let us first deal with the initial phases of the movement. Structural considerations and examination of our material have led us to the hypothesis that *there is a certain fundamental incompatibility between commitment to*

London: Routledge and Kegan Paul, 1949; L. A. Coser, "Some Aspects of Family Policy," *American Journal of Sociology*, Vol. 52 (1951); K. Geiger, "Changing Political Attitude in a Totalitarian Society," *World Politics*, Vol 8 (1956) and his "Deprivation and Solidarity in the Soviet Urban Family," *American Sociological Review*, Vol. 20 (1955); N. S. Timashef, "An Attempt to Abolish the Family in Russia," in N. W. Bell and E. F. Vogel (Eds.), *Modern Introduction to the Family*. New York: Free Press of Glencoe, 1961, pp. 55–64. For material on China, see C. Yang, *The Chinese Family in the Communist Revolution*. Cambridge, Mass.: Harvard University Press, 1959; M. L. Chin, Women in Communist China. Cambridge, 1962 (mimeographed). Cf. also W. J. Goode, *World Revolution and Family Patterns*. New York: Free Press of Glencoe, 1963.

[3] M. Spiro. *Kibbutz: Venture in Utopia*. Cambridge, Mass.: Harvard University Press, 1956; M. Holloway. *Heavens on Earth! Utopian Communities in America, 1680–1880*. London: Turnstile Press, 1951.

a radical revolutionary ideology and intense collective identification on the one hand and family solidarity on the other.[4] Kinship is based on maintenance of intergenerational ties and a certain basic continuity of transmitted tradition. A total rejection of this continuity leads to revolt against the authority of the former generation and disrupts cross-generational kinship ties. Kinship is essentially non-selective and non-ideological. For the ascriptive "natural" kinship ties members of a revolutionary elite substitute a *Wahlverwandschaft* based on a spontaneous communion of kindred souls and on an identification with a common mission. Ideology becomes the dominant unifying factor. Relatives and friends who do not share this commitment become outsiders, almost strangers.

The urge to emigrate to the new country and establish a Kibbutz was an outcome of a kind of conversion which entailed a total change of world view and way of life. This overpowering urge did not affect either whole communities or whole families. It cut through and disrupted both kinship and local ties. The pioneering ideology appealed mainly to the young and unattached, and induced them to sever their relations with parents, to discard their former attachments and disentangle themselves from their social setting altogether. The young pioneers emigrated either on their own or with a group of comrades. The disposition to establish very cohesive communities and relegate the family to a secondary position is closely related to this radical dissociation from former ties and to familial discontinuity. The intimate person-to-person relations, the intense togetherness and the unity of purpose which permeated all contracts were more significant than kinship loyalties. External ties and conflicting loyalties were not allowed to interfere with internal cohesion.

The formation of families of procreation within the Kibbutz confronted the collectives with the problem of internal family attachments. New families are a source of centrifugal tendencies. Family ties are based on an exclusive and particularistic loyalty which sets the members of the family more or less apart from the rest of their comrades. The new elementary families may easily become competing foci of intense emotional involvement and infringe on the loyalties to the collective. Deep attachment to one's spouse and children based on purely expressive interpersonal relations may gain precedence over the more ideological and more task-oriented relations with comrades. Families are considered divisive factors also because they are intermediate units which interpose and come between the individual and the community. Inasmuch as they act as buffers and protect the individual from the direct impact of public opinion, they reduce the effectiveness of informal collective control over members.

The anti-familistic tendencies inherent in the revolutionary and collectivist ideology of the Kibbutz were enhanced by the conditions in which it de-

---

[4] A more or less strong anti-familistic bias seems to be typical of both religious and socialist communal settlements established in America. See W. A. Hinds, *American Communal and Cooperative Colonies.* Oneida, N.Y.: Office of the American Socialist, 1878. A. E. Bestor, *Backwoods Utopias.* Philadelphia: University of Pennsylvania Press, 1959.

veloped and by the nature of the functions it performed for the society as a whole. The Kibbutzim acted as an avant-garde of the emergent society. They were therefore a unique combination of agricultural settlements, training centers and military outposts. Each new community served as a spearhead of the advancement of settlement into more outlying and more arid frontier regions and had to fight its way against great odds — eroded and barren soil, severe scarcity of water, lack of adequate training and experience, very little capital resources for basic investment and the heavy burden of self-defense in a hostile environment. Settlement entailed in most cases a long preparatory period of entrenchment, land reclamation and experimentation, during which cultivation did not yield any profit. The Kibbutzim could overcome the almost insurmountable difficulties facing them only by means of channeling most of their resources of manpower and capital into production and by restricting their input into consumption and services to the bare minimum. Centralized communal organization of the non-productive branches of their economy enabled the Kibbutzim to reduce their investment in these spheres and to utilize fully the productive capacity of their members.

The tendency to attend to the needs of its members directly on the community level rather than by means of family households was strongly reinforced by the demographic characteristics of the Kibbutz and by its function as a training center for the youth movements. The presence of a considerable number of young members without families of their own in the Kibbutz and the constant turnover of temporary trainees made development of communal service institutions imperative.

Last but not least of the factors operating in the same direction was the function of the Kibbutz as a first defense line in outlying regions and around more vulnerable types of settlements.[5] Settlement in remote frontier areas was a semi-military undertaking which required a flexible combination of activities directed towards economic development on the one hand and defense on the other. The social organization and physical layout of the Kibbutz resembled in many respects that of an army camp. Settlements composed of organizationally and ecologically independent family farms were much more difficult to tend and to defend in times of emergency. The non-familistic structure of the Kibbutz facilitated the task of merging the semi-military and economic functions.[6]

[5] Material on military organization indicates clearly that there is a certain inherent incompatibility between a strong emphasis on military duties and family commitments. The tension is sometimes resolved by prohibition of marriage until completion of army service. For an interesting case in point see M. Gluckman, "The Kingdom of the Zulu," in M. Fortes and E. E. Evans-Pritchard (Eds.), *African Political Systems*. New York: Oxford University Press, 1950; and A. T. Bryant, *Olden Times in Zululand and Natal*. London: Longmans, Green, 1929.

[6] In our analysis of the position of the family in the revolutionary phase we put the main emphasis on inherent ideological and structural tendencies on the one hand and on situational factors on the other. For an analysis which derives this anti-familism almost exclusively from an over-reaction against Jewish tradition, see S. Diamond, "Kibbutz and Shtetl," *Social Problems*, Vol. 5 (1957).

Family Functions

The inherent tension between the collective and the family and the pressure of situational exigencies led to a far-reaching limitation of the functions of the family. The Kibbutzim curtailed family obligations and attachments and took over most of its functions. Husband and wife were allotted independent jobs. There was a strict ban on assigning members of the same family to the same place of work. Division of labor in the occupational sphere was based on a denial of sex-differentiation. Women participated to a considerable extent in hard productive labor as well as in defense activities. All meals were taken in the common dining hall. Communal institutions and stores supplied goods and catered services on an equalitarian basis. There was a very small personal cash allowance and standards of consumption were extremely austere and, by and large, uniform. The spouses looked after their small and simply furnished rooms but had few other household responsibilities. Interaction between the sexes in the economic sphere occurred on the level of the community as a whole and not directly between mates.

There was during this stage a far-reaching limitation of the functions of the family in the sphere of replacement as well.[7] The birth rate in the Kibbutzim was for a long time far below the level of replacement. Life in the Kibbutz leveled and standardized the fertility norms of all families within it. This seems surprising if we take into consideration the fact that the attitude toward children was very positive and that they symbolized the promise of the future. This apparent discrepancy between this child-centered position and the tendency to limit fertility drastically can be partly accounted for if we take into consideration the hazardous environmental conditions in which the Kibbutzim developed and their severe economic difficulties. Yet this is only partial explanation and there are many indications that ideological and structural pressures enhanced the tendency towards limitation of family size. During the revolutionary phase of development, the Kibbutzim emphasized recruitment by means of ideological conversion.[8] They ensured their continuity and growth by drawing reinforcements of volunteers from external sources rather than by means of natural increase. The role model of both men and women required a wholehearted devotion to work and active participation in communal activities. The emphasis on activities outside the family orbit and the masculine role prototype prevented any intense identification with the role of mother and curbed the desire for children.

A partial abdication of the parents in the sphere of socialization is another

[7] See Y. Talmon-Garber, "Social Structure and Family Size," *Human Relations*, Vol. 12 (1959).

[8] The history of both religious and socialist communes supply us with many analogies in this respect. Such communes are faced with a dilemma. They tend to limit the family in this respect, yet they cannot ensure their continuity without internal natural increase. See B. M. Shambaugh, *Amana — The Community of True Inspiration.* Iowa City, Iowa: State Historical Society of Iowa, 1908. For an interesting discussion of the same problem in a different setting, see H. C. Lea, *Historical Sketch of Sacerdotal Celibacy in the Christian Church.* Philadelphia: Lippincott, 1867.

aspect of the re-structuring of family roles. The whole system was organized on a basis of relative separation between family and child. The physical care and rearing of the children were basically the responsibility of the Kibbutz, not so much of their parents. In most Kibbutzim children lived apart from their parents. From birth they slept, ate and later on studied in special children's houses. Each age group led its own life and had its autonomous arrangements. Parents were not completely excluded. Children met their parents and siblings in off-hours and spent the afternoons and early evenings with them. On Saturdays and holidays they stayed with their parents most of the time. In most Kibbutzim, parents put their young children to sleep every night. There were thus frequent and intensive relations between parents and children. The main socializing agencies were, however, the peer age-group and the specialized nurses, instructors and teachers. The age-groups substituted for the sibling group. It duplicated the structure of the community and mediated between children and adults.[9]

This system of socialization can be partly accounted for by situational pressures, and it developed at first by trial and error. It enabled mothers to continue their work in communal institutions and reduced the number of workers engaged in the upbringing and education of the children. It enabled the Kibbutz to isolate the children and protect them from the ill effects of the low standard of living of their parents. Children could be accorded far better living conditions than those for adults and get specialized care. The children's houses were in more than one way an economical and convenient solution of practical problems, yet there is much more to it than just that. At the root of the matter lies the intent to transfer the main responsibility for socialization from the parents to the community. Basically, the children belonged to the community as a whole. The core of internal family activities which looms so large in other types of family has thus diminished considerably. The family almost ceased to be an autonomous unit from the point of view of division of labor.

The Sexual Ethic

Another important aspect of the process is the change of patterns in the sphere of sexual relations and in internal family affairs. A number of ideological, structural and situational factors operate in this field.[10] There was, first of all, the contemptuous reaction against the set patterns of the bourgeois way of life and the attempt to do away with such restrictive conventional norms as the demands of chastity and lifelong fidelity and double standards for women and men. It was felt that sexuality should be anchored in spontaneous love. Marriage was to be a voluntary union between free persons and

[9] Cf. M. Spiro, *Children of the Kibbutz.* Cambridge, Mass.: Harvard University Press, 1958; also Y. Talmon-Garber, "The Family and Collective Socialization in the Kibbutz," *Niv Hakvotsah*, Vol. 8 (1959) (in Hebrew).

[10] For a partly analogous development, see Vera S. Dunham, "Sex — From Free Love to Puritanism" in A. Inkeles and K. Geiger (Eds.), *Soviet Society.* Boston: Houghton Mifflin, 1961, pp. 540–546.

was to be binding on the marital partners only as long as it continued to be based on sincere and deep attachment and as long as both partners desired to maintain it. Premarital relations were considered legitimate and were not censured. The union between a couple did not require the sanction of the marriage ceremony. A couple who maintained a stable relationship for some time and decided to establish a family applied for a room of their own and started to live together without ceremonies or celebrations. The formal wedding was usually deferred until the birth of the first child, and was performed mainly because it was the only way to legitimize children according to the law of the land. Marriage did not change the status of the wife. Wives remained members in their own right and many retained their maiden names. The right of separation and divorce was not restricted in any way.

This extremely liberal position, which put such a strong emphasis on personal autonomy and erotic gratification, was counterbalanced and checked by the deep-seated sexual modesty and reticence instilled in the members by their traditional Jewish upbringing and by the asceticism and collectivism of the Kibbutz. Members who came from comparatively small communities and traditional milieus could not eradicate the attitudes toward sex cultivated in them during childhood and adolescence. These attitudes were reinforced by the strong puritan strains in the revolutionary world view and way of life. A high evaluation of sexual gratification ran counter to the pervasive emphasis on ascetic dedication and voluntary self-abnegation. Love was problematical in this type of community also because it is anchored in the specifically personal and private sphere and, inasmuch as it leads to preoccupation with innermost emotional states, it might detract from the task-oriented concentration in collective goals.[11] Inasmuch as it evokes intense emotion, it is not very amenable to social control and tends to get out of hand.

Last but not least of all factors operating in their field was the scarcity of women. In most Kibbutzim, women were during this stage a minority — 20–35 per cent of the total membership. This disequilibrium between the sexes had a double effect. Inasmuch as the serious scarcity of sexual partners resulted in competition, it enhanced the tendency towards shifting relations and instability. At the same time, in an indirect way, it had the opposite effect and enhanced the deep-seated asceticism prevalent in the Kibbutz. Under such circumstances, an unequivocal emphasis on sexual gratification was bound to breed bitter frustration and destructive rivalry. Demographic disequilibrium increases the disruptive potentiality of free love and necessitates the fostering of restraint and moderation.

In spite of the situational exigencies and the counterbalancing ideological pressures, the doctrine of free love was the dominant one and had a very strong impact on the emerging institutional patterns. Yet while maintaining

[11] Cf. Philip E. Slater, "On Social Regression," *American Sociological Review*, Vol. 28 (1936), pp. 339–364; and W. R. Bion, "Experiences in Groups III," *Human Relations*, Vol. 2, No. 1 (1949), pp. 13–22.

their positive attitude towards erotic attraction, the Kibbutzim developed many ingenious mechanisms which toned it down and checked its disorganizing effects. Relations between the sexes were de-eroticized and neutralized by dealing with sexual problems in a straightforward, objective and "rational" manner and by minimizing the differentiation and distance between the sexes. Women adopted male style of dress and male patterns of behavior. Beauty care and personal adornment which play up and enhance femininity were completely eliminated. The Kibbutzim de-emphasized physical shame between the sexes. Larger rooms which accommodate three or more occupants were often assigned to unattached men and women, who shared their room as a matter of course. They were expected to take one another for granted and in most cases there was little erotic tension between them. Couples attempted to keep the special ties between them secret as long as they could. They tried to be as inconspicuous and as discreet as possible even when their being a "couple" was common knowledge and fully approved by public opinion. They avoided appearing together in public and when in sight of their comrades refrained from any overt signs of affection.

The emphasis on free love and the emphasis on restraint and reticence operated simultaneously and checked each other. This accounts for the fact that in spite of the complete absence of institutionalized restrictions sexual relations were, generally speaking, not taken lightly. There was hardly any promiscuous and indiscriminate mating or wild and irresponsible experimentation. A very high incidence of shifting relations, separation and divorce occurred only in a minority of Kibbutzim.

Family Role Relationships

Internal relations between members of the elementary family were patterned to a large extent on relations between co-members and emphasized equality and companionship. Execution of family tasks was based on a tenet of strict sex equality. Husbands were expected to participate in looking after the family flat and taking care of the children equally with their wives. Spouses cooperated closely and were in most respects interchangeable. Both conjugal and parents-children relationships were exceedingly non-authoritarian. Spouses had no right to impose their authority on each other, and there was hardly any differentiation between their spheres of special competence. The attitude toward children was very permissive and there were hardly any distancing mechanisms. Children were not required to approach their parents with reticence or special deference; the relationship was easygoing and uninhibited. The dominant pattern in internal family interaction was comradeship on equal terms.

The changes in family relations were mirrored to some extent in the emerging kinship terminology. The terms for husband and wife were abandoned since they were indicative of the conception of the family as a legally binding paternalistic institution. The term for establishing a family was "to enter a family room." The husband was referred to as "my young man"

(*Habachur Sheli*). By the same token the wife was called "my young woman" (*Habachura Sheli*). Even these terms were often felt to be too familistic and members would try to circumvent and avoid them by using proper names for reference as well as for address. Children were encouraged to use their parents' proper names for both reference and address instead of "father" and "mother."[12] The terms "son" and "daughter" were extended to all children of the Kibbutz and the only distinguishing mark was the occasional use of the personal possessive pronoun when the parent was referring to his own children and the personal plural when referring to children of the Kibbutz.

The Family and the Collective

Segregation of family life was made almost impossible by the housing policy. Capital was invested mainly in expansion of productive enterprises, and in construction of communal institutions. Couples often had to wait for many months before they were allocated a room of their own. Families were requested to accommodate an additional member in their one-room apartments for some time, whenever the scarcity of housing became very acute. This was only a temporary emergency measure, yet the recurring violation of conjugal privacy expresses very clearly the precedence of collective over personal considerations. Examination of the type of houses built in the first Kibbutzim affords another indication of the same tendency. The dwelling unit consisted of one single room. A number of rooms were arranged in a row and led to one long narrow corridor or veranda. Bathrooms and sanitary facilities were built in the center of the compound and were shared by all members. The public baths and showers were important meeting places in which members exchanged information, conducted informal discussions of local problems and gossiped. Privatization of family life was made almost impossible by this type of housing policy and physical layout of the community.

Any tendency to stay away in the family rooms and to build up a segregated family life was strongly condemned. Private radios and electric kettles were banned for a long time because, among other reasons, they enhanced the attraction of the home and undermined full participation in communal affairs. There was little regard for family relationships in work allocation. Husband and wife were often assigned to jobs with different timetables and consequently did not see much of each other. There was also very little coordination of vacations and holidays. Even the weekly day off of husband and wife often fell on different days. There was hardly any family entertainment or family visiting. All members of the family func-

---

[12] On the use of personal names instead of or in conjunction with kinship terms in order to de-emphasize ascriptive kinship affiliations and in order to negate an indication of asymmetrical distribution of authority, see David M. Schneider and G. C. Homans, "Kinship Terminology and the American Kinship System," *American Anthropologist*, Vol. 57, No. 6, December 1955, pp. 1194–1208.

tioned independently and were pulled in different directions.[13] Much of life in the Kibbutz was lived in the public view. Members spent most of their free time together. They met every evening in the communal dining hall, in the reading room or the central lawn, and spent their time in committee work and heated discussions. Spontaneous community singing and folk dancing were the main recreational activities. Public opinion discouraged constant joint appearance of the couple in public. Husband and wife who stuck together and were often seen in each other's company were viewed with ridicule.

Patterns of celebrating festive occasions symbolized the overall importance of the community. There were hardly any family-centered celebrations. Weddings were as short and informal as possible and the ceremonies were performed in most cases outside the community. Wedding anniversaries and birthdays meant very little and were usually not commemorated. The Kibbutzim curtailed the functions of the family in all communal and national festivities. The family ceased to function as an independent and active unit in all ceremonies.

It should be noted that while the Kibbutzim limited the functions of the family drastically and emphasized the predominance of the Collective, they did not abolish the family altogether.[14] The anti-familistic policy was not based on a preconceived or fully worked out anti-familistic ideology. Most early formulations of ideological position did not propose to do away with the family completely. Justification for the restrictive norms was couched in terms of liberation of the family rather than of its negation and elimination. It should be stressed also that even during the earliest phases, when the anti-familistic bias was at its strongest, the family remained an identifiable unit. Families were regarded by their own members and by outsiders as distinct subgroups. There were socially regulated patterns of mating and children were recognized as offspring of particular parents. While premarital sexual relations were permitted, there was a clear-cut distinction between casual sexual experimentation, love affairs and the more durable and publicly sanctioned unions. By asking for a room of their own, the couple made public their wish to have permanent relations and eventually have children. Residence in a common bedroom-livingroom allocated by the Kibbutz conferred legitimacy to the couple. While children did not actually share a common domicile with their parents, they visited their parents' room and it was their home by reference. The life of the child alternated between the two ecological centers and both nursery and his parents' room were in a real sense home to him.

[13] For a fuller analysis of the process described here, see Y. Talmon-Garber, "The Family in Collective Settlements," *Transactions of the World Congress of Sociology*, 1957; and "Family Structure and Social Change," *International Social Science Journal*, Vol. 14, No. 3 (1962), pp. 500–522.

[14] See M. Spiro, "Is the Family Universal? — The Israeli Case," in N. W. Bell and E. Vogel (Eds.), *op. cit.*, pp. 55–64; also K. Gough, "The Nayar Kinship System," *Journal of the Royal Anthropological Institute*, Vol. 89, Part 1 (1959); E. R. Leach, "Polyandry, Inheritance and the Definition of Marriage," *Man*, Vol. 55, No. 199 (1955), pp. 182–185.

The family did not relinquish its communal functions completely either. Parents contributed to the economic support of their children indirectly by working jointly rather than separately. Similarly, though educators were the designated representatives of the Kibbutz rather than of the parents, parents exercised a direct and continuous influence on the trained personnel in charge of their children. Since children's institutions were not segregated from the community either ecologically or socially, parents were able to supervise closely the way their children were raised there. They exercised a considerable direct influence on their children during the time they spent together every day.[15] While interaction of family members with one another was in many cases less frequent than interaction with outsiders, internal ties remained more continuous, more meaningful and more intense. The emotional ties that bound husband and wife and parents and children were much more intimate and more exclusive than their ties with other members of the community.

The Process of Routinization

Expansion and stabilization of the Kibbutzim reinforce the family's position and bring about a partial restoration of its lost functions. As the Kibbutzim grow and establish themselves in the area, they become less vulnerable to attacks, and defense considerations lose some of their prominence. Military training and guard duty become less time- and effort-consuming. The Kibbutzim gradually manage to consolidate their economic position as well. The dynamic drive, the ascetic dedication and perseverance inspired by the intense identification with collective values enable the settlers to overcome the enormous environmental obstacles. The Kibbutzim become ongoing economic concerns and sometimes even attain modest prosperity. The situational exigencies which put a premium on a non-familistic division of labor are less pressing and allow a certain amount of internal decentralization and flexibility. In some spheres, there is even a reversal of trends and practical considerations of efficiency lead to more familistic patterns.

Consolidation and economic expansion reduce the intensity of collective identification. The fusion between personal and collective aspirations occurs during a period of revolutionary ferment, in a situation of emergency. Normalization blunts the sense of utmost urgency and blurs the vision which makes such fusion possible. During the initial phases, economic activity

[15] Cf. M. Spiro, 1958, *op. cit.;* also R. Bar Yoseph, "The Patterns of Early Socialization in the Collective Settlements in Israel," *Human Relations,* Vol. 12, No. 4 (1959), pp. 345–360; E. E. Irvine, "Observations in the Aims and Methods on Child-Rearing in Communal Settlements in Israel," *Human Relations,* Vol. 5, No. 3 (1952), pp. 247–275; Helen Faigin, "Social Behavior of Young Children in the Kibbutz," *Journal of Abnormal Social Psychology,* Vol. 56, No. 1 (1958), pp. 117–129; A. I. Rabin, "Infants and Children under Conditions of Intermittent Mothering," *American Journal of Orthopsychiatry,* Vol. 28, No. 3 (July 1958), pp. 577–586; and "Attitudes of Kibbutz Children to Parents and Family," *American Journal of Orthopsychiatry,* Vol. 29, No. 3 (January 1959), pp. 172–179.

serves as an instrument for the realization of socialist and national ideals and is therefore imbued with deep seriousness and dignity. Development of large-scale and specialized economic enterprises entails partial emancipation of the economic sphere from its subordination to the ideals of pioneering. By loosening its direct connection with the paramount values, economic activity is divested of its special aura and turns into matter-of-fact routine. Routinization of everyday activity leads to a certain dissociation between the individual and the community. Work is no longer as all-absorbing, deeply meaningful and inherently satisfying as it used to be. Purely personal aspirations and purely expressive interpersonal relations attain partial autonomy.[16]

Development and consolidation effect the position of the family in yet another way. Differentiation of functions and the concomitant crystallization of the groups which perform these functions disrupt the original homogeneity of the newly established Kibbutz. The various groups of settlers which join the core of founders of the community at different stages of its development do not assimilate fully and continue to maintain their internal solidarity. The community is gradually subdivided by distinct, overlapping and cross-cutting subgroups which mediate between the individual and the collective and partly take over control of him. The Kibbutzim become more tolerant towards internal differentiation. The family is accorded a certain amount of autonomy and assigned a place among the subgroups.

The appearance of the second generation is of crucial importance in this context because children are the main focus of semi-segregated family life in the Kibbutzim. Marriage does not entail a redefinition of roles and a new division of labor nor cause a clearly perceptible cleavage between the couple and the rest of the community. The birth of children makes manifest the partial independence of the family, and introduces a gradual shift of emphasis from disruption of inter-generation ties to continuity. Children are expected to settle in the Kibbutzim founded by their parents and continue their lifework there. The family of orientation is no longer an external and alien influence. Parents and children are members of the same Kibbutz, who live in close proximity and share, at least to some extent, the same ideals. Identification with one's family may thus reinforce identification with the collective.

Internal processes of routinization within the Kibbutzim are intensified by external processes of routinization in the society as a whole. Acquisition of state power lessened the dependence of the social structure on voluntaristic-charismatic movements oriented to collective service. Implementation of collective goals has been increasingly relegated to bureaucratic organizations such as the army, the Settlement Agency and the Civil Service. Coupled with the functional shift came an ideological reformulation. The emphasis on long-term collective goals was superseded by concern with short-term

[16] For a fuller analysis, see Y. Talmon and E. Cohen, "Collective Settlements in the Negev," in Joseph Ben-David (Ed.), *Agricultural Planning and the Village Community in Israel*. Paris: UNESCO, 1964, pp. 58–95.

tasks and immediate personal satisfactions. The limitation of avant-garde functions and the partial alienation from the society at large have a corrosive effect on the Kibbutzim and undermine their assurance in the final outcome of their revolutionary venture. Members are often assailed by self-doubt and insecurity. Dissociation between the Collective movement and Israeli society enhances the dissociation between individual members and their Kibbutz.

Family Functions

The shift of emphasis from discontinuity to continuity in more differentiated and less cohesive Collectives and the change of their position in the society as a whole account for the partial "emancipation" of the family. The family regains some of its lost functions in the *sphere of housekeeping*. Most families have their afternoon tea at home with their children. In some Kibbutzim, families sometimes eat their evening meal at home too. Most families do it only occasionally, as a special treat for the children, while some eat at home regularly almost every evening. Though most clothing still goes to the communal laundry, many families tend to look after their best clothes at home so that there is a little extra washing, mending and ironing now and then. The typical dwelling unit now consists of a semidetached flat containing one or two rooms, kitchenette and private sanitary facilities. While the style of the internal decoration has remained on the whole functional and uncluttered, the standard of equipment and the number of items of furniture supplied to each unit have increased considerably. The flat now requires more elaborate and more systematic care. It is in many cases an important symbol of the togetherness of the family and a physical manifestation of its separateness. Members usually tend it with care and have a strong desire to make it as neat and pleasant as possible.

The attenuation of the ascetic ideology and the change of patterns of distribution of certain items of consumption have a direct effect on the family. Many Kibbutzim have recently abolished the allocation of certain goods according to fixed and very specific standards and introduced a more flexible distributional system. Every member has a claim on an average per capita share of the allowance for clothing, for instance, and within the limits of this allowance is entitled to choose items of clothing according to his own taste and personal predilections. Freedom of choice is narrowly circumscribed within the limits of an allowance for a specified type of consumer goods, but some of the responsibility for planning in this sphere is transfered to the family.[17] Increased autonomy in the sphere of consumption has brought about the need for systematic and careful budgeting.

There is a considerable increase of the family's functions in the *sphere of reproduction*. Examination of demographic data indicates a considerable

[17] See E. Rosenfeld, "Institutional Change in the Kibbutz," *Social Problems*, Vol. 5 (1957), pp. 110–136. Cf. also the research report which summarizes the results of our project in this respect; "Patterns of Allocation in the Sphere of Consumption" (in Hebrew, mimeographed, 1959).

increase in the birth rate in the Kibbutzim. Economic considerations in favor of restriction of family size lose part of their weight in longer established Kibbutzim. We witness also a considerable change of the attitude towards fertility. As long as the main emphasis was on conversion and as long as reinforcements to the Kibbutzim came mainly from the youth movement and training centers, natural increase had only secondary importance. The dwindling of external recruiting sources and the difficulties experienced by the Kibbutzim in absorption of new emigrants have greatly enhanced the importance of natural increase. Emphasis has shifted from recruitment of volunteers from outside to expansion from within. The emergence of a more feminine role prototype for women and the partial emancipation of the family reinforce the tendency towards a higher birth rate. It is felt that children consolidate the position of the family in the community and contribute to a richer and more varied family life.

Parents tend to take a more active part in the *socialization of their children*. There is much closer cooperation between nurses, instructors, teachers and parents. Parents help in looking after their young children; they take turns in watching them at night and nurse them when they are ill. They help in the preparation of festivals arranged for the children and attend most of them. There is considerably more parental supervision of the children's behavior, choice of friends and reading habits. Parents try to influence their choice of future occupations and insist on their right to be consulted on this matter. Some Kibbutzim have introduced a more radical reorganization. Children in these Kibbutzim no longer sleep in the children's houses. They stay with their age-groups during the day but return home every afternoon. Duties of child care and socialization have thus partly reverted to the family.

Sex Role-Differentiation in the Occupational Sphere

The line dividing internal and external family activities has shifted considerably in all spheres except for the occupational. There is a considerable pressure to reduce the number of hours that women work in communal enterprises but only small concessions have been made in this sphere; mothers of babies get more time off from work now and aging women start to work part-time earlier than the men. The Kibbutzim put the main emphasis on the occupational role and it has remained the major focus of activity for both men and women. Yet even here we witness considerable modifications. There is now a fairly clear-cut sex role-differentiation in work organization. Women are mainly concentrated in occupations more closely allied to traditional housekeeping such as cooking, laundry service, nursing and teaching.[18] There are a number of intermediate spheres in

[18] For a more detailed analysis of the emergence of sex-role differentiation, see Y. Talmon-Garber, "Sex-role Differentiation in an Equalitarian Society," in Lasswell, Burma and Aronson (Eds.), *Sociology and Life.* Chicago: Scott, Foresman, 1964.

which women participate alongside men, yet many occupations are completely or almost completely sex-segregated. Women participate in predominantly masculine occupations more than men do in predominantly feminine occupations. Interchangeability is thus limited and asymmetrical.

Sex differentiation in the occupational sphere was kept at a minimum as long as the women were young and had few children, and as long as all efforts were concentrated on production and the standard of living was kept very low. Communal institutions replace the mother very early but they cannot eliminate the special ties between the mother and her baby. Pregnant women are transferred to lighter tasks and nursing mothers work only part-time. As they have to nurse and feed their babies every few hours, it is more convenient for them to work in one of the communal service institutions situated near the children's houses, and they usually take a leave of absence from productive labor. The births of more children entail recurrent interruptions and discontinuity. With age, mothers usually find it increasingly difficult to return to physical labor in outlying orchards and fields. The birth of children affects work allocation in yet another way. It entails a growing need for more workers for services and child care. This process is further enhanced by the rise in the standard of living. Non-productive work now requires about 50 per cent of all workers and absorbs most of the women, who usually number less than half the population of the Kibbutz. Since women cannot replace men fully in hard productive labor, it seems a waste to allow them to work in agriculture and, at the same time, to assign able-bodied men to the services. When practical considerations of utility gain precedence, considerable sex differentiation in job allocation comes to be regarded as inevitable.

The Sexual Ethic and Family Stability

So far, we have dealt with the relations between the family and other institutions. Let us now turn to internal role-relationships. There are significant changes in the norms pertaining to sexual relations and marriage. During the first phases of the development, the movement combined an extremely permissive attitude toward erotic attachment with far-reaching neutralization of relations between the sexes. The Kibbutzim do not now resort so much to de-eroticization. At the same time, their attitude towards sexual relations has become considerably less permissive. Most of the de-eroticizing mechanisms have been modified or completely discarded. The Kibbutzim now refrain from assigning members of both sexes to the same room. The emerging sex-role differentiation and the attenuation of the ascetic ideology have resulted in considerable differentiation of styles of dress and demeanor. Inconspicuous beauty care and personal adornment which discreetly underline femininity are permissible and are becoming increasingly prevalent. Couples are considerably less reticent and are not embarrassed when seen together in public.

Modifications of the doctrine of free love develop in the opposite direction. The general ideological position has remained basically liberal, yet when it comes to more specific and more practical norms, there are many reservations. Practically all feel very strongly that adolescents should not be preoccupied with sexual matters and should refrain from sexual relations altogether. After graduating from school, young members may engage in sexual relations with impunity, yet they are enjoined not to be indiscriminate and not to treat such matters in a frivolous, off-hand manner. Promiscuous experimentations are frowned upon and viewed with open disapproval. There is a considerable decrease in the age at marriage and in many cases premarital relations are just a short prelude to marriage. The time interval between commencement of sexual relations and foundation of a family is much shorter than it used to be. Normally, marriage now precedes the beginning of life together in a family apartment. Quite a number of couples postpone regular sexual relations until they marry. Most couples attach considerable importance to their marriage and want it to be a meaningful and memorable event. Wives tend now to discard their maiden names and adopt their husbands' names.

The attitude towards extra-marital relations is more critical and restrictive. While feeling that spouses should be understanding and tolerant and should not make too much fuss about a passing fancy or a temporary lapse, most members maintain that extra-marital liaisons endanger the stability and cohesion of the community and should be avoided as much as possible. They regard the right of divorce as inalienable but feel that it should be exercised only in cases of very serious and persistent estrangement. Divorce of couples who already have children is severely censured and condemned by public opinion. Officially, the Kibbutz has no right to interfere in these matters and members may do as they please, but many informal pressures are brought to bear on parents who contemplate divorce. The image of the ideal family has changed radically. Life-long companionship, mutual trust and understanding are emphasized much more than intensity of erotic attachment. Responsibility and loyalty are considered more important than spontaneity.

Both the community and the family have a vested interest in stability. Informal communication in such a closely-knit and cohesive community makes it virtually impossible to keep an extra-marital liaison secret and segregated — it soon becomes common knowledge. Since life in the Kibbutz entails close cooperation and frequent contacts between all members, the neglected spouse is exposed to recurrent encounters with the rival. Bitter jealousies which tear members apart and breed long-drawn enmities have a corrosive effect on interpersonal relations and impair the functioning of the system as a whole. A divorce is experienced by members of the family concerned as a major upheaval in their lives, since it cuts them loose from their most important source of emotional support and security. If both husband and wife stay on in the Kibbutz, they cannot possibly avoid each other. This is very irksome in cases in which the dissolution of the family left an aftermath of strong resentment. Small wonder that in most cases one spouse tends to withdraw from the Kibbutz and to leave it for good. In spite of the fact that children in the Kibbutz have a number of major socializers and a host of secondary ones, the rift between their parents and the loss of one is felt to be very harmful. It is significant that in spite of the absence of legal restrictions and economic hindrances, the rate of divorce has dropped drastically even in Kibbutzim which originally had a comparatively high rate of family dissolution. In most Kibbutzim, divorce has become a rare occurrence, and some have not had a divorce in their community for years. Families are on the whole cohesive and stable and cases of severe and protracted conflict are not common.[19]

Internal Division of Labor

Sex-role differentiation in work assignment impinges on the family. Productive labor and overall administration draw men far afield. Women's work does not take them far from their apartment or the children's houses. Since they are concentrated in occupations closely allied to housekeeping and child care, they find it easier to cope with their tasks at home. This process is accelerated when deeply-rooted sex-role images gain precedence and undermine the equalitarian ideology. The emergent division of labor is flexible and fluctuating. The husband usually helps his wife clean the flat and prepare the afternoon tea. Some husbands do it regularly, some do it now and then and some do it rarely, only in case of emergency when their wife is either very tired, ill or away. Clothes are exclusively the wife's concern. In most families the wife does most of the housekeeping and it is mainly her responsibility. Her husband is regarded as her assistant or as her temporary stand-in but not as co-worker on equal terms.[20] Budgeting of personal allowances of the whole family is almost invariably the responsibility of the wife. Officially, these allowances are personal and not transferable, but in practice this injunction is overruled and the allowances are pooled and treated as a family allowance. Since men are less concerned about scarcity of clothing and other consumer goods, a considerable part of their allowance is in fact transferred to their wives. They are usually not

[19] The data on the stability of the family in the Kibbutz does not corroborate the hypothesis that limitation of the role of the father in the maintenance and placement of his children leads to instability. Cf. R. Smith, *The Negro Family in British Guiana.* New York: Humanities Press, 1956.

[20] Cf. E. Bott, *Families and Social Networks.* London: Tavistock Publications, 1957, Ch. 5. The data presented here seems to indicate that Bott's hypothesis, which relates conjugal role-segregation to degree of network connectedness, needs re-examination and revision. In the Kibbutz growing differentiation between different types of social relations and loosening of social control over the family enhance sex-role differentiation rather than diminish it.

much interested in this small-scale budgeting and leave the planning and management of the family "finances" to their wives entirely.

Authority Pattern

The consolidation of the family unit and the emerging sex-role differentiation within it have a direct effect on the family internal authority structure. Internal discussions and disagreements are usually kept within the family, and there is a strong tendency to maintain a common front towards outsiders. We witness the emergence of a "regional" division of spheres of authority. Family authority is determined by the manner in which obligations and responsibilities are distributed between marital partners. There are also many indications that while the wife has more say in routine matters, the husband exercises more influence in matters of principle. Analysis of family decisions shows that husbands are usually more strict in their adherence to community norms and that they exert pressure on their wives in this respect. Public opinion ridicules a "weak" husband who gives way to his wife and does not prevail on her not to deviate from the accepted norms. It should be stressed that while the emergent pattern indicates a certain division of spheres of authority and favors a husband who takes a firm stand in matters of principle, it is not a clear-cut pattern, and it does not enforce an institutionalized position of pivotal authority for either spouse.

Informal Relations and Leisure-time Activities of Husband and Wife

The tendency towards a more familistic pattern may be clearly discerned in the subtle transformation of informal relations and leisure-time activities of husband and wife. Free time spent in public has diminished considerably. There is still much organized activity on the community level and most members participate in committees, in work group discussions and in various cultural interest groups. Yet they are not as eager as they used to be to participate in public discussions or attend public meetings. Spontaneous dancing and community singing sessions are rare. Husband and wife spend much of their free time together at home. They usually sit near each other during evening meals and on all public occasions. There is a far better coordination of their work schedules, vacations and holidays. Families get special consideration in this respect so that husbands and wives are able to spend their free time together. Much of the informal interchange between members occurs within the homes and entertaining and visiting are becoming joint family affairs. It is now considered impolite to invite only one of the spouses. Both husband and wife may have close friends of their own but if any of their special friends are uncongenial to the other spouse, they are gradually dropped. It is significant that increasing sex-role differentiation is accompanied by an increase in joint leisure-time activities and not by increasing segregation.

Child Care

In the sphere of child care, there is considerably more cooperation and interchangeability than in housekeeping.[21] This is clearly the effect of the system of socialization. As parents do not carry the main responsibility for either maintenance or socialization of their children, the main emphasis is put on affective ties. Parents handle their small children in an affectionate, gentle and warm way. Expressions of affection are restrained and grow less overt as the children grow up, yet the parents continue to lavish them with loving attention and do their best to be fully available to them while they are at home. The petty quarrels and persistent disagreements which often pester parent-children relationships in other types of families are quite rare here. Parents endeavor to make the few hours their children spend with them as pleasant and carefree as possible. They abstain from making too many demands on their children, and from severely penalizing misdemeanors, so as not to mar the happy hours of their daily reunion. Their main function is to minister to their children's need for security and love. Both of them interact with their children in much the same way and play a common protective role. Fathers usually take a lively interest in their children and participate actively in looking after them. Mothers have closer contacts with babies and small children but fathers come into the picture very early. Sex of the children has no marked effect either.

In spite of the considerable blurring of differences between the father role and the mother role, there are some signs of differentiation even here. The mother is as a rule more concerned with the bodily well-being of the children and takes care of them while they are at home. She usually has more contact with the children's institutions and the school and supervises the upbringing of her children there. There is not much routine disciplining in the family but, such as there is, is more often than not the mother's responsibility. The source of this responsibility is primarily in her duties as housekeeper and part-time caretaker of her children. The child has to conform to certain standards of cleanliness and order. The living quarters of the family in the Kibbutz are small: in many cases one room serves all purposes. While standards of order are by no means very strict and exacting, there is a concern with the neatness of the flat. Even with a maximum of permissiveness the child has to be controlled and restricted to some extent. There are also the problems of personal cleanliness and health preservation. The father is less involved in these problems and the child may find him an ally in cases of exaggerated concern with them on the part of the mother. The father's main responsibilities are outside the home — in the yard, on the farm, in dealing with communal affairs which concern the Kibbutz as a whole. In the eyes of the growing child, the father emerges gradually as the repre-

[21] For the factors which enhance the tendency to de-differentiation of parental roles in the modern family, see P. E. Slater, "Parental Role-Differentiation," *American Journal of Sociology*, Vol. 67 (1961), pp. 296–308.

sentative of the Kibbutz and its values within the family, while the mother acts primarily as the representative of the family in the Kibbutz.[22]

Parents emphasize the unity of the family and promote closer contacts between siblings. Older children are not burdened with heavy duties and are not compelled to look after younger ones regularly, yet they are encouraged to assume some responsibility and participate at least to some extent in the care of their younger siblings. The sibling relations are not devoid of tension and rivalry. Constant sharing in the peer group often breeds a craving for a complete monopoly over the parents and persistent demands for individual attention. Yet it seems that the atmosphere at home is less competitive than in the nursery. The sibling group is as a rule smaller than the age group and, unlike it, is age-graded. Births are usually planned and an interval of at least two years is considered desirable. Thus the parents have enough time for intensive care of each child during the first years of his life, and needs and claims for attention can be graded according to age. Conflict situations are minimized by the segregation and differentiation of activities in different age groups and in different children's houses. Having siblings enhances the prestige of the older child in his age group. He will often assume a protective role towards his younger siblings and take care of them of his own accord.

We witness a "dialectical" process in the sphere of parent-children relations. The extreme limitation of the family functions in the sphere of maintenance and socialization of its children have not led to disruption of family solidarity. Paradoxically, the curtailment of obligations reinforced rather than weakened parent-children relationships and enhanced the importance of the emotional ties between them. Insofar as the family has ceased to be the prime socializing agency, it avoids to some extent the inevitable ambivalence towards the agents of socialization. Parents do not have to play the two-sided role of ministering to the children's needs for care and security on the one hand, and of thwarting their wishes in various ways on the other. Since they do not carry the main responsibility for disciplining their children, they can afford to be easy and loving partners. Interaction with the parents is restricted and intermittent, yet it is continuous and consistently warm and permissive.

The role system in the children's houses is from several points of view the reverse of the role system of the family. There is a considerable turnover of

[22] Our data disprove the hypothesis that the mother figure is always the more permissive and supportive and the father more denying and demanding as far as the administering of specific disciplines and everyday relations are concerned. It reinforces the hypothesis of "positional" differentiation. The mother is the representative of the family, while the father is the representative of the community at large. For the distinction between role and position, see B. J. Berger's "Comment on Slater's Paper," *American Journal of Sociology,* Vol. 67 (1961), pp. 308–311; cf. also T. Parsons and R. Bales, *Family, Socialization and Interaction Process.* New York: The Free Press of Glencoe, 1955, Ch. 2 & 6.

child-care workers. This prevents the child from forming a strong and permanent identification with any of them. The relations in the nursery are, in addition, less affectively toned. They focus on the maintenance of a certain routine and are regulated primarily by professional criteria of competence. Diffuse general friendliness is emphasized more than love. Any attempt to monopolize the nurse must fail and the child has to learn to wait his turn and share with his peers. While the family is focused on diffuse gratification and tension release, the nursery and the school are task-oriented and emphasize performance. The child is encouraged to do things for himself and is pushed towards learning and early maturation. There is in the family a permissiveness towards slow development which is a kind of latency for the accelerated process of maturation in the nursery. Each child has an ascribed place in his family and receives his share of uncontested love and attention. The position of the child in the age group is ascribed only to a limited extent. In spite of the fact that the educators emphasize coordination of needs and cooperation, competition is not eliminated. The age group furnishes a stage for acting out dominance-submission problems. The child tests his powers in his relations with his age peers. He competes with them for his position in the group and for the approval of adults in charge of it. The family keeps the socializing situation balanced by providing the child with unconditional love and loyalty which are his right irrespective of his status in his group and which he does not have to share with his age mates.[23]

The countervailing functions of the family in the socialization process account for the overall importance of the parent-child relationship. Young children are deeply dependent, and very often over-dependent, on their parents. The children have come very often to occupy the emotional center of the parents' life. They eventually outgrow the intense involvement with their parents, and gradually become attached to their age-mates with whom they share uninterruptedly all their formative experiences of infancy, childhood and adolescence. Solidarity in the Kibbutz is focused primarily on horizontal ties between age equals, rather than on vertical ties between successive generations.[24] Adolescents gradually become firmly embedded in their group and drift away to a certain extent from their parents. The relationship with them remains straightforward, unconstrained and, in many cases, also exceedingly friendly, but it is no longer very intense and intimate. Parents resent the partial estrangement and often blame it on the usurpation of communal institutions. It is this process which is at the root of the recent reorganization of patterns of socialization.[25]

[23] Cf. R. Bar Yoseph, op. cit.

[24] For the effect of the emphasis on horizontal ties on family relationships in modern society, see E. Cummings and D. M. Schneider, "Sibling Solidarity," American Anthropologist, Vol. 63 (1961).

[25] See Y. Talmon-Garber, "The Family and Collective Education in the Kibbutz," Niv-Hekvutsah, Vol. 8, No. 1, pp. 2–52 (in Hebrew). Cf. also H. Faigin, op. cit.; and A. I. Rabin, op. cit.

Kinship Terms

The emerging role-relationships in the elementary family are partly mirrored in the change of terminology. The terms "my young man" and "my young woman" are felt to be inappropriate, especially when the couples concerned are past their prime. There are no fixed fully legitimized terms, but there is a growing tendency to refer to a husband as "my man" (*Haish Sheli*) and for the wife there are alternative terms: "my woman" (*Haisha Sheli*), "the woman" (*Haisha*). Sometimes members employ in a joking manner the rather poetic biblical *Raayati*. Quite often one notices a reversal to the traditional terms "husband" and "wife," which were strictly taboo in the past. These terms are employed self-consciously in a half-apologetic, half-defiant way. Almost invariably children now address and refer to their parents as father (*Aba*) and mother (*Ima*), adding the personal possessive pronoun when using the terms for reference. Small children tend to add this personal possessive pronoun now and then also when they use the parental term for address, thus emphasizing the intimacy and exclusiveness of the relationship. Parents often use the kinship terms "son" (*Ben*) and "daughter" (*Bat*) when addressing and referring to their children instead of their proper names.[26] Another significant change is the development of technonymic patterns. Children refer and address other childrens' parents by adding the name of the child to the parental term. Most adults are designated by the children as father of . . . or mother of. . . . The children use either the name of the adult's child they know best or the name of his first-born. So prevalent is this pattern that children will often refer to unmarried or childless adults as "father (or mother) of no one." This tendency to identify a person by underlining his role as parent to a certain child is not confined only to the children; it often penetrates to adult society as well.

Wider Kinship Ties

The most important feature of the process of change from the point of view of future development is the gradual re-emergence of wider kinship ties. As long as the generational structure of the Kibbutz remained truncated, most members did not have any kin besides members of their own elementary family living in the same community. A gradual process of change sets in when the children of the founders establish families and the Kibbutz develops into a full-scale three-generational structure. The Kibbutzim have in addition accepted social responsibility for aging or sick parents[27] and transfer many of them to their children in the Kibbutz. Old parents live either in separate blocks of dwellings or in a semi-detached little flat adjoin-

[26] Since proper names are used for address and reference in interaction between all members of the community, the use of such personal names becomes undifferentiated and neutralized and ceases to denote special intimacy or exclusiveness.

[27] See Y. Talmon-Garber, "Aging in a Planned Society," *American Journal of Sociology*, Vol. 67, No. 3 (1961), pp. 286–295.

ing their children's flat. Relatives who live in the same community maintain close contacts through frequent visiting and mutual help. There are many indices of the emergence of cohesive kinship groupings. Relatives very often tend to cluster and form united blocks which have a considerable influence on communal affairs.

Members tend to renew their contact with relatives who live outside the Kibbutz as well. They will stay with their relatives when they go to town and will invite them to visit. They accept personal presents from kin and reciprocate by sending farm produce from time to time. There is thus a considerable interchange between members and their relatives outside the Kibbutz. The wider kinship categories have, however, remained amorphous and fluid.[28] There is a vague sense of obligation to maintain amicable relations with all kin but actually contacts with kin outside the Kibbutz remain largely selective.[29] Congeniality of a relative is determined by many factors: political allegiance and sympathy towards the collective movement; potential of mutual help; accessibility in terms of propinquity; and, last but not least, mutual liking and compatibility on a purely personal basis.

The structure and function of the emerging kinship groupings are largely determined by patterns of mate-selection prevalent in the second generation. The most significant factor here is the spontaneous "exogamous" tendencies manifested by members of the second generation. There is hardly any erotic attraction between them and with very few exceptions they seek their marriage partners outside their own subgroup. They tend to marry (a) members who joined their Kibbutz at later stages of its development, (b) members of other Kibbutzim, (c) members of training groups of prospective settlers organized by the youth movements and (d) outsiders who are not affiliated with the collective movement.[30]

The predilection of members of the second generation for out-group relations in the erotic sphere stems at least in part from the system of socialization. The peer group is based on diffuse and all-embracing solidarity and discourages exclusive dyadic attachments within it. The exogamous tendencies are further enhanced by the ambivalent attitude of the second generation towards local continuity.[31] Most members of the second generation have a strong loyalty to their native Kibbutz but at the same time they often feel hemmed in and isolated. The exogamous pattern expresses their craving for new experiences and their groping for new contacts.

The exogamous tendencies manifested by the second generation have

[28] It is perhaps significant that, unlike the kin terms denoting relationships within the elementary family, wider kinship terms remain undifferentiated and classificatory.
[29] On selectivity in the contacts with relatives, cf. R. Firth (Ed.), *Two Studies of Kinship in London.* London: Athlone Press, 1956; see also E. Bott, *Families and Social Network.* London: Tavistock Publications, 1957, Ch. 5.
[30] For a fuller analysis, see Y. Talmon, "Mate Selection in Collective Settlements," *American Sociological Review*, August 1964, pp. 491–509.
[31] Cf. M. Sarell, "The Second Generation in Collective Settlements," *Megamoth*, Vol. 4 (1961), pp. 123–132 (in Hebrew).

far-reaching structural consequences. The prevalent patterns check the growth and consolidation of kinship blocks within the Kibbutz. Extra second-generation marriage gives rise to a less extended and less interconnected web of intra-collective kinship affiliations than intra second-generation marriage. Normally only one of the spouses in such an out-group union is likely to have his parents and siblings living with him in the same Kibbutz. No less important is the function of out-group marriage in counteracting the tendency of the old-timers to consolidate their position as a separate and dominant group. Through their children, the established old-timers are linked to less established and more marginal members. Kinship affiliations cut across the divisions between the subgroups and link them.

Exogamous patterns of mate-selection make an important contribution on the level of the movement as well. Inter-collective unions counteract the strong separatist tendencies of the local communities and foster cooperation between them. Marriages with members of training groups strengthen the ties between the Kibbutzim and the youth movements. Such unions often create a conflict of loyalties and threaten local continuity but the gains for the movement outweigh the losses for the local community. Marriage with outsiders who do not belong and do not identify with the collective movement is more problematical and occurs less frequently. Extra-movement unions link the Kibbutzim with other sectors of the society and provide valuable connections with other elite groups, but they often lead to desertion from the Kibbutz and dissociation from the movement. It is significant that the intra-collective, inter-collective and intra-youth movement unions are the most prevalent. These patterns maintain a flexible balance between in-group unity and closure and inter-group connectedness. It should be noted that marriage patterns have come to serve as integrating mechanisms of major importance.

The change of the position of the family and the growing importance of the kinship groups are symbolized and made manifest by the patterns of celebrating festive occasions. Weddings have become important events both for the families concerned and the community as a whole. They are celebrated by the whole Kibbutz and are made the occasion of big, joyous parties. There is a tendency in most Kibbutzim to celebrate a number of marriages together but the couples which participate in this joint communal celebration are entitled to an additional, more exclusive party for their friends and relatives. Many families celebrate wedding anniversaries and birthdays regularly and attach considerable importance to them. Relatives gather on all important family reunions. Celebrations of communal and national festivals have become much more kinship-typed. Members of each family tend to cluster and sit near one another. Members are entitled to invite relatives who are not members of the Kibbutz to these festivals. Hundreds of such guests come to each Kibbutz from far and wide and spend their holidays with relatives there.

Supplementary Institutional Mechanics — Checks on Familism

The transformation described above indicates clearly that the Kibbutz has moved far away from the anti-familistic pole.[32] It should be stressed, however, that there are powerful internal pressures which block the trend towards familism. The tendency to revert to a familistic division of labor is held in check by two major restraining factors: (a) the collectivistic emphasis; and (b) the tendency to extension of organizational units of rationalization and specialization. The attenuation of the collectivist ideology and the shift to intergenerational continuity ease the tension between family and community but the basic rivalry does not disappear. Inasmuch as the family accepts the primacy of collective consideration, it may become a valuable ally. Inasmuch as it resents a subordinate position and disputes the authority of collective institutions, it is still a potential source of conflict and competition. The collectivistic emphasis is now much more moderate and more tolerant towards differentiation, but the tendency to limit and control the family is still operative. Furthermore, the attentuation of the collectivistic restraints is partly counterbalanced by a considerable increase in the emphasis on rationalization and specialization of the economic structure of the Kibbutz. This accelerated process of rationalization counteracts the tendency to reversal to a non-specialized and small-scale domestic pattern.

The presence of such internal restraining factors accounts for the fact that, structurally speaking, the Kibbutz has remained basically non-familistic. Both husband and wife work full time in communal institutions and most goods and services are supplied directly to members by the community. Parents make an extremely significant and indispensable contribution to the socialization of their children, but the center of gravity has remained in communal institutions. The main responsibility for preparing the children for their roles as adult members in their Kibbutz rests with the educators. Parents have only a limited influence on the process of placement of their children and on their choice of occupation.[33] The family in the Kibbutz has a strong affective orientation; it emphasizes intimacy and exclusiveness. In itself, it is hardly fit to prepare the child for life in the Kibbutz, with its emphasis on togetherness and sharing and its highly rationalized work-centered economic system.

[32] It should be noted that the purpose of this case study is to underline the general trends. For lack of space we cannot present here our data on variation as to the extent and rate of change. Comparative data on different types of Kibbutzim and different categories of members indicate that there is considerable and patterned variation in this respect. For a comparative analysis of men versus women, first versus second generation members, leaders versus the rank and file and long established versus recently established Kibbutzin, see Y. Talmon-Garber, "Social Structure and Family Size." *ibid.* The Family and Collective Socialisation in the Kibbutz, *ibid.*

[33] On the problems of placement, see Y. Talmon-Garber, "Occupational Placement of the Second Generation in Collective Settlements," *Megamoth*, Vol. 8 (1957), pp. 352–369 (in Hebrew).

There is also the problem of social control in adult society. The Kibbutz makes many demands on its members, but employs only a few formal means of control. Allocation of material rewards is unrelated to position or performance and there are hardly any formal sanctions in cases of faulty execution of tasks or deviance. The proper functioning of the system depends primarily on the voluntary identification of the members of the Kibbutz with collective aims and ideals. The family represents the private sphere. If it becomes an independent, largely self-sufficient and powerful unit, it is bound to undermine the primacy of collective considerations. Comprehensive ties between co-members which are based on a shared ideology and common objectives may easily be superseded by divisive and narrow loyalties based on kinship affiliation.

The Kibbutzim are very much aware of the dangers inherent in the disengagement of the family from the collective. They have tried to check this trend by reinforcing the non-familistic division of labor and have gone about it in two seemingly opposed ways.\ Most important is the drive to improve the efficiency of the services by means of an intensive process of rationalization, mechanization and professionalization of service branches. Until recently, collective organization of consumption lagged far behind production and did not get a fair trial in this respect. At least part of the discontent which led to the reversal of functions to the family stemmed from the fact that the service institutions were allocated very limited resources and were not effectively organized. Most service branches operated with a minimal budget and inadequate, outdated equipment. The Kibbutzim are now reorganizing and mechanizing them all. In doing so, they draw on experience accumulated in the Kibbutzim and on the advice of various outside experts. They make a persistent effort to develop scientifically tested techniques in the sphere of housekeeping and child care and to turn these occupations into semi-professions. Workers in these fields are sent for professional training in institutions outside the community. The Federations organize seminars and refresher courses in home economics, nursing and child care, in which members get some theoretical grounding and practical guidance. Training is kept up and continued by extensive reading in semi-scientific literature and by occasional lectures. These efforts have a considerable effect on service and children's institutions. A process of gradual but cumulative improvement sets in and communal institutions are able to render much more satisfactory services.

The efficiency drive leads to the formulation of precisely defined, fixed regulations and to a certain formalization of communication and control. While increasing efficiency, this process entails standardization and often leads also to rigidity and imposed uniformity. Specialized bureaucratic agencies are effective in coping with repetitive routine tasks, but are not as well fitted to solve idiosyncratic personal problems.[34] There is an inherent tendency

[34] E. Litwak. "Complementary Functions of Bureaucratic and Family Organizations" (mimeographed); see also B. Moore, Jr., *Political Power and Social Theory*. Cambridge, Mass.: Harvard University Press, 1958.

in such agencies to treat situations and people "by the book," as if they were alike. They tend to assume sameness of needs and disregard differentiation of individual inclinations and tastes. The Kibbutzim make a special effort to avoid undue uniformization and inflexibility. They have counteracted the dysfunctions entailed in the process of bureaucratization by widening the margin of permitted variation and by allowing their members more freedom of choice. Workers in charge of the communal kitchen and dining hall make special efforts to cater to different tastes by diversifying their menus and offering as many alternative courses as possible. The range of consumer choice has become much wider than it used to be and personal predilections and idiosyncrasies are not disregarded. To cite another important example, the schedule in the children's houses has become much more flexible, and parents have more free access to them. Within certain circumscribed limits, parents are given a free hand. Communal institutions consciously cultivate a home-like, pleasant atmosphere, and the workers in charge are enjoined to treat members in a considerate and attentive manner. Disinterest in personal problems, impatience and brusqueness are severely censured. The task of inducing a process of bureaucratization and starting a counteracting process of de-bureaucratization, simultaneously, is difficult, but not insurmountable. Kibbutzim in which this policy was implemented in a systematic and determined way have managed to formalize their institutional structure, yet avoid many of the disfunctions entailed in such a process.

The familistic trend is very strong in most Kibbutzim and in many it seems to be gathering momentum. It is not easily curbed, yet the reorganization and the host of supplementary mechanisms evolved lately are not without avail. In some notable cases, the reorganization has brought about a partial reversal of trends. The families relinquish some of their newly acquired tasks and communal institutions are taking over again. This partial reversal of trends is particularly noticeable in the case of the relationship between the family and the communal kitchen and dining hall. In a number of Kibbutzim in our sample we were able to witness a partial comeback to the dining hall. Before the reorganization, it was very sparsely attended during the evening meal and looked almost deserted at times. The prompt service, the clean, comfortable and cheerfully decorated new hall and the good, varied food made communal dining much more attractive than it used to be and won over many of the adherents of the domestic pattern. Cooking and eating at home have not disappeared completely even after the reorganization, but most families now eat most of their meals in the communal dining hall. The familistic pattern serves as a complementary rather than a competing solution.

Reorganization and progressive professionalization check to some extent the familistic trend in the sphere of child-rearing as well. The mistrust and discontent which parents feel towards the communal children's institutions stem primarily from the tensions inherent in the collectivistic pattern itself, but the uneasiness and resentment are enhanced by faulty organization and a shortage of skilled and fully trained personnel. Collective socialization has been tried out under conditions which were far from optimal. Maintenance of educational institutions on a high level and unflagging efforts to develop and improve them bolster the confidence of parents in communal socialization and decrease the pressure for familistic innovations. Building of children's houses which are fully equipped and fully adapted to the needs of the children, careful calculation of the size of the groups and the adult-children ratio, modification of methods of recruitment and training of educators and critical appraisal and revision of educational methods increase the chances of success. Of considerable importance here are the attempts to regularize the contacts and improve communication between parents and the specialized personnel in charge of their children. Special efforts are made now to draw them into active participation in activities in the children's houses, and to enlist their cooperation in their contacts with their children at home.

The anti-familism of the revolutionary phase has thus abated, but has not disappeared altogether. It has been superseded by a moderate collectivism which regards the family as a useful though dangerous ally. The Kibbutzim still try to control and limit the family and direct it towards the attainment of collective goals. The main problem of the Kibbutzim from a dynamic point of view is how to allow the family more privacy and a certain internal autonomy without harming the cohesion of the community.

Selected Readings

Bentwich, N. (Ed.) *A New Way of Life: The Collective Settlements of Israel.* London: Shindles and Golomb, 1949.

Buber, M. *Paths in Utopia.* London: Routledge and Kegan Paul, 1949.

Darin-Drabkin, H. *The Other Society.* London: Gollancz, 1962.

Deroche, H. *Au pays du Kibbutz.* Paris: Union Suisse des Coopératives de Consommation, 1960.

Friedmann, G. "L'aventure kibbutsique et les défis du siècle," *Revue française de sociologie*, Vol. 5 (1964), pp. 259–289.

Infield, H. F. *Cooperative Living in Palestine.* London: Kegan Paul, Trench, Trubner, 1946.

————. *Cooperative Communities at Work.* London: Kegan Paul, Trench, Trubner, 1947.

Landshut, S. *The Kvutza.* Jerusalem, The Zionist Library, 1944. (In Hebrew.)

Spiro, M. E. *Kibbutz: Venture in Utopia.* Cambridge, Mass.: Harvard University Press, 1956.

————. *Children of the Kibbutz.* Cambridge, Mass.: Harvard University Press, 1958.

Talmon-Garber, Y., and E. Cohen. "Collective Settlements in the Negev," in J. Ben-David (Ed.), *Agricultural Planning and Village Community in Israel.* Paris: UNESCO, 1964.

Kibbutz and Parental Investment
(*Women in the Kibbutz* Reconsidered)

Joseph Shepher and Lionel Tiger

On 15 September 1975, two books waited for the Israeli author in his mailbox at the University of Haifa: the first copy of *Women in the Kibbutz*, just arrived from New York, and the heavy volume of E. O. Wilson, *Sociobiology: A New Synthesis* (1975). Shepher browsed with satisfaction through the pages of his recently published book with Lionel Tiger, but did not read it: he knew it almost by heart from the repeated proofreadings. Instead, he began to study Wilson's book. When after several days, he finished chapters 15 and 16, on parental investment, he was as though struck by lightning: the lightning of overwhelming evidence. But it was too late. The book was out and had run its course. Its three editions provoked some forty-odd reviews and created a scientific debate. Most of the reviewers praised the well organized data and the sophistication of their analysis but disagreed with the authors' interpretation. Especially the feminists— Bernard (1976), Shapiro (1976), Somerville (1979), and Syrkin (1976) accused the authors with selectiveness of analysis of different data, of internal contradictions and of biological determinism. Others, like Cohen (1976), Peres and Russkin (1977), Rosner and Palgi (1976) were more balanced in their criticism. Interestingly, none of the critics claimed that Tiger and Shepher were wrong in their *biological* argument, that their use of the vague concept of "biogrammar" is theoretically vulnerable and guilty of group selectionist aberrations. Most sociobiologists praised the book and quoted it repeatedly: Wilson (1979), van den Berghe (1979).

It is only fair that after five years, the authors themselves should reconsider their own arguments and put them in the correct theoretical perspective. In fact, we, the authors, can hardly excuse our ignoring parental investment theory as the right theoretical framework for our argumentation by the synchrony of the publication of our book with that of Wilson's. All his enormous contribution to the formulation of sociobiological theory notwithstanding, E. O. Wilson was, to a certain extent, codifying earlier pieces of the theoretical framework: especially that of Hamilton (1964) and Trivers (1972). Whereas Hamilton's papers were published in a highly professional biological journal, Trivers' article (1972) was published in a volume much more accessible to social scientists: Campbell's *Sexual Selection and the Evolution of Man (1871–1971)* (1972). In fact, both authors read this volume during the hectic days of the writing of their own book, but apparently did not realize the relevance of Trivers' paper (that was based mainly on ornithological evidence) to their own human case. Moreover, as most social scientists, the authors were too slow in adjusting themselves to the new forms of evolutionary thinking and in keeping up with the burgeoning literature of the early 1970s. Be as it may, it is never too late to admit one's shortcomings and to try to set them aright.

Trivers' theory of parental investment is as simple as it is powerful. It is, in fact, a specific case of Hamilton's (1964) inclusive fitness theory. Hamilton, in his effort to answer the question whether altruism is a plausible evolutionary strategy, convincingly proves that an animal can increase its fitness (the relative number of its surviving offspring) not only by breeding itself, but, instead, by helping its close relatives to breed. This help—consentaneously called altruism— is proportional to the degree of relatedness of the benefactor to the beneficiary. The question of whether an animal should breed itself or should act altruistically to its relatives is a question of individual strategy highly dependent on environmental factors.

Another problem of strategy arises between males and females in sexually reproducing species. In order to have offspring, a sexually reproducing creature has to combine its genes with those of the opposite sex. In some species, the offspring is created by the very fact of fertilization and no additional care is needed to bring the offspring to maturation. In others, different energetic efforts are needed to achieve the same purpose, such as gestation, feeding, protecting, teaching, etc. All these efforts may collectively be called parental investment, although in many species the biological parents do not perform them (the best examples are the hymenoptera).

In most birds and mammals, parental investment is highly asymmetric. The greatest part of parental investment is done by the female, and in some avian and mammal species, the male only contributes his sex cells. The disproportionate parental investment is the basis of different sexual strategies of males and females. Since the female usually is the high investor, she becomes a limiting resource for the low investor males. Males usually fight for females and the latter are cautious and selective. Males usually tend to mate polygynously, being able to genetically benefit from mating with every female, mainly because they count on the high investment of the female which would prevent her from deserting the offspring. On the other hand, females are not usually prone to being polyandrous because they cannot, thereby, increase their fitness. Consequently, it is hardly surprising that in the whole mammalian class, polygyny is usual and polyandry is highly exceptional. So it is with humans. More than 70 percent of human societies are polygynous, whereas only 1 percent are polyandrous.

Parental investment and inclusive fitness explain not only male-female strategies, but also parent-child conflict and sibling conflict (Trivers 1974), and several problems of courtship, kinship and marriage (Chagnon and Irons 1979; Symons 1979).

Let us now review our findings in the light of the parental investment (pi) theory. We summarized them on pages 262–263 of our book:

1. Early in kibbutz history, more than half the women worked for a considerable time in production. Then came a long, gradual process of sexual polarization of work. Today the sexual division of labor has reached about 80 percent of maximum.

2. Sexual division of labor is more polarized in the second and kibbutz-bred generations than it is in the first generation, and more polarized in younger kibbutzim than in older ones.

3. Despite complete formal equality in political rights, women are less active in the General Assembly than men are, as measured both by their presence in the Assembly and by the incidence of their participation. Women are somewhat overrepresented in committees dealing with social, educational, and cultural problems; they are seriously underrepresented in committees dealing with economy, work, general policymaking, and security.

4. The higher the authority of an office or committee, the lower the percentage of women in it. At the highest level of the kibbutz, women make up only 14 percent of the personnel.

5. Women seem to have special problems sustaining all-female work groups; they usually prefer mixed-sex groups or male leadership.

6. Men and women receive nearly the same number of years of education; in fact, women have a slight edge. Advanced schooling, however, differs in kind for each sex. Women are overrepresented in higher nonacademic education leading to such jobs as elementary-school teaching, kindergarten teaching, and medical nursing. Men are overrepresented in higher academic education leading to such jobs as agriculture, engineering, economics, and management.

7. From the ninth grade on, women consistently fall below men in scholarly achievement. This discrepency between sexes seems to be wider here than in comparable modern societies.

8. Although women, like men, are drafted into the army, the overwhelming majority of kibbutz girls (like other Israeli girls) do secretarial and service jobs there; few do characteristically male work or occupy command positions. The conception of the women's army as essentially a substitute unit, also providing back-up aid and encouragement for the fighting men, is completely accepted by the kibbutz girls. There has, however, been a steady expansion of the range of noncombat tasks for women.

9. Even the long, demanding Yom Kippur War did not substantially change the division of labor in the kibbutzim, even though almost half the men were called up by the army for a long period.

10. The family has risen from its initial shadowy existence to become the basic unit of kibbutz social structure. It now fulfills important functions in consumption and education, and there are demands for further expanding its function. Increased familization is indicated by high and growing rates of birth and marriage, and by a decreasing divorce rate. The status of singles, especially of women, is becoming more and more problematic, to the extent that the family, the kibbutz and even the federations now try to help them marry.

11. The main instigators of familization are women, whose attitude toward familism is more positive than men's.

12. Attitudes toward equality have always been more egalitarian than actual behavior has. The discrepancy causes recurrent soul-searching within the kibbutzim and federations.

How is sexual division of labor connected with parental investment theory? Obviously, the higher parental investment of the female is energetically extremely demanding. The very asymmetry of parental investment between male and female is the foundation of sexual division of labor. Assuming that every individual has the ability to expend a limited and equal amount of energy to all the possible endeavors and purposes, the female, by investing generously in the offspring, has to forego investments in alternative tasks. Assuming that amount of energy expended is not limited but flexible because of possible time differences in energy investment, the female has to work more hours than the male if she wants to perform the same tasks in addition to those of her high parental investment. Thus, if we take the first assumption that is $\Sigma e_m = \Sigma e_f$ (total available energy is equal in both sexes) and we know that $pi_f > pi_m$ then the free energy fe of the male must be greater than that of the female.

Thus, $fe_m = \Sigma e - pi_m$ and

$fe_f = \Sigma e - pi_f$ and since:

$pi_f > pi_m$ therefore, obviously:

$fe_m > fe_f$

In the case of the second assumption, the total available energy will be a linear function of time:

$\Sigma e_m = t_m e$ Where e is the unit of energy expended in t time:

$\Sigma e_f = t_f e$ and therefore, free energy:

$fe_m = t_m e - pi_m$

$fe_f = t_f e - pi_f$ therefore $fe_m = fe_f$ is possible only if $t_f > t_m$

Assuming that fe_m should be equal to fe_f, we have:

$t_m e - pi_m = t_f e - pi_f$

$pi_f - pi_m = t_f e - t_m e$ or:

$\Delta pi = \Delta te$ that is, the higher the difference in parental investment between the female and the male, the higher the difference between the time she and the male have to work in order to have the same "free energy."

All this concerns the quantitative aspects of division of labor between the sexes. The size of parental investment depends on the number of children, their ages and spacing of births. Δpi is uninfluenced by pi_m until after delivery, except the male's contribution to the female's feeding and thereby, to the nutrition of the offspring. After delivery, Δpi is highly dependent on the propensity of the male to invest in the offspring directly or indirectly, although the flexibility of Δpi is much lower in preindustrial cultures where lactation is simply part of the natural order of things.

Sexual division of labor is not less dependent on asymmetry of parental investment from the qualitative point of view. Not only is the female able to expend less "free energy" than the male, but the free energy she does expend must be devoted to tasks, that in order to be fulfilled, have to be in close propinquity to the tasks of parental investment. Hence, the "domestic" character of "female" tasks. Guarding the fire, home making, cooking, washing, or alternatively any work that can be carried out without unduly moving, transferring or otherwise disturbing the baby.

All this assumes that only the two parents can share the parental investment. But parents can and do delegate their parental investment activities, first of all to relatives, such as siblings, grandparents, uncles, aunts, who themselves, are interested in the wellbeing of the offspring according to Hamilton's inclusive fitness principle. Since in most cases, maternal investment is thereby alleviated, we usually speak of "allomothering." Allomothering can be part of inclusive fitness altruism, but it can be undertaken by an unrelated individual if she can profit thereby, by training herself in mothering for her future tasks.

In the case of the kibbutz, we witness *an institutionalized allomothering*. In the "classical" collective system of housing (see Tiger and Shepher 1975, pp. 56, 162–165) the parents spent from $1^1/_2$ to 3–4 hours per day with their child, according to the child's age: the older the child, the longer the time spent with him. The "real" parental investment—feeding (after weaning), washing, dressing, toilet training, playing, teaching, walking—was carried out mainly by a nurse or nurses, absolutely unrelated to the child. (Normatively, the policy was to prevent sisters, grandmothers, or aunts from working with the children in order to maintain the universalistic standards between the nurses and the children.) During the night, the children sleeping in the children's houses—usually situated in the ecological heart of the kibbutz—were watched by a female nightwatch.

Such a far reaching delegation of parental investment to nonrelatives, especially in early childhood, is extremely rare in human societies. Under what conditions would one expect such a strategy? If the parental investment theory makes good sense, one has to hypothesize that such a strategy would be chosen only in extreme situations, in which all the energy is needed in order to provide the basic needs of life such as food, shelter, and security. Such situations arise, for instance, during war, extreme difficulties in production, and during scarcity of manpower. In the early kibbutz, all these elements were present, with two additional factors: this was a self-selected group of unrelated youngsters, and they believed that they could substitute friendship relations for family relations (see pp. 37–38, 59, 206–210). Therefore, no relatives for allomothering were available. Even if there were, the ideology stemming largely, but not exclusively, from the extreme situations, and their having nicely adjusted to them, prevented "nepotistic" allomothering. Not that the whole process of the collectivization was very smooth (see p. 161) and, at least partially, the origin of the Moshav Movement can be traced back to the disputes on parental investment in the first kibbutz (Bein 1945, pp. 166–168, 230–232). Moreover, the general attitude was not to hasten with marriage, and when married, to postpone having children (see pp. 206–210). Thus, the group had decided to change the composition of total free energy available to all tasks except parental investment to:

$$\Sigma fe_1 = fe_m + fe_f = (\Sigma e - pi_m) + (\Sigma e - pi_f)$$

By having only a few children (let us assume 25 percent of the women) we shall have:

$$\Sigma fe_2 = (\Sigma e - pi_m) + 0.75 (\Sigma e - pi_m) + 0.25 (\Sigma e - pi_f)$$
$$\Sigma fe_2 = 1.75 (\Sigma e - pi_m) + 0.25 (\Sigma e - pi_f)$$

whence it is obvious that:

$$\Sigma fe_2 > \Sigma fe_1$$ where Σfe_1 represents a situation in which all adult females have children.

Moreover, instead of letting all the mothers freely invest in their offspring, the kibbutz instituted groups of five children nursed by a single nurse, thereby cutting total parental investment by 80 percent and increasing the free available energy considerably. That was not easy either, but it was rendered possible because of the dire environmental conditions, the powerful ideology and the tight solidarity of the group.

From the point of view of the individual, this strategy was acceptable as long as he or she considered his or her attachment to the group as mentally, emotionally and economically better for parent and offspring than in another social form. There were expectable differences between males and females. The latter had more difficulties in accepting the strategy than the former, because of their higher initial parental investment. The long and obstinate fight to return to personal, and not delegated, parental investment is largely the fight of women.

Of course, not all members of the kibbutz were prepared to delegate parental investment to others. Many left the kibbutz and are still leaving because of the collectivistic parental investment strategy. Recently, the Kibbutz Artzi federation stood up in its convention against the pressure of legitimately introducing the familistic housing system of the children. One of the results: couples leave the kibbutzim of the Artzi federation and join kibbutzim of the Ichud federation, where the housing system is familistic.

In view of the system of delegated parental investment, one can easily understand the quasi-underground existence of the family in the early kibbutz, as well as the impressive process of gradual familization.

The nuclear monogamous family, as was known in the cultures where most kibbutz founders were socialized, was a result of high paternal investment in the offspring. The economic existence of the female and her children was dependent on the male's work. Bulwarked by religious sanctions, this created either a very strong social control, negatively sanctioning males who neglected their paternal duties, and/or the romantic love complex which was largely the outcome of atomization of the productive system, the dependence of sexual outlet on marriage, and the competition among males for the most desirable females. The traditional sexual division of labor between the providing male and the home-making socializing female broke down in the early kibbutz. Everyone had to provide. There were few children and few home services. Hence, the nuclear family was also unimportant. Couples were slowly formed, there was a high rate of divorce and a lot of talk of free love. Marriages were informally contracted and even the privacy of the couple was intruded upon by the "primus" custom (see pp. 207–210). Since the investment of the male was not needed or at least not individually, it was not necessary for the nuclear family to be an important and stable unit. This explains the comparatively large percentage of singles (not divorced or widowed!), both males and females, who have children in the kibbutz:

	Males %	N	Females %	N
Kibbutz Artzi	1.73	(17)	3.22	(17)
Ichud	3.69	(61)	3.73	(27)
Total		78		44

	Males %	N	Females %	N
Comparable* data for Israel	2.95	9,100	1.96	4,500

* Not strictly comparable because those singles are not necessarily the parents of the children in the household.
Source: Statistical Abstracts, 1979.

Also a very large percentage of divorced and widowed singles have children:

	Males %	N	Females %	N
Kibbutz Artzi	91.04	(216)	95.84	(578)
Ichud	83.63	(181)	93.68	(595)
Total		397		1,173

Source: Tiger and Shepher (1975). Computed from tables 2, 50a, 51a.

Obviously, if the parental investment is delegated to the collective, the marital status of the parents does not have a decisive impact on the socialization of the children.

But when the economic and security situation improved, and starting from the late 1930s, more and more children appeared (Shepher 1977, pp. 38–41), even the delegated system of parental investment created a sexual divjision of labor. Since an increasing number of women were extracted from the labor pool of production in order to handle the growing number of young children (nobody suggested that men should do this), and since the growing population needed more services, more women who wanted to be close to their children, first reluctantly and later willingly, agreed to supply the services of cooking, washing, ironing, mending and health care.

However, it was a change of degree, not of kind. It was not until the mid-1950s, after the War of Liberation was over, when security was much better and the economic situation had greatly improved, that the twin process of polarization of sexual division of labor and "familization" achieved momentum. With the amazing force of an irresistible social movement, the women of the Ichud federation won their case: the familistic system of housing was legitimized in 1967, and today there are almost no kibbutzim left in the Ichud federation with the collectivistic system. The Kibbutz Meuchad federation followed, and with the impending fusion between the two federations, the last obstacles were to be removed before the full introduction of the familistic system. The Kibbutz Artzi federation, in which such an "iconoclastic" proposal could not even be mentioned earlier, was compelled to deal in its national convention recently, with the formal request of one of its kibbutzim to introduce the familistic system of housing. In spite of a very effective informal pressure of the young women in many kibbutzim, the convention rejected the request, trying to block the way of the growing social movement within its cohorts exactly as the Ichud federation did in 1950 and 1964, and probably with no greater chance of success.

The defenders of the ideology, mainly males, found consolation in the illusion that the change in the housing system is not more than a technical matter. What happened though was nothing but the *reindividuation of the parental investment*. Instead of 1–3 hours, mothers now spent 15 hours per day with their children. They bathed them, put them to bed, woke them up in the morning, bathed them again, dressed them, brought them back to the children's house, and visited them there once or twice during the day-care hours between 7:00 a.m. and 4:00 p.m. The nursing mother kept her baby at home 24 hours a day for the first 3 to 6 months and only thereafter brought it to the babies' house for the day. In acknowledgement of the fact that females take the greatest part of this new individual parental investment, the working hours of the mothers were formally cut from 12.5–37.5 percent, no matter where those mothers worked. Since most of them, however, worked in the children's houses, the cut is an obvious change in the direction of the individuation of parental investment. The corollaries of this sweeping change strengthened the nuclear family tremendously. The familistic system of housing necessitated a large apartment. Instead of the 1–1½ room apartment allotted to a couple whose children spent the night in the children's houses, the new system provided the family 2–3 bedrooms, a large living room complete with a kitchenette, and an open or closed patio. The big apartment required much housework, and the kitchenette was an attracting factor for the family to have its evening meals there instead of in the communal dining hall.

Having more housework, the woman needs more help from her mate. More paternal investment strengthens the nuclear family. All the indicators of its growing importance appear: the romantic love complex, early dating and early sex life of the young females, early marriage, great formal ceremonialism of the wedding, stability of the marriage, descending divorce rates, ascending remarriage rates, almost unbearable social status of singles, especially of females in the age of fertility, institutionalized and informal matching for singles, and rising fertility rates reaching a new modal average of four children per couple.

The males, indeed, invest much more than before in their children and in the family home. Seeing his mate almost collapsing under her self-imposed heavy burden of five to seven hours of work, housework, preparation of meals, nursing and nurturing the children, the male takes upon himself the heavy work of gardening, removing the garbage, bringing and taking the laundry, and occasionally substituting for the tired wife by bringing food and washing the children, etc.

The strong nuclear family constantly attracts new functions to itself: it is a central unit of consumption, it has an important say in matters of education, it becomes a focus of rites de passage of all its members. Bowing to this general tendency, the kibbutz transfers functions that were once characteristically collective, to the family: care for the children during Sabbath, care for the sick, and care for the aged. Especially in cases of manpower shortage, the kibbutz readily finds solutions in the general atmosphere of inclusive fitness and parental investment. This development pushes the kibbutz to the extreme limit of its uniqueness—it becomes more and more like the *moshav shitufi*, a kolchoz-like form of cooperation, where production is collective but consumption is individual.

In what sense is the present explanation superior to what we used in our book (see pp. 269–281)? There we used a very inarticulate and, even at the time of its English publication (1973), completely outdated biological paradigm—that of Count (1973). Count's essays on the biogram were first published in German and English (Count 1958a and 1958b). In his elaboration of the vague concept of biogram, Count (1973, pp. 25–26) devoted two pages to the concept of "parentalism" and actually spoke of parental investment, but surprisingly, he did not reach the conclusion that there might generally be some differences between the sexes in parental investment. Even in dealing with the mammalian biogram, he had only this to say:

> The peculiar mammalian physiological pattern of coitus-uterine gestation-lactation has its psychological corollary. The female always possesses a double reproductive orientation: an erotic orientation toward a male partner and a broody orientation toward her offspring; while the male possesses but one: an erotic orientation toward a female partner. Hence the monopoly of familialism by the female sex.

Count completely misses the point: the problem is not single and double orientation, but basically higher female parental investment and high variability of male parental investment. The question is—generally and especially in the human case—under what conditions will a strategy of higher parental investment "pay" for a male. Shepher (1978) tried to explain how the human male became a reluctant monogamist deviating, thereby, from the usual mammalian pattern.

Tiger and Fox (1971, p. 6) criticized the concept of biogram: "the total repertoire of possible behaviors of any species." They argued that such a repertoire would be a static list, and in order to understand how the elements in the list are related, one had to know the rules that governed the relationships between the different items of the repertoire. These rules being similar to those of the grammar of a language, can therefore be called "biogrammar." Thus the human biogrammar would be then the set of ground rules according to which the repertoire of universally human behavioral traits is organized.

Let us now return to *Women in the Kibbutz*. We presented our main argument on page 272:

> We have already cited evidence that sex differences in political and economic activity are universal, that the care of young children is virtually everywhere a female monopoly, and that some widely argued explanations for this universality are weak, improbable, or partial. Our data show that although some 10 to 15 percent of the women in the kibbutz express dissatisfaction with their sociosexual roles, the overwhelming majority not only accept their situations but have sought them. They have acted against the principles of their socialization and ideology, against the wishes of the men of their communities, against the economic interest

of the kibbutzim, in order to be able to devote more time and energy to private maternal activities rather than to economic and political public ones. Obviously these women have minds of their own; despite obstacles, they are trying to accomplish what women elsewhere have been periodically urged to reject by critics of traditional female roles. Our biogrammatical assertion is that the behavior of these mothers is ethologically probable: they are seeking an association with their own offspring, which reflects a species-wide attraction between mothers and their young. Usually women have no choice but to have close contact with their children; in the kibbutz, the opposite is true. So, what kibbutz women choose to do may be significantly related to what other women elsewhere routinely do under similar circumstances, if also apparently more constraining ones. A single case cannot define a species, but given the experimental style of kibbutz society, the result is certainly revealing.

All this is true but the argument that kibbutz women act in an "ethologically probable" way is a theoretically free-swaying assertion. Kibbutz women act as they do because they are mammals and, therefore, are predisposed to a high and direct parental investment. They, being cultural animals, are able to subdue this predisposition as long as the environmental situation makes such a postponment and suppression the only viable alternative. No sooner is the pressure removed, the behavior predictable through parental investment theory inexorably returns.

Then too: in our handling the double phenomenon of polarization of sexual division of labor and familization, we argued that the two processes were parallel, but we did not show why. Parental investment theory explains both, and in fact, argues that the two phenomena are the different facets of the same process, namely, the reindividuation of parental investment.

We rather agree with our own critics. We accept the data, but we criticize the interpretation, only for different reasons.

References

Bein, A., 1945. *The History of Zionist Settlement*. Tel-Aviv: Masada (Hebrew).

Bernard, J., 1976. "Maternal Deprivation: a New Twist." *Contemporary Psychology* 23: 172–74.

Chagnon, N. A., and G. I. Irons, 1979. *Evolutionary Biology and Human Social Behavior*. North Scituate, Mass.: Duxberry.

Cohen, Erik, 1976. Review in *American Journal of Sociology*: 708–9.

Count, Earl W., 1973. *Being and Becoming Human: Essays on the Biogram*. New York: Van Nostrand Reinhold.

Count, Earl W., 1958a. "The Biological Basis of Human Sociality." *American Anthropologist* 60: 1049–85.

Count, Earl W., 1958b. "Eine Biologische Entwicklungsgeschichte der Menschlichen Socialität." *Homo* 9: 129–46.

Hamilton, W. D., 1964. "The Genetical Evolution of Social Behavior." *Journal of Theoretical Biology* 7: 1–52.

Peres, Y., and Russkin, L., 1977. Review in *Journal of Marriage and Family* 39: 627–28.

Rosner, M., and M. Palgi, 1976. "Sexual Equality in the Kibbutz: A Retreat or a Change of Significance?" *Kibbutz* 3–4: 149–85 (Hebrew).

Shapiro, J. R., 1976. "Determinants of Role Differentiation: The Kibbutz Case." *Reviews in Anthropology* (Nov.–Dec. 1976): 682–92.

Shepher, Joseph, 1977. *Introduction to the Sociology of the Kibbutz.* Ruppin Institute (Hebrew).

Shepher, Joseph, 1978. "Reflections on the Origin of the Human Pair Bond." *Journal of Social and Biological Structures* 1: 3.

Sommerville, M. R., 1979. Review in *Contemporary Sociology* 8(2).

Symons, Donald, 1979. *The Evolutionary Theory of Human Sexuality.* New York and Oxford: Oxford University Press.

Syrkin, Marie, 1976. Review in *The New Republic* (November): 25–27.

Tiger, L., and R. Fox, 1971. *The Imperial Animal.* New York: Holt, Rinehart and Winston.

Tiger, L., and J. Shepher, 1975. *Women in the Kibbutz.* New York: Harcourt, Brace & Jovanovich.

Trivers, R. L., 1972. "Parental Investment and Sexual Selection." In B. Campbell (ed.), *Sexual Selection and the Descent of Man, 1871–1971.* Chicago: Aldine-Atherton.

Trivers, R. L., 1974. "Parent-Offspring Conflict." *American Zoologist* 14.

Van den Berghe, Pierre, 1979. *Human Family Systems.* New York: Elsevier.

Wilson, E. O., 1975. *Sociobiology: A New Synthesis.* Cambridge, Mass.: Harvard-Belknap.

Wilson, E. O., 1978. *On Human Nature.* Cambridge Mass: Harvard University Press.

Relations between Generations
in the Israeli Kibbutz

Erik Cohen and Menachem Rosner

The Israeli kibbutz is approaching social maturity; most kibbutzim were founded more than twenty years ago, the oldest have been in existence for fifty to sixty years. New membership today is drawn mostly from children of the kibbutz, whereas in the past most recruits came from outside.[1] In the oldest kibbutzim the second generation already account for one third to one half of the membership; they form the largest single social group and fill some of the central roles in the community.[2] The second generation are well on the way to taking over the economic, public, and social direction of the kibbutz from the founders and other groups of members who joined after its establishment.

Second generation members upon reaching maturity tend to remain in the kibbutz in which they were born, except those who transfer to another kibbutz on marriage or abandon the kibbutz way of life altogether.[3] The second generation member is, indeed, expected to continue to live in his kibbutz of origin, though he may spend a year or two helping a younger kibbutz.[4] However, he is

[1] On the second generation see M.E. Spiro, *Children of the Kibbutz* (Harvard University Press, 1958). In 1967 there were 45,000 members of Kibbutzim of whom 22 per cent belonged to the second generation.

[2] For example: in one of the two mature kibbutzim recently studied, there were 107 members of the second generation out of a total of 298; in another, 176 out of 437.

[3] On marriage patterns of the second generation see Y. Talmon-Garber, 'Mate Selection in Collective Settlements', *American Sociological Review*, 1964, 491–508. No reliable information exists on the percentage of second generation members who left the kibbutz movement as a whole. In one of the movements 16·1 per cent out of 3000 second generation members had left by 1967.

[4] On patterns of assistance between older and younger kibbutzim see Y. Talmon and E. Cohen, 'Collective Settlements in the Negev', in J. Ben-David (ed.), *Agricultural Planning and Village Community in Israel* (UNESCO, 1964).

not expected to stay on in the younger one and he usually prefers to return to his kibbutz. Until recently only one new kibbutz had been actually founded by second generation youngsters. Though some of the kibbutz federations admit the necessity of new kibbutzim founded by the second generation, it was not until the Six Day War, when new problems of national defence were created in the conquered areas, that several new kibbutzim were established by the second generation in the Golan heights and in northern Sinai.

Superficially, it seems that there is an orderly transition in the kibbutzim, each community being self-perpetuating. However, such a conclusion glosses over a most important issue: what does continuity in the kibbutz actually mean? It may mean two quite different things: continuity of ideologically anchored norms and behaviour, or continuity, as an ongoing social concern, of an ecologically based social group. The mere fact that the second generation stay where they were born does not in itself guarantee the continuity of the kibbutz as a utopian society based on a distinct ideology. Indeed, the crucial problem in any analysis of continuity in the kibbutz is to understand the attitudes of the second generation towards kibbutz life.

Students of the kibbutz framed this problem in terms of the 'inheritance of a revolution'[5]: the paradox of people who had revolted against their own parents and who transmit their revolutionary ideology to their children, who in their turn are expected to continue peacefully the life work of their parents. The empirical question which most investigators have studied is: are the institutional arrangements of the kibbutz adequate to create in the second generation the personality, attitudes, and skills necessary for a successful economic, social, or ideological transmission from one generation to the next?[6] Their answers to these questions were affirmative or negative, according to their own attitudes, methodology, and the type of community or federation in which they happened to have worked; no conclusive evidence in either direction has yet been presented.

[5] Particularly by Y. Talmon-Garber in lectures and private conversation. A similar approach, though differently formulated, characterized M. Spiro's *Children of the Kibbutz, op. cit.*; and, on a different and somewhat abstract level, S. Rettig and B. Pasamanick, 'Some Observations on the Moral Ideology of First and Second Generation Collective and Non-Collective Settlers in Israel', *Social Problems*, No. 2, 1963.

[6] Ibid.; see also Spiro, *op. cit.*

This muddled state of affairs invites a new look, not only at the empirical data, but also at the underlying theoretical problem. Its reformulation may provide a new insight into the generational dynamics and the broader forces of change at work in the kibbutz.

The underlying assumption of most investigators has apparently been that the original ideology of the kibbutz was a solid and well-integrated body of values, which the parents tried to inculcate in their children. When the parent generation was not successful in such an attempt, various extra-ideological factors were called upon to account for the failure. Particularly prominent among these was the drifting away of the parent generation from the original values, which created a discrepancy between the official teaching and the actual experience of second generation members when observing the everyday behaviour of their elders. Influences extraneous to the kibbutz were also often invoked: the second generation's contact with peers from the cities and other settlements, while in the army or on their visits to towns, as well as with mass communication media – newspapers, radio, films.[7] Less often, the second generation's structural position within the community is used as a clue to explain their acceptance or rejection of a value-precept.[8]

Interpretations of this kind may go some way to explain the ideological attitude of the second generation. However, they overlook a point which is crucial to the transmission process in the kibbutz: the original ideology, far from being a solid and well integrated whole, actually contains many inconsistencies and contradictions; these permit an elastic and many-sided interpretation of the original values of the kibbutz, all of which might be considered legitimate. Thus the very body of ideas and ideals which is to be transmitted is in itself complex and problematic,[9] and the extent of success of the transmission cannot be adequately established by simply finding out whether the second generation accepts or rejects any particular item of some 'original ideology'. The problem is often not one of acceptance or rejection but just of

[7] See particularly M. Sarell, 'Shamranuth' Ve'Hidush' Be'dor Hasheni Be'kibbutzim ('Conservatism' and 'Innovation' in the second generation in the Kibbutz), *Megamot*, No. 2, 1961.
[8] See Y. Talmon-Garber, 'Social Structure and Family Size,' *Human Relations*, 1959.
[9] For an example of this approach, see E. Cohen, 'Progress and Communality: Value Dilemmas in the Collective Movement', *International Review of Community Development*, 1966.

differing interpretation. And the crucial theoretical question is, which factors influence the second generation members to prefer one of the possible interpretations of the basic values to any other. Such an approach enables us to look upon the ideology in a dynamic, undogmatic way, with the second generation playing a creative role in the process of ideological reformulation.

In order to answer this question, our point of departure will be similar to that of other studies: the structural position of the second generation in the kibbutz as heir to a revolution, and we shall try to show how this position influences the second generation's ideological preferences in the various spheres of kibbutz life.

The first generation of kibbutz members chose kibbutz life voluntarily and deliberately as an alternative to the bourgeois way of life of their parents which they had rejected. Although they may have been living on a kibbutz for a quarter of a century or more, their approach to kibbutz life is still what we call an 'outside-in' approach: their basic frame of reference is society outside the kibbutz, as it is or as they imagine it to be, and they look upon the kibbutz as a social experiment within this society. The second generation, being born into the kibbutz and almost automatically accepted into membership, have a different approach, one which we call 'inside-out'. The kibbutz for them is a fact, a way of life as any other; the world outside is mostly unknown and they are curious to encounter it and compare it with the kibbutz. The revolutionary struggle of their parents has little meaning for them. They struggle with a different problem: to endow their own life with meaning within the setting of a revolutionary movement, the course of which has in fact not been set by themselves. While trying to come to terms with this problem they formulate their own interpretation of kibbutz life and its ideology. The differences between the first and second generations in their interpretations of kibbutz life could be formulated in terms of five central dilemmas:

1. *The kibbutz as a social experiment vs. the kibbutz as a home*: for the first generation the kibbutz is still something strange and not wholly self-evident; it is a conscious social creation and has to be constantly regulated, interpreted, and evaluated. For the second generation, on the other hand, it is a natural way of life, a home, which in itself does not cause astonishment or inner elation. The first generation often see the kibbutz as a social form which is

wholly different from any other, not comparable with ordinary forms of human existence. The second generation look upon it more as another form of human organization and feel free to compare it to forms of life outside the kibbutz.

2. *Cognitive vs. emotional emphasis*: for the first generation the choice of kibbutz life was a matter of profound personal conviction; they might be emotionally deeply bound to their community, but the intellectual conviction that they chose the 'right' way of life is predominant in their orientation; the second generation are predominantly emotionally attached to the kibbutz, but less concerned with it intellectually. This point often comes to the fore in discussions between the generations: 'The second generation who grow up in the kibbutz are not able to explain the ideological value of kibbutz life. There is a great danger in this. There are values which should be taught.'[10] First generation members assert that the second generation 'do not know why' they live in the kibbutz. A second generation member answered these charges in an incisive article by stating: 'Those who doubt and say: "You (the second generation) have no value-conviction but only habit and love, and these give no security in the world" . . . should be told: "The love of life is the love of man . . . Let us not forget that equality and cooperation are only means, but the love of man and aspiration to a meaningful life are ends in themselves.'[11] This exchange demonstrates the inter-generational conflict in terms of conviction vs. emotion.

3. *Emphasis on values and concepts vs. emphasis on persons*: here lies possibly the most far-reaching difference between the generations. The first generation conceived of an ideal community which the members are expected to live up to; if they cannot do so they are at fault. S. Diamond emphasized this point when he quoted the typical reaction of old-time members to the inadequacies of life in the kibbutz: 'The kibbutz . . . is excellent; it is men who are not worthy'.[12] The second generation, however, concern themselves with real living persons, not with ideal constructs. 'Our parents made an anti-religious revolution. They removed God from his

10 G.R. in, 'Chaverim Mesichim – Hakibbutz Be'e'inei Hador Hasheni' (Members talk – the Kibbutz in the eyes of the second generation), *Hedim*, 1967.
11 O. Lulav, 'Atem Ve'ilu Anachnu' (You! And We?) *Hedim*, 1968.
12 S. Diamond, 'Kibbutz and Shtetl: The History of an Idea', *Social Problems*, 1957, 98.

throne and in His place they put the values of the kibbutz. They created a religion of the kibbutz. They have a great zeal for values but not for human beings. The parents have turned the values of their life into God's words and have stopped seeing man in his pettiness and weakness. They probably felt that human beings in themselves do not measure up to its obligations, but instead of trying to discover the defects in the framework, they disowned the humanness in their hearts'.[13]

4. *Emphasis upon institutional form vs. emphasis on human content:* originally, the kibbutz was intended to be a free, uninstitutionalized collective of equals. However, the terms of collective living were gradually spelled out in formal rules; this is particularly so in the highly complex, mature kibbutzim which contain most of the second generation members. The second generation react against the formalization introduced by the first generation by demanding that kibbutz life be based on freely developing relationships between members, not on the frozen precepts of original kibbutz dogma.

5. *Emphasis upon the collective vs. emphasis upon the individual:* the initial ideal of the kibbutz sought to achieve self-realization of the individual through his participation in the collective effort. In fact, self-realization of the individual was often impaired by heavy emphasis on self-sacrifice. The common reaction against this has been individualism, which in the first generation took the form of an excessive concern with material consumption and high living standards. Between these extremes, self-realization as a spiritual goal was often forgotten. The second generation are not much concerned with the long-range dreams of the kibbutz movement but have a high stake in the attainment of their own aspirations within the movement. So individual self-realization, whether in work, education, or leisure, may become of paramount importance even as against collective goals. In the words of the second generation member quoted above: 'The goals of the renaissance of [Jewish] statehood and the creation of a new society did not leave you [the parents] time for yourselves, and so the individual in each of you was pushed aside by the importance of the collective enterprise. And we? When we grow up we shut ourselves up in the family. We aspire to studies which are not necessarily of use

---

[13] O. Lulav, *loc. cit.*

to the collective. We do not take less account of personal than of social considerations. You will say that we are selfish. And I would say that we are not cut off from ourselves.'

An important point to note about these five dilemmas is that almost equal ideological justification could be found for the attitude of each generation on any one of them. The kibbutz sought to encompass simultaneously both horns of each dilemma – to be a social experiment *and* a home, a 'right' social order *and* an emotional experience, etc. It was unable to realize these aims simultaneously, and so each generation embrace that interpretation of kibbutz life which better suits their perspective, interests, and structural position within the community. But the second generation do not necessarily deviate by not accepting the orthodox interpretation of the kibbutz. The situation is more complex. Among the first generation people often stick obstinately to the orthodox concepts or deviate from them completely, with only few attempts at mediation or reinterpretation. The second generation, less constrained by the experiences and obligations of the past, feel free to reinterpret and by so doing reformulate the ideology and actually recreate kibbutz life.

The foregoing analysis helps us to understand the position of the second generation in the various spheres of kibbutz life. We shall restrict our remarks to four central areas of collective life: work, public activity, education, and consumption.

Work has always been regarded as the most important area of kibbutz life, both for the individual and for the collective. Members are usually deeply devoted to their work, and this devotion has been transmitted to the second generation. One often hears older members remark that 'everything would be fine if the second generation were behaving as properly in every sphere as they do at work'. However, the second generation approach work slightly differently from the first; to put it briefly: for the first generation, work was a pioneering sacrifice; for the second, it is a means of self-realization. For members of the first generation work was almost a ritual of self-purification or a means of self-assertion; often arduous and monotonous, in itself it offered little reward[14]; it was a sacred or a moral obligation. The second generation, on

[14] See e.g. Spiro's description of the devotion of a woman member to a difficult and unrewarding task, in M. Spiro, *Kibbutz, Venture in Utopia* (Harvard University Press, 1956), 17–18.

the other hand, have a zest for work; they 'enjoy' agricultural work where the first generation would just 'value it highly'. The value of work was internalized and became part of their emotional set-up. The second generation are also more demanding; they do not devotedly and unquestioningly agree to perform arduous and non-professional jobs. Looking at work as a means of self-realization, they seek jobs with responsibility, scope, and a broad perspective, opportunities to realize abilities and apply knowledge. This creates pressure upon the first generation to cede positions of responsibility to the younger one. The extent to which the first generation are willing to do so is a major influence on generational relations; the first generation's unwillingness to abandon such positions is the most common cause of clashes or at least of strained relations between the generations. However, the rapid expansion of the kibbutz economy is often an alleviating factor; new positions are being created which absorb persons of ambition without others having to be removed from their positions. The system of rotation of roles also helps, in that some turnover, particularly in central roles, is expected, and young members may be moved into positions which older members will in any case abandon. In some rare cases a reverse process is at work; first generation members are only too happy to abandon positions which the second generation members are rather reluctant to take over. In these cases a leadership vacuum results.

But even when the transfer of roles between generations is smooth, many problems remain. Although the kibbutz has developed a modern and dynamic organization, relatively few positions of really broad scope and responsibility actually exist in it; and these are fiercely – if covertly – contested. In particular, there is a scarcity of professional and managerial positions for women of the second generation, most of whom have to be satisfied with relatively simple and monotonous jobs. Difficulties in placing younger second generation members of both sexes become particularly acute in older kibbutzim, where the pace of economic development is slower and where the younger members of the second generation find most positions of interest occupied by the older members of their generation. In this case, intra-generational tensions may arise; these can be somewhat eased by the mechanism of rotation, but the difficulties may also multiply as the third generation appears on the scene in large numbers.

This state of affairs may generate strong pressure for some institutional changes in the sphere of work, particularly an increase in the number and scope of professional roles within the kibbutz, as well as employment of kibbutz members outside the settlement in regional, national, and other enterprises and institutions. An expansion of professional roles accords also with the broader trend of industrialization in the kibbutz. The repercussions of such developments on the social structure of the kibbutz remain to be seen.

The second generation are not as a rule very active in the public life of the kibbutz. As our investigation has shown,[15] the second generation consistently participate less in the institutions of direct democracy than the first generation, and markedly less than the younger members of the first generation who are close in age to the second generation but were not born on a kibbutz. The second generation fill fewer and less responsible public offices than the others; they also attend the collective assembly less frequently. It still remains to be seen whether this trend will change as the second generation grow older. They may then possibly start to move from positions of responsibility at work into public offices. Some indications in this direction can indeed be observed in the older kibbutzim. However, even when members of the second generation become active publicly they are selective in the type of public activity they engage in: they are more prone to perform public roles involving economic rather than other matters, and they are unresponsive to demands for public activity outside the kibbutz, in the kibbutz movement, the party, or the government. (An exception would be the army, where many second generation youngsters tend to remain as officers on active duty.) This unwillingness is clearly related to the general perspective of the second generation; considering their kibbutz as their 'home' in the ordinary sense of the term, they tend to disregard the importance of the broader political framework of which the kibbutz, as a cell of a 'revolutionary' movement, is a part. This lack of commitment to the broader framework is a matter of much concern to the first generation, who fear that the kibbutz will lose its revolutionary ideological content when the second generation finally take over. It also serves to encourage them to stick to roles and positions with

[15] See E. Cohen, *A Comparative Study of the Political Institutions of Collective Settlements in Israel*, (Hebrew University, Jerusalem, 1968), (mimeo).

an ideological content in order that the movement's basic goals should not be debased by the youngsters. As a result, the second generation members become even more uninterested than they would otherwise be.

Since the second generation get more and more involved in the economic sphere, while the first generation still dominate the public sphere, a 'vertical differentiation' between the generations results. This may have important structural consequences for the future development of the kibbutz, since different spheres of kibbutz life would be guided by the varying and sometimes conflicting interests and ideas of the generations.

In regard to consumption, the kibbutz in its early days manifested marked features of 'secular asceticism'; the importance of consumption was largely disregarded and its level held to a minimum. With increasing affluence and the gradual change in the original commitment of the members, the level of consumption started to rise; it also became one of the members' chief concerns, in particular of the women members.[16]

The second generation were not brought up on ascetic principles and in conditions of scarcity. The children of the kibbutz have always been well cared for and even in hard times did not suffer from any deficiencies. This preferential treatment for the children was rooted in kibbutz ideology; as a future-oriented society, the children were the promise of its success. It also legitimized a relatively high level of expenditure for child care.[17] As a result of this treatment, the second generation had no need to react to early deprivation with an inordinate emphasis on consumption, as had occurred in the first generation. Rather they are not content with no more than a reasonably high level of consumption; they also strive to develop a distinctive style of life which would set the kibbutz apart from other groups in Israeli society. This emphasis differs markedly from the earlier tendency of the founders of the kibbutz to develop a uniform style of life with no distinctions, or only minimal ones, between individuals. Whereas the first generation were self-absorbed, virtually dismissing the world

16 On this development, see Y. Talmon and Z. Stup, 'Histapkut Be'mu'at: D'fusei T'murah Ideologit' (Secular asceticism: Patterns of ideological change) in Sh. Wurm (ed.), *Sefer Bussel* (Tel-Aviv).

17 Ibid. Of particular interest in this respect is the fact that those who worked in child-care were particularly prone to reject the ascetic ideology in consumption.

outside and dissociating themselves from it, the second generation's quest for a style of their own is inwardly directed although it is not intended to stifle individual variation within; this is, within broad limits, rather encouraged. The second generation thus occupy in the sphere of consumption an intermediate position, between the original asceticism now abandoned, and the outright consumer attitude which can now be found among many members of the first generation.

Problems of education have given rise to serious strains between the generations. The first generation of the kibbutzim were mainly well-educated; a minority even had academic training. Many of them had renounced academic studies and a professional career to seek their vocation as farmers or as workers in Israel. This background serves to explain their negative ideological attitude to formal education. Schooling beyond the secondary level was disregarded. Examinations, and particularly academic degrees, were despised. The original kibbutz ideology conceived of the member as a 'cultured worker', but he was expected to continue his education in his spare time, mostly by individual study, or as a participant in local study groups or short-term courses. Until recently, the kibbutz movements made only sparse use of institutions of higher learning and tried to cope with the rising demand for education through the development of a complex of educational facilities managed and staffed by their own members.

However, the demand of the second generation for increased educational opportunities goes much beyond anything that the kibbutz is willing or able to supply. A large number of second generation members would like to attend universities, and though the number of university students has increased greatly recently, it still falls short of the demand. The main problem is that the kibbutzim cannot and will not grant a large number of their youngsters a leave of absence which would increase the time which a second generation member spends outside his own community to 6–7 years: three years in military service, about one year of assistance in another kibbutz, and then two or three years at the university.

The inter-generational conflict over education is not solely a technical one; it has to do with the conception of the role and content of formal education in kibbutz life. First generation members consider such education mainly as a tool for the better performance of collective, and particularly economic, tasks. For them, the determining factor in a decision concerning higher education is whether the kibbutz needs a certain kind of professional expertise or not. The second generation, however, consider higher education chiefly as a means of individual development or as a way to achieve a vocational or professional career in the kibbutz. The needs of the collective often take second place in their considerations; some indeed assert that higher education is an end in itself and should be divorced from considerations of practical need. This attitude clearly reflects the second generation's emphasis on individual self-fulfilment as a central value in kibbutz life.

In conclusion a few general points on the nature of continuity and conflict between the generations in the kibbutz which emerge from this presentation. Inter-generational continuity in the kibbutz can be studied on three levels: the family, the individual settlement, and the kibbutz movement as a whole. Family continuity would be expressed by sons of the first generation taking over their parents' roles, particularly in the economic and political activities of the kibbutz. Though continuity on this level sometimes exists, it is not typical. Parents may wield some covert influence on the occupational placement of their offspring,[18] but it is by no means decisive and is in any case much weaker than the influence of urban parents, for example, in the occupational placing of their children.

Nor is there much continuity in the movement as a whole; the second generation show little interest in it and have little to do with the activities of the political party to which it is attached; they are reluctant to work for the movement or the party or to accept posts of responsibility within these larger formations.

The level at which continuity does exist is that of the individual community. Children are expected to stay on in the kibbutz of their parents and to continue their life-work, and the expectation is reinforced by the institutional arrangement through which the movement stops sending newly recruited members to an old-established kibbutz when its children begin to reach the age of membership. The continuity of the kibbutz is thus largely depen-

18 See Y. Talmon, 'Hamishpacha Ve'hahatzava Hachevratit Shel Hador Hasheni Be'kibbutz' (The family and the social placement of the second generation in collective settlements), *Megamot*, 1957.

dent upon internal growth, and the founders are understandably eager for their children to stay where they were born. They are asked to assist in a younger kibbutz for a year or two as an expression of movement-wide solidarity, but are not expected to settle there permanently; those who do wish to stay run into difficulties with their parent settlement. Marriage between members of the second generation from different kibbutzim causes similar problems. The young couple usually stays provisionally in the settlement of one of the spouses for six months or more before deciding in which to settle permanently.

Most second generation members are not particularly eager to settle in a young kibbutz or to establish a new one. Until 1967 only one new kibbutz was founded by members of the second generation, and even this only under the prodding of the older leaders of the movement. Few second generation youngsters actually stay on after the year or two of assistance to a younger kibbutz. However, there are some who would like to free the younger generation from the control of the older in an attempt at revolution-cum-continuity. These might find scope in the present trend to establish new kibbutzim on the Golan heights and in the northern Sinai peninsula. Though this trend obviously derives from military necessities and is inspired by nationalist motives, it may nevertheless mark a turning point in the accepted pattern of inter-generational continuity in the kibbutz movement.

To conclude our argument: at first sight, it seems that the kibbutz offers little ground for a conflict between generations. It is expected to be an open and fluid society with a great deal of internal mobility between roles and no vested interests, personal or generational. However, a further look reveals several sources of possible conflict: one is the great difference in perspective between the generations, originating in their differing experience and their differential structural position in the kibbutz; as a result the two interpret the kibbutz ideology differently, and this gives rise to mutual accusations of 'dogmatism' and 'deviation'. The conflict is intensified by the division of labour in the kibbutz, in which the second generation often find their avenues of mobility blocked as first generation members, still young and vigorous, occupy most positions of importance and responsibility in the economic and public fields. Though the kibbutz continues to grow and new positions are constantly created, it is often unable to satisfy the aspirations of the second generation which it itself encouraged. Generations often clash on these matters, and kibbutzim in which transmission between generations is smooth are few in number. Nevertheless, the process of transmission is, in general, successful: as we have seen, most second generation members continue to live in the settlement of their parents, and though their outlook may be rather different from the original conception of kibbutz life, it is a further development of, and not a deviation from, the movement's ideology. The main problem which the kibbutz faces is whether it will be able to contain in the future the tendencies to innovate and to change, so as to accommodate the aspirations of the second generation. As the kibbutz is a highly self-concerned society, constantly probing and criticising itself, there is no doubt that efforts will be made to meet the new exigencies. The volume of social research on the second generation going on at present is witness to this effort. However, as the second generation gradually take over, numerically and functionally, a rather different kind of kibbutz community from that known up to now is bound to emerge. But the kibbutz has evolved through many different forms in the past as well.

This essay has necessarily been kept in very general terms, ignoring the many variations between individual kibbutzim as well as between kibbutz movements. There are differences not only between generations but also between the older and younger members of the second generation, and a third generation is gradually reaching the age of membership in the oldest kibbutzim. We have little information on these intra-generational differences or on the third generation itself. However, the younger members of the second generation and the third generation will encounter a very different situation from that which confronted the older second generation when they came of age. Whether more strife or more continuity is to be expected is a question which awaits investigation.

Socialization Practices of Parents, Teachers, and Peers in Israel: The Kibbutz Versus the City

Edward C. Devereux, Ron Shouval,
Urie Bronfenbrenner, Robert R. Rodgers,
Sophie Kav-Venaki, Elizabeth Kiely, Esther Karson

About 600 Israeli preadolescents, half from 29 kibbutzim and half from 9 classrooms in the city of Tel Aviv, were asked to describe the frequency of certain socializing behaviors of their mothers, fathers, teachers, peers, and, in the kibbutz, care givers as well. Kibbutz and city parents were seen as equally supportive, but the latter were much more salient as disciplinarians. Even more striking was the finding that the role of the kibbutz teacher more closely resembled that of the parent, particularly as a provider of emotional security. Contrary to expectations, neither the peer group nor the metapelet emerged as supportive figures, but both were salient as agents of discipline and disapproval. The implications of these patterns for personality development are discussed.

Although a great deal has been written about the children of the kibbutz, curiously there has been relatively little systematic research on the topic. Most studies until now have dealt either with one or with very few kibbutzim, rather than with systematic sam-

The study of socialization in Israel, of which the present report forms a part, was initiated as a component in a long-term research program being carried out in the Department of Human Development and Family Studies, in the New York State College of Human Ecology at Cornell University, under a grant from the National Science Foundation, and continued under a grant from the U.S. Office of Education. In the present project, the Cornell Group (Devereux, Bronfenbrenner, Rodgers, Kiely, & Karson) is collaborating with an Israeli group (Shouval, Kav-Venaki) from the Department of Psychology at Tel-Aviv University. The Tel-Aviv group has assumed full responsibility for the field work in Israel and a shared responsibility for the analyses and reports. Permission to conduct tests in Israeli schools and kibbutzim was granted by the Israel Ministry of Education and the Institute of Research on Kibbutz Education at Oranim. Special thanks are extended to Dr. Menachem Gerson, Dr. Maish Reeb, and to Michael Nathan, of the Oranim Institute, for their constructive help and assistance at all stages of the study, and to our many students in Tel Aviv and at Cornell who helped in the field and in the office. Author Bronfenbrenner's address: Department of Human Development and Family Studies, Cornell University, Ithaca, New York 14850.

ples. Many have relied more upon impression-istic observations and clinical insights than upon operationally defined measures. And many have lacked any explicit control groups with which to compare kibbutz child-rearing practices and outcomes.

The present paper represents the first in a projected series of reports growing out of a 4-year research project assessing socialization experiences and outcomes in representative samples of kibbutzim, moshavim, city families, and particular ethnic groups living in Israel, for example, Oriental Jews, Jews from English-speaking countries, the Soviet Union, Latin America, etc., and sabras (native-born Israelis).

In this initial report, we examine how children living in the children's houses in a systematic sample of kibbutzim describe the behaviors of the principal socialization agents in their daily lives: their mothers and fathers, their teachers, their peers, and their meta-pelet.[1] We shall ask in what specific ways the behavior of these agents, as described by the kibbutz children, differs from or resembles that of their urban counterparts, as described by children attending schools in Tel Aviv.

Socialization in the Kibbutz

The most distinctive feature of kibbutz upbringing lies in the fact that the children live, not with their own parents, but in special "children's houses" nearby, with a cohort of age-mates, under the care of a trained meta-pelet. Typically, the kibbutz has a whole colony of such houses, divided by age level from the infants' and toddlers' houses up to those for the teenagers. This system was planned both to allow the mothers to participate fully in the extrafamilial work and citizenship duties of the kibbutz and to contribute to the goal of assigning equal responsibilities to both husband and wife for the home and family (Rabin 1970; Rosner 1969; Talmon-Garber 1965). However, the principal reason for the adoption of this special child-training insti-tution probably lay in the special kinds of goals the kibbutzim had for their children. Rather than emphasizing conventional aca-demic achievement and the encouragement of mobility aspirations among the learners, kib-

butz education was to be focused on fostering such values as cooperation, responsibility, de-votion to work—including manual labor—and the need for selfless dedication to the goals of the collective.

For two reasons, the kibbutz style of child rearing was thought to be appropriate for achieving these goals. First, collective up-bringing seemed an effective way of overrid-ing the more traditional and idiosyncratic values and child-rearing styles of individual families. Second, it was believed that trained child-care specialists, the metaplot and teach-ers, functioning as agents of the total commun-ity, might be able to inculcate community goals with more skill and impartiality than the parents (Golan 1958, 1959; Rabin 1971; Shepher 1969; Talmon-Garber 1956, 1964).

The education of the kibbutz child was not to be confined to the classroom alone; rather, the entire life space of the child was to be shaped with specific educational pur-poses in view. In this process, the child's peer group was expected to play a central role. Ex-cept for a few hours in the late afternoon, the child spends his entire day in the company of the same small group of age-mates. Together they eat, sleep, go to classes, work on the gar-den, and engage in recreational activities. Moreover, the membership of this peer group remains substantially unchanged, year after year. In the children's-house setting, there is little opportunity for privacy, escape, or pair-ing off. Necessarily, the children must some-how learn to cooperate and get along with one another. If any are shirkers, unwilling to carry their fair share of the work load, or if any are bullies or spoilsports, the natural processes of peer interaction can be counted upon to apply powerful and appropriate sanctions. All this can happen quite naturally, without the more formal structures of peer government em-ployed in the children's collectives in the Soviet Union (Bronfenbrenner 1970).

Having the classroom right in the same house where the children are living permits a great deal of flexibility in scheduling, so that the school and nonschool parts of the child's day can be blended together with no abrupt breaks. The kibbutz child does not have to "go" to school, because he is already there. It

---

[1] We retain the Hebrew word *metapelet* (pl. metaplot) to refer to this child-care agent, because the English word "nurse" carries inappropriate connotations and "care giver" seems awkward.

is the teachers who come to the children, and spend much of the day with them.

The teacher is concerned not just with book learning in the classroom but with the educational values of the entire regime. In the kibbutz classroom, a free and relaxed atmosphere is encouraged, with the teacher guiding rather than pressing the children. Kibbutz education is noncompetitive; there is little pressure for grades or other quantified measures of achievement, especially in the earlier years of school.

For the very young children, the metapelet is clearly the most central person in the children's house. Although she continues to play a prominent role with the older children as well, her importance appears to recede a bit as the teacher gains in salience. While the teacher's role is somewhat more specialized, the metapelet is the general-purpose mother substitute in the children's house.

While a major part of the socialization process in the kibbutz has been extended to other agents—to the peer group, the teacher, and the metapelet—the plan also allows for close contact between parents and their own children. In the late afternoon, after the day's work is done, the children return to their parents' apartments for the customary "four o'clock meal" where they spend the time until supper together. Since the parents have little need to be engaged in household tasks and meal preparation at this time, they usually give the children their full time and attention during these hours.

At supper time, the children return to their children's house to eat with their peers, while the parents eat with other adults in the community dining hall. Afterward, the children may play together in or near their children's house; or they may wander once more into the parents' area, wherein formal games involving adults and children may develop on the lawns. But at bedtime, it is the parents, rather than the metapelet or teacher, who spend the final period of the day with the children in the children's house, reading to them, talking quietly with them on their beds, and tucking them in for the night.

While this kind of pattern may be "typical," in fact there is a good deal of planned and unplanned variation. Since both parents are working in the immediate vicinity, they frequently drop by to visit the children's houses at odd times throughout the day. During their free time, older children wander over to visit their younger siblings in the toddler's house, or their parents at their place of work. While the work assignments for the younger children are usually centered in and around their own children's house, older children spend an hour or more, depending on their age, working along with their parents and other adults on the farm or workshop. On weekends the children are free to spend the whole time with their families. In sum, both the educational philosophy of the kibbutz and the ecology of the setting appear to provide ample scope for parents and children to maintain close and warm contact with one another.

While we have focused here on the separate roles of parents, teachers, and metaplot, we should note that, in the closed network setting of the kibbutz, these are all members of the same system. They live close by in the same little community, share the same broad core of common values, see each other often, and know each other well. And so, of course, do all the other adults and children in the kibbutz. Children often have an opportunity to know and interact with the parents of all of their peers. And the parents see and know not just their own children, but all their children's peers as well. While the major concern of this paper is the special roles of parents, teachers, and metaplot, it must not be forgotten that in the kibbutz community all adults are actively concerned with the socialization of all children.

Kibbutz versus City

The basic parameters in the life space of children growing up in Tel Aviv, or in most any other major urban area, contrast sharply with those which shape the world of the kibbutz child. The city children in our sample live with their parents and siblings, share family meals, and spend much of their free time at home with the family. Their parents maintain a primary responsibility for their socialization, including whatever disciplinary controls are deemed appropriate.

The schools city children attend are relatively large; they tend to serve several neighborhoods and encompass a more heterogeneous population. The classrooms in the city average 35 children each in contrast to the 10–12 in the kibbutz, and there are generally several classrooms for each grade level. After school hours, the children disperse to several different neighborhood areas. Thus, whereas the kibbutz child is fated to spend much of his time with the same small group of age-mates, not necessarily of his own choosing, we may speculate that a much larger element of mutual selectivity operates in the formation of urban peer groups. Here groups of differing size and character will develop in schools and in neighborhoods; some children may be excluded from any of them, and all have ample opportunities to escape for a while if they choose—to pursue solitary activities or to enjoy the company of a single reliable buddy.

The situation of the city teacher also contrasts sharply with that of the teacher on the kibbutz. She may come from a quite different background from that of the children she teaches, and live in a different part of the city. In addition, she has little basis for contact with her pupils' parents, and almost never sees the children outside the classroom setting.

Some Research Questions

The contrasting socialization patterns in kibbutz and city raise a number of questions. For example: Does the fact that kibbutz children live in a house of their own under the care of a metapelet substantially change their relationships with parents, teachers, and peers? Do relationships with parents in the kibbutz become less affectionate, or perhaps only less ambivalent? Does the kibbutz peer group become a more powerful force in the socialization of the child? Do kibbutz teachers find themselves in a different role because the parents no longer have an exclusive responsibility for the upbringing of the child?

With questions like these in mind, let us turn now to the data from our present research to see how children in the two settings actually describe the behavior of the principal socializing agents in their lives.

Methods and Research Design

Sample design and subjects.—Israeli kibbutzim differ from each other in a number of ways which may be expected to have conse-

quences for the socialization of children. In the present research, we have attempted to take some of these into account by employing a stratified sampling procedure, controlling for ideological movement, size, and generation. Within each of the three major federations,[2] kibbutzim were selected of three different sizes: small (less than 100 adult members), medium (100–300 members), and large (more than 300 members). Among the available kibbutzim from each movement and size, settlements were further stratified by generation. Approximately half were taken from older, third-generation kibbutzim, in which most of the parents were themselves kibbutz born and reared; the rest from second-generation kibbutzim, in which our subjects were usually the children of the founders. We had hoped to include at least two kibbutzim in each cell of the resulting $3 \times 3 \times 2$ matrix, but some cells could not be filled because some combinations proved to be rare or nonexistent. After the elimination of a few settlements in which the children were found to be living at home with their parents, we retained 29 kibbutzim for the present analysis.

Subjects for the kibbutz sample consisted of all the sixth-grade children, and some of the fifth-grade children,[3] living in these 29 kibbutzim, a total of 162 boys and 152 girls. The number of subjects per kibbutz ranged from five to 19, averaging about 12.

The urban sample consisted of all the sixth-grade children in three schools in Tel Aviv, with three classrooms in each school averaging 35 children per classroom, a total of 149 boys and 138 girls. To provide an approximate match with the background of the kibbutz parents, city schools were chosen from predominantly middle-class neighborhoods in which most residents were from families of European origin. In both samples, most of the children were 11 or 12 years of age, but because the kibbutz sample contained some fifth graders, the average age of the kibbutz group was slightly younger than the city group. For this reason, all relationships reported below have been controlled for age by means of a covariance design.

Instruments   and   administration.—The

---

[2] Most of the kibbutzim in present-day Israel are affiliated with one of the three principal federations—Artzi, Meuchad, and Ichud—which differ from each other in their degree of commitment to radical socialist ideology, Artzi being most, and Ichud least, radical.

[3] Fifth graders were included only in a few settlements where they were needed to help complete the sample design.

data for the present report stem entirely from the responses of the children in the two samples to a series of questionnaires dealing with their perceptions of the behavior of their fathers, mothers, teachers, and peers, and, for the kibbutz children, of the metaplot as well. These questionnaires were included with other instruments in a testing session lasting about 1 hr and 20 min. All the children in each classroom or kibbutz were tested together as a group. Instructions and test items were read orally by trained administrators from our Tel-Aviv research staff, in the absence of other adults.

Among the instruments employed in these testing sessions, the only one of concern in the present report was a specially adapted short form derived from the Cornell Parent Behavior Inventory (Devereux, Bronfenbrenner, & Rodgers 1969). In this short form, a single item was selected to represent each of 12 different dimensions of behavior measured by clusters of items in the longer form; in a few cases minor revisions of wording were introduced so that the descriptions could be applied to the behaviors of teachers and peers as well as of parents. Except for appropriate

pronoun changes, the rating forms were identical for each of the agents; the children were asked to report how often the agent being rated had engaged in the particular kind of behavior described by the item during the past year. Responses were recorded on a five-step rating scale, ranging from "never" to "very often."

Prior work with the longer form of this instrument has shown that each of the dimensions included in the questionnaire represents a different and relevant dimension in the behavior of various socializing agents. For example, physical punishment and deprivation of privileges appear to have quite different consequences for children's behavior. There exists, however, an extensive pattern of low but significant correlations among two broad clusters of items on the questionnaire, here labeled "support" and "discipline." Our technique for handling the special problem presented by these correlations will be discussed shortly. In table 1, we present the actual wording of each of the items employed in the short form, together with the label of the more general variable each was used to index.

TABLE 1

VARIABLES AND ITEMS USED TO DESCRIBE BEHAVIOR OF MOTHER, FATHER, TEACHER, PEERS, AND METAPELET

Cluster and Original Variable Name	Questionnaire Order and Wording of Items
Support:	
Nurturance	1. I can count on her to help me out if I have some kind of problem.
Achievement demands	3. She keeps pushing me to do my best in whatever I do.
Independence demands	5. She keeps pushing me to think independently.
Instrumental companionship ...	6. She helps me with my schoolwork, if there is something I don't understand.
Consistency	8. I know what she expects of me and how she wants me to act.
Autonomy	9. She lets me make my own plans for things I want to do.
Principled discipline	10. When she wants me to do something, she explains why.
Discipline:	
Physical punishment	2. She says she will hit me or smack me if I do something she doesn't like.
Social isolation	7. She won't let me do things with her when I do something she doesn't like.
Affective punishment	11. She acts cold and unfriendly when I do something she doesn't like.
Strictness	12. She is very strict toward me, if I don't do what is expected of me.
Indulgence (not in either cluster)	4. She lets me off easy when I do something she doesn't like.
Response alternatives:	
1—Never	
2—Hardly ever	
3—Sometimes	
4—Fairly often	
5—Very often	

NOTE.—Wording given here is that employed for the mother. Except for changes in pronouns (he, they, etc.), identical questions were used for other agents.

It should be kept in mind that our data deal not with the actual behaviors of these socializing agents but only with the children's perceptions and reports of these behaviors.

Method of analysis.—Preliminary analyses revealed that the mean of the responses of the children in our samples to the various items on the questionnaire differed significantly from kibbutz to kibbutz, and also from classroom to classroom in the city sample. Because of the existence of these "classroom effects" in both samples, a decision was made to treat classrooms and kibbutzim, rather than individual children, as the units of analysis, taking classroom means on our various items as the basic measured variables.[4] City-kibbutz differences were then tested for statistical significance against the variance among groups within the city and kibbutz samples. This analytical procedure has the effect of requiring that, to arrive at any generalization about differences between the behavior of socialization agents in the kibbutz and the city, we must be able to demonstrate that such differences clearly override the within-sample variation among the kibbutzim and among the classrooms in our two sampled populations.

As noted above, although the 12 items included in the questionnaire here employed were intended to represent analytically and empirically distinguishable aspects of behavior, in fact an extensive pattern of low but significant intercorrelations exists among them. Such intercorrelations may reflect empirical realities of the world we are examining: for example, parents who punish in one way may in fact be more inclined to punish in other ways as well. But such correlations may also contain an element of artifact: for example, children may differ in a general tendency to give socially acceptable responses, or to see some agents in more favorable terms than others. In the presence of such "halo" responses, individual items would not be meaningfully discriminated.

Because of the existence of such intercorrelations, the item-by-item significance tests presented below are not all statistically independent of each other, and may in fact tend to

exaggerate the number of apparent differences between the two samples. In order to control for these correlated findings and to obtain a clearer picture regarding which items or clusters of items were independently discriminating between the two samples, we employed a specially adapted technique of multiple regression analysis which permits assessing the extent to which a difference across settings in one variable still obtains after control for other variables. The details of this method have been fully described in a separate technical appendix available upon request (Bronfenbrenner 1973).

While the results of this multiple regression analysis are presented in the familiar form of means, mean differences, and corresponding significance levels, they differ from those obtained by conventional analyses of variance in having been subjected to a double test. They are significant not only as they stand, but after control for all other mean differences reported in the same analysis; in other words, the findings are statistically independent of each other.

Results

Similarities in the two settings.—Our main focus in the present report is upon the ways in which the socialization experiences of children in the kibbutz and city samples are different from each other. To clear the way for this discussion, let us begin by noting a few ways in which the two samples did not differ significantly.

Parental role differentiation.—In our own earlier studies of child rearing in other cultures (Devereux, Bronfenbrenner, & Rodgers 1969; Devereux, Bronfenbrenner, & Suci 1962), we have noted a pattern in which mothers are seen as generally more active than fathers on virtually all child-rearing practices, and especially so on the variables in the supportive cluster. This general pattern held in Israel as well, with mothers significantly exceeding fathers in reported readiness to help children when they have problems, in pushing them to do their best, in letting them know how she expects them to act, and in em-

[4] Classroom means were defined as the means for the boys and girls in each group, computed separately. This procedure has the effect of assigning equal weight to each sex, thus balancing out differences stemming from differing sex ratios in the various classrooms. The use of the mean of classroom means as a basis for determining the overall mean for the kibbutz and the city samples also balances out size differences, by assigning equal weight to each sample unit.

ploying withdrawal of companionship as a control technique. Israeli fathers were perceived as exceeding mothers only in their greater willingness to help children with their school work. These patterns of parental role differentiation were virtually the same in the kibbutz and city samples. While they were generally similar to those observed in other cultures, the differences between the two parents were generally smaller than those observed, for example, in England and Germany.

Sex-role differentiation.—Another area in which the reports of the kibbutz and city children were substantially similar was in the ways boys and girls described the behaviors of the various socializing agents. As in our earlier studies in other cultures, boys in both Israeli samples saw their fathers as being more active with them than did girls. This greater involvement of fathers with boys occurred both in the areas of support and of discipline. In contrast, in both samples, the girls saw their fathers as somewhat more indulgent. Again, in both settings mothers were seen as distributing their attentions more evenly between boys and girls on all the supporting variables, while being somewhat more strict and punitive with boys than with girls.

In the descriptions of the behavior of teachers and of peers, moreover, the experiences of boys and girls were nearly alike, and what few sex differences were found tended to be substantially the same in city and kibbutz. For example, in both settings boys were more likely than girls to report that their peers were ready to resort to physical force and social isolation in dealing with disapproved behaviors.

Since there were no differences across settings with respect to sex of parent or child, the ratings made by boys and girls have been pooled in all subsequent analyses, and descriptions made of fathers and mothers have been combined to yield a more general "parental" profile.

Differences between the two settings.—Let us turn next to a consideration of the ways in which the roles of the various socialization agents, as described by the children in the city and in the kibbutz, differed between the two settings. The results obtained by the analysis-of-variance method are shown in table 2; those obtained by the multiple regression analysis, in table 3.

Differences in teacher behavior.—Both

TABLE 2

MEANS AND MEAN DIFFERENCES IN RATINGS BY CITY VS. KIBBUTZ CHILDREN OF BEHAVIOR OF TEACHERS, PARENTS, AND PEERS: ANALYSIS OF VARIANCE

VARIABLES AND CLUSTERS	TEACHERS			PARENTS			PEERS		
	City	Kibbutz	Difference	City	Kibbutz	Difference	City	Kibbutz	Difference
Support:									
1. Nurturance	3.65	4.25	−.60***	4.73	4.66	.07	4.22	4.06	.16
3. Achievement demands	3.84	4.39	−.55***	4.59	4.51	.08	3.75	3.66	.09
5. Independence demands	3.57	4.26	−.69***	4.33	4.24	.09	3.48	3.35	.13
6. Instrumental companionship ..	3.02	3.86	−.84***	3.43	3.75	−.32**	3.28	3.32	−.04
8. Consistency	3.65	3.53	.12	4.04	3.76	.28*	3.32	3.20	.12
9. Autonomy	4.04	3.86	.18	4.27	4.34	−.07	4.21	4.14	.07
10. Principled discipline	3.60	4.03	−.43***	4.19	4.14	.05	3.85	3.93	−.08
Discipline:									
2. Physical punishment	1.03	1.14	−.11**	1.65	1.28	.37***	1.33	1.63	−.30**
7. Social isolation ..	1.41	1.85	−.44***	1.93	1.52	.41***	1.79	2.01	−.22*
11. Affective punishment	2.58	2.34	.24	1.80	1.73	.07	2.07	2.38	−.31**
12. Strictness	2.46	2.26	.20	2.13	1.87	.26**	1.78	1.91	−.13
4. Indulgence	2.36	2.46	−.10	2.78	2.77	.01	2.91	2.85	.06

* $p \leq .10$.
** $p \leq .05$.
*** $p \leq .01$.

TABLE 3

INDEPENDENTLY SIGNIFICANT DIFFERENCES IN RATINGS BY CITY AND KIBBUTZ CHILDREN OF BEHAVIOR OF
TEACHERS, PARENTS, AND PEERS: MULTIPLE REGRESSION ANALYSIS

		MEANS AND MEAN DIFFERENCES						
		Main Effects[a]			Interactions			
VARIABLES	Item[b] Numbers	City	Kibbutz	City-Kibbutz	Inter-action Effect	City	Kibbutz	City-Kibbutz
Teacher:								
A. Independence demands	5	3.57	4.25	−.69**	...	...	...	...
B. Support cluster	1,3,6,10	3.53	4.13	−.60**	...	...	...	...
C. Disciplinary acts	2,7	1.22	1.50	−.28**	...	...	...	...
D. Autonomy ...	9	(4.04	3.86	.18)	B–D	−0.51	0.27	−.78*
Parent:								
C. Disciplinary acts	2,7	1.79	1.40	.39**	...	...	...	...
E. Instrumental companionship	6	3.43	3.75	−.32*	...	...	...	...
F. Support cluster	1,3,5,9,10	(4.42	4.38	.04)	C–F	−2.63	−2.98	.35*
G. Disciplinary attitudes	11,12	(1.97	1.80	.17)	C–G	−0.18	0.40	.22*
Peer:								
H. Overall discipline cluster	2,7,11,12	1.74	1.98	−.24**	...	...	...	...

[a] Values in parentheses are means involved in significant interactions but not in main effects.
[b] For text of reference items see table 1.
* $p \leq .05$.
** $p \leq .01$.

observation and theoretical speculation had led us to expect that the role of the teacher in the kibbutz would be more salient than that of the teacher in the city. The results clearly support this expectation. On seven of the items, taken singly, kibbutz children assigned significantly higher scores to their teachers than did the city children. Furthermore, there seemed to be more consensus among kibbutz children in the ways each particular group described their teachers: on 11 of the 12 scales, within-class variance in teacher descriptions was smaller on the kibbutz than in the city classrooms, and significantly so on eight of the 12 items.

When these means were processed by our multiple regression procedure to control for the intercorrelations among them, several statistically independent differences emerged. The strongest effect was the greater encouragement of independent thinking by kibbutz teachers. The kibbutz teacher was also seen as more likely to engage in other behaviors implying strong support for the child and his

achievement, as evidenced by her greater perceived willingness to help the children not only with school work but with other kinds of problems as well, her encouragement of the children to do their best in everything they try, and her willingness to explain her reasons for desired behaviors.

The kibbutz teachers were also described as more ready than city teachers to assume an active disciplinary role when necessary. While kibbutz teachers were not seen as generally more strict or unfriendly, they were seen as somewhat more likely than city teachers to react to misconduct by withdrawing their companionship or threatening physical punishment.

Finally, the regression analysis revealed one significant interaction effect involving a relationship between encouragement of autonomy and the general support cluster (line D in table 3). While children in the kibbutz and in the city did not differ in their reports of their teachers' willingness to let them make their own plans, for the city children this particular kind of supporting behavior was seen as relatively more common than all other kinds of support provided by their teachers; but for kibbutz children encouragement of autonomy was indistinguishable from other patterns of teacher support.

On all the other items in the questionnaire—those dealing with consistency, rejection, strictness, and indulgence—there were no significant differences between city and kibbutz teachers.

Differences in parent behavior.—Our prior speculations and analyses had led us to expect that the role of the parents on the kibbutz might involve considerably less in the way of discipline and control than is demanded of city parents. The results impressively confirm this expectation. While city parents tended to exceed their kibbutz counterparts on all the discipline variables, by far the largest difference occurred in their larger role in imposing specific punishments when children misbehave: in withdrawing their companionship for a while, or in threatening physical punishment. Given this general trend, there is nevertheless a significant interaction effect (line G of table 3) indicating that general disciplinary attitudes, such as acting cold and unfriendly or strict when children misbehave, play a relatively more prominent part in the total disciplinary repertoire of the kibbutz parents than of city parents.

In the domain of supporting behaviors, kibbutz parents do not fall short of their city counterparts; in fact, on one variable (helping children with schoolwork), they were significantly more active. Finally, a significant interaction effect (line F of table 3) indicates that the ratio of supportive to punitive behaviors was reliably greater for kibbutz parents than for city parents. The overall balance of the parent role in the kibbutz thus tends to be more positive and supportive.

Differences in peer behavior.—Our prior observations and speculations suggested that the peer group in the kibbutz might play a generally more prominent role than the peer group in the city, and especially so in the area of discipline and control. The evidence from the present research only partially supports these expectations. The only significant main effect pertained to the set of variables we have designated as the discipline cluster.

Compared to their age-mates in the city, peers in the kibbutz were more likely to react to behavior they did not like by acting cold and unfriendly, by refusing to play with the offending child for a while, by threatening physical harm, or by other expressions of generally negative attitudes (line H in table 3).

In all other respects the accounts of peer behavior in city and kibbutz were statistically indistinguishable. What this means is that the kibbutz children were neither more nor less likely to behave supportively toward each other than were children in the city. A separate analysis, moreover, revealed that differences in the behavior of teachers and of parents accounted for a great deal more of the total variance between city and kibbutz than did differences in peer behavior.

On the role of the metapelet.—To conclude our account, we must say a word about the special role of the metapelet as a socializing agent. While we have no direct counterpart in the city with whom to compare the metapelet, we may gain some perspective on her role by comparing her profile with that of mothers and teachers, both in the kibbutz and in the city. The relevant results of these comparisons are presented in table 4.

In our introductory discussion, we had pictured the metapelet as a general-purpose mother substitute, especially for the very little children; but our observations led us to the speculation that the metapelet role may recede in salience for the older children, by whom she might tend to be seen primarily in the role of household drudge and disciplinarian.

Our results generally confirm these impressions. In comparison with the kibbutz mother, the metapelet is rated as significantly higher on all of the items in the discipline cluster, and as significantly lower on all of the items in the support cluster. When we compare the role of the kibbutz metapelet with that of the city mothers, the results for the supportive behaviors are substantially the same as for kibbutz mothers; thus, mothers in both settings are seen as significantly more supportive on every single item. On matters of discipline, however, the metapelet and the city mother are more nearly alike. Both agents are equally active in providing discipline and occasional punishments for the children under their care, the only significant differences

TABLE 4

MEAN DIFFERENCES IN CHILDREN'S RATINGS OF METAPELET VS. MOTHERS AND TEACHERS IN CITY AND KIBBUTZ: ANALYSIS-OF-VARIANCE METHOD

VARIABLES AND CLUSTERS	Mean for Metapelet	MEAN DIFFERENCES			
		Metapelet— Kibbutz Mother	Metapelet— City Mother	Metapelet— Kibbutz Teacher	Metapelet— City Teacher
Support:					
1. Nurturance	3.89	−0.83**	−0.95**	−0.36**	0.24
3. Achievement demands	3.77	−0.81**	−0.94**	−0.62**	−0.07
5. Independence demands	3.47	−0.74**	−0.92**	−0.79**	−0.10
6. Instrumental companionship ..	1.97	−1.58**	−1.33**	−1.89**	−1.05**
8. Consistency	3.43	−0.44**	−0.71**	−0.10	−0.22
9. Autonomy	3.76	−0.61**	−0.49*	−0.10	−0.28
10. Principled discipline	3.80	−0.36**	−0.43*	−0.23*	−0.20
Discipline:					
2. Physical punishment	1.55	0.29**	−0.11	0.41**	0.52*
7. Social isolation	1.86	0.28*	−0.14	0.01	0.45*
11. Affective punishment	2.50	0.75**	0.69*	0.16	−0.08
12. Strictness	2.49	0.61**	0.32	0.23*	0.03
4. Indulgence	2.64	−0.08	−0.04	0.18	0.28

* $p \leq .05$.
** $p \leq .01$.

being in the somewhat greater use of affective punishment by the metapelet; she is more inclined to act cold and unfriendly toward a child who has misbehaved. City parents, as noted earlier, are evidently more ready to handle misconduct by specific disciplinary actions.

The kibbutz teacher is perceived as generally more supportive than the metapelet; but on matters of discipline, and especially in the domain of maintaining strict control of the children and of administering occasional punishments, the kibbutz teacher is surpassed by the metapelet. A comparison of the role of the city teacher with that of the kibbutz metapelet reveals that both of them play substantially similar roles in the area of support, in which they both fall far short of the levels of support provided by mothers in both settings and by teachers in the kibbutz. The only significant difference between the two agents is found in the greater readiness of city teachers to help children with their schoolwork, duties the metapelet leaves to parents and the teacher. On the discipline side, the profiles for the two agents are also similar, except that the metapelet exceeds the city teacher in her

readiness to employ specific punishments when the children misbehave. The multiple regression analysis also revealed one interaction effect, indicating that policies of "principled discipline" figure more prominently in the total disciplinary profile of the city teacher than in that of the kibbutz metapelet.

Discussion

Before considering the implications of the results reported above, readers should be reminded of some of the limitations of the present research. Our results deal not with the actual behavior of the various socialization agents considered, but rather with the children's reports of such behavior, as recorded on a simple, short-form questionnaire. Our present report provides no data regarding possible differences in child behavior associated with the different socialization experiences of kibbutz versus city children. Although our samples are sufficiently large to assure statistical reliability, our urban sample is drawn entirely from a single Israeli city, Tel Aviv. Our kibbutz sample, on the other hand, represents a fairly adequate cross-section of all the different kinds of kibbutzim found in Israel, but the analyses here reported ignore the possible consequences of such differences for socialization on the kibbutz. Subjects in the present study are all in a fairly narrow age range, being mostly 11 or 12 years old, and hence no light can be shed on changes in socialization experiences at various other developmental stages. Finally, from the data at hand, we cannot say to what extent the kibbutz-city differences here reported may in fact reflect more general rural-urban differences. Future phases of the present research program have been designed to overcome some of these limitations.

Summary and Commentary

In general, our findings lend support to expectations derived both from our own observations and those of others. With respect to parents on the kibbutz, our data make it clear that it is primarily the disciplinary responsibilities, especially those involving specific punishment, which have been delegated to other agents. Kibbutz parents are seen as no less nurturant and supportive than their city counterparts, and maintain close and warm contact with their children. Our study thus provides no support for those who have interpreted the kibbutz experiment as involving the risks and maladjustments thought to be associated with parental separation and institutionalized child rearing (Bettelheim 1969; Neubauer 1965).

The intriguing question remains whether kibbutz parents have more or less influence than parents of home-reared children in shaping the personalities and values of their children. The present study makes it abundantly clear that the ratio of support to control, in the profile of kibbutz parents, is skewed very heavily on the support side. This leads to the expectation that parent-child relationships may be characterized by less ambivalence than that which generally prevails between parents and children reared at home.

One might speculate that kibbutz parents would therefore make more attractive models for identification. The question arises, however, whether parental values and standards will be modeled and internalized if the parents do not also punish their children when they fall short of their expectations. Perhaps, as Burton and Whiting (1961) have argued in their status-envy theory, identification will

not really work unless the model uses his power occasionally to withhold valued resources from the child.

Still other problematics in the parent-child relationship in the kibbutz revolve about the possibility that affectional ties, bolstered perhaps by vague feelings of guilt on the part of the parents and by separation anxieties on the part of the children, run some risk of becoming too close and binding. If this were so, the kibbutz children might be expected to manifest some of the kinds of disturbances described by Levy (1943) in his account of overprotected children. The fact that the kibbutz child is forced to cope with the separate world of the children's house, however, probably minimizes this risk.

Ultimately, of course, the intensity of the tie between parents and children in the kibbutz is affected by the role of other key socializing agents in the child's life space. Particularly in the early years, one might speculate that the metapelet could become a real rival of the mother for the child's affections. Unfortunately, our present sample does not include any preschool children; but our results for the preadolescents make it abundantly clear that, by this age, the metapelet is no rival at all. As we have seen, her relationships to the children, whatever they may have been before, seem to concentrate very heavily in the realm of discipline and punishment. In virtually all spheres of behavior she is seen as significantly more punitive than the mother, and also less supportive. Under these circumstances, it is doubtful that the metapelet will figure as a likely model for identification, and we may even wonder how much influence she will have in shaping the values and character of the children in her care.

The role of the teacher in the kibbutz is more interesting and complex. As we have seen, she is far more salient than the city teacher, and especially so in the area of support; indeed, her supportive role, on many dimensions, approaches that of the kibbutz parents. In contrast to the parents, the kibbutz teacher also takes a more active part in discipline and control, with the result that her profile more closely resembles that of the traditional mother of home-reared children. But unlike the mother of home-reared children, the kibbutz teacher's disciplinary role is mitigated in one very important respect by the continued presence of the metapelet in the same house: it is clear that much of the burden of nagging and scolding devolves upon the metapelet. Whenever a child needs to be disciplined, it is likely to be she, rather than the teacher or mother, who most often has to carry it through.[5] Under these circumstances, the teachers on the kibbutz may be able to exploit their strong affective bonds with the children and employ psychological discipline techniques, such as withdrawing companionship and affection, quite effectively.

In contrast, because of their generally lower support profile, city teachers may experience more difficulty in controlling the children in their care, and are probably less likely to figure as potential models for childhood identification. In the kibbutz, however, if there is sufficient continuity over time in the relationship, our data suggest that the teacher might become a major target for identification and modeling for school-age children. Her influence in this respect is probably also increased over that of the city teacher by the fact that she is also a member of the same community as the parents and an accepted representative of the same consensus values. City teachers may have quite a different status, either below or above that of the parents whose children they teach, and may represent quite different values.

Finally, our data confirm the expectation that the members of the kibbutz peer group play an especially prominent role in disciplining and controlling each other's behavior. Such punitive techniques as threatening violence, withdrawing companionship, or acting cold and unfriendly, as devices for controlling deviant behavior, are far less frequent in urban peer groups, perhaps because these groups are formed through processes of mutual self-selection and can more easily employ the ultimate sanction of exclusion. The kibbutz peer group is a relatively closed network, and like siblings in a large family, they must somehow manage to get along. This fact, coupled with the cooperative, egalitarian ideology of the kibbutz, might lead one to expect that the kibbutz collective would develop into an especially cohesive, solidary band. The evidence from the present research lends no support to this notion. All we can say, at this point, is that the

kibbutz peer group is neither more nor less supportive than its urban counterpart. Perhaps the felt need continually to police each other's behavior places a damper on the development of high group cohesiveness among these preadolescent kibbutz children. A previous study by Shapira and Madsen (1969), however, has demonstrated that kibbutz children tend. to be more cooperative and less competitive than urban children in Israel.

Among the unanticipated findings of the present research, we should note the relatively greater stress on independent thinking and academic achievement attributed to the kibbutz teachers. This may reflect a response to recent changes in the educational goals of kibbutz education, since more and more kibbutz children are now being prepared to enter the universities. But perhaps this stress on independence and achievement has long been present. For as recent Israeli history has impressively demonstrated, there is something about the kibbutz educational system which is capable of producing not only committed, cooperative kibbutzniks, but also a very large share of the nation's political and military leadership.

So much for our preliminary mapping of the differential forces at play in the "socialization space" of children growing up on Israeli kibbutzim and in Israeli cities. Obviously the crucial question must be: What are the consequences of these differences for the behavior and development of children? This will be our central concern in subsequent papers in this series.

References

Bettelheim, B. *The children of the dream.* New York: Macmillan, 1969.

Bronfenbrenner, U. *Two worlds of childhood: U.S. and U.S.S.R.* New York: Russell Sage Foundation, 1970.

Bronfenbrenner, U. Testing group differences among correlated variables: an application of multiple regression. Mimeographed. Cornell University, Department of Human Development and Family Studies, Ithaca, N.Y., 1973.

Burton, R. V., & Whiting, J. W. M. The absent

---

[5] In fairness, we must add that even threats of physical punishment are relatively rare on the kibbutz, and that the children may be inclined to overestimate the punitive behaviors of the metapelet vis-à-vis those of parents, because in the children's-house setting they are aware, not just of the own punishments, but also of those received by their peers.

father and cross-sex identity. *Merrill-Palmer Quarterly*, 1961, **7**, 85–95.

Devereux, E. C.; Bronfenbrenner, U.; & Rodgers, R. R. Child-rearing in England and the United States: a cross-cultural comparison. *Journal of Marriage and the Family*, 1969, **31**, 257–270.

Devereux, E. C.; Bronfenbrenner, U.; & Suci, G. Patterns of parent behavior in the United States of America and the Federal Republic of Germany: a cross-national comparison. *International Social Science Journal*, 1962, **14**, 488–506.

Golan, S. Collective education in the kibbutz. *American Journal of Orthopsychiatry*, 1958, **28**, 549–556.

Golan, S. Collective education in the kibbutz. *Psychiatry*, 1959, **22**, 167–177.

Levy, D. *Maternal overprotection*. New York: Columbia University Press, 1943.

Neubauer, P. B. (Ed.) *Children in collectives: child rearing norms and practices in the kibbutz*. Springfield, Ill.: Thomas, 1965.

Rabin, A. I. The sexes—ideology and reality in the Israeli kibbutz. In G. H. Seward & R. C. Williamson (Eds.), *Sex roles in changing society*. New York: Random House, 1970.

Rabin, A. I. *Kibbutz studies*. East Lansing: Michigan State University Press, 1971.

Rosner, M. Changes in the conception of equality of women in the kibbutz. Givat Haviva: Institute for Research of Kibbutz Society, 1969. (In Hebrew)

Shapira, A., & Madsen, M. C. Cooperative and competitive behavior of kibbutz and urban children in Israel. *Child Development*, 1969, **40**, 609–617.

Shepher, J. The child and the parent-child relationship in kibbutz communities in Israel. Extrait des carnets de l'enfance, Assignment Children, No. 10, June 1969,. United Nations Fund.

Talmon-Garber, Y. The family in collective settlements. *Third World Congress of Sociology*, 1956, **4**, 116–126.

Talmon-Garber, Y. The family in a revolutionary movement—the case of the kibbutz in Israel. In M. Nimkoff (Ed.), *Comparative family systems*. Boston: Houghton Mifflin, 1964.

Talmon-Garber, Y. Sex-role differentiation in an egalitarian society. In T. G. Lasswell, J. Burma, & S. Aronson (Eds.), *Life in society*. Chicago: Scott Foresman, 1965.

The Committed: Preliminary Reflections on the Impact of the Kibbutz Socialization Pattern on Adolescents

Reuven Kahane

INTRODUCTION

Many educational systems face the problem of socializing the young into patterns of commitment and obligation while at the same time directing them towards social change and innovation rather than conformity or deviancy.[1] The kibbutz educational system provides us with an example which has succeeded in simultaneously generating value commitment and innovative capacity while minimizing social deviancy and anti-social manifestations.

The kibbutz educational system has been defined as being essentially collectively oriented. However, closer examination of this system indicates that structurally it is based on a fusion of collectivistic and individualistic components. In other words, the system establishes some kind of balance between elements which encourage collectivism and those reinforcing individualism. This unique mixture probably explains many of the qualities attributed to the native-born kibbutz members.

Certain characteristics of the second and third generations of the kibbutz recently have become increasingly salient.[2] First, a strong collectivistic value commitment is discernible in their tendency to volunteer for various roles which are central to the society, as well as in their performance in 'routine' career patterns. What is unique to kibbutz youth is that many of them, before entering into specialized occupations in their kibbutz or outside of it, serve an additional year in national service, such as in border settlements, developing towns or youth movements. To some degree, their participation in these activities indicates a pragmatic value commitment, that is, the tendency to translate value orientations into concrete roles and actions. In other

This article is dedicated to the memory of J. Mesinger, one of the most distinguished theoreticians of kibbutz education. I wish to thank Dr Chaim Adler and Mr Y. Dar both of the Hebrew University for their beneficial comments on this paper.

words, in most cases kibbutz youth do not display mere formal commitment to abstract ideals, but translate their ideals into practice. Thus, for these youth, the gap between value and reality (or performance) is relatively narrow, and values gain meaning through their implementation.

Secondly, these youth seem to display a large capacity for innovation and flexible adaption in adjusting to changing physical and social conditions. This capacity has been revealed in an active adaption to day-to-day reality—a style in which one activates all the resources at one's disposal in order to cope with different situations and current problems.[3] An important aspect of this pattern of active adaption is that it is accompanied by an innovative capacity—or a strong tendency towards entrepreneurship. Proof of the prevalence of this characteristic may be found in the fact that a large number of native-born kibbutz members hold positions as officers or pilots in the army, out of proportion to kibbutz population, holding age and education constant.[4]

Another area in which the impact of the kibbutz movement is well recognized is the cultural field, especially in writings, dance and folk music. Large parts of the secular culture, as opposed to religious culture in Israel, have originated in the kibbutz and have spread throughout the country. The most salient attempts in this direction have been the reconstitution of traditional Jewish holidays by giving them a new flavour.

A further and very important area of innovation and entrepreneurship of the second generation in the kibbutz is in the field of economic modernization, represented primarily in the promotion of industrialization. This advance is the result of the attempt to gain power and prestige in the new climate flourishing in Israel, where wealth has become an important factor. From the internal point of view, economic entrepreneurship gives the new generation an opportunity for self-fulfilment in an area in which one can prove himself as an individual as well as contribute to the welfare of the collective.[5]

This last characteristic is closely related to the final quality: the tendency to strive for high achievements in collective and individual fields. This orientation has often been described as the will to succeed, to achieve prominence, and to be 'better than everybody else' in every possible sphere of endeavour; the propensity to strive for achievement usually in areas in which it is possible to combine individual success with response to central socially important needs.[6]

Two major explanations have been given for the development of the above characteristics: the first explanation is advanced in research conducted in the fifties and the early sixties by Yonina Talmon[7] which concentrated on the value system of the kibbutz and its institutional position in Israeli society. These studies claim that the interaction between the internal ethic of the kibbutz and its elitistic position in the broader society caused it to activate its resources in almost every area central to Israeli society. A different explanation is a more psychological one and concentrates on the personality traits, the motivational patterns and the need achievement of the second generation of the kibbutz. It focuses on the psychological mechanisms by which several personality traits are developed, but, to some degree, neglects the structural factors underlying their development.[8]

Most writers on the kibbutz consider its socialization system an essential mechanism for transmission of value orientations and patterns of behaviour to the younger generation;[9] however, they have rarely attempted to analyse the structural components of the adolescent educational system and to relate them to the characteristics of kibbutz youth mentioned above. This paper will make a preliminary attempt to explain how these qualities have been developed through the media of education. Education is defined here as the entire complex of agents, formal and informal, by which adolescents are socialized in the kibbutz.

Since the nature of the kibbutz educational system has been well-documented, we shall deal here only with those characteristics which are relevant to our analysis.[10] Further, we will not take into account different variations and recent changes in this system, but instead we will deal with the past pattern (as it was for the second kibbutz generation) almost as an 'ideal type'.

I   THE DEVELOPMENT OF PRAGMATIC VALUE COMMITMENT

The development of commitment to national and universal values and of the tendency to translate this commitment into pragmatic conduct can be attributed to the fact that the educational system in the kibbutz operated within a framework in which the emphasis was on symmetrical-egalitarian relations and in which the principles of self-government were basic. These principles found their most salient expression in the children's society. Since each member had a relatively equal position and resources, no one had the power to force his terms on another. Consequently, the participants had to mutually adjust their expectations and evaluations. Under these conditions, they were inculcated with the importance of rules stressing the need to take other people's rights into account. Thus, in a system of symmetrical interaction, kibbutz youth learns and commits itself to the norm of reciprocity—that is, to more universal values.[11] Equality was possible because of the relative homogeneity of the population, and reinforced within the educational framework by a special arrangement in which a broad spectrum of activities was offered with no one particular type of activity being dominant. This multi-dimensional pattern of activity provided youngsters with an opportunity to exhibit capabilities other than the usually emphasized intellectual ones, such as physical strength, athletic ability, artistic talent, etc. Here one may argue that differentiation in performance led to multi-dimensional scales of evaluation. This process, in turn, operated as a mechanism providing alternative quasi-equivalent statuses for the participants. The equivalent status system (which was almost an 'organic division of labour') functioned both quantitatively and qualitatively. First, it offered the opportunity of achieving status to a greater number of actors, and secondly, it encouraged a balanced reciprocal pattern of interaction, thus indirectly increasing participation in the children's society and reinforcing commitment to principles of reciprocity.

Power in the children's society was wielded by its institutions, the 'secretary' and various committees, which are all managed by the adolescents themselves.[12] These institutions had the power to enforce rules and norms of conduct and thus might have had the capacity to destroy the symmetric pattern of relationship and to reduce the potential for free decision. However, this possibility was held in check by the existence of strict, almost legal, rules by which the boundaries of these institutions were defined. Even more significant is the fact that active participation in the direct democracy in the children's society gave each child the opportunity to express criticism before the 'general assembly' regarding the operation of the institutions. Hence, the dependence of the central roles and institutions of the children's society on its members was quite extensive, thus reducing the possibility of institutional coercion. However, here, too, lay the seeds of lack of discipline and rejection of authority which often characterized the children's society of the kibbutz.

A factor no less decisive for the development of symmetric relations was the extent of authority granted to the children's society by adults. Kibbutz society opposed the central assumption, basic—implicitly or explicitly—to most educational systems, that children are incomplete beings who are too immature either to be responsible or to enter into the adult roles incumbent on them. Instead, the underlying assumption of the kibbutz educational system was that children are responsible beings upon whom the adult society cannot impose authority from above but with whom they must interact on a basis of mutual understanding.[13] The translation of this assumption into practice led to the minimization of adult interference in the children's society. Furthermore, when adults activated their authority they did so mainly by justifiable persuasion rather than through coercion. In this way, the acceptance of principles and rules was based on mutual understanding, and therefore they were perceived as fair and legitimate. As a result, commitment to social rules was achieved and norms were relatively easily internalized and institutionalized in the children's society.

Furthermore, within their 'mini-society' children were given the opportunity to experiment through the process of trial and error in a framework which was semi-serious and semi-game-like, i.e., in a context which might be defined as structural moratorium. In this context, youth tests the application of different rules and modes of behaviour before committing themselves to specific value patterns and role models. Since almost every rule was subject to the children's test of direct experience, the main criterion developed to evaluate values and norms was their applicability, a criterion which was essential for the promotion of the pragmatic value-commitment of kibbutz youth.

II THE DEVELOPMENT OF ADAPTIVE CAPACITY

The development of the ability to flexibly adapt to different situations and tasks or of the ability to effectively manipulate existing resources and to cope with current difficulties can largely be attributed to the value postulates underlying kibbutz society in the educational system. The self-definition of kibbutz society as different, 'Utopian' and vanguard separated it from all that surrounded it.[14] It urged that the repudiation of an extensive part of the content and methods of conventional instruction was necessary for the creation of a 'new personality' and a new society. This conviction led, for example, to the rejection of the examination and grades system as a mechanism of pupil differentiation and selection and in general as a means for reinforcing achievement and motivation. Instead, kibbutz educationalists attempted to construct an original alternative educational paradigm based on informal codes of control. A similar attempt had been made to revise the content of education so that it would be based on progressive-socialist ideology.[15]

However, in reality, even though it aimed at removing itself from conventional educational traditions, this alternative model did not have the resources nor the institutional equipment to constitute a substitute. The result was an eclectic educational system which was neither well-structured nor systematic.[16]

In the kibbutz educational system, the autodidactic intellectuals of the kibbutz often became the teachers, some lacking any kind of teacher training and others having undergone training in a special kibbutz teachers' college. What they taught was an aggregation of ideas and new discoveries which they compiled from available books and journals. With their rejection of established textbooks and of 'conventional wisdom', they encouraged pupils to express their own ideas and to be innovative in their approach. This philosophy rarely contributed to the development of intellectual discipline; instead, it reinforced tendencies towards speculative thinking. However, this style of thinking was accompanied by a clear value orientation which integrated, on the ideological level, various eclectic patterns of knowledge and resulted in the development of a comprehensive *Weltanschauung*. Further, since this ideological form of education succeeded in conveying the highes societal values it paradoxically legitimized criticism of concrete modes of behaviour even in the kibbutz system and encouraged different interpretations of how values could be translated into behaviour and institutional arrangements. Within this pattern of education it seems that one may find at least part of the explanation for both the value commitment and the flexible adjustment capacity of kibbutz youth.

Yet two other factors need to be mentioned. Generally speaking, in the kibbutz system, the second generation was exposed to many dilemmas or unsolved conflicts which compelled them to act as almost constant 'decision makers'.[17] These decisions frequently involved a choice between an individualistic or collective orientation. As Talmon hinted, the strain between these orientations and the need to decide in specific situations contributed to the reduction of ideological rigidity and increased behavioural flexibility.[18]

Differentiation and conflict among socialization agents in the kibbutz were other factors contributing to the development of flexibility and rationality in decision-making.[19] Youth on the kibbutz were exposed to multiple agents of socialization which, on the one hand, were highly interdependent, but, on the other hand, were highly differentiated.

Thus, for example, the family acted as an expressively oriented agent.[20] In contrast, the school was aimed primarily at the development of knowledge and skills mixed with socio-moral orientations. The 'nurse' (*metapelet*) in the collective children's home aimed at adjusting the children to routine habits. The youth society was fundamentally oriented towards ideological and moral socialization. This functional differentiation encouraged a rational form of education, because each agent specialized in a particular function and most educational activity occurred outside the family framework. However, this functional differentiation was never absolute in reality and the roles of different socialization agents overlapped; hence, one finds many reports of conflict between them. The system as a whole can be defined as a total structure, not only because it encompasses all aspects of life, but mainly because different inconsistent patterns of socialization are fused therein.[21] This inconsistency eventually resulted in increasing the behavioral flexibility of kibbutz youth who were forced many times to adjust to cross-pressures from different agents of socialization.

III   THE DEVELOPMENT OF EXCESSIVE NEED ACHIEVEMENT

In reference to the ambitiousness of native-born kibbutz youth, three points can be argued. First, while the fostering of élite consciousness was an integral element of kibbutz education, i.e., emphasizing the superiority of the kibbutz as a way of life,[22] it was also stressed that this superiority was bound up with duties and obligations, rather than with privileges—a type of *noblesse oblige*. Moreover, privileges were defined as the opportunity to fulfil central societal roles. Many times what was perceived in the wider society as a duty was defined as a privilege for the kibbutz member. For example, an extra year of military service to work in developing towns was perceived as a privilege by kibbutz youth.[23] Thus, the norm of *noblesse oblige* encouraged a unique pattern of collective need-achievement.

This norm was fostered by the very structure of the kibbutz society. Because of the collective egalitarian system of the kibbutz, opportunities to gain either power or economic standing were very limited and, as a result, prestige became a central reward.[24] Prestige was allocated in the educational system (as well as in the general kibbutz society) according to performance of roles benefiting the collectivity. Examinations and a grading system were substituted by a system in which prestige was allocated not only according to educational achievement but also according to performance in the service of the kibbutz or in the service of the children's society. This pattern discouraged, to some degree, intellectual achievement making kibbutz youth 'middle-reachers' in conventional educational terms,[25] while at the same time encouraging other qualities. Since prestige became an important factor in establishing self-identity, status and satisfaction, and since the principal way of achieving prestige was by means of activity which served the collectivity as a whole, a collective-oriented achievement need was developed.

The second factor which explains the exaggerated achievement need of kibbutz youth is related to the self-image of the kibbutz; the kibbutz defined itself as an 'incomplete' society, as a good society in the making, and as 'an experiment which has not failed'.[26] In accordance with this self-definition, youth were socialized to continually strive for perfection. This constant struggle strengthened elements of discontent and criticism of both self and kibbutz. The result was the institutionalization of a norm of dissatisfaction as well as aspirations towards perfection.

Thirdly, the educational system of the kibbutz was highly competitive. Because of the collective boarding system the child was planted in the peer group at a very early age. Within this context, children were forced simultaneously to compete bitterly as well as to co-operate with each other. The persisting tension between these two demands produced a pattern of conduct which contained both individualistic orientations based on competition and collective orientations based on joint co-operative effort.[27] The competitive element inserted strong individualistic achievement impetus. The co-operative element restrained and directed this impetus into channels which were more collectively oriented. The disposition towards achievement in collective tasks was a conscious attempt to compromise between these two antagonistic orientations, that is, to gain individual status by success in the performance of collective goals.

CONCLUSIONS

The kibbutz educational system, at least that within which the second generation was socialized, provides us with the opportunity to analyse a collective educational system in which individualistic orientations were fused producing committed, but still innovative, patterns of behaviour. Hence, if the kibbutz educational system really operated in the way in which it is analysed in this paper, it provides us with a model of a system which successfully mitigated basic educational dilemmas through a combination of autonomy and control.[28]

Three points from a comparative perspective have to be mentioned. First, it seems that the kibbutz educational system has much in common with various 'elitistic' schools. This is especially true regarding the English public schools which are not only similar in some structural elements, but also, to a certain extent, in the nature of their product.[29] Thus a broad study on this dimension seems to be useful.

A second aspect for comparison is the structural totality which characterizes both the English public schools and the kibbutz socialization system. An interesting point to be considered in this comparison is how different or even contradictory educational patterns, formal and informal, are fused.

A third comparison might examine the fusion of co-operative and competitive structural elements and the resulting balance between collectivistic and individualistic orientations.[31]

With these perspectives in mind, a comprehensive study of different educational systems designed to isolate social and cultural variables which have an impact on the educational context would be useful. By means of this research, one may be able to discern to what extent an educational system may succeed in nurturing value commitment and responsible behaviour while at the same time increasing innovative capacity as a response to cultural pluralism and rapid social change.

Notes

1. The most relevant studies of this problem are those by Keniston. See, for example, K. Keniston, 'Youth and Violence: the Contexts of Moral Crisis', in R. T. Sizer (ed.), *Moral Education: Five Lectures*, Cambridge, Mass., Harvard University Press, 1973.

2. To some degree, these characteristics are common to a large number of the second generation Israelis who grew up in either the moshav or in the youth movements, two systems which were heavily influenced by the kibbutz. How-

ever, they appear to be more salient in the second kibbutz generation, including those sons who have left the kibbutz.

3. Bettelheim claimed the opposite. 'Despite great courage and devotion ... they are lacking in that immediate and flexible evaluation, a spontaneous adjustment to ever-changing situations that make for the most useful soldier today.' Bruno Bettelheim, *Children of the Dream*, London, Paladin, 1971, p. 237. It is hard to discern from what sources he collected these findings as they are in

complete contradiction to other analyses. See, for example, Yehuda Amir, 'The Effectiveness of the Kibbutz-born Soldier in the Israel Defence Forces', *Hum. Relat.*, vol. 22 (1969), pp. 333–44; and M. Gal, 'Military Unit as a Social Group', *Shdemot*, no. 50 (Spring 1973), pp. 34–50 (Hebrew).

4. In 1972 there were 227 kibbutzim with a total population of 90,000 which constituted about 3·3 per cent of the Jewish population in Israel. *C.B.S. Statistical Abstract of Israel*, no. 24 (1973), Table II/9, pp. 30–1. No data have been published as to the exact numbers of kibbutz members among the officers and select units of the army. However, according to unpublished data collected by the kibbutz movement, kibbutz members constituted between 15 and 20 per cent of the casualties of both the Six Day War in 1967 and the October 1973 War.

5. See Ch. Adler and R. Kahane, 'Values, Religion and Culture', in S. N. Eisenstadt, *et al.* (eds.), *Israel— Society in the Making*, vol. II, Jerusalem, Academon, 1974 (Hebrew); and Z. Goldberg, *Kibbutz, Society and State*, Beit Berl, 1974, pp. 76–7 (Hebrew).

6. These orientations can be detected in the writings and diaries of kibbutz sons who were killed in the wars. Our principal sources are R. Avi-Noam (ed.), *Gviley-Aish*, Tel Aviv, Ministry of Defence, 3 vols, 1953, 1958 and 1970; and various diaries of kibbutz-born youth who were killed during the wars.

7. Yonina Talmon, *The Kibbutz: Sociological Studies*, Jerusalem, The Magnes Press, 1970 (Hebrew). This volume has been recently published in English with some changes: Yonina Talmon, *Family and Community in the Kibbutz*, Cambridge, Mass., Harvard University Press, 1972.

8. Amir, op. cit., and Albert I. Rabin, *Growing Up in the Kibbutz*, New York, Springer Publishing Company, 1965.

In general it seems that personality traits typical of kibbutz youth were not delineated clearly; see Aharon Antonovsky, Josefh Marcus and J. Kiatz, *An Investigation of Leadership Qualities of Kibbutz-raised Young Men*, Tech. Report, European Research Office, U.S.A., Project No. DA J 3768-0765, 1969, quoted in Julius Zellermayer and Josefh Marcus, 'Kibbutz Adolescence: Relevance to Personality Development Theory', *J. Youth and Adolescence*, vol. 1 (June 1972), pp. 143–54.

It was found that kibbutz youth 'possess an identity distinctly independent from the social environment' and that they make a relatively smooth transition into adult society (Zellermayer and Marcus, ibid., p. 148). However, the samples employed were too small to draw any significant conclusions for this study.

9. Rivka Bar-Yoseph, 'The Pattern of Early Socialization in the Collective Settlements in Israel', *Hum. Relat.*, vol. 12 (1959), pp. 345–60; Bettelheim, op. cit., 1971; Talmon, op. cit., 1970; and Melford E. Spiro, *Children of Kibbutz*, New York, Schocken Books, 1971.

10. The primary documents on the kibbutz educational system are mostly in Hebrew. Among them the most important are: Shevach Eden, 'Children's Society in Kibbutz', in *Encyclopedia of Education*, I, Jerusalem, The Ministry of Education and Culture and Bialik Institute, 1961 (Hebrew); S. Golan, 'Collective (Co-operative) Education', in *Encyclopedia of Education*, Jerusalem, The Ministry of Education and the Bialik Institute, 1961b (Hebrew); Jehuda Mesinger, *The Education of the Second Generation*, Tel Aviv, Am Oved, 1973 (Hebrew); Yehuda Ron-Polani, *The Children's Society in Israel*, Tel Aviv, Ihud HaKvuzot ve HaKibbutzim, 1964 (Hebrew); Reuven Shapira (ed.), *From Generation to Generation: The Book of the Educational Institute of Hashomer Hatzair Mishmar HaEmek*, Merhavia, Hakibbutz HaArzi, 1948 (Hebrew).

11. The importance of symmetric relationships for the development of value commitment has been discussed in another paper, which was based to a large degree on the theory of Piaget. In this paper, it was claimed that it is not

the involvement with peers *per se* which influences youth, but the symmetric structure of peer groups which has the impact of furthering commitment to universal law. Jean Piaget, *The Moral Judgement of the Child*, New York, The Free Press, 1965; Reuven Kahane, *Structure and Uses of Informal Youth Educational Organizations: An Analytical Framework*, Jerusalem, The Hebrew University, Department of Sociology, 1974 (mimeo).

12. There is no doubt that these institutions, controlled by the youth themselves, many times took a hard line towards children, and adult interference became necessary. However, these institutions also prevented, to some extent, the possibility that powerful youth would attempt to dictate their wishes.

13. Ron Polani, op. cit., 1964.

14. H. Darin-Drabkin, *The Other Society*, New York, Brace and World, 1963.

15. Golan, op. cit., 1961; Mesinger, op. cit., 1973; Ron-Polani, op. cit., 1964.

16. An electic non-systematic pattern of education in the kibbutz reinforced by free, undisciplined methods of teaching was experienced by almost every 'product' of this educational system until recently. It was discussed in various meetings on education held by the kibbutz movement. See, for example, *Igeret Le-Hinuch* (Letter of Education), nos. 1–2, 26–27 (June 1963) and nos. 6, 32 (March 1966). Recently, however, both content and teaching methods employed in the kibbutz have become more similar to those common to the rest of Israeli society. See Yechescael Dar, 'Social Changes in the Kibbutz School', in S. N. Eisenstadt, *et al.* (eds.), *Education and Society in Israel*, Jerusalem, Academon, 1968 (Hebrew).

17. See Chaim Adler and Reuven Kahane, 'Pattern of Youth in Israel', in C. Ormian (ed.), *Education in Israel*, Jerusalem, The Ministry of Education, 1973 (Hebrew); Yosef Ben David, 'Occupational Problems in the Kibbutz: Second Generation', *Niv HaKvutza*, vol. 20 (February 1972), pp. 481–92

(Hebrew); Erik Cohen and Menachem Rosner, 'Relation Between Generations in the Israeli Kibbutz', *J. Contemp. Hist.*, vol. 5 (1970), pp. 76–86; Moshe Sarel, 'Conservatism and Orientation Toward Change in the Kibbutz Second Generation', *Megamot*, vol. 11 (1961), pp. 99–123 (Hebrew); Talmon, op. cit., 1970, p. 180.

18. Talmon, op. cit., 1970, p. 154. Perhaps the best illustration of the strain between individualistic and collective orientations (or inner and outer directed orientations, to use Riesman's phrase), can be found in *Diary of a Young Man* with an Introduction by S. Golan, Merhavia, Poalim Library, 1954 (Hebrew).

19. Golan, op. cit., 1961.

20. S. Kugelmass and Shlomo Breznitz, 'Perceptions of Parents by Kibbutz Adolescents: a Further Test of the Instrumentality–Expressivity Model', *Hum. Relat.*, vol. 19 (February 1966), pp. 117–22.

21. Bar Yosef, op. cit., 1959; Mesinger, 1973, op. cit.; Talmon, op. cit., 1970; and Menachem Gerson, 'Family', in A. Jarus *et al.* (eds.), *Children and Families in Israel: Some Mental Health Perspectives*, New York, Gordon and Breach, The Henrietta Szold Institute, 1970.

Both Spiro and Bettelheim emphasized the 'monastic' form of the kibbutz educational system. Both claimed that resulting from this structure the second generation is characterized by a non-individualistic orientation and by ideological rigidity and, therefore, rarely adjusts flexibly to changing conditions (see Bettelheim, op. cit., 1971, pp. 199 ff.). These observations are not supported by the above research and also not by a recent study: *Problem of Collective Education: Partial Findings from the Research on the Sons of Kibbutz*, Givat Haviva, 1971 (Hebrew), mimeo.

22. In one research project it was found that kibbutz youth score high on the self-esteem scale, i.e., the importance attributed to the self in comparison with others. If this research is valid, it indicates that psychologically kibbutz youth are conscious of their élite status in Israeli

society. See B. H. Long, E. H. Henderson and L. Platt, 'Self–Other Orientations of Israeli Adolescents reared in Kibbutzim and Moshavim', *Developmental Psychol.*, vol. 3 (March 1973), pp. 300–8.

23. Gal, op. cit., 1973.

24. Menachem Rosner, 'The Balance of Rewards of Branch Managers', *Hedim*, vol. 29 (February 1964), pp. 46–57; June, pp. 67–80 (Hebrew).

25. Bettelheim, op. cit., 1971, p. 257.

26. Talmon, op. cit., 1970, pp. 223 ff.

27. In her study of children's games on the kibbutz, Eiferman found that 'single party games are scarcely played at all among kibbutz children while group games which demand co-operation towards the achievement of a common aim, but within an overall competitive framework, are far more popular'. Her inference is that if the games reflect general patterns of behaviour, then one can conclude 'that co-operation and competition cannot be looked upon as opposite poles'. The strain between co-operation and competition is closely related to the conflict between collectivism and individualism in the kibbutz—a dilemma which is never solved, but is usually mitigated by various mechanisms. Rivka Eifermann, 'Co-operativeness and Egalitarianism in Kibbutz Children's Games', *Hum. Relat.*, vol. 23 (1970), pp. 579–87. See also A. Shapira and M. C. Madsen, 'Co-operative and Competitive Behavior of Kibbutz and Urban Children in Israel', *Child Development*, vol. 40 (1969), pp. 609–18.

28. Recently, with the institutionalization of the kibbutz system, the differences between the kibbutz and the state educational system in Israel have tended to diminish. This trend will probably have the effect of increasing the similarities between kibbutz youth and other young members of Israeli society (Dar, op. cit., 1968).

29. See for example Ian Weinberg, *The English Public Schools*, New York, Atherton Press, 1967.

30. For further discussion on the differences between collective and individualistic educational patterns see Uri Bronfenbrenner, *Two Worlds of Childhood: U.S. and U.S.S.R.*, New York, Touchstone Book, Simon and Schuster, 1972.

WORK AND PRODUCTION

Structural Differentiation, Production Imperatives, and Communal Norms: The Kibbutz in Crisis

Ivan Vallier

ABSTRACT

This paper is a multi-level explanation of the "kibbutz crisis." Due to widespread structural differentiation in Israel since 1948 the kibbutzim, as a group of concrete collectivities, have been "specialized" relative to the adaptive problem and are now primarily units of the economy. Pressures are placed on the kibbutzim to subordinate communal moral-integrative norms to rational criteria and production effectiveness. The diverse repercussions of this dilemma are described and analyzed in kibbutz Mayeem Kareem.

INTRODUCTION

The societal-subsystem relationship, a major point of articulation between macroscopic social

processes and concrete systems, is a promising but relatively undeveloped area of sociological inquiry.

* Revised version of one part of the author's unpublished doctoral dissertation, "Production Imperatives in Communal Systems: A Comparative Study with Special Reference to the 'Kibbutz Crisis'", Harvard University, 1959. I should like to thank the

This paper deals with one such relationship, the Israeli society and the agricultural communes (*kibbutzim*). The focus is on an empirical pattern of internal difficulties that presently characterizes these communes, frequently referred to as the "kibbutz crisis", and takes into account two levels of social structure: a level between the kibbutzim and the wider society and a level between one kibbutz and its several subsystems. The basic hypothesis underlying the analysis is that the "kibbutz crisis" is intimately related to the processes of structural differentiation and functional specialization occurring in all spheres of the society. The kibbutzim, very much involved in these changes, have been rapidly stripped of certain key functions that tended to promote their integration and viability. The vigorous moves of the new state toward economic stability, political unity, and social progress have pushed the kibbutzim into a primary production role and placed on them the burden of maximizing production outputs. This specialized instrumental role in a rapidly industrializing society demands internal adjustments that are incongruent with the communal-solidary norms that dominate role-relationships in the kibbutz community. The consequences of this incongruence between an instrumental position in the society and the unique communal norms are serious internal strains.

Several questions point up the problem of the paper: How has the kibbutzim's position been altered? What are the consequences of placing a communal-type system in a conspicuously important production role? And, how do required adjustments in kibbutz norms affect other processes and relationships in the communal system? The answers attempted hinge on a clear understanding of the historical role of the kibbutzim, the sociological features of the kibbutz, and the ways in which these features relate to the operating requirements of an effective production enterprise.

THE SOCIOLOGICAL FEATURES OF THE KIBBUTZ

The kibbutz is a unique small-scale[1] system dominated by the values of fraternity and equality.

The fraternal, horizontal emphasis encourages close, informal relationships. The equality standard discourages hierarchy and privilege, thereby reducing vertical social differentiation. The key institutional patterns (collective property, cooperative labor, shared distribution, direct democracy, communal dining, collective nurseries, and mutual responsibility) articulate the central values with the exigencies of daily life. Solidarity and informality are the expected bases of member-member relationships.

The kibbutz's way of life is comprehensive for the individual. All of his social relationships (except for occasional trips to the city) are consummated with others who occupy the same formal status position: member-comrade or member-equal. Spiro refers to the kibbutz as a *gemeinschaft*.[2] It is a system viewed by the members as morally right, therefore a set of institutional arrangements valued as an end in itself.

Structurally these systems are highly interdependent.[3] Small modifications in any key rela-

Communal Settlements," *Scripta Hierosolymitana*, III (Jerusalem, Israel: The Hebrew University Press, 1956); Eva Rosenfeld, "Stratification in a 'Classless' Society," *American Sociological Review*, 16 (December 1951), pp. 766–774; Richard D. Schwartz, "Functional Alternatives to Inequality," *American Sociological Review*, 20 (August 1955), 424–430; entire issue of *Social Problems*, V (Fall 1957); Elizabeth Irvine, "Observations on the Aims of Methods of Child Rearing in Communal Settlements in Israel," *Human Relations*, 5 (1952), 247–275.

[2] "The kibbutz is a *gemeinschaft*, not only because of its small size and the opportunity this affords for the frequency and intimacy of interaction. It is a *gemeinschaft*, rather, because it functions *as if* it were united by bonds of kinship, *as if* it were a lineage or a large extended family. In their own eyes, as well as in the eyes of the outside observer, the chaverim (members) constitute a family, psychologically speaking, bound by ties of common residence, common experience, a common past, and a common fate, and mutual aid—all the ties which bind a family—as well as a common ideology". Melford E. Spiro, *Kibbutz: Venture in Utopia* (Cambridge, Mass.: Harvard University Press, 1956), pp. 90–91.

[3] Russ makes the following statement: "The structure of the kibbutz is not haphazard. It has its own logic. Its fundamental principles are interwoven and bound up with one another. When one is undermined, there is a danger to the entire structure". A. Russ, "Crisis in Kibbutz Hameuhad," *Israel* (June–July 1951), p. 51; and Oded notes that the kibbutz "is the

members of the American Christian Palestine Committee, New York City, who provided the fellowship making possible a year's study in Israel.

[1] Several different but more extended descriptions of the kibbutz's sociological features may be found in Yonina Talmon-Garber, "Social Differentiation in

tional area have important repercussions throughout the total system. Consequently the kibbutz's normative base restricts the types of structural solutions that can be effected for solving the system problems under changing conditions.[4] Innovations that create status differences, power positions, and unequal privileges have to be carefully guarded against. It is true, however, that some required activities are more problematic for the integration and stability of the norms than others.[5] Production, for instance, is one of the most threatening activities in its sociological implications for it requires the instrumental organization of resources, the legitimation of hierarchically-arranged leadership roles, the disciplining of a labor force, and the routine assignment of differentially rewarding tasks. Various mechanisms, including task rotation, have been instituted to minimize the potentially disruptive consequences of production work. But with the use of these integrative devices, some sacrifice in production effectiveness has to be accepted.[6] To follow a policy of strict rotation means, in actuality, that members not especially qualified to assume key instrumental positions eventually take a turn. Weber has pointed to the

relationship between communal norms and instrumental activities as follows: "Communistic systems for the communal or associational organization of work are unfavorable to calculation and to the consideration of means for obtaining optimum production; because ... they tend to be based on the direct feeling of mutual solidarity".[7]

STATEHOOD AND CHANGE: THE KIBBUTZ'S DILEMMA

The 225 communes, with a membership of more than 80,000, are a fully integrated sector of the society's institutional order and have contributed positively in many ways to Israel's growth and international distinction.[8] However, the kibbutz members have always faced to some degree the dilemma of maintaining a unique normative base and, at the same time, maximizing production goals.[9] Yet the intensity of this dilemma has varied with the change in the kibbutzim's relationship to the larger society.

In the period preceding statehood, 1918 to 1948, this internal dilemma was largely latent owing to the fact that the kibbutzim (as defense posts, immigrant training depots, cultural centers, models of grass-roots communism, and agricultural proving grounds) served a strategic multifunctional role.[10] Hence they were not evaluated by strict standards of economic rationality. During this intense colonization period the kibbutzim

---

most interdependent of human associations, and its effectiveness and efficiency are a direct function of cooperation. Unless personal relations are perfect between all members and none ever suffers from lapses of responsibility—both utopian requirements—some friction and waste are inevitable". Y. Oded, "Kibbutz Needs Fresh Challenge," *Jerusalem Post*, April 30, 1954.

[4] On the principle of "structural compatibility," see Parsons' section entitled "The Structural Imperatives of a Given Social System," *The Social System* (Glencoe, Ill.: The Free Press, 1951), pp. 177–180.

[5] A theoretical statement on the implications of instrumental activities or the adaptive phase for social structure is set forth by Parsons in the *Working Papers* (Glencoe, Ill.: The Free Press, 1951), pp. 183 ff.; see also Morris Zelditch, Jr., "Role Differentiation in the Nuclear Family: A Comparative Study," in T. Parsons and Robert F. Bales, *Family, Socialization and Interaction Process* (Glencoe, Ill.: The Free Press, 1955), pp. 309–312.

[6] Rosenfeld's statement pinpoints this idea: "A young group is able to sacrifice efficiency for the sake of a principle it deems more noble. As the group increases in size . . . as its investments grow . . . , the risks entailed in maintaining turnover of managers becomes too great". Eva Rosenfeld, "Institutional Change in Israeli Collectives" (Unpublished doctoral dissertation, Columbia University, 1952), p. 72.

[7] Max Weber, *The Theory of Social and Economic Organization*, trans. by A. M. Henderson and Talcott Parsons (New York: Oxford University Press, Inc., 1947), p. 265.

[8] On the history and development of the kibbutzim, see especially: J. Elazari-Volcani, *The Communistic Settlements in the Jewish Colonization in Palestine* (Tel-Aviv, Palestine: Palestine Economic Society, 1927); Edwin Samuel, *Handbook of the Jewish Communal Villages* (Jerusalem: Zionist Organization, Youth Department, ca. 1935); Shalom Wurm, *The Kvutza* (New York: Habonim Labor Zionist Youth Organization, 1942); R. Bentwich, ed., *A New Way of Life: The Collective Settlements of Israel* (London: Shindler and Golomb, 1949); Henrik Infield, *Cooperative Living in Palestine* (London: Kegan Paul, Trench, Trubner and Co., 1944); Alex Bein, *The Return to the Soil* (Jerusalem, Israel: The Youth and Hechalutz Department of the Zionist Organization, 1952).

[9] Elazari-Volcani, *ibid*.

[10] See G. Muenzner, *Jewish Labour Economy in Palestine* (London: Victor Gollanz, Ltd., 1945) and Samuel Kurland, *Cooperative Palestine* (New York: Sharon Books, 1947).

were valued for their contribution to diverse goals and correspondingly received great amounts of financial support and positive prestige rewards without having to meet standards of production effectiveness. Land, long-term credit, trained personnel, wholesale trading stores and co-operative markets were made available to the kibbutzim through the wider co-operative structure that formed the basis of the Jewish community.[11] As Barber rightly argues, the kibbutzim benefited greatly from this external support.[12]

With the establishment of the Israeli state in 1948, major structural changes took place in rapid sequence.[13] The Israeli society, geared to reaching major goals effectively, entered a phase of widespread structural differentiation.[14] In this period of major change, the original multifunctional kibbutz was placed in a more specialized role. The bulk of the kibbutzim's quasi-military duties were transferred to the newly-formed Defense Force and their immigrant-training responsibilities were given to units developed for this purpose. In like manner, the kibbutzim's important symbolic role, as pioneer elite, was generalized to the society as a whole. By virtue of their significant land holdings and the agricultural know-how of the members, the kibbutzim's functional position was pared down to one of economic primacy.

In the competitive, instrumentally-oriented post-state period, pressures from the higher councils of government planning and economic policy-

making have been placed on all production units.[15] Efficiency teams and productivity institutes were formed to iron out production problems in order to raise levels of output.[16] The kibbutzim, dominating the agricultural sector, were caught in this instrumental push.

The responses of the individual kibbutzim to these pressures have varied. Those aligned with the moderate political parties have attempted to integrate their activities with the trend of events in the larger society. In other cases, particularly among the kibbutzim of the more radical Mapaam group, the communal institutions have been held to with vigor.[17] Nevertheless, the over-all picture is one of developing internal strains with several observable results: intermember conflicts, chronic dissatisfactions, moral disillusionment, and membership withdrawals. Serious commentators on this state of affairs speak of "the kibbutz crisis". In a review of these evaluations which attempt to spell out the reasons for this crisis,[18] three major points of view can be discerned: (1) the "evolutionists," who argue that the communal settlement was a good idea at one time but now it has served its purpose and must therefore be replaced with other social forms; (2) the "perfectionists," who claim that the "crisis" is due to a change in the

---

[11] Muenzner, ibid., pp. 82–85; S. Kurland, ibid., p. 199, ff.; Avraham Granovsky, Land Policy in Palestine (New York: Bloch Publishing Co., 1940); I. Meriminski, "Hechalutz: Tasks and Duties," in What Is Hechalutz? (New York: Hechalutz Organization of America, Hechalutz Library, No. 2, n.d.).

[12] Bernard Barber, Social Stratification: A Comparative Analysis of Structure and Process (New York: Harcourt and Brace, 1957), p. 13, ff.

[13] S. N. Eisenstadt, The Absorption of Immigrants (London: Routledge and Kegan Paul, Ltd., 1954), especially Chapters II and III; and by the same author, "The Social Conditions of the Development of Voluntary Associations," in Scripta Hierosolymitana, III (Jerusalem, Israel: The Hebrew University Press, 1956).

[14] On the sociological aspects of structural differentiation, see T. Parsons and Neil J. Smelser, Economy and Society (Glencoe, Ill.: The Free Press, 1956), pp. 255–274; Neil J. Smelser, Social Change in the Industrial Revolution (Chicago: University of Chicago Press, 1959).

[15] For a detailed, excellent discussion of this program, see H. Fish, "Raising Productivity in Israel," International Labour Review, 68 (October-November 1953), 377, ff.

[16] For a summary of the changes and balance related to the export-import problem of deficits, see the Israel Economist, Annual: 1948–1949 (Jerusalem, Israel: Ahva Press, 1950); see also the same publication for the years 1950–1960; Ben Nathan, "Economic Factors Behind the Israel Government Crisis," Jewish Frontier (March 1951), pp. 16–17; David Horowitz, "Fundamental Trends in Israel's Economy," Middle Eastern Affairs, 3 (May 1952), p. 144.

[17] For an analysis of the internal strains in one kibbutz, see Melford E. Spiro, ibid., Chapter 7, "The Crisis in the Kibbutz," pp. 201–239.

[18] Ben Halpern, "The Kibbutz Comes of Age," Jewish Frontier, 16, No. 6 (June 1949), p. 19; Toby Shafter, "The Kibbutz in Transition," Jewish Frontier, 18 (January 1954), pp. 16–18; Y. Oded, "Kibbutz Needs Fresh Challenge," Jerusalem Post, April 30, 1954; Melford E. Spiro, op. cit., 1956, chapter 7; A. A. Kulmus, "Background of the Kibbutz Crisis," Zionist News Letter, 4, No. 1, p. 25; Maurice Samuel, Level Sunlight (New York: Alfred Knopf, Inc., 1953); Moshe Sharett, "Israel's Position and Problems," Middle Eastern Affairs, 3 (May 1952).

moral fabric of the kibbutz member, that he has changed from a strong idealist to a satisfied family man; and (3) the "anti-collectivists," who see the "crisis" as a result of an inherent incongruity between man's needs and the closed, restrictive, communal life.

These several explanations do not, from my point of view, take into account sufficiently the sociological setting of the "crisis," *viz.*, the relationship between the functional position of the kibbutzim in the larger society and the implications of this instrumental role for their internal functioning. Fortunately, a prolonged field study[19] of one kibbutz made by the author during this "crisis" period provides first-hand materials that bear importantly on a fuller understanding of the consequences of a changing societal-subsystem relationship.

PRODUCTION IMPERATIVES IN THE KIBBUTZ

Mayeem Kareem,[20] the kibbutz studied, is a typical communal settlement of the middle Mandate period. This settlement was established in the 1930's by a group of young German Jews who had trained for agricultural work in the European youth organization of the Jewish Federation of Labour. Membership of Mayeem Kareem in 1954 totalled 375: 160 adult members, 150 children, 20 grandparents, and the remainder, youth groups and agricultural trainees.

Mayeem Kareem's economy consisted of intensive agriculture and several service operations. Ten major divisions, including cereal crops, a dairy, banana plantations, fish ponds, a grain mill, poultry houses, and vegetable gardens, formed the focus of the production operation. In the few years preceding the study, Mayeem's economy had developed both in size and complexity, requiring differentiation along both the skill and power dimensions.[21]

In the course of the year's field work, nine months were spent living and working in the commune.[22] Although intensive interviews were ob-

[19] The study was made possible through a fellowship received from the Blanche Shepard Memorial Fund administered by the American Christian Palestine Committee, New York City.

[20] Mayeem Kareem is a pseudonym for the kibbutz.

[21] The labor force of 167 adults included 32 skilled specialists and managers, 29 semi-skilled workers and 106 unskilled.

[22] The field study was carried out in 1953-1954 under the direction of Dr. Yonina Garber-Talmon and the

tained from a sample of 30 adult members, most of the information pertinent to this article was gained through continuous observation and indirect questioning during actual work in various branches of the economy.

Throughout the study, two main problems focused the research: (1) changes occurring in the institutional patterns having to do with increasing production effectiveness and (2) the consequences of these changes for other important aspects of the kibbutz system. The success of the complex economic enterprise required the effecting of several structural changes that contradicted the basic normative expectations of the members. Five of the most important changes are here described.

Criteria For Allocating Personnel To Work Roles

As the economic organization of the kibbutz grew increasingly complex and specialized, the standards for assigning members to occupational roles were modified. The work preferences of the members were increasingly subordinated to the instrumental requirements of the production program. Priority was increasingly placed on the members' differentiated skills, special training and general performance capacity. One of the most important managers made this principle explicit: "The community must give the jobs to the most capable".

The Decision-Making Process

The kibbutz general assembly, consisting of the entire adult membership, is the institutional arena for discussing and deciding on all matters that affect the total system. All members are equally privileged to present a point of view in the weekly meetings. Decisions are reached by a majority of those present.

With the multiplication of occupational activities and production divisions, issues frequently arise from day to day that demand immediate attention and/or appraisal in light of specialized knowledge. In these cases, referral to the general assembly means considerable delay. To avoid this drag, many decisions are made outside the assembly. A veteran member put it this way: "When

members of the Research Seminar in Sociology at the Hebrew University in Jerusalem. The questionnaire used was developed by the seminar. Grateful acknowledgement is made especially to Dr. Garber-Talmon and to her course assistant, Amitai Etzioni, now Associate Professor of Sociology, Columbia University.

the farm was small, there were many problems put before the general assembly which would be impossible now. Taking out five pounds used to be a decision of the members, now one thousand can be taken out by a special committee". The acceptance of responsibility for making *minor* decisions outside the general assembly in the interest of settling an issue and sustaining the production work has led to the making of *more important* decisions in a similar way. In Mayeem Kareem the bulk of decision-making regarding the planning and policy of the economy were being made in a few small committees which had earlier functioned as advisory or implementing groups. One member commented as follows: "The *meshek* (farm operation) has changed and the various committees get more rights". In the interest of effectiveness, the executive farm committee, the secretariat, and several "ad hoc" committees were assuming a larger and larger role in areas of importance that were legitimately the responsibility of the general assembly. As one member volunteered, "Last year important decisions were being made by the farm committee 'unofficially'". Clearly, the demands of the production operation placed considerations of decision-making efficiency over those of equality and diffuse responsibility. Mayeem Kareem had not only created new production divisions and new occupational roles but had also shifted functional responsibilities to structures not originally intended to carry them.

The Incipient Formation Of An Elite Leadership Group

In kibbutz ideology, all members are equal. This equality means, among other things, that all members have equal responsibilities to serve both as leaders and as ordinary laborers. Rosenfeld has shown,[23] however, that even in the kibbutzim talent rises to the top because of the demand for leadership capacity. In Mayeem Kareem the development of an elite group among top coordinating and managerial positions was in evidence. However, this group was not a solid, exclusive, self-conscious stratum.[24]

The members who occupied these top roles were identified for a five year period, 1949–1954. From a membership of more than 150 adults, Mayeem

[23] Eva Rosenfeld, *op. cit.*, 1952.
[24] Yonina Garber-Talmon's excellent article on social differentiation in the kibbutzim supports this statement. See Y. Garber-Talmon, *op. cit.*, 1956.

Kareem had given the top leadership responsibilities for the five-year period to 31 members, less than a fifth of those eligible. And among these 31 top leaders, one person had seven key roles in the five year period, five members had each held five roles, three had had four key roles, and five others had occupied three key roles.

Adoption Of Formal Communication Techniques

The publication of a weekly news sheet, "The Yomim", represented another innovation in Mayeem Kareem. This news sheet provided the members with pertinent information on decisions made or developments pending. The news sheet gave an account of the main topics currently under consideration by the central committee and a break down of the members' votes. Other topics included were crop sales, production results, and equipment acquisitions. This news sheet functioned to provide the members with a wider understanding of the production activities in the kibbutz. In earlier years the members had known "what was going on". Increases in complexity of operation and the segmentation of work activities led to communication gaps. Members of one economic division were often unaware of the problems and/or accomplishments of other divisions. The kibbutz in a period of rapid expansion had grown beyond the sphere of comprehension of the individual member.[25] Specialization, hurried schedules, and an increase in production efforts worked against the informal patterns which had functioned effectively only a few years earlier.

Hired Laborers

The fifth change Mayeem Kareem was making in this post-state production era centered on the recruitment of additional laborers. Mayeem, at the time of the study, had practiced the policy of hired laborers[26] for one year. It represented, therefore, a

[25] For an analysis of the informal control patterns in the kibbutz, see Richard D. Schwartz, "Social Factors in the Development of Legal Control: A Case Study of Two Israel Settlements," *Yale Law Journal*, 63 (February 1954), pp. 471–491.
[26] The "hired laborer question" raises one of the most important controversies surrounding the kibbutz today. The value premises of the kibbutzim, including the self-labor principle, prevent them from accepting the policy even though many immigrants are unemployed and government officials have urged co-operation. The kibbutzim have received strong negative criticism for their reluctant stand even though they differ among

very recent change, but one that was most conspicuous. Since the principle of self-labor was so dominant in the kibbutz value system, this form of exploitation had been avoided in every way.

The number of hired laborers working in Mayeem Kareem varied with the season. For example, during the harvest period as many as 25 or 30 were employed. About 15 men were hired on a more permanent basis. However, even these were not contracted for a specific time. They were strictly defined as "temporary" help. These hired laborers made up a very valuable, low-status, mobile work force for the commune. The hirelings were expected to work a full nine-hour day in any division which needed them. At all times there existed a clear-cut division between the members and the hired laborers with respect to the type of work assigned.

TYPES OF COMPLICATIONS AND STRAINS ATTENDING CHANGES

Periods of change are inevitably periods of stress and strain. Modifications in social structure have unanticipated consequences, not all of which are positive for the system.[27] Under pressure to raise production effectiveness, steps were taken in Mayeem Kareem to allocate resources more effectively. This entailed changes, the most important of which have been briefly described above.

The second focus of the field work was on the difficulties and problems that followed from the adjustments in the instrumental sub-system. These

are defined as a series of complications attending the changes in the production operation. The four most important ones are as follows:

Inflexibility Of The Labor Force

With increased specialization, the chances for occupational tenure increased. Under these conditions, members became attached to their jobs and to the differential privileges gained from them. When the production schedule had to be changed and members reallocated, the members assigned to the more specialized and rewarding jobs showed an unwillingness to move quickly into other work roles critical for the completion of a job. Tractor drivers, for example, demonstrated strong resistance when the work manager assigned them to uncompleted manual work.

The need for occupational specialization in the production operation led to worker-job identifications which interfered with the redistribution of the labor force when the work schedule had to be shifted unexpectedly. The exigencies of agricultural production require a flexible work force, yet if this operation is large and complex, specialization is also needed. By emphasizing the latter imperative, Mayeem Kareem indirectly encouraged a set of worker attitudes blocking labor mobility and quick reassignment.

Reduction Of Worker Satisfactions For the Unskilled Member

Paralleling the semi-skilled and skilled workers' attachments and satisfactions were the dissatisfactions on the part of the members who lacked special training or leadership ability. Increasingly, the unskilled workers found themselves members of a labor reservoir viewed as a ready source of energy for the many difficult and less attractive jobs that seemed to abound in the kibbutz. These members realized the implications of this status: that their opportunities for assignment to more rewarding jobs were very small. On those occasions when an unskilled member asked for a less difficult job he would receive the answer: "But you can't handle it well". If he asked for the privilege of learning the skill, the usual answer was "We can't take the time now. Maybe next year". For the most part the kibbutz had to informally postpone this kind of on-the-job training for this would take away a needed laborer and would generally complicate the reassignment of jobs to members who were already proficient. It was not

themselves as to what the policy means and how far it can be tolerated. The Mapaam settlements, attached to the Kibbutz Ha'artzi Federation, are the strongest ideologically and have refused to accept the policy. Hakibbutz Hamehaud, a second federation, is the most liberal. Certain kibbutzim of this group have accepted the policy fully. Mayeem Kareem, a member of a third federation, Hever Hakvutzot, has shown great reluctance to use hired laborers but has indirectly legitimated it as a temporary practice. For an analysis of the consequences of the use of hired laborers as compared to other types of auxiliary laborers, see Ivan Vallier, "Social Change in the Kibbutz Economy," *Economic Development and Cultural Change* (forthcoming).

[27] Richard McCleery's *Policy Change in Prison Management* (East Lansing, Mich.: Michigan State University, 1957), is an excellent case study of the problem of "unanticipated consequences". For the theoretical discussion of "unanticipated consequences," see Robert K. Merton, "The Unanticipated Consequences of Purposive Social Action," *American Sociological Review*, 1 (1936), pp. 894–904.

simply a decision to hold the aspirant back but rather that the system did not allow the degree of "resource waste" necessary for training the new man.

Dissatisfaction Of Women

A third consequence of the more rational use of production resources was the gradual exclusion of women from direct production tasks. Although the kibbutzim's ideology places unusual emphasis on sexual equality in all spheres excepting the reproductive, it is gradually recognized that women cannot carry the same burden of work in the field as the men. This pattern in the Israeli communes has been discussed elsewhere,[28] but not in the context of the theoretical problem examined here. Hence, the characteristics of the pattern in Mayeem Kareem should be noted. Out of a total of 84 adult women, only one worked regularly in the field. A second woman assisted with the poultry, a third worked in the dairy. Other than these, the women's occupations were limited to one of the following spheres: laundry, kitchen, dining room, serving room, children's houses (including teaching and nursing).

The symptoms of the women's dissatisfactions came out in direct verbal criticisms, through a pattern of work tardiness, in heated conflicts with the work assigner, and in worker-worker squabbles during the day. The women, socialized to an equality-dominated system, were consistently faced with facts to the contrary. This discrepancy was given a semblance of meaning by relating the pattern to the requirements of the economy and to the "good of the whole kibbutz". But this surface explanation did not prove strong enough to suppress the negative feelings many of the women expressed.

The "Refusal Pattern"—Responsibility Without Power

Paralleling the dissatisfactions and tensions arising from the emergence of divisions in Mayeem Kareem's labor force of equals is the problem of exercising delegated authority and its implications for motivating members to fulfill key leadership positions having to do with management, organizing production activities, allocating scarce resources, and assigning members to work tasks.

[28] Spiro, op. cit., 1956, Chapter 7, "The Crisis in the Kibbutz," pp. 201–209.

This is a phenomenon of serious proportions and one which appears to be on the increase.

The members who serve as leaders occupy positions which are legitimated but not fully institutionalized, viz., the positions are only reluctantly accorded a place in a system based on equality and voluntary co-operation. As the force of production goals makes greater inroads on the kibbutz's internal activities, these leaders gain increased responsibility. Yet the added burdens of leadership are not accompanied by proportional increases of formal power.[29] Even though a manager is given full responsibility to delegate, sanction, and direct, he is empirically involved in a web of solidary, affective, equalitarian expectations which dampen the sharp, straightforward exercise of authority.

The members who accept the task of directing community operations are made responsible for successful achievement and yet are limited in the use of controls. A branch manager cannot lower a member's wages if he fails to perform. Nor can he "fire" him. The responsibility of balancing heavy work requirements with communal norms, i.e., "expected solidarity and equality," complicates the effectiveness of the leader's efforts. This is essentially the problem of discipline versus affectivity, a latent dilemma in all communal systems but a major source of strain when an attempt is made to increase an accustomed pace of instrumental performance.

Strains attend leadership in the kibbutz because leaders experience contradictory expectations, "You should be responsible and effective, but you should not exercise power". If the leader fails to guide his division or activity to success, he is criticized for incompetence. Similar responses from others occur, on the other hand, if the leader is "authoritarian" and severe. This leadership dilemma and the concurring strain leads many members to withdraw from community responsibility. This reluctance to accept public positions may be referred to as the "refusal pattern".

The refusal pattern takes shape when the general assembly meets to elect members to the central positions. The members who are unwilling to accept these posts use a variety of excuses: lack of

[29] For a discussion of the problem of "responsibility without power" and its implications for system instability, see T. Parsons and Neil J. Smelser, op. cit., 1956, p. 268 and Marion J. Levy, Jr., The Structure of Society (Princeton, New Jersey: Princeton University Press, 1952), p. 472, ff.

ability ("someone else can do it better than I"); commitment to other responsibilities ("I am already serving on the Housing Committee"); health, family troubles, or the lack of a replacement ("who will do the job I now have?"). Interviews covering this topic of community responsibility indicated the following characteristics of the pattern: (1) there was unanimous agreement among the members questioned that the refusal pattern existed; (2) the members noted that the refusal pattern had increased over the recent years both in frequency and scope; and (3) the amount of refusal varied with the type of position that was being reassigned. Refusals were principally related to positions which required the member to take action or make decisions which had consequences for the whole community and thereby placed the occupant in "the public's eye" where his everyday actions and long-term efforts were easy to evaluate. These positions, in addition, usually required the member to give up or sacrifice some of his non-occupational interests, including after-hours time and family associations. In short, criticism is feared and leadership responsibility is perceived as separating one from the informal community and his family-leisure hours.

Those who were willing to fulfill leadership roles, meaning that they had the capacity to tolerate public disapproval and evaluation, were constantly or continually allocated by the community to the public hot spots. In this pattern there tended to be a tacit agreement on the part of the refusing members that those in charge could go ahead and run the show. This led to a withdrawal of support from the leaders and to a retreat from an equal share of communal responsibility. The over-all picture of these central positions indicated that only a minority of the members were willing to undertake the heavy responsibilities and this increased the rank-and-file versus elite cleavage in the community. The nonleaders were apprehensive about accepting responsibility yet resented the pattern that was emerging. This pattern of political apathy and its stratification consequences increased in turn both the responsibility and the strain of the occupants. The basic principles of the kibbutz were being violated, and no easy solution was at hand.

A SOCIOLOGICAL INTERPRETATION OF THE CRISIS

Mayeem Kareem during the post-state period is encountering serious internal problems. The research points clearly to these difficulties as having developed in relation to increased task responsibilities connected to the pressures for raising the effectiveness of production activities. Mayeem Kareem's economy requires a complex division of labor. The intensity and scope of the total production operation are forcing changes in the structure of power, in the organization of work, and in the occupational role system. These adjustments are helping the kibbutz achieve its short-run production goals. But since these developments toward formality, hierarchy, specialization, and diversity have taken place within a communal institutional framework, the entire system has been affected. Basic changes in the instrumental subsystem have had repercussions for other aspects of the collective life. Intermember tensions have developed in those instances where the communal norms are subordinated to more instrumental considerations. Communication patterns on an informal level are breaking down. Cliques are developing in the wider community along lines that reflect the various members' positions in the occupational system. Leaders in the work situation tend to seek the companionship of other division leaders during leisure hours. The over-all solidarity of the kibbutz can no longer be taken for granted. *Mayeem Kareem is attempting to carry out a complex production operation within the institutional limits of an extreme communal pattern.* The crucial relationship between the instrumental requirements of the commune and its ideal institutional basis has become a major source of strain.

It is the conclusion of this paper that the kibbutzim's complex internal strains are closely related to the incongruence between the communal norms governing the kibbutzim and their functional position in the wider society. It does not appear that the sociological problem of the kibbutzim can be understood by limiting the analysis to the internal features. The kibbutzim are, from the wider society's standpoint, mainly production units. The new structures that were established in the period following the formation of the Israeli state in 1948 took over many of the more expressive functions that the kibbutzim had helped to carry during the Mandate period. Structural differentiation led to the specialization of concrete groups or collectivities along key functional lines. The kibbutzim, as a group of units, were "specialized" relative to the adaptive problem and are now primarily units of the economy.

In discussing the problem of structural differentiation, Parsons states that with respect to the value pattern of a societal subsystem "Its direction of differentiation is defined by the primary function of the subsystem for the larger system of which it is a part".[30] A business firm, for example, belongs to the economy and, on a higher level, to the adaptive or instrumental subsystem. The business firm's function is to produce a certain type of goods or services. The roles that are institutionalized within this production unit are those which stress performance, specificity, discipline, and universalism. The business firm's main value pattern is, therfore, appropriate to the subsystem in which it is located. The business firm, in its instrumental role, is integrated in terms of norms which stress "economic rationality". The kibbutz, in its present instrumental role, is a communal system integrated on the basis of "moral-integra-

[30] T. Parsons and R. Bales, *op. cit.*, 1955, p. 160.

tive" values, the polar opposite of those functional for the firm. In explaining the difficulties that are presently being encountered by the kibbutzim, it is important to consider this difference. These communes, because of a unique historical situation, illustrate a sociological problem which may be referred to as "value pattern inappropriateness". The norms or values governing role relationships in the kibbutzim are not appropriate to the production tasks they are now emphasizing.

I interpret this incongruity or inappropriateness between the kibbutzim's functional role and their institutionalized value patterns as one of the basic sociological factors which has given rise to the difficulties or "crisis" within the kibbutz. Production imperatives, hypothetically, always pose problems for communal systems. In the kibbutz, however, these production imperatives are exaggerated. This emphasis has increased the potential for conflict between the values and the instrumental subsystem.

Kibbutz and Colony: Collective Economies and the Outside World

David Barkin and John W. Bennet

In an increasingly integrated world social system, the communitarian society must guard its autonomy while it simultaneously adjusts to external institutions in order to survive. In this paper we are concerned with the ways in which two of the most successful or at least enduring examples of collective agriculture and communal living, the kibbutz communities of Israel and the colonies of Hutterian Brethren in North America, are adapting to the pressures of the external society in order to retain their cultural integrity.[1] Although the ideologies of these groups are linked in the distant past, from the standpoint of cultural background one could hardly find two more disparate cases: the sixteenth-century Anabaptist Hutterites with their Christian brotherhood, and the kibbutzniks, with their secular socialism and Zionist zeal. These are real differences, but these communities also have two important things in common: a dedication to the principles of communal property and communal living, and making a living by operating large, diversified agricultural enterprises. These similarities create a common need on the part of both Hutterites and kibbutzniks to maintain a certain distance from the surrounding society and its prevailing individualistic organization; to calculate the advantages and disadvantages of an agrarian economy in an industrial age; and to experience virtually identical problems of management and social organization created by large-scale agrarian diversification.

Since both kibbutz and colony are 'intentional communities' that is, with institutions deliberately planned to differ from those of the majority in their respective national societies, ideology is unusually important to

The authors wish to thank the following persons for reading and commenting on the manuscript of this paper: Yehuda Landau, Michael Keren, Erik Cohen, Dov Weintraub, John Hostetler, and Eli Leshem. The paper is much better for their attention, but the authors are, of course, solely responsible for its contents.

[1] For further information about the kibbutz see the following: Weintraub *et al.* (1969); Darin-Drabkin (1962); Kanovsky (1966). A valuable discussion of the dilemmas produced by social and economic change in Israel is found in Cohen (1966). For information on the Hutterites see: Bennett (1967); Peters (1965); Hostetler and Huntington (1967); Spiro (1956); Friedmann (1961); Ridemann (1565).

them. Their charters of social organization and action are based on a set of beliefs of what is right, proper, and good in society and personality, and these charters both facilitate and limit economic action. In the second place, since the agrarian collective must survive in a socioeconomic system different from its own, it must strike a careful balance between its necessary adherence to certain features of the external system and its need to retain its own institutions. Whether or not this balance is expressed in formal ideology, the collective it required to make continual adjustments in order to survive.

The emphasis in this paper on economic matters is based partly on the professional interests of the writers, and partly upon a conviction that in these particular cases the economic sphere is particularly significant. This is so because both collectives are remarkably intensive and efficient producers: economics is their business, and their ideologies stress work, frugality, consumption, the nature of property, decision-making and planning. In the second place, economics is important because in order to survive, both collectives must observe or adhere to rules established by the external society concerning labor, costs, taxes, and modes of production. This necessity often creates strain and requires complex internal adjustments.

The purpose of this paper is to suggest a frame of reference for the analysis of the efforts of these communal societies to balance internal and external forces. This frame is derived from the concept of 'opportunity costs',[2] which is no more than the economist's way of recognizing that people make comparative judgments of profitability and gain between their present activities and other possible activities. Opportunity costs can be computed quantitatively, in dollars or cents, or they can be rendered in terms of qualitative factors, like value preferences. The concept is simply a way of calling attention to the fact that communal societies do not exist in isolation, but rather in a world of alternative opportunities. Their members are required to make decisions about these alternatives, whether to change the traditional activities of the community, and whether the individual members should leave the community to try another occupation and way of life.

In both the kibbutz and the Hutterian colonies, ideology and culture function to define and also restrict the range of possible alternative responses to given situations. But when the objective milieu changes, pressures may be created by the attractiveness of outside opportunities. To meet these

---

[2] Opportunity cost is a basic concept underlying economic theory and is an essential part of the methodology of economic analysis. Like some other economic concepts, it is derived from a basic aspect of human behavior; in this case, the making of comparisons. By focusing on the alternative uses of given resources, the concept forces the economic analyst to study explicitly the process of making choices among competing goals. For a discussion of the concept, see: Ferguson (1969), p. 185. It should be noted that our opportunity cost analysis bears a resemblance to the 'social-exchange' approaches of Blau (1964) and Homans (1961) or, in anthropology, Frederik Barth (1967).

challenges, and assuming that the group cannot be kept in total ignorance of them, alternative activities must be found to counteract the outside attractions, or internal rules must be eased or modified or some combination of the two must be available. Thus, although the communities may seek to retain their cultural, economic, and ideological identity, they are constantly confronted with the institutions and opportunities of the surrounding societies. The community may try to reduce undesirable effects of such comparisons on its members, but to the extent that the comparisons are invidious, there will be strong pressures on the community to initiate some changes.

An understanding of 'opportunity cost' phenomena, therefore, should make a contribution to our knowledge of the basic forces for change and conservatism in local communities and regions. If the costs of shifting to new opportunities are high, and/or if these opportunities are barred to the members of such societies, then the opportunity cost of one's present and available activities is low, since little or nothing is lost by continuing to engage in them. On the other hand, if for one reason or another there is a loss by continuing in these available undertakings ('loss' can be understood as either or both financial or social status, self-esteem, prestige, etc.), then the opportunity cost of these existing undertakings is high, and the proclivity to seek alternatives will exist.

There is, of course, a question as to what extent the members of such societies think objectively in opportunity-cost terms. Obviously people do not consciously calculate gains and losses all the time, nor make decisions always or exclusively on the basis of such calculations. However, we hold that since there are social and economic survival issues involved in these processes of evaluation of alternatives, there will always be a strong tendency for opportunity-cost factors to influence behavior.[3] The two groups

[3] Opportunity costs underlie a great many phenomena of change in peasant communities, and have been reported in a number of studies without, however, full realization of the pervasiveness and regularity of the process. For example, Henry Rosenfeld (1958; 1968) reports that despite increasing tendencies toward 'fission' of the Arab village family (out-migration of sons) the patrilineal extended family remains the 'structural unit' of the society since, due to the low skills and poor education of the migrating sons, they must frequently return and rely on the family and village resources. Thus the apparently better opportunities of the outside turn out to be spurious; or, in opportunity-cost terms, the attractions of external opportunities seemed to make local activities 'high' in cost, whereas in fact the alternative costs of local opportunities were 'low' due to the lack of educational accreditation. Another common observation made by students of peasant families is that the richer the family, the greater the tendency of sons to remain at home, neatly illustrating the principle of low costs of available opportunities (i.e., one can make more by staying at home) (Friedl, 1962; 1964 for Greece; and Goldberg, 1968; 1969 for Israel and Lebanon). Frederik Barth (1961) reports for the Basseri nomads still another opportunity-cost phenomenon: as flocks grow in size, productivity declines, due to inability to control animals, cheating by shepherds, etc. This diminishes the ability of the family economy to supply needs at the desired consumption level, and automatically makes external opportunities—in this case, landed agriculture—more attractive. As the family invests in land, it becomes sedentary. Thus opportunity-cost processes result in a considerable change in the cultural ecology of the group. It can be seen from these examples that opportunity cost can be a tool for the understanding of the presence or absence of change

346   The Sociology of the Kibbutz

examined in this paper are well aware that the perennial problem at issue is whether or not they can retain their distinctive communal institutions in the face of changes necessary in order to survive.

Out-migration of members of the communities is involved in this process of adaptation in the following manner: since retention of traditional institutions can be furthered by permitting the movement out of the community of the most dissident individuals, under certain circumstances strong cost differentials favoring external opportunities may serve to strengthen the community by removing the human foci of discontent. On the other hand, the process of out-migration can be, and usually is perceived as a danger, regardless of possible desirable effects, since it injures morale: the ideologically chartered community does not like to acknowledge breakup. Departure of members is often defined as *defection*.

Consequently the enclaved community will typically seek a balance between the migration response and responses involving internal adjustments and changes, the combination of the two constituting an adaptive response or adaptive strategy.[4] It is our contention that the adaptive responses demonstrated by the kibbutz and the colony differ only in intensity and clarity from those found in all other human groups and communities exposed to the influence of a macrosocial system.

The paper begins with a description of the kibbutz and the Hutterian colony, their cultural antecedents and contemporary position. It proceeds to a description of the economics of these two communities, and the ideological guidelines of the economies. The paper concludes with a consideration of patterns of adaptation to external pressures.

HISTORY, CULTURE, AND IDEOLOGY

The principal difference between kibbutz and colony communalism is that the first is based on secular utopian socialist doctrines, and the second on a Christian religious tradition. Of the two, the Hutterian is the older by far, being a modern representative of the ancient Christian practices of communal withdrawal and collective property, rooted in pre-Christian Jewish sectarianism (the Essenic sects), and embodies in Jesus' commands for charity and the sharing of property as related in the Book of Acts.[5]

and migration in agrarian societies whose opportunities differ from those available on the outside. George Foster's concept of 'limited good' would be, in our terms, a case where the external opportunities are perceived as less rewarding than the available internal ones. There is no question that purely 'cultural' or valuational factors can influence economic change or growth, but it is probably safe to assume that realistic economic factors of alternative opportunity risk, and social abilities to accept these or not, lie somewhere in the background of every instance of conservatism or change. As in Rosenfeld's cases, frequently cultural or psychological factors can falsify the actual structure, but sooner or later the realities of opportunity will assert themselves.

[4] For a discussion of adaptive strategy and process, see: Bennett (1969) Ch. 1. This book also contains discussions of Hutterian adaptive postures and opportunity costs (Ch. 8, 10).

[5] For accounts of the 'radical' stream in Christianity which adhered to communal doctrines, see the following: Pascal (1936); Williams (1962); Cohn (1947).

Sects advocating these communal ideals of the apostolic church have repeatedly arisen through the centuries, making communalism the oldest social dissent movement in Western civilization.

The kibbutz is a living version of the socialist communitarian ideal which developed out of the eighteenth-century pre-Marxist utopian movements, themselves secularized versions of the old Judeo-Christian communalism. Kibbutz origins are traced to practical experiments in agriculture in desert Palestine in the early years of the twentieth century, when the Zionist movement commenced its program of colonization. The high costs and needs for labor in creating irrigation and other techniques required to farm in this forbidding environment encouraged collective, risk-spreading solutions, which were reinforced by socialist ideology brought to Palestine by European and particularly Russian Jewish immigrants. Kibbutz ideology, in keeping with its pragmatic and idealistic bases, stresses the virtues of hard work and self-help, as well as communal property and general collective sharing.

Hutterian beliefs put less emphasis on work and self-help for their own sake, and more on them as instruments to accomplish the ideal of a true Christian community. However, the ideology of both collectives deplores individual selfishness, competition, and aspiration, and both generally regard the pursuit of pleasure and luxury as corrupting. The Hutterites refuse to engage in politics or to hold political office; the kibbutz has no such prohibition, due basically to the secular socialist background of the ideology. Thus the one major difference between the two ideologies is the strong set of injunctions in the Hutterian against dealing with the 'world system', which is seen as corrupt and hence to be avoided, not reformed. Kibbutz ideology seeks more actively to participate in and to change the world. However, since the kibbutz, like the colony, is a separatist experiment, it, too, must be careful of its involvements, and a few carefully administered means of controlling contact with the outside world have evolved.

The Hutterites reinforce their ideological demands by an intricate system of institutions, beginning with carefully supervised child socialization in special schools, and continuing through adult life with various disciplinary methods. Individuality is discouraged in the colony nursery and 'German school', and brotherhood and equality are encouraged, although patriarchalism and respect for the aged are also taught. Job progression, sharing in responsibility, and rotation of interesting tasks, along with the practice of dividing the colony when its population reaches about 130, permit nearly every man to experience the rewards of the system—constituting a covert and marginal recognition of the 'individualistic' need for rewards and incentives—an example in its own right of Hutterian adaptability or ability to make sensible compromises with uncompromising ideals. Perhaps the deepest level of Hutterian adaptability is manifested in the fact that while the ideological design preaches austere communal brotherhood, its reiteration and reinforcement simultaneously instruct Hutterites in the opposite, the individualistic hedonism of the 'outside' but as something to avoid, rather than to embrace.

The kibbutz system of reinforcements and social controls is much more ambivalent. In the first place, the kibbutz seeks to engage with the outside world, and even to maintain its political influence over it, although at the same time, to avoid its individualistic contaminations and hedonistic drives. This means that the kibbutz is not in a position to socialize or discipline its members as strenuously as the colony, since the boundaries between approved and disapproved behavior are vague. In place of this, the kibbutz practices a degree of social pressure—gossip, shunning—but perhaps more importantly seeks to reward its members on a scale more nearly approximating that obtained on the outside. There is greater toleration of deviant behavior in the kibbutz than in the colony, aside from social pressure, and often the only proviso is that the person fulfil his regular work quota. More so than the colony, the kibbutz willingly permits its dissatisfied members to leave the community, or to find jobs outside for prolonged periods, and engages in many other compromises. Penalties for obvious infractions of the rules are relatively mild.[6]

Both of the communities practice a degree of separation of family members; the children are raised by the collective, and return to the parents' domicile only at intervals. The basic reason for this device is to be found in the evident need to socialize the members in the stringent ideals and behavior patterns of communalism (especially critical for the early kibbutz, with its original population derived from noncommunal society), and also in the need to free the women for labor (women work in both colony and kibbutz). Another or related reason is that both share in the ancient communal ideal of egalitarian brotherhood (though with varying emphases, as already noted), which requires a certain amount of suppression of the individuality and factionalism deriving from strong nuclear or extended kin family groups.

The organizational structures of the two collective communities are substantially similar, differences existing mainly in a bias toward egalitarianism on the part of the kibbutz, and a greater respect for hierarchal patriarchalism in the case of the colony. Thus, kibbutz affairs are supervised by committees whereas Hutterian affairs are guided solely by elected officers

---

[6] With respect to contacts with the outside, the separate kibbutz federations have differing policies, although the differences are not important at the level of generality of the paper. The most 'isolationist' federation is the left-wing or most strictly communal: *Kibbutz Ha'artzi.* The others rank in this order: *Ihud, Meuchad, Dati*—the last, the least isolationist, is an orthodox Jewish kibbutz movement. This is interesting since one might expect the most religious group to display the most tendency to withdraw. However, since Judaism is a state religion in Israel it is a symbol of identity with the national entity.

and benevolent authoritarian elders. However, all Hutterite colonies, and most kibbutzim, are essentially diversified farming enterprises, and the organizational pattern is dominated by the instrumental needs of this form;[7] recently, however, the kibbutzim have expanded their industrial activities which now employ a sizable proportion of the labor force. In both groups there is a top echelon of executives who conduct community affairs, and a second echelon of managers of the several economic activities or branches. In both communities, most issues are discussed in the general assembly, and officers and managers are elected by majority vote. The reality of ongoing social life in both societies regularly falls short of the ideals of human personality and spiritual or ideological conviction expressed in their ideologies. However, the two movements have been highly successful experiments when compared to other communal groups, most of which have had short lives.

The persistence of the kibbutz and the Hutterian movements is due to many things, including ideological commitment, adaptability, and historical accidents. One expression of adaptability is sheer technical and organizational efficiency. The Hutterites survived because they knew how to manage during periods of economic decline and in economically hostile environments.[8] Historically, these skills were developed in an important sixty-year period in the sixteenth century, when the Lords Kaunitz of Moravia brought the persecuted Brethren in from the Tyrol to manage their estates. This stewardship experience provided them with basic techniques of organization and management still followed today. Various economic experiments and social exigencies in early Palestine Zionist agriculture likewise provided the kibbutzniks with a practical background that has served them in good stead. Also to be emphasized is the presence in both movements of searing experiences that helped build commitment: the persecutions and martyrdoms of the Hutterites, and the frontier fighting and heroism of the embattled kibbutzniks in the warfare which has accompanied the establishment of the Israeli state.

KIBBUTZ AND COLONY TODAY

We are dealing here with numerous and well-established populations, not a handful of utopian communities struggling to find and maintain a unique way of life. The very numbers of colonies and kibbutzim help to sustain the movements and to provide a reference group for comparative judg-

[7] For Hutterian farm and colony organizational structure, see Bennett (1967), Ch. 6. For the kibbutz see Kanovsky (1966), pp. 23–6. For considerations of Hutterian and Anabaptist economics, see Sommer (1954); Klassen (1964); and Riley and Stewart (1966).

[8] It should be noted that during the last fifty years of Hutterian residence in the Ukraine, the colonies were in serious trouble, and the movement may well have survived because Mennonites extended considerable aid. The reasons for the decline are obscure. However, the Hutterites suffered extreme hardships and persecution repeatedly in their history, and more often than not pulled through on their own.

ments between the movements and the outside. With the formalized co-operation provided by the federations and service centers of the kibbutzim, and the informal intercolony cooperation of the Hutterites, economic support can be provided for weak members, and reliance on the outside lessened to some extent. Thus the demographic strength of both Hutterian and kibbutz societies provides psychological and economic reinforcements for the continuity and social health of the two systems.

The Hutterian Brethren grew from the original group of about 800, who came to North America from the Ukraine, to a 1970 population of between 19,500 and 22,000. The present number of colonies is placed between 170 and 180. These colonies are located in the Great Plains of the United States and Canada; about 80 percent of all Hutterites live in Canada. Hutterites first appeared in North America in the 1870s, as part of the 'Volga German' migration, along with Anabaptist Mennonites and Protestant groups. The Brethren selected the Great Plains for two reasons: first, they closely resembled the Ukraine, where Hutterites had spent the past century, becoming accustomed to its semiaridity or subhumidity and the combined grain-and-livestock regimes suitable to that environment. Secondly, very large tracts of cheap land were available and far removed from cities, the latter regarded by the Hutterites as disruptive.

Hutterian population grows at a rate of about 2.5 percent per year, which is the highest rate found for European-derived, relatively well educated populations in the United States and Canada. This expanding population is housed in colony-communities of between 60 and 140 persons. Currently, colonies divide when their population reaches between 115 and 130 persons, at which time a new tract of land is acquired and developed for a new colony. The population is split down the middle of the age pyramid when the 'new farm', as Hutterites call it, is ready for occupancy.

The rate of permanent out-migration from Hutterian colonies is below their population growth rate; most students obtain figures of no more than 1 percent from localized studies. The rate of temporary out-migration, confined to young men, is higher, from 2 to 5 percent. These men stay away for a period ranging from six months to two years, then return to the colony to stay. Departure of women is virtually zero: the Hutterites are especially restrictive with their female population.[9]

In 1967 there were 232 kibbutzim, with a total population of 83,310. Although this represented a 54 percent increase in membership since the formation of the Israeli state in 1948, the relative proportion of kibbutzniks in Israel declined from almost 8 percent at the time of partition to about 3 percent in 1967. This occurred because in only five of the twenty years

[9] There is no single authoritative study of Hutterian out-migration, but the 'localized studies' mentioned in the text all agree on the figure of 1 percent or lower. Available information is found in Hostetler (1965); Eaton and Hayer (1955a); Eaton and Weil (1955); Eaton and Mayer (1955b); Pratt (1969); and a summary of all data: Baden (1968).

since statehood and not once since 1962 has the natural population growth (births minus deaths) plus new recruits to existing and new kibbutzim been sufficient to offset those who choose to abandon the kibbutzim. In the 1960s, average out-migration was about 1 percent per year. In 1962, however, there was actually a net migration of people into the kibbutzim while in the other years out-migration fluctuated between about zero in 1967 and an exodus of 3 percent in 1961. We are suggesting that these variations depend to a large extent on the political and economic climate in the country as a whole; external conditions have varied greatly in the past decade as political tensions increased and employment levels changed.[10] The losses have principally been to the city, as educated young people (men and women) seek more lucrative jobs and the excitement of urban living. Before the establishment of the state, and even for a period after partition, the kibbutz was the symbol of Zionist courage and determination, and many incoming refugees and pioneers chose to settle in or establish kibbutzim. After a while the fervor subsided, and the majority of the settlers in agriculture chose other types of agrarian settlements.

While the Hutterian colony remains small—rarely more than 130 persons—kibbutzim are all sizes from 300 or so to 2,000. Originally, in the prekibbutz *kvutza* stage, the ideal stressed very small groups, even smaller than the modern Hutterian colony. However, the needs for labor in the Palestine environment forced a change, and the kibbutz movement proper was founded on the idea of larger groups. Kibbutzniks are well aware of problems associated with their relatively large size—large, that is, for sustaining communal social interaction at the intimate levels considered effective.

The worlds in which the kibbutzim and the colonies live as enclaved entities are very different. The Hutterites live in the northern Great Plains, the most sparsely populated and least urbanized and industrialized part of settled North America. The kibbutzniks, on the other hand, live in the midst of a densely populated country with pervasive urban standards and economic integration. Kibbutz communities also adjoin one another; they are not isolated, as are many Hutterian colonies.

Kibbutzniks consider themselves Israeli super-citizens, in light of the heroic frontier and pioneer role of the kibbutz movement. They are loyal to their ideals, but are also fiercely loyal to Israel, and are accepted by other Israelis as such. The Hutterites have a more detached identity: they are, first of all, Christian Brethren, and secondly, Canadian or U.S. citizens. They obey laws, local and otherwise, but their loyalties to the state are

---

[10] Computed from data in the Central Bureau of Statistics, Vols. 1–19. Recently the moshav population has also declined relative to the national population, as Israel has moved from a rural to an urbanized society. The decline is less apparent, however, because of the very rapid growth of this settlement type during the early years of statehood. (See Weintraub *et al.* [1969] for discussions of the relative postures of various Israeli settlements and their populations.)

ambiguous and are viewed as practical necessities, although in recent years Hutterian attitudes in some colonies have changed toward a somewhat greater attachment to the nation and the locality.

The distinction between the relative roles of the kibbutz and the colony in the external society is of paramount importance in understanding their adaptive processes. The Hutterites are politically unimportant and socially marginal elements in North American society. The kibbutzim, on the other hand, play a disproportionately large role in their nation. Although the political influence of the kibbutz has been declining as Israeli society has developed, the kibbutzim still retain an important measure of influence in governmental decision-making. The diminution of political influence of the kibbutz, however, is one of the sources of conflict as national economic development causes increasing strains on the cohesiveness of the community.

A GENERAL DESCRIPTION OF THE KIBBUTZ ECONOMY

The kibbutz can be defined economically as a semiautonomous unit functioning in a highly integrated national market economy. As such it receives market signals about the prices of goods and services which it purchases and sells to others, and it is also limited in its scope of action by the test of profitability of its operations. While in general terms, the kibbutz must sell goods at prices equal to or greater than production costs in order to obtain consumption goods, it enjoys a number of 'subsidies', or advantages, which permit it to take risks and suffer losses that would injure a more independent enterprise. Actually the kibbutz is entitled to no more subsidy than other units (e.g. *moshavim*) but the superior level of planning and promotion in the kibbutz tends to attract more than its share.

Thus the kibbutz is not really a free competitive unit in a market economy. In the first place, it cannot own its own land, since in Israel most land is the property of the state. Moreover the kibbutz production is regulated by a government quota system which affects all producers.[11] The individual kibbutz is expected to develop specific annual plans for the use of its labor and capital equipment in order to implement the quotas and use resources effectively. These plans are the basis for the assignment of labor and machinery within the kibbutz as well as for the calculation of the costs of production in each of the several activities in which the kibbutz engages. Capital funds for these activities are available for most agricultural

---

[11] For a discussion of the broad outlines of agricultural development policy in Israel, see Weitz and Rokach (1968). For specific information on the application of national agricultural policy to the kibbutz economy, see Kanovsky (1966), especially Ch. 6. The increasing emphasis on national agricultural planning and on the twin goals of production limitation and income maintenance for the individual entrepreneuring farm sector has created problems for the kibbutzim. On the one hand, many of the most profitable agricultural ventures are limited by production controls, while other products are supported at price levels which often do not reflect the extra costs of collective consumption and services in the kibbutz.

enterprises at reduced interest rates. Although the kibbutzim do have the obligation to repay these capital grants, much easier terms are provided and it appears that the sanctions against default are less severe than in the private sector.[12]

In addition to productive efficiency, kibbutzniks have another extremely important goal: the desire to ensure that they and their children will remain in the forefront of leadership of the nation and that they will be an important factor in its further development. The implication of this generalized aspiration is a commitment, on the one hand, to as much education as possible for the young people, and, on the other hand, to an active participation in national political and intellectual life.

This poses some conflict for the kibbutz, as we shall see below, because of the high cost of providing higher education and the problems of incorporating highly trained people into the traditional kibbutz structure. At present, most kibbutzim provide a twelfth-grade education for all of their children, in contrast to the eighth-grade education provided elsewhere; the government does not pay the cost of the four additional years. This places the kibbutznik in a very favorable position in the job market—at least in that market requiring high school training.[13]

[12] In spite of their declining influence in national political and economic life, the kibbutzim find their interests well represented by organizations like the Jewish Agency. Since the early 1960s, the Agency has taken under its wing practically all the kibbutzim founded since 1948 and some of the older ones as well, in an attempt at reorganization pointing toward greater financial independence. The effort involves plans to subsidize the capital costs of development and to provide more adequate technical assistance. The effort has also reduced the burden of the newer kibbutz communities on the older ones, by the practice of the federations of supplying unpaid kibbutzniks to manage the newer communities. The Agency efforts have supplied paid managers and training programs for technical and management personnel. Needless to say, there is nothing comparable to this in the case of the Hutterites, who must finance their own managerial training and services, and also prefer to do so because of their exclusionist ideology.

[13] In the absence of specific data on the educational achievements of kibbutzniks, the following table is suggestive of the relative position of the various groups in the national population. The average educational level for the Jewish population in Israel was thus about 7.5 years of schooling (1967). This level is 'low' if one considers that the figure includes large numbers of immigrants from North Africa and the Levant (about one quarter of the total population represented in the table).

Jewish Population Aged 14 and Over by Number of Years of Schooling and Continent of Birth, 1967 (percentages)

Number of years of schooling	0	1–4	5–8	9–12	13+	Total
Total population over 14	11.3	7.6	31.9	37.9	11.3	100.0
Born in Israel	1.5	1.2	23.2	58.7	15.4	100.0
Born in Africa–Asia	26.7	9.6	36.4	23.7	3.6	100.0
Born in Europe–America	3.1	9.3	32.9	38.8	15.9	100.0

Source: Central Bureau of Statistics, Israel, *Statistical Abstract of Israel*, 1968, Table T/35, p. 551.

The kibbutznik is likely to be at least as well educated as the average figure for all Israeli-born people. The youthful member of a collective settlement may be even better educated than

The kibbutzim also bear the costs of university training for selected members. These opportunities are increasing in response to pressures from several directions, although college training is not so prevalent as in similar classes in the urban population. However, the young people themselves are increasingly strident in their requests for higher education, and plans for a kibbutz university are under way (1970). The mechanization of agricultural enterprises and the industrialization efforts require skilled personnel and lead the settlements to send people to school for specialized education. Thus, the kibbutzim are encouraging members to obtain technical training in business, engineering, and related fields as part of their efforts to increase productivity and to satisfy the demands of their members for greater personal fulfillment of intellectual and productive potential.

The belief in the equality of man, an important element in kibbutz ideology, is often referred to in discussions about the desirability of hiring outsiders to satisfy the labor needs of the kibbutz. In many circumstances this question is resolved in the negative: men are not hired if it is at all possible to manage without them, since it tends to violate the equality principle. But expansion is necessary and when undertaken often requires the creation of a permanently employed labor force. Kibbutzniks are concerned and are apt to be quite apologetic about this but almost 60 percent of those employed in kibbutz industry were not members of kibbutz communities. Most of them, however, were in unskilled or low-skill positions (Shatil, 1968: 15).

The kibbutzim are faced with a dilemma in view of their ideological distaste for hired labor; there is a shortage of labor in many kibbutzim, due both to increased production and to out-migration, and this is limiting the possibilities for growth and diversification. Several devices are used to obtain the needed labor in addition to hiring nonmembers. Children are released from school at harvest time so that they may work in the fields; this labor is anticipated in the annual economic plan and generally taken into account when planning the school program. Voluntary labor from the cities and from abroad provides another fill-up for the critical shortages when crops have to be harvested or picked. Such labor is low-cost, since expenditure on it is lower than for members (e.g. they often sleep in tents).

The decision-maker in the kibbutz must also take account of the actual conditions in the rest of the country which influence the kibbutz. This is especially important in a country like Israel where economic growth has been rapid. As a consequence of this development, attractive, well-paid,

a contemporary *sabra* in Israeli society because of barriers to secondary school education—it is not yet entirely free though partly subsidized by the state. In the kibbutz, high school training is extended to all young people and increasing numbers are attending post-high school training courses and universities. The situation strongly suggests that the young kibbutznik is more likely to have a high school education than the average Israeli youth outside the settlements, and that this differential is likely to continue. However, as noted in the text, college education is probably less prevalent than in middle-class urban groups.

high-level employment opportunities are relatively plentiful in the new industries and the demand for labor sometimes outstrips the growth of the qualified labor force. In Israel these conditions are heightened by the small size of the country and the rapid flow of information about economic opportunities from one part of the nation to another.[14]

Prosperity and development affect the kibbutz by attracting members away from the communal way of life to the rewards offered by the private sector. This is especially true for the younger people who are clamoring for more education on the one hand, and complaining about their inability to use it effectively within the kibbutz, on the other. Everyone is aware of the differences between kibbutz consumption levels and those in the rest of the country, and comparisons are constantly made because of the mobility of the people between the two sectors. Thus while the kibbutz is required to expand production to meet quotas and to support its rising level of collective consumption, it risks alienation and restlessness on the part of its better educated members.[15]

This combination of factors has created pressures for two different kinds of adjustments in kibbutz life to take account of outside events and ideas. On the one hand, the kibbutzim have greatly raised the level of collective consumption by adding amenities such as art centers, ranch-type housing, swimming pools, social centers, and paid vacations. Weekly motion picture programs and frequent lectures are standard features in most communities. Higher community incomes have undoubtedly led to many of these improvements, but their volume and the rapidity with which they have sprung up is testimony to the effectiveness of pressure from the private economy to improve the living conditions of the kibbutzniks. It is clear that these projects often compete with investments in new productive activities for both capital and labor and this choice further confirms the increasingly high value placed on consumption.

In spite of these improvements and the greater diversity now emerging in kibbutz life, consumption levels are still below those which might be expected by members if they were working in private economy. Although figures for *average* consumption levels in the nation belie this finding. It seems clear that this is *not* the relevant comparison. Since the kibbutznik often compares himself with the *upper* strata of Israeli society, his antici-

[14] As suggested in the text, the better-educated kibbutznik (something beyond high school) does not compare himself with the general agricultural population in Israel but rather with the upper strata of urban society. Although wage data for industrial jobs would be difficult to use for purposes of comparison here, some data on wages in the private sector of agriculture and other occupations might be of value. In 1967 the average annual salary for employees in agriculture was I£4,580; in industry, I£6,780; in public services, I£7,300 (data from Central Bureau of Statistics 1968, Table K/36, pp. 292–3). It does not seem unreasonable to suggest that a kibbutznik could obtain at least a 50 percent monetary premium for working in the private economic sector, because the figures just given understate the differentials: the newer and more dynamic the business or industrial field, the higher the wages.

[15] For discussions of these problems, see Cohen (1966); Weintraub *et al.* (1969).

pated potential consumption level in the individualistic culture to which he might move would be significantly greater than that which he enjoys as a member of a collective settlement.[16]

On the other hand, the kibbutz offers advantages which the figures for consumption levels mask. One of the most important of these is the complete provision for education, medical care, and old age. The kibbutznik need not worry about having sufficient reserves for any of these purposes and this is often cited as an important offsetting factor to higher individual consumption. A second problem is the lack of comparability between living conditions in the two type of worlds; the kibbutz still deemphasizes competition among individuals for higher consumption which may reduce the need to purchase some items.

Communal living does, however, reduce the range for individual expression and this has been considered an essential part of the kibbutz lifestyle. Shatil (1968: 38) argues that invidious comparisons with external consumption levels are not the reasons for rising kibbutz expenditures and the exodus from the kibbutz, because the out-migration figures establish no direct correlation of this type. It seems to us, however, that 'limitative competition' for consumption among kibbutzim and the generally rising incomes have, in fact, played important roles in pressuring the kibbutzim to raise living standards even at the expense of their basic financial structures which have sometimes suffered as a result (Kanovsky, 1966: 100).

The second adjustment in kibbutz structure is the movement to add industry and services to the agrarian regime, also stimulated by the course of national economic progress. There are several forces pushing the kibbutzim in this direction. One is the increasingly large numbers of older people living in kibbutzim whose usefulness in agriculture is limited. Industrialization is at least a partial solution to the problems of the aged because the kibbutz cannot pay pensions, and the productivity of older persons need be only sufficiently high to produce competitive returns on the capital equipment that they use.

[16] There is no consensus among students of the kibbutz as to the relative levels of individual welfare and consumption gratification in the settlements and Israeli society generally. The original ideological commitment to austerity was abandoned soon after statehood with increasing prosperity and relaxation of rationing (Spiro, 1956: 67 ff.). Current debate centers on whether kibbutz consumption levels have reached average levels in the urban society; there is little disagreement on the point that the typical kibbutz provides a higher level of living than that available to the average private entrepreneur farmer. Available data suggest that the 'net income' of an average kibbutz 'family' (two adults with an appropriate number of children up to 18 years) has recently varied between I£6,000 and I£6,700 (Shatil, 1968: 26). Some argue that such high income-equivalent levels are better or at least as good as those available elsewhere, while others suggest that the kibbutzniks usually view themselves as somewhat poorer than urban peers. The income figures given in the preceding footnote do not provide a clear answer, but the weight of our analysis would indicate a preference for the latter opinion. Personal experience of the writers bears out the conclusion that the average kibbutznik, when questioned on this point, almost always considers his own level of living to be below that now attainable for an increasing number of urban dwellers.

At the other end of the spectrum, the young people are clamoring for better education and opportunities to work in jobs which are more technically and intellectually challenging. The opportunities offered these new entrants into the labor force by the private economy are often very attractive and the kibbutzim are beginning to react to this challenge by adding new lines of production which require some of the skills acquired by the young people.

Population growth in individual kibbutzim also creates pressures for further diversification, especially in view of the quota system which places limitations on the potential growth of the most lucrative agricultural activities. Finally, the desire for higher communal incomes places additional pressure on the kibbutz to make additional investments which will raise labor productivity so as to permit further increases in the standard of living.

The response to all these pressures has been the relatively rapid introduction of industrial enterprises into the kibbutzim. These industrial plants are small because of the reluctance to hire outside workers and the unavailability of investment funds. They do, however, represent an important use for the accumulating profits from existing activities and claim a large part of the capital available for investment in the kibbutzim.

Another response to these pressures has been the development of service centers and agencies for the kibbutzim within the framework of the national kibbutz federations. These service organizations provide labor and technical knowledge for many jobs ranging from construction to industrial planning. Although all kibbutzim are expected to contribute a certain amount of manpower for these central service depots through a taxing system, there is a compensation scheme to take account of those units which provide more or less their due share. These jobs provide another opportunity for highly trained people to use their skills productively while remaining within the kibbutz framework.

In summary, the kibbutz movement has developed in response to the economic pressures imposed on it by the larger economy in which it functions. Specifically, as the opportunities for more lucrative jobs improve in the private sector, the kibbutz has responded by improving its own collective consumption standards and diversifying its productive base to provide more satisfying jobs for those who could not work well within the traditional agricultural framework and to improve the productivity of labor to finance the higher living standards. Although the ideology of the kibbutz has constrained the growth of its activities, it has not halted the industrial diversification of the kibbutz economy—had this happened it is likely that the pressures to break down the kibbutz structure would have been much more effective.

358   The Sociology of the Kibbutz

A GENERAL DESCRIPTION OF THE HUTTERIAN ECONOMY

The Hutterian colony can be defined economically as an autonomous unit functioning in a national agrarian economy of varying degrees of integration. The colony must make its own living; it does not receive subsidies from government to the extent of many kibbutzim, and it does not govern its production on the basis of quotas established by government agencies. The Hutterian colonies are organized in three groups or *leute*, but these are social and religious groupings and lack formalized economic functions (the kibbutz federations have somewhat more, with their service centers and cooperatives, although government subsidies and assistance are not channelled through the federations).

Capital for agricultural operations comes from three sources: (1) internal cash savings; (2) other colonies, as loans; and (3) private banks. In Canada, government resources are unavailable to Hutterites except in the form of a few indirect benefits, such as discounts on seeds and fertilizer through government distribution channels, or shared costs on irrigation development. In the United States, government benefits (such as farm subsidies) available to Hutterites are somewhat more abundant. However, most Hutterites prefer to avoid obligations to government and everywhere seek to provide their own capital through savings or to borrow from each other or local banks. In a Canadian region including about forty colonies studied by one of the authors, 96 percent of all capital was generated from within colony system or borrowed from private sources.

Hutterites need capital for development of their enterprises, and also for financing the constant splitting of the colonies and the establishment of new colonies. This fission process is the major difference between Hutterian and kibbutz socioeconomy.[17] Hutterites limit the population of the colony community to between 115 and 130 persons since they believe that collective living is too difficult (or impossible) with more, and also because the resources ordinarily available to them in the Northern Plains make it possible to support this number easily at the desired level of collective consumption. However, Hutterites resist diversification and further development, which might permit larger colonies, since they fear prosperity, and in any event have beliefs preventing them from engaging in industry.

Despite their control of growth, the Hutterian colony is not usually starved for capital. The high productivity, frugal consumption level and access to bank credit at the current prime interest rates provide most colonies with most of the money they need to operate the economy at the

17 Only one kibbutz divided by plan: Daganiya, also considered to be the pioneer kibbutz community. A few had factional disputes and then split into two or more. Others have remained unitary and most, though now static, have experienced population growth; new kibbutzim are formed from immigrants or volunteer membership selected from various kibbutzim.

desired level, or to bring it to this level. Colonies with 'excess' capital are required to loan much of their surplus to other colonies in need of capital. Production is ideally defined for living and furthering the existence of the sect, not for profit.

Since the Hutterites are independent entrepreneurial producers, not geared into quotas and other planned systems,[18] their own level of planning is much more variable than that of the kibbutz. Planning is, in fact, one way of distinguishing the degrees of efficiency among colonies. Changes in emphasis on certain crops or activities is made on the basis of particular resource problems or on current market conditions, not on the basis of government quotas, as in the Israeli case.

In both Canada and the United States, Hutterites pay income taxes on the basis of corporate or cooperative organizations, not as individuals. This provides them with certain advantages since their *per capita* income level is low, and the laws governing corporation or cooperative taxation provide for relatively liberal deductions. They also benefit from discounts available to bulk commodity purchasers, extensive machinery users, and the like. The collective organization of the colony, to some extent like the case of the kibbutz and its preferential treatment by the state of Israel, thus provides savings[19]—a factor which earns the colonies considerable resentment from non-Hutterian agriculturalists and townspeople.

The effective external milieu for the colonies is dual: (1) the immediate region or locality; and (2) the larger nation, with its market economy and government bureaus. Nearly all Hutterites deliberately choose to live in relatively isolated regions of the northern Plains, lacking in industry and urban occupational opportunities, and in these regions, the colonies are often the most affluent agrarian economic enterprises. Thus many or most Hutterites can enjoy a position of relative superiority over their neighbors and can have considerable confidence in their own institutions. The little towns of the northern Plains have only a few, low-paying jobs, and the other agricultural enterprises of the region (ranches and farms) pay even lower wages. This seems unrewarding to an able young Hutterite who can be confident of eventually rising to become a manager of one of the economic activities and eventually an executive or Elder. Lacking high school or

[18] The only possible qualification of this statement would arise from a consideration of Hutterian participation in pooled marketing or other agricultural support systems. Probably 70 percent of the grains produced by Canadian colonies are sold to the Wheat Pool; a much lower percentage of their livestock is likewise marketed through Pool facilities. Since the Wheat Pool arranges, through the Canadian Wheat Board, to sell grain abroad, grain prices are in effect subsidized, although this system has not completely prevented gluts and price fluctuation. If this represents a degree of subsidization, it is no more than that enjoyed by all other Western Canadian private producers. In the U.S., the colonies benefit no more or less than other producers. Many colonies in the U.S. deliberately choose to remain outside of such programs, if they can do so legally, for reasons mentioned in the text.

[19] See Bennett (1967), Ch. 9, for some comparative data on Hutterian and individual agricultural enterprise, showing the savings afforded by the colony's diversified economy of scale, and its austerity program.

college accreditation, Hutterites are barred from certain outside managerial jobs that might otherwise be open to them by virtue of their impressive experience; thus their eighth-grade educations have a very low opportunity cost compared to their earning power in the colony. A Hutterite could expect to earn at best about $150 a month as a mechanic; in a developed colony, on its plateau of affluence, as a manager his labor can produce up to $250 per month, and as a field hand, at least $200, although he would not receive the full amounts in cash, consumption goods, or services. Nevertheless, Hutterian collective consumption often provides a greater range of goods and services than the incomes of the typical small under-capitalized local farmer and rancher.

The national economy and culture has many implications for Hutterian economy and life, and we have already noted some of these. To these we can add the fact that the consumer economy and its pressures constitute a major danger for the Bretheren since they can create desires among the population, especially the young people, for a more luxurious and expensive life. It is not only the increased cost of consumption that the Brethern fear, but the divisive effect of the individual consumption aspiration and ownership.

Although individual consumption is tightly controlled, the Hutterites resemble the kibbutz in that *collective* consumption has slowly but steadily increased, and will probably continue on this course. Although Hutterian taboos limit this growth and it is less noticeable because restricted to necessities (no swimming pools or 'luxuries' as in the case of the kibbutz), it is for the same reasons: the need for meeting, in some degree, the standards of the outside world in order to cope with rising desires, especially on the part of the young people. In the past decade or so changes have been particularly noticeable: the introduction of central propane heating and hot running water by many colonies; instances of indoor flush toilets; more elaborate and expensive kitchen and food storage facilities; more frequent trade-ins of the large station wagons used for personal transportation, as well as a keener interest in the appearance of these vehicles and other things. However, these introductions and changes have been relatively modest, and have not seriously cut into capital resources needed to finance production.[20]

The changes have enabled colonies to maintain a consumption level for the individual nuclear family units which is at least on a par with that of their neighbors in most northern Plains districts, with the exception of

[20] Consumption often rises in the colonies due to the process of fission (explained in Bennett [1967], pp. 184–98, and Diagram 4, where the pattern of colony economic growth is also compared to that of the kibbutz). When a colony divides, the old colony in effect transfers its indebtedness to the new colony, and the old colony, with its agricultural regime established, and retaining most of its machinery and tools, with its population halved, is in the position of relative affluence. Frequently such colonies use their new 'surplus' to provide collective consumption benefits, like central heating systems, although they must do this very cautiously, or suffer censure.

things like private automobiles, vacations, and in general, the many small personal possessions of the non-Hutterites. The Hutterites regularly compare their consumption level with that of their farmer–rancher neighbors, and derive considerable satisfaction with the general parity or even superiority, although there is always the secret admiration of personal possessions. This means that unlike the kibbutznik, who compares his consumption level with that of the highest strata in Israeli society, the Hutterite is making his comparison with lower income levels of the Canadian and U.S. nations.

There is one context of 'consumption' expenditures in the Hutterian economy that needs special recognition. This concerns the increasing tendency to purchase expensive powered machinery and labor-saving gadgets of all kinds. While these machine purchases are defended on grounds of efficiency, there is also no doubt that to some extent they are a substitute for personal consumption. The gleaming automatic milking machinery, automatic animal feeding systems, stainless steel-walled showers, or the grain combine with an air conditioned cab, are proudly displayed to the visitor, with open pleasure and pride.

The desire to avoid the consequences of individual consumption and its psychological and cultural accompaniments leads the Brethren to restrict contact with mass circulation media, secular books in general, to forbid radio and television, and to restrict greatly movement of the population, especially travel to towns and cities. Education is likewise controlled: Hutterian children receive a thorough 'German schooling' in the colony school through age fifteen, a period of intense indoctrination in communal ways and education in the religious principles of Anabaptism. At the same time, the Brethren permit the outside community to give the children eight years of education, with the school building built by the colony on the premises.[21]

[21] For information on Hutterian schooling, see the following sources on which our own discussion is based (plus personal observations by J.W.B.): Hostetler (1965); Hostetler and Redekop (1962); Knill (1958); Hostetler and Huntington (1967), especially pp. 98–100. As Hostetler and Huntington remark, 'The farther a child goes in school, the less he is said to learn' (100). This sentence summarizes the interpretation made by every student of Hutterian education: that the 'English school' (public school built by the Brethren on the colony premises and staffed by a local school teacher assigned to the colony) is simply tolerated by the Brethren for the purposes of providing basic instruction in reading, writing and arithmetic. Any other influence the school may have on the children—for example, their interest in consumption, the pleasures of the outside world, or too-great concern for learning—will be openly or covertly combated by the colony, and especially by the German school teacher, in his regular instruction sessions with the children. 'Thus the English school is encapsulated by the colony pattern, and ideally its influence cannot go beyond the bounds set by the culture' (Hostetler and Huntington, 1967: 99). As we note in the text, however, the deficiencies of this training are made up in considerable part by informal study and practical learning. The colony, with its complex diversification, management, and mechanization is an ideal place for such supplementary learning. Hutterites have made a few experiments in higher education for their teachers and technicians—high school, and in a few cases, teachers' colleges. These experiments have all failed from the Hutterian point of view, since few of the trainees returned to Hutterian life. Two U.S. states and one Canadian province now require ninth- and tenth-grade education as compulsory for Hutterites, but as yet this requirement is either being ignored, or substitutes are put together in the form of asking the English school teacher to supply additional instruction.

In spite of the formal deficiencies, which reduce its value to many, the educational level of perhaps half of the male Hutterians appears to be about equal to or better than that of the average farmer or rancher (but not the local middle-income townsman, in most cases), especially in the technical and managerial sphere as a result of private study and on-the-job training in the colony. However, this education lacks much of the cultural and academic content of those trained fully in the public schools, and limits the ability of Hutterites to assimilate themselves into secular society and also, therefore, their potential occupational mobility.[22]

While the Hutterites do unusually well on their limited formal education, there is no doubt that the deficiencies, particularly in such spheres as advanced arithmetic and mathematics, are functioning as a check on production decisions, given the increasing sophistication of the economy and agronomy. Hutterites are aware of this problem, and thus far have responded only by encouraging self-training. Hutterites thus are beginning to feel the need for more formal education and this will be an increasingly important adaptive problem for them. Along with consumption pressures, it could become a major cause of basic change in Hutterian society in the next generation.

While both Hutterian colonies and kibbutzim use a full range of mechanical and power equipment in their production, the Hutterites have avoided industrial development, unlike the kibbutzniks. However, the Hutterites, like the kibbutzniks, resist the hiring of outside labor, even though they occasionally find it necessary. The Hutterites are not as concerned as the kibbutzniks with the equality issue, since their ideology qualifies it and permits a strong patriarchal element, but they are deeply concerned about the corrupting influence of outsiders on their young people.

The colony system is able to reduce the problem of the aged by the fission process, which always splits the colony population pyramid down the middle. Hutterites also have deep respect for the aged built into their ideology, which blends egalitarian brotherhood ideas with patriarchal hierarchalism and seniority. Their deliberate preservation of many handicraft skills also provides satisfying small tasks for the aged and resembles the kibbutz alternative of using the older people in the small industries.

Young kibbutzniks are generally restless and openly demand new opportunities for education and employment. Young Hutterites are generally much more committed to the traditional system, although discontent and passive rebellion often simmer beneath the surface in many colonies. However, the Hutterite young people do not openly demand new opportunities and education, since it is officially barred to them, whereas it is a more or

[22] The intensive socialization in the colony, the thorough indoctrination with the use of German and Hutterian Tyrolese dialect in the German school mean that the Hutterite has a distinctive accent, often perceived by outsiders as slightly comic or at best rustic.

less official alternative to kibbutz existence. If a Hutterian youth wishes a different life, he must simply depart; the community will not provide opportunities for training. The isolation of the colonies in a relatively poor

CHART 1

Kibbutz	Colony
All institutions communal in nature, few changes	All institutions communal, no changes
Partly subsidized entrepreneurial unit, geared to partly planned economy	Independent entrepreneurial unit, with little or no subsidy; not part of a planned economy
Capital acquired by own operations and by government subsidies	Capital acquired by own operations and by loans from private sources
Development and diversification tends to expand, producing ideological strain	Development controlled by ideology and by fission process (need to save)
Industry being added to increase output and income	No industry; little likelihood at present; mechanization of agriculture aids productivity
Recurrent labor shortages, hire labor, with consequent ideological strain	Little or no labor shortage; rarely hire labor due to less need, and also fear strain and influence
Alternative job opportunities plentiful in skilled and semi-skilled occupations in urban economy; possible to earn more than individual consumption on kibbutz	Limited alternative job opportunities mostly in unskilled agricultural and service industries in rural areas; wages don't permit higher living standard than in colony
Steady out-migration	Very little out-migration
Formalized intercommunity cooperation organizations	Informal intercommunity cooperative networks and relationships
Expanding education—minimum of 12 years as compared to national average of 7.5; college and technical education available to some	Restricted education—minimum of 8 years compared to 6-year regional average; culturally different than prevailing education; no college or technical education
Problem of supporting the aged	No problem of the aged
Consumption changes largely collective but approval of a degree of individual consumption aspiration; individual consumption less than that of groups with whom kibbutznik compares himself	Consumption changes entirely collective; strong disapproval of individual aspiration; little difference between colony and surrounding area in consumption standards, or colony superior to average
Collective and individual consumption levels rising steadily	Collective consumption level rising slowly, and carefully controlled
Ideology approves relatively high degree of political and intellectual involvement with outside, and it is increasing	Ideology strongly disapproves political and intellectual involvement with outside, and there is little
Accepted by non-kibbutz Israelis	Resented or viewed with ambivalence by non-Hutterites

region also means that invidious comparisons are blunted and the 'pull' of the outside is diffuse, often confined to wistful desires for a few prized personal possessions.[23]

Those few colonies located near large cities (in South Dakota and Manitoba) experience more serious problems with their young people than the more isolated majority, for obvious reasons. A few colonies, considered to be only marginal or doubtful members of the sect by the others, have experimented with town high school education for some of their young, and in most such cases the students do not return to the colony. Still, every colony, isolated or not, will have two or three young men who finally obtain permission from the Elders to leave the colony for a year or so to experience the 'outside'; Hutterian Elders grant these requests in the well-founded belief that it is better to do so in order to remove a possible troublemaker, and in the security of their knowledge that these young men will eventually return to stay.

The differences and similarities between the two types of settlements described in the preceding sections are summarized in chart 1.

PATTERNS OF ADAPTATION

We have discussed the changes made by two types of collective, 'intentional' human communities in response to external pressures and demands. We have visualized this process in terms of the ways these communities have handled their economics and personnel policies in order to retain their basic core of institutions and at the same time cope with the external forces requiring adaptation. The distinctive cultures of the kibbutz and the colony tell us much about the differing patterns of adaptation and change, but on the whole we have found considerable similarity, due basically to the comparable positions, in both cases, of diversified economic enterprises which practice a degree of withdrawal and boundary maintenance concerning the social and economic system of their respective nations.

Thus, the kibbutz has gone farther down the path of internal change than the colony, partly because of its more tolerant and accepting approach to the outside world. The colony, due to its sacred, exclusionistic ideology,

---

[23] Complex psychodynamic issues underlie this paragraph, on which there exists very little information. Hutterian socialization is more drastic than that of the kibbutz in the sense that the child is presented with fewer alternatives, and threats of punishment are used extensively as inducements to conformity. Kibbutz socialization appears to use rewards more than punishment (Bettleheim. 1969). These differences can mean that since fewer Hutterites leave the community than kibbutzniks, there is more covert violation of the community rules by them than in the case of the kibbutznik who would be more prone to depart, but less inclined to engage in petty theft, clandestine violation of rules of behavior and consumption, and the like. We cannot be sure if this is the case, but our personal experiences in both types of communities would make this interpretation a plausible one. To stretch the argument a bit further, it can be suggested that the colony, which at one level is more resistant to change and dissolution than the kibbutz, may at other levels be more friable, and the whole Hutterite system more prone to radical changes if opportunity costs reach a certain level. That is, defection could reach large proportions in a very short time.

seeks out isolated and minimally incorporated parts of North America, and thus can avoid undesirable influences and the need for extensive change. However, the forces operating on the colony seem similar, and it is easy to predict changes of the kibbutz type, given increasing economic development of the Great Plains milieu.

Although there have been changes in the kibbutz system, both communities have been successful in retaining the essential and basic institutions of communal property, living, and decision-making. They have done so while accepting extensive mechanization and rationalization of their operations. The kibbutz has gone even further in these directions than the colony, owing to its more exposed economic position, but its internal social arrangements have retained most of their chartered design. This suggests that communal economics and social organization *can* survive in an individualistic, capitalistic world, and accept much of the instrumental frame of that world with minimal compromise of basic tenets and practices—at least up to a point.

However, the data also indicate that the communal frame, if worked out so as to guarantee basic resources, and basic operating efficiency, actually confers an advantage on the community. The contemporary experimental 'youth communes' can take heart, but at the same time, one must point again to the impressive efficiency and rationality of the successful cases. One must point also to another key factor: the large population base enjoyed by both colonies and kibbutzim, and the possibilities this affords of risk-spreading, mutual cooperation, and loans of capital to the temporarily ailing or immature communities. The Hutterian accomplishment stands out over the kibbutz in this respect, perhaps, since the Brethren achieve their success with minimal outside aid, whereas the kibbutz enjoys a certain amount of subsidy, especially in its formative years and when in economic straits.

In our analysis we focused on the types of comparisons individuals in each community make with the external milieu. In effect, we were examining the opportunity costs of the collective economic solution to survival. Since membership in a communal society embraces all aspects of life, it was necessary to include extra-economic considerations in our evaluations of the way in which each controls defection while not losing its uniqueness. Thus, in addition to the usual considerations of alternative wage earnings, we also had to discuss the problem of economic and social security, which wages are generally assumed to encompass in a private enterprise economy, at least in the usual sense of the concept of opportunity costs.

In both societies we found that adjustments were being made in consumption patterns as production rose. However, this increase takes different forms in the two communities. The Israelis find it necessary to improve individual standards of living and have little hesitancy (and are under greater pressure) to abandon their former austerity. The Hutterites are also raising collective living standards but have made few or no concessions to individual tastes, and we suggest that the Hutterites are helped in this procedure by the spartan quality of life of all people living in the northern Plains and the relative security for members provided by collective living.

This outcome is not independent of other features of the two societies. When looking at the occupational opportunities available inside the two communities and on the outside, it became evident that the kibbutzniks were in a much better position to take advantage of the rapid growth of new industries than the Brethren.

The Brethren provide a restricted education which is well suited to supply people for the agricultural tasks of the colony, but too parochial to prepare young people to cope with the challenges of the competitive North American world. Yet the internal 'earning power' of this limited education is extraordinary, because the low formal accreditation bars Hutterites from lucrative jobs on the outside. The kibbutz, on the other hand, encourages development of human potential within the limits of its financial resources, and provides at least as good an education through high school as other Israeli schools. This education permits the kibbutz to compete with outside attractions, but has its dangers since it also equips young people to accept outside opportunities.

While the colony out-migration rate is lower than the kibbutz, the Hutterites do have to cope with 'defection' and when their colonies are in proximity to urban centers, they have problems comparable to those of the kibbutz. In both cases members showing extreme dissidence are permitted to leave—permanently in extreme cases, temporarily in others. Recognition is shown in both of the need to remove dissatisfied people from the corporate body, but at the same time, such removal is opposed and everything possible is done to bring the person around to accepting the sanctioned lifeways.

The Hutterian ideology itself is an explanation for the slowness of change in the traditional system. By deliberately isolating themselves as much as possible from the influence of the outer world and limiting the training of their members, the colonies have insulated themselves against the forces of change which might otherwise threaten their present form of life. On the other hand, this posture contains dangers of inflexibility in the face of rapid change in the surrounding milieu, and it is adaptable primarily to an intensely rural environment. Evidence from urbanized areas suggests great vulnerability in the face of urban pressures and temptations.

Kibbutz ideology was both spartan *and* accessible in the beginning. The kibbutz movement was one of the moving forces behind the creation of the Israeli state and it has always identified itself with the nation's progress. When Israeli economic policy changed from agricultural development to industrialization, accompanied by a rapid rise in living standards, the kibbutz followed suit, although often reluctantly. As a result, there have been changes in the meaning and practices of collective life, although there are also differences among kibbutzim in the degree of change. The future of change will depend on the outcome of the competition between the private sector and its demands for the kibbutzniks as members of the labor force, and the kibbutz' ability to continue modifying its structure to provide jobs and other opportunities to complement the attractiveness of communal living. The volume of resources required for this task is a prime concern of organizations like the Jewish Agency which are committed to strengthening the kibbutzim.[24]

Thus, by focusing on the opportunity costs of labor in two collective societies, we were compelled to examine the ways in which each is coping with the challenge of dissatisfaction among its members. We stressed only those aspects of community life which seem to have greatest influence in inducing people either to remain in the community or to leave. The decision-making process is obviously strongly influenced by alternative opportunities available in the rest of the society for members of the community.

We are not arguing that all communal societies operate similarly or that they are influenced by the same pressures from the larger societies of which they are a part. On the contrary, our analysis suggests that ideology and environment both have important roles to play in determining the pace and the type of adaptive mechanisms. We tried to demonstrate, however, that by examining similar types of data in two different cultures a meaningful analysis of the dynamics of social change could emerge and provide the basis for a generalized approach to this problem.

Many 'foreign observers ... question the future of the kibbutz. ... Intuitively, they tend to consider that their future will be similar to that of other "utopian societies" which arose in various parts of the world and then disappeared' (Kanovsky, 1966: 142). Our analysis suggests that the kibbutz is a dynamic institution in a developing economy and that quite likely it will be able to meet the challenges of the larger society by adapting itself as rapidly as possible to the requirements of that society while retaining its essential communal character. However, the original utopian frontier agrarian image of the kibbutz will become increasingly unrealistic as Israel transforms itself into an urban-industrial state. Perhaps the analysis also suggests ways in which change will have to be managed by government poli-

---

[24] Bruno Bettleheim's (1969) analysis of the kibbutz society tends to confirm our analysis of the reasons for leaving. While he concentrates on psychological factors in the migration decision, he confirms the private society's ability to offer 'greater freedom to develop emotionally or otherwise' (280). He adds that the past subsidies will have to continue since 'even the most cursory inspection convinces one that kibbutz society could not survive economically without drawing upon the highly developed technology of surrounding Israel' (283).

cies if some of the original characteristics of the institution are to be retained; that is, an approach to economic development which considers the costs of preserving traditional institutions of moral and social value.

One can predict that as the northern Great Plains environment becomes more urbanized, more firmly tied to national entities, the Hutterites will experience changes comparable to those already visible for the kibbutz. Colonies already show various departures from the traditional model: some are becoming more specialized in production, to take advantage of market opportunities; many are spending more on consumption, especially on domestic establishment, to permit a more comfortable life; others are contemplating new educational schemes, perhaps even some tentative industrial experiments. While predictions are hazardous for this intricately institutionalized society, there is some reason to believe that over the next generation, the Hutterian movement may diversify into a variety of types.

Still, Hutterian ideology is adamant on one point: that the search for profit and pleasure is the road to evil and to human divisiveness; and that economics is a way of life, and a means to life, and not an end in itself. Not all Hutterian colonies are or will be able to withstand the pressures toward prosperity, but the majority probably will. It is too much to ask the rest of the world to follow this path, but perhaps its lessons can serve as a desirable moderating influence.

BIBLIOGRAPHY

Baden, John A. (1968), 'The Management of Social Stability: A Political Ethnography of the Hutterites of North America'. Unpublished Ph.D. dissertation, Department of Political Science, Indiana University, Bloomington.

Barth, Frederik (1961), *Nomads of South Persia: The Basseri Tribe of the Khamsem Confederacy*. New York: Humanities Press.

—— (1967), 'On the Study of Social Change', *American Anthropologist*, 69: 661–9.

Bennett, John W. (1967), *Hutterian Brethren: The Agricultural Economy and Social Organization of a Communal People*. Stanford: Stanford University Press.

—— (1969), *Northern Plainsmen: Adaptive Strategy and Agrarian Life*. Chicago: Aldine Publishing Company.

Bestor, Arthur E. (1950), *Backwoods Utopias: The Sectarian and Owenite Phases of Communitarian Socialism in America*. Philadelphia: University of Pennsylvania Press.

Bettleheim, Bruno (1969), *The Children of the Dream*. New York, Philadelphia: Macmillan.

Blau, Peter (1964), *Exchange and Power in Social Life*. New York: Wiley.

Boguslaw, Robert (1968), *New Utopians: A Study of System Design and Social Change*. Englewood Cliffs, New Jersey: Prentice-Hall.

Central Bureau of Statistics, Israel, *Statistical Abstract*. Tel Aviv.

Cohen, Eric (1966), 'Progress and Communality: Value Dilemmas in the Collective Movement', *International Review of Community Development*, Nos. 15, 16.

—— and M. Rosner (1968), 'Relations Between Generations in the Israeli Kibbutz', unpublished manuscript, Hebrew University and Givaat Haviva.

Cohn, Norman (1947), *The Pursuit of the Millenium*. New York: Essential Books (Republished by Harper & Row, 1962).

Kibbutz and Colony: Collective Economics and the Outside World   369

Darin-Drabkin, Haim (1962), *The Other Society*. New York: Harcourt, Brace & World.
Eaton, Joseph W., and A. J. Mayer (1955a), 'Demography of the Hutterites in North Dakota', *Geographic Review*, 45: 573.
—— (1955b), *Man's Capacity to Reproduce: A Demography of a Unique Population*. Glencoe, Illinois: Free Press.
Eaton, Joseph W., and R. J. Well (1955), *Culture and Mental Disorders: A Comparative Study of Hutterites and Other Populations*. Glencoe, Illinois: Free Press.
Ferguson, Charles E. (1969), *Microeconomic Theory*. Homewood, Illinois: Irwin.
Foster, George M. (1967), *Tzintzuntzan: Mexican Peasants in a Changing World*. Boston: Little, Brown & Co.
Friedl, Ernestine (1962), *Vasilika: A Village in Modern Greece*. New York: Holt, Rinehart & Winston.
—— (1964), 'Lagging Emulation in a Post-Peasant Society', *American Anthropologist* 66: 574–5.
Friedmann, Robert (1961), *Hutterite Studies*. Scottdale, Pennsylvania: Herald Press.
Goldberg, Harvey (1968), 'Elite Groups in Peasant Communities. A Comparison of Three Near Eastern Villages', *American Anthropologist*, 70: 718–31.
—— (1969), 'Domestic Organization and Wealth in an Israeli Immigrant Village', *Human Organization*, 28: 59–63.
Homans, George (1961), *Social Behavior: Its Elementary Forms*. New York: Harcourt, Brace & World.
Hostetler, John A. (1965), 'Education and Marginality in the Communal Society of the Hutterites, mimeographed monograph, Pennsylvania State University.
Hostetler, John A. and G. E. Huntington (1967), *The Hutterites in North America*. New York: Holt, Rinehart & Winston.
Hostetler, John A., and C. Redekop (1962), 'Education and Assimilation in Three Ethnic Groups', *Alberta Journal of Educational Research*, 8: 189–203.
Kanovsky, Eliyahu (1966), *The Economy of the Israeli Kibbutz* (Harvard Middle Eastern Monographs 13). Cambridge, Mass.: Harvard University Press.
Klassen, Peter (1964), *The Economics of Anabaptism: 1525–1560*. The Hague: Mouton & Co.
Knill, William D. (1958), 'Hutterian Education: A Descriptive Study Based on the Hutterian Colonies within Warner County, Alberta, Canada'. Unpublished Ph.D. dissertation, Montana State University, Bozeman, Montana.
Nordoff, Charles (1875), *The Communistic Societies of the United States*, New York: Harper & Brothers (reprinted by Dover Publications, 1966).
Noyes, John H. (1870), *History of American Socialisms*. New York (reprinted by Hillary House, 1961).
Pascal, R. (1936), 'Communism in the Middle Ages and the Reformation: Waldenses and Anabaptists', in J. Lewis, ed., *Christianity and the Social Revolution*. New York: Scribners.
Peters, Victor (1965), *All Things Common: The Hutterian Way of Life*. Minneapolis: University of Minnesota Press.
Pratt, William F. (1969), 'The Anabaptist Explosion'. *Natural History*, 78: No. 2.
Ridemann, Peter (1565), *Account of our Religion, Doctrine, and Faith* (translated by K. Hasenberg, Bungay). Suffolk: Hodder & Stoughton, Ltd., in conjunction with Plough Publishing House, 1950.
Riley, Marvin P., and J. R. Stewart (1966), *The Hutterites: South Dakota's Communal Farmers. Brookings: South Dakota State University*.
Rosenfeld, Henry (1958), 'Processes of Structural Change within the Arab Village Extended Family', *American Anthropologist*, 60: 1127–39.

—— (1968), 'Change, Barriers to Change, and Contradictions in the Arab Village Family', *American Anthropologist*, 70: 732–52.

Rosner, Menachem (1967), 'Women in the Kibbutz: Changing Status and Concepts', *Asian and African Studies* (Annual of the Israel Oriental Society), 3: 35–68.

Shatil, Joseph E. (1968), *Criteria for Socioeconomic Efficiency of the Kibbutz: The Point of View of an Economist*. Processed paper, Givaat Haviva (Research Center for the kibbutz).

Sommer, Donald (1954), 'Peter Ridemann and Menno Simons on Economics', *Mennonite Quarterly Review*, 28: 205–23.

Spiro, Milford (1956), *Kibbutz: Venture in Utopia*. Cambridge, Mass.: Harvard University Press.

Talmon-Garber, Yonina (1963), 'Social Change and Family Structure', *International Social Science Journal*, 14: 468–87.

—— (1965), 'The Family in a Revolutionary Movement: The Case of the Kibbutz in Israel', in M. Nimkoff, ed., *Comparative Family Systems*. New York: Houghton Mifflin.

Weintraub, D., M. Lissak and Y. Asmon (1969), *Moshava, Kibbutz, and Moshav: Patterns of Jewish Rural Settlement and Development in Palestine*. Ithaca: Cornell University Press.

Weitz, R., and Avshalom Rokach (1968), *Agricultural Development: Planning and Implementation* (Israel Case Study). Dordracht, Holland: D. Reidel Publishing Co.

Williams, George H. (1962), *The Radical Reformation*. Philadelphia: Westminster Press.

Industrialization in Advanced Rural Communities: The Israeli Kibbutz

Yehuda Don

I

The concept of rural industrialization has in the last decade gradually gained ground as a leading socio-economic option to combat undesirable effects of attempts to obtain economic growth through focusing development efforts on the major urban centers. Such disparity between the rate of growth of economic and social opportunities, real or imaginary, in the cities, vis-a-vis the usually dormant and often declining rural areas, led to a constant drift of rural population to urban centers. Such migration, if unchecked, will, according to World Bank sources, increase urban population at twice the rate of general demographic growth and bring about uncontrollable sprawling urban conglomerates. The introduction of industrialization to rural areas has been considered as one possible instrument towards the obtainment of a more balanced development, under conditions of declining demand for labor in agriculture, due to mechanization or to the lack of additional employment opportunities for the large rural families. And indeed, a group of experts was convened in September 1973 in Bucharest, to explore the case of Rural Industrialization. Its brief report, which has now become a major document on the issue[1], concentrates on the developing countries and their particular set of conditions and requirements. However, industrial development in rural areas, geared towards the rural population, has been going on in Eastern and Western Europe, as well as in other developed regions, for the last two decades.

The industrialization of the Israeli collective settlement, the Kibbutz, is one unique example of building industry in small, highly developed and rather sophisticated rural communities.

371

II

At the end of 1973 there were, according to the Annual Report of the Israeli Registrar of Cooperatives (1974, p. 412) 238 Kibbutzim with an average population of about 430, 260 of whom belong to the labor force[2]. Only a handful of Kibbutzim have more than 600 working members, and a Kibbutz with a labor force of less than 100 is usually not regarded viable in the long run.

In 1974 there were 248 industrial plants in the Kibbutzim with a labor force of 10,800 and an output of IL 1,575 million ($ 262 million appx.) They produced 5.7 per cent of the country's industrial output, and invested IL 197 million, 9.8 per cent of the total industrial investment that year[3]. The Kibbutz has thus become a distinctly agro-industrial settlement, in contrast to its overwhelmingly agricultural character in the past.

This process of industrialization took place in less than twenty years. Industrial labor force increased from 1958 to 1974 by about 260 per cent, from 3,000 to nearly 11,000 workers. From 1958 onwards virtually the total increment to the Kibbutz labor force has been assigned to industry. Output growth greatly outstripped that of labor force, increasing by about 2500 per cent, from IL 15.7 million in 1958 to over IL 400 million in 1974 (all in constant 1958 prices)[4]. Obviously, such disparity in growth rates can only be explained by heavy investment in industry, as well as by rapid technological progress, entailing an increase in total productivity.

The rate of growth of the industrial sector in the Kibbutz movement was considerably faster than that of the Israeli industry in general. As a result the share of the Kibbutzim in total industrial output increased from 4.9 per cent in 1970 to 6.0 per cent in 1974[5]. Among the main reasons for this development was the fact that the rate of growth of investment in industry was considerably faster in the Kibbutz than in the economy in general[6].

These developments changed the relative position of industry in the Kibbutz economy. Industry/agriculture ratio of labor grew from 0.21 in 1958 to 0.65 in 1973. Industry/agriculture ratio of capital grew also impressively from 0.14 in 1958 to 0.30 fifteen years later[7]. Beyond increasing its share in labor and capital, the Kibbutz industry also outstripped agriculture in the rate of growth of its Total Productivity Index[8], despite the fact that in these years Kibbutz agriculture developed into one of the most productive agricultural systems in the world.

III

The Kibbutz model of industrialization is focused on the individual rural settlement. This conception is in sharp contradiction to the recommended models of inter-village industrial centers, leaning on already existing "... locations, which possessed a higher degree of social organization than the rural agricultural settlements" and which "... could become the module upon which the programme of regional development was constructed"; and in another passage "... rural industrialization was not the setting up of one or more industrial undertakings in every village, or as one participant put it, at every crossroad"[9]. This is exactly what Kibbutz industrialization has been doing. It is introspective, aiming at the solution of the specific problems in each Kibbutz, which embarks on the establishment of industrial plants[10].

The reasons for the widespread and rapid industrialization of the Israeli Kibbutzim during the last two decades are complex.

The main motive has probably been economic. The first and fundamental task of the rural sector, after 1948, was the provision of food for the rapidly growing population. This task was accomplished towards the end of the 1950's, with most massive development projects completed, increasing greatly the production potentials of agriculture, and bringing cultivable land, and, particularly water reserves, close to full exploitation. On the other hand, the rate of growth of the Israeli population slowed down at that time, so that agriculture was capable of handling the slowly growing demand for produce with reasonably stable quantities of land and water.

In addition, during the 1950's, to encourage production, the government maintained a policy of easy credit and an artificially low rate of exchange for imported agricultural machinery. Relative prices of imported mechanized input were thus greatly reduced and thereby encouraged Kibbutz agriculture to adopt capital intensive production patterns. Such high capital intensity enabled Kibbutz agriculture to easily meet the gradually expanding demand for its produce, with a constant and even slightly reduced labor force.[11]

Thus two processes had to be encountered:
1. a relative decline in the profitability of agriculture.
2. a relative surplus of high priced Kibbutz labor, released from agriculture.

Under such conditions, and in view of the high priority given by the government from the late 1950's onward to industrialization (backed

by due policies), many Kibbutzim turned to industry. They did so
mainly because they realized that the utilization of both capital and
labor, was more profitable in industry than in agriculture[12]. It is
suggested, therefore, that the prime motivation for industrialization
was economic[13]. Additional reasons emphasized in the literature are:
a) The necessity to find suitable employment solutions for the aged
   and the physically limited members for whom agriculture is too
   straining[14].
b) The demand for employment opportunities for female members in
   "productive" branches, outside the service – catering – education
   nexus[15].
c) To provide technologically challenging economic functions for the
   young and ambitious members.

IV

The Kibbutz industrial enterprise is a unique blend of economic
rationality and a rigidly confined set of ideological restrictions. Though
the objective function of its plant is by no means the ordinary profit
maximization paradigm, economic targets form a prime constraint for
any industrial initiative. The Kibbutz economy is operated by a
remarkably high quality labor force, the average standard of education
is probably the highest in the country[16], ". . . as virtually every child is
given 12 years of institutionalized full time education." (Don, 1975,
p. 13) The average standard of living of this population – measured
by disposable income per capita – places it between the 6th and the
7th upper decile of the entire population.
    Shadow price of labor in the kibbutz is at least $2\frac{1}{2}$ times higher than
the price of industrial labor. Consequently, no kibbutz plant survives
unless it fulfills the condition of very high return to labor.
    The non-economic constraints originate from:
1. the kibbutz constitution;
2. the welfare conceptions of the kibbutz towards its members.

1. The constitutional constraints are, in fact, the transplantation of
the kibbutz principles into the field of industrial relations.
a) Operating within an equalitarian society, work on the plant, in
   whichever function, carries no direct remuneration.
b) Almost none of the customary motivational means exist in the
   kibbutz plant. There is no promotion, very little status remuneration to directors is acknowledged, there is a constant pressure for

continuous rotation in all managerial functions, and the hierarchical relations created within the plant disappear outside of it.

c) The kibbutz is considered sovereign over the plans and policies of its plant. Its elected directors (the Secretariat) are expected to exercise full authority over the management of the plant and the supreme body over its fortunes is the members' assembly.

d) Operating in a voluntary society, the plant's management has neither tools nor authority to effectuate disciplinary or coercive measures against non-cooperating member-workers. Likewise, authoritarian managerial methods, as compared to authority based on professional skill and experience, are not only disliked, but also ineffective[17].

e) The principle of self labor (no hired workers on the plant), when applied, becomes a limitation on the expansibility of production.

f) No disciplinary action concerning the manipulation of the wages or the employment of the members is conceivable.

2. The welfare constraints confine the range of the socially acceptable industrial activities, in view of the characteristics of the labour force involved in all stages of production and in view of its expectations from its work in industry.

a) Production processes entailing widespread and continuous physical strain are unaccepted.

b) The same applies to particularly monotonous processes.

c) At least some stages of the production must involve technologically challenging activities.

Without due considerations given to these constraints, the plant faces the perils of either losing its unique character or jeopardizing its entire existence, due to the reluctance of its member-workers to go along with its industrial practices.

All these constraints operate under the shadow of the fundamental requirement of a high rate of return for labor.

It seems obvious that by the standard paradigms of microeconomic analysis, all ideological constraints are limiting factors, artificially narrowing the scope of profit maximization. Restrictions created by welfare requirements are handled in a market economy by the relative wages mechanism. The principle of two way rotation seems to contradict the advantages of specialization[18]. Democratization of the decision making procedures through shop-floor assemblies and management-workers committees, introduces elements of inefficiency into management. Equalized remuneration violates the principle of distribution according to marginal product. The implementation of kibbutz sovereignty may hinder the exploitation of opportunities for profit making or expansion. Finally, the reluctance to hire labor up to the level where its marginal product equals the ongoing wage rate, reduces the possibility of resolving problems of welfare constraints and reduces the profit making utilization of the plant.

However, these self-imposed restrictions indicate a lack of rationality only under the assumption that the objective function of the kibbutz is identical to that of market enterprises. However, it is not. The kibbutz plant aims at simultaneously obtaining a wide facet of welfare objectives. Satisfaction at work, a sense of involvement and responsibility are as important objectives of the plant as profitability.

The basic analytical difference between the profit oriented and the kibbutz plant seems to be in the inverse logical sequence of the main variables and the opposite direction of their functional relationships.

In a profit maximizing plant[19] branch and location are simultaneously determined by their direct effect on profitability (in view of perspective marketing opportunities – regarded as a parameter for the entrepreneur). Branch selection has a decisive effect on technology[20], which, together with marketing considerations, determines size. Technology also determines – together with size and relative price structure of production factors (influenced itself by location), the method of production[21]. Method of production and size jointly determine the managerial structure and hierarchy. Labor relations and social organization are the results of this sequence, and are brought to optimum through the price mechanism. (There are, of course, additional social and political institutions of great influence, operated by the State, the Trade Unions, etc., but they are exogenous for our analysis of the course of decision making.)

The course of decisions in the kibbutz plant is different. The objective function is complex and seeks solution for at least three separate, through not necessarily independent, objectives:

1. Profitability – providing for the accepted standard of living.
2. Satisfaction of members at work – depending on psychological factors.
3. Industrial solution to employment problems – result of excess labor of given quality, limitations and ambitions.

Satisfaction (welfare) and employment considerations simultaneously determine production method and managerial system, both of which

have a decisive influence on size. Also present are ideological parameters, such as self labor and considerations with regard to the balance
between the plant and the kibbutz. They also effect decisions on size.
Managerial and production methods, together with size, determine
technology, which, along with profit considerations and market parameters, determine branch. Location is no variable in the kibbutz flow
chart.

The following are the graphic presentations of the two flow charts.

CHART I: *Flow Chart of a Market Oriented Profit Maximizing Plant*

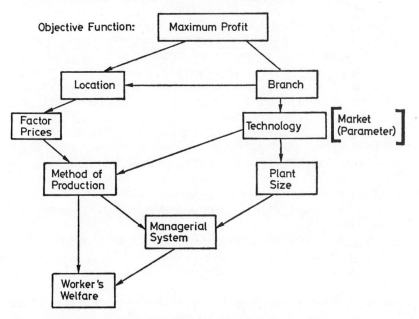

Probably the most significant difference between the two flow charts
is the place of "Branch" and "Technology", which are prime determining factors in profit maximizing plants and derivatives of size and
methods of production and management in the kibbutz plant. This
fact was eloquently emphasized by Melman who, by describing what
he called "managerial mode of organization" wrote: "... responsibility
for the character of the industrial corporation and its consequences, is
assigned to technology"; ... "Man individually, and in groups, is
viewed as the servant of the machine." (1970-1, p. 47)

CHART II: *Flow Chart of a Kibbutz Plant*

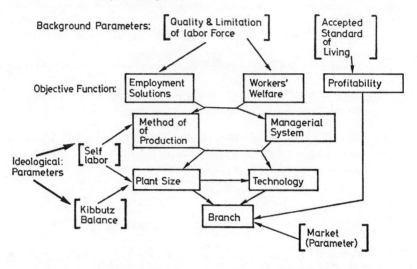

In the kibbutz plant, however, the three critical decisions of size, technology and branch are the result of considerations, aiming at a simultaneous solution of:

1. optimum utilization of the available member's labor force;
2. maximum employment of non hierarchical, democratic management methods;
3. maximum possible observation of the ideological constraints of the kibbutz principles;
4. profitability, at least for the accepted standard.

Welfare and ideological considerations led to the preference of small units, to prevent the plant from outgrowing the kibbutz and also to ease the application of appropriate managerial methods. On the other hand, kibbutz industry in general operates under increasing returns to scale[22].

The issue of size for new plants seems now settled. In 1974 nearly 80 per cent of the plants had 50 or less employees and 93 per cent had 100 or less.

TABLE I: *Distribution of size of kibbutz plants by employees in 1974*[23]

No. of employees	10 or less	11-30	31-50	51-100	100 or more
Per cent of plants	27	32	20	14	7
Accumulated percentage	27	59	79	93	100

Technology employed in most plants is highly capital intensive and sophisticated machinery substitute for size in maintaining high productivity.

Branch composition has gone through significant changes during the last thirty years. The changes indicate a pattern of losing contact with agriculture and a movement towards high technology activities.

TABLE II: *The development of branch composition in kibbutz Industry*[24]

Branch Year:	Percentage of Plants			
	1946-7	1952	1963	1973
Metal and Printing	36.5	33.1	34.6	30.9
Electronics	–	–	4.6	10.2
Timber and Furniture	34.1	16.9	11.5	7.7
Plastics and Rubber	–	–	9.2	21.5
Food	11.1	18.2	13.0	8.9
Textile and Leather	7.9	8.8	6.9	5.7
Building Material	2.4	8.8	5.4	4.5
Chemicals	2.4	3.4	3.1	1.6
Misc.	5.6	10.8	11.5	10.2
Total	100	100	100	100

The outstanding trends are:
1. a remarkable growth in plastics, rubber and electronics;
2. a drastic and persistent decline in timber and furniture;
3. a smaller decline in food, textiles, leather and chemicals;
4. rapid responses to temporary increases of demand; (food and building material in 1952)
5. a continuous primacy of the metal industry.

Generally, a movement towards sophisticated technology and high capital intensity is clearly observable. Such shifts necessitated large volumes of capital, which were raised without particular difficulties, also as a result of the easy transferability of capital released in agriculture (itself more capital intensive than industry).

This solution of relatively small highly capital intensive plants, which pay reasonably great attention to ideological constraints, has also proved economically remunerative. The kibbutz plant is probably more efficient than its non kibbutz counterpart[25]. Return to labor is considerably higher, and return to capital, even at the margin, is not lower than the ongoing market rates. The difference must be attributed to qualitative factors, such as managerial efficiency, high quality of labor and stronger motivation of the labourer. It is therefore obvious that measures, which cater for quality and strengthen motivation are positively corelated with profitability[26].

The most problematic ideological constraint is the objection to hired labor. In spite of long efforts to eradicate it, 47 per cent of all employees in kibbutz industry were hired in 1974. Regarding its effects, it was suggested and statistically supported, if not proved, that member labor in plants with hired labor was of a lower quality[27].

It is also suggested that hired labor is negatively corelated with capital intensiveness and technology, yet it is not stated unequivocally which of the two is the independent variable. In other words, we do not know whether hired labor itself serves as an alternative to capital, or branch selection with rather rigid technology has determined the labor intensiveness of the production function[28]. The corelation of hired labor with profitability has not yet been conclusively stated. Though there are certain indications to a negative coefficient, they can also be interpreted as the results of intervening variables[29].

There is no doubt that the industrializing experiment of the kibbutz has been successful. It has succeeded because it has had at its disposal:
1. high standard and strongly motivated manpower;
2. well run-in democratic institutions;
3. sufficient capital;

This reasoning leads back to the U.N. experts' recommendation that rural industrialization be viewed as an integral part of a comprehensive development process which also includes ingredients such as land reform and appropriate legislation. In this respect the kibbutz model is in harmony with recommended patterns. Industry reached the kibbutz in most cases after agricultural and social consolidation, and after it had a satisfactory social and physical infrastructure.

The experience of the kibbutz in rural industrialization may be of some value for similar experiments in spheres such as:
1. experimentations with the adaptation of small and medium-sized plants to branches;

2. experimentations in different fashions of integration between agricultural and industrial activities;
3. experimentation in the democratization of management methods.

NOTES

[1] See (17).
[2] This extraordinarily high ratio of 60 p.c. despite the reasonably high birth rate, is the result of a statistical definition, which considers every inhabitant between 18 years and retirement age automatically as belonging to the labor force, irrespective of his occupation.
[3] See (1) various pages.
[4] Sources for 1958 taken from (4) and for 1974 (1) ibid.
[5] Growth indices for the years 1970-1974 for the two industrial sectors are the following:

Year		1970	1971	1972	1973	1974
I	Kibbutz Industry	100	114	142	170	171
II	General Industry	100	111	125	133	140
$\frac{I \times 100}{II}$		100	103	114	128	122

Data from (1) ibid. p. 45. In view of lack of reliable time series on output for the Kibbutz industry, sales figures substituted for output figures. It created for 1974 an upward bias for the Kibbutz industry of about 6 per cent.
[6] Investment index figures for 1970-1974 are the following:

Year		1970	1971	1972	1973	1974
I	Kibbutz Industry	100	100	158	186	180
II	General Industry	100	111	122	115	129
$\frac{I \times 100}{II}$		100	90	130	162	140

Data from (1) ibid p. 57.
[7] Data from (4) ibid.
[8] Total Productivity Index of agriculture and industry showed the following development:

Year	Agriculture	Industry	100 × Industry/ Agriculture
1957	100	100	100
1965	146	157	107
1973	190	215	113

Data from (5) ibid.
[9] See (17) ibid, p. 5.
[10] There exists a parallel highly developed regional network of industrial plants, serving groupings of Kibbutzim- or Moshavim – in most rural areas of the country. These "regional centers" however, do not accomodate production oriented plants. The regional center plants aim at serving, following the patterns of routine central productive cooperatives of multipurpose primary agricultural cooperatives, the agricultural and consumption objectives of their members' patrons, the kibbutzim in the respective regions. For a comprehensive analysis of this network of regional centers, see (12).

[11] Labor force index in agriculture declined from 100 in 1958 to 95 in 1969.

[12] This contention seemed to be true. A three years moving average calculated on Barkai's figures (4) p. 11 gave the following results:

Marginal Product of Capital

	In percentage			Index		
Years	Agric.	Indus.	Ind./Agr.	Agric.	Indus.	Ind. × 100/Agric.
*1958-60	0.102	0.221	2.16	100	100	100
*1960-62	0.102	0.228	2.24	100	103	103
1961-63	0.110	0.214	1.95	108	97	90
1962-64	0.103	0.229	2.23	101	104	103
1963-65	0.123	0.227	1.85	121	103	85

Marginal Product of Labor

	In constant IL per day			Index		
Years	Agric.	Indus.	Ind./Agr.	Agric.	Indus.	Ind. × 100/Agric.
*1958-60	24.80	29.06	1.19	100	100	100
*1960-62	27.29	37.79	1.38	111	130	117
1961-63	28.74	44.24	1.54	117	152	130
1962-64	32.61	45.11	1.38	133	155	117
1963-65	37.44	48.35	1.29	153	166	109

(*) Figures for 1959 were not available.

The following conclusions are derived from the tables:

1. Rate of Return on capital in Industry as represented by Marginal Product was and remained higher than in Agriculture.
2. Rate of Return on labor grew rapidly at the expense of little or no growth in the Rate of Return on Capital.
3. No clear pattern can be observed in the Industry/Agriculture ratios on capital. In labor the ratio increased until 1961-3 and then slid back.

[13] The author accepts thus the views of Barkai over those of Leviatan (13), Golomb (11) and Schtanger (18), who place economic and other considerations on equal footing. The approach of Barkai is preferred as it explains more satisfactorily the time factor and the rhythm of the industrializing process.

[14] D. Atar forecast that by 1980, 15.4 per cent of the population at the veteran kibbutzim (established until 1936) and 9.8 percent at the medium ones (established between 1936 and 1948) will be above the age of 65. See (3) p. 63.

[15] Despite efforts of "productivization" the ratio of female workers in agriculture and industry remains low (15.5 percent of the "young" and 10 percent of the "old" generation). See (7) p. 31.

[16] In a recent study on the second generation (7), the schooling standard of the investigated second generation population was the following:

Years of formal education:	8 or less	9-11	12	13+	Total
Percentage of the population:	1	6	78	15	100

See ibid p. 34.

Regarding student population ratio, returns are contradictory According to M. Chizik

(8), in one of the major kibbutz movements – Kibbutz Artzi – there were in 1972 – 1000 students, out of a population of about 36 000.

In another study of the other two great movements – Hameuchad and Ichud – G. Mossinsohn (16) found in 1971 – 1084 students, out of a population of about 60 000. The crude student/population ratios are unexplicably different (2.77 percent by Chizik and 1.60 percent by Mossinsohn) though they are both higher than the national average (1.17 per cent).

[17] The extent of professional versus authoritarian managerial styles were analysed on a 5 steps ordered scale. Average results for the industrial management in the kibbutz were high (3.54), though not as high as in kibbutz agriculture (3.91). See (19) p. 16.

[18] Rotation in the kibbutz plant is a two-way affair, with both upward and downward movements. It differs from the basically one-way (upward) rotation in market enterprises. The average rotation pattern in the kibbutz industry was 3-4 years (like in agriculture), though it had a larger variance. See (14). In a study on the aged members in industry (3), it was found that of all industrial workers who had served in the past on the Board of Secretariat, 53 percent worked at the time of the study as ordinary laborers. ibid. p. 66.

[19] The following analysis assumes that both the profit seeking and the kibbutz plants are "pure" models.

[20] J. Woodward in her classical work (20) distinguished between three industrial systems:
1) Production in small units;
2) mass production;
3) processing industries. For each system which may even cut through two digit branch definitions, the technological implications are rather rigid.

[21] With size and technology given, there seems to be little leeway for substitutability of factors in production proper. It is, however, possible in various supporting activities.

[22] Barkai estimated that with a Cobb Douglas production function, using two inputs, returns to scale were increasing in nine of the ten investigated years. See (6).

[23] Source (1) p. 68. Analysing figures from 1971 shows a slight tendency of decline in size.

Accumulated percentage of employees

Year	30 or less	50 or less	100 or less	Median
1971	49	75	92	30.6
1972	55	75	92	27.2
1973	56	76	93	26.0
1974	59	79	93	24.4

[24] Data from various sources.

[25] Melman found significant differences in a group of six pairs of kibbutz and non kibbutz plants in six separate branches, in favour of the kibbutz plants. He found that "the cooperative (i.e. kibbutz / Y.D. /) enterprises showed higher productivity of labor (26 per cent), higher productivity of capital (67 and 33 percent), larger net profit per production worker (115 percent) and lower administrative cost (13 percent)". See (15) p. 52. This author is not convinced that the sample and the statistical methods used by Melman justify outright quantitative statements, however, the overall results are also impressive.

[26] The variables: 1) "sense of involvement and entrepreneurial behaviour", 2) "motivations" and 3) "quality of labor force" are positively corelated to profit indicators ($r = 0.50$, 0.34 and 0.35 respectively). The explaining coefficient of these variables (R^2) with profit indicators, using multiple correlation, was 0.40. See (13) p. 19. A comparative study on agricultural cooperatives in Eastern Europe came to similar conclusions. See (10).

[27] See (20).

[28] The second hypothesis is supported by the very great difference between branches with regard to their hired labor ratio. It is the highest in timber and furniture (74.5 percent), in building materials and quarries (73.4 percent), and in food (71.5 percent). It is the lowest in plastics and rubber (16.4 percent), in electronics (20.5 percent), and in chemicals (20.6 percent). See (1) p. 66.
[29] See (13) pp. 18-19.

REFERENCES

1. Annual Report of the Interkibbutz Association for Industry for the Year 1974, (1975), Tel-Aviv (Hebrew).
2. Annual Report of the Registrar of Cooperative Societies for 1973, (1974), Labor & National Insurance, (Hebrew).
3. ATARI, D. (1975), Gerontological Aspects of the Kibbutz Industry Study, The Kibbutz, 2, 63-68, (Hebrew).
4. BARKAI, H. (1972), Industrial Revolution in the Kibbutz – Clarifications and Notes, Falk Institute Research Series No. 31, (Jerusalem), (Hebrew).
5. BARKAI, H. (1975), The Kibbutz and the Economic Realities of the 1970-ies, The New Economic Policy and the Kibbutz, ed. Y. Don, (Tel Aviv: CIRCOM), (Hebrew).
6. BARKAI, H. (1974), An Empirical Analysis of Productivity and Factor Allocation in Kibbutz Farming and Manufacturing, Falk Institute Discussion Paper 748, (Jerusalem), (Mimeographed).
7. BEN-DAVID, Y. Continuity and Change in the Sphere of Work – the Second Generation in the Kibbutz, The Kibbutz, 28-46, (Hebrew).
8. CHIZIK, M. (1973), Studies at the Kibbutz' Expense, Hedim, (Hebrew).
9. DON, Y. (1975), Dynamics of the Development of the Israeli Kibbutz, Dept. of Economics, Bar Ilan University, Discussion Paper 7512, (Ramat Gan).
10. DON, Y. (1973), Management Patterns and Economic Results in Agricultural Cooperatives, Journal of Rural Cooperation, 1, (1-2), 21-30.
11. GOLOMB, N. (1975), Social and Organizational Structure of the Industrial Plant in the Kibbutz, Rupin College, (Mimeographed), (Hebrew).
12. KELLERMAN, A. (1976), Spatial Aspects of Interrural Centers of Israel, Journal of Rural Cooperation, 4, 51-71.
13. Leviatan, U. Industrialization and the Kibbutz Values – Contradiction and Completion, The Kibbutz, 11-27, (Hebrew).
14. LEVIATAN, U. (1973), The Industrial Revolution in the Kibbutz Movement, Givat Haviva, (Mimeographed), (Hebrew).
15. MELMAN, S. (1970/1), Managerial Versus Cooperative Decision Making in Israel, Studies in Comparative International Development, 4, 47-57.
16. MOSSINSOHN, G. Higher Education of the Younger Generation in the Kibbutz, The Kibbutz, 210-217, (Hebrew).
17. Rural Industrialization: Report of an Expert Group, (1974), U.N. Publication ST/ESA/4 N.Y.
18. SCHTANGER, S. (1971), The Kibbutz Industry, (Tel Aviv: The Interkibbutz association for industry), (Mimeographed), (Hebrew).
19. TANNENBAUM, A. S. et al (1974), Hierarchy in Organization.
20. WOODWARD, J. (1965), Industrial Organization – Theory and Practice, (London).
21. ZAMIR, D. (1972), The Effect of Hired Labor on the Kibbutz Plant, (Mimeographed), (Hebrew).

Organizational Effects of Managerial Turnover in Kibbutz Production Branches

Uri Leviatan

The phenomenon of institutionalized general turnover and internal rotation of managerial personnel and its effects upon the conduct of the organizations involved is examined with data from production branches of Israeli kibbutzim. Arguments for and against the effectiveness of such a norm are presented. Four specific hypotheses are formulated. About 60 productive organizations were involved: 33 farm branches and 27 industrial plants. Data were collected by way of questionnaires to all workers at each organization and by way of documents and interviews with informants. The major findings are the following: The potential for managerial positions is larger than needed for a given time; in the branches studied the median time in office was about 2-3 years. Organizations that practice rotation are not less (and maybe more) effective than those that do not practice rotation. This is because their workers are more involved, knowledgable, and creative than those in the latter. Length of time in office sometimes appeared to have adverse effects for the functioning of organizations.

INTRODUCTION

Every formal organization faces the problem of managerial turnover. Sooner or later every manager has to be replaced. This is true of most

[1] This study is a secondary analysis of data collected for a larger study concerning the industrialization processes in the Kibbutz society at the Center for Social Research on the Kibbutz at Givat Haviva. Support for the original study was granted by the Fritz Naphtali Foundation, the American Council for the Behavioral Sciences in the Kibbutz, and the Kibbutz Artzi movement.

[2] Uri Leviatan was at the Center for Social Research on the Kibbutz at Givat Haviva when conducting this study. The Center has now moved to the University of Haifa and changed its name to The Institute for Research of the Kibbutz and the Cooperative Idea. Requests for reprints should be sent to Dr. Uri Leviatan, University of Haifa, Haifa 31 999, Israel.

385

offices at every level of management. Different organizations have different rates of turnover among their managerial personnel. Trow (1961) reported that in a sample of small plants in the U.S.A. (each up to 100 workers) involved in the production of shoes, cars, and beer, the rate of turnover of company presidents was 12% during a period of 10 years. The rate of turnover for larger companies in the same branches of production was 15% during that same period. In another study, reported by Trow in the same paper, the median time in office for founders of businesses was 30 years and over. For nonfounders the median time was 20-25 years. Trow also reported data from the Soviet Union that indicated that the length of time in office of managers there (at that time, 1954) was usually only 2-3 years. It is evident, therefore, that a great variability exists in the rate of turnover of managers. This raises a question that should be explored: What are the various organizational effects that are the outcomes of variability in managerial turnover?

This paper deals with managerial turnover in the production branches of the kibbutz society. In it, rotation of top managers of production branches (as well as other civic office holders) is a normative dictum. For instance, the kibbutz Artzi[3] convention on industrial problems (February 1976) reiterated previous recommendations that top managers should be replaced after a period of 3-5 years in office. This is realized in various kibbutzim in a variety of ways. One survey (Rosner, 1977) found that the mean time in office for industrial top managers was 3.5 years, but a large variability existed since the standard deviation was 2.6 years.

Turnover of managers in the kibbutz setting has a unique aspect and could be labeled as "internal rotation." Central office holders are rotated out of their offices and assigned to other roles, usually in lower managerial levels, *within* the same organization, while other workers take up positions of managerial offices. Only a few formal organizations practice this method as used by the kibbutzim. One could cite academic faculties in universities where administrative positions are rotated; the same is true for some unions of professionals (Lipset, 1954) and to a small extent within political parties. Never is it practiced in business organizations.

There is relatively little research literature dealing with replacement of managers, but the evidence available indicates that managerial turnover in formal organizations has an adverse effect on the efficient functioning of the organization (e.g., Grusky, 1969, 1970). No research, besides a few case studies, is available concerning the topic of internal rotation.

[3]The Kibbutz Artzi is one of the three large kibbutz movements in Israel. It consists of about a third of all kibbutz population. It is assumed that the reader has a basic knowledge of kibbutz life and history. The interested reader is directed to general descriptive books such as Darin's (1962).

The focus of this paper will be, therefore, on the following two topics: The effects of the periodic replacement of managers and the effects of internal rotation on organizational efficiency and effectiveness.

Rotation of Managers in Kibbutz Society

The kibbutz movement was always in favor of the internal rotation of high-level office-holders. The reasons were mainly of an ideological nature:

A desire to prevent the monopolization of rewards by high-ranking officers, and to keep a certain social equality among the members.

Preserving the principle of the integration of mental and manual work.

The wish to enhance the relationship among members as whole individuals and not as office- or role-holders, and the belief that permanency in office would create the latter.

A fair distribution of the office load among more individuals for those offices in which the balance of rewards is negative (Rosner & Abend, 1968).

Since the emphasis of the above points is upon ideological aspects that are related to the rotation principle and not upon the effective functioning of the organizations in which rotation is practiced, this whole principle has come under attack by an important fraction of the kibbutz society. This change of attitude has resulted, to some extent, from the very intensive industrialization process occurring in the kibbutz movement (Leviatan, 1976) as well as from the general increase in the complexity of its economic functioning. Opponents of the rotation principle point out that top office-holders now receive a very long training. Their roles are very complex and becoming proficient in them takes time. Mistakes are very costly to the organization, and the skills needed for success in managing are relatively rare. All this, so goes the argument, makes the upholding of the ideological principle of rotation after short periods (3-5 years) a very costly decision and exacts an economic price which is too high. The change in attitude that had occurred during the late 1960s was exemplified by the following research findings.

Cohen (1965) found in the kibbutz Artzi movement in 1960 that 22% of the respondents who worked in industry opposed the principle of rotation in the office of plant manager. This was also more or less the case in the other two kibbutz movements. In a study of the second generation in the kibbutzim in 1969, we find that although the kibbutz Artzi movement did not change (21% were against the application of the principle to plant managers), the other two movements (the Ichud and the Meuchad movements) did undergo a dramatic change: 60% in one and 63% in the second opposed rotation in this office. (Rosner, Ben-David, Avnat, Cohen, & Leviatan, 1978).

The arguments raised by kibbutz members against the use of the rotation principle are not more than specific ones in the more general, theoretical group of arguments that are raised by researchers and others in this field. In what follows I will discuss the arguments that are raised for and against the use of the rotation principle. I will also emphasize the unique conditions in the kibbutz movements that may modify some of the arguments.

The main focus of this paper is upon the organizational effects of turnover and of internal rotation. In several other places (Leviatan, 1969, 1970, 1975) a more comprehensive treatment of the topic was stated but this cannot be repeated here due to space limitations.

The following paragraphs consist of statements pro and con regarding the benefits to an organization from the concept of replacement of managers.

Accumulation of Experience

An individual who serves longer in office gains more experience and learns to solve more problems. When such a person is confronted with a problem, he should have more means for its solution than a person without experience and it is probable that his solution would be more effective. Veterans should also not repeat mistakes, since their lessons have already been learned. This would not be the case with a novice.

Since all organizational theories postulate managerial effectiveness as a prime factor in determining organizational effectiveness, an organization with veteran management should be more effective than organizations with novice management. Hence there should be a monotonic (perhaps even linear) relationship between the length of time of a manager in office and his effective functioning.

This hypothesis provokes the following contrary arguments:

First, although experience with many previous solutions is an advantage, it carries with it a price tag. When the external conditions surrounding a social organization change, solutions to the new, as well as the old, problems should be adapted to the new situation. If a person is in an office a long time it is probable that he will be tied, mentally, to habits of thinking and acting that were successful in the past but are not necessarily appropriate for the present. In such a case, he has, first, to overcome old habits and, second, to acquire new ways of thought and action that are appropriate to the new situation. A new person in an office has to go through the second phase only. Therefore, his adaptation to the new conditions should be much easier. The psychology of learning teaches that old habits serve as inhibitors to new learning and that the more rooted they are, the stronger their inhibiting effect (Kimble, 1961).

I would like, therefore, to postulate that up to a certain point in time the cost and the difficulty stemming from adherence to old, inappropriate ways of thinking are less than the advantage stemming from the accumulation of experience. From that point on, the marginal contribution of experience decreases, while stagnation on inappropriate reactions and irrelevant routine increases. This is where the effectiveness of an office-holder decreases from its peak. The prediction is, therefore, a nonmonotonic and perhaps even a curvilinear relationship between the length of time a person serves in a central managerial position and his effectiveness in that position.

In organizations based on modern technology, where the environmental changes are most frequent and potent, an office-holder should be at his most effective from the point in time when he has already mastered his work and learned all the problems related to it up to the point when changes in the external environment call for new solutions. Before and *after* this optimum period the effectiveness of the office-holder should be lower. Second, a person who stays for a very long time in a managerial position loses his contact with those who are at the rank and file level; his communication lines with them are disrupted and he does not feel their problems as he did at the beginning of his climb up the hierarchical ladder. Since organizational research has proved the importance of free and intensive communication in determining organizational effectiveness (e.g., Likert, 1967), we could expect that at a certain point in time the contribution of a manager's accumulating experience is not enough to compensate for the disadvantages that stem from his estrangement from the true nature of the organization.

The above arguments are summarized in the following hypotheses:

Hypothesis Ia. There is no linear, or even monotonic, relationship between the length of time that a person serves in a central managerial office and the extent to which he is successful in it.

Hypothesis Ib. This should be true in variables expressing the economic success of the organization. It would also be expressed in variables expressing the adaptability of managers to changes in the environment.

Hypothesis Ic. The communication lines between a manager and other organization members would deteriorate with the number of years that he serves in his office.

The next set of arguments relates to the unique effects of internal rotation and the existence of ex-top-officers within the current lower hierarchical levels of the workers of a productive organization.

When Replaced Managers Stay Within the Organization

One could expect negative behavior of a replaced manager who stays within the organization because his new role definition does not allow him, in many cases, to utilize his skills, abilities, and experience to a maximum. This leads to frustration and aggressive behavior. It is possible to prevent the frustration and at the same time achieve positive results for the organization by a new role definition that would use the skills of the replaced central individuals and at the same time would upgrade the whole job structure of the organization. By doing this, the quality of teamwork and the quality of the decision-making process should also be upgraded because the team would be composed of many individuals who have acquired the relevant skills in their formal positions.

The result of internal rotation should also bring a decrease in the time invested by managers in overseeing, guiding, and training their underlings. This is because workers with previous managerial experience in the same organization could take upon themselves some of the overseeing functions and perhaps need no training at all. The new manager should be able then to dedicate more of his time to planning of the work, coordination, and the relationships with outside systems. Indeed, Melman (1971) found that in kibbutz industrial plants the proportion of managers to workers was lower than that of comparable industrial plants in Israeli towns.

Hypothesis II. An organization composed of a high proportion of members who held central managerial positions in it in the past would be more effective than an organization in which the proportion of such ex-office-holders is lower. This relationship should be stronger in organizations in which ex-office-holders are making more use of their skills, abilities, and experience in their present jobs.

Hypothesis III. In an organization in which there is a large proportion of ex-office-holders, the present office-holders should have to invest less time, relatively, in the functions of training and overseeing than in organizations in which this proportion is smaller.

More Benefits from Internal Rotation

1. By applying the principle of internal rotation an organization should reach a stage where a large number of its members would possess knowledge relevant to the efficient functioning of the organization (that is—current office-holders as well as recent ex-officers). This is a necessary condition for the effective behavior of organization members not only because it brings about a high level of satisfaction from membership in the

organization, but also because it enables them to initiate efforts where they are most needed for the accomplishment of the organization's goals.

2. Possession of relevant information serves also as a necessary condition for the application of influence on what happens within the organization, which in turn increases its effectiveness (Likert, 1967; Katz & Kahn, 1966; Indik, 1963; Tannenbaum, 1968).

3. In an organization in which internal rotation of office-holders exists we would expect more feeling of equality among members of all ranks. When a feeling of equality prevails in an organization the participation of its members in contributing to its goal achievement rises (Bridges, 1968; Strodtbeck, 1957).

4. When internal turnover is the norm, the probability that members will advance is higher. The need for achievement is realized and a higher level of satisfaction among members should be expected.

Figure 1 explains schematically the ideas raised in the above paragraphs. Two hypothetical organizations are shown, each of which consists of three members (the "round," the "triangular," and the "square"

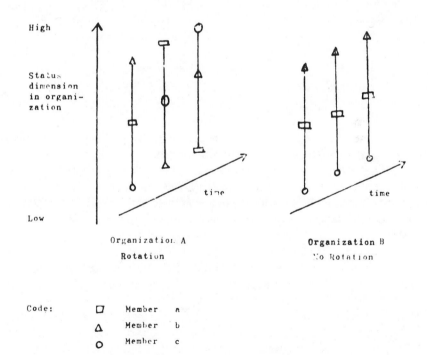

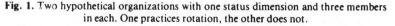

Fig. 1. Two hypothetical organizations with one status dimension and three members in each. One practices rotation, the other does not.

members) and one status dimension only. Organization A exercises the internal rotation norm at the end of every unit of time. After three units of time, all three members should have acquired skills, experience, and knowledge because they have served in positions of high status. In Organization B only one person (the triangular) should have developed such experience and acquired managerial skills and knowledge.

5. Of particular theoretical relevance to the problem of internal rotation is the concept of "total amount of influence (control)" as defined and used by Tannenbaum and others (e.g., Tannenbaum, 1968). This aspect of rotation is developed in some detail in the following paragraphs.

I start with several assumptions that have both theoretical and empirical backing:

a. Organizations with larger amounts of influence are more effective.
b. Individuals who are higher up on an organization's managerial status dimensions are accorded more influence in their organizations.
c. There exists a time-lag effect with regard to the relationship between a position of a person on a status dimension at a given time and his influence in the organization in later periods. The loss of influence is gradual and a person who held an office in the past, but not at present, would have influence, the level of which is intermediate between that of present office holders and that of persons who never held an office. The level of influence at any given time stands in negative linear relation to the length of time since serving in office. It reaches the level of influence of those who never held an office after a period of 3-4 years (Leviatan, 1970).

The reasoning for this statement is based on two arguments: Past office holders still possess relevant information and they would be consulted by current decision makers; and many members still consider them to be experts in their respective fields and, therefore, continue to seek their help and advice. These two resources deteriorate as time elapses.

Given the above three assumptions it follows that the total amount of influence should be higher in organizations in which internal rotation is practiced than in those where it is not practiced. If jobs are upgraded in their content for ex-officers, one would expect that, on the average, the organization would be characterized by higher levels of opportunities for self-realization.

Possession of information, having influence (control), probability for advancement, and feeling of equality are all contributors to a sense of higher motivation to contribute to the achievement of organizational goals. They are also facilitators of initiative-taking behavior in the direction of those goals. Hence, we should expect that in organizations with a high proportion of ex-officers there would be higher levels of motivation and initiative-taking behavior.

The next hypothesis summarizes the above arguments in a formal way.

Hypothesis IV: Organizations that practice the norm of internal rotation in central offices would be characterized (a) by a greater number of members who possess relevant information and (b) by a greater amount of members' influence on what is happening in the organization. (c) They would offer more chances for advancement, (d) would be characterized by more feeling of equality, (e) and their members would show more motivation and more initiative-taking behavior towards the achievement of the organization's goals.

METHOD

The present study was part of a research program on kibbutz industrialization undertaken by the Center for Social Research on the Kibbutz. Previous analyses of some of the data have been reported by Leviatan (1970, 1976) and Eden and Leviatan (1974).

Population and Sample

The population was defined as all industrial plants that, in 1970, (a) were members of the Kibbutz Industrial Association (K.I.A.), (b) were owned by individual kibbutzim (and not by interkibbutz conglomerates), (c) employed at least five workers, no more than 30% of whom were hired laborers (i.e., nonmember wage-earners), and (d) had been established at least 1 year prior to the study.

Of the 157 plants affiliated with the K.I.A. in 1970, 97 met the combined criteria for selection. Ten of these were barred from the sample since they had participated in a somewhat similar study only a year earlier. The detailed sampling procedure for the industrial plants in the sample is described in Eden and Leviatan (1974).

In addition to the sample of industrial plants another sample of 33 farm branches[4] was selected from the same kibbutzim and thus 60 organizations could potentially be included in the study. Questionnaires were distributed to all kibbutz members employed in each selected factory or farm branch. The total number of members working in the 60 organizations was about 800. In all, about 600 workers returned usable questionnaires, for a response rate of about 75%.

In addition to the questionnaire, interviews were conducted with the managers and "hard" data on economic performance were collected. The

[4]One of the main goals for the original study was a comparison of farm branches to industrial plants in terms of workers' reaction to their environment, while holding constant the global environmental variables.

economic data were available only from 21 industrial plants and from none of the farm branches. Since the farm branches were small (sometimes only 3-5 workers) some of them had to be deleted from certain analyses, thereby reducing the sample. The comparison between farm branches and industrial plants is not shown in this paper but is exhibited in Leviatan (1975). Here all organizations were treated together.

Procedure

The top manager of each site sampled was informed in advance about the research project; a letter from the K.I.A. and the Center for Social Research on the Kibbutz was sent soliciting his cooperation. Field workers from the Center arrived at each plant on a prearranged date and appeared before the workers' assembly to describe the research and administer the questionnaires. Absent workers received envelopes for mailing back their completed questionnaires directly to the Center. All questionnaires were anonymous except in the eyes of the researchers. Individual questionnaires and managers' interviews were completed during the spring of 1970. Performance data of industrial plants were collected during the autumn of 1970.

Measurements

The research upon which the data and the findings of this study are based was not directed toward the testing of the hypotheses in this paper. The data analyses are secondary and the operation of theoretical hypotheses could not always be accomplished with the measures available. Some of the theoretical hypotheses could not even be tested.

The measurements of the variables in use in the analyses that follow are listed in the order of their introduction in the next section.

1. *Length of time in office* (*of the manager*) was taken from organization records and informants.

2. *Economic effectiveness* was measured by the rate of capital recovery (RCR). This index was available for 21 industrial plants only and for none of the farm branches.

3. *Success of the manager in his office* was indexed by the mean score from three questions on five category scales and over all workers, evaluating the perceived adaptability of a manager to changes, his perceived quality as a manager, and his perceived performance in his office.

4. *Communication effectiveness* was measured by an index of Likert-type questions concerning the amount of knowledge possessed by workers

with regard to five spheres: investment, production plans, economic results, technological problems, integration of own work in organization.

5. *Proportion of past and present central office holders.* This variable is indicative of the extent of internal turnover. There are two measures: (a) The proportion was calculated and weighted by the average status level of all office-holders during the time of 5 years (for details see Leviatan, 1970). (b) The percentage of organization members who served in office during the last 2 years preceding the study.

6. *Time devoted by manager to training others and overseeing others' work.* An estimate given by each top manager of the average percentage of his weekly work time.

7. *Opportunities for self-realization in the job* was measured by answers to five questions about the content of the job, opportunities for learning, self-development, utilization of skill, knowledge, and experience. An index was composed of these questions.

8. *Influence in organization* was measured by an index composed of answers to three questions probing this aspect. The amount of influence in the organization was the calculated mean of all members.

9. *Participation of workers* in the decision-making process was measured by calculating the mean score, on a five-point scale, of the workers' perception of the authority of the general assembly in six selected areas.

10. *Length of training* given to workers was measured by calculating the mean length of job-relevant training (in months) received by an average worker in each organization.

11. *Opportunities for advancement* was measured by two questions directed to all respondents asking them about their perceived probability of advancing and having higher-level jobs and offices in the organization.

12. *Motivation* was measured by an index of three questions concerning the degree of commitment of respondents to their own job, group job, and organization goals.

13. *Initiative-taking* behavior was measured by an index of five questions measuring the degree to which a person works more than prescribed by rules, solves problems, tries new ways and methods, and reads professional material.

FINDINGS

Our data show that a large variance exists among managers with regard to the length of time that they serve in office. The mean length of time was 3.3 years. The median was between 2 and 3 years. Table I shows the exact distribution for present and recent past top managers. It is also in-

Table I. Distribution of Past and Present Managers by Length of Time in Office

	No. years in office								Total	Mean
	1	2	3	4	5	6	7	+8		
Present managers	12	17	7	2	6	4	2	3	53	3.1
Past managers	4	25	14	5	9	–	–	7	64	3.4
Total past and present	16	42	21	7	15	4	2	10	117	3.3
Total (%)	14	36	18	6	13	3	2	9	101	

teresting to note that the potential for rotation in the top offices indeed exists, at least as viewed by current managers. When asked about the percentage of organizational members that, in their opinion, could successfully fill in the top roles, the answer was an average of about 15%. Given this background, I now turn to the testing of the hypotheses.

Tests of Hypotheses

Hypothesis Ia was tested by relating variable 1 (length of time in office) to variable 2 (economic effectiveness of organization) as expressed by rate of return on capital. The test was conducted for 20 organizations only, all of them industrial plants, since no data on both variables were available for the rest. These 20 plants were broken into three groups according to variable 1 and with similar numbers of plants in each of them (eight plants with managers 1 or 2 years in office, six plants with managers 3 or 4 years in office, and six with managers 5 or more years in office). The mean scores on variable 2 are, respectively, 19.5%, 36.2%, and 29%. This difference among the groups does not reach an accepted level of significance of $p < .05$, probably due to the smallness of the sample, but it clearly supports the hypothesis in its weak form (that is, no monotonic relationship was shown) and is even indicative of the stronger notion of a curvilinear relationship between the two variables.

Hypothesis Ib was tested by relating the length of time in office of current managers (variable 1), with the perceived success of the manager in his role (variable 3). No linear relationship was found ($r = -.050$ for 51 organizations). When the organizations were broken into three groups—those in which managers served 1-2 years; those with managers in office 3-5 years; and those with managers in office 6 years or more—no statistically significant differences were found among the three groups. The mean scores on variable 3 were 4.19, 4.28, and 4.33, respectively. It seems that the hypothesis in its weak form is supported (no relationship) but no support is given to the notion of a curvilinear relationship.

Hypothesis Ic was tested by relating variable 1 to variable 4 (communication effectiveness). A negative relationship was hypothesized but the data did not support it. No statistically significant relation was found ($r = -.050$) for the total group of organizations. [When the organizations were tested separately for industrial plants and farm branches the correlation was much higher, though still not significant, for the plants ($r = -.27$, $N = 27$) but stayed low for the farm branches ($r = .02$).] One more relevant point is in order: One could conceive variables 8 (workers' influence), 9 (workers' participation in decision-making through the general assembly), and 10 (average length of job-relevant training) as other indicators of open channels of communication and influence between management and workers. It is interesting to note that additional calculations show that there exists a negative relationship between the length of time of a manager in his office and variable 8 ($r = -.49$, $p < .01$), between the first variable and variable 9 ($r = -.38$, $p < .05$), and between the same independent variable and the length of training offered to workers, variable 10 ($r = -.44$, $p < .01$).

Although findings show only partial support for the hypotheses, they should be considered encouraging. One has to remember that the data are biased in the direction *opposite* to the research hypothesis because the data are cross-sectional. It is very possible that those managers who stayed many years in their office remained there because they were the most successful. If that were the case, then one could expect that those very managers should be more successful as compared to those who serve an average length of time; yet results are as they are.

Hypothesis II was tested by relating variable 2 (the measure of economic effectiveness) as a dependent variable, to variable 5a (proportion of past and present office-holders) as the independent variable. (The part of the hypothesis that deals with the moderating effect on the above relationship that comes from the level of the skill utilization of ex-officers could not be tested with our data due to technical problems with its handling.) Only 21 industrial plants were put to this test. For the nine plants where 36% or more of their workers held any office during the 2 years preceding the study, the mean rate of capital recovery was 35.3% (SD = 30.1) and for the 12 plants where only 35% or less were in office during those years, the mean rate of capital recovery was 21.7% (SD = 19.5). The *t* was at the 1.26 level, which is too low for a significant difference, although in the right direction. This hypothesis cannot be considered as supported but one could be justified in speculating that a larger sample could show the difference as statistically significant.

Hypothesis III was tested by relating variable 5b to variable 6 (time devoted by manager to training and overseeing others). Here too, only 22 industrial plants were available for the analysis. A correlation coefficient yielded a score of $r = -.46$ ($p < .05$). This hypothesis is supported.

Table II. Relationships (r) Between Proportion of Past and Present Office-Holders and Various Dependent Variables

	Correlation coefficient	Number of organizations
Initiative-taking behavior	.35[a]	55
Psychological involvement at work	.36[a]	55
Influence at work place	.63[a]	55
Information about work-relevant objects	.62[a]	55
Chances for advancement in organization	.30[a]	55

[a] $p < .01$.

Hypotheses IVa through IVe were tested by relating variable 5 to variables 4 (communication effectiveness), variable 8 (influence at work place), variable 9 (chances for advancement in organization), variable 10 (psychological commitment to organization's and job goals), and variable 11 (initiative-taking behavior). All relations are significant at the .01 level of probability, as can be seen in Table II. The level of the correlations is not only statistically significant, but also meaningful in its magnitude, ranging from about 10 to about 40% of the common variance.

SUMMARY AND DISCUSSION

The major questions dealt with in this paper were the following: Is a policy of managerial turnover in general and of internal turnover (rotation) of managers in kibbutz production branches in particular, of any detrimental effect to an organization's effectiveness or is it beneficial to its effective functioning? Four formal hypotheses were tested. In summarizing the findings, one could state as follows:

a. A manager's length of time in office was not related monotonically to the economic success of the organization and a trend toward a curvilinear relationship was indicated.

b. The quality of management was not affected by the length of time in office. It did not deteriorate, but *also* did not improve.

c. For industrial plants a trend toward a negative relationship was discovered between the length of time in office of top managers and the effectiveness of communication channels between management and workers. Negative relations were also found between the manager's length of time in office and organization variables such as influence, participation in decision-making, and training of workers.

d. Trends were found showing that organizations with higher proportions of present officers plus ex-office-holders were more effective with regard to their economic functioning.

e. In such organizations, managers could devote less time to functions such as training and overseeing (and more to planning, coordinating, administration, and public relations).

f. Organizations with higher proportions of present officers and ex-officers were characterized by more opportunities for advancement, greater total amount of control, more knowledge by its members about itself.

g. As a result of (f), those organizations were also characterized by higher levels of motivation and commitment by their members.

On the face of it, it seems that the answer to the major questions is straightforward. The least that can be said is that managerial turnover does not cause any harm to the organization. Indications are in the direction that when a manager *is not* replaced after some optimal period, detrimental effects start to show (points a-c above).

A more solid finding regards the practice of internal turnover and specifically the effects associated with the staying of the ex-officers at lower hierarchical levels within the organization (points d-g above). Hypotheses II-IV show that the effects are all in the positive direction. All these findings seem to be in conflict with the few previous findings reported by other researchers and the theoretical reasoning cited in the introduction. Since all theoretical arguments against turnover and internal turnover of managers were attacked by counter-arguments in the introduction, we would perhaps be satisfied with the simple statement that the "real world" "had spoken" its judgment through the data, yet other data "had spoken" differently. Could the two be incorporated into a coherent model?

It is possible that findings such as those reported here are relevant for kibbutz organizations only. As long as no other study along the lines of this one is made with other organizations, no definite answer to this possibility can be given. Indeed, we know from data collected in the same study but not reported here that some characteristics that are more manifest in kibbutz organizations than in other organizations influence the relation between turnover and factors that contribute to effectiveness. For example, in those organizations in which a stronger legitimation for periodic managerial turnover existed and where the membership participated more strongly in picking a replacement for the manager, the relationships between the new management and the workers were less conflict-ridden and more harmonious. Although kibbutz organizations are on the average higher on these variables (e.g., Tannenbaum, Kavĉiĉ, Rosner, Vianello, & Weiser, 1974), they by no means have a theoretical monopoly in it. In principle, every organization could practice the same norms. And so it is possible to introduce those variables (legitimation, participation) as modifiers in a theoretical model.

Another point that is relevant regarding the generalizability of these and other kibbutz findings: Research with kibbutz work organizations has shown that the pattern of relationships among various variables (structural, attitudinal, behavioral, emotional) is not different in its essence from that found in studies with similar organizations in the U.S.A. and Europe (Leviatan, 1976). The differences lie in the absolute levels of the variables' scores but not in their intercorrelations. Variables related to the turnover phenomenon are no more than a single case in point of the general cluster of structural variables of social organizations. It is legitimate, then, to assume that their pattern of relationships with other variables—in a population outside the kibbutz—would be similar to the pattern within the kibbutz. In this respect, the kibbutz can serve as an experimental laboratory in the organizational research sphere.

Finally, similar results to those reported in this research were found in a few studies conducted in organizations outside the kibbutz (Trow, 1961); it seems that when the conditions in formal organizations are like the conditions in kibbutz organizations (legitimation for rotation, no relationship between the status level of the office and level of rewards), the findings would be like those within the kibbutz organizations.

The findings reported here seem all the more promising in view of some of the methodological problems that affected this study and worked *against* the support of its hypotheses. These problems were manifest mainly because it is a secondary analysis of data collected primarily for other purposes.

1. The small number of organizations made it difficult to reach results that were statistically significant and it was at times impossible to break down the data into more than one dimension.

2. The organizations studied varied from each other on almost any conceivable relevant dimension with regard to the dependent variables, especially the economic effectiveness index: size of organization, production technology, age, geographical location, etc. This variation was intentional and was designed for the purposes of the original study for which the data were collected. For our purposes this variation could be considered as error variance or "noise" in the system. A better planned study should have a control for all these variables either by sampling or by statistical controls. Neither solution was possible in this case.

3. The major independent variable, length of time in top management, was measured cross sectionally. This again should have worked against the hypotheses tested; "longevity" in office could be the result of success (only the successful managers stayed in office). A better plan would have been a longitudinal study in which managers and their performance were followed through several years and trends of changes measured.

It is surprising that after all these methodological difficulties, most of them working against the research hypotheses, the findings supported most hypotheses. In no case was there found support for any of the opposite hypotheses raised by other researchers and practitioners. In some cases a more precise positive hypothesis could be supported or at least its trend was indicated in the data.

In conclusion, it seems that the best attitude to assume toward the question of the effect of rotation and planned turnover of management is an empirical one. Only a well-planned program of research can supply valid answers. The small number of available studies in this sphere is in no way justifiable in light of the findings from this research.

REFERENCES

BRIDGES, E. M., DOYLE, D. J., & MAHAN, D. J. Effects of hierarchical differentiation on group productivity. *Administrative Science Quarterly,* 1968, *13*(2), 305-320.
COHEN, E. *A Study of the work sphere in the kibbutz Artzi movement.* Minhal Hadracha, 1965 (in Hebrew).
DARIN, H. *The other society.* London: Victor Golanez, 1962.
EDEN, D., & LEVIATAN, U. Farm and factory in the kibbutz—A study in agrico-industrial psychology. *Journal of Applied Psychology,* 1974, *59*(4), 596-602.
GRUSKY, O. *Succession and organizational innovation: Some experimental findings.* Mimeo, Dept. of Sociology, UCLA, 1970.
GRUSKY, O. Succession with an ally. *Administrative Science Quarterly,* 1969, *14*(2), 155-171.
HAKIBBUTZ HAARTZI. *Takanot hakibbutz* (kibbutz regulations), no date (in Hebrew).
INDIK, B. P. Some effects of organization size on members' attitudes and behavior. *Human Relations,* 1963, *16,* 369-384.
KATZ, D., & KAHN, R. *The social psychology of organizations.* New York: Wiley, 1966.
KIMBLE, G. A. *Hilgard and Marquis conditioning and learning* (2nd ed.). New York: Appleton-Century-Crofts, 1961.
LEVIATAN, U. *Status structure in social systems as a causal variable to individual mental health and performance, and to the systems' performance and effectiveness.* Mimeographed paper, Department of Psychology, University of Michigan, 1969.
LEVIATAN, U. *Status in human organization as a determinant of mental health and performance.* Doctoral dissertation, University of Michigan, 1970.
LEVIATAN, U. *Turnover of office holders in kibbutz production branches.* Center for Social Research on the Kibbutz, 1975 (in Hebrew).
LEVIATAN, U. The process of industrialization in the Israeli kibbutzim. In J. Nash, et al. (Eds.), *Popular participation in the social change.* The Hague: Mouton, 1976, pp. 521-547.
LIKERT, R. *The human organization.* New York: McGraw-Hill, 1967.
LIPSET, S. M. The political process in trade unions: A theoretical statement. In M. Berger et al. (Eds.), *Freedom and control in modern society.* New York: Van Nostrand, 1954, chapt. 4, 82-124.
MELMAN, S. Managerial vs. cooperative decision making in Israel. *Studies in Comparative International Development,* 1971, *6*(3), 17-32.
ROSNER, M. Ideology and organisation—The case of kibbutz industrialisation. Paper read at the International conference on social change and organisational development, Dubrovnik, February 1977.
ROSNER, M., & ABEND, A. Factors that affect willingness to take on social offices. *Hedim,* 1968, 88 (in Hebrew).
ROSNER, M., BEN-DAVID, Y., AVNAT, A., COHEN, N., & LEVIATAN, U. *The second generation—Between continuity and change.* Sifriat Poalim, 1978 (in Hebrew).

STRODTBECK, F. L., JAMES, R. M., & HAWKINS, C. Social studies in jury deliberations. *American Sociological Review,* 1957, *22,* 713-719.

TANNENBAUM, A. *Control in organisation.* New York: McGraw-Hill, 1968.

TANNENBAUM, A., KAVČIČ, B., ROSNER, M., VIANELLO, M., & WEISER, G. *Hierarchy in organization.* San Francisco: Jossey-Bass, 1974.

TROW, D. B. Executive succession in small companies. *Administrative Science Quarterly,* 1961, *6*(2), 222-239.

Statistical Appendix

Eliette Orchan

The major difficulty in dealing with statistical data about the kibbutz movement is the lack of uniformity in data gathered by different sources for different purposes and by different methods, which often causes an inconsistency of data about the same objects.

The following statistical data is divided into two sections—population, and industry and agriculture. Data on the kibbutz Hameuchad is lacking or has not been brought up-to-date.

I would like to emphasize a few trends that have been clarified by the following tables:

Table 1

The data reveals that the kibbutz population increased each year from 1914 to 1947, in comparison with the general Jewish population in Israel at that time. After 1947 it decreased consistently from 7.5% in 1947 to 3.3% in 1977. The general Jewish population grew at a much faster rate than the kibbutz population in that period, even though the kibbutz population continued to grow consistently.

The ratio of kibbutz population to rural population was at its highest in 1950, at 42%. In 1955 it decreased to 21%, but since then it has been increasing steadily—to 36% in 1977.

Table 2

The population of the kibbutzim was more than 110,000 in 1978. The largest share of the population is distributed equally between the Kibbutz Ichud and Artzi movements; the Kibbutz Meuchad movement is the smallest of the first three in population and in number of kibbutzim; the Ichud has the largest number of kibbutzim and number of children.

Table 3

The rate of growth of the kibbutz population during the last years in all of the different movements is more or less the same (14%), excluding the religious kibbutzim and Pagi (19%). The rate is a little lower than the rate of growth of the Jewish population in Israel (17%) for the same period.

Table 4

The principal trend is that approximately 30% of new kibbutz members today are born in the kibbutz and 40–45% are educated in youth movements in Israel and abroad. Kibbutz Artzi especially has more members who are educated in the kibbutz framework from an early age.

The nonmovement joiners (people who joined the kibbutz from outside as adults and who did not receive a kibbutz education) stood at 20% in 1973. During the last years their share of new members has been increasing constantly.

Table 5

The Kibbutz Artzi movement accepted more new members during the last years than did the Ichud movement, but more members left as well. During the last ten years the rate of leaving from all joiners was approximately 40%; and from kibbutz-born members almost 60%.

Table 6

The distribution of kibbutz population by age is very similar to the distribution of the general population, except for those 65 years old and over: 6% versus 8%.

Tables 8 and 9

Tables 8 and 9 show the agricultural and industrial contribution of the kibbutzim to the country's output and export. Although the kibbutz movement is only approximately 35% of the rural population, its output in different sectors of agriculture is much more than this. If we compare the industrial output to the share of kibbutz movement in the general population (3.3%), we can also see the large percentage of the kibbutz output in different industrial branches, especially in plastics (55%).

It is hard in such a short appendix to show all the aspects of kibbutz life and development over the years, but we can see that these different settlements expanded and increased their population despite the number of leavers and succeeded in many areas of life, such as financial development, more than other sectors of the population.

TABLE 1

Kibbutz Population in relation to General and Rural Jewish Population

Year	Kibbutz Population in Relation to General Jewish Population (%)	Absolute Numbers	Kibbutz Population in Relation to Rural Jewish Population (%)	Growth Index
1914	0.21	180		
1922	0.88	735		
1927	2.64	3,909		
1932	2.51	4,391		
1936	4.43	16,444		
1941	5.85	27,738		
1947	7.52	47,408		100
1948	7.14	54,208		114
1950	5.55	66,708	42.11	141
1955	4.79	76,115	21.11	160
1960	4.08	77,890	24.26	164
1965	3.51	80,800	30.22	170
1970	3.30	84,500	31.08	178
1973	3.53	91,600	34.61	193
1976	3.3	98,700	35.58	208
1977	3.3	101,400	35.79	214
1978	3.3	103,700	36.03	218
1979	3.3	105,800	36.35	223

Sources: Until 1973—Shepher, J., *Introduction to the Sociology of the Kibbutz*, 1977, Rupin Institute, p. 39.

From 1976 to 1979—*Statistical Abstract of Israel*, 1978, p. 40.

TABLE 2

Kibbutz Population by Categories and Movement (December 1978)

	All	Ichud	Artzi	Meuchad	Religious	Other
Total population	114,836	38,711	38,375	30,557	6,321	807
Number of Kibbutzim	246	90	77	62	14	3
Permanent population	96,702	32,631	32,712	25,655	5,083	621
Members and candidates	61,633	20,762	21,301	16,429	2,797	344
Children	35,069	11,869	11,411	9,226	2,286	277
Members' parents	2,314	840	840	527	96	11
Youths and Outside children	3,915	1,026	1,170	1,367	293	79
Others	11,905	4,214	3,653	3,028	849	65

Source: Publication of the kibbutz movement (January 1, 1979).

TABLE 3
Recent Growth of Kibbutz Population in the Different Movements

	1973[1]	1978[2]	% of Growth
Kibbutz Artzi	33,831	38,375	13
Ichud	33,840	38,711	14
Meuchad	27,100	30,557	13
Others (Religious, Pagi)	6,001	7,128	19
Total Kibbutz Population	100,772	114,836	14
General Jewish Population	2,686,700	3,141,200	17

1. Shepher, J., *Introduction to the Sociology of the Kibbutz*, p. 73.

2. Internal publications of the kibbutz movement.

TABLE 4
Sources of Kibbutz Membership and Candidacy, 1973 (percent)

Movement	Number of members	Kibbutz-born members	Kibbutz-educated members	Graduate of youth movements in Israel	Graduate of youth movements abroad	Non-movement joiners
Ichud	17,839	29	6	18	30	0.7
Artzi	19,861	29	13	9	28	21
Meuchad	13,321	32	10	13	22	23

Source: Shepher, J., *Introduction to the Sociology of the Kibbutz*, p. 58.

TABLE 5
Turnover of Members in Kibbutz Artzi and Ichud Movements, 1970-1979

	Artzi[1]	Ichud[2]	Meuchad[3]
Total number of kibbutz joiners	13,553	12,703	
Total number of people who left the kibbutz	8,457	7,468	
Number of kibbutz-born joiners	4,907	4,086	1,992
Number of kibbutz-born who left	2,807	2,290	1,162
Percentage of kibbutz-born who left	57	56	58
Net absorption	5,096	5,235	

1. Orchan, E., *Demographic Process During 10 Years in Kibbutz Artzi Movement*, published at 13th Congress of Kibbutz Artzi, December 1980.

2. *Population Census of Ichud and Religious Movements in 1979*, published by Ichud.

3. Levy, Amir, *Kibbutz-born Members Who Left: 1970–1977*.

TABLE 6

Distribution of Kibbutz Population versus Israel's Total Jewish Population, by age, 1976
(percent)

Age	Kibbutz Movement	Israel
0–14	28.3	29.8
15–29	30.1	27.7
30–44	19.6	15.6
45–64	16.2	18.6
65+	5.8	8.3
Total (%)	100	100

Source: Hechev, *Know the Kibbutz Movement*. Ben-Ami, S., (ed.) 1977, p.8.

TABLE 7

Development of Kibbutz Industries

	1970	1979	Increase (%)
Number of kibbutz industries	170	306	80
Number of employees	8,050	13,918	70
Sales (IL. millions current prices)	976	14,595	132.3

Source: 1. *Encyclopedia of Social Sciences*, vol. 6, D. Knooni, (ed.). Tel-Aviv: El Hamishmar, 1981, p. 825 (Hebrew).

TABLE 8

Contribution of Kibbutz Movement to Total Israeli Agricultural Output and Export, 1978

	OUTPUT		EXPORT	
	Absolute Numbers*	Percentage	Absolute Numbers	Percentage
Wheat	88.21	50.4		
Cotton	63.1	80.4	41.5	77.1
Potatoes	156.9	71.1		
Bananas	41.9	76.8		80.0
Avocados	14.5	61.9	1.0	84.0
Citrus	224.8	15.2		14.8
Milk (liters)	327.9	51.8		
Meat	22.4	55.2		
Fish	13.8	96.5		

*Absolute numbers is in thousands of tons.

Source: Heshev, *Know the Kibbutz Movement*, Sokolosky, M., (ed.), 1980, pp. 11, 14, 16, 17.

TABLE 9

Contribution of Kibbutz Movement to Total Israeli Indusrial Output and Export, 1978

	OUTPUT (millions of IL., prices 1978)		EXPORT (millions of U.S. $)	
	Absolute Numbers in the Country	Kibbutz Production (%)	Absolute Numbers in the Country	Kibbutz Production (%)
Metal Products	26,350	7.8	386.1	7.9
Wood and By-products	6,950	13.5	33.1	32.1
Plastic Products	4,150	54.8	46.0	60.8
Quarrying, Mining	3,120	9.3	78.5	–
Food	36,135	3.3	214.9	15.9

Source: Heshev, *Know the Kibbutz Movement*, 1980.

The Kibbutz: Selected Bibliography

Shimon Shur and David Glanz

Introductory Note

The kibbutz has attracted a very considerable amount of attention since the early 1950s. Consequently, the number of publications, both popular and scientific, on the subject of this uniquely Israeli social invention is enormous.

The present bibliography of over 240 items, is a selected bibliography of social research on the kibbutz. The articles listed were published in English, or languages other than Hebrew, in refereed academic journals or books. Scholarly works which appeared as books, or chapters within books, were also included. Unpublished dissertations, theses, research reports, or conference papers, encyclopedia articles, and nonscientific articles were excluded. Primarily, only items of sociological and social concern were included. But selected articles on the economic, psychological, and educational aspects of the kibbutz were also included, as well as articles of a comparative nature. In the first section, the items are presented in alphabetical order by author's name and date of publication, while in the second section, the references are classified and cross-referenced by subject categories.

1. ALON, Moni
   1970   "The child and his family in the kibbutz: second generation." In A. Jarus et al. (eds.), *Children and Families in Israel*. New York: Gordon & Breach.
2. AMIR, Yehuda
   1969   "The effectiveness of the kibbutz-born soldier in the Israel Defense Forces." *Human Relations* 22(4): 333–44.
3. ANTONOVSKI, Aharon; ARIAN, Alan
   1972   "Living in a collective sub-society." In A. Antonovski and A. Arian, *Fears of Israelis: Consensus in a New Society*. Jerusalem: Academic Press.

4. ARIAN, Alan
   1966   "Utopia and politics: the case of the Israeli kibbutz." *Journal of Human Relations* 14(3): 391–403.
5. ATAR, David
   1975   "Das Altern in der Kibbutzgesellschaft." *Geriatrie* 5(4): 98–102.
6. AVGAR, A.; BRONFENBRENER, U.; HENDERSON, A.
   1977   "Socialization practices of parents, teachers and peers in Israel: kibbutz, moshav and city." *Child Development* 48(4): 1219–27.
7. BAR-YOSEPH, Rivka
   1959   "The pattern of early socialization in the collective settlements in Israel." *Human Relations* 12(4):345–60.
8. BARINBAUM, Lea
   1972   "Role confusion in adolesence." *Adolescence* 7(25): 121–27.
9. BARKAI, Haim
   1972   "The kibbutz—an experiment in microsocialism." In I. Howe and C. Gersham (eds.), *Israel, the Arabs, and the Middle East.* New York: Bantam.
10. BARKIN, D.; BENNET, J. W.
    1972   "Kibbutz and colony: collective economics and the outside world. *Comparative Studies in Society and History* 14(4): 456–83.
11. BARTOLKE, Klaus; BERGMANN, Theodor; LIEGLE, Ludwig (eds.)
    1980   *Integrated Cooperatives in the Industrial Society: The Example of the Kibbutz.* Assen: Van Corcum.
12. BARTOLKE, Klaus
    1980   "Introduction: motivations and challenges of an international symposium on the kibbutz." In K. Bartolke et al. (eds.), op. cit.
13. BARZEL, Alexander
    1980   "Some outlines for a social philosophy of the kibbutz." In K. Bartolke et al. (eds.), op. cit.
14. BEIT-HALLAHMI, Benjamin; RABIN, Albert I.
    1977   "The kibbutz as a social experiment and as a childrearing laboratory." *American Psychologist* 32(7): 533–41.
15. BEIT-HALLAHMI, Benjamin; NEVO, Baruch; RABIN, Albert
    1979   "Family and community raised (kibbutz) children 20 years later: biographical data." *International Journal of Psychology* 14(4) 215–23.
16. BEN-DAVID, Joseph
    1964   "The kibbutz and the moshav." In J. Ben-David, *Agricultural Planning and Village Community in Israel.* Paris: U.N.E.S.C.O.
17. BEN-RAFAEL, Eliezer
    1973   "Problèmes sociaux d'une société collective: le kibboutz." *Archives Internationales de Sociologie de la Cooperation et le Dévelopement* 34: 174–80.
18. BEN-RAFAEL, Eliezer; TAGLIACOZZO, A.; KRAUS, Vered
    1975   "L'abandon du kibboutz par les jeunes." *Sociologia Ruralis* 15(3): 31–41.

19. BEN-RAFAEL, Eliezer
    1976   "The stratification system of the kibbutz." In Y. Landau et al. (eds.),
            Rural Communities: Inter-cooperation and Development. New York:
            Praeger.

20. ———
    1980   "Dynamics of social stratification in kibbutzim." *International Journal
            of Comparative Sociology* 21(1–2): 88–100.

21. BERGMANN, Theodor
    1980a   "The kibbutz in the continuum of forms of cooperation." In K.
            Bartolke et al. (eds.), op. cit.

22. ———
    1980b   "The replicability of the kibbutz experiment." In K. Bartolke et al.
            (eds.), op. cit.

23. BERMAN, Yitshak
    1974   "Some problems of the aged in the rural milieu in Israel: moshav,
            kibbutz and village." *International Journal of Aging and Human
            Development* 5(3): 257–63.

24. BETTELHEIM, Bruno
    1969   *The Children of the Dream: Communal Childrearing and American
            Education*. New York: Macmillan.

25. ———
    1973   "Some reflections on the kibbutz." In M. Curtis and M. Chertoff
            (eds.), *Israel: Social Structure and Change*. New Brunswick, N. J.:
            Transaction.

26. BIERVERT, Bernard; GAARLAND, Hans Peter
    1980   "Theoretical approaches to consumption and leisure in kibbutzim."
            In K. Bartolke et al. (eds.), op. cit.

27. BLASI, Joseph R.
    1976   "The kibbutz as a learning environment." In O. K. Oliver (ed.),
            Education and Community. Berkeley, Calif.: McCutchen.

28. BLASI, Joseph R.; MURRELL, Diana L.
    1977   "Adolescence and community structure: research on the kibbutz of
            Israel." *Adolescence* 12(46): 165–73.

29. BLASI, Joseph R.
    1977   "The Israeli kibbutz: economic efficiency and justice." *Community
            Development Journal* 12(3): 201–11.

30. ———
    1978   *The Communal Future: The Kibbutz and the Utopian Dilemma*.
            Kibbutz, Communal Society, and Alternative Social Policy Series,
            vol. 1, Norwood, Pa.: Norwood Editions.

31. ———
    1980   "Some aspects of quality of life in a kibbutz." In K. Bartolke et
            al. (eds.) op. cit.

32. BLITSTEN, Dorothy R.
    1963   "Experiments with family life in Russia and Israel." In Dorothy R.
            Blitsten, *The World of the Family: A Comparative Study of Family*

Organizations in Their Social and Cultural Settings. New York: Random House.

33. BLUMBERG, Rae L.
    1976a   "Erosion of sexual equality in the kibbutz. Structural factors affecting the status of women." In Joan Roberts (ed.), *Beyond Intellectual Sexism: A New Woman, A New Reality.* New York: D. McKay.

34. ———
    1976b   "Kibbutz women: from the fields of revolution to laundries of discontent." In Lynn Iglitzin and Ruth Ross (eds.), *Women in the World: A Comparative Study.* Santa Barbara, Calif.: Clio Books.

35. BRANDOW, Selma Koss
    1979   "Illusion of equality: kibbutz women and the ideology of the new Jew." *International Journal of Women Studies* 2(3): 268–86.

36. BUBER, Martin
    1949   "An experiment that did not fail." In M. Buber, *Paths in Utopia.* Boston: Beacon Press.

37. BUBER-AGASSI, Judith
    1980   "The status of women in kibbutz society." In K. Bartolke et al. (eds.), op. cit.

38. CANTRIL, Hadley
    1965   "What people are concerned about: kibbutzim." In H. Cantril, *The Pattern of Human Concerns.* New Brunswick, N.J.: Rutgers University Press.

39. CHERNS, Albert (ed.)
    1980a   *Quality of Working Life and the Kibbutz Experience. Proceedings of an International Conference in Israel, June 1978.* Kibbutz, Communal Society, and Alternative Social Policy Series, vol. 2, Norwood, Pa.: Norwood Editions.

40. ———
    1980b   "The quality of working life and the community." In A. Cherns (ed.), op. cit.

41. CLARK, Peter
    1980   "Organization theories, quality of working life and organization choices for the kibbutz." In A. Cherns (ed.), op. cit.

42. COHEN, Erik
    1966   "Progress and communality: value dilemmas in the collective movement." *International Review of Community Development* 15–16: 3–18.

43. COHEN, Erik; ROSNER, Menachem
    1970   "Relation between generations in the kibbutz." *Journal of Contemporary History* 5(1): 73–86.

44. COHEN, Erik
    1976   "The structural transformation of the kibbutz." In G. K. Zollschan and W. Hirsch (eds.), *Social Change.* Cambridge, Mass.: Schenkman.

45. CURTIS, Michael
    1973   "Utopia and kibbutz." In M. Curtis and M. Chertoff (eds.), *Israel: Social Structure and Change*. New Brunswick, N.J.: Transaction.
46. DANIEL, Abraham
    1975   "The kibbutz movement and hired labor." *Journal of Rural Co-operation* 3(1): 31–40.
47. DARIN-DRABKIN, Haim
    1962   *The Other Society*. London: Gollanz.
48. DAVIS, Ann; OLESEN, Virginia
    1971   "Communal work and living: notes on the dynamics of social distance and social space." *Sociology and Social Research* 55(2): 191–202.
49. DEVEREUX, E. C.; SHUVAL, R.; BRONFENBRENNER, U.; RODGERS, R. R.; KAV-VENAKI, S.; KIELY, E.; KARSON, E.
    1974   "Socialization practices of parents, teachers and peers in Israel: the kibbutz vs. the city." *Child Development* 45(2): 269–81.
50. DIAMOND, Stanley
    1957   "Kibbutz and shtetl: the history of an idea." *Social Problems* 5(2): 71–99.
51. ———
    1975   "Personality dynamics in an Israeli collective: a psychohistorical analysis of two generations." *History of Childhood Quarterly* 3(2): 1–41.
52. DON, Yehuda
    1977   "Industrialization in advanced rural communities: The Israeli kibbutz." *Sociologia Ruralis* 17(1–2): 59–72.
53. EATON, J. W.; CHEN, M.
    1970   "Kibbutz viability." In Joseph W. Eaton and Michael Chen, *Influencing the Youth Culture: A Study of Youth Organizations in Israel*. Beverly Hills, Calif.: Sage.
54. EDEN, Dov
    1975   "Intrinsic and extrinsic rewards and motives: replication and extension with kibbutz workers." *Journal of Applied Social Psychology* 5(4): 348–61.
55. EIFERMAN, R. R.
    1970   "Cooperativeness and egalitarianism in kibbutz children's games." *Human Relations* 23(6): 579–87.
56. EISENSTADT, S. N.
    1979   "Some observations on historical changes in the structure of kibbutzim." *The Kibbutz—Interdisciplinary Research Review* (Hebrew), vol. 6–7. The section in English 1979: XVI–XX.
57. ERIKSON, Erik H.
    1968   "Identity confusion in life history and case history; examples on development of kibbutzniks." In E. H. Erikson (ed.), *Identity: Youth and Crisis*. New York: Norton.

58. ETZIONI, Amitai
    1957   "Solidaric work-groups in collective settlements (kibbutzim)." *Human Organization* 16(3): 2–6.
59. ———
    1959   "The functional differentiation of elites in the kibbutz." *American Journal of Sociology* 64(5): 476–87.
60. FEIN, A.; GAL, D; ROSENMAN, H.; ROSNER, M.
    1971   "The transition from agriculture to industry within a full cooperative village: the case of the kibbutz." In J. Y. Klatzman, B. Y. Ilan, and Y. Levi (eds.), *The Role of Group Action in the Industrialization of Rural Areas.* New York: Praeger.
61. FISHMAN, A. (ed.)
    1957   *The Religious Kibbutz Movement: The Revival of the Jewish Religious Community.* Jerusalem: Religious Section of the Youth and Hehalutz Department of Zionist Organization.
62. FOLLING-ALBERS, Maria
    1980   "Sociostructural change of the kibbutz and its impact on preschool education." In K. Bartolke et al. (eds.), op. cit.
63. FRANK, Michael Joseph
    1968   *Cooperative Land Settlements in Israel and Their Relevance to African Countries.* Basel: Kyklos.
64. FRIEDMANN, George
    1967   "The kibbutz adventure and the challenges of the century." In G. Friedmann, *The End of the Jewish People?* London: Hutchinson.
65. GABOVITCH, B.
    1956   "Les kibboutzim d'inspiration religieuse." *Archives de Sociologie des Religions* 1(2): 96–101.
66. GAMSON, Zelda
    1975   "The kibbutz and higher education: cultures in collision?" *Jewish Sociology and Social Research* 2(1): 10–28.
67. GERSON, Menachem
    1970   "The child and his family in the kibbutz: the family." In A. Jarus et al. (eds.), op. cit.
68. ———
    1978   *Family, Women and Socialization in the Kibbutz.* Lexington, Mass.: Lexington Books.
69. ———
    1980   "The family in the kibbutz." In K. Bartolke et al. (eds.), op. cit.
70. GOLAN, Shmuel
    1958   "Collective education in the kibbutz." *American Journal of Orthopsychiatry* 28(3): 549–56.
71. GOLDENBERG, Sheldon; WEKERLE, Gerda R.
    1972   "From utopia to total institution in a single generation: the kibbutz and the Bruderhof." *International Review of Modern Sociology* 2(2): 224–32.

72. GOLOMB, Naphtali
    1980   "The relations between the kibbutz and its industry." In A. Cherns
                (ed.), op. cit.
73. GUREVITCH, Michael; LOEVY, Zipora
    1973   "The diffusion of television as an innovation: the case of the kib-
                butz." *Human Relations* 25(3): 181–97.
74. HELMAN, Amir
    1980   "Income-consumption relationship within the kibbutz system." In
                K. Bartolke et al. (eds.), op. cit.
75. ICHILOV, Orit; BAR, Shmuel
    1980   "Extended family ties and the allocation of social rewards in veteran
                kibbutzim in Israel." *Journal of Marriage and the Family* 42(2):
                421–26.
76. INFIELD, Henrik F.
    1955   "Pains of growth in Israel: the kvutza faces change." In H. F.
                Infield, *Utopia and Experiment: Essays in the Sociology of Coop-
                eration*. New York: Praeger.
77. JARUS, A; MARCUS, J.; OREN, J.; RAPAPPORT, Ch. (eds.)
    1970   *Children and Families in Israel: Some Mental Health Perspectives.*
                New York: Gordon & Breach.
78. KAFFMAN, Mordechai
    1965   "A comparison of psychopathology: Israeli children from kibbutzim
                and from urban surroundings." *American Journal of Orthopsychia-
                try* 35(3): 509–20.
79. ———
    1976   "Kibbutz adolescents today—changes and trends." *Israel Annals
                of Psychiatry and Related Disciplines*. 14(2): 145–54.
80. ———
    1977   "Sexual standards and behavior of the kibbutz adolescent." *Amer-
                ican Journal of Orthopsychiatry* 47(2) 207–17.
81. ———
    1978a   "Adolescent rebellion in the kibbutz." *Journal of the American
                Academy of Child Psychiatry* 17(1): 154–64.
82. ———
    1978b   "Kibbutz adolescents—changing aspects of behaviour and atti-
                tudes." In Y. Anthony (ed.), *The Child and His Family: Children
                and Their Parents in a Changing World*. International Yearbook of
                Child Psychiatry and Allied Professions. New York: Wiley.
83. KAHANE, Reuven
    1975   "The committed; preliminary reflections on the impact of the kibbutz
                socialization pattern on adolescents." *British Journal of Sociology*
                26(3): 343–53.
84. KATZ, Daniel; GOLOMB, Naphtali
    1974–75   "Integration, effectiveness and adaptation in social systems: a com-
                parative analysis of kibbutzim communities." *Administration and
                Society* 6(3): 283–315; 1975, 6(4) 389–421.

85. KAV-VENAKI, Sophie; LEVIN, Iris; ESFORMES, Yehuda; KARSON, Esther
    1978   "Patterns of self- and intragroup evaluations in two different Israeli
                preadolescent peer groups: the kibbutz and the city." *Journal of
                Cross-Cultural Psychology* 9(2): 237–52.

86. KELLER, Suzanne
    1973   "The family in the kibbutz: what lessons for the United States?" In
                M. Curtis and M. Chertoff (eds.), *Israel: Social Structure and Change.*
                New Brunswick, N.J.: Transaction.

87. KEREM, Moshe
    1970   "The child and his family in the kibbutz: the environment." In A.
                Jarus et al. (ed.), op. cit.

88. KLEIN, Hilel
    1972   "Holocaust survivors in kibbutzim: readaptation and reintegration."
                Israel Annals of Psychiatry and Related Disciplines 10(1): 78–91.

89. KRASILOWSKY, Davis; GINAT, Yigal; LANDAU, Rita; BODENHEIMER,
    Myriam
    1972   "The significance of parent-role substitution by society in various
                social structures." *American Journal of Orthopsychiatry* 42(4): 710–
                18.

90. KRESSEL, G.
    1976   "Ethnic duality in the kibbutz." *Ethnic Groups* 1(1): 241–62.

91. KROOK, Dorothea
    1968   "Rationalism triumphant: an essay on the kibbutzim of Israel." In
                Preston King and B. C. Parekh (eds.), *Politics and Experience:
                Essays Presented to Michael Oakeshott.* Cambridge, England: Cam-
                bridge University Press.

92. KUGELMASS, S.; BREZNITZ, S.
    1966   "Perception of parents by kibbutz adolescents: a further test of the
                instrumentality-expressivity model." *Human Relations* 19(1): 117–
                22.

93. KURZWEIL, Zwi E.
    1964   "Some aspects of kibbutz education." In Z. E. Kurzweil, *Modern
                Trends in Jewish Education.* New York: Thomas Yoseloff.

94. ———
    1974   "Kibbutzerziehung." In Z. E. Kurzweil, *Vorläufer Progressiver
                Erziehung.* Dusseldorf: A Henn.

95. LESHEM, E.; COHEN, E.
    1968   "Public participation in collective settlements in Israel." *Interna-
                tional Review of Community Development* 19–20: 251–70.

96. LEVI, Yair
    1967   "Coopération et microsocieté: le secteur kibboutzique Israélien de-
                vant la 'loi de transformation de Franz Oppenheimer'." *Coopération*
                37(4): 34–36.

97. LEVIATAN, Uri
    1973   "The industrial process in Israeli kibbutzim: problems and their
                solution" In M. Curtis and M. S. Chertoff (eds.), *Israel: Social
                Structure and Change.* New Brunswick, N.J.: Transaction.
98. ———
    1976   "The process of industrialization in the Israeli kibbutzim." In J.
                Nash et al. (eds.), *Popular Participation in Social Change.* The
                Hague: Mouton.
99. ———
    1978   "Organizational effects of managerial turnover in kibbutz production
                branches." *Human Relations* 31(11): 1001–1018.
100. LEVIATAN, Uri; ROSNER, Menachem (eds.)
    1980   *Work and Organization in Kibbutz Industry.* Norwood, Pa.: Nor-
                wood Editions.
101. LEVIATAN, Uri
    1980a   "Hired labor in the kibbutz: ideology, history and social psycho-
                logical effects." In U. Leviatan and M. Rosner (eds.), op. cit.
102. ———
    1980b   "Human factors and economic performance in kibbutz plants." In
                U. Leviatan and M. Rosner (eds.), op. cit.
103 ———
    1980c   "Importance of knowledge—intensive occupations for the kibbutz
                society." In U. Leviatan and M. Rosner (eds.), op. cit.
104. ———
    1980d   "Individual effects of managerial rotation: the case of the 'demoted'
                office holder." In U. Leviatan and M. Rosner (eds.), op. cit.
105. ———
    1980e   "The work sphere in kibbutz society." In K. Bartolke et al. (eds.)
                op. cit.
106. ———
    1980f   "Work and age: centrality of work in the life space of older kibbutz
                members." In U. Leviatan and M. Rosner (eds.), op. cit.
107. LEVIATAN, Uri; ROSNER, Menachem
    1980   "Lessons from research on kibbutz industrialization—summary."
                In U. Leviatan and M. Rosner (eds.), op. cit.
108. LEVIATAN, Uri; EDEN, Dov
    1980   "Structure, climate, members' reactions and effectiveness in kibbutz
                production organizations." In U. Leviatan and M. Rosner (eds.),
                op. cit.
109. LIEGLE, Ludwig
    1971a   *Familie und Kollektiv im Kibbutz: Eine Studie über die Funktionen
                der Familie in einem Kollektiven Erziehungsystem.* Berlin and Basel:
                Beltz.
110. ———
    1971b   *Kollektiv Erziehung im Kibbutz. Texte zur Vergleichenden Sozial-
                isation Forschung.* Munich: Piper, Erziehung in Wissenschaft und
                Praxis.

111. LIFSHITZ, Michaela; BAUM, Ronie; BALGUR, Irith; COHEN, Channa
     1975   "The impact of the social milieu upon the nature of adoptees' emo-
                   tional difficulties." *Journal of Marriage and the Family* 37(1): 221–
                   28.
112. LILKER, Shalom
     1977   "Martin Buber and the kibbutz." In A. Yassour (ed.), *Kibbutz
                   Members Analyze the Kibbutz*. Cambridge, Mass.: Institute for Co-
                   operative Community.
113. MACAROV, David
     1972   "Work patterns and satisfactions in an Israeli kibbutz: a test of the
                   Herzberg hypothesis." *Personnel Psychology* 25(3): 483–93.
114. ———
     1975   "Work without pay: work incentives and patterns in a salaryless
                   environment." *International Journal of Social Economics* 2(2): 106–
                   14.
115. MALRAUX, Clara
     1964   *Civilisation du kibboutz*. Geneva: Gonthier.
116. MARCUS, Joseph
     1971   "Kibbutz group care." *Early Child Development and Care* 1(1):
                   67–98.
117. MARIAMPOLSKI, Hyman
     1976   "Changes in kibbutz society." *International Review of Modern So-
                   ciology* 1(1): 201–16.
118. MARKOVIC, Mihailo
     1980   "The quality of working life and self-determination." In A. Cherns
                   (ed.), op. cit.
119. MEDNICK, Martha T. Shuch
     1975   "Social change and sex-role inertia: the case of the kibbutz." In
                   M. T. Sh. Mednick, S. Sch. Tangri, and L. W. Hoffman, *Women
                   and Achievement: Social and Motivational Analyses*. New York:
                   Wiley & Sons.
120. MEIER-CRONEMEYER, H.
     1969   *Kibbutzim-Geschichte, Geist und Gestalt; Teil 1, Geschichte*. Han-
                   over: Verlag für Literatur und Zeitgeschehen.
121. MELMAN. S.
     1971   "Managerial vs. cooperative decision making in Israel." *Studies in
                   Comparative International Development* 6(3): 47–62.
122. MOLHO, Sara; KATZ, Elihu
     1970   "Personal and other factors in the adoption of agricultural innova-
                   tions in the kibbutz and the old-established moshav." In S. Molho
                   (ed.), *Agricultural Extension*. Jerusalem: Keter.
123. NACHMIAS, Chava
     1977   "The status attainment process: a test of a model in two stratification
                   systems." *The Sociological Quarterly* 18(4): 589–607.
124. NAGLER, Shmuel
     1970   "The child and his family in the kibbutz: mental health." In A.
                   Jarus et al. (eds.), op. cit.

125. NATHAN, Michael
      1980   "Sex-roles in the kibbutz: some implications of the conflict between
                  reality and ideology." In K. Bartolke et al. (eds.), op. cit.
126. NEUBAUER, P. B. (ed.)
      1965   *Children in Collectives: Childrearing Aims and Practices in the
                  Kibbutz.* Springfield, Ill.: Thomas.
127. NEVO, B.
      1977   "Personality differences between kibbutz-born and city-born adults."
                  Journal of Psychology 96(2): 303–8.
128. NIV, Amitai
      1977   "Internal paradoxes and conflicts in the interface." In A. Yassour
                  (ed.), op. cit.
129. NIV, Amitai; BAR-ON, Dan
      1980   "Quality of work life in the kibbutz: the use of applied behavioral
                  sciences in training programmes for managers and field workers."
                  In A. Cherns (ed.), op. cit.
130. NONELL, Caroline
      1972   "Los kibbutzim: sociedades comunitarias. *Revista Internacional de
                  Sociología* 30(1–2): 226–30.
131. PADAN-EISENSTARK, Dorit
      1973   "Girls' education in the kibbutz." *International Review of Education*
                  19(1): 120–25.
132. PALGI, Michal
      1980   "Women members in the kibbutz and participation." In K. Bartolke
                  et al. (eds.), op. cit.
133. PARAN, Uzi
      1970   "Kibbutzim in Israel: their development and distribution." *Jeru-
                  salem Studies in Geography* 1: 1–36.
134. PERES, Jochanan
      1963   "Youth and youth movements in Israel." *Jewish Journal of Soci-
                  ology* 5(1): 94–110.
135. PERLMUTTER, Amos
      1970   "The agricultural collective settlement system: Hityashvut." In A.
                  Perlmutter, *Anatomy of Political Institutionalization: The Case of
                  Israel and Some Comparative Analyses.* Cambridge, Mass.: Harvard
                  University Center for International Affairs.
136. PIROJNIKOFF, Lee; HADAR, Ilana
      1973   "Self-perception differences among kibbutz and city adults in Israel
                  and Jewish and non-Jewish adults in the United States." *Journal of
                  Psychology* 84: 105–10.
137. PRAG, ALEX
      1962   "Some demographic aspects of the kibbutz life in Israel." *Jewish
                  Journal of Sociology* 4(1): 39–46.
138. PREALE, J.; AMIR, Y.; SHARAN, S.
      1970   "Perceptual articulation and task effectiveness in several Israel sub-
                  cultures." *Journal of Personality and Social Psychology* 15(3): 190–
                  95.

139 RABIN, A. I.
    1957   "The Israeli kibbutz as a laboratory for testing psychodynamic hy-
                potheses." *Psychological Record* 7: 111–15.
140. ———
    1958   "Kibbutz children: research findings to date." *Children* 5: 179–85.
141. ———
    1959   "Attitudes of kibbutz children to family and parents." *American
                Journal of Orthopsychiatry* 29(3): 172–79.
142. ———
    1961a   "Kibbutz adolescents." *American Journal of Orthopsychiatry* 31(3):
                493–504.
143. ———
    1961b   "Personality study in Israeli kibbutzim." In B. Kaplan (ed.), *Study-
                ing Personality Cross-Culturally*. New York: Harper and Row.
144. ———
    1964   "Kibbutz mothers view collective education." *American Journal of
                Orthopsychiatry* 34(1): 140–42.
145. ———
    1965   *Growing Up in the Kibbutz: Comparison of the Personality of Chil-
                dren Brought Up in the Kibbutz and of Family-Reared Children*.
                New York: Springer.
146. ———
    1968   "Some sex differences in the attitudes of kibbutz adolescents."
                Israel Annals of Psychiatry 6(1): 62–69.
147. ———
    1970   "The sexes: ideology and reality in the Israeli kibbutz." In G. H.
                Seward and R. C. Williamson (eds.), *Sex Roles in a Changing So-
                ciety*. New York: Random House.
148. ———
    1971   *Kibbutz Studies: A Digest of Books and Articles on the Kibbutz by
                Social Scientists, Educators, and Others*. East Lansing, Mich.:
                Michigan State University Press.
149. RABIN, A. I.; HAZAN, Bertha (eds.)
    1973   *Collective Education in the Kibbutz—From Infancy to Maturity*. New
                York: Springer.
150. RABIN, A. I.; BEIT-HALLAHMI, Benjamin
    1981   *Twenty Years Later: Kibbutz Children*. New York: Springer.
151. RABKIN, Leslie Y.; SPIRO, M. E.
    1971   "Postscript: the kibbutz in 1970." In M. Spiro, *Kibbutz: Venture
                in Utopia*. New York: Schocken.
152. RABKIN, Leslie Y.
    1975   "Superego processes in a collective society: the Israeli kibbutz."
                International Journal of Social Psychiatry 21(2): 79–86.
153. RETTIG, S.; PASSAMANIC, B.
    1963   "Some observations on the moral ideology of first and second gen-
                eration collective and noncollective settlers in Israel." *Social Prob-
                lems* 11(2): 165–78.

154. RETTIG, S.
    1966   "Relation of social systems to intergenerational changes in moral attitudes." *Journal of Personality and Social Psychology* 4(4): 409–14.
155. ———
    1972   "Anomie in the kibbutz." *International Journal of Group Tensions* 2(4): 37–52.
156. RON-POLANY, Yehuda
    1965   "The parent-child relationship in collective education in Israel." *International Review of Education* 11(2): 224–28.
157. RONEN, S.
    1978   "Personal values—a basis for work motivational set and work attitudes." *Organizational Behavior and Human Performance* 21(1): 80–107.
158. ROSENFELD, Eva
    1951   "Social stratification in a classless society." *American Sociological Review* 16(6) 766–74.
159. ———
    1957   "Institutional change in the kibbutz." *Social Problems* 5(2): 110–36.
160. ROSENFELD, Henry
    1971   "The culture of kibbutz Ein-Harod: an anthropological perspective." *Ariel* 28: 14–25.
161. ROSNER, MENACHEM
    1967   "Women in the kibbutz: changing status and concepts." *Asian and African Studies* 3: 35–68.
162. ———
    1970   "Communitarian experiment, self-management experience and the kibbutz." *Group Process* 3(1): 79–101.
163. ROSNER, Menachem; KAVČIČ, B.; TANNENBAUM, A. S.; VIANELLO, M.; WIESER, G.
    1970   "Worker participation and influence in five countries." *Industrial Relations* 9(2): 148–60.
164. ROSNER, Menachem
    1972   "Women in the kibbutz." In Judith Bardwick (ed.), *Readings on the Psychology of Women*. New York: Harper and Row.
165. ———
    1973   "Worker participation in decision making in kibbutz industry." In M. Curtis and M. Chertoff (eds.), *Israel: Social Structure and Change*. New Brunswick, N.J.: Transaction.
166. ———
    1974   "L'autogestion industrielle dans les kibboutzim." *Sociologie du Travail* 16(1): 25–64.
167. ROSNER, Menachem; PALGI, Michal
    1977   "Ideology and organization; the case of the kibbutz industrialization." *Mens en Onderneming* (Men and Enterprise) 31: 323–44.

168. ROSNER, Menachem
      1979   "Changes in the leisure culture of the kibbutz." *Leisure and Society*
                  2(2): 451–83.
169. ROSNER, Menachem; AVNAT, Alexander
      1979   "Seven years later." *Journal of Rural Cooperation* 7(1–2): 65–95.
170. ROSNER, Menachem
      1980a   "Hierarchy and democracy in kibbutz industry." In U. Leviatan and
                  M. Rosner (eds.), op. cit.
171. ——
      1980b   "The quality of working life in the kibbutz." In A. Cherns (ed.),
                  op. cit.
172. ——
      1980c   "Self management in kibbutz industry: organization patterns as de-
                  terminants of psychological effects." In U. Leviatan and M. Rosner
                  (eds.), op. cit.
173. ROSNER, Menachem; PALGI, Michal
      1980   "Ideology and organizational solutions: the case of the kibbutz in-
                  dustrialization." In U. Leviatan and M. Rosner (eds.), op. cit.
174. ROSNER, Menachem; COHEN, Nissim
      1980   "Is direct democracy feasible in modern society? The lesson of the
                  kibbutz experience." In K. Bartolke et al. (eds.) op. cit.
175. ROSOLIO, Daniel
      1974   "Patterns of interrelations between the government and the kibbutz
                  as an economic and ideological entity." In *3rd International Sym-
                  posium on Dynamics of Interrelations between Agricultural Coop-
                  eratives and the Government*. Tel-Aviv: C.I.R.C.O.M.
176. SCHLESINGER, Benjamin
      1970   "Family life in the kibbutz of Israel: utopia gained or paradise lost?"
                  International Journal of Comparative Sociology 11(4): 251–71.
177. SCHLESINGER, Yaffa
      1977   "Sex roles and social change in the kibbutz." *Journal of Marriage
                  and the Family* 39(4): 771–79.
178. SCHWARTZ, R. D.
      1954   "Social factors in the development of legal control: a case study of
                  two Israeli settlements." *Yale Law Journal* 63(4): 471–91.
179. ——
      1955   "Functional alternatives to inequality." *American Sociological Re-
                  view* 20(4): 424–30.
180. ——
      1957   "Democracy and collectivism in the kibbutz." *Social Problems* 5(2):
                  137–47.
181. SEGAL, Mordechai
      1970   "The child and his family in the kibbutz: school age." In A. Jarus
                  et al. (eds.), op. cit.
182. SELIER, F.
      1972   "Kibbutz-family research and the outsider: a commentary." *Inter-
                  national Journal of Comparative Sociology* 13(3–4): 223–24.

183. ———
1978 "Some functional and structural aspects of family life in a communal society: the financial sector of the kibbutz family." In B. Misra and J. Preston (eds.), *Community, Self and Identity*. The Hague: Mouton.
184. ———
1980 "Family and family tasks in a communal society." In K. Bartolke et al. (eds.), op. cit.
185. SHAPIRA, Ariella; LOMRANZ, Jacob
1975 "The kibbutz: growing up in a society of peers." *Psychology* 12(2): 53–69.
186. SHAPIRA, Ariella
1976 "Developmental differences in competitive behavior of kibbutz and city children in Israel." *Journal of Social Psychology* 98(1): 19–26.
187. SHAPIRO, Allan E.
1976 "Law in the kibbutz: a reappraisal." *Law and Society Review* 10(3): 415–38.
188. SHATIL, Joseph
1969–70 "Criteria for socio-economic efficiency of the kibbutz." *Archiv für Oeffentliche und Freigemeinnutzige Unternehmungen*. Part 1: 9(1), 1969. Part 2: 9(3), 1970.
189. SHELHAV, Moshe; BAR-ON, Dan
1980 "Innovative teams." In A. Cherns (ed.), op. cit.
190. SHELHAV, Moshe; GOLOMB, Naphtali
1980 "The sociotechnical projects in kibbutz industries." In A. Cherns (ed.), op. cit.
191. SHEPHER, Israel
1980 "Social boundaries of the kibbutz." In E. Marx (ed.), *A Composite Portrait of Israel*. London: Academic Press.
192. SHEPHER, Joseph
1969 "Familism and social structure: the case of the kibbutz." *Journal of Marriage and the Family* 31(3): 567–73.
193. ———
1970 "Organizational effectiveness in kibbutz society in the light of a new theory." *Sociologia Ruralis* 10(1): 21–37.
194. ———
1971 "Mate selection among second generation kibbutz adolescents and adults: incest avoidance and negative imprinting." *Archives of Sexual Behavior* 1(4): 293–307.
195. ———
1973 "Services publiques hors kibboutz." *Archives Internationales de la Coopération et du Développement* 34: 181–96.
196. ———
1974a "The kibbutz." In L. Weller, *Sociology in Israel*. Westport, Conn.: Greenwood.
197. SHEPHER, Joseph; TIGER, Lionel
1978 "Female hierarchies in a kibbutz community." In L. Tiger and H. Fowler (eds.), *Female Hierarchies*. Chicago: Aldine.

198. SHEPHER, Joseph
    1980   "The message of the kibbutz." In M. Kranzberg (ed.), *Ethics in a Pervasive Technology*. Boulder Col.: Westview.
199. SHEPHER, Joseph; TIGER, Lionel
    1981   "Kibbutz and parental investment." In P. A. Hare, H. H. Blumberg, V. Kent, and M. Davies (eds.), *Small Groups: Social-Psychological Processes, Social Action and Living Together*. London: Wiley.
200. SHOUVAL, Ron; KAV-VENAKI, S.; BRONFENBRENNER, U.; DEVEREUX, E.; KIELY, E.
    1975   "Anomalous reactions to social pressure of Israel and Soviet children raised in family vs. collective settings." *Journal of Personality and Social Psychology* 32(3): 477–89.
201. SHUR, Shimon
    1972   *Kibbutz Bibliography*. Tel Aviv: Higher Education and Research Authority of the Federation of Kibbutz Movements.
202. ———
    1978a   *The Kibbutz: Selected Bibliographical Entries*. Haifa: The Institute for Research of the Kibbutz and the Cooperative Idea, Haifa University.
203. ———
    1978b   "Research on the culture of leisure in the kibbutz in Israel." *Loisir Information* 6(3): 7.
204. ———
    1980   "Success in application and strategies of diffusion: the case of the kibbutz industry research findings." In A. Cherns (ed.), op. cit.
205. SHUR, Shimon; BEIT-HALLAHMI, Benjamin; BLASI, Joseph Raphael; RABIN, Albert L.
    1981   *The Kibbutz: A Bibliography of Scientific and Professional Publications in English*. Norwood. Pa.: Norwood Editions.
206. SPIRO, Melford E.
    1954   "Is the family universal?" *American Anthropologist* 56: 839–46.
207. ———
    1956   *Kibbutz: Venture in Utopia*. Cambridge, Mass.: Harvard University Press.
208. ———
    1957   "The Sabras and Zionism: a study in personality and ideology." *Social Problems* 5(2): 100–110.
209. ———
    1958   *Children of the Kibbutz*. New York: Schocken.
210. ———
    1979   *Gender and Culture. Kibbutz Women Revisited*. Durham, N.C.: Duke University Press.
211. TALMON-GARBER, Yonina
    1952   "Social differentiation in cooperative communities." *British Journal of Sociology* 3(4): 339–57.

212. ———
        1954   "The family in Israel." *Marriage and Family Living* 16(4): 343–
                    49.
213. ———
        1956   "Differentiation in collective settlements." *Scripta Hierosolymitana*
                    3: 153–78.
214. ———
        1959   "Social structure and family size." *Human Relations* 12(2): 121–
                    46.
215. ———
        1962   "Aging in collective settlements in Israel." In C. Tibbits and W.
                    Donehue (eds.), *Social and Psychological Aspects of Aging*. New
                    York: Columbia University.
216. ———
        1963   "Social change and family structure." *International Social Science
                    Journal* 14(3): 468–87.
217. TALMON-GARBER, Yonina; COHEN, Erik
        1964   "Collective settlements in the Negev." In J. Ben-David (ed.), *Ag-
                    ricultural Planning and Village Community in Israel*, Paris: Unesco.
218. TALMON-GARBER, Yonina
        1964   "Mate selection in collective settlements." *American Sociological
                    Review* 29(4): 491–508.
219. ———
        1965a   "Experiment in utopia: the lesson of the Israeli kibbutz." In Y. L.
                    Talmon, *The Unique and the Universal*. London: Seeker and War-
                    burg.
220. ———
        1965b   "The family in a revolutionary movement, the case of the kibbutz
                    in Israel." In M. Nimkoff (ed.), *Comparative Family Systems*. New
                    York: Houghton, Mifflin & Co.
221. ———
        1965c   "Sex-role differentiation in an equalitarian society." In T. G. Las-
                    swell, J. Burma, and S. Aronson (eds.), *Life in Society*. Chicago:
                    Scott, Foresman & Co.
222. TALMON-GARBER, Yonina; STUPP, L.
        1970   "Secular asceticism: patterns of ideological change." In S. N. Ei-
                    senstadt et al. (eds.), *Integration and Development in Israel*. Jeru-
                    salem: Israel University Press.
223. TALMON-GARBER, Yonina
        1972   *Family and Community in the Kibbutz*. Cambridge, Mass.: Harvard
                    University Press.
224. TANNENBAUM, Arnold S.; KAVČIČ, Bogdan; ROSNER, Menachem;
        VIANELLO, Mino; WIESER, George
        1974   *Hierarchy in Organizations*. San Francisco: Jossey-Bass.
225. TIGER, Lionel; SHEPHER, Joseph
        1975   *Women in the Kibbutz*. New York: Harcourt, Brace & Jovanovich.

226. VALLIER, Ivan A.
       1962a   "Social change in the kibbutz economy." *Economic Development and Cultural Change* 10(4): 337–52.
227. ———
       1962b   "Structural differentiation, production imperatives and communal norms: the kibbutz in crisis." *Social Forces* 40(3): 233–42.
228. VITELES, Harry
       1967   *The Evolution of the Kibbutz Movement*. London: Valentine, Mitchell. Vol. 2 of H. Viteles, *A History of the Cooperative Movement in Israel*.
229. ———
       1968   *An Analysis of the Four Sectors of the Kibbutz Movement*. London: Valentive, Mitchell. Vol. 3 of H. Viteles, *A History of the Cooperative Movement in Israel*.
230. WEINGARTEN, Murray
       1962   "The individual and the community." In E. Josephson and M. Josephson, (eds.), *Man Alone*. New York: Dell.
231. WEINGROD, Alex; GUREWITSCH, Michael
       1977   "Who are the Israeli elites?" *Jewish Journal of Sociology* 19(1): 67–77.
232. WEINTRAUB, D.; LISSAK, M.; AZMON, Y.
       1969a   "Growth of the kibbutz movement: Hakibbutz Hameuchad." In D. Weintraub et al., *Moshava, Kibbutz, and Moshav Patterns of Jewish Rural Settlement and Development in Palestine*. Ithaca: Cornell University Press.
233. ———
       1969b   "Kibbutz: Ein-Harod." In D. Weintraub et al. op. cit.
234. WERSHOW, Harold J.
       1969   "Aging in the Israeli kibbutz." *The Gerontologist* 9(4): 300–304.
235. ———
       1973a   "Aging in the Israeli kibbutz: growing old in a mini-socialist society." *Jewish Social Studies* 35(2): 141–48.
236. ———
       1973b   "Aging in the Israeli kibbutz: some further investigations." *International Journal of Aging and Human Development* 4(3): 211–27.
237. WILLNER, Dorothy
       1969   *Nation Building and Community in Israel*. Princeton, N.J.: Princeton University Press.
238. YASSOUR, Avraham (ed.)
       1977   *Kibbutz Members Analyze the Kibbutz*. Cambridge, Mass.: The Institute for Cooperative Community.
239. YASSOUR, Avraham
       1977   "The sorcerer's apprentice: the dangers inherent in the success of industry in the kibbutz." In A. Yassour (ed.), op. cit.
240. YINON, Yoel; FREEDMAN, Nili.
       1977   "The social needs of kibbutz and urban Israeli youth." *Journal of Social Psychology* 103(2) 319–20.

241. YUCHTMAN, Ephraim
     1972   "Reward distribution and work-pole attractiveness in the kibbutz:
                reflections on equity theory." *American Sociological Review* 37(5):
                581–95.
242. ZILLER, R. C.
     1973   "Self-other orientations of kibbutz children." In R. C. Ziller, *The
                Social Self.* New York: Pergamon.
243. ZIV, Avner; GREEN, David; GUTTMAN, Joseph
     1978   "Moral judgement differences between city, kibbutz, and Israeli
                Arab preadolescents on the realistic-relativistic dimension." *Journal
                of Cross-Cultural Psychology* 9(2): 215–25.
244. ZIV, Avner; SHULMAN, Shmuel; SCHLEIFER, Hedy
     1979   "Moral development: parental and peer-group influence on kibbutz
                and city children." *Journal of Genetic Psychology* 134(2): 233–40.

Bibliographical Subject Index

HN 660 .A8 S83 v.2

Studies of Israeli society

ר.ש.ראו.נ

MAY 0 9 '00